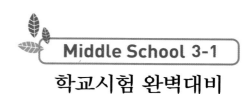
KB100526

1학기 전과정

적중 100 plus⁺

영어 기출문제집

중 3

천재 | 이재영

Best Collection

구성과 특징

교과서의 주요 학습 내용을 중심으로 학습 영역별 특성에 맞춰 단계별로 다양한 학습 기회를 제공하여
단원별 학습능력 평가는 물론 중간 및 기말고사 시험 등에 완벽하게 대비할 수 있도록 내용을 구성

Words & Expressions

Step1   Key Words 단원별 핵심 단어 설명 및 풀이
Key Expression 단원별 핵심 숙어 및 관용어 설명
Word Power 반대 또는 비슷한 뜻 단어 배우기
English Dictionary 영어로 배우는 영어 단어

Step2   실력평가 단원별 수시평가 대비 주관식, 객관식 문제풀이

Step3   서술형 대비 학업성취도 및 수행능력평가 대비 서술형 문제풀이

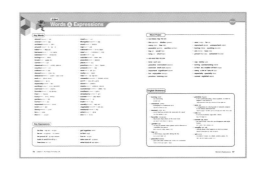

Conversation

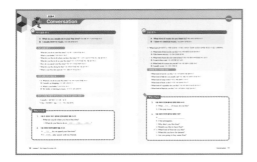

Step1   핵심 의사소통 소통에 필요한 주요 표현 방법 요약
핵심 Check 기본적인 표현 방법 및 활용능력 확인

Step2   대화문 익히기 교과서 대화문 심층 분석 및 확인

Step3   교과서 확인학습 빈칸 채우기를 통한 문장 완성 능력 확인

Step4   기본평가 시험대비 기초 학습 능력 평가

Step5   실력평가 단원별 수시평가 대비 주관식, 객관식 문제풀이

Step6   서술형 대비 학업성취도 및 수행능력평가 대비 서술형 문제풀이

Grammar

Step1   주요 문법 단원별 주요 문법 사항과 예문을 알기 쉽게 설명
핵심 Check 기본 문법사항에 대한 이해 여부 확인

Step2   기본평가 시험대비 기초 학습 능력 평가

Step3   실력평가 단원별 수시평가 대비 주관식, 객관식 문제풀이

Step4   서술형 대비 학업성취도 및 수행능력평가 대비 서술형 문제풀이

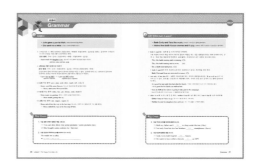

Reading

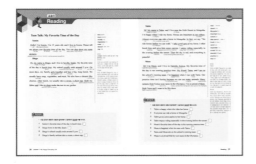

Step1   구문 분석 단원별로 제시된 문장에 대한 구문별 분석과 내용 설명
확인문제 문장에 대한 기본적인 이해와 인지능력 확인

Step2   확인학습A 빈칸 채우기를 통한 문장 완성 능력 확인

Step3   확인학습B 제시된 우리말을 영어로 완성하여 작문 능력 키우기

Step4   실력평가 단원별 수시평가 대비 주관식, 객관식 문제풀이

Step5   서술형 대비 학업성취도 및 수행능력평가 대비 서술형 문제풀이
교과서 구석구석 교과서에 나오는 기타 문장까지 완벽 학습

Composition

|영역별 핵심문제|

단어 및 어휘, 대화문, 문법, 독해 등 각 영역별 기출문제의 출제 유형을 분석하여 실전에 대비하고 연습할 수 있도록 문제를 배열

|단원별 예상문제|

기출문제를 분석한 후 새로운 시험 출제 경향을 더하여 새롭게 출제될 수 있는 문제를 포함하여 시험에 완벽하게 대비할 수 있도록 준비

|서술형 실전 및 창의사고력 문제|

학교 시험에서 점차 늘어나는 서술형 시험에 집중 대비하고 고득점을 취득하는데 만전을 기하기 위한 학습 코너

|단원별 모의고사|

영역별, 단계별 학습을 모두 마친 후 실전 연습을 위한 모의고사

교과서 파헤치기

- **단어Test1~3** 영어 단어 우리말 쓰기, 우리말을 영어 단어로 쓰기, 영영풀이에 해당하는 단어와 우리말 쓰기
- **대화문Test1~2** 대화문 빈칸 완성 및 전체 대화문 쓰기
- **본문Test1~5** 빈칸 완성, 우리말 쓰기, 문장 배열연습, 영어 작문하기 복습 등 단계별 반복 학습을 통해 교과서 지문에 대한 완벽한 습득
- **구석구석지문Test1~2** 지문 빈칸 완성 및 전문 영어로 쓰기

Contents

What Matters to You?

의사소통 기능

- 감정 표현하기

  A: It's going to rain all day long.

  B: Really? I'm glad I can wear my new raincoat.

- 동의하기

  A: I think the most boring day of the week is Monday.

  B: You can say that again.

언어 형식

- 관계대명사 what

  They didn't tell me **what** I wanted to know.

- 지각동사+목적어+동사원형

  I **saw** Mom **come** into my room.

Words & Expressions

Key Words

- **allowance** [əláuəns] 명 용돈
- **amazing** [əméiziŋ] 형 놀라운
- **animation** [æ̀nəméiʃən] 명 애니메이션, 만화 영화
- **appear** [əpíər] 동 나타나다
- **boring** [bɔ́ːriŋ] 형 지루한
- **chase** [tʃeis] 동 추적하다
- **chest** [tʃest] 명 상자, 가슴
- **chew** [tʃuː] 동 씹다
- **delighted** [diláitid] 형 기쁜
- **faraway** [fɑ́ːrəwèi] 형 멀리 떨어진
- **goods** [gudz] 명 상품
- **greatly** [gréitli] 부 매우
- **hurry** [hə́ːri] 동 서두르다
- **include** [inklúːd] 동 포함하다
- **invention** [invénʃən] 명 발명, 발명품
- **jealous** [dʒéləs] 형 질투하는
- **jewel** [dʒúːəl] 명 보물
- **kitten** [kítn] 명 새끼 고양이
- **merchant** [mə́ːrtʃənt] 명 상인
- **pack** [pæk] 동 짐을 꾸리다, 가득 채우다
- **palace** [pǽlis] 명 궁전

- **pleased** [pliːzd] 형 기쁜
- **prepare** [pripέər] 동 준비하다
- **present** [prizént] 동 주다, 선사하다
- **priceless** [práislis] 형 소중한
- **puzzled** [pʌ́zld] 형 당황스러운
- **raincoat** [réinkòut] 명 비옷
- **rat** [ræt] 명 쥐
- **realize** [ríːəlàiz] 동 깨닫다
- **relax** [rilǽks] 동 쉬다
- **repay** [ripéi] 동 갚다
- **servant** [sə́ːrvənt] 명 하인
- **serve** [səːrv] 동 음식을 날라 주다
- **speechless** [spíːtʃlis] 형 말문이 막힌
- **spice** [spais] 명 향료
- **subject** [sʌ́bdʒikt] 명 과목
- **tool** [tuːl] 명 도구, 연장
- **trade** [treid] 동 무역하다, 교역하다
- **valuable** [vǽljuəbl] 형 소중한
- **whisper** [hwíspər] 동 속삭이다
- **wonder** [wʌ́ndər] 동 놀라워하다
- **worthless** [wə́ːrθlis] 형 가치 없는

Key Expressions

- **a walking dictionary** 살아 있는 사전, 만물박사
- **after a while** 잠시 후에
- **all day long** 하루 종일
- **be sure that** ~ ~을 확신하다
- **Break a leg!** 행운을 빌어!
- **chase A away** A를 쫓아내다
- **get a chance to** ~ ~할 기회를 얻다
- **get over** 극복하다
- **Good for you.** 잘했다.
- **have two left feet** 동작이 어색하다
- **in history** 역사적으로

- **student card** 학생증
- **support ~ by trading** 무역으로 ~을 부양하다
- **take a picture** 사진을 찍다
- **take care of** ~ ~을 돌보다
- **take ~ hard** ~을 심각하게 받아들이다
- **tell the time** 시간을 알아보다
- **thanks to** ~ ~ 덕택에
- **weather report** 일기예보
- **What a surprise!** 정말 놀랍구나!
- **You can say that again.** 네 말이 맞아.

Word Power

※ 서로 비슷한 뜻을 가진 어휘

- □ **amazing** 놀라운 : **surprising** 놀라운
- □ **chase** 추적하다 : **follow** 뒤따르다
- □ **delighted** 기쁜 : **pleased** 기쁜
- □ **jealous** 질투하는 : **envious** 부러워하는
- □ **merchant** 상인 : **dealer** 상인
- □ **play** 연극 : **drama** 연극
- □ **present** 주다, 선사하다 : **give** 주다
- □ **puzzled** 당황스러운 : **embarrassed** 당황한
- □ **tool** 도구, 연장 : **device** 기구

- □ **boring** 지루한 : **dull** 지루한
- □ **chest** 상자 : **box** 상자
- □ **goods** 상품 : **product** 상품
- □ **jewel** 보물 : **treasure** 보물
- □ **pack** 가득 채우다 : **fill** 채우다
- □ **pleased** 기쁜 : **glad** 기쁜
- □ **priceless** 소중한 : **valuable** 소중한
- □ **relax** 휴식을 취하다 : **rest** 쉬다
- □ **worthless** 가치 없는 : **valueless** 가치 없는

※ 서로 반대의 뜻을 가진 어휘

- □ **appear** 나타나다 ↔ **disappear** 사라지다
- □ **delighted** 기쁜 ↔ **sorrowful** 슬퍼하는
- □ **include** 포함하다 ↔ **exclude** 제외하다
- □ **happy** 행복한 ↔ **unhappy** 불행한
- □ **priceless** 소중한 ↔ **worthless** 가치 없는

- □ **boring** 지루한 ↔ **exciting** 흥미진진한
- □ **glad** 기쁜 ↔ **sad** 슬픈
- □ **pack** 짐을 꾸리다 ↔ **unpack** 짐을 풀다
- □ **popular** 인기 있는 ↔ **unpopular** 인기 없는

English Dictionary

□ **allowance** 용돈
→ an amount of money that you are given regularly or for a special purpose
규칙적으로 또는 특별한 목적을 위하여 주어지는 상당한 양의 돈

□ **animation** 만화 영화
→ a film, television programme, computer game, etc that has pictures, clay models, etc that seem to be really moving
실제로 움직이는 듯한 그림, 점토 모형 등을 가진 영화, TV 프로그램, 컴퓨터 게임 등

□ **chase** 추적하다
→ to quickly follow someone or something in order to catch them
붙잡기 위하여 어떤 사람 또는 무엇인가를 빠르게 쫓아가다

□ **chest** 상자
→ a large strong box that you use to store things in or to move your personal possessions from one place to another
물건을 옮기거나 보관하기 위하여 사용하는 크고 튼튼한 상자

□ **include** 포함하다
→ to make someone or something part of a larger group
무엇인가를 더 큰 집단의 한 부분으로 만들다

□ **merchant** 상인
→ someone who buys and sells goods in large quantities
대량으로 물건을 사고파는 사람

□ **pack** 짐을 꾸리다
→ to put things into cases, bags, etc ready for a trip somewhere
어딘가로 여행할 준비로 물건을 상자, 가방 등에 넣다

□ **servant** 하인
→ someone, especially in the past, who was paid to clean someone's house, cook for them, answer the door, etc
집을 청소하기, 요리하기, 손님맞이 등을 위하여 고용된 사람

[01~02] 다음 대화의 빈칸에 들어갈 말을 고르시오.

01

A: It's going to rain all day long.
B: Really? I'm glad I can _____ my new raincoat.

① wash   ② choose
③ repay   ④ wear
⑤ wonder

02

A: I think the most boring day of the week is Monday.
B: You can _____ that again.

① speak   ② say
③ talk   ④ hear
⑤ wonder

[03~04] 다음 빈칸에 들어갈 말로 적절한 것을 고르시오.

03

The merchant went to different places to _____ his family by trading.

① support   ② call
③ move   ④ communicate
⑤ visit

04

One day, the merchant filled his ship with _____ and visited a faraway island.

① consumers   ② values
③ goods   ④ lists
⑤ areas

05 다음 중 밑줄 친 부분의 뜻풀이가 바르지 않은 것은?

① It's going to <u>rain</u> all day long. (비가 내리다)
② I think the most <u>boring</u> day of the week is Monday. (지루한)
③ The food looks so <u>delicious</u>. (맛있는)
④ I don't <u>agree</u> with you on that issue. (동의하다)
⑤ I didn't know you didn't <u>like</u> the plan. (~같은)

06 다음 빈칸에 알맞은 말이 바르게 짝지어진 것은?

• Some servants chased rats _____ with sticks.
• Rix got a rabbit from a friend and did his best to take good care _____ it.

① on – for   ② along – in
③ back – with   ④ off – on
⑤ away – of

07 다음 영영풀이에 해당하는 단어를 고르시오.

to bite food several times before swallowing it

① punch   ② chase
③ chew   ④ trade
⑤ present

서답형
08 다음 주어진 단어를 이용해 빈칸을 완성하시오.

There are many great _____ around us.

➡ _____ (invent)

01 다음 짝지어진 단어의 관계가 같도록 빈칸에 알맞은 말을 쓰시오. (주어진 철자로 시작할 것)

> amazing : s_____ = boring : dull

02 다음 영어 풀이에 해당하는 단어를 주어진 철자로 시작하여 쓰시오.

> an amount of money that you are given regularly or for a special purpose

➡ a_____

03 다음 짝지어진 단어의 관계가 같도록 빈칸에 알맞은 말을 쓰시오. (주어진 철자로 시작할 것)

> appear : disappear = b_____ : exciting

[04~05] 다음 대화의 빈칸에 들어가기에 적절한 단어를 주어진 철자로 시작하여 쓰시오.

04
> Many people will agree that paper is the greatest invention. T_____ _____ paper, we all can read books and write things down.

05
> • I need some time to relax. We all need to do something to g_____ _____ stress.
> • I will g_____ _____ this difficulty by myself.
> • He will help you to g_____ your broken heart.

[06~07] 내용상 다음 주어진 빈칸에 들어가기에 적절한 단어를 쓰시오. (주어진 철자로 시작할 것)

06
> Antonio asked, "Are there no cats on this island?" The queen looked p_____. "What is a cat?" she asked.

07
> After a while, the servant returned with a box, and the queen p_____ it to Luigi. When Luigi opened the box, he was speechless.

08 다음 밑줄 친 단어와 의미가 같은 단어를 쓰시오. (주어진 철자로 시작할 것)

> You can say that again! Mom would love it as a birthday present.

➡ g_____

09 다음 우리말에 맞게 빈칸에 알맞은 말을 쓰시오.

(1) 우리는 목요일에 어려운 과목이 모두 있어.
➡ We have all the difficult _____ on Thursday.

(2) 너는 서둘러서 돌아가야 해.
➡ You must _____ to go back.

(3) 너는 어떤 종류의 학교를 염두에 두고 있니?
➡ What kind of school do you have in _____?

Conversation

교과서

① 감정 표현하기

> • I'm glad I can wear my new raincoat. 새로 산 비옷을 입게 되어 기뻐.

■ 'I'm glad I can wear my new raincoat.'는 자신의 감정 상태를 나타내는 표현이다. 'I'm 감정 형용사 ~'로 표현하며 'I feel 감정 형용사 ~'로 나타낼 수도 있다.

■ '~에 대해 …하다'의 뜻으로 'I'm 감정 형용사 ~' 또는 'I feel 감정 형용사 ~'에서 감정 형용사는 glad, delighted, pleased, worried 등을 쓴다.

■ 감정을 표현할 때 'I'm glad 감정 형용사 ~' 또는 'I feel 감정 형용사 ~'에서 사용하는 감정 형용사 뒤에는 접속사 that과 함께 '주어+동사~'가 이어져서 감정의 원인을 나타낸다. 여기에 사용되는 접속사 that은 보통 생략한다.

감정 표현하기

• I'm glad ~. ~하게 되어 기뻐.
= I feel glad ~.

• I'm worried ~. ~하게 되어 걱정이야.
= I feel worried ~.

• I'm pleased ~. ~하게 되어 기뻐.
= I feel pleased ~.

• I'm delighted ~. ~하게 되어 기뻐.
= I feel delighted ~.

감정 표현에 대한 응답

• Good for you. 잘 됐구나.

• Don't worry. 걱정하지 마.

• Don't take it so hard. 너무 심각하게 생각하지 마.

핵심 Check

1. 다음 우리말과 일치하도록 빈칸에 알맞은 말을 쓰시오.

   A: It's going to rain all day long. (하루 종일 비가 올 거야.)

   B: Really? I'm _____ I can wear my new raincoat.

   (정말? 나는 새로 산 비옷을 입을 수 있어 기뻐.)

2. 다음 대화의 순서를 바르게 배열하시오.

   (A) Good for you

   (B) Yes. It's going to rain all day long.

   (C) Really? I'm glad I can use my new umbrella.

   (D) Did you hear the weather report?

   ➡ _____

② 동의하기

> • **You can say that again.** 네 말이 맞아.

■ 상대방의 말이나 의견에 동의할 때는 'You can say that again.'이라고 한다. 'I agree with you.'라고 할 수도 있다. 상대방의 말에 동의하지 않을 때는 'I don't agree.'라고 한다.

■ 상대방의 표현에 동의할 때는 '나도 그래.'의 의미로 'Me, too.' 또는 'So+동사+주어.'의 형태를 쓴다. 이때 사용하는 동사는 be동사, do, does, did를 포함하는 조동사들이다. 부정문에 이어지는 경우에는 so 대신 neither를 사용하여 'Neither+동사+주어.'라고 하거나 'Me neither.'라고 할 수 있다.

동의하기

• You can say that again. 네 말이 맞아.
• I agree with you. 동의해.
• So am/do I. 나도 마찬가지야.

• Neither am/do I. 나도 그래.
• Me, too./Me, neither. 나도 그래.

반대하기

• I don't agree with you. 나는 동의하지 않아.
• I have a different idea. 나는 생각이 달라.

• I don't think so. 나는 그렇게 생각하지 않아.

핵심 Check

3. 다음 우리말과 일치하도록 빈칸에 알맞은 말을 쓰시오.

(1) **A:** That man looks just like Ben. (저 사람은 꼭 Ben처럼 보여.)

   B: You can _____ that again. (네 말이 맞아.)

(2) **A:** I think I have time to eat a snack. (나는 간식 먹을 시간이 있다고 생각해.)

   B: I don't _____. You must hurry to go back. (그렇지 않아. 너는 서둘러 돌아가야 해.)

4. 다음 주어진 문장을 자연스러운 대화가 되도록 배열하시오.

G: Hey, Minjun. What a surprise!

B: Hi, Sora. I'm glad we're in the same class.

(A) I'm a little worried that there'll be more schoolwork.

(B) I'm thinking of an animation high school. I love painting.

(C) I am, too. We're now in our last year in middle school. How do you feel?

(D) Me, too. We also have to think about our high school.

(E) Which kind of school do you have in mind?

➡ _____

Listen – Listen & Answer Dialog 1

G: Hey, Minjun. ❶What a surprise!

B: Hi, Sora. ❷I'm glad we're in the same class.

G: ❸I am, too. We're now in our last year in middle school. How do you feel?

B: I'm a little worried ❹that there'll be more schoolwork.

G: Me, too. We also have to think about our high school.

B: ❺Which kind of school do you ❻have in mind?

G: I'm thinking of an animation high school. I love painting.

G: 야, 민준아. 정말 놀랍다!
B: 안녕, 소라야. 우리가 같은 반에 있어서 기뻐.
G: 나도 그래. 우리 이제 중학교의 마지막 학년이야. 기분이 어떠니?
B: 공부할 게 더 많을 것 같아서 조금 걱정이야.
G: 나도 그래. 고등학교에 대해서도 생각해야 하지.
B: 너는 어떤 학교를 마음에 두고 있니?
G: 나는 애니메이션 고등학교를 생각하고 있어. 내가 그림 그리는 걸 좋아하거든.

❶ 'What a surprise!'는 감탄문으로 '주어+동사'가 생략되었다.
❷ 'I am glad'는 감정을 나타내는 표현으로 감정 형용사 뒤에는 감정의 이유를 나타내는 종속절을 유도하는 접속사 that이 생략되었다.
❸ 'I am, too.'는 동의하는 표현으로 am 뒤에는 앞 문장에 있었던 glad가 생략되었다. 동의를 나타내는 표현은 'I agree.' 또는 'Me, too.'를 쓸 수도 있다.
❹ that은 접속사로 쓰여서 감정을 나타내는 worried의 원인을 유도하고 있다.
❺ 'Which kind of school'이 문장의 목적어 역할을 한다.
❻ have A in mind: A를 염두에 두다

Check(√) True or False

(1) Minjun and Sora are in the same class.　　T ☐ F ☐

(2) Minjun is thinking of an animation high school.　　T ☐ F ☐

Listen – Listen & Answer Dialog 2

G: Oliver, what club are you going to join?

B: I'm not sure. ❶How about you, Sora?

G: I want to join the school dance club.

B: Really? But I heard you're preparing for an animation high school.

G: Right, but I need some time to relax. We all need to do something to get over stress.

B: You can say that again.

G: Why don't you join me? It'll be fun.

B: No, thanks. Dancing is not for me. I ❷have two left feet.

G: Oliver, 넌 어느 동아리에 들어갈 거니?
B: 잘 모르겠어. 소라, 너는?
G: 난 학교 춤 동아리에 가입하고 싶어.
B: 정말? 하지만 네가 애니메이션 고등학교를 준비하고 있다고 들었는데.
G: 그렇긴 한데, 좀 쉴 시간이 필요해. 우리 모두 스트레스를 극복하려면 뭔가를 할 필요가 있잖아.
B: 전적으로 동의해.
G: 너 나랑 함께하는 게 어때? 재미있을 거야.
B: 고맙지만 사양할게. 춤은 내게 맞지 않아. 난 몸치야.

❶ 'How about ∼?'는 상대에게 제안하는 표현으로 'What about ∼?'라고 할 수도 있다.
❷ 'have two left feet'은 '동작이 서툴다'는 의미이다.

Check(√) True or False

(3) Sora is preparing for an animation high school.　　T ☐ F ☐

(4) Oliver will join the dance club.　　T ☐ F ☐

(5) Sora thinks she has two left feet.　　T ☐ F ☐

Listen More – Listen and say

B: Jimin, look! That red phone case ❶looks nice!

G: You can say that again! Mom would love it ❷ as a birthday present.

B: I wonder how much it costs.

G: Let me see. It costs 40,000 won.

B: Really? That's so expensive!

G: I don't agree. Look! It works as a wallet, too.

B: Oh, I didn't see that. Then let's buy it for Mom.

G: Okay. I'm delighted to buy something special for Mom.

B: ❸So am I.

❶ 자동사 look은 주격보어 형용사가 필요하다.
❷ as는 전치사로 쓰였다.
❸ 'So am I.'는 동의하는 표현이다.

Speak – Talk in pairs.

A: Did you hear ❶the weather report?

B: Yes. It's going to rain all day long.

A: Really? I'm ❷glad I can wear my new raincoat.

B: Good for you.

❶ 'the weather report'는 '일기예보'이다.
❷ glad 뒤에는 접속사 that이 생략되었다.

Speak – Rap Time

A: I'm really worried I can't find my ❶student card.

B: You can make another one. ❷Don't take it so hard.

❶ student card: 학생증
❷ 동사 take는 '받아들이다, 생각하다'의 의미로 'Don't take it so hard.'는 '심각하게 생각하지 마.'에 해당한다.

Speak – Talk in groups.

A: I think the most ❶boring day of the week is Monday.

B: ❷You can say that again.

C: I don't think so. Thursday is the most boring.

D: I agree. We have all the difficult subjects on Thursday.

❶ boring은 '사람을 지루하게 하는'의 뜻으로 분사형용사이다.
❷ 'You can say that again.'은 상대의 말에 동의한다는 의미이다.

My Speaking Portfolio.

1. B1: What do you do in your free time? I listen to music. I think it's the greatest invention. I can't ❶live without it.

2. G: I think chocolate is the greatest invention. It makes me feel good. It also helps me focus better when I study.

3. B2: Many people will agree that paper is the greatest invention. ❸Thanks to paper, we all can read books and write things down.

❶ live without: ~ 없이 살다
❷ thanks to ~: ~ 덕택에

Wrap Up – Listen & Speaking ❺

B: You ❶look so serious. What's going on?

G: Oh, I'm just practicing for the school play tomorrow.

B: How do you feel about it?

G: I'm worried ❷I may make a mistake.

B: I'm sure you'll do well. ❸Break a leg!

G: Thanks.

❶ 자동사 look의 보어는 형용사이다.
❷ 접속사 that이 생략되었다.
❸ 'Break a leg!'는 상대에게 행운을 빌어주는 표현이다.

Wrap Up – Listen & Speaking ❻

G: ❶Have you heard about Mr. Oh?

B: No. What about him?

G: He ❷won first prize in the TV quiz show.

B: It's not surprising. He ❸seems to know about everything.

G: You can say that again! He's ❹a walking dictionary.

❶ 경험의 의미를 가지는 현재완료이다.
❷ win의 과거 won은 '(상을) 받았다'의 의미로 쓰였다.
❸ seem은 보어로 to부정사를 가진다.
❹ 'a walking dictionary'는 '걸어 다니는 사전, 박식한 사람, 살아 있는 사전'이라는 의미이다.

● 다음 우리말과 일치하도록 빈칸에 알맞은 말을 쓰시오.

Listen – Listen and Answer – Dialog 1

G: Hey, Minjun. _____ a _____!

B: Hi, Sora. I'm _____ we're in the _____ class.

G: I _____, too. We're now in our _____ year in middle school. _____ do you feel?

B: I'm a little _____ that there'll be more schoolwork.

G: Me, too. We also _____ _____ think about our _____ school.

B: _____ kind of school do you _____ in _____?

G: I'm _____ of an animation high school. I love _____.

Listen – Listen and Answer – Dialog 2

G: Oliver, _____ club are you _____ to _____?

B: I'm not _____. How _____ you, Sora?

G: I want to _____ the school dance club.

B: Really? But I _____ you're _____ for an animation high school.

G: Right, but I _____ some time to _____. We all _____ to do something to _____ _____ stress.

B: _____ _____ _____ that again.

G: _____ _____ you join me? It'll be fun.

B: No, thanks. Dancing is not _____ _____. I have _____ _____ feet.

Listen More – Listen and say

B: Jimin, look! That red phone _____ _____ nice!

G: You can _____ _____ again! Mom would love it _____ a birthday present.

B: I _____ _____ _____ it costs.

G: _____ me see. It _____ 40,000 won.

B: Really? That's so _____.

G: I don't _____. Look! It _____ _____ a wallet, too.

B: Oh, I didn't see that. Then let's _____ it for Mom.

G: Okay. I'm _____ to buy something _____ for Mom.

B: _____ _____ I.

G: 야, 민준아. 정말 놀랍다!

B: 안녕, 소라야. 우리가 같은 반에 있어서 기뻐.

G: 나도 그래. 우리 이제 중학교의 마지막 학년이야. 기분이 어떠니?

B: 공부할 게 더 많을 것 같아서 조금 걱정이야.

G: 나도 그래. 고등학교에 대해서도 생각해야 하지.

B: 너는 어떤 학교를 마음에 두고 있니?

G: 나는 애니메이션 고등학교를 생각하고 있어. 내가 그림 그리는 걸 좋아하거든.

G: Oliver, 넌 어느 동아리에 들어갈 거니?

B: 잘 모르겠어. 소라, 너는?

G: 난 학교 춤 동아리에 가입하고 싶어.

B: 정말? 하지만 네가 애니메이션 고등학교를 준비하고 있다고 들었는데.

G: 그렇긴 한데, 좀 쉴 시간이 필요해. 우리 모두 스트레스를 극복하려면 뭔가를 할 필요가 있잖아.

B: 전적으로 동의해.

G: 너 나랑 함께하는 게 어때? 재미있을 거야.

B: 고맙지만 사양할게. 춤은 내게 맞지 않아. 난 몸치야.

B: 지민아, 봐! 저 빨간 전화기 케이스 멋지다!

G: 정말 그렇다! 생신 선물로 어머니께서 좋아하실 거야.

B: 난 가격이 얼마인지 궁금해.

G: 어디 보자. 가격은 40,000원이야.

B: 정말? 그거 너무 비싸다!

G: 난 동의하지 않아. 봐! 이건 지갑 역할도 해.

B: 아, 그건 못 봤어. 그럼 어머니를 위해 그걸 사자.

G: 알았어. 어머니께 뭔가 특별한 것을 사 드리게 되어 기뻐.

B: 나도 그래.

Speak – Talk in pairs.

A: Did you hear the _____ _____?

B: Yes. It's _____ _____ _____ all day long.

A: Really? I'm _____ I can _____ my new raincoat.

B: _____ for you.

Speak – Talk in groups.

A: I think the most _____ day of the _____ is Monday.

B: You _____ _____ that again.

C: I _____ _____ so. Thursday is the most boring.

D: I _____. We have all the _____ _____ on Thursday.

My Speaking Portfolio.

1. B1: _____ do you do in your _____ time? I _____ to music.
I think it's the _____ _____. I can't _____ without it.

2. G: I think chocolate is the _____ _____. It makes me _____
_____. It also helps me _____ better when I study.

3. B2: Many people will _____ that paper is the greatest invention.
_____ _____ paper, we all can _____ books and
_____ things down.

Wrap Up - Listening & Speaking ❺

B: You look so _____. What's _____ on?

G: Oh, I'm just _____ for the school play tomorrow.

B: How do you _____ _____ it?

G: I'm _____ I may _____ a mistake.

B: I'm _____ you'll do well. _____ a _____!

G: Thanks.

Wrap Up - Listening & Speaking ❻

G: Have you _____ about Mr. Oh?

B: No. _____ about him?

G: He _____ first _____ in the TV quiz show.

B: It's not _____. He _____ to know about everything.

G: You can say that again! He's a _____ dictionary.

해석

A: 일기예보 들었니?
B: 들었어. 하루 종일 비가 올 거야.
A: 정말! 새 비옷을 입을 수 있어 기뻐.
B: 좋겠다.

A: 나는 가장 지루한 날이 월요일이라고 생각해.
B: 네 말이 맞아.
C: 나는 그렇게 생각하지 않아. 목요일이 가장 지루해.
D: 나도 동의해. 우리는 목요일에 어려운 과목이 모두 있어.

1. B1: 여러분은 여가 시간에 무엇을 하나요? 나는 음악을 듣습니다. 나는 음악이 가장 위대한 발명품이라고 생각합니다. 나는 음악 없이는 살 수 없습니다.
2. G: 나는 초콜릿이 가장 위대한 발명품이라고 생각합니다. 초콜릿은 내가 기분이 좋아지도록 해 줍니다. 그것은 또한 내가 공부할 때 더 잘 집중하도록 도와줍니다.
3. B2: 종이가 가장 위대한 발명품이라는 데 많은 사람이 동의할 것입니다. 종이 덕분에 우리는 모두 책을 읽고 무언가를 적을 수 있습니다.

B: 너 진지해 보인다. 무슨 일이니?
G: 아, 그냥 내일 있을 학교 연극을 연습하는 중이야.
B: 기분이 어때?
G: 실수할까 봐 걱정돼.
B: 너는 틀림없이 잘할 거야. 행운을 빌어!
G: 고마워.

G: 오 선생님에 관해 들었니?
B: 아니. 선생님에 관해 뭘?
G: 선생님이 TV 퀴즈 쇼에서 우승하셨대.
B: 놀랄 일도 아니지. 선생님은 모든 것에 관해 알고 계신 것 같아.
G: 맞아! 걸어 다니는 사전이시지.

[01~02] 다음 대화의 빈칸에 들어갈 말로 알맞은 것은?

01

> A: It's going to rain all day long.
> B: Really? I'm _____ I can wear my new raincoat.

① glad   ② surprised   ③ tired
④ worried   ⑤ missed

02

> A: I'm glad I can go to the zoo.
> B: You're going to the zoo? _____ for you.

① Good   ② Well   ③ Rather
④ Yet   ⑤ Sad

03 다음 주어진 단어를 이용하여 우리말에 해당하는 영어 문장을 쓰시오.

> B: I heard you're preparing for an animation high school.
> G: Right, but I want to join the school dance club to have some time to relax. We all need to do something to get over stress.
> B: 전적으로 동의해. (say, again)
> G: Why don't you join me? It'll be fun.

➡ _____

04 다음 대화의 순서가 바르게 배열된 것을 고르시오.

> B: You look so serious. What's going on?
> G: Oh, I'm just practicing for the school play tomorrow.
> (A) Thanks.
> (B) How do you feel about it?
> (C) I'm worried I may make a mistake.
> (D) I'm sure you'll do well. Break a leg!

① (A) – (C) – (D) – (B)   ② (D) – (B) – (A) – (C)
③ (B) – (C) – (D) – (A)   ④ (C) – (A) – (B) – (D)
⑤ (C) – (B) – (D) – (A)

[01~02] 다음 대화를 읽고 물음에 답하시오.

B: Jimin, look! That red phone case looks nice!

G: _____ (A) _____ Mom would love it as a birthday present.

B: I wonder how much it costs.

G: Let me see. It costs 40,000 won.

B: Really? That's so expensive.

G: I don't agree. Look! It works as a wallet, too.

B: Oh, I didn't see that. Then let's buy it for Mom.

G: Okay. I'm delighted to buy something special for Mom.

B: So am I.

01 위 대화의 빈칸 (A)에 들어가기에 적절하지 <u>않은</u> 것은?

① I think so, too!

② You can say that again!

③ Me, neither!

④ I agree with you!

⑤ Me, too!

02 According to the dialogue, which one is NOT true?

① Jimin thinks her mom will love the phone case.

② The boy didn't know the phone case works as a wallet, too.

③ Jimin thinks the phone case is too expensive.

④ The boy agrees to buy the phone case as a birthday present for his mother.

⑤ The boy is delighted to buy something special for his mom.

[03~04] 다음 대화를 읽고 물음에 답하시오.

G: Hey, Minjun. What a surprise!

B: Hi, Sora. I'm ____ (A) ____ we're in the same class.

G: I am, too. We're now in our last year in middle school. How do you feel?

B: I'm a little worried that there'll be more schoolwork.

G: ____ (B) ____ , too. We also have to think about our high school.

B: Which kind of school do you have in mind?

G: I'm thinking of an animation high school. I love painting.

03 빈칸 (A)에 들어갈 가장 알맞은 말을 고르시오.

① worried   ② glad   ③ tired

④ nervous   ⑤ sad

서답형

04 빈칸 (B)에 알맞은 말을 쓰시오.

➡ _____

05 다음 대화의 빈칸에 들어갈 말로 알맞은 것은?

> **A:** I'm really worried I can't find my student card.
>
> **B:** You can make another one. Don't _____ it so hard.

① leave   ② play   ③ take

④ wear   ⑤ enjoy

06 다음 대화의 빈칸에 들어갈 말로 알맞은 것은?

> G: I'm worried I may make a mistake.
> B: I'm sure you'll do well. Break a _____!
> G: Thanks.

① stick   ② leg   ③ dish
④ waist   ⑤ chair

[07~08] 다음 대화의 순서가 바르게 배열된 것을 고르시오.

07

> A: Did you hear the weather report?
> (A) Yes. It's going to rain all day long.
> (B) Good for you.
> (C) Really? I'm glad I can wear my new raincoat.

① (A) – (C) – (B)   ② (B) – (A) – (C)
③ (B) – (C) – (A)   ④ (C) – (A) – (B)
⑤ (C) – (B) – (A)

08

> B: Hi, Sora. I'm glad we're in the same class.
> G: I am, too. We're now in our last year in middle school. How do you feel?
> B: I'm a little worried that there'll be more schoolwork.
> (A) Which kind of school do you have in mind?
> (B) Me, too. We also have to think about our high school.
> (C) I'm thinking of an animation high school. I love painting.

① (A) – (C) – (B)   ② (B) – (A) – (C)
③ (B) – (C) – (A)   ④ (C) – (A) – (B)
⑤ (C) – (B) – (A)

09 다음 짝지어진 대화가 <u>어색한</u> 것을 고르시오.

① A: I love cheese pizza.
    B: Me, too.
② A: I think history is an interesting subject.
    B: I think so, too.
③ A: That man looks just like Ben.
    B: You can say that again.
④ A: What is the greatest invention in history?
    B: I'd say the clock. We can't tell the time without it.
⑤ A: Did you hear the weather report?
    B: No. It's going to rain all day long.

서답형

10 다음 대화의 빈칸에 들어갈 말을 <보기>에서 골라 순서대로 배열하시오.

> G: Oliver, what club are you going to join?
> B: I'm not sure. How about you, Sora?
> G: I want to join the school dance club.
> B: _____
> G: _____
> B: _____
> G: _____
> B: _____

┌─── 보기 ───┐

(A) Why don't you join me? It'll be fun.
(B) No, thanks. Dancing is not for me. I have two left feet.
(C) Really? But I heard you're preparing for an animation high school.
(D) You can say that again.
(E) Right, but I need some time to relax. We all need to do something to get over stress.

➡ _____

[01~02] 다음 대화의 빈칸에 들어갈 말로 알맞은 말을 한 단어로 쓰시오.

01

A: I think I have _____ to eat a snack.
B: I don't agree. You must hurry to go back.

➡ _____

02

B: Hi, Sora. I'm glad we're in the same class.
G: I am, too. We're now in our last year in middle school. How do you feel?
B: I'm a little _____ that there'll be more schoolwork.
G: Me, too. We also have to think about our high school.

➡ _____

[03~05] 다음 대화를 읽고 물음에 답하시오.

B: You look so serious. __(A)__'s going on?
G: Oh, I'm just practicing for the school play tomorrow.
B: How do you feel about it?
G: I'm worried I may make a __(B)__.
B: I'm sure you'll do well. (C)행운을 빌어!
G: Thanks.

03 빈칸 (A)에 알맞은 의문사를 쓰시오.

➡ _____

04 내용상 빈칸 (B)에 들어가기에 적절한 한 단어를 주어진 철자로 시작하여 쓰시오.

➡ m_____

05 밑줄 친 (C)의 우리말을 괄호 안의 단어를 포함하여 영작하시오.

➡ _____ (leg)

[06~07] 다음 대화를 읽고 물음에 답하시오.

G: Have you heard about Mr. Oh?
B: No. What about him?
G: He __(A)__ first prize in the TV quiz show.
B: It's not surprising. He seems to know about everything.
G: You can say that again! (B)그는 만물박사야.

06 내용상 위 대화의 (A)에 들어가기에 적절한 한 단어를 쓰시오.

➡ _____

07 위 대화의 밑줄 친 (B)의 우리말에 어울리는 영어 문장을 완성하시오. (dictionary 포함)

➡ _____

08 다음 밑줄 친 우리말을 영작하시오. (don't really 포함)

A: What is the greatest invention in history?
B: I'd say the clock. We can't tell the time without it.
C: 나는 동의할 수 없어. I think the cell phone is the greatest invention.

➡ _____

Grammar

교과서

① 관계대명사 what

• They didn't tell me **what** she wanted to know.
그들은 그녀가 알기를 원하는 것을 내게 말하지 않았다.

■ 형태: what+주어+동사

의미: ~하는 것

■ 관계대명사 what은 선행사를 포함한 관계대명사로 형용사절이 아니라 명사절을 유도한다. 선행사가 별
도로 없기 때문에 해석할 때는 '~하는 것' 등으로 해석한다.

• what I saw 내가 본 것

• what she heard 그녀가 들은 것

• I want to read **what** she wrote. (what she wrote는 동사 read의 목적어)

• She told me **what** she had heard at the meeting. (what she had heard ~는 동사 told의 직접목적어)

■ 명사절을 유도하는 관계대명사 what은 명사절 속에서 주어나 목적어 역할을 한다.

• He picked up **what** was on the table. (관계대명사 what은 동사 was의 주어 역할을 하는 주격이다.)

• He doesn't like **what** she sent to him. (관계대명사 what은 동사 sent의 목적어 역할을 하는 목적격이다.)

관계대명사 what이 포함된 관용적인 표현

• what one has (사람이) 가진 것, 그의 재산

• what one is 현재의 그 사람 (사람 됨됨이, 인격)

• what one was 과거의 그 사람

• what is better 더욱 좋은 것은

• what is worse 더욱 나쁜 것은

핵심 Check

1. 다음 주어진 문장에서 적절한 것을 고르시오.

(1) He didn't show me (that / what) she had brought.

(2) I don't understand (that / what) he said.

(3) (That / What) he had painted made us surprised.

(4) He didn't read the message (that / what) she had sent to him.

(5) Did you see (that / what) he had put on the table?

❷ 지각동사의 목적격보어 – 원형부정사

> • I **saw** Mom **come** into my room. 나는 엄마가 방에 들어오시는 것을 보았다.

■ 형태: 지각동사+목적어+동사원형

의미: ~가 …하는 것을 보다/듣다/느끼다

■ allow, ask, cause 등의 동사 뒤에서 목적어의 행위를 설명하는 목적격보어를 쓸 때는 to부정사를 쓰지만, see, watch, notice, hear, listen to, feel 등의 지각동사는 목적어의 행위를 나타내는 목적격보어로 부정사를 쓸 때는 to가 없는 원형부정사를 쓴다.

  • We **saw** him **move** the table. 우리는 그가 테이블을 옮기는 것을 보았다.

  • She **heard** the baby **cry** in the room. 그녀는 아기가 방에서 우는 것을 들었다.

  • He **felt** someone **touch** his shoulder. 그는 누군가가 그의 어깨를 만지는 것을 느꼈다.

  • She **listened to** someone **open** the door. 그녀는 누가 문을 여는 것을 들었다.

  cf. She **allowed** us **to watch** TV. 그녀는 우리가 TV를 보는 것을 허락했다.

■ 지각동사의 목적격보어로 원형부정사를 쓰지만, 목적어의 행위가 진행 중임을 강조할 때는 현재분사를 쓰기도 한다.

  • I **saw** them **playing** on the ground. 나는 그들이 운동장에서 놀고 있는 것을 보았다.

  • We **heard** her **singing** in the room. 우리는 그녀가 방에서 노래하고 있는 것을 들었다.

  • I **noticed** him **turning** on the TV. 나는 그가 TV를 켜는 것을 보았다.

핵심 Check

2. 다음 주어진 문장에 어울리는 것을 고르시오.

  (1) Mary watched the artist (to draw / draw) a picture.

  (2) They watched the sun (to set / set) in the west.

  (3) He saw the sun (to rise / rising) in the east.

  (4) She felt a drop of water (to fall / falling) on the head.

  (5) I watched her (to make / making) some food.

  (6) She allowed us (to go / going) out for a walk.

  (7) He advised them (to take / take) some rest.

  (8) I saw the dog (to run / running) in the garden.

  (9) She was listening to the rain (to fall / falling) on the roof.

  (10) Mary heard him (to fall / fall) on the stairs.

01 다음 빈칸에 들어갈 알맞은 것은?

> Did you tell him _____ you had heard?

① that   ② which   ③ what
④ about what   ⑤ who

02 다음 중 밑줄 친 부분의 쓰임이 <u>어색한</u> 것을 고르시오.

① I asked him move the bag.
② She heard him call her name.
③ I didn't allow him to go out.
④ He saw the dog run out of the room.
⑤ I felt him touch my back.

03 다음 우리말에 맞게 괄호 안에 주어진 어휘를 바르게 배열하시오. (필요하면 어형을 바꿀 것)

(1) 그는 시장에서 많은 사람들이 소리 지르는 것을 들었다. (many people, at the market, hear, shout, he)

➡ _____

(2) 유나는 그들이 운동장에서 놀고 있는 것을 보았다. (Yuna, on the ground, see, play, they)

➡ _____

04 다음 빈칸에 들어갈 말로 알맞은 것은?

> When I opened the door, I found _____ he had sent to me.

① that   ② which   ③ what
④ about what   ⑤ who

05 다음 빈칸에 들어가기에 적절한 것으로 짝지어진 것은?

> She listened to them _____ the violin.

① to play – play   ② to play – playing
③ play – playing   ④ playing – played
⑤ have played – to play

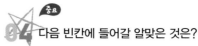
01 다음 중 밑줄 친 부분의 쓰임이 나머지 넷과 다른 것은?

① I saw them <u>climb</u> the tree to catch a bird.
② I can't allow you <u>to behave</u> like that.
③ I went to the place <u>to meet</u> my friends.
④ We heard him <u>get</u> out of the room to catch the bus.
⑤ He felt her <u>push</u> his back in the crowded bus.

02 다음 주어진 문장의 빈칸에 들어가기에 어색한 것은?

He _____ her to come early after the class.

① told
② asked
③ saw
④ expected
⑤ wanted

03 빈칸에 들어갈 말을 순서대로 바르게 연결한 것은?

• She told them _____ quiet in the class.
• They advised him _____ some rest after the work.
• We saw him _____ some rest after he finished the work.

① be　 – take　 – take
② be　 – to take – take
③ to be – to take – take
④ to be – take　 – to take
⑤ be　 – to take – to take

04 다음 빈칸에 들어갈 알맞은 것은?

Did you hear anyone _____ you?

① to call
② called
③ call
④ have called
⑤ being called

05 다음 중 밑줄 친 부분의 쓰임이 어색한 것을 고르시오.

① I found <u>what</u> he had lost.
② She knew <u>what</u> he wanted to buy.
③ She knew <u>that</u> he was busy.
④ She told me <u>that</u> she wanted.
⑤ We understand <u>what</u> he said.

06 다음 빈칸에 들어갈 말이 바르게 짝지어진 것은?

• John heard a man _____ about the picture.
• I saw John _____ in the living room.

① talking – dancing
② to talk – dancing
③ talked – danced
④ talking – to dance
⑤ talk – to dance

07 다음 중 어법상 어색한 문장을 고르시오.

① We expect him to send the letter on his way to school.
② His mother told him to study law at the college.
③ He saw them to walk on the street this afternoon.
④ I heard the phone ringing in the room.
⑤ They watched us play after the class.

서답형

08 다음 괄호 안에서 알맞은 말을 고르시오.

(1) He doesn't like the gift (that / what) she gave him.

(2) She was pleased with (that / what) he had given her.

(3) (That / What) made me pleased was his kindness.

(4) We heard him (to play / play) the piano.

(5) They saw the students (to run / running) across the road.

서답형

09 다음 우리말에 맞게 괄호 안에 주어진 어휘를 바르게 배열하시오.

(1) 그는 내가 설명하는 것을 이해하지 못했다. (didn't, what, he, understand, explained, I)

　➡ _____

(2) 그녀는 내가 그녀에게 사준 것을 좋아하지 않았다. (didn't, like, had bought, I, for her, what, she)

　➡ _____

(3) 그는 그가 그린 것을 나에게 보여주었다. (he, he, me, showed, had painted, what)

　➡ _____

(4) 나는 그녀가 방에서 우는 것을 들었다. (I, her, in the room, cry, heard)

　➡ _____

(5) 우리는 그가 제시간에 오기를 기대한다. (we, him, to, expect, come, on time)

　➡ _____

 10 빈칸에 들어갈 말을 순서대로 바르게 연결한 것은?

> • They are constructing the building _____ is the tallest in the city.
> • He is now trying to make _____ I asked him to make for my brother's birthday party.

① that – that
② that – which
③ that – what
④ what – that
⑤ what – which

11 다음 중 어법상 틀린 문장을 모두 고르면? (정답 3개)

① He watched some people live in tents.
② Can you smell something burning?
③ She felt someone touches her arm.
④ I saw your sister takes the subway.
⑤ I could hear her to sing her favorite song.

 12 다음 우리말을 영어로 바르게 옮긴 것은?

> 중요한 것은 너의 계획이다.

① What is important is you planned.
② That is important is your plan.
③ What is important is your plan.
④ Your plan is that is important
⑤ Your plan is the thing what is important.

13 빈칸에 들어갈 말을 순서대로 바르게 연결한 것은?

• His father listened to him _____ on the phone.

• The teacher told him _____ to school on time.

① to talk – to come
② talk – to come
③ talking – come
④ talking – came
⑤ talk – coming

14 다음 우리말을 영어로 바르게 옮긴 것은?

나는 그가 말하는 것을 이해했다.

① I understood that he said.
② I understood what he said.
③ I understood which he was saying.
④ I understood what he said it.
⑤ I understood the thing what he said.

15 다음 중 밑줄 친 부분의 쓰임이 어색한 것을 고르시오.

① We expect the weather to be fine.
② He saw her prepare dinner.
③ I heard him open the case.
④ He told her to send the letter.
⑤ She ordered them get up early.

16 다음 중 어법상 어색한 문장을 고르시오.

① I saw the car that he was driving.
② She knew the boy that I was talking about.
③ That is the most important is your choice.
④ He is reading the book that I gave him.
⑤ Jenny lives in the house that her grandfather built.

17 다음 빈칸에 들어갈 수 있는 말이 다른 것을 두 개 고르시오.

① I cannot find _____ he gave me.
② She showed me the photos _____ she had taken.
③ We need to pay attention to _____ she is saying.
④ She read the message _____ he had sent to her.
⑤ I have something _____ I want to tell you.

서답형

18 주어진 어휘를 이용하여 다음 우리말을 영어로 쓰시오.

우리는 인사동에서 우리가 즐길 수 있는 것을 발견했다. (find, enjoy)

➡ _____ in Insa-dong

19 다음 중 밑줄 친 부분의 쓰임이 어색한 것을 고르시오.

① He allowed them to play in the room.
② She asked me to leave the room.
③ She saw them enter the room.
④ I heard him to sing a song.
⑤ He felt her touch his hand.

20 다음 빈칸에 들어갈 말로 알맞은 것은?

She won't tell me _____ you talked about the accident.

① what   ② which
③ who   ④ that
⑤ how

01 다음 우리말에 맞게 괄호 안에 주어진 어휘를 바르게 배열하시오. (필요한 어휘 변형 및 추가 가능)

(1) 나를 놀라게 한 것은 그의 불친절한 대답이었다. (I, he, answer, rude, be, what, surprised)

➡ _____

(2) 그는 학교에서 들은 것을 나에게 말했다. (told, had heard, he, I, what, at school)

➡ _____

(3) 너는 네가 말하는 것에 책임을 져야 한다. (you, you, have to, are saying, responsible for, what)

➡ _____

(4) 우리는 지난여름에 그가 집을 짓는 것을 보았다. (we, he, saw, the house, build, last summer)

➡ _____

(5) 그녀는 나에게 문을 열어 달라고 요청했다. (she, me, asked, open the door)

➡ _____

(6) 그녀는 우리가 집 밖으로 나가는 소리를 들었다. (hear, go, she, out of the house, us)

➡ _____

(7) 우리는 그가 우리에게 가지고 온 것을 너에게 줄 것이다. (will give, bring, what, we, you, to us)

➡ _____

02 다음 문장에서 잘못된 부분을 바르게 고쳐, 전체 문장을 다시 쓰시오.

(1) I heard him to talk on the phone.

➡ _____

(2) She felt the man to pull her by the hand.

➡ _____

(3) They expected him being quiet during the class.

➡ _____
_____

(4) That is important is to finish the work before dinner.

➡ _____
_____

03 다음 중 어법상 어색한 문장 2개를 골라 번호를 쓰고, 올바른 형태로 고쳐서 다시 쓰시오.

ⓐ I can hear the bell ring.
ⓑ I feel my body getting cold.
ⓒ She heard the child cries.
ⓓ He hears the students laughing.
ⓔ They saw he wearing that hat.

번호　　　　올바르게 고친 문장
(1) _____ ➡ _____
(2) _____ ➡ _____

04 다음 우리말을 관계대명사 what과 함께 괄호 안에 주어진 단어를 사용하여 영작하시오.

그는 나에게 내가 가진 것에 만족하라고 조언했다.
(advise / be satisfied with)

➡ He _____.

05 다음 우리말과 같은 의미가 되도록 괄호 안의 단어를 이용하여 5단어로 영작하시오.

그녀는 그들이 축구하고 있는 것을 보았다.
(watch)

➡ _____

06 다음 〈보기〉에서 빈칸에 들어가기에 적절한 말을 골라 쓰시오. (필요한 경우 단어 추가)

┌─ 보기 ─┐
what   that   exercise   walk   drawing
└────────┘

(1) Mary watched the artist _____ the picture.

(2) What do you think about _____ she said?

(3) Will you move the bag _____ is on the chair?

(4) Did you advise him _____ every day?

(5) Who heard the boy _____ up the stairs?

07 〈보기〉를 참고하여 주어진 두 문장을 부정사를 이용하여 한 문장으로 연결하여 쓰시오.

┌─ 보기 ─┐
• My sister sang a song at the party.
• I heard her.
➡ I heard my sister sing a song at the party.
└────────┘

(1) • He stopped at the traffic light.
  • I watched it.
  ➡ _____

(2) • He was swimming in the pool.
  • When I turned my head, I saw it.
  ➡ When I turned my head, _____.

(3) • He laughed loudly at the table.
  • My mother heard him.
  ➡ _____

(4) • She pushed me on the back.
  • I felt it.
  ➡ _____

(5) • He was pulling my hand.
  • I felt it.
  ➡ _____

08 다음 주어진 단어를 적절하게 배열하여 주어진 문장을 완성하시오.

(1) Mary _____ in the kitchen. (her brother / cook / watched)

(2) He wants to _____. (she / eat / what / cooked)

(3) James _____. (his mother / open / heard / the window)

(4) He told me to _____. (what / had sent / read / she / to me)

09 다음 문장에 공통으로 들어가기에 적절한 한 단어를 쓰시오.

┌─────────────────────────┐
• Would you tell me _____ you have in mind?
• She showed me _____ she had bought.
└─────────────────────────┘

➡ _____

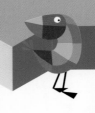
A Priceless Gift

Long ago, an honest merchant lived in Genoa, Italy. His name
　　　　　　　　　　　　　　　　　　　　좁은 장소+넓은 장소

was Antonio, and he went to different places to support his family
　　　　　　　　　　　　　　　　　　　　　부사적 용법(목적)

by trading. One day, he filled his ship with goods and visited a faraway
by ~ing(전치사+동명사): ~함으로써　　　fill A with B: A를 B로 채우다　상품

island. There he traded tools for spices and books for nuts. Thanks to
　　　　trade A for B: A와 B를 교환하다　　　　　　　　~ 덕분에(= because of, owing to, due to)

Antonio, the islanders could get what they needed.
　　　　　　　　　　　　　　= the things which

One night, Antonio had dinner with the island's queen at her
　　　　　　　　had a dinner(×)

palace. When dinner was served, rats appeared, and some servants
　　　　　　　served(×)　　　were appeared(×): appear는 수동태로 쓸 수 없다.

chased them away with sticks.
chased away them(×): 이어동사에서 목적어가 인칭대명사일 때는 목적어를 동사와 부사 사이에 써야 함.

Antonio was greatly surprised that there were rats in the palace.
　　　　　　　형용사 surprised 수식　　　이유를 나타내는 부사절을 이끄는 접속사

He asked, "Are there no cats on this island?" The queen looked
　　　　　　　　　　　　　　　　　　　　　look+형용사: ~하게 보이다

puzzled. "What is a cat?" she asked.
감정을 나타내는 동사는 사람을 수식할 때 보통 과거분사를 사용

honest 정직한	
merchant 상인	
different 다른	
support 부양하다, 지원하다	
trade 교역, 교역하다	
faraway 멀리 떨어진	
tool 도구, 공구	
spice 향신료	
islander 섬사람	
appear 나타나다	
servant 하인	
stick 막대기	
puzzled 당황한, 어리둥절한	

확인문제

● 다음 문장이 본문의 내용과 일치하면 T, 일치하지 <u>않으면</u> F를 쓰시오.

1 Antonio was an honest merchant who lived in Genoa, Italy. ☐

2 Antonio traded tools for spices and books for nuts in his village. ☐

3 Thanks to Antonio, the islanders could get what they needed. ☐

4 When Antonio had dinner with some servants, rats appeared. ☐

5 Antonio was surprised that there were rats in the palace. ☐

6 The queen knew what a cat was. ☐

The merchant said to himself, "What the islanders here need is
주어와 목적어가 같을 때는 재귀대명사를 쓴다.

not tools or books, but cats." He brought two cats from his ship and
not A but B: A가 아니라 B

let them run free. "What amazing animals!" cried the queen when she
사역동사 let+목적어+원형부정사   *= How amazing the animals are!*

saw all the rats run away. She gave Antonio a chest that was filled with
지각동사 saw+목적어+원형부정사(running도 가능함)   *주격 관계대명사*   *be filled with = be full of: ~로 가득 차다*

jewels.

Back in Italy, Antonio told his friends about his good fortune.
= (When he came) Back in Italy

Luigi, the richest merchant in Genoa, heard the story and was jealous.
동격   *= envious*

"Cats are worthless," Luigi thought. "I'll bring the queen what is really
= valueless   *= the thing which*

valuable. I'm sure that the queen will give me more jewels."
= It is certain

Luigi packed his ship with wonderful paintings and other works of
pack A with B: A를 B로 가득 채우다   *(문학·예술 따위의) 작품, 저작물, 제작품*

art. He took the gifts to the island. To get a chance to meet the queen,
부사적 용법(목적)   *형용사적 용법*

he told the islanders a lie that he was a good friend of Antonio's. When
동격의 접속사   *한정사(관사/소유격/지시형용사)끼리 중복해서 쓸 수 없으므로 이중소유격(of+소유대명사/~'s) 사용*

the queen heard about Luigi, she invited him to her palace for dinner.

Before sitting down at the table, Luigi presented the queen with all his
= Before he sat   *present+사람+with+사물= present+사물+to+사람*

gifts, and the queen thanked him again and again. "I'll repay you with
= over and over

a priceless gift," said the queen.
값진

---

run free 마음대로 돌아다니다
run away 달아나다
chest 상자
jewel 보석
fortune 행운, 재산
jealous 질투하는, 시샘하는
worthless 가치 없는, 쓸모없는
valuable 가치 있는, 귀중한, 소중한
pack 짐을 싸다
gift 선물
present 주다, 제시하다
again and again 여러 번, 반복하여
reply 보답하다, (돈을) 갚다

📎 확인문제

● 다음 문장이 본문의 내용과 일치하면 T, 일치하지 않으면 F를 쓰시오.

1 The islanders didn't need tools or books. ☐

2 The queen gave Antonio a chest that was filled with jewels. ☐

3 Luigi was the richest merchant in Genoa. ☐

4 Luigi thought that cats were priceless. ☐

5 Luigi packed his ship with wonderful paintings and other works of art. ☐

6 Luigi was a good friend of Antonio's. ☐

Luigi watched the queen whisper in a servant's ear. He became
_{지각동사 watched+목적어+원형부정사(whispering도 가능함)}

excited and hopeful. He was sure that he would receive more jewels
_{감정을 나타내는 동사는 사람을 수식할 때 보통 과거분사를 사용}

than Antonio.

After a while, the servant returned with a box, and the queen
_{잠시 후에}

presented it to Luigi. When Luigi opened the box, he was speechless.
_{present+사물+to+사람 = present+사람+with+사물}   _{speechless: (특히 너무 화가 나거나 놀라서) 말을 못하는}

There was a kitten in the box. "Antonio gave us the priceless
_{→ (3형식) Antonio gave the priceless cats to us}

cats, and we now have some kittens," said the queen. "In return
_{in return for: ~의 답례로}

for the wonderful gifts you gave us, we want to give you what is
_{= that you gave us}   _{the thing which}

most valuable to us."
_{valuable의 최상급}

Luigi realized that, in the queen's mind, the kitten was worth

far more than all the jewels in the world. He tried to look pleased with
_{= much. even. still. a lot: 비교급 강조(훨씬)}   _{감정을 나타내는 동사는 사람을 수식할 때 보통 과거분사를 사용}

the gift. He knew that was the right thing to do.
_{to look pleased with the gift}   _{형용사적 용법}

Luigi did not return home a richer man. But he was surely a wiser
_{= When Luigi returned home. he was not a richer man.}

one.
_{= man}

---

whisper 속삭이다. 귓속말을 하다

hopeful 희망에 찬

receive 받다

speechless 말이 안 나오는, 말을 못하는

kitten 새끼 고양이

worth ~의 가치가 있는

pleased 기뻐하는, 만족한

valuable 귀중한

right 옳은

surely 확실히, 분명히

📎 **확인문제**

● 다음 문장이 본문의 내용과 일치하면 T, 일치하지 않으면 F를 쓰시오.

1 Luigi was sure that he would receive more jewels than Antonio. ☐

2 When Luigi opened the box that the queen presented to him, he was satisfied. ☐

3 There was the gift that Luigi expected to receive in the box. ☐

4 Luigi realized that, in the queen's mind, the kitten was worth far more than all the jewels in the world. ☐

5 Luigi tried to look pleased with the gift. ☐

6 Luigi did not become a wise man. ☐

• 우리말을 참고하여 빈칸에 알맞은 말을 쓰시오.

1 A _____ Gift

2 Long ago, _____ _____ _____ lived in Genoa, Italy.

3 His name was Antonio, and he went to different places _____ _____ _____ _____ by trading.

4 One day, he _____ his ship _____ goods and visited a faraway island.

5 There he _____ tools _____ spices and books _____ nuts.

6 _____ _____ Antonio, the islanders could get _____ they needed.

7 One night, Antonio _____ _____ _____ the island's queen at her palace.

8 When dinner _____ _____, rats _____, and some servants _____ _____ _____ with sticks.

9 Antonio was _____ _____ that there were rats in the palace.

10 He asked, "_____ _____ _____ _____ _____ on this island?"

11 The queen _____ _____.

12 "What is a cat?" _____ _____.

13 The merchant _____ _____ _____, "_____ the islanders here need is _____ tools or books, _____ cats."

14 He _____ two cats _____ his ship and _____ _____ _____ free.

15 "_____ amazing animals!" cried the queen when she saw all the rats _____ away.

16 She gave Antonio a chest that _____ _____ _____ jewels.

17 _____ in Italy, Antonio told his friends about his _____ _____.

18 Luigi, _____ _____ _____ in Genoa, heard the story and was _____.

19 "Cats are _____," Luigi thought.

20 "I'll bring the queen _____ is really valuable.

1 소중한 선물

2 먼 옛날 이탈리아 제노바에 정직한 상인 한 명이 살았다.

3 그의 이름은 Antonio로, 그는 교역으로 가족을 부양하기 위해 여러 곳을 다녔다.

4 어느 날 그는 배에 상품을 가득 싣고 머나먼 섬으로 갔다.

5 거기서 그는 공구를 향신료와 바꾸었고, 책을 견과류와 바꾸었다.

6 Antonio 덕에 섬사람들은 필요한 것을 얻을 수 있었다.

7 어느 날 밤, Antonio는 궁전에서 그 섬의 여왕과 저녁 식사를 했다.

8 식사가 나왔을 때 쥐들이 나타났고, 하인 몇 명이 막대기로 쥐를 쫓아내었다.

9 Antonio는 궁전에 쥐가 있다는 사실에 무척 놀랐다.

10 그는 "이 섬에는 고양이가 없습니까?"라고 물었다.

11 여왕은 어리둥절한 것처럼 보였다.

12 "고양이가 뭔가요?"라고 그녀가 물었다.

13 상인은 "여기 섬사람들이 필요로 하는 것은 공구나 책이 아니라 고양이야."라고 혼자 중얼거렸다.

14 그는 배에서 고양이 두 마리를 데리고 와서, 자유롭게 돌아다니도록 풀어놓았다.

15 "정말 놀라운 동물이네요!" 쥐가 모두 도망가는 것을 보자 여왕이 감탄하였다.

16 그녀는 Antonio에게 보석이 가득한 상자를 주었다.

17 이탈리아로 돌아와서, Antonio는 자신에게 일어난 행운을 친구들에게 이야기했다.

18 제노바에서 가장 부유한 상인인 Luigi는 그 이야기를 듣고 시샘이 일었다.

19 "고양이는 쓸모없어." Luigi가 생각했다.

20 "난 여왕에게 정말로 귀중한 것을 가지고 갈 거야.

21 _____ _____ that the queen will give me more jewels."

22 Luigi _____ his ship _____ wonderful paintings and other _____ of art.

23 He _____ the gifts _____ the island.

24 To get a chance to meet the queen, he told the islanders a lie that he was _____ _____ _____ _____ _____.

25 When the queen heard about Luigi, she _____ him _____ her palace for dinner.

26 Before _____ down at the table, Luigi _____ the queen _____ all his gifts, and the queen thanked him _____ _____ _____.

27 "I'll _____ you _____ a priceless gift," said the queen.

28 Luigi watched the queen _____ in a servant's ear.

29 He became _____ and _____.

30 He was sure that he would receive _____ _____ _____ Antonio.

31 After a while, the servant returned with a box, and the queen _____ it _____ Luigi.

32 When Luigi opened the box, he was _____.

33 There was a _____ in the box.

34 "Antonio gave us the _____ cats, and we now have some kittens," said the queen.

35 "_____ _____ _____ the wonderful gifts you gave us, we want to give you _____ _____ _____ _____ to us."

36 Luigi realized that, in the queen's mind, the kitten was worth _____ _____ _____ all the jewels in the world.

37 He tried to _____ _____ with the gift.

38 He knew that was the _____ _____ _____ _____.

39 Luigi did not return home a _____ man.

40 But he was surely _____ _____ _____.

21 틀림없이 여왕이 내게 더 많은 보석을 줄 거야."

22 Luigi는 멋진 그림들과 다른 예술 작품을 배에 실었다.

23 그는 선물을 섬으로 가지고 갔다.

24 여왕을 만날 기회를 얻기 위해서, 그는 자신이 Antonio의 친한 친구라고 섬사람들에게 거짓말을 했다.

25 Luigi에 관해 듣고, 여왕은 그를 궁전으로 저녁 식사에 초대했다.

26 식탁에 앉기 전에 Luigi는 여왕에게 자신이 가져온 온갖 선물을 전했고, 여왕은 그에게 여러 차례 감사하다고 했다.

27 "당신께 값진 선물로 보답하겠습니다."라고 여왕이 말했다.

28 Luigi는 여왕이 하인의 귀에 대고 속삭이는 것을 지켜보았다.

29 그는 흥분되고 기대에 부풀었다.

30 그는 Antonio보다 많은 보석을 받게 될 거라고 확신했다.

31 잠시 후에 하인이 상자 하나를 가지고 돌아왔고, 여왕은 그것을 Luigi에게 주었다.

32 상자를 열어본 Luigi는 말문이 막혔다.

33 상자 안에는 새끼 고양이가 한 마리가 들어 있었다.

34 "Antonio가 우리에게 매우 귀한 고양이들을 줬는데, 이제 새끼 고양이 몇 마리가 생겼어요."라고 여왕이 말했다.

35 "당신이 우리에게 준 멋진 선물에 보답하는 뜻에서, 우리에게 가장 값진 것을 당신에게 드리고 싶어요."

36 여왕의 생각에는 세상의 온갖 보석보다 새끼 고양이가 훨씬 더 가치 있다는 것을 Luigi는 깨달았다.

37 그는 선물에 대해 기뻐하는 표정을 지으려고 애썼다.

38 그게 올바른 행동이라는 것을 그는 알았다.

39 Luigi는 더 부유한 사람이 되어 집으로 돌아오지는 않았다.

40 하지만 그는 분명히 더 현명한 사람이 되었다.

우리말을 참고하여 본문을 영작하시오.

1 소중한 선물
➡ _____

2 먼 옛날 이탈리아 제노바에 정직한 상인 한 명이 살았다.
➡ _____

3 그의 이름은 Antonio로, 그는 교역으로 가족을 부양하기 위해 여러 곳을 다녔다.
➡ _____

4 어느 날 그는 배에 상품을 가득 싣고 머나먼 섬으로 갔다.
➡ _____

5 거기서 그는 공구를 향신료와 바꾸었고, 책을 견과류와 바꾸었다.
➡ _____

6 Antonio 덕에 섬사람들은 필요한 것을 얻을 수 있었다.
➡ _____

7 어느 날 밤, Antonio는 궁전에서 그 섬의 여왕과 저녁 식사를 했다.
➡ _____

8 식사가 나왔을 때 쥐들이 나타났고, 하인 몇 명이 막대기로 쥐를 쫓아내었다.
➡ _____

9 Antonio는 궁전에 쥐가 있다는 사실에 무척 놀랐다.
➡ _____

10 그는 "이 섬에는 고양이가 없습니까?"라고 물었다.
➡ _____

11 여왕은 어리둥절한 것처럼 보였다.
➡ _____

12 "고양이가 뭔가요?"라고 그녀가 물었다.
➡ _____

13 상인은 "여기 섬사람들이 필요로 하는 것은 공구나 책이 아니라 고양이야."라고 혼자 중얼거렸다.
➡ _____

14 그는 배에서 고양이 두 마리를 데리고 와서, 자유롭게 돌아다니도록 풀어놓았다.
➡ _____

15 "정말 놀라운 동물이네요!" 쥐가 모두 도망가는 것을 보자 여왕이 감탄하였다.
➡ _____

16 그녀는 Antonio에게 보석이 가득한 상자를 주었다.
➡ _____

17 이탈리아로 돌아와서, Antonio는 자신에게 일어난 행운을 친구들에게 이야기했다.
➡ _____

18 제노바에서 가장 부유한 상인인 Luigi는 그 이야기를 듣고 시샘이 일었다.
➡ _____

19 "고양이는 쓸모없어." Luigi가 생각했다.
➡ _____

20 "난 여왕에게 정말로 귀중한 것을 가지고 갈 거야.
➡ _____

21 틀림없이 여왕이 내게 더 많은 보석을 줄 거야."
➡ _____

22 Luigi는 멋진 그림들과 다른 예술 작품을 배에 실었다.
➡ _____

23 그는 선물을 섬으로 가지고 갔다.
➡ _____

24 여왕을 만날 기회를 얻기 위해서, 그는 자신이 Antonio의 친한 친구라고 섬사람들에게 거짓말을 했다.
➡ _____

25 Luigi에 관해 듣고, 여왕은 그를 궁전으로 저녁 식사에 초대했다.
➡ _____

26 식탁에 앉기 전에 Luigi는 여왕에게 자신이 가져온 온갖 선물을 전했고, 여왕은 그에게 여러 차례 감사하다고 했다.
➡ _____

27 "당신께 값진 선물로 보답하겠습니다."라고 여왕이 말했다.
➡ _____

28 Luigi는 여왕이 하인의 귀에 대고 속삭이는 것을 지켜보았다.
➡ _____

29 그는 흥분되고 기대에 부풀었다.
➡ _____

30 그는 Antonio보다 많은 보석을 받게 될 거라고 확신했다.
➡ _____

31 잠시 후에 하인이 상자 하나를 가지고 돌아왔고, 여왕은 그것을 Luigi에게 주었다.
➡ _____

32 상자를 열어본 Luigi는 말문이 막혔다.
➡ _____

33 상자 안에는 새끼 고양이 한 마리가 들어 있었다.
➡ _____

34 "Antonio가 우리에게 매우 귀한 고양이들을 줬는데, 이제 새끼 고양이 몇 마리가 생겼어요."라고 여왕이 말했다.
➡ _____

35 "당신이 우리에게 준 멋진 선물에 보답하는 뜻에서, 우리에게 가장 값진 것을 당신에게 드리고 싶어요."
➡ _____

36 여왕의 생각에는 세상의 온갖 보석보다 새끼 고양이가 훨씬 더 가치 있다는 것을 Luigi는 깨달았다.
➡ _____

37 그는 선물에 대해 기뻐하는 표정을 지으려고 애썼다.
➡ _____

38 그게 올바른 행동이라는 것을 그는 알았다.
➡ _____

39 Luigi는 더 부유한 사람이 되어 집으로 돌아오지는 않았다.
➡ _____

40 하지만 그는 분명히 더 현명한 사람이 되었다.
➡ _____

[01~03] 다음 글을 읽고 물음에 답하시오.

Long ago, an honest merchant lived in Genoa, Italy. His name was Antonio, and he went to different places (A)to support his family by trading. One day, he filled his ship ⓐ goods and visited a faraway island. There he traded tools ⓑ spices and books ⓑ nuts. Thanks to Antonio, the islanders could get what they needed.

One night, Antonio had dinner with the island's queen at her palace. When dinner was served, rats appeared, and some servants chased them away with sticks.

01 위 글의 빈칸 ⓐ와 ⓑ에 들어갈 전치사가 바르게 짝지어진 것은?

① of – from
② with – to
③ with – for
④ for – to
⑤ of – for

02 아래 〈보기〉에서 위 글의 밑줄 친 (A)to support와 to부정사의 용법이 같은 것의 개수를 고르시오.

┌─ 보기 ├─
① English is difficult to learn.
② He had the fortune to be born with a silver spoon in his mouth.
③ My ultimate goal is to become a great scientist.
④ He promised me to be here at ten o'clock.
⑤ This plan leaves nothing to be desired.

① 1개 ② 2개 ③ 3개 ④ 4개 ⑤ 5개

03 According to the passage, which is NOT true?

① Antonio was an honest merchant who lived in Genoa, Italy.
② Antonio supported his family by trading goods.
③ Antonio traded tools for spices and books for nuts.
④ Antonio had dinner with the island's queen at his ship.
⑤ Some servants chased rats away with sticks.

[04~05] 다음 글을 읽고 물음에 답하시오.

Antonio was greatly surprised that there were rats in the palace. He asked, "Are there no cats on this island?" The queen looked puzzled. "What is a cat?" she asked.

The merchant said to himself, "ⓐ the islanders here need is not tools or books, but cats." He brought two cats from his ship and let them run free. "ⓑ amazing animals!" cried the queen when she saw all the rats run away. She gave Antonio a chest that was filled with jewels.

서답형
04 위 글의 빈칸 ⓐ와 ⓑ에 공통으로 들어갈 알맞은 말을 쓰시오.

➡ _____

중요
05 위 글의 제목으로 알맞은 것을 고르시오.

① How Many Cats Do You Have?
② Rats in the Palace? How Wonderful!
③ How Lovely the Cats Are!
④ What They Really Need Are Cats!
⑤ The Queen Gave Antonio Jewels.

[06~08] 다음 글을 읽고 물음에 답하시오.

Back in Italy, Antonio told ①his friends about his good fortune. Luigi, the richest merchant in Genoa, heard the story and was jealous. "Cats are ⓐworthless," Luigi thought. "I'll bring the queen what is really valuable. I'm sure that the queen will give ② me more jewels."

Luigi packed his ship with wonderful paintings and other works of art. He took the gifts to the island. To get a chance to meet the queen, ③he told the islanders a lie that he was ⓑAntonio의 친한 친구. When the queen heard about Luigi, she invited ④him to her palace for dinner. Before sitting down at the table, Luigi presented the queen with all his gifts, and the queen thanked him again and again. "I'll repay ⑤you with a priceless gift," said the queen.

06 위 글의 밑줄 친 ①~⑤ 중에서 가리키는 대상이 나머지 넷과 <u>다른</u> 것은?

①   ②   ③   ④   ⑤

07 위 글의 밑줄 친 ⓐworthless와 바꿔 쓸 수 있는 말을 고르시오.

① priceless   ② invaluable
③ precious   ④ valuable
⑤ valueless

08 위 글의 밑줄 친 ⓑ의 우리말에 맞게 5단어로 영작하시오.

➡ _____

[09~11] 다음 글을 읽고 물음에 답하시오.

Luigi watched the queen whisper in a servant's ear. He became excited and hopeful. He was sure that he would receive more jewels than Antonio.

After a while, the servant returned with a box, and the queen presented it ___ⓐ___ Luigi. When Luigi opened the box, he was speechless.

There was a kitten in the box. "Antonio gave us the priceless cats, and we now have some kittens," said the queen. "In return for the wonderful gifts you gave us, we want to give you ⓑ우리에게 가장 값진 것."

09 위 글의 빈칸 ⓐ에 알맞은 것은?

① on   ② for   ③ to
④ at   ⑤ with

10 위 글의 밑줄 친 ⓑ의 우리말에 맞게 6단어로 영작하시오.

➡ _____

11 위 글을 읽고 알 수 <u>없는</u> 것을 고르시오.

① What present did Luigi expect?
② What present did the queen give to Luigi?
③ How did Luigi react when he saw the queen's present?
④ How many cats did Antonio give to the queen?
⑤ Why did the queen give such a present to Luigi?

[12~14] 다음 글을 읽고 물음에 답하시오.

Back in Italy, Antonio told his friends about his good fortune. Luigi, the richest merchant in Genoa, heard the story and was ①jealous. "Cats are worthless," Luigi thought. "I'll bring the queen (A)[who / what] is really valuable. I'm sure that the queen will give me more jewels."

Luigi ②packed his ship with wonderful paintings and (B)[other / another] works of art. He took the gifts to the island. To get ③a chance to meet the queen, he told the islanders a lie that he was a good friend of (C)[Antonio / Antonio's]. When the queen heard about Luigi, she ④invited him to her palace for dinner. Before sitting down at the table, Luigi presented the queen with all his gifts, and the queen thanked him ⑤again and again. "I'll repay you with a priceless gift," said the queen.

12 위 글의 괄호 (A)~(C)에서 어법상 알맞은 낱말을 골라 쓰시오.

➡ (A) _____ (B) _____ (C) _____

13 위 글의 밑줄 친 ①~⑤와 바꿔 쓸 수 있는 말로 옳지 않은 것을 고르시오.

① envious   ② filled
③ an opportunity   ④ visited
⑤ over and over

14 According to the passage, which is NOT true?

① Luigi was the richest merchant in Genoa.
② Luigi thought that cats were valueless.
③ Luigi was Antonio's good friend.
④ The queen invited Luigi to her palace for dinner.
⑤ Luigi presented all his gifts to the queen.

[15~17] 다음 글을 읽고 물음에 답하시오.

Luigi watched the queen whisper in a servant's ear. He became ____ⓐ____ and ____ⓑ____. He was sure that he would receive more jewels than Antonio.

After a while, the servant returned with a box, and the queen presented it to Luigi. When Luigi opened the box, he was speechless.

There was a kitten in the box. "Antonio gave us the priceless cats, and we now have some kittens," said the queen. "ⓒIn spite of the wonderful gifts you gave us, we want to give you what is most valuable to us."

15 위 글의 빈칸 ⓐ와 ⓑ에 들어갈 알맞은 말을 고르시오.

① nervous – upset
② excited – hopeful
③ excited – hopeless
④ upset – bored
⑤ disappointed – surprised

16 다음 질문에 대한 알맞은 대답을 주어진 단어로 시작하여 빈칸에 쓰시오. (7단어)

> Q: Why was Luigi speechless when he opened the box?
>
> A: Because _____
> instead of more jewels than Antonio had received.

17 위 글의 밑줄 친 ⓒ에서 흐름상 어색한 부분을 찾아 고치시오.

_____ ➡ _____

[18~20] 다음 글을 읽고 물음에 답하시오.

There was a kitten in the box. "Antonio gave us the priceless cats, and we now have some kittens," said the queen. "In return for the wonderful gifts you gave us, we want to give you (A)[that / what] is most valuable to us."

Luigi realized that, in the queen's mind, the kitten was worth far (B)[more / less] than all the jewels in the world. He tried to look (C)[pleasing / pleased] with the gift. He knew that was the right thing to do.

Luigi did not return home a richer man. But he was surely a wiser ___ⓐ___.

18 위 글의 빈칸 ⓐ에 들어갈 알맞은 대명사를 쓰시오.

➡ _____

19 위 글의 괄호 (A)~(C)에서 문맥이나 어법상 알맞은 낱말을 골라 쓰시오.

➡ (A) _____ (B) _____ (C) _____

20 Luigi에 대한 묘사로 가장 알맞은 것은?

① rude　　　　② thoughtful
③ brave　　　　④ lonely
⑤ humorous

[21~23] 다음 글을 읽고 물음에 답하시오.

Long ago, an honest merchant lived in Genoa, Italy. (①) His name was Antonio, and he went to different places to support his family by trading. (②) One day, he filled his ship with goods and visited a faraway island. (③) There he traded tools for spices and books for nuts. (④)

One night, Antonio had dinner with the island's queen at her palace. (⑤) When dinner ___ⓐ___, rats appeared, and some servants chased ⓑthem away with sticks.

21 위 글의 빈칸 ⓐ에 serve를 알맞은 형태로 쓰시오.

➡ _____

22 위 글의 흐름으로 보아, 주어진 문장이 들어가기에 가장 적절한 곳은?

> Thanks to Antonio, the islanders could get what they needed.

①　　　②　　　③　　　④　　　⑤

23 위 글의 밑줄 친 ⓑthem이 가리키는 것을 본문에서 찾아 쓰시오.

➡ _____

[24~26] 다음 글을 읽고 물음에 답하시오.

Antonio was greatly surprised that there were rats in the palace. He asked, "Are there no cats on this island?" The queen looked puzzled. "(A)What is a cat?" she asked.

The merchant said to himself, "(B)What the islanders here need is ___ⓐ___ tools or books, ___ⓑ___ cats." He brought two cats from his ship and let them run free. "(C)What amazing animals!" cried the queen when she saw all the rats run away. (D)She gave Antonio a chest that was filled with jewels.

24 위 글의 빈칸 ⓐ와 ⓑ에 들어갈 알맞은 말을 고르시오.

① either – or 　　② neither – nor
③ not – but 　　④ both – and
⑤ at once – and

25 위 글의 밑줄 친 (A)~(C)의 What과 문법적 쓰임이 같은 것을 모두 골라 쓰시오.

① That's not what I meant to say.
② What a fool you are!
③ What can I do for you?
④ What I said is true.
⑤ What a charming girl she is!
➡ (A)와 쓰임이 같은 것: _____ ,
　(B)와 쓰임이 같은 것: _____ ,
　(C)와 쓰임이 같은 것: _____

26 위 글의 밑줄 친 문장 (D)에서 생략할 수 있는 부분을 생략하고 문장을 다시 쓰시오.

➡ _____

[27~29] 다음 글을 읽고 물음에 답하시오.

There was a kitten in the box. "Antonio gave us the priceless cats, and we now have some kittens," said the queen. "In return for the wonderful gifts you gave us, we want to give you what is most valuable to us."

Luigi realized that, in the queen's mind, the kitten was worth (A)far more than all the jewels in the world. He tried to look pleased with the gift. He knew that was the right thing (B)to do.

Luigi did not return home a ___ⓐ___ man. But he was surely a ___ⓑ___ one.

27 위 글의 빈칸 ⓐ와 ⓑ에 들어갈 알맞은 말을 고르시오.

① richer – more foolish
② poorer – wiser
③ wiser – poorer
④ richer – wiser
⑤ poorer – more foolish

28 위 글의 밑줄 친 (A)far와 바꿔 쓸 수 없는 말을 고르시오.

① much 　　② even 　　③ very
④ still 　　⑤ a lot

29 아래 〈보기〉에서 위 글의 밑줄 친 (B)to do와 문법적 쓰임이 같은 것의 개수를 고르시오.

┌─ 보기 ─┐
① I got up early to catch the train.
② There was not a moment to lose.
③ It is difficult to know oneself.
④ He was kind enough to lend me the money.
⑤ He has many children to look after.
└──────┘

① 1개　② 2개　③ 3개　④ 4개　⑤ 5개

[01~03] 다음 글을 읽고 물음에 답하시오.

Long ago, an honest merchant lived in Genoa, Italy. His name was Antonio, and he went to different places to support his family by trading. One day, he filled his ship with goods and visited a faraway island. There he traded tools for spices and books for nuts. ⓐThanks to Antonio, the islanders could get what they needed.

One night, Antonio had dinner with the island's queen at her palace. ⓑWhen dinner was served, rats were appeared, and some servants chased them away with sticks.

01 위 글의 밑줄 친 ⓐ를 enable을 사용하여 고칠 때, 빈칸에 들어갈 알맞은 말을 쓰시오.

➡ Antonio enabled the islanders _____ what they needed.

02 위 글의 밑줄 친 ⓑ에서 어법상 틀린 부분을 찾아 고치시오.

_____ ➡ _____

03 다음 빈칸 (A)와 (B)에 알맞은 단어를 넣어 섬사람들이 필요한 물건을 구한 방법을 완성하시오.

The islanders could get what they needed such as tools and books by trading __(A)__ for tools and __(B)__ for books with Antonio.

➡ (A) _____ (B) _____

[04~06] 다음 글을 읽고 물음에 답하시오.

Back in Italy, Antonio told his friends about his good fortune. Luigi, the richest merchant in Genoa, heard the story and was jealous. "Cats are worthless," Luigi thought. "ⓐI'll bring the queen what is really valuable. I'm sure that ⓑthe queen will give me more jewels."

Luigi packed his ship with wonderful paintings and other works of art. He took the gifts to the island. To get a chance to meet the queen, he told the islanders ⓒa lie that he was a good friend of Antonio's. When the queen heard about Luigi, she invited him to her palace for dinner. ⓓBefore sitting down at the table, Luigi presented the queen with all his gifts, and the queen thanked him again and again. "I'll repay you with a priceless gift," said the queen.

04 위 글의 밑줄 친 ⓐ와 ⓑ를 3형식 문장으로 고치시오.

➡ ⓐ _____
  ⓑ _____

05 위 글의 밑줄 친 ⓒa lie의 내용을 본문에서 찾아 쓰시오.

➡ _____

06 위 글의 밑줄 친 ⓓ를 다음과 같이 바꿔 쓸 때 빈칸에 들어갈 알맞은 말을 두 단어로 쓰시오.

➡ Before _____ down at the table,

[07~10] 다음 글을 읽고 물음에 답하시오.

Antonio was (A)[great / greatly] surprised that there were rats in the palace. He asked, "Are there no cats on this island?" The queen looked (B)[puzzling / puzzled]. "What is a cat?" she asked.

The merchant said to (C)[him / himself], "ⓐ여기 섬사람들이 필요로 하는 것은 공구나 책이 아니라 고양이야." He brought two cats from his ship and let them run free. "ⓑWhat amazing animals!" cried the queen when she saw all the rats run away. ⓒShe gave Antonio a chest that was filled with jewels.

중요

07 위 글의 괄호 (A)~(C)에서 어법상 알맞은 낱말을 골라 쓰시오.

➡ (A) _____ (B) _____ (C) _____

08 위 글의 밑줄 친 ⓐ의 우리말에 맞게 한 단어를 보충하여, 주어진 어휘를 알맞게 배열하시오.

but / need / tools or books / is / cats / here / not / the islanders / ,

➡ _____

_____

09 위 글의 밑줄 친 ⓑ를 다음과 같이 바꿔 쓸 때 빈칸에 들어갈 알맞은 말을 쓰시오.

➡ _____ amazing the animals are!

10 위 글의 밑줄 친 ⓒ를 다음과 같이 바꿔 쓸 때 빈칸에 들어갈 알맞은 말을 쓰시오.

➡ She gave Antonio a chest that _____

_____ _____ jewels.

[11~14] 다음 글을 읽고 물음에 답하시오.

Luigi watched the queen whisper in a servant's ear. He became excited and hopeful. He was sure that he would receive more jewels than Antonio.

After a while, the servant returned with a box, and ⓐthe queen presented it to Luigi. When Luigi opened the box, he was speechless.

There was a kitten in the box. "ⓑAntonio gave us the worthless cats, and we now have some kittens," said the queen. "In return for the wonderful gifts you gave us, we want to give you ⓒwhat is most valuable to us."

11 위 글의 밑줄 친 ⓐ를 다음과 같이 바꿔 쓸 때 빈칸에 들어갈 알맞은 말을 쓰시오.

➡ the queen presented Luigi _____

_____.

중요

12 위 글의 밑줄 친 ⓑ에서 흐름상 어색한 부분을 찾아 고치시오.

_____ ➡ _____

13 위 글의 밑줄 친 ⓒ가 가리키는 것을 본문에서 찾아 쓰시오.

➡ _____

14 본문의 내용과 일치하도록 다음 빈칸 (A)와 (B)에 알맞은 단어를 쓰시오.

Luigi gave the queen (A)_____

_____ and he was sure that he would receive more jewels than Antonio, but the queen presented a kitten to Luigi in return because a kitten was (B)_____

_____ to them.

My Speaking Portfolio

A: What is <u>the greatest</u> invention in history?
최상급에 the가 쓰였다.

B: <u>I'd say</u> the clock. We can't <u>tell the time</u> without it.
= I would say   시간을 알다

C: I don't really agree with you. I think the cell phone is the greatest invention.
동사 think 다음에 접속사 that 생략

D: You can say that again.

구문해설 · You can say that again. 네 말이 맞아.

All Ears

M: 1. I don't agree with you on that issue.

2. I didn't know you didn't like the plan.
동사 know의 목적어가 되는 명사절을 이끄는 접속사 that 생략

A: I'm glad I can go to the zoo.

B: You're going to the zoo? Good for you.
평서문의 형태이지만 의미상 질문을 나타낸다.

A: I think I have time to eat a snack.
형용사적 용법의 부정사

B: I don't agree. You must hurry to go back.

구문해설 · Good for you. 좋겠다. 잘되었구나. · hurry 서두르다

Wrap Up – Reading

Isabel lives in a small village near Kakamega, Kenya. In the past, she

had to walk a long distance every day to get clean water. She sometimes got
must의 과거   부사적 용법(목적)

sick because of the dirty water she drank. Three months ago, she received a
because of+명사구   dirty water (that) she drank

valuable gift from a volunteer worker. It looks like a thick straw. Dirty water
= precious   looks like+명사

goes into the straw, and clean water comes out of it. Isabel carries the straw
= the straw

everywhere. Now, she does not get sick anymore. She can go to school every
더 이상 ~ 아닌

day. So, the straw is what is most valuable to Isabel.
the thing which

구문해설 · village: 마을 · past: 과거 · distance: 거리 · receive: ~을 받다
· volunteer: 자원 봉사자 · straw: 빨대

해석

A: 무엇이 역사상 가장 위대한 발명품이니?

B: 나는 시계라고 말하겠어. 그것이 없으면 시간을 알 수 없어.

C: 나는 동의하지 않아. 나는 휴대전화가 가장 위대한 발명품이라고 생각해.

D: 네 말이 맞아.

M: 1. 나는 그 문제에 대하여 너에게 동의하지 않아.

2. 나는 네가 그 계획을 좋아하지 않는다는 것을 알지 못했어.

A: 나는 동물원에 갈 수 있어서 기뻐.

B: 동물원에 가니? 좋겠구나.

A: 나는 간식을 먹을 시간이 있다고 생각해.

B: 나는 동의하지 않아. 너는 서둘러 돌아가야 해.

Isabel은 케냐의 Kakamega 인근 마을에 살고 있다. 예전에 그녀는 깨끗한 물을 구하기 위해 매일 먼 거리를 걸어야 했다. 그녀는 가끔 그녀가 마신 더러운 물로 인해 병에 걸리기도 했다. 석달 전 그녀는 자원봉사자 한 명에게서 귀한 선물을 받았다. 그것은 두꺼운 빨대처럼 생겼다. 더러운 물이 빨대로 들어가면 깨끗한 물이 나온다. Isabel은 그것을 어디나 가지고 다닌다. 이제 그녀는 더 이상 병에 걸리지 않는다. 매일 학교에 갈 수 있다. 그래서 그 빨대는 Isabel에게 가장 귀중한 것이다.

영역별 핵심문제

01 다음 영영풀이에 해당하는 단어를 고르시오.

> to quickly follow someone or something in order to catch them

① drive   ② chase   ③ order
④ walk   ⑤ look after

02 다음 문장의 빈칸에 들어가기에 적절한 것은?

> A: We're now in our last year in middle school. Which kind of school do you _____?
> B: I'm thinking of an animation high school.

① want to visit   ② take care of
③ want to draw   ④ appear to get
⑤ have in mind

03 다음 빈칸에 들어가기에 적절한 것을 고르시오.

> There the merchant _____ tools for spices and books for nuts. Thanks to Antonio, the islanders could get what they needed.

① supported   ② visited   ③ got
④ invited   ⑤ traded

04 다음 밑줄 친 단어와 의미가 같은 단어를 고르시오.

> We can't <u>tell</u> the time without the clock.

① know   ② repay   ③ set
④ talk   ⑤ present

05 다음 대화의 빈칸에 들어가기에 알맞은 말은?

> A: I think the most boring day of the week is Monday.
> B: You can say that again.
> C: I don't _____ so. Thursday is the most boring.
> D: I agree. We have all the difficult subjects on Thursday.

① think   ② agree   ③ say
④ tell   ⑤ intend

06 다음 대화의 순서가 바르게 배열된 것을 고르시오.

> A: Did you hear the weather report?
> (A) Really? I'm glad I can wear my new raincoat.
> (B) Yes. It's going to rain all day long.
> (C) Good for you.

① (A) – (C) – (B)   ② (B) – (A) – (C)
③ (B) – (C) – (A)   ④ (C) – (A) – (B)
⑤ (C) – (B) – (A)

07 다음 대화의 빈칸에 들어갈 말로 알맞은 것은?

> G: Have you heard about Mr. Oh? He won first prize in the TV quiz show.
> B: It's not surprising. He seems to know about everything.
> G: You can say that again! He's a _____ dictionary.

① walking   ② useful   ③ surprising
④ wise   ⑤ large

08 다음 짝지어진 대화가 <u>어색한</u> 것을 고르시오.

① A: I think I have time to eat a snack.
B: I don't agree. You must hurry to go back.

② A: I think the most boring day of the week is Monday.
B: You can say that again.

③ A: I think the cell phone is the greatest invention.
B: You can say that again.

④ A: It's going to rain all day long.
B: Really? I'm sad I can wear my new raincoat.

⑤ A: Did you hear the weather report?
B: Yes. It's going to rain all day long.

[09~11] 다음 대화를 읽고 물음에 답하시오.

B: Jimin, look! That red phone case looks nice!
G: You can say that again! Mom would love it as a birthday present.
B: I __(A)__ how much it costs.
G: Let me see. It costs 40,000 won.
B: Really? That's so expensive.
G: I don't agree. Look! It works as a wallet, too.
B: Oh, I didn't see that. Then let's buy it for Mom.
G: Okay. I'm delighted to buy something special for Mom.
B: (B)나도 마찬가지야.

09 빈칸 (A)에 들어갈 가장 알맞은 말을 고르시오.

① wonder   ② know
③ tell   ④ recognize
⑤ think

10 밑줄 친 (B)의 우리말을 영작하시오. (so를 포함하시오.)

➡ _____ (3단어)

11 위 대화를 읽고 대답할 수 <u>없는</u> 것은?

① What would they like to buy?
② Who thinks the red phone case is too expensive?
③ What are they going to buy?
④ What does their mother want as a birthday present?
⑤ Does the boy agree to buy the red phone case?

Grammar

12 다음 우리말을 영어로 바르게 옮긴 것은?

> 그녀는 자기가 만든 것을 나에게 주었다.

① She made what I had given to her.
② She gave me what I had made for her.
③ I gave her what I had made.
④ I gave her what she had made.
⑤ She gave me what she had made.

13 빈칸에 들어갈 말을 순서대로 바르게 연결한 것은?

> • Can you imagine _____ he describes?
> • I saw the boy _____ along the street yesterday.

① that – walk
② that – to walk
③ what – walk
④ what – to walk
⑤ that – walking

14 다음 중 밑줄 친 부분의 쓰임이 어색한 것을 고르시오.

① I don't know <u>what</u> she bought.
② We saw <u>what</u> she had put on the table.
③ She learned <u>what</u> he had some time to rest.
④ We should know <u>what</u> is the most important.
⑤ I don't understand <u>what</u> he told me.

15 다음 중 밑줄 친 부분의 쓰임이 어색한 것을 고르시오.

① I expect him <u>to win</u> the match.
② He told them <u>to come</u> early.
③ She asked him <u>to move</u> the bag.
④ He saw her <u>to take</u> the book.
⑤ They allowed him <u>to swim</u> there.

16 다음 중 어법상 어색한 문장을 고르시오.

① I asked him to be quiet during dinner.
② She told him to clean the room.
③ He listened to her to explain the situation.
④ We allowed them to go to the beach.
⑤ They expected him to be quiet.

17 다음 빈칸에 들어갈 말로 알맞은 것은?

> Jack told me _____ early after the school was over.

① coming   ② come
③ to come   ④ comes
⑤ came

18 다음 괄호 안에서 알맞은 말을 고르시오.

(1) He was reading (that / what) she had sent to him.
(2) We saw them (to swim / swimming) across the river.
(3) You should carefully listen to (that / what) the teacher is saying.
(4) His mother asked him (to take / take) the waste out.
(5) Mary's mother saw her (to study / study) for the exam.

19 다음 중 밑줄 친 부분의 쓰임이 어색한 것을 고르시오.

① She heard him <u>to break</u> the window.
② He asked us <u>to take</u> some rest.
③ She expected him <u>to call</u> her.
④ She told him <u>to get</u> up early.
⑤ He advised us <u>to exercise</u> every day.

20 빈칸에 들어갈 말을 순서대로 바르게 연결한 것은?

> • She told me _____ she had heard at the library.
> • Did she tell you _____ she had in mind?

① that – that
② that – what
③ what – which
④ what – what
⑤ what – that

Reading

[21~23] 다음 글을 읽고 물음에 답하시오.

Long ago, an honest merchant lived in Genoa, Italy. His name was Antonio, and he went to different places to support his family by ⓐtrading. One day, he filled his ship with goods and visited a faraway island. There he traded tools for spices and books for nuts. ⓑThanks to Antonio, the islanders could get ⓒwhat they needed.

21 위 글의 밑줄 친 ⓐtrading과 문법적 쓰임이 같은 것을 모두 고르시오.

① He is collecting stamps.
② My hobby is swimming.
③ I heard him playing the piano.
④ We enjoy watching action movies.
⑤ Keeping a diary every day is not easy.

22 위 글의 밑줄 친 ⓑThanks to와 바꿔 쓸 수 없는 말을 모두 고르시오.

① Because of   ② Instead of
③ Owing to   ④ Due to
⑤ In spite of

23 위 글의 밑줄 친 ⓒwhat을 선행사와 관계대명사로 나눠 세 단어로 바꿔 쓰시오.

➡ _____

[24~26] 다음 글을 읽고 물음에 답하시오.

Antonio was greatly surprised (A)that there were rats in the palace. He asked, "Are there no cats on this island?" The queen looked puzzled. "What is a cat?" she asked.

The merchant said to himself, "What the islanders here need is not tools or books, but cats." He brought two cats from his ship and let them ___ⓐ___ free. "What amazing animals!" cried the queen when she saw all the rats ___ⓑ___ away. She gave Antonio a chest (B)that was filled with jewels.

24 위 글의 빈칸 ⓐ와 ⓑ에 공통으로 들어갈 알맞은 말을 고르시오.

① run   ② ran
③ to run   ④ running
⑤ were running

25 위 글의 밑줄 친 (A)와 (B)의 that과 문법적 쓰임이 같은 것을 각각 아래 〈보기〉에서 모두 골라 쓰시오.

┌─── 보기 ───┐
① He is the greatest novelist that has ever lived.
② He was the first man that came here.
③ I'm glad that you like it.
④ We will discuss all that matters.
⑤ I am sorry that he is gone.
└────────────┘

➡ (A)의 that과 쓰임이 같은 것: _____
(B)의 that과 쓰임이 같은 것: _____

26 According to the passage, which is NOT true?

① Antonio asked the queen if there were no cats on that island.
② At first, the queen didn't know what a cat was.
③ The islanders didn't need tools or books.
④ Antonio brought two cats from his ship and let them run free.
⑤ The queen gave Antonio a chest full of jewels.

[27~28] 다음 글을 읽고 물음에 답하시오.

Luigi packed his ship with wonderful paintings and other ⓐworks of art. He took the gifts to the island. To get a chance ⓑto meet the queen, he told the islanders a lie that he was a good friend of Antonio's. When the queen heard about Luigi, she invited him to her palace for dinner. Before sitting down at the table, Luigi presented the queen with all his gifts, and the queen thanked him again and again. "I'll repay you with a priceless gift," said the queen.

27 위 글의 밑줄 친 ⓐworks와 같은 의미로 쓰인 것을 고르시오.

① Look at the works of a clock.
② I like the works of Picasso.
③ He works 40 hours a week.
④ The ice works aren't closed even in winter.
⑤ This pill works on you.

28 위 글의 밑줄 친 ⓑto meet과 to부정사의 용법이 같은 것을 모두 고르시오.

① He has no money to buy the book with.
② He is the last man to tell a lie.
③ It is not easy to write good English.
④ I went to the airport to see him off.
⑤ I don't know what to do next.

[29~30] 다음 글을 읽고 물음에 답하시오.

Dear future Jihun,
  How are you doing? You are now a writer, ⓐ
_____ _____?
  I have included two things in the time capsule for you. The first thing is a pair of basketball shoes. They helped me make many friends in the basketball club. The other thing is my favorite book. I wanted to become a writer after I read it.
  I hope these things will bring back happy memories of your middle school days.

Jihun

29 위 글의 빈칸 ⓐ에 들어갈 알맞은 부가의문문을 쓰시오.

➡ _____

30 Fill in the blanks (A) and (B) with the suitable words.

In the time capsule, Jihun has included a pair of (A)_____ _____ because they helped him make many friends in the basketball club, and his favorite book because it gave him a dream to become (B)_____ _____.

31 주어진 글 다음에 이어질 글의 순서로 가장 적절한 것은?

One night, Antonio had dinner with the island's queen at her palace.

(A) Antonio was greatly surprised that there were rats in the palace. He asked, "Are there no cats on this island?"
(B) The queen looked puzzled. "What is a cat?" she asked.
(C) When dinner was served, rats appeared, and some servants chased them away with sticks.

① (A) – (C) – (B) ② (B) – (A) – (C)
③ (B) – (C) – (A) ④ (C) – (A) – (B)
⑤ (C) – (B) – (A)

단원별 예상문제

[01~02] 다음 빈칸에 들어갈 말로 적절한 것을 고르시오.

01 출제율 90%

I have _____ two things in the time capsule for you.

① found
② included
③ repayed
④ realized
⑤ counted

02 출제율 95%

Rix got a rabbit from a friend and did his best to take good _____ of it.

① help
② look
③ fun
④ care
⑤ delight

[03~04] 다음 영영풀이에 해당하는 단어를 쓰시오. (주어진 철자로 시작할 것)

03 출제율 90%

a large strong box that you use to store things in or to move your personal possessions from one place to another

➡ c_____

04 출제율 85%

things that are produced in order to be sold

➡ g_____

[05~06] 다음 빈칸에 들어갈 말로 적절한 것을 고르시오.

05 출제율 95%

A: Did you hear the _____ report?
B: Yes. It's going to rain all day long.

① advice
② weather
③ school
④ homework
⑤ cloud

06 출제율 95%

A: I'm really _____ I can't find my student card.
B: You can make another one. Don't take it so hard.

① worried
② delighted
③ glad
④ surprised
⑤ pleased

07 출제율 90%

짝지어진 단어의 관계가 같도록 빈칸에 알맞은 말을 쓰시오.

delighted : pleased = p_____ : valuable

08 출제율 90%

다음 대화의 빈칸에 알맞은 것을 고르시오.

I heard you will join the school dance club but I don't want to join you because I have _____. Dancing is not for me.

① right hands
② too much work
③ a good eye
④ no friends there
⑤ too left feet

09 출제율 95%

다음 대화의 순서가 바르게 배열된 것을 고르시오.

G: Have you heard about Mr. Oh?
B: No. What about him?
(A) You can say that again! He's a walking dictionary.
(B) He won first prize in the TV quiz show.
(C) It's not surprising. He seems to know about everything.

① (A) – (C) – (B)
② (B) – (A) – (C)
③ (B) – (C) – (A)
④ (C) – (A) – (B)
⑤ (C) – (B) – (A)

[10~12] 다음 대화를 읽고 물음에 답하시오.

> G: Oliver, what club are you going to join?
> B: I'm not sure. How ___(A)___ you, Sora?
> G: I want to join the school dance club.
> B: Really? But I heard you're preparing for an animation high school.
> G: Right, but I need some time to relax. We all need to do something to get over stress.
> B: You can say that again.
> G: Why don't you join me? It'll be fun,
> B: No, thanks. (B)춤은 나와 맞지 않아. I am really poor at dancing.

10 위 대화의 빈칸 (A)에 들어가기에 적절한 것은?

① for
② with
③ from
④ about
⑤ against

11 밑줄 친 (B)의 우리말을 영작하시오. (dancing, for를 포함할 것)

➡ _____ (5단어)

12 위 대화의 내용과 일치하지 <u>않는</u> 것은?

① Oliver is going to join the school dance club.
② Sora is preparing for an animation high school.
③ Sora wants to do something to get over stress.
④ Sora wants Oliver to join her.
⑤ Oliver thinks he has two left feet.

13 다음 빈칸에 들어갈 말로 알맞은 것은?

> I was listening to the rain _____ on the ground.

① to fall
② falling
③ falls
④ fell
⑤ fallen

14 빈칸에 들어갈 말을 순서대로 바르게 연결한 것은?

> • We will discuss the plan _____ he suggested.
> • She didn't like _____ I had given her.

① what – what
② what – that
③ what – which
④ that – that
⑤ that – what

15 다음 우리말을 영어로 바르게 옮긴 것은?

> 나는 그가 담을 넘는 것을 보았다.

① He saw me to cross the fence.
② He saw me crossing the fence.
③ I saw him crossed the fence.
④ I saw him to cross the fence.
⑤ I saw him cross the fence.

16 다음 빈칸에 들어갈 말로 알맞은 것은?

> She was pleased with _____ he had heard from me.

① that
② what
③ which
④ from which
⑤ in which

17 다음 중 밑줄 친 부분의 쓰임이 어색한 것을 고르시오.

① She asked him to turn on the TV.
② He advised them to study hard.
③ I saw him to drive the car.
④ He expected her to tell the truth.
⑤ I told him to go home early.

[18~20] 다음 글을 읽고 물음에 답하시오.

Long ago, an honest merchant lived in Genoa, Italy. His name was Antonio, and he went to different places to support his family by trading. One day, he (A)filled his ship with goods and visited a faraway island. There he traded tools for spices and books for nuts. Thanks to Antonio, the islanders could get (B)what they needed.

One night, Antonio had dinner with the island's queen at her palace. When dinner was served, rats appeared, and some servants ⓐ_____ them away with sticks.

18 주어진 영영풀이를 참고하여 빈칸 ⓐ에 철자 c로 시작하는 단어를 쓰시오. (어법에 맞게 어형 변화를 할 것)

to run after something or follow it quickly in order to catch or reach it

➡ _____

19 위 글의 밑줄 친 (A)filled와 바꿔 쓸 수 있는 단어를 고르시오.

① full   ② packed
③ picked   ④ gathered
⑤ chose

20 위 글의 밑줄 친 (B)what they needed가 가리키는 것을 본문에서 찾아 쓰시오. (두 개)

➡ _____, _____

[21~23] 다음 글을 읽고 물음에 답하시오.

Antonio was greatly surprised that there were rats in the palace. He asked, "Are there no cats on this island?" The queen looked puzzled. "What is a cat?" she asked.

The merchant said to himself, "What the islanders here need is not tools or books, but cats." He brought two cats from his ship and let ⓐthem run free. "What amazing animals!" cried the queen when she saw all the rats run away. She gave Antonio a chest that was filled with jewels.

21 위 글을 읽고 고양이에 대한 여왕의 심경 변화로 가장 알맞은 것을 고르시오.

① bored   → surprised
② nervous   → pleased
③ confused → nervous
④ satisfied → confused
⑤ puzzled   → amazed

22 위 글의 밑줄 친 ⓐthem이 가리키는 것을 본문에서 찾아 쓰시오.

➡ _____

23 본문의 내용과 일치하도록 다음 빈칸 (A)와 (B)에 알맞은 단어를 쓰시오.

When the queen saw two cats that Antonio had brought from his ship run free and all (A)_____ _____ run away, she gave Antonio a chest that was filled with (B)_____ in return for his help.

[24~26] 다음 글을 읽고 물음에 답하시오.

Luigi watched the queen ___ⓐ___ in a servant's ear. He became excited and hopeful. He was sure that he would receive more jewels than Antonio.

After a while, the servant returned with a box, and the queen presented it to Luigi. When Luigi opened the box, he was speechless.

There was a kitten in the box. "Antonio gave us the priceless cats, and we now have some kittens," said the queen. "In return for the wonderful gifts you gave us, we want to give you what is most valuable to us."

출제율 90%

24 위 글의 빈칸 ⓐ에 들어갈 알맞은 말을 <u>모두</u> 고르시오.

① to whisper ② would whisper
③ whispering ④ whispered
⑤ whisper

출제율 100%

25 위 글의 제목으로 알맞은 것을 고르시오.

① Wow! I'll Surely Receive More Jewels!
② Poor Luigi's Unrealized Expectation
③ It Turned Out as Expected
④ A Kitten, a Perfect Present
⑤ How to Give Wonderful Gifts

출제율 95%

26 Which question canNOT be answered after reading the passage?

① When did Luigi become excited and hopeful?
② Did Luigi receive what he wanted as gifts?
③ When Luigi opened the box, was he satisfied with what was in the box?

④ When did Antonio give the queen the priceless cats?
⑤ What was most valuable to the queen?

[27~28] 다음 글을 읽고 물음에 답하시오.

Isabel lives in a small village near Kakamega, Kenya. In the past, she had to walk a long distance every day to get clean water. She sometimes got sick ⓐbecause of the dirty water she drank. Three months ago, she received ⓑa valuable gift from a volunteer worker. It looks like a thick straw. Dirty water goes into the straw, and clean water comes out of it. Isabel carries the straw everywhere. Now, she does not get sick anymore. She can go to school every day. So, the straw is what is most valuable to Isabel.

출제율 90%

27 위 글의 밑줄 친 ⓐ를 다음과 같이 바꿔 쓸 때 빈칸에 들어갈 알맞은 말을 쓰시오.

➡ _____ she drank dirty water

출제율 100%

28 위 글의 ⓑa valuable gift에 관한 내용으로 적절하지 <u>않은</u> 것은?

① 자원봉사자가 3개월 전에 Isabel에게 주었다.
② 두꺼운 빨대처럼 생겼다.
③ 더러운 물이 빨대 속으로 들어가면, 깨끗한 물이 그 밖으로 나온다.
④ Isabel은 그것을 집에 소중하게 간직해 두었다.
⑤ 그것은 Isabel에게 가장 귀중한 것이다.

01 다음 우리말에 맞게 빈칸에 알맞은 말을 쓰시오.

(1) 춤은 나와 어울리지 않아. 나는 동작이 서툴러.
→ Dancing is not for me. I have two _____ feet.

(2) 그는 무역으로 가족을 부양하기 위하여 여기저기 다녔다.
→ He went to different places to _____ his family by trading.

(3) Antonio 덕택에 그 섬사람들은 그들이 원하는 것을 얻을 수 있었다.
→ _____ to Antonio, the islanders could get what they needed.

(4) 몇몇 하인들이 막대기로 쥐를 쫓아냈다.
→ Some _____ chased the rats away with sticks.

02 다음 영영풀이에 해당하는 단어를 쓰시오. (주어진 철자로 시작할 것)

someone, especially in the past, who was paid to clean someone's house, cook for them, answer the door, etc

→ s_____

[03~04] 다음 대화를 읽고 물음에 답하시오.

G: Hey, Minjun. What a surprise!
B: Hi, Sora. I'm glad we're in the same class.
G: I am, too. We're now in our last year in middle school. How do you feel?
B: (A)나는 학교 공부가 더 많을 것 같아서 좀 걱정이 돼.
G: (B)Me, too. We also have to think about our high school.
B: Which kind of school do you have in mind?
G: I'm thinking of an animation high school. I love painting.

03 밑줄 친 (A)의 우리말을 영어로 옮기시오.

필수 어휘: a little, that, there, schoolwork

→ _____
_____

04 밑줄 친 (B)와 같은 의미가 되도록 다음 빈칸을 채우시오.

→ _____ _____ _____.

05 다음 우리말에 맞게 괄호 안에 주어진 어휘를 바르게 배열하시오. (어형 변화 가능 / 필요한 어휘 추가)

(1) 나는 비가 창문에 떨어지는 것을 들었다. (I, the rain, fall, hear, on the window)
→ _____

(2) 우리는 그가 운동장에서 공을 차고 있는 것을 보았다. (we, he, kicking, saw, the ball, on the ground)
→ _____

(3) 그녀는 내가 말한 것을 이해할 수 없었다. (I, her, she, told, understand, what, couldn't)
→ _____

06 다음 대화의 빈칸에 들어갈 말을 고르시오. (주어진 철자로 시작할 것)

A: I think I have time to eat a snack.
B: I don't agree. You must _____ to go back.

→ h_____

Back in Italy, Antonio told his friends about his good fortune. Luigi, the richest merchant in Genoa, heard the story and was jealous. "Cats are worthless," Luigi thought. "I'll bring the queen what is really valuable. ⓐI'm sure that the queen will give me more jewels."

Luigi packed his ship with wonderful paintings and other works of art. He took the gifts to the island. To get a chance to meet the queen, he told the islanders a lie that he was a good friend of Antonio's. When the queen heard about Luigi, she invited him to her palace for dinner. Before sitting down at the table, ⓑLuigi presented the queen with all his gifts, and the queen thanked him again and again. "I'll repay you with a priceless gift," said the queen.

07 위 글의 밑줄 친 ⓐ를 다음과 같이 바꿔 쓸 때 빈칸에 들어갈 알맞은 말을 쓰시오.

➡ It is _____ that the queen will give me more jewels. = The queen will _____ give me more jewels.

08 위 글의 밑줄 친 ⓑ를 다음과 같이 바꿔 쓸 때 빈칸에 들어갈 알맞은 말을 쓰시오.

➡ Luigi presented all his gifts _____ _____ _____ .

Long ago, an honest (A)[consumer / merchant] lived in Genoa, Italy. His name was Antonio, and he went to different places (B)[to support / supporting] his family by trading. One day, he filled his ship with (C)[good / goods] and visited a faraway island. There he traded tools for spices and books for nuts. ⓐAntonio 덕에 섬사람들은 필요한 것을 얻을 수 있었다.

One night, Antonio had dinner with the island's queen at her palace. ⓑWhen dinner was served, rats appeared, and some servants chased away them with sticks.

09 위 글의 괄호 (A)~(C)에서 문맥이나 어법상 알맞은 낱말을 골라 쓰시오.

➡ (A) _____ (B) _____ (C) _____

10 위 글의 밑줄 친 ⓐ의 우리말에 맞게 주어진 어휘를 이용하여 10 단어로 영작하시오.

Thanks to, the islanders

➡ _____

_____

11 위 글의 밑줄 친 ⓑ에서 어법상 틀린 부분을 찾아 고치시오.

_____ ➡ _____

01 빈칸에 알맞은 말을 넣어 Antonio와 Luigi의 이야기를 정리해 봅시다.

Antonio visited an island for trading. → He gave _____ to the queen, so the rats ran away. → The queen gave him _____. → Luigi heard about Antonio's good fortune. → He gave expensive gifts to the _____. → The queen _____.

02 빈칸에 알맞은 표현을 넣어 〈보기〉처럼 자신의 생각을 말해 봅시다.

| 보기 |

What I want to do the most is to take a trip to Africa.

(1) What I want to eat now is _____.
(2) _____ is what I usually do in my free time.
(3) I will never forget what _____.

03 다음 내용을 바탕으로 지훈이가 타임 캡슐에 넣을 편지를 쓰시오.

미래의 나에게 궁금한 점: You are now a writer, aren't you?
타임 캡슐에 넣을 물건: • a pair of basketball shoes   • my favorite book
이유: • helped me make many friends in the basketball club
     • gave me a dream to become a writer

Dear future Jihun,
How are you doing? You are now (A)_____, aren't you?
I have included two things in the time capsule for you. The first thing is a pair of (B)_____. They helped me make (C)_____ in the basketball club.
The other thing is my (D)_____. I wanted to become (E)_____ after I read it.
I hope these things will bring back happy memories of your middle school days.

Jihun

단원별 모의고사

[01~02] 다음 짝지어진 두 단어의 관계가 같도록 빈칸에 알맞은 말을 쓰시오. (주어진 철자로 시작할 것)

01

tool : device = amazing : s_____

02

delighted : sorrowful = include : e_____

03 다음 우리말에 맞게 빈칸에 알맞은 말을 쓰시오. (주어진 철자로 시작할 것)

(1) 상인은 "이곳 섬사람들이 필요한 것은 고양이들이야."라고 혼잣말을 했다.
➡ The merchant said to _____, "What the islanders here need is cats."

(2) 그녀는 Antonio에게 보물로 가득 찬 상자를 주었다.
➡ She gave Antonio a c_____ that was filled with jewels.

(3) Luigi는 그의 배를 훌륭한 그림으로 가득 채웠다.
➡ Luigi p_____ his ship with wonderful paintings.

04 다음 중 밑줄 친 부분의 뜻풀이가 바르지 않은 것은?

① Did you hear the weather report? (일기예보)
② I'm glad I can wear my new raincoat. (입다)
③ It's all right. Don't take it so hard. (가지고 가다)
④ We have all the difficult subjects on Thursday. (과목들)
⑤ That man looks just like Ben. (~ 같은)

05 다음 영영풀이에 해당하는 단어를 쓰시오. (주어진 철자로 시작할 것.)

someone who buys and sells goods in large quantities

➡ m_____

06 다음 밑줄 친 단어와 의미가 같은 단어를 고르시오.

I'll bring the queen what is really valuable.

① priceless
② valueless
③ worthless
④ expensive
⑤ terrible

07 다음 대화의 순서가 바르게 배열된 것을 고르시오.

B: Jimin, look! That red phone case looks nice!
G: You can say that again! Mom would love it as a birthday present.
B: I wonder how much it costs.
G: Let me see. It costs 40,000 won.
B: Really? That's so expensive.

(A) Okay. I'm delighted to buy something special for Mom.
(B) I don't agree. Look! It works as a wallet, too.
(C) Oh, I didn't see that. Then let's buy it for Mom.

B: So am I.

① (A) – (C) – (B)
② (B) – (A) – (C)
③ (B) – (C) – (A)
④ (C) – (A) – (B)
⑤ (C) – (B) – (A)

[08~10] 다음 대화를 읽고 물음에 답하시오.

G: Oliver, what club are you going to join?

B: I'm not sure. How about you, Sora?

G: I want to join the school dance club.

B: Really? But I heard you're preparing for an animation high school.

G: Right, but I need some time to relax. We all need to do something to ___(A)___ over stress.

B: You can say that again.

G: Why don't you join me? It'll be fun.

B: No, thanks. Dancing is not for me. I have two left ___(B)___.

08 빈칸 (A)에 들어갈 가장 알맞은 말을 고르시오.

① take ② get ③ make
④ turn ⑤ grow

09 빈칸 (B)에 알맞은 말을 쓰시오.

➡ _____

10 위 대화를 읽고, 대답할 수 없는 질문은?

① What does Sora want to do to get over stress?
② What kind of high school is Sora preparing for?
③ What club is Oliver going to join?
④ Why doesn't Oliver agree to join the dance club?
⑤ Does Oliver think Sora needs some time to relax?

[11~13] 다음 대화를 읽고 물음에 답하시오.

B: Jimin, look! That red phone case looks nice!

G: You can say that again! Mom would love it as a birthday present.

B: I ___(A)___ how much it costs.

G: Let me see. It costs 40,000 won.

B: Really? That's so expensive.

G: I don't agree. Look! It works as a wallet, too.

B: Oh, I didn't see that. Then let's buy it for Mom.

G: Okay. I'm delighted to buy something special for Mom.

B: ___(B)___ am I.

11 빈칸 (A)에 들어갈 가장 알맞은 말을 고르시오.

① guess ② know ③ ask
④ say ⑤ wonder

12 빈칸 (B)에 알맞은 말을 쓰시오.

➡ _____

13 위 대화의 내용과 일치하는 것은?

① Jimin doesn't agree that the red phone case looks nice.
② They are looking for a cheap phone case.
③ Jimin doesn't think the red phone case is too expensive.
④ The boy doesn't want Jimin to buy the phone case.
⑤ The boy isn't delighted to buy the phone case.

14 다음 빈칸에 들어갈 말로 알맞은 것은?

He told me _____ he had in mind.

① what ② which ③ that
④ how ⑤ who

15 다음 빈칸에 들어갈 말로 알맞은 것은?

He likes the picture _____ he took during the holiday.

① that
② what
③ in which
④ in that
⑤ with which

16 다음 중 밑줄 친 부분의 쓰임이 어색한 것을 고르시오.

① I heard him <u>talk</u> on the phone.
② She saw them <u>sit</u> on the bench.
③ They listened to him <u>sing</u> a song.
④ She expects them <u>arrive</u> on time.
⑤ He felt her <u>touch</u> his hand.

17 다음 우리말을 영어로 바르게 옮긴 것은?

우리는 그가 그 사건을 설명하는 것을 들었다.

① We heard him explain the accident.
② He explained what we heard about the accident.
③ We heard his explain the accident.
④ We heard him to explain the accident.
⑤ He heard us explain the accident.

18 다음 중 어법상 어색한 문장을 고르시오.

① My father told me to do my homework.
② I heard him play the violin in the yard.
③ She didn't read the letter what he had sent to her.
④ He liked the painting that she had given to her.
⑤ He knew what he had to buy on his way home.

19 다음 괄호 안에서 알맞은 말을 고르시오.

(1) He took pictures of (that / what) he saw during the travel.
(2) I couldn't find the money (that / what) he had put on the table.
(3) He heard the children (to talk / talk) about the animation.
(4) He noticed the players (to take / taking) a rest.

[20~21] 다음 글을 읽고 물음에 답하시오.

Long ago, an honest merchant lived in Genoa, Italy. His name was Antonio, and he went to different places to support his family by trading. One day, he filled his ship with goods and visited a faraway island. There he traded tools for spices and books for nuts. Thanks to Antonio, the islanders could get ⓐ _____ they needed.

One night, Antonio had dinner with the island's queen at her palace. When dinner was served, rats appeared, and some servants chased them away with sticks.

20 위 글의 빈칸 ⓐ에 들어갈 알맞은 말을 고르시오.

① which
② what
③ that
④ when
⑤ where

21 Which question canNOT be answered after reading the passage?

① Where did Antonio live?
② How did Antonio support his family?
③ How long did it take for Antonio to reach a faraway island?
④ What did Antonio trade on the island?
⑤ When did rats appear?

[22~23] 다음 글을 읽고 물음에 답하시오.

Antonio was greatly surprised that there were rats in the palace. He asked, "Are there no cats on this island?" The queen looked puzzled. (①) "What is a cat?" she asked. (②)

The merchant said to himself, "What the islanders here need is not tools or books, but cats." (③) "What amazing animals!" cried the queen when she saw all the rats run away. (④) She gave Antonio a chest that was filled with jewels. (⑤)

22 위 글의 흐름으로 보아, 주어진 문장이 들어가기에 가장 적절한 곳은?

> He brought two cats from his ship and let them run free.

① ② ③ ④ ⑤

23 주어진 영영풀이에 해당하는 단어를 본문에서 찾아 쓰시오.

> a large, heavy box used for storing things

➡ _____

[24~26] 다음 글을 읽고 물음에 답하시오.

Back in Italy, Antonio told his friends about his good fortune. Luigi, the richest merchant in Genoa, heard the story and was jealous. "Cats are (A)[priceless / worthless]," Luigi thought. "I'll bring the queen what is really (B)[valuable / valueless]. I'm sure that the queen will give me more jewels."

Luigi packed his ship with wonderful paintings and other works of art. He took the gifts to the island. ⓐTo get a chance to meet the queen, he told the islanders a lie ⓑthat he was a good friend of Antonio's. When the queen heard about Luigi, she invited him to her palace for dinner. Before sitting down at the table, Luigi presented the queen with all his gifts, and the queen thanked him again and again. "I'll repay you with a (C)[priceless / worthless] gift," said the queen.

24 위 글의 괄호 (A)~(C)에서 문맥상 알맞은 낱말을 골라 쓰시오.

➡ (A) _____ (B) _____ (C) _____

25 위 글의 밑줄 친 ⓐTo get과 to부정사의 용법이 다른 것을 모두 고르시오.

① You will find it difficult to read the novel.
② I am sorry to hear that.
③ He grew up to be a great doctor.
④ There was nothing to be seen.
⑤ He must be foolish to believe such a thing.

26 위 글의 밑줄 친 ⓑthat과 문법적 쓰임이 같은 것을 모두 고르시오.

① This is the dress that she bought yesterday.
② No one can deny the fact that you are guilty.
③ My arm doesn't reach that far.
④ The climate of this country is like that of Italy.
⑤ There was no hope that she would recover her health.

Lesson 2

Animals, Big and Small

 의사소통 기능

- 선호 묻고 답하기

  A: Which do you like better, dogs or cats?

  B: I like dogs better.

- 설명 요청하기

  A: It's an animal.

  B: Can you tell me more about it?

언어 형식

- 명사를 뒤에서 꾸미는 분사

  Look at the sun **rising** over the sea.

- 접속사 since

  Since it rained heavily, the station was closed.

Words & Expressions

Key Words

- □ **appear**[əpíər] 동 나타나다, (글 속에) 나오다
- □ **Arctic**[áːrktik] 형 북극의 cf. **Antarctic** 남극의
- □ **beehive**[bíːhàiv] 명 벌집
- □ **billion**[bíljən] 명 십억
- □ **breathe**[briːð] 동 호흡하다
- □ **chemical**[kémikəl] 명 화학물질
- □ **chestnut**[tʃésnʌt] 명 밤
- □ **choose**[tʃuːz] 동 고르다, 정하다 (= **pick**, **select**)
- □ **colony**[káləni] 명 군락, 군집
- □ **defend**[difénd] 동 방어하다
- □ **endangered**[indéindʒərd] 형 위험에 처한, 멸종 위기의
- □ **entire**[intáiər] 형 전체의
- □ **except**[iksépt] 전 ~을 제외하고
- □ **exchange**[ikstʃéindʒ] 명 교환 동 교환하다
- □ **extremely**[ikstríːmli] 부 극심하게
- □ **faraway**[fáːrəwèi] 형 멀리 떨어진
- □ **female**[fíːmeil] 형 여성의, 암컷의
- □ **flesh**[fleʃ] 명 살, 고기
- □ **insect**[ínsekt] 명 곤충
- □ **hardly**[háːrdli] 부 거의 ~ 않다
- □ **hold**[hould] 동 수용하다, 지니다
- □ **including**[inklúːdiŋ] 전 ~을 포함하여
- □ **last**[læst] 동 지속되다

- □ **lung**[lʌŋ] 명 폐
- □ **male**[meil] 형 남성의, 수컷의
- □ **million**[míljən] 명 백만
- □ **nap**[næp] 명 낮잠
- □ **offer**[ɔ́ːfər] 동 제공하다
- □ **polar bear** 북극곰
- □ **prefer**[prifə́ːr] 동 선호하다
- □ **produce**[prədjúːs] 동 생산하다, 만들어 내다
- □ **protect**[prətékt] 동 보호하다
- □ **resident**[rézədnt] 명 거주자
- □ **rub**[rʌb] 동 문지르다, 비비다
- □ **scary**[skɛ́əri] 형 무서운
- □ **sensitive**[sénsətiv] 형 ~에 민감한, 예민한
- □ **share**[ʃɛər] 동 공유하다
- □ **skinny**[skíni] 형 여윈, 두께가 얇은
- □ **social**[sóuʃəl] 형 사회적인, 사교적인
- □ **stripe**[straip] 명 줄무늬
- □ **talent show** 장기 자랑
- □ **unbelievable**[ənbəlívəbəl] 형 믿을 수 없는
- □ **underwater**[əndərwɔ́tər] 형 수중의, 물속의
- □ **watermelon**[wɔ́tərmelən] 명 수박
- □ **weigh**[wei] 동 무게가 나가다
- □ **wild**[waild] 형 야생의, 자연 그대로의

Key Expressions

- □ **a big fan of** ~ ~의 열렬한 지지자
- □ **as of** ~ 현재, ~일자로
- □ **be all ears** 경청하다
- □ **by the way** 그런데
- □ **cost an arm and a leg** 비싼 값을 치르다
- □ **decide on** ~을 결정하다
- □ **have a hard time** 어려움을 겪다
- □ **have a long face** 표정이 우울하다
- □ **have fun** 재미있게 보내다
- □ **keep an eye on** ~을 지켜보다, ~을 감시하다

- □ **lay eggs** 알을 낳다
- □ **learn by heart** 암기하다
- □ **look after** ~을 돌보다
- □ **one another** 서로
- □ **out of nowhere** 어디선지 모르게, 느닷없이
- □ **pass on** 전달하다
- □ **seem to** ~인 것 같다
- □ **take a look at** ~을 보다
- □ **turn one's nose up at** ~을 거절하다
- □ **What is/are ~ for?** ~의 용도는 무엇이니?

Word Power

※ 서로 비슷한 뜻을 가진 어휘

- □ **hold** 수용하다, 지니다 : **contain** 포함하다
- □ **choose** 고르다 : **select** 선택하다
- □ **offer** 제공하다 : **provide** 제공하다
- □ **protect** 보호하다 : **defend** 방어하다
- □ **appear** 나타나다 : **show up** 나타나다
- □ **hardly** 거의 ~ 않다 : **scarcely** 거의 ~ 않다
- □ **entire** 전체의 : **whole** 전체의

- □ **exchange** 교환하다 : **trade** 교환하다
- □ **difference** 차이점 : **variety** 다양함
- □ **prefer** 선호하다 : **like** 좋아하다
- □ **social** 사회적인, 사교적인 : **sociable** 사교적인
- □ **extremely** 극심하게 : **highly** 매우
- □ **resident** 거주자 : **dweller** 거주자
- □ **unbelievable** 믿을 수 없는 : **incredible** 믿을 수 없는

※ 서로 반대의 뜻을 가진 어휘

- □ **wild** 야생의 ↔ **tamed** 길들여진
- □ **difference** 차이점 ↔ **similarity** 닮은 점
- □ **sensitive** 예민한 ↔ **insensitive** 둔한
- □ **social** 사교적인 ↔ **unsociable** 사회성이 없는
- □ **resident** 거주자 ↔ **nonresident** 비거주자
- □ **defend** 방어하다 ↔ **attack** 공격하다
- □ **unbelievable** 믿을 수 없는 ↔ **credible** 믿을 만한

- □ **Arctic** 북극의 ↔ **Antarctic** 남극의
- □ **prefer** 선호하다 ↔ **dislike** 싫어하다
- □ **faraway** 멀리 떨어진 ↔ **near** 가까운
- □ **appear** 나타나다 ↔ **disappear** 사라지다
- □ **male** 남성의, 수컷의 ↔ **female** 여성의, 암컷의
- □ **regularly** 규칙적으로 ↔ **irregularly** 불규칙하게

English Dictionary

□ **beehive** 벌집
→ a structure where bees are kept for producing honey
꿀 생산을 위해 벌이 길러지는 구조물

□ **choose** 고르다
→ to decide which one of a number of things or people you want
많은 사람이나 사물 중에서 어느 것을 원하는지 정하다

□ **Arctic** 북극의
→ relating to the most northern part of the world
지구의 가장 북쪽과 관련된

□ **prefer** 선호하다
→ to like someone or something more than someone or something else
다른 어떤 사람이나 어떤 것보다 어떤 사람이나 어떤 것을 더 좋아하다

□ **watermelon** 수박
→ a large round fruit with hard green skin, red flesh, and black seeds
초록 껍질, 빨간 과육, 검정 씨앗을 가진 둥근 과일

□ **insect** 곤충
→ a small creature such as a fly or ant, that has six legs, and sometimes wings
여섯 개의 다리와 때로는 날개를 가진 파리나 개미 같은 작은 생물

□ **colony** 군락, 군집
→ a group of animals or plants of the same type that are living or growing together
함께 살거나 자라는 같은 종류의 동물 또는 식물의 집단

□ **resident** 거주자
→ someone who lives or stays in a particular place
특정한 장소에 살거나 머무르는 사람

□ **exchange** 교환
→ the act of giving someone something and receiving something else from them
무엇인가를 다른 사람에게 주거나 그들로부터 받는 행위

□ **nap** 낮잠
→ a short sleep, especially during the day
낮 동안 짧게 자는 잠

01 다음 영영풀이에 해당하는 단어를 고르시오.

> a structure where bees are kept for producing honey

① flower   ② cave
③ chestnut   ④ beehive
⑤ camp

[02~03] 다음 대화의 빈칸에 들어갈 말을 고르시오.

02

> A: Can you tell me about your dream?
> B: _____ My dream is to make a fantastic team.

① No way.   ② Don't mention it.
③ Not at all.   ④ Really?
⑤ Sure.

03 중요

> B: Mike, how do you like the camp?
> G: It's great. I'm having a lot of _____.

① trouble   ② fun
③ time   ④ difficulty
⑤ problem

[04~05] 다음 빈칸에 들어갈 말로 적절한 것을 고르시오.

04

> People come to the woods and _____ the forest. Many of my friends have lost their homes.

① destroy   ② keep
③ cross   ④ grow
⑤ visit

05

> I get scared whenever I have to cross a big street. This morning I was almost hit. I don't understand why people are in such a _____.

① danger   ② house
③ hurry   ④ plan
⑤ camp

06 중요 다음 주어진 우리말에 어울리는 문장으로 빈칸에 가장 적절한 것은?

> 우리는 종종 개미가 느닷없이 나타나는 것을 본다.
> ➡ We often see ants come _____.

① from time to time
② somewhere near
③ without noticing
④ out of nowhere
⑤ off the corner

07 다음 밑줄 친 단어와 의미가 가장 가까운 단어를 고르시오.

> Can you guess how many bees live there?

① estimate   ② count
③ measure   ④ weigh
⑤ tell

서답형

08 다음 주어진 단어를 이용해 빈칸을 완성하시오.

> Can you tell me about their _____?

➡ _____s (differ)

01 다음 짝지어진 단어의 관계가 같도록 빈칸에 알맞은 말을 쓰시오. (주어진 철자로 시작할 것)

defend : attack – r_____ : irregularly

02 다음 밑줄 친 단어와 의미가 같은 단어를 쓰시오. (주어진 철자로 시작할 것)

The beehive can <u>hold</u> over 50,000 bees.

➡ c_____

03 다음 영영풀이에 해당하는 단어를 쓰시오. (주어진 철자로 시작할 것)

relating to the most northern part of the world

➡ A_____

04 다음 우리말에 맞게 빈칸에 알맞은 말을 쓰시오. (주어진 철자가 있는 경우에는 주어진 철자로 시작할 것)

(1) 나는 배가 몹시 아파요.
  ➡ I have a t_____ stomachache.
(2) 때때로 나는 너무 어두워서가 아니라 너무 밝아서 길을 잃어요.
  ➡ Sometimes I get _____ not because it's too dark but because it's too bright.
(3) 불빛이 너무 밝으면 나는 어디로 날아가야 할지 분간할 수 없어요.
  ➡ When lights are too bright, I can't t_____ which way to fly.
(4) 우리는 종종 느닷없이 개미가 나오는 것을 본다.
  ➡ We often see ants come out of n_____.

05 다음 문장의 빈칸에 〈보기〉에 있는 단어를 넣어 자연스러운 문장을 만드시오.

┌─ 보기 ─┐
after   breathe   shy   common

(1) The air was so fresh, and the hikers started to _____ slowly.
(2) I had few friends in elementary school since I was extremely _____.
(3) Mother Teresa spent her entire life looking _____ the poor.
(4) A washing machine is a _____ machine that you can see at home.

06 다음 우리말을 영어로 옮길 때 주어진 철자로 시작하여 빈칸에 적절한 말을 완성하시오.

(1) 네가 없는 동안 내가 개를 지켜볼 것이다.
  ➡ I will k_____ an e_____ o_____ your dog while you are away.
(2) Mike는 오늘 표정이 우울하다.
  ➡ Mike h_____ a l_____ f_____ today.

07 다음 문장의 빈칸에 들어가기에 적절한 단어를 주어진 철자로 시작하여 쓰시오.

Dogs are more s_____ to smells than humans are.

Conversation

교과서

1 선호 묻고 답하기

> **A** Which do you like better, dogs or cats?
> **B** I like dogs better.

- 선호를 물어보는 표현은 '더 좋아하다'에 해당하는 'like better'를 사용하여 'Which do you like better, A or B?' 또는 'Which one do you like, A or B?'의 형태로 나타낸다.

- 제한된 범위 안에서 '어느 것을 더 좋아하니?'라고 할 때는 의문사 which 또는 which one을 쓴다. '더 좋아하다'의 의미인 'like better'는 동사 'prefer = 선호하다'를 써서 'Which (one) do you prefer, A or B?'라고 할 수 있다.

- 대답할 때는 'like A better than B' 또는 'prefer A to B'라고 한다.

선호 묻기

- Which do you like better, fish or birds? 물고기와 새 중에서 어느 것을 더 좋아하니?
- Which do you prefer, fish or birds?

선호 답하기

- I like fish better than birds. = I prefer fish to birds. 나는 새보다 물고기를 더 좋아한다.

핵심 Check

1. 다음 우리말과 일치하도록 빈칸에 알맞은 말을 쓰시오.

   (1) **A:** _____ do you like better, ice cream or milk?

   (아이스크림과 우유 중에서 어느 것을 더 좋아하니?)

   B: Ice cream is more delicious, I think.

   (2) **A:** Which do you _____ to take, the bus or the subway?

   (버스와 지하철 중에서 어느 것을 타는 것을 선호하니?)

   B: I _____ to take the subway every weekday. (나는 주중에는 지하철 타는 것을 선호해.)

2. 다음 대화의 순서를 바르게 배열하시오.

   (A) Me, too.

   (B) Which do you like better, hot weather or cold weather?

   (C) I like hot weather better. I like going swimming in the sea.

   (D) I like cold weather better. I'm sensitive to hot temperatures. How about you?

   ➡ _____

② 설명 요청하기

> **A** It's an animal. 그것은 동물이야.
>
> **B** Can you tell me more about it? 그것에 대해 더 말해 줄 수 있니?

■ 상대방의 말을 듣고 추가로 더 설명해 달라고 할 때는 'Can you tell me more about it?'이라고 한다. 좀 더 공손하게 표현하여 Can 대신에 Could나 Would를 사용할 수도 있다. tell 대신에 explain을 써서 'Can you explain that more, please?'라고 할 수 있다.

■ 상대방의 말을 잘 알아듣지 못해서 다시 물어볼 때는 'What do you mean (by that)?'이라고 한다. '잘 이해하지 못했습니다.'의 의미로 'I don't get it.' 또는 'I'm not following you.'라고 할 수도 있다.

설명 요청하기

- Can you tell me more about it? 그것에 대해 더 설명해 주시겠습니까?
- Could/Would you tell me more about it?
- Can you explain it more, please?

다시 설명 요청하기

- I don't get it. 잘 이해하지 못했습니다.
- I'm not following you. 이해를 못했어요.

핵심 Check

3. 다음 우리말과 일치하도록 빈칸에 공통으로 알맞은 말을 쓰시오.

A: Can you _____ me about your plan? (너의 계획에 대해 말해 줄 수 있니?)

B: Okay. I'll _____ you as soon as I can. (알았어. 가능한 한 빨리 말해 줄게.)

4. 다음 주어진 문장을 자연스러운 대화가 되도록 배열하시오.

(A) That's too bad. Is there anything we can do to help them?

(B) Those are good points. I think it's time to get serious about protecting birds.

(C) I heard birds are having a hard time these days. Can you tell us more?

(D) Sure. The cities are too bright at night. Many birds lose their way.

(E) Yes. First, we should turn off unnecessary lights at night. Also we should hold the Earth Hour campaign regularly.

➡ _____

 Listen – Listen & Answer Dialog 1

B: Amber, how do you like the camp?

G: It's great. I'm ❶having a lot of fun.

B: Me, too. The ❷talent show last night was really great.

G: Yeah. ❸By the way, did you decide on the afternoon program?

B: No, I haven't ❹yet. Which ❺do you think is better, hiking or swimming?

G: I'll go hiking because we can see wild birds and insects in the woods.

B: I'll join you. I like birds and insects.

G: Great. I heard we'll have a hiking guide.

B: Sounds good.

B: Amber, 캠프 어때?

G: 좋아. 아주 재미있어.

B: 나도 그래. 어젯밤 장기 자랑은 정말 멋졌어.

G: 맞아. 그런데 너는 오후 프로그램 결정했니?

B: 아니. 아직 못했어. 너는 산행과 수영 중에 뭐가 낫다고 생각해?

G: 숲에서 야생 조류와 곤충을 볼 수 있으니까 난 산행을 할 거야.

B: 나도 같이할게. 나는 새와 곤충을 좋아하거든.

G: 좋아. 산행 가이드가 있을 거라고 들었어.

B: 잘됐다.

❶ have a lot of fun = 매우 재미있게 보내다

❷ talent show = 장기 자랑

❸ 'by the way'는 대화의 화제를 바꾸어 이야기할 때 '그건 그렇고, 그런데' 등의 의미로 사용한다.

❹ 부정문에 쓰인 yet은 '아직'의 의미이다.

❺ 'do you think'에 이어지는 간접의문문이 의문사로 시작할 때는 의문사를 문장 첫 자리에 써야 한다.

Check(√) True or False

(1) The girl didn't decide on the afternoon program.　　　　T ☐ F ☐

(2) The boy will go hiking.　　　　T ☐ F ☐

Listen – Listen & Answer Dialog 2

W: Everyone, look at this chestnut tree. This is the oldest tree in these woods.

B: Can you tell me ❶how old it is?

W: It's about 150 years old.

B: Wow! It's ten ❷times my age.

G: Ms. Oh, is that a beehive up in the tree?

W: Yes. Can you guess how many bees live there?

G: 500 bees?

W: Good guess, but it's big enough to hold over 50,000 bees.

B, G: Unbelievable!

W: 여러분, 이 밤나무를 보세요. 이것은 이 숲에서 가장 오래된 나무랍니다.

B: 그 나무가 몇 살인지 알려 주실 수 있나요?

W: 150살쯤 되었어요.

B: 와! 제 나이의 열 배군요.

G: 오 선생님. 나무 위에 있는 저것은 벌집인가요?

W: 맞아요. 벌이 저곳에서 몇 마리나 사는지 짐작할 수 있겠어요?

G: 500마리요?

W: 좋은 추측입니다. 하지만 저것은 5만 마리 이상을 수용할 만큼 커요.

B, G: 믿을 수 없어요!

❶ 'how old it is'는 의문사로 시작하는 간접의문문이다. 간접의문문은 "의문사+주어+동사"의 어순이다.

❷ times는 횟수와 배수를 나타낸다. 여기에서는 배수로 쓰여서 'ten times'는 '열 배'이다.

Check(√) True or False

(3) The tree is ten times older than the boy.　　　　T ☐ F ☐

(4) The tree is 500 years old.　　　　T ☐ F ☐

(5) We can't guess how many bees live in a beehive.　　　　T ☐ F ☐

Listen More – Listen and choose.

B: Sora, can you ❶take a look at these pictures?
G: ❷What are these for?
B: I'm ❸trying to choose a picture for my story in the school newspaper.
G: What's your story about?
B: Nature's future.
G: ❹Can you tell me more about it?
B: It's about ❺endangered animals in the Arctic areas.
G: That sounds interesting.
B: ❻Which picture do you think is better?
G: I like the one showing a skinny polar bear.

❶ take a look at ~ = ~을 보다
❷ What ~ for? = 무슨 용도로 ~?
❸ try to ~ = ~하려고 노력하다
❹ 'Can you tell me more about it?'은 상대방에게 더 많은 설명을 요청하는 말이다.
❺ endangered = 멸종 위기에 처한
❻ Which ~는 정해진 범위 안에서 '어느 것 ~'이라고 물어보는 것이다.

Speak – Talk in groups.

A: Which do ❶like better, dogs or cats?
B: I like dogs better. They are more friendly. ❷How about you?
C: I like cats better.
D: ❸Me, too. Cats are much cleaner than dogs.

❶ like better = prefer 더 좋아하다, 선호하다
❷ 'How about you?'는 상대의 의견을 물어보거나 권유 또는 제안을 하는 표현이다.
❸ 'Me, too.'는 동의하는 표현으로 'So+동사+주어'의 형태로 나타내기도 한다.

Speak – Talk in pairs.

A: What ❶are you drawing?
B: An elephant.
A: What's an elephant?
B: It's an animal.
A: ❷Can you tell me more about it?
B: It's a big animal that has a long nose and big ears.

❶ 현재진행 시제로 현재 진행되고 있는 동작에 대한 질문이다.
❷ 'Can tell me more about it?'은 추가적인 설명을 요청하는 것으로 tell 대신 explain을 쓸 수도 있다.

My Speaking Portfolio Step 3

A: I heard whales are ❶having a hard time these days. Can you tell me more?
B: Sure. There's lots of trash in the sea. Many whales eat it and ❷get sick.
A: That's too bad. Is there anything we can do ❸to help them?
B: Yes. First, we should try to clean up the sea. Also, ...

❶ 'have a hard time'은 '어려움이 있다'는 표현으로 'have a difficult time' 'have trouble'이라고 할 수 있다.
❷ 'get sick'은 '병에 걸리다'의 의미로 get은 '~하게 되다'의 의미이다.
❸ 'to help them'은 목적을 나타내는 to부정사로 '돕기 위하여'에 해당하는 의미이다.

Wrap Up – Listening & Speaking ❺

G: What do you do in your free time?
B: I listen to music ❶like EDM or hip-hop.
G: Which do you like better?
B: I prefer hip-hop.
G: Why?
B: Well, it ❷sounds more exciting.

❶ like는 '~처럼'의 의미로 사례를 덧붙일 때 사용한다.
❷ sound는 형용사 보어를 사용하여 'sound+형용사'이다.

Wrap Up – Listening & Speaking ❺

G: Guess what I'm talking about.
B: Okay. ❶Go ahead.
G: It's a common machine ❷that you can see at home.
B: Well, can you tell me more?
G: It helps you wash clothes.
B: Now I know what it is.

❶ 'Go ahead.'는 '계속해.'라는 의미이다.
❷ that은 목적격 관계대명사로 선행사는 a common machine이다.

● 다음 우리말과 일치하도록 빈칸에 알맞은 말을 쓰시오.

Listen – Listen and Answer – Dialog 1

B: Amber, _____ do you like the camp?

G: It's _____. I'm _____ a lot of fun.

B: _____, too. The talent _____ last night was really _____.

G: Yeah. _____ the way, did you _____ on the afternoon program?

B: No, I haven't _____. _____ do you _____ is _____, hiking or swimming?

G: I'll go _____ because we can _____ _____ birds and _____ in the woods.

B: I'll _____ you. I like _____ and insects.

G: Great. I _____ we'll have a hiking _____.

B: Sounds good.

Listen – Listen and Answer – Dialog 2

W: Everyone, _____ at this _____ tree. This is the oldest tree in these _____.

B: Can you _____ me _____ _____ it is?

W: It's _____ 150 years old.

B: Wow! It's _____ _____ my age.

G: Ms. Oh, is that a _____ _____ in the tree?

W: Yes. Can you _____ how many _____ _____ there?

G: 500 bees?

W: Good _____, but it's _____ to _____ over 50,000 bees.

B, G: _____!

Listen More - Listen and choose.

B: Sora, can you _____ a _____ at these pictures?

G: _____ are these _____?

B: I'm _____ to _____ a picture for my _____ in the school newspaper.

G: _____ your story _____?

B: Nature's future.

G: Can you _____ me _____ _____ it?

B: It's about _____ _____ in the _____ areas.

G: That _____ interesting.

B: _____ _____ do you think is better?

G: I like the one _____ a _____ polar bear.

Speak – Talk in groups.

A: Which do _____ _____, dogs or cats?

B: I _____ dogs better. They are more _____. _____ _____ you?

C: I like cats better.

D: _____, too. Cats are _____ _____ than dogs.

Speak – Talk in pairs.

A: What are you _____?

B: An _____.

A: What's an elephant?

B: It's an _____.

A: Can you _____ _____ _____ about it?

B: It's a _____ animal _____ _____ a long nose and big ears.

My Speaking Portfolio Step 1

1. People _____ to the _____ and _____ the forest. Many of my friends have _____ their homes. I don't know _____ to go.

2. I get _____ _____ I have to _____ a big street. This morning I was _____ hit. I don't _____ _____ people are in _____ a hurry.

3. I have a _____ _____. I _____ something strange. I think it's _____ someone _____ into the sea.

4. Sometimes I _____ _____ not because it's _____ _____ but because it's _____ _____. When lights are too bright, I can't tell which way to fly.

Wrap Up - Listening & Speaking ❺

G: What do you _____ in your _____ _____?

B: I _____ to music _____ EDM or hip-hop.

G: _____ do you _____ _____?

B: I _____ hip-hop.

G: Why?

B: Well, it _____ more _____.

해석

A: 개와 고양이 중에 어느 것을 더 좋아하니?

B: 개를 더 좋아해. 그들이 더 친절해. 너는 어떠니?

C: 나는 고양이를 더 좋아해.

D: 나도 그래. 고양이가 개보다 훨씬 더 깨끗해.

A: 너는 무엇을 그리고 있니?

B: 코끼리.

A: 코끼리가 뭐니?

B: 그것은 동물이야.

A: 그것에 대하여 더 말해 줄 수 있니?

B: 그것은 긴 코와 큰 귀를 가진 덩치 큰 동물이야.

1. 사람들이 숲에 와서 삼림을 파괴해요. 내 친구들 중 많은 수가 집을 잃었어요. 나는 어디로 가야 할지 모르겠어요.

2. 나는 큰 길을 건너야 할 때마다 겁이 나요. 오늘 아침 나는 차에 치일 뻔했다고요. 사람들이 왜 그리 급한지 이해가 안 돼요.

3. 나는 배가 몹시 아파요. 나는 이상한 것을 먹었어요. 내 생각에 그것은 누군가 바다에 버린 것 같아요.

4. 때때로 나는 너무 어두워서가 아니라 너무 밝아서 길을 잃어요. 불빛이 너무 밝으면 나는 어디로 날아가야 할지 분간할 수 없어요.

여: 너는 한가한 시간에 뭐 하니?

남: 나는 EDM이나 힙합 같은 음악을 들어.

여: 어떤 것을 더 좋아하는데?

남: 나는 힙합을 더 좋아해.

여: 왜?

남: 글쎄. 그게 더 신나거든.

[01~02] 다음 대화의 빈칸에 들어갈 말을 고르시오.

01

B: Amber, how do you like the camp?

G: It's great. I'm having a lot of fun.

B: Me, too. The talent show last night was really _____.

① terrible　　　② worrying　　　③ disappointing

④ great　　　⑤ sorry

02

W: Everyone, look at this chestnut tree. This is the oldest tree in these woods.

B: _____ how old it is?

W: It's about 150 years old.

① Did you ask　　　② When did you say

③ Can you tell me　　　④ Would you ask

⑤ Can I tell you

[03~04] 다음 대화를 읽고 물음에 답하시오.

A: Which do like better, dogs or cats?

B: I like dogs better. They are more friendly. _____(A)_____ you?

C: I like cats better.

D: Me, too. _____(B)_____

03 빈칸 (A)에 들어갈 가장 알맞은 말을 고르시오.

① How about　　　② Why are　　　③ Which are

④ Which do　　　⑤ Why don't

04 다음 중 빈칸 (B)에 들어가기에 가장 적절한 것은?

① Cats are more difficult to grow.

② Cats are much cleaner than dogs.

③ Dogs are more active and cute.

④ Dogs are more cute than cats.

⑤ Cats and dogs are all scary.

[01~02] 다음 대화의 빈칸에 들어갈 말로 알맞은 것은?

01

B: Sora, can you take a look at these pictures?

G: What are these _____?

B: I'm trying to choose a picture for my story in the school newspaper.

G: What's your story about?

B: Nature's future.

① for   ② about
③ with   ④ by
⑤ in

02

A: Which do like better, dogs or cats?

B: I like dogs better. They are more friendly. How about you?

C: I like cats better.

D: _____ Cats are much cleaner than dogs.

① Why don't you like them?
② How about you?
③ Why not?
④ Neither am I.
⑤ Me, too.

 03 다음 빈칸에 들어갈 말이 순서대로 바르게 짝지어진 것은?

G: What do you do in your free time?

B: I listen to music __(A)__ EDM or hip-hop.

G: Which do you like better?

B: I __(B)__ hip-hop.

G: Why?

B: Well, it sounds more __(C)__.

	(A)	(B)	(C)
①	like	prefer	boring
②	like	prefer	exciting
③	about	dislike	boring
④	about	dislike	exciting
⑤	with	listen	boring

[04~05] 다음 대화의 순서가 바르게 배열된 것을 고르시오.

04

A: What are you drawing?

B: Sunglasses.

(A) Can you tell me more about them?

(B) They are things that you wear on your face.

(C) What are sunglasses?

B: They are a pair of lenses that protect your eyes from strong sunlight.

① (A) – (C) – (B)   ② (B) – (A) – (C)
③ (B) – (C) – (A)   ④ (C) – (A) – (B)
⑤ (C) – (B) – (A)

 05

G: Guess what I'm talking about.

B: Okay. Go ahead.

G: It's a common machine that you can see at home.

(A) Now I know what it is.

(B) Well, can you tell me more?

(C) It helps you wash clothes.

① (A) – (C) – (B)   ② (B) – (A) – (C)
③ (B) – (C) – (A)   ④ (C) – (A) – (B)
⑤ (C) – (B) – (A)

[06~09] 다음 대화를 읽고 물음에 답하시오.

> B: Amber, how do you like the camp?
> G: It's great. I'm ___(A)___ a lot of fun.
> B: (B)Me, too. The talent show last night was really great.
> G: Yeah. (C)그런데 넌 오후 프로그램을 결정했니?
> B: No, I haven't yet. Which do you think is better, hiking or swimming?
> G: I'll go hiking because we can see wild birds and insects in the woods.
> B: I'll join you. I like birds and insects.
> G: Great. I heard we'll have a hiking guide.
> B: Sounds good.

06 빈칸 (A)에 들어갈 가장 알맞은 말을 고르시오.

① giving
② having
③ going
④ thinking
⑤ wondering

07 밑줄 친 (B)와 바꿔 쓸 수 있는 것을 고르시오.

① Neither am I.
② Nor do I.
③ So am I.
④ So do I.
⑤ Neither do I.

서답형

08 아래 주어진 단어를 포함하여 밑줄 친 (C)에 어울리는 영어 문장을 완성하시오.

> on, by, decide, did, way

➡ _____

_____

09 위 대화의 내용과 일치하지 <u>않는</u> 것은?

① Amber is satisfied with the camp program.
② Amber likes hiking better than swimming.
③ The boy didn't decide on the afternoon program.
④ Amber wants to join the boy.
⑤ The afternoon program will have a hiking guide.

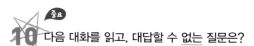

10 다음 대화를 읽고, 대답할 수 <u>없는</u> 질문은?

> G: Which do you like better, hot weather or cold weather?
> B: I like cold weather better. I'm sensitive to hot temperatures. How about you?
> G: I like hot weather better. I like going swimming in the sea.
> W: Me, too.
>
> G = Girl, B = Boy W = Woman

① Which does the girl like better, hot weather or cold weather?
② Why does the boy like cold weather?
③ Does the woman like hot weather?
④ Which does the boy like better, hot weather or cold weather?
⑤ Does the boy like going swimming?

[01~02] 다음 대화를 읽고 물음에 답하시오.

B: Sora, can you take a look at these pictures?
G: What are these for?
B: I'm trying to choose a picture for my story in the school newspaper.
G: What's your story about?
B: Nature's future.
G: Can you tell me more about it?
B: It's about endangered animals in the Arctic areas.
G: That sounds interesting.
B: Which picture do you think is better?
G: I like the one showing a skinny polar bear.

01 Why does the boy want to choose a picture? Complete the sentence.

➡ He _____

_____ .

02 What is the boy's story about? Complete the sentence.

➡ It is about _____ .

03 주어진 단어를 사용하여 밑줄 친 우리말에 해당하는 영어 문장을 완성하시오.

I get scared whenever I have to cross a big street. This morning I was almost hit. 사람들이 왜 그토록 급한지 이해가 안 돼요.

such, why, understand, in, people, a, hurry

➡ _____

_____

04 다음 대화의 문맥상 또는 어법상 어색한 것을 찾아 고치시오.

A: What do you prefer, pizza or fried chicken?
B: I like pizza better. I can choose the toppings I like. How about you?
A: I like fried chicken better.
C: Me, too. I'm a meat lover.

_____

➡ _____

[05~06] 다음 대화를 읽고 물음에 답하시오.

W: Everyone, look at this chestnut tree. This is the oldest tree in these woods.
B: Can you tell me how old it is?
W: It's about 150 years old.
B: Wow! It's ten times my ___(A)___ .
G: Ms. Oh, is that a beehive up in the tree?
W: Yes. Can you guess how many bees live there?
G: 500 bees?
W: Good guess, but (B)그것은 5만 마리 이상을 수용할 만큼 커요. (hold, enough, over, big)
B: G: Unbelievable!

05 빈칸 (A)에 들어가기에 적절한 단어를 쓰시오.

➡ _____

06 주어진 단어를 포함하여 밑줄 친 (B)의 우리말을 영작하시오.

➡ _____

Grammar

① 명사를 뒤에서 꾸미는 분사

> • Look at the sun **rising over the sea**. 바다 위로 떠오르는 해를 봐.

■ 형태: 명사+현재분사[과거분사]+수식어구

　의미: ~하는 … / ~된 …

■ 분사는 현재분사와 과거분사가 있다. 분사는 문장 안에서 형용사 역할을 하여 명사를 수식할 수 있다. 분사가 수식어구와 함께 사용될 때는 명사 뒤에서 수식한다. '명사+분사'는 '명사+주격 관계대명사+ be동사+분사'에서 '주격 관계대명사+be동사'가 생략된 것이라고 볼 수 있다.

　• Look at the boy **dancing on the stage**. 무대 위에서 춤을 추는 소년을 보아라.

　• Look at the picture **painted by a parrot**. 앵무새에 의해서 그려진 그림을 보아라.

■ 분사가 명사를 수식할 때 현재분사는 능동이나 진행의 의미를 가져서 '~하는, ~하고 있는'의 의미가 된다. 과거분사는 수동이나 완료의 의미를 나타내어 '~해진, ~하게 된'의 의미가 된다.

　• Do you know the child **crying at the door**? 문에서 울고 있는 아이를 아니?

　• Look at the man **climbing the tall building**. 높은 건물을 올라가고 있는 사람을 봐.

　• I like every food **cooked by my grandmother**. 나는 할머니에 의해서 요리된 모든 음식을 좋아해.

　• He is carrying a basket **filled with cherries**. 그는 체리로 가득 채워진 바구니를 운반하고 있다.

핵심 Check

1. 다음 주어진 문장에서 적절한 것을 고르시오.

　(1) He visited the doctor (was working / working) at the hospital.

　(2) The woman (is sleeping / sleeping) in the room will wake up in an hour.

　(3) Do you know the girl (is walking / walking) along the street?

　(4) The man sitting by the window (is waiting / waiting) for his wife.

　(5) Those books lying on the desk (are / being) very interesting.

　(6) Tom was taking out some chairs (were broken / broken) during the earthquake.

　(7) The idea (was discussed / discussed) yesterday will be important for your plan.

2. 다음 빈칸에 주어진 단어를 적절한 형태로 쓰시오.

　(1) The people in the town love the church _____ in 1890. (build)

　(2) The book _____ in 1940 has many interesting stories. (write)

　(3) Harry has been _____ to watch TV for an hour. (allow)

　(4) Look at the girl _____ the tall building. (climb)

　(5) This picture _____ at the top of the mountain shows wonderful scenery. (take)

② 접속사 since와 though

> • **Since** it rained heavily, the station was closed. 심하게 비가 와서 역이 문을 닫았다.

■ 형태: **Since/Though** + 주어+동사 ~, 주어+동사
  주어+동사 ~ **since/though** + 주어+동사

  의미: **since** = ~이기 때문에, ~한 이래로
   though = 비록 ~이지만

■ since는 종속접속사로 주절의 이유나 근거를 나타내어 '~이기 때문에, ~해서'의 의미를 나타낸다. since는 부사절을 유도하며 since가 유도하는 부사절은 주절의 앞이나 뒤에 쓰인다.

  • **Since** I ate a whole pizza, I am full.
   = I am full since I ate a whole pizza. 피자 한 판을 다 먹었기 때문에 나는 배가 부르다.

  • **Since** it is hot, I want to drink something cold.
   = I want to drink something cold since it is hot. 날씨가 더워서 나는 차가운 것을 마시고 싶다.

  cf. She has lived here **since** she moved to this city. 그녀는 이 도시로 이사한 이후로 여기에서 살고 있다.
   (since = ~한 이래로)

■ 접속사 though는 although와 함께 '비록 ~이기는 하지만, ~할지라도'의 의미로, 주절과 대조되거나 상반되는 내용을 나타내는 양보의 접속사이다. though와 although는 부사절을 유도한다.

  • **Though** I ate a whole pizza, I am still hungry.
   = I am still hungry **though** I ate a whole pizza. 비록 내가 피자 한 판을 다 먹었지만, 나는 여전히 배가 고프다.

  • I am tired **though** I slept enough last night.
   = **Though** I slept enough last night, I am tired. 비록 어젯밤에 충분히 잤지만, 나는 피곤하다.

핵심 Check

3. 다음 주어진 문장에 어울리는 것을 고르시오.

  (1) (Since / Though) you finished your homework, you may go out and play.

  (2) (Since / Though) he had prepared a lot, he failed at the tryout.

  (3) I don't want to go to the party (though / since) I have no one to talk with.

  (4) (Though / Since) he was smiling, he didn't look that happy.

  (5) It is sunny (though / since) it is cold.

01 다음 빈칸에 들어갈 말로 알맞은 것은?

> Who is the man _____ by the door?

① stand　　　② stood　　　③ to stand

④ standing　　⑤ is standing

02 다음 중 밑줄 친 부분의 쓰임이 어색한 것을 고르시오.

① The boy wearing a baseball cap is my brother.

② Do you know the child crying in the room?

③ Look at the man climbing the high mountain.

④ I like every food cooking by my grandmother.

⑤ He is carrying a basket filled with cherries.

03 다음 〈보기〉의 밑줄 친 부분과 쓰임이 같은 것은?

┤ 보기 ├

> This is a photo taken last weekend.

① He has a lovely daughter named Elizabeth.

② I helped her clean the cage made of wood.

③ The cat watched us from a chair painted green.

④ Ants produced a special chemical for communication.

⑤ Mary used the smartphone for three years.

04 다음 우리말을 영어로 바르게 옮긴 것은?

> 비록 날씨가 춥지만 나는 차가운 것을 마시고 싶다.

① It is cold though I want to drink something cold.

② Though it is hot, I want to drink something hot.

③ Since it is cold, I want to drink something cold.

④ Though it is cold, I want to drink something cold.

⑤ Though I want to drink something cold, it is cold.

05 다음 괄호 안에서 알맞은 말을 고르시오.

(1) The man [wears / wearing] a white shirt is my uncle.

(2) I ate the whole cake [though / since] I really liked cake.

서답형

01 〈보기〉를 참고하여 주어진 두 문장을 한 문장으로 연결하여 쓰시오.

> ─┤ 보기 ├─
> • The book was written by her.
> • The book is easy to read.
> ➡ The book written by her is easy to read.

(1) • The man was running along the road.
   • The man was asking for help.
   ➡ _____

   _____

(2) • The boy was eating lunch.
   • He was sitting on the floor.
   ➡ _____

   _____

(3) • The man was reading a book.
   • He told us to be quiet.
   ➡ _____

   _____

(4) • The boys were allowed to watch TV.
   • They were eating snacks.
   ➡ _____

   _____

02 다음 중 밑줄 친 부분의 쓰임이 어색한 것을 고르시오.

① I am tired though I slept enough last night.
② Though I ate a whole pizza, I am still hungry.
③ I stayed home though I felt tired.
④ Since I am tired, I will stop working.
⑤ Though he was full, he ate more cake.

서답형

03 다음 괄호 안에서 알맞은 말을 고르시오.

(1) The photos [taken / taking] by him show some sailing boats.
(2) The kid [walk / walking] across the garden is my brother.
(3) Do you know the man [inviting / invited] to the party?
(4) [Though / Since] I met him before, I was pleased to see him again.
(5) [Though / Since] I had lunch, I am still hungry.

04 다음 중 밑줄 친 부분의 쓰임이 어색한 것을 고르시오.

① The story is about endangered animals in the Arctic areas.
② I like the picture showing a skinny polar bear.
③ A watermelon is a ball-shaped fruit that has sweet and juicy flesh in it.
④ Look at the sun rising over the sea.
⑤ Though it rained heavily, he didn't go out.

05 다음 우리말을 영어로 바르게 옮긴 것은?

> 저기에서 노래하는 사람을 보아라.

① Look at the man sings over there.
② Look at the man singing over there.
③ Singing over there the man looking.
④ Looking at the man singing over there.
⑤ Look at the man to sing over there.

06 다음 중 밑줄 친 부분의 쓰임이 다른 하나를 고르시오.

① Those books <u>written</u> by James are very interesting.
② We saw the picture <u>taken</u> at the top.
③ He <u>found</u> a picture showing the image of a person.
④ Animals <u>found</u> in the mountain were eating grass.
⑤ The <u>frightened</u> child ran into the room.

07 다음 중 밑줄 친 부분의 쓰임이 어색한 것을 고르시오.

① An airplane is a <u>flying</u> machine that can take you to a faraway place.
② The girl <u>singing</u> over there is Nancy.
③ I helped her clean the cage <u>made</u> of glass.
④ The woman <u>moving</u> the table is my sister.
⑤ There is a picture <u>paint</u> by a parrot.

08 다음 빈칸에 들어갈 말로 알맞은 것은?

> _____ it rained heavily, the station was closed.

① Although   ② While
③ Whether   ④ Since
⑤ If

09 다음 우리말을 영어로 바르게 옮긴 것은?

> 나는 그녀가 요리한 음식을 모두 좋아한다.

① I like every food cooked by her.
② She likes all the food I cooked.
③ She likes every food cooked by her.
④ I like every food cook by her.
⑤ I like every food cooking by her.

서답형
10 다음 우리말에 맞게 괄호 안에 주어진 어휘를 바르게 배열하시오. (필요하면 어형을 바꿀 것)

(1) 아이 한 명이 해변에서 놀고 있었다. (was, playing, the beach, there, a boy, on)
➡ _____

(2) 나는 나무로 만들어진 벤치에 앉았다. (the bench, wood, make, of, sat, on, I)
➡ _____

(3) 나는 너무 어리기 때문에 그 영화를 볼 수 없다. (I, watch, too young, am, the film, can't, I, since) (since로 시작할 것)
➡ _____

서답형
11 다음 괄호 안에서 알맞은 말을 고르시오.

(1) This is a cake (make / made) by him this morning.
(2) I visited a castle (built / building) a hundred years ago.
(3) I cleaned the wall (painting / painted) yellow.
(4) The taxi driver (moving / moved) the bag is very kind.
(5) The woman watched us from a car (wash / washed) this morning.

12 다음 중 밑줄 친 부분의 쓰임이 어색한 것을 고르시오.

① The children wearing a baseball cap are my friends.
② Do you know the girl playing in the room?
③ Look at the man running over the hill.
④ An essay wrote carefully will receive a high grade.
⑤ Since it was raining, we didn't go out.

13 다음 중 밑줄 친 부분의 쓰임이 다른 하나를 고르시오.

① The boy singing a song is my nephew.
② I know the child crying loudly.
③ The parrot sitting on the tree said, "Hurry up."
④ She enjoyed talking to her friends after the class.
⑤ The man walking into the room said hello to me.

14 다음 중 밑줄 친 부분의 쓰임이 어색한 것을 고르시오.

① In the room, I saw a picture drawn by him.
② That is the tower built by her last year.
③ The girl sitting under the tree called my name.
④ I like every book written by him.
⑤ I don't like the gift gave to me.

[15~16] 다음 빈칸에 들어갈 말로 알맞은 것은?

15

> Like humans, they live almost everywhere in the world, except a few extremely cold places _____ Antarctica.

① include
② included
③ includes
④ including
⑤ have included

16

> _____ he knows how to drive a car, he doesn't like to drive a car.

① Though
② Since
③ While
④ Whether
⑤ Unless

17 다음 밑줄 친 것 중에서 쓰임이 다른 하나는?

① Tom was tired since he walked for a long distance.
② Since it was very cold, I had to put on the jacket.
③ My mother made a cake since it was my birthday.
④ She has lived here since 2005.
⑤ I won't travel by train since I don't like the noise.

18 다음 빈칸에 들어가기에 적절한 것은?

> Jane is _____ though she slept enough last night.

① free
② glad
③ busy
④ tired
⑤ happy

01 다음 우리말에 맞게 괄호 안에 주어진 어휘를 바르게 배열하시오. (필요한 어휘 변형 및 어휘 추가 가능)

(1) 그는 그에게 보내진 메시지를 읽지 않았다. (read, send, the message, to him, he, didn't)

➡ _____

_____

(2) 농구하고 있는 아이들은 내 친구들이다. (be, the children, my friends, play basketball)

➡ _____

_____

(3) 그는 내 동생에 의해 그려진 그림을 보고 있었다. (was looking at, by, paint, he, the picture, my brother)

➡ _____

_____

(4) 그 책이 너무 재미있어서 나는 그 책을 어젯밤에 읽기를 끝냈다. (the book, so, finished, was, reading the book, interesting, since, I, last night) (since로 시작할 것)

➡ _____

_____

(5) 나는 배가 고팠지만 음식을 먹지 않았다. (I, hungry, eat, was, didn't, though, I, the food) (though로 시작할 것)

➡ _____

_____

02 다음 밑줄 친 단어 대신 쓸 수 있는 단어를 쓰시오. (한 단어)

Though he was busy, he helped me.

➡ _____

03 다음 문장에 주어진 단어를 적절한 형태로 빈칸에 쓰시오.

(1) The man _____ by the tree was Ann's husband. (sit)

(2) Those books _____ on the desk are very difficult to read. (lie)

(3) He has to fix the door _____ a few days ago. (break)

(4) A picture _____ the top of the mountain was wonderful. (show)

(5) He was eating cookies _____ by his mother. (make)

04 다음 주어진 문장의 빈칸에 접속사 since와 though 중에서 적절한 것을 쓰시오.

(1) _____ it is cold, I want to drink something hot.

(2) _____ it rains, I'll go out with my friends.

(3) _____ I am tired, I want to go home early.

(4) _____ I am tired, I will stay up late and enjoy Friday night.

05 다음 우리말과 의미가 같도록 영작할 때 빈칸에 알맞은 말을 〈조건〉에 맞게 쓰시오.

┌─ 조건 ┤
'bark'를 사용하여 문장을 완성할 것.

거리에서 짖고 있는 개 한 마리가 있다.
= There is _____ _____ _____
on the street.

06 다음 문장에서 어법상 어색한 부분을 바르게 고쳐 문장을 다시 쓰시오.

> The man walked his dogs is a famous singer.

➡ _____

07 다음 우리말에 맞게 빈칸에 알맞은 말을 쓰시오.

> 나는 방금 먹었기 때문에 배고프지 않다.
> ➡ I'm not hungry _____ I have just eaten.

➡ _____

08 다음 주어진 문장을 〈보기〉와 같이 분사가 있는 한 문장으로 다시 쓰시오.

> ┤ 보기 ├
> • The children are watching TV.
> • They will help you.
> ➡ <u>The children watching TV will help you.</u>

(1) • The church was built 100 years ago.
　　• It has beautiful stained glass.

➡ _____

_____

(2) • The car was rolling down the road.
　　• It made a loud noise.

➡ _____

_____

(3) • The woman is cooking apple pies.
　　• She will give them to you.

➡ _____

_____

(4) • The photos were taken by Ann.
　　• They show some wild birds.

➡ _____

_____

(5) • The message was sent to him.
　　• He was reading the message.

➡ _____

_____

09 다음 대화의 우리말에 해당하는 문장을 영어로 옮길 때 빈칸에 들어가기에 적절한 단어를 쓰시오.

> B: Which picture do you think is better?
> G: 나는 여윈 북극곰을 보여 주는 사진이 마음에 들어.(= I like the one _____ a skinny polar bear).

➡ _____

10 다음 문장에서 어색한 것을 바로 잡으시오.

(1) Mike was reading the newspaper send to him this morning.

_____ ➡ _____

(2) Did the children like the actor sung on the stage?

_____ ➡ _____

(3) The animals eaten plants are called beavers.

_____ ➡ _____

Reading

 교과서

The Amazing Ants

For the science project, our group has chosen very special insects.
현재완료

• They are very social.

• They are as old as the T-Rex.
as+형용사/부사+as: '~만큼 …한', 원급 비교 표현

• They appear in Aesop's stories.

• They use a special chemical to communicate.
'의사소통하기 위해', to부정사의 부사적 용법(목적)

Can you guess what they are? Yes, the answer is ants. We want to
guess의 목적어 역할을 하는 간접의문문, '의문사+주어+동사'의 어순
share with you what we have learned about these insects.
관계대명사 what(선행사 포함): '~하는 것'   현재완료   = ants

How Many Ants Are on Earth?

We often see ants come out of nowhere. Like humans, they live
지각동사+목적어+목적보어(동사원형)
almost everywhere in the world, except a few extremely cold places
a little(×)
including Antarctica. As of 2018, there were over 7 billion people on
billions(×)
Earth. Then, how about ants? According to scientists, there are about
= what about   ~에 의하면   약
one million ants for every human in the world. Though each ant hardly
'비록 ~이지만'(양보를 나타내는 접속사)   거의 ~ 않다
weighs anything, one million ants are as heavy as a human being
비교하는 두 대상의 특성이 동등함을 나타내는 원급 비교 구문
weighing about 62 kilograms.
명사를 뒤에서 수식하는 분사구 = who weighs about 62 kilograms

insect 곤충

social 사회적인, 사교적인

appear 나타나다. (글 속에) 나오다

chemical 화학물질

share 공유하다

out of nowhere 어디선지 모르게. 느닷없이

except ~을 제외하고

extremely 극심하게

including ~을 포함하여

as of ~ 현재. ~일자로

billion 십억

million 백만 (1,000,000)

hardly 거의 ~ 않다

human being 사람, 인간

weigh 무게가 나가다

확인문제

● 다음 문장이 본문의 내용과 일치하면 T, 일치하지 않으면 F를 쓰시오.

1 Ants are very social. ☐

2 The T-Rex is older than ants. ☐

3 Ants often come out of nowhere. ☐

4 Ants live almost everywhere in the world including Antarctica. ☐

5 There are about one million ants for every human in the world. ☐

6 One million ants are heavier than a human being weighing about 62 kilograms. ☐

What Is the Ant Society Like?

Ants live in colonies which have lots of residents living together.
<small>which의 선행사 / 주격 관계대명사 / = many / = that live</small>
Within a colony, there are usually three different types of ants. There
is the queen, and what she does her entire life is lay eggs. The second
<small>선행사를 포함하는 관계대명사('~하는 것') / during이 생략된 부사적 대격(시간, 거리, 방법, 정도를 나타낼 때, 전치사가 생략되고 남은 명사(구)가 부사구 역할을 하는 것) / be동사 뒤에서 to부정사가 보어로 쓰일 때 to가 종종 생략된다. 주어가 관계대명사 what이고 do[does] 동사를 포함하는 경우</small>
type of ant is the male that helps the queen produce these eggs. The
<small>주격 관계대명사 / help(준사역동사)+목적어+목적보어(원형부정사)</small>
third type of ant is the worker. Worker ants are all female and do
very important jobs, like caring for eggs, defending the colony, and
<small>전치사 like의 목적어(동명사) / like의 목적어(동명사)</small>
collecting food.
<small>like의 목적어(동명사)</small>

How Do Ants Communicate?

Though ants do not speak like humans, they actually have
<small>= Although</small>
a "language." Ants produce a chemical called a pheromone
<small>앞의 명사 a chemical을 수식하는 분사구. = which is called a pheromone</small>
to communicate with one another. By using the chemical, they can
<small>to부정사의 부사적 용법(목적) / ~을 사용함으로써</small>
exchange information about food or danger. Ants also use touch for
communication. For example, if an ant finds food, it passes on the
<small>예를 들면</small>
good news by rubbing its body on its neighbor. Since an ant has legs
<small>이유를 나타내는 부사절을 이끄는 접속사</small>
covered with very sensitive hairs, it can sense even the smallest touch.
<small>= which are covered with very sensitive hairs</small>

colony (동식물의) 군락, 군집
resident 거주자
entire 전체의
lay eggs 알을 낳다
male 남성의, 수컷의
produce 생산하다, 만들어 내다
female 여성의, 암컷의
defend 방어하다
one another 서로
exchange 교환하다
pass on 전달하다
rub 문지르다, 비비다
sensitive 예민한, 민감한

확인문제

● 다음 문장이 본문의 내용과 일치하면 T, 일치하지 <u>않으면</u> F를 쓰시오.

1 Within a colony, there are usually three different types of ants. ☐

2 What the queen does her entire life is care for eggs. ☐

3 The male helps the queen produce the eggs. ☐

4 Worker ants are all male. ☐

5 Ants produce a chemical called a pheromone to communicate with one another. ☐

6 Since an ant has wings covered with very sensitive hairs, it can sense even the smallest touch. ☐

FUN FACTS ABOUT ANTS

01 Some Queen ants live up to 30 years.

02 Some ants can carry things that are 50 times their own body
<u>= which</u>   <u>50배</u>
weight.

03 Ants do not have lungs but breathe through small holes in their
<u>~을 통해서</u>
bodies.

04 An ant has two stomachs. One stomach holds food for itself, and
<u>둘 중 하나</u>   <u>재귀대명사</u>
the other holds food to share with others.
<u>둘 중 다른 하나</u>   <u>= other ants</u>

05 Most ants can swim and live 24 hours underwater.
<u>물속에서(부사)</u>

up to ~까지
weight 몸무게, 체중
lung 폐
breathe 호흡하다
hole 구멍
stomach 위
underwater 수중에서

📎 **확인문제**

● 다음 문장이 본문의 내용과 일치하면 T, 일치하지 <u>않으면</u> F를 쓰시오.

1 Most Queen ants live up to more than 30 years. ☐

2 Ants have small holes in their bodies. ☐

3 An ant has another stomach to share food with other ants. ☐

● 우리말을 참고하여 빈칸에 알맞은 말을 쓰시오.

1 The _____ Ants

2 _____ _____ _____ _____ , our group _____
   _____ very special insects.

3 They are very _____ .

4 They are _____ _____ _____ the T-Rex.

5 They _____ in Aesop's stories.

6 They use _____ _____ _____ to communicate.

7 Can you guess _____ _____ _____ ?

8 Yes, _____ _____ is ants.

9 We want to _____ _____ you _____ we have learned
   about these insects.

10 _____ _____ _____ Are on Earth?

11 We often see ants come _____ _____ _____ .

12 _____ _____ , they live almost everywhere in the world,
   _____ a few extremely cold places _____ _____ .

13 _____ _____ _____ , there were over 7 billion people on
   Earth.

14 Then, _____ _____ ants?

15 _____ _____ _____ , there are about one million ants
   _____ _____ _____ in the world.

16 Though each ant _____ _____ _____ , one million ants
   are _____ _____ _____ a human being weighing about 62
   kilograms.

17 What _____ the Ant Society _____ ?

18 Ants live in colonies _____ _____ lots of residents _____
   together.

19 _____ a colony, there are usually _____ _____ _____
   of ants.

1 놀라운 개미

2 과학 프로젝트를 위해, 우리 모
   둠은 매우 특별한 곤충을 선택
   했습니다.

3 그들은 매우 사회적입니다.

4 그들은 티라노사우루스만큼 오
   래되었습니다.

5 그들은 이솝 이야기에 등장합니
   다.

6 그들은 의사소통하기 위해 특별
   한 화학물질을 사용합니다.

7 그들이 어떤 곤충인지 추측할
   수 있나요?

8 네. 정답은 개미입니다.

9 저희들은 이 곤충에 관해 알게
   된 것을 여러분과 함께 나누고
   싶습니다.

10 지구상에는 얼마나 많은 개미가
   있을까?

11 우리는 종종 난데없이 나타나는
   개미들을 본다.

12 인간처럼, 개미도 남극을 포함
   한 일부 극도로 추운 곳을 제외
   한 전 세계 거의 모든 곳에 살고
   있다.

13 2018년 현재, 지구상에 70억이
   넘는 인구가 있었다.

14 그렇다면, 개미는 어떨까?

15 과학자들에 의하면, 세상에는
   사람 한 명당 약 백만 마리의 개
   미가 있다.

16 개미 한 마리는 거의 무게가 나
   가지 않지만 백만 마리의 개미
   는 체중이 약 62kg인 사람 한
   명과 무게가 같다.

17 개미 사회는 어떠할까?

18 개미는 많은 거주자가 함께 사
   는 군집을 이루어 산다.

19 군집 안에는 보통 세 가지 다른
   종류의 개미가 있다.

20 There is the queen, and _____ _____ _____ her entire life is lay eggs.

21 The second type of ant is the male that helps the queen _____ _____ _____.

22 _____ _____ _____ of ant is the worker.

23 Worker ants are all female and do very important jobs, _____ _____ for eggs, _____ the colony, and _____ food.

24 _____ Do Ants Communicate?

25 Though ants do not speak _____ _____, they _____ _____ a "language."

26 Ants produce a chemical _____ a pheromone _____ _____ _____ one another.

27 _____ _____ the chemical, they can _____ _____ about food or danger.

28 Ants also use touch _____ _____.

29 _____ _____, if an ant finds food, it passes on the good news _____ _____ its body _____ its neighbor.

30 Since an ant has legs _____ _____ very sensitive hairs, it can sense _____ _____ _____ _____ _____.

31 _____ _____ ABOUT ANTS

32 01 Some Queen ants live _____ _____ 30 years.

33 02 Some ants can carry things that are _____ _____ _____ _____ _____ _____.

34 03 Ants do not have lungs but _____ _____ _____ _____ in their bodies.

35 04 An ant has _____ _____.

36 _____ stomach holds food _____ _____, and _____ _____ holds food to share with others.

37 05 _____ _____ can swim and live 24 hours _____.

---

20 여왕개미가 있고, 그녀가 평생 하는 일은 알을 낳는 것이다.

21 두 번째 종류는 여왕이 알을 낳는 것을 돕는 수개미이다.

22 세 번째 종류는 일개미이다.

23 일개미는 모두 암컷인데, 알을 돌보고, 군집을 방어하며, 먹이를 모으는 것과 같은 매우 중요한 일을 한다.

24 개미는 어떻게 의사소통할까?

25 개미들이 인간처럼 말을 하는 것은 아니지만, 그들은 실제로 '언어'를 가지고 있다.

26 개미는 서로 소통하기 위해 '페로몬'이라고 불리는 화학물질을 분비한다.

27 그 화학물질을 사용하여 그들은 먹이나 위험에 관한 정보를 교환할 수 있다.

28 개미는 또한 의사소통을 위해 접촉을 이용한다.

29 예를 들어, 먹이를 발견할 경우 개미는 자기 몸을 이웃의 개미에게 문질러서 좋은 소식을 전달한다.

30 개미는 (자극에) 매우 민감한 털로 덮인 다리가 있기 때문에, 아주 미세한 접촉도 감지할 수 있다.

31 개미에 관한 재미있는 사실

32 01 어떤 여왕개미는 30년까지 살 수 있다.

33 02 어떤 개미들은 자기 몸무게의 50배에 달하는 것을 들 수 있다.

34 03 개미는 폐가 없지만, 몸에 있는 작은 구멍을 통해 호흡한다.

35 04 개미는 위가 두 개 있다.

36 하나에는 자신의 먹이를 저장하고 다른 하나에는 다른 개미들과 함께 나눌 먹이를 저장한다.

37 05 대부분의 개미는 수영할 수 있고 물속에서 24시간 동안 살 수 있다.

우리말을 참고하여 본문을 영작하시오.

1 놀라운 개미
➡ _____

2 과학 프로젝트를 위해, 우리 모둠은 매우 특별한 곤충을 선택했습니다.
➡ _____

3 그들은 매우 사회적입니다.
➡ _____

4 그들은 티라노사우루스만큼 오래되었습니다.
➡ _____

5 그들은 이솝 이야기에 등장합니다.
➡ _____

6 그들은 의사소통하기 위해 특별한 화학물질을 사용합니다.
➡ _____

7 그들이 어떤 곤충인지 추측할 수 있나요?
➡ _____

8 네. 정답은 개미입니다.
➡ _____

9 저희들은 이 곤충에 관해 알게 된 것을 여러분과 함께 나누고 싶습니다.
➡ _____

10 지구상에는 얼마나 많은 개미가 있을까?
➡ _____

11 우리는 종종 난데없이 나타나는 개미들을 본다.
➡ _____

12 인간처럼, 개미도 남극을 포함한 일부 극도로 추운 곳을 제외한 전 세계 거의 모든 곳에 살고 있다.
➡ _____

13 2018년 현재, 지구상에 70억이 넘는 인구가 있었다.
➡ _____

14 그렇다면. 개미는 어떨까?
➡ _____

15 과학자들에 의하면, 세상에는 사람 한 명당 약 백만 마리의 개미가 있다.
➡ _____

16 개미 한 마리는 거의 무게가 나가지 않지만 백만 마리의 개미는 체중이 약 62kg인 사람 한 명과 무게가 같다.
➡ _____
_____

17 개미 사회는 어떠할까?
➡ _____

18 개미는 많은 거주자가 함께 사는 군집을 이루어 산다.
➡ _____

19 군집 안에는 보통 세 가지 다른 종류의 개미가 있다.

➡ _____

20 여왕개미가 있고. 그녀가 평생 하는 일은 알을 낳는 것이다.

➡ _____

21 두 번째 종류는 여왕이 알을 낳는 것을 돕는 수개미이다.

➡ _____

22 세 번째 종류는 일개미이다.

➡ _____

23 일개미는 모두 암컷인데, 알을 돌보고, 군집을 방어하며, 먹이를 모으는 것과 같은 매우 중요한 일을 한다.

➡ _____

_____

24 개미는 어떻게 의사소통할까?

➡ _____

25 개미들이 인간처럼 말을 하는 것은 아니지만, 그들은 실제로 '언어'를 가지고 있다.

➡ _____

26 개미는 서로 소통하기 위해 '페로몬'이라고 불리는 화학물질을 분비한다.

➡ _____

27 그 화학물질을 사용하여 그들은 먹이나 위험에 관한 정보를 교환할 수 있다.

➡ _____

28 개미는 또한 의사소통을 위해 접촉을 이용한다.

➡ _____

29 예를 들어, 먹이를 발견할 경우 개미는 자기 몸을 이웃의 개미에게 문질러서 좋은 소식을 전달한다.

➡ _____

30 개미는 (자극에) 매우 민감한 털로 덮인 다리가 있기 때문에, 아주 미세한 접촉도 감지할 수 있다.

➡ _____

31 개미에 관한 재미있는 사실

➡ _____

32 01 어떤 여왕개미는 30년까지 살 수 있다.

➡ _____

33 02 어떤 개미들은 자기 몸무게의 50배에 달하는 것을 들 수 있다.

➡ _____

34 03 개미는 폐가 없지만, 몸에 있는 작은 구멍을 통해 호흡한다.

➡ _____

35 04 개미는 위가 두 개 있다.

➡ _____

36 하나에는 자신의 먹이를 저장하고 다른 하나에는 다른 개미들과 함께 나눌 먹이를 저장한다.

➡ _____

37 05 대부분의 개미는 수영할 수 있고 물속에서 24시간 동안 살 수 있다.

➡ _____

[01~03] 다음 글을 읽고 물음에 답하시오.

For the science project, our group has chosen very special insects.

- They are very social.
- They are as old as the T-Rex.
- They appear in ⓐAesop's stories.
- They use a special chemical ⓑto communicate.

Can you guess what they are? Yes, the answer is ants. We want to share with you what we have learned about these insects.

01 위 글의 밑줄 친 ⓐAesop's stories가 속하는 문학 장르로 알맞은 것을 고르시오.

① poem　　　　② essay
③ fable　　　　④ play
⑤ scenario

02 아래 〈보기〉에서 위 글의 밑줄 친 ⓑto communicate와 to부정사의 용법이 다른 것의 개수를 고르시오.

┌─── 보기 ├───
① You have to study hard to pass the exam.
② He tried to help the poor man.
③ She was surprised to hear the news.
④ She awoke to find herself famous.
⑤ Her dream is to be a dancer.

① 1개　② 2개　③ 3개　④ 4개　⑤ 5개

03 위 글의 뒤에 올 내용으로 가장 알맞은 것을 고르시오.

① 과학 프로젝트 과제 선택 과정 설명
② 과학 프로젝트 과제 조사 방법 설명
③ 개미와 티라노사우르스의 비교
④ 의사소통에 필요한 매체 발표
⑤ 모둠이 개미에 관해 알게 된 것 발표

[04~06] 다음 글을 읽고 물음에 답하시오.

What Is the Ant Society Like?

(A)Ants live in colonies which has lots of residents living together. Within a colony, there are usually three different types of ants. There is the queen, and what she does her entire life is ＿ⓐ＿ eggs. The second type of ant is the male that helps the queen produce these eggs. The third type of ant is the worker. Worker ants are all female and do very important jobs, like caring for eggs, defending the colony, and collecting food.

04 위 글의 빈칸 ⓐ에 들어갈 알맞은 말을 모두 고르시오.

① to lay　　　　② laid
③ lie　　　　　④ lay
⑤ lying

서답형
05 위 글의 밑줄 친 (A)에서 어법상 틀린 부분을 찾아 고치시오.

＿＿＿＿＿ ➡ ＿＿＿＿＿

서답형
06 주어진 영영풀이에 해당하는 단어를 본문에서 찾아 쓰시오.

a group of organisms of the same type living or growing together

➡ ＿＿＿＿＿＿＿＿＿

[07~09] 다음 글을 읽고 물음에 답하시오.

How Many Ants Are on Earth?

We often see ants come out of nowhere. Like humans, they live almost everywhere in the world, ___ⓐ___ a few extremely cold places including Antarctica. As of 2018, there were over 7 billion people on Earth. Then, how about ants? According to scientists, there are about one million ants ___ⓑ___ every human in the world. Though each ant hardly weighs anything, one million ants are as heavy as a human being ⓒweighing about 62 kilograms.

07 위 글의 빈칸 ⓐ와 ⓑ에 들어갈 전치사가 바르게 짝지어진 것은?

      ⓐ   ⓑ   ⓐ   ⓑ
① for   – from   ② except – for
③ in   – for   ④ for   – to
⑤ except – from

08 위 글의 밑줄 친 ⓒweighing과 문법적 쓰임이 같은 것을 모두 고르시오.

① My hobby is collecting stamps.
② The boy reading a book in the room is Ben.
③ Do you know the girl speaking English over there?
④ She left without saying a word.
⑤ Who is the boy playing baseball?

09 According to the passage, which is NOT true?

① Ants can live even in very cold places.
② As of 2018, over 7 billion people were living on Earth.
③ The number of ants is about one million times more than that of humans.
④ Each ant hardly weighs anything.
⑤ The weight of one million ants is about 62 kilograms.

10 다음 주어진 글 다음에 이어질 글의 순서로 가장 적절한 것은?

> Though ants do not speak like humans, they actually have a "language."

(A) Ants also use touch for communication. For example, if an ant finds food, it passes on the good news by rubbing its body on its neighbor.

(B) Ants produce a chemical called a pheromone to communicate with one another. By using the chemical, they can exchange information about food or danger.

(C) Since an ant has legs covered with very sensitive hairs, it can sense even the smallest touch.

① (A) – (C) – (B)   ② (B) – (A) – (C)
③ (B) – (C) – (A)   ④ (C) – (A) – (B)
⑤ (C) – (B) – (A)

[11~12] 다음 글을 읽고 물음에 답하시오.

How Do Ants Communicate?

Though ants do not speak like humans, they actually have a "language." Ants produce a chemical called a pheromone to communicate with one another. By using the chemical, they can exchange information about food or danger. Ants also use touch for communication. For example, if an ant finds food, it passes on ⓐthe good news by rubbing its body on its neighbor. Since an ant has legs covered with very sensitive hairs, it can sense even the smallest touch.

11 위 글의 주제로 알맞은 것을 고르시오.

① the way in which ants communicate

② how to produce a pheromone

③ various kinds of chemicals

④ the reason ants exchange information

⑤ the right way to use touch

서답형

12 위 글의 밑줄 친 ⓐthe good news의 내용을 우리말로 쓰시오.

➡ _____

[13~15] 다음 글을 읽고 물음에 답하시오.

We often see ants come out of nowhere. Like humans, they live almost everywhere in the world, except a few extremely cold places including Antarctica. As of 2018, there were over 7 billion people on Earth. Then, how about ants? According to scientists, there are about one million ants for every human in the world. (A)Though each ant hardly weighs anything, one million ants are as heavy as a human being ___ⓐ___ about 62 kilograms.

13 위 글의 빈칸 ⓐ에 weigh를 알맞은 형태로 쓰시오.

➡ _____

14 위 글의 밑줄 친 (A)Though와 바꿔 쓸 수 있는 말을 <u>모두</u> 고르시오.

① In spite of　② Although

③ Even though　④ Despite

⑤ As though

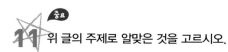

15 위 글의 제목으로 알맞은 것을 고르시오.

① How Do Ants Communicate?

② Have You Ever Seen Ants?

③ What Is the Ant Society Like?

④ How Many Ants Are There on Earth?

⑤ Can Ants Live in Antarctica?

[16~18] 다음 글을 읽고 물음에 답하시오.

What Is the Ant Society Like?

Ants live in colonies (A)[where / which] have lots of residents living together. Within a colony, there are usually three different types of ants. There is the queen, and ⓐ <u>what</u> she does her entire life is lay eggs. The second type of ant is the male that helps the queen (B)[produce / producing] these eggs. The (C)[third / three] type of ant is the worker. Worker ants are all female and do very important jobs, like ⓑcaring for eggs, defending the colony, and collecting food.

16 위 글의 괄호 (A)~(C)에서 문맥이나 어법상 알맞은 낱말을 골라 쓰시오.

➡ (A) _____ (B) _____ (C) _____

17 위 글의 밑줄 친 ⓐwhat과 문법적 쓰임이 같은 것을 모두 고르시오.

① What do you think of that film?

② What I said is true.

③ I always do what I believe is right.

④ What a beautiful house!

⑤ Do you know what this is?

18 위 글의 밑줄 친 ⓑcaring for와 바꿔 쓸 수 있는 말을 모두 고르시오.

① looking after   ② taking after

③ making sure   ④ taking care of

⑤ looking for

[19~21] 다음 글을 읽고 물음에 답하시오.

FUN FACTS ABOUT ANTS

01 Some Queen ants live ⓐup to 30 years.

02 Some ants can carry things that are 50 (A) [hours / times] their own body weight.

03 Ants do not have lungs but breathe through small holes in their bodies.

04 An ant has two stomachs. One stomach holds food for itself, and (B)[others / the other] holds food to share with (C)[others / the other].

05 Most ants can swim and live 24 hours underwater.

19 위 글의 밑줄 친 ⓐup to와 가장 가까운 의미로 쓰인 것을 고르시오.

① He's not up to the job.

② What's she up to?

③ The temperature went up to 35℃.

④ It's up to her to finish the work.

⑤ Her latest book isn't up to her usual standard.

20 위 글의 괄호 (A)~(C)에서 문맥이나 어법상 알맞은 낱말을 골라 쓰시오.

➡ (A) _____ (B) _____ (C) _____

21 위 글을 읽고 알 수 없는 것을 고르시오.

① 여왕개미의 수명

② 개미의 몸무게

③ 개미의 호흡 방법

④ 개미의 위의 개수

⑤ 개미가 물속에서 살 수 있는 시간

[22~23] 다음 글을 읽고 물음에 답하시오.

How Do Ants Communicate?

 Though ants do not speak like humans, they actually have a "language." Ants produce a chemical called a pheromone to communicate with one another. By (A)using the chemical, they can exchange information about food or danger. Ants also use touch for communication. ___ⓐ___, if an ant finds food, it passes on the good news by rubbing its body on its neighbor. Since an ant has legs covered with very sensitive hairs, it can sense even the smallest touch.

22 위 글의 빈칸 ⓐ에 들어갈 알맞은 말을 고르시오.

① Therefore   ② For example

③ In fact   ④ However

⑤ In other words

23 아래 〈보기〉에서 위 글의 밑줄 친 (A)using과 문법적 쓰임이 다른 것의 개수를 고르시오.

┌─ 보기 ┐
① Why are you using the chemical?
② When did you finish using the chemical?
③ How about using the chemical?
④ I saw him using the chemical.
⑤ She stopped using the chemical.
└─────┘

① 1개　② 2개　③ 3개　④ 4개　⑤ 5개

[24~25] 다음 글을 읽고 물음에 답하시오.

Mosquito	
Home	Mosquitoes like warm weather and they are easily found in places with still water.
Life Span	Males usually live for about five ⓐ_____ seven days, while females can live for two weeks ⓐ_____ a month.
Food	Mosquitoes mainly feed ⓑ_____ fruit and plant nectar, but the female mosquitoes also drink the blood of other animals.
Fun Facts	• A mosquito can drink blood up to three times its weight. • Female mosquitoes can lay up to 300 eggs at a time.

24 위 글의 빈칸 ⓐ와 ⓑ에 들어갈 전치사가 바르게 짝지어진 것은?

　　　ⓐ　ⓑ　　　　　　ⓐ　ⓑ
① for – on　　　② to　– by
③ to　– on　　　④ for – to
⑤ on　– by

25 Which question CANNOT be answered after reading the passage?

① Where can we find mosquitoes easily?
② How long do male mosquitoes usually live?
③ Why can female mosquitoes live longer than males?
④ Do male mosquitoes drink the blood of other animals?
⑤ How many eggs can female mosquitoes lay at a time?

[26~28] 다음 글을 읽고 물음에 답하시오.

FUN FACTS ABOUT ANTS
01 Some Queen ants live up to 30 years.
02 Some ants can carry things ⓐ자기 몸무게의 50배에 달하는.
03 Ants do not have lungs but breathe through small holes in their bodies.
04 An ant has two stomachs. One stomach holds food for itself, and the other holds food to share with others.
05 Most ants can swim and live 24 hours underwater.

26 위 글의 밑줄 친 ⓐ의 우리말에 맞게 주어진 어휘를 이용하여 8단어로 영작하시오.

┌─────────────────────┐
│　　　that, body weight　　　│
└─────────────────────┘

➡ _____

27 개미가 호흡하는 법을 우리말로 쓰시오.

➡ _____

28 개미의 위의 역할을 우리말로 쓰시오.

➡ _____
_____

[01~03] 다음 글을 읽고 물음에 답하시오.

For the science project, our group has chosen very special insects.

- They are very social.
- They are as old as the T-Rex.
- They appear in Aesop's stories.
- They use a special chemical (A)to communicate.

(B)그것들이 무엇인지 추측할 수 있나요? Yes, the answer is ants. We want to share with you ___ⓐ___ we have learned about these insects.

01 Fill in the blank ⓐ with a suitable word.

➡ _____

02 위 글의 밑줄 친 (A)to communicate를 다음과 같이 바꿔 쓸 때 빈칸에 들어갈 알맞은 말을 쓰시오.

➡ _____ _____ to communicate

= _____ _____ to communicate

= _____ _____ _____ they _____ communicate

= _____ _____ they _____ communicate

03 위 글의 밑줄 친 (B)의 우리말에 맞게 주어진 어휘를 알맞게 배열하시오.

what / you / guess / they / can / are / ?

➡ _____

[04~06] 다음 글을 읽고 물음에 답하시오.

How Many Ants Are on Earth?

We often see ants come ⓐ난데없이. Like humans, they live almost everywhere in the world, except a few extremely cold places including Antarctica. ⓑ2018년 현재, there were over 7 billion people on Earth. Then, ⓒhow about ants? According to scientists, there are about one million ants for every human in the world. ⓓSince each ant hardly weighs anything, one million ants are as heavy as a human being weighing about 62 kilograms.

04 위 글의 밑줄 친 ⓐ와 ⓑ의 우리말에 맞게 각각 3단어로 영작하시오.

➡ ⓐ _____ ⓑ _____

05 위 글의 밑줄 친 ⓒhow about ants?를 다음과 같이 바꿔 쓸 때 빈칸에 들어갈 알맞은 말을 쓰시오. (3단어)

➡ _____ _____ _____ are there on Earth?

06 위 글의 밑줄 친 ⓓ에서 흐름상 어색한 단어를 찾아 고치시오.

_____ ➡ _____

[07~09] 다음 글을 읽고 물음에 답하시오.

What Is the Ant Society Like?

Ants live in colonies which have lots of residents ⓐliving together. Within a colony, there are usually ⓑthree different types of ants. There is the queen, and what she does her entire life is lay eggs. The second type of ant is the male that helps the queen produce these eggs. The third type of ant is the worker. Worker ants are all female and do very important jobs, ⓒlike caring for eggs, defending the colony, and collecting food.

07 위 글의 밑줄 친 ⓐliving을 관계대명사를 사용하여 두 단어로 고치시오.

➡ _____

08 위 글의 밑줄 친 ⓑthree different types of ants가 가리키는 것을 본문에서 찾아 쓰시오.

➡ _____, _____, _____

09 위 글의 밑줄 친 ⓒlike를 두 단어로 바꿔 쓰시오.

➡ _____

[10~12] 다음 글을 읽고 물음에 답하시오.

How Do Ants Communicate?

ⓐThough ants do not speak like humans, they actually have a "language." Ants produce a chemical (A)[calling / called] a pheromone to communicate with one another. By using the chemical, they can (B)[change / exchange] information about food or danger. Ants also use touch for communication. For example, if an ant finds food, it passes on the good news by rubbing its body on its neighbor. Since an ant has legs (C)[covering / covered] with very sensitive hairs, it can sense even the smallest touch.

10 위 글의 괄호 (A)~(C)에서 문맥이나 어법상 알맞은 낱말을 골라 쓰시오.

➡ (A) _____ (B) _____ (C) _____

11 위 글의 밑줄 친 ⓐ를 다음과 같이 바꿔 쓸 때 빈칸에 들어갈 알맞은 접속사를 쓰시오.

➡ Ants do not speak like humans, _____ they actually have a "language."

12 위 글의 내용을 다음과 같이 정리하고자 한다. 빈칸 (A)와 (B)에 들어갈 알맞은 단어를 본문에서 찾아 쓰시오.

> Ants can communicate with one another by using the (A)_____ called a pheromone and (B)_____.

Communicate: Speak

A: Which do you prefer, pizza or fried chicken?
선호를 묻는 말로 'Which do you like. A or B?' 형태이다.

B: I like pizza better. I can choose the toppings I like. How about you?
'the toppings I like'는 '내가 좋아하는 토핑'이라는 뜻으로 목적격 관계대명사가 생략되었다.

A: I like fried chicken better.

C: Me, too. I'm a meat lover.
'Me. too.'는 동의하는 말로 'So do I.'라고 할 수 있다.

구문해설 · How about you? 너는 어떠니? (권유, 제안, 상대의 의견 요청)

해석

A: 피자와 치킨 중 어느 것을 좋아하니?

B: 피자를 더 좋아해. 나는 내가 좋아하는 토핑을 고를 수 있어. 너는 어떠니?

A: 나는 프라이드 치킨을 더 좋아해.

C: 나도 그래. 나는 고기를 좋아해.

My Speaking Portfolio

M: Honeybees are easily found in warm places which have many plants
　　　　　　　be+과거분사: 수동태　　　　　　　　　주격관계대명사
and flowers. A queen lives up to five years, but worker bees only live for
　　　　　　　　　　　　　　～까지
about seven weeks. Honeybees go from flower to flower to collect food. A
약　　　　　　　　　　　　　　from A to B: A에서 B로　　to부정사의 부사적 용법-목적(～하기 위하여)
worker bee makes hundreds of trips to produce a small amount of honey.
　　　　　　　　　　　　　　　　to부정사의 부사적 용법-목적(～하기 위하여)
By moving around, honeybees help plants grow.
move around: 옮겨 다니다　　　　　　help+목적어+동사원형

구문해설 · collect: 모으다　· hundred: 백, 100　· hundreds of: 수백의　· amount: 양
· grow: 성장하다

남: 꿀벌은 식물과 꽃이 많은 따뜻한 곳에서 쉽게 발견된다. 여왕벌은 5년까지 살지만, 일벌은 겨우 7주 정도만 산다. 꿀벌은 먹이를 모으기 위해 꽃에서 꽃으로 옮겨 다닌다. 일벌은 적은 양의 꿀을 만들기 위해 수백 번의 이동을 한다. 여기저기 옮겨 다니면서 꿀벌은 식물이 성장하는 것을 돕는다.

Wrap Up – Reading

Ants seem to be busy all the time and never rest. But this is not true. Worker
　～인 것처럼 보인다　　　　　　　　　　　개미는 항상 바쁘고 전혀 휴식을 취하지 않는 것처럼 보이는 것
ants rest by taking very short naps about 250 times a day. Each of these naps
　　　　　　　　　　　　　　　　　　　= per(～당, ～마다)
lasts only about a minute. This means that the worker ants sleep for about four
　　　　　　　　　　앞의 내용, 즉 일개미는 하루에 약 250번의 짧은 잠을 자며 이 잠은 불과 1분 정도 이어진다는 사실을 가리킨다.
hours each day. On the other hand, queen ants fall asleep 90 times a day, and
　　　　　　　　　　반면에　　　　　　　　　　　　잠들다
they sleep for about six minutes at a time. This means that they sleep for about
　　　　　　　　　　　　　　　　　　동사 means의 목적어를 이끄는 접속사로, 생략할 수 있다.
nine hours each day. In short, ants sleep and rest just like us though they do so
　　　　　　　　　　= In brief: 즉, 간단히 말해서　　　　　　양보를 나타내는 접속사(비록 ～이지만)　　= sleep
in a different way.　　　　　　　　　　　　　　　　　　　　　　　　　　　and rest

구문해설 · seem to: ～인 것처럼 보이다　· nap: 낮잠　· last: 지속되다　· all the time: 항상

개미는 항상 바쁘고 전혀 휴식을 취하지 않는 것처럼 보인다. 하지만 이것은 사실이 아니다. 일개미는 하루에 약 250번의 짧은 잠을 자며 휴식을 취한다. 이 잠은 불과 1분 정도 이어진다. 이것은 일개미가 하루에 4시간 정도 잠을 잔다는 의미이다. 반면에, 여왕개미는 하루에 90번 잠을 자고, 한 번에 약 6분 동안 잠을 잔다. 이것은 여왕개미가 하루에 약 9시간 동안 잠을 잔다는 것을 의미한다. 즉, 방식이 다르기는 하지만 개미도 우리처럼 잠을 자고 휴식을 취한다.

Words & Expressions

01 다음 영영풀이에 해당하는 단어를 고르시오.

> to try to answer a question or form an opinion when you are not sure whether you will be correct

① guess   ② chase   ③ decide
④ defend   ⑤ produce

02 다음 대화의 빈칸에 들어갈 말을 고르시오.

> B: Amber, how do you like the camp?
> G: It's great. I'm having a lot of fun.
> B: Me, too. The talent show last night was really _____.

① boring   ② sad   ③ worried
④ great   ⑤ disappointed

03 다음 빈칸에 들어갈 말로 적절한 것을 고르시오.

> Sometimes I get lost not because it's too _____ but because it's too bright.

① shiny   ② heavy   ③ dark
④ colorful   ⑤ extreme

04 다음 중 밑줄 친 부분의 뜻풀이가 바르지 않은 것은?

① By the way, did you decide on the afternoon program? (결정하다)
② They had a talent show. (장기 자랑)
③ Frank saw wild birds and insects in the woods. (야생의)
④ Can you guess how many bees live there? (꿀벌)
⑤ I don't like noisy music. (~ 같은)

Conversation

[05~06] 다음 대화의 빈칸에 들어갈 말을 고르시오.

05
> B: Sora, can you take a look at these pictures?
> G: What are these for?
> B: I'm trying to _____ a picture for my story in the school newspaper.

① choose   ② take   ③ draw
④ give   ⑤ like

06
> A: Which do like better, dogs or cats?
> B: I like dogs better. They are more friendly. How about you?
> C: _____
> D: Me, too. Cats are much cleaner than dogs.

① I like dogs better.
② I like cats better.
③ I play more often with my dogs.
④ Why do you like cats better?
⑤ I kept dogs in my house.

07 다음 대화에 이어지는 순서가 바르게 배열된 것을 고르시오.

> B: The talent show last night was really great.
> G: Yeah. By the way, did you decide on the afternoon program?

(A) Great. I heard we'll have a hiking guide.

(B) No, I haven't yet. Which do you think is better, hiking or swimming?

(C) I'll go hiking because we can see wild birds and insects in the woods.

(D) I'll join you. I like birds and insects.

① (A) – (C) – (D) – (B)
② (D) – (B) – (A) – (C)
③ (B) – (C) – (D) – (A)
④ (C) – (A) – (B) – (D)
⑤ (C) – (B) – (D) – (A)

[08~11] 다음 대화를 읽고 물음에 답하시오.

A: I heard birds are having a _____(A)_____ these days. Can you tell us more?

B: Sure. The cities are too bright at night. Many birds lose their way.

A: _____(B)_____ Is there anything we can do to help them?

B: Yes. First, we should turn off unnecessary lights at night. Also we should hold the Earth Hour campaign regularly.

A: Those are good points. I think (C)새를 보호하는 것에 관하여 진지해져야 할 시간이라고. (time, it's, get, protect, serious)

08 빈칸 (A)에 들어갈 알맞은 말을 고르시오.

① flying chance   ② hard time
③ great friend   ④ new mate
⑤ wonderful time

09 빈칸 (B)에 알맞은 말을 고르시오.

① Me, too.
② You can say that again.
③ I'm pleased with it.
④ How nice of you!
⑤ That's too bad.

10 밑줄 친 (C)의 우리말을 영어로 옮기시오. (주어진 단어를 이용할 것.)

➡ _____

11 위 대화의 내용과 일치하지 <u>않는</u> 것은?

① Many birds are having trouble finding their way.
② Many birds lose their way due to the bright cities during the day.
③ For the birds, we should turn off unnecessary lights at night.
④ Holding the Earth Hour campaign regularly will be helpful for the birds.
⑤ They are talking about protecting birds.

Grammar

12 다음 빈칸에 들어갈 말로 알맞은 것은?

> Do you know the child _____ on the bed?

① to sleep   ② sleep
③ slept   ④ sleeping
⑤ be sleeping

13 다음 우리말을 영어로 바르게 옮긴 것은?

> 나는 나이가 어리기 때문에 차를 운전할 수 없다.

① Since I cannot drive a car, I am young.
② Since I am young, I cannot drive a car.
③ I am young since I cannot drive a car.
④ Though I am young, I cannot drive a car.
⑤ Though I cannot drive a car, I am young.

14 다음 〈보기〉의 밑줄 친 부분과 쓰임이 다른 것은?

> ┤ 보기 ├
> Who is the lady <u>playing</u> tennis with Mark?

① I like the picture <u>showing</u> wonderful mountain tops.
② The man <u>talking</u> on the phone is my teacher.
③ I don't mind your brother <u>talking</u> in this room.
④ She met a man <u>speaking</u> Italian.
⑤ There was a car <u>running</u> on the road.

[15~16] 다음 빈칸에 들어가기에 적절한 것은?

15
> _____ ants do not speak like humans, they actually have a "language."

① Though ② Since ③ Because
④ Unless ⑤ After

16
> Ants produce a chemical _____ a pheromone to communicate with one another.

① calls ② calling ③ called
④ to call ⑤ is called

17 다음 우리말에 맞게 괄호 안에 주어진 어휘를 바르게 배열하시오. (필요하면 어형을 바꿀 것)

(1) 나는 그 가수에 의해서 불리는 모든 노래를 좋아한다. (like, song, sing, every, I, the singer, by)

➡ _____

(2) 그는 침대에서 자는 아이를 깨우지 않으려고 애썼다. (he, to wake up, not, tried, the baby, on the bed, sleep)

➡ _____
_____

18 다음 〈보기〉의 밑줄 친 부분과 쓰임이 같은 것은?

> ┤ 보기 ├
> The kid <u>wearing</u> a baseball cap is my nephew.

① He enjoyed <u>meeting</u> them.
② Do you know the child <u>crying</u> at the door?
③ His hobby is <u>listening</u> to music.
④ I don't mind your <u>making</u> noises.
⑤ He finished <u>reading</u> the book.

19 다음 대화를 읽고 어법상 틀린 부분을 찾아 알맞게 고쳐 쓰시오.

> B: Sora, can you take a look at these pictures?
> G: What are these for?
> B: I'm trying to choose a picture for my story in the school newspaper.
> G: What's your story about?
> B: Nature's future.
> G: Can you tell me more about it?
> B: It's about endangering animals in the Arctic areas.
> G: That sounds interesting.

_____ ➡ _____

20 다음 우리말을 영어로 올바르게 옮긴 것은?

> 나는 조심스럽게 일하는 그 여자를 좋아한다.

① I like the woman works very carefully.
② I like carefully the woman working.
③ The woman likes my working very carefully.
④ The woman I like works very carefully
⑤ I like the woman working very carefully.

21 다음 중 밑줄 친 부분의 쓰임이 어색한 것을 고르시오.

① An essay written carefully will receive a high grade.
② Though it rained heavily, we had to stop playing soccer.
③ Though it was very warm, she didn't take off her coat.
④ Since I am a middle school student, I cannot drive a car.
⑤ Since you don't have any evidence, you cannot punish him.

22 잘못된 부분을 바르게 고쳐 문장을 다시 쓰시오.

(1) He is carrying a basket filling with cherries.

➡ _____

(2) Though it is cold, I want to drink something hot.

➡ _____

(3) I am tired since I slept enough last night.

➡ _____

[23~25] 다음 글을 읽고 물음에 답하시오.

How Many Ants Are on Earth?

We often see ants come out of nowhere. (①) ⓐLike humans, they live almost everywhere in the world, except a few extremely cold places including Antarctica. (②) As of 2018, there were over 7 billion people on Earth. (③) According to scientists, there are about one million ants for every human in the world. (④) Though each ant hardly weighs anything, ⓑone million ants are as heavy as a human being weighing about 62 kilograms. (⑤)

23 위 글의 ①~⑤ 중 다음 주어진 문장이 들어갈 알맞은 위치는?

> Then, how about ants?

①   ②   ③   ④   ⑤

24 위 글의 밑줄 친 ⓐLike와 의미가 같은 것을 고르시오.

① He is very like his father.
② Do you like swimming?
③ There are fruits like apples and pears.
④ She responded in like manner.
⑤ I, like everyone else, want to live long.

25 다음 중 밑줄 친 ⓑ의 의미를 바르게 이해한 사람을 고르시오.

① 진수: A human being weighing about 62 kilograms is heavier than one million ants.
② 희라: The weight of one million ants is about 62 kilograms.

③ 민규: One million ants are less heavy than a human being weighing about 62 kilograms.

④ 영진: A human being weighing about 62 kilograms isn't so heavy as one million ants.

⑤ 송미: One million ants are heavier than a human being weighing about 62 kilograms.

[26~28] 다음 글을 읽고 물음에 답하시오.

How Do Ants Communicate?

Though ants do not speak like humans, they actually have a "_____ⓐ_____." Ants produce a chemical called a pheromone to communicate with one another. By using the chemical, they can exchange information about food or danger. Ants also use touch for communication. For example, if an ant finds food, it passes on the good news by rubbing its body on its neighbor. ⓑSince an ant has legs covered with very sensitive hairs, it can sense even the smallest touch.

26 위 글의 빈칸 ⓐ에 들어갈 알맞은 말을 고르시오.

① letter   ② rule
③ symbol   ④ language
⑤ culture

27 위 글의 밑줄 친 ⓑSince와 같은 의미로 쓰인 것을 모두 고르시오.

① Since she is attractive, she is loved by many people.
② She's been off work since Tuesday.
③ We've lived here since 1994.
④ Since I'm busy, I can't go there.
⑤ I haven't eaten since breakfast.

28 According to the passage, which is NOT true?

① Ants do not speak like humans.
② Ants can communicate with one another by using a pheromone.
③ Ants also use touch for communication.
④ The legs of an ant are covered with very sensitive hairs.
⑤ Ants can't sense the smallest touch.

[29~30] 다음 글을 읽고 물음에 답하시오.

ⓐHoneybees are easily found in warm places where have many plants and flowers. A queen lives up to five years, but worker bees only live for about seven weeks. Honeybees go from flower to flower to collect food. A worker bee makes hundreds of trips to produce a small amount of honey. By moving around, honeybees help plants grow.

29 위 글의 밑줄 친 ⓐ에서 어법상 틀린 부분을 찾아 고치시오.

_____ ➡ _____

30 본문의 내용과 일치하도록 다음 빈칸 (A)와 (B)에 알맞은 단어를 쓰시오.

To produce a small amount of (A)_____, a worker bee makes (B)_____ _____ _____, and by doing so helps plants pollinate.

*pollinate: 수분(受粉)하다, 가루받이를 하다

단원별 예상문제

01 출제율 90%
다음 짝지어진 단어의 관계가 같도록 빈칸에 알맞은 말을 쓰시오. (주어진 철자로 시작할 것)

> choose : select – offer : p_____

02 출제율 95%
다음 주어진 단어를 이용해 빈칸을 완성하시오.

> G: What's your story about?
> B: It's about _____ animals in the Arctic areas.

➡ _____ (danger)

03 출제율 90%
다음 밑줄 친 단어와 의미가 가장 가까운 단어를 고르시오.

> The photograph of the insects was underline{unbelievable}.

① incredible ② colorful
③ wonderful ④ worried
⑤ puzzled

[04~05] 다음 대화의 빈칸에 들어갈 말을 고르시오.

04 출제율 95%

> G: What do you do in your free time?
> B: I listen to music like EDM or hip-hop.
> G: Which do you like better?
> B: I _____ hip-hop.
> G: Why?
> B: Well, it sounds more exciting.

① decide ② write
③ make ④ prefer
⑤ support

05 출제율 95%
내용상 다음 빈칸에 들어가기에 적절한 것은?

> Ants also use touch for communication. For example, if an ant finds food, it _____ the good news by rubbing its body on its neighbor.

① gives up ② gets over
③ passes on ④ looks after
⑤ waits for

06 출제율 85%
다음 영영풀이에 해당하는 단어를 고르시오.

> to decide which one of a number of things or people you want

① take ② bring
③ choose ④ call
⑤ reside

[07~08] 다음 빈칸에 들어갈 말로 적절한 것을 고르시오.

07 출제율 95%

> Bees live together in a _____. It usually has a large number of residents in it.

① support ② colony
③ forest ④ village
⑤ society

08 출제율 90%

> Elephants are social animals. _____ elephants help each other look after their babies.

① Kind ② Careful
③ Female ④ Male
⑤ Adult

[09~10] 다음 대화를 읽고 물음에 답하시오.

B: ⓐAmber, how do you like the camp?

G: It's great. I'm having a lot of fun.

B: Me, too. ⓑThe talent show last night was really terrible.

G: Yeah. By the way, did you decide on the afternoon program?

B: ⓒNo, I haven't yet. Which do you think is better, hiking or swimming?

G: ⓓI'll go hiking because we can see wild birds and insects in the woods.

B: I'll join you. I like birds and insects.

G: Great. ⓔI heard we'll have a hiking guide.

09 밑줄 친 ⓐ~ⓔ 중에서 흐름상 어색한 문장을 고르시오.

① ⓐ   ② ⓑ   ③ ⓒ   ④ ⓓ   ⑤ ⓔ

10 위 대화를 읽고, 대답할 수 없는 것은?

① Where are they at the moment?

② What was last night's program?

③ What will they do this afternoon?

④ Where can they swim?

⑤ Who will help them hike this afternoon?

[11~12] 다음 대화의 빈칸에 들어갈 말을 고르시오.

11

A: Which do you like better, sci-fi movies or horror movies?

B: I like sci-fi movies better. How about you?

A: I like horror movies better.

C: _____ Horror movies are more exciting.

① So am I.   ② Nor am I.

③ I don't agree.   ④ Me, too.

⑤ I like sci-fi movies.

12

G: Guess what I'm talking about.

B: Okay. Go ahead.

G: It's a common machine that you can see at home.

B: Well, can you tell me more?

G: _____

B: Now I know what it is.

① It helps you wash clothes.

② I don't know much about it.

③ Would you ask me more?

④ How about asking someone else?

⑤ You can guess what I am saying.

13 다음 〈보기〉의 밑줄 친 부분과 쓰임이 같은 것은?

┌─── 보기 ───┐

We saw a big eagle <u>flying</u> above us.

① <u>Learning</u> English is very important.

② His wish is <u>traveling</u> around the world.

③ I hate <u>speaking</u> in front of other people.

④ A police officer is <u>guarding</u> the entrance.

⑤ What is your secret for <u>winning</u> the contest?

14 주어진 단어를 이용하여 빈칸에 적절한 형태로 쓰시오.

Since an ant has legs _____ with very sensitive hairs, it can sense even the smallest touch. (cover)

15 다음 중 밑줄 친 부분이 어법상 어색한 것은?

① Be careful with the boiling water.
② What is the language speaking in Mexico?
③ The boy playing basketball is my brother.
④ Look at the sleeping baby. He's so cute!
⑤ These are the pictures painted by Picasso.

16 다음 빈칸에 알맞은 것은?

> This is the novel _____ by Albert Camus.

① write　　② wrote　　③ written
④ writing　　⑤ to write

17 다음 빈칸에 들어갈 말로 알맞은 것은?

> _____ he was ill, he had to cancel the appointment.

① Whether　　② Since　　③ Unless
④ Until　　⑤ Although

18 다음 빈칸에 들어갈 말로 알맞은 것은?

> (A) I ate a whole pizza _____ I was on a diet.
> (B) _____ it is hot, I want to drink something cold.

	(A)	(B)
①	since	Though
②	since	Although
③	unless	Since
④	though	Since
⑤	though	Unless

[19~21] 다음 글을 읽고 물음에 답하시오.

What Is the Ant Society Like?

Ants live in colonies which have lots of residents living together. Within a colony, there are usually three different types of ants. There is the queen, and what she does her entire life is lay eggs. The second type of ant is the male (A)that helps the queen produce these eggs. The third type of ant is the worker. Worker ants are all female and do very important jobs, like ____ⓐ____ for eggs, ____ⓑ____ the colony, and ____ⓒ____ food.

19 위 글의 빈칸 ⓐ~ⓒ에 care, defend, collect를 각각 알맞은 형태로 쓰시오.

➡ ⓐ _____ ⓑ _____ ⓒ _____

20 아래 〈보기〉에서 위 글의 밑줄 친 (A)that과 문법적 쓰임이 같은 것의 개수를 고르시오.

> ┤ 보기 ├
> ① The climate of Seoul is like that of Paris.
> ② He is the first man that came here.
> ③ This is the watch that I bought yesterday.
> ④ This is my sister and that is my cousin.
> ⑤ Is this the farm that they spoke of?

① 1개　② 2개　③ 3개　④ 4개　⑤ 5개

21 According to the passage, which is NOT true?

① In ants' colonies, there are lots of residents living together.
② Usually three different types of ants are within a colony.
③ The queen lays eggs during her entire life.

④ The male helps the queen to produce the eggs.

⑤ Worker ants are all male.

[22~24] 다음 글을 읽고 물음에 답하시오.

How Do Ants Communicate?

Though ants do not speak like humans, they actually have a "language." Ants produce a chemical called a pheromone ⓐto communicate with one another. By using the chemical, they can exchange information about food or danger. Ants also use touch for communication. For example, if an ant finds food, it passes on the good news by rubbing its body on its neighbor. Since an ant has legs covered with very sensitive hairs, ⓑit can sense even the smallest touch.

출제율 95%

22 위 글의 밑줄 친 ⓐto communicate와 to부정사의 용법이 같은 것을 모두 고르시오.

① The girl grew up to be an artist.

② It isn't easy to remember all the rules.

③ Kate must be stupid to believe Jake.

④ We need a house to live in.

⑤ His job is to take pictures.

출제율 95%

23 위 글의 밑줄 친 ⓑit이 가리키는 것을 본문에서 찾아 쓰시오.

➡ _____

출제율 90%

24 본문의 내용과 일치하도록 다음 빈칸에 알맞은 단어를 쓰시오.

An ant can sense even the smallest touch thanks to its _____ covered with very sensitive hairs.

[25~26] 다음 글을 읽고 물음에 답하시오.

Ants seem to be busy all the time and never rest. But (A)this is not true. Worker ants rest by taking very short naps about 250 times a day. Each of these naps lasts only about a minute. (B)This means that the worker ants sleep for about four hours each day. ____ⓐ____, queen ants fall asleep 90 times a day, and they sleep for about six minutes at a time. (C)This means that they sleep for about nine hours each day. ____ⓑ____, ants sleep and rest just like us though they do so in a different way.

출제율 90%

25 위 글의 빈칸 ⓐ와 ⓑ에 들어갈 알맞은 말을 고르시오.

① Thus – To sum up

② On the other hand – In short

③ As a result – In brief

④ Therefore – In short

⑤ On the other hand – However

출제율 100%

26 위 글의 밑줄 친 (A)this, (B)This, (C)This가 가리키는 내용을 각각 우리말로 쓰시오.

➡ (A) _____

_____

(B) _____

_____

(C) _____

01 다음 영영풀이에 해당하는 단어를 쓰시오.

> a small creature such as a fly or ant, that has six legs, and sometimes wings

➡ _____

02 다음 밑줄 친 단어와 의미가 같은 단어를 쓰시오. (주어진 철자로 시작할 것)

> I'm trying to <u>choose</u> a picture for my story in the school newspaper.

➡ s_____

03 다음 우리말에 맞게 빈칸에 알맞은 말을 쓰시오.

(1) 그런데 너는 오후 프로그램을 결정했니?
   ➡ By the way, did you _____ on the afternoon program?
(2) 좋은 추측입니다. 하지만 저것은 5만 마리가 넘는 벌을 수용할 만큼 커요.
   ➡ Good guess, but it's big enough to _____ over 50,000 bees.

04 다음 중 〈보기〉에 있는 단어를 사용하여 자연스러운 문장을 만드시오.

┌─── 보기 ───┐
chemical ants information language
└──────────────┘

(1) _____ live in colonies.
(2) Though ants do not speak like humans, they actually have a "_____."
(3) Ants produce a _____ called a pheromone to communicate with one another.
(4) By using the chemical, they can exchange _____ about food or danger.

05 다음 대화의 빈칸에 들어갈 말로 알맞은 것은?

> A: Which do you like better, soccer or baseball?
> B: I like soccer better. Soccer is more exciting. How about you?
> A: I like baseball _____. I'm a big fan of the Lions.
> C: Are you? I'm a big fan of the Lions, too.

➡ _____

06 다음 우리말과 의미가 같도록 빈칸에 알맞은 말을 쓰시오. (단, 괄호 안에 주어진 단어가 있을 경우 활용할 것)

(1) 벽을 파란색으로 칠하는 남자를 보아라.
   ➡ Look at the man _____ the wall blue. (paint)
(2) John은 Tom이 만든 피자를 먹고 있다.
   ➡ John is eating the pizza _____ by Tom. (make)
(3) 파티에 초대된 사람들이 파티를 즐기고 있다.
   ➡ The people _____ to the party are enjoying themselves.

07 다음 우리말을 영어로 옮길 때 빈칸에 적절한 단어를 쓰시오. (주어진 철자로 시작할 것)

> 나이가 아주 많지만 그녀는 음식을 직접 요리한다.
> = T_____ she is very old, she cooks food herself.

How Many Ants Are on Earth?

We often see ants come (A)[into / out of] nowhere. Like humans, they live (B)[most / almost] everywhere in the world, except a few extremely cold places including Antarctica. As of 2018, there were over 7 billion (C)[people / peoples] on Earth. Then, how about ants? According to scientists, there are about one million ants for every human in the world. ⓐ각각의 개미는 거의 무게가 나가지 않지만, one million ants are as heavy as a human being weighing about 62 kilograms.

08 위 글의 괄호 (A)~(C)에서 문맥상 알맞은 낱말을 골라 쓰시오.

➡ (A) _____ (B) _____ (C) _____

09 위 글의 밑줄 친 ⓐ의 우리말에 맞게 주어진 어휘를 이용하여 6단어로 영작하시오.

each, hardly, anything

➡ _____

10 How many ants are there for each person in the world? Answer in English in a full sentence. (6 words)

➡ _____

How Do Ants Communicate?

Though ants do not speak like humans, they actually have a "language." Ants produce a chemical (A)called a pheromone to communicate with one another. By _____ⓐ_____ the chemical, they can exchange information about food or danger. (B)Ants also use touch for communication. For example, if an ant finds food, it passes on the good news by _____ⓑ_____ its body on its neighbor. Since an ant has legs (C)covered with very sensitive hairs, it can sense even the smallest touch.

11 위 글의 빈칸 ⓐ와 ⓑ에 use와 rub를 각각 알맞은 형태로 쓰시오.

➡ ⓐ _____ ⓑ _____

12 위 글의 밑줄 친 (A)와 (C) 앞에 생략된 말을 각각 쓰시오.

➡ (A) _____ (C) _____

13 위 글의 밑줄 친 (B)의 예를 우리말로 설명하시오.

➡ _____

_____

01 신체를 나타내는 말이 포함된 표현을 찾아 문장을 만들어 봅시다.

eye	nose	ear	face	heart	arm

(1) I'll _____ your dog while you're away. ~을 지켜보다, ~을 감시하다

(2) Mike _____ today. 표정이 우울하다

(3) When the teacher talked about the camp schedule, everyone _____. 경청했다

(4) I'll _____ this offer. ~을 거절하다

(5) Try to _____ these English idioms. 암기하다

(6) It will _____ to buy a new car. 비싼 값을 치르다

02 다음 문장의 빈칸에 since나 though를 쓰시오.

(1) _____ it rained heavily, the soccer match was canceled.

(2) I don't want to go to the party _____ I have no one to talk with.

(3) _____ he was smiling, he didn't look that happy.

(4) It is sunny _____ it is cold.

03 다음 내용을 바탕으로 꿀벌에 관한 보고서를 쓰시오.

> **Home:** Honeybees are found in warm places around the world.
>
> **Life Span:** A queen lives up to five years, but worker bees only live for about seven weeks.
>
> **Food Collection:** Honeybees visit flowers to collect food.
>
> **Fun Facts:**
> • A worker bee makes hundreds of trips to produce a small amount of honey.
> • By moving around, honeybees help plants grow.

> Honeybees are easily found in (A)_____ which have many plants and flowers. A queen lives up to (B)_____, but worker bees only live for (C)_____. Honeybees go from flower to flower (D)_____. A worker bee makes (E)_____ to produce a small amount of honey. By moving around, honeybees help plants (F)_____.

단원별 모의고사

01 다음 짝지어진 단어의 관계가 같도록 빈칸에 알맞은 말을 쓰시오. (주어진 철자로 시작할 것)

> defend : attack = male : f_____

02 다음 짝지어진 단어의 관계가 같도록 빈칸에 알맞은 말을 쓰시오. (주어진 철자로 시작할 것)

> unbelievable : incredible =
> choose : s_____

03 다음 영영풀이에 해당하는 단어를 고르시오.

> to provide something that people need or want

① offer
② receive
③ make
④ buy
⑤ produce

04 다음 대화의 빈칸에 들어갈 말을 고르시오.

> A: Which do you prefer to take, the bus or the subway?
> B: I _____ to take the subway better.

① select
② offer
③ prefer
④ like
⑤ choose

05 다음 빈칸에 들어갈 말로 적절한 것을 고르시오.

> Within a _____, there are usually three different types of ants.

① village
② value
③ colony
④ forest
⑤ tree

06 다음 〈보기〉에서 적절한 단어를 골라 주어진 문장을 완성하시오.

> ┤ 보기 ├
> exchange sensitive colonies weighs

(1) Each ant hardly _____ anything.
(2) Ants live in _____ which have lots of residents living together.
(3) By using the chemical, ants can _____ information about food.
(4) An ant has legs covered with very _____ hairs.

07 다음 중 밑줄 친 부분의 뜻풀이가 바르지 <u>않은</u> 것은?

① Some ants can carry things that are <u>50 times</u> their own body weight. (50배)
② Most ants can swim and live 24 hours <u>underwater</u>. (수중에서)
③ Ants <u>breathe</u> through small holes in their bodies. (숨 쉬다)
④ The machine can take you to a <u>faraway</u> place. (멀리 떨어진)
⑤ What <u>chemical</u> do ants use to communicate? (화학적인)

08 다음 밑줄 친 단어와 의미가 가장 가까운 단어를 고르시오.

> This beehive is big enough to <u>hold</u> over 50,000 bees.

① contain
② produce
③ chase
④ provide
⑤ prefer

[09~11] 다음 대화를 읽고 물음에 답하시오.

A: I heard birds are having a hard time these days. Can you tell us more?

B: Sure. The cities are too bright at night. Many birds lose their way.

A: That's too bad. (A)우리가 그들을 돕기 위해 무언가 할 수 있는 것이 있니?(can, is, there, do, anything, we, help, them, to)

B: Yes. First, we should _____ (B) _____ unnecessary lights at night. Also we should hold the Earth Hour campaign regularly.

A: Those are good points. I think it's time to get serious about protecting birds.

09 주어진 단어를 배열하여 (A)의 우리말에 해당하는 영어 문장을 완성하시오.

➡ _____

10 대화의 흐름으로 보아 (B)에 들어가기에 가장 적절한 것은?

① catch on   ② turn around
③ get over   ④ care for
⑤ turn off

11 According to the dialogue, which one is NOT true?

① Birds are having trouble finding food.
② Birds lose their way because the cities are too bright at night.
③ We should turn off unnecessary lights at night.
④ We should get serious about protecting birds.
⑤ We should hold the Earth Hour campaign regularly.

12 다음 대화의 순서가 바르게 배열된 것을 고르시오.

W: Everyone, look at this chestnut tree. This is the oldest tree in these woods.

B: Can you tell me how old it is?

W: It's about 150 years old.

B: Wow! It's ten times my age.

G: Ms. Oh, is that a beehive up in the tree?

(A) Good guess, but it's big enough to hold over 50,000 bees.

(B) Yes. Can you guess how many bees live there?

(C) 500 bees?

B: G: Unbelievable!

① (A) – (C) – (B)   ② (B) – (A) – (C)
③ (B) – (C) – (A)   ④ (C) – (A) – (B)
⑤ (C) – (B) – (A)

13 짝지어진 대화가 어색한 것을 고르시오.

① A: Which picture do you like better?
   B: I like the one showing a mountain.
② A: I like dogs better. They are more friendly. How about you?
   B: Why do you like dogs better?
③ A: What are you drawing?
   B: An elephant.
④ A: What are sunglasses?
   B: They are things that you wear on your face.
⑤ A: Can you tell me more about it?
   B: It's a flying machine that can take you to a faraway place.

[14~16] 다음 대화를 읽고 물음에 답하시오.

B: Amber, how do you like the camp?

G: It's great. I'm having a lot of fun.

B: Me, too. The talent show last night was really great.

G: Yeah. _____(A)_____, did you decide on the afternoon program?

B: No, I haven't yet. Which do you think is better, hiking or swimming?

G: I'll go hiking because we can see wild birds and insects in the woods.

B: _____(B)_____ I like birds and insects.

G: Great. I heard we'll have a hiking guide.

B: Sounds good.

14 빈칸 (A)에 들어갈 알맞은 말을 고르시오.

① However
② By the way
③ For example
④ In the end
⑤ First of all

15 위 대화의 빈칸 (B)에 들어가기에 알맞은 것은?

① Neither am I.
② So am I.
③ I don't agree.
④ I'll join you.
⑤ You can say that again.

16 위 대화의 내용과 일치하지 <u>않는</u> 것은?

① 소녀의 이름은 Amber이다.
② 소년은 어젯밤 장기 자랑이 재미있었다.
③ 소녀는 오후 프로그램을 결정하지 못했다.
④ 소년은 새와 곤충을 좋아한다.
⑤ 산행 가이드가 있을 것이다.

17 다음 〈보기〉의 밑줄 친 부분과 쓰임이 <u>다른</u> 것은?

┤ 보기 ├
I know a woman <u>working</u> at the bank.

① All the windows <u>facing</u> the street were shut.
② Do you know the boy <u>walking</u> around the garden?
③ The baby <u>sleeping</u> in the room will wake up in an hour.
④ They enjoyed <u>jogging</u> in the park.
⑤ We will take the train <u>arriving</u> at platform.

18 다음 우리말을 영어로 바르게 옮긴 것은?

시간이 별로 없지만 너를 도와줄게.

① Though I have time, I can't help you.
② Though I help you, I don't have much time.
③ Since I don't have much time, I won't help you.
④ Since I don't have much time, I will help you.
⑤ Though I don't have much time, I will help you.

19 다음 중 밑줄 친 부분의 쓰임이 <u>어색한</u> 것을 고르시오.

① <u>Since</u> it rained heavily, the soccer match was canceled.
② <u>Since</u> she was ill, she didn't go to the party.
③ I don't want to go to the party <u>though</u> I have no one to talk with.
④ <u>Though</u> you don't like him, you must be polite.
⑤ <u>Though</u> he was young, he was not afraid at all.

[20~21] 다음 글을 읽고 물음에 답하시오.

How Many Ants Are on Earth?

We often see ants ___ⓐ___ out of nowhere. Like humans, they live almost everywhere in the world, except a few extremely cold places including Antarctica. As of 2018, there were over 7 (A)[billion / billions] people on Earth. Then, (B)[how about / why don't you] ants? According to scientists, there are about one million ants for every human in the world. Though each ant (C)[hard / hardly] weighs anything, one million ants are as heavy as a human being weighing about 62 kilograms.

20 위 글의 빈칸 ⓐ에 들어갈 알맞은 말을 <u>모두</u> 고르시오.

① to come　　　　② come
③ came　　　　　④ will come
⑤ coming

21 위 글의 괄호 (A)~(C)에서 문맥이나 어법상 알맞은 낱말을 골라 쓰시오.

➡ (A) _____ (B) _____ (C) _____

[22~23] 다음 글을 읽고 물음에 답하시오.

Ants live in colonies which have lots of residents living together. Within a colony, there are usually ⓐ<u>three different types of ants</u>. There is the queen, and what she does her entire life is lay eggs. The second type of ant is the male that helps the queen produce these eggs. The third type of ant is the worker. Worker ants are all female and do very important jobs, like caring for eggs, defending the colony, and collecting food.

22 위 글의 제목으로 알맞은 것을 고르시오.

① Funny Facts About Ants
② What Is the Ant Society Like?
③ How Do Ants Communicate?
④ Why Do Ants Live in Colonies?
⑤ How Many Ants Are on Earth?

23 위 글의 밑줄 친 ⓐ가 하는 일을 각각 우리말로 쓰시오.

➡ 여왕개미: _____
　 수개미: _____
　 일개미: _____
　 _____

[24~25] 다음 글을 읽고 물음에 답하시오.

How Do Ants Communicate?

Though ants do not speak like humans, they actually have a "language." Ants produce a chemical called a pheromone to communicate with one another. By using ⓐ<u>the chemical</u>, they can exchange information about food or danger. Ants also use touch for communication. For example, if an ant finds food, it passes on the good news by rubbing its body on its neighbor. ⓑ<u>Since an ant has legs covered with very sensible hairs, it can sense even the smallest touch.</u>

24 위 글의 밑줄 친 ⓐthe chemical이 가리키는 것을 본문에서 찾아 쓰시오.

➡ _____

25 위 글의 밑줄 친 ⓑ에서 문맥상 낱말의 쓰임이 적절하지 <u>않은</u> 것을 찾아 알맞게 고치시오.

_____ ➡ _____

Lesson

Special

Reading for Fun 1

The Full Jar

Words & Expressions

Key Words

☐ **fill** [fil] 동 채우다, 메우다

☐ **full** [ful] 형 가득 찬

☐ **health** [helθ] 명 건강

☐ **jar** [dʒɑːr] 명 병, 항아리

☐ **lose** [luːz] (**lost–lost**) 동 잃어버리다

☐ **matter** [mǽtər] 동 중요하다

☐ **open** [óupən] 형 열려 있는, 막혀 있지 않은

☐ **pour** [pɔːr] 동 붓다, 따르다

☐ **raise** [reiz] 동 ～을 들어 올리다

☐ **reply** [riplái] 동 대답하다

☐ **roll** [roul] 동 굴러가다

☐ **room** [ruːm] 명 공간, 여지

☐ **same** [seim] 형 같은

☐ **seem** [seim] 동 …으로 보이다, …(인 것) 같다, …(인 것)으로 생각되다

☐ **shake** [ʃeik] (**shook–shaken**) 동 흔들다

☐ **space** [speis] 명 (비어 있는) 공간

☐ **spend** [spend] 동 소비하다, 쓰다

☐ **stand** [stænd] (**stood–stood**) 동 서 있다

☐ **suddenly** [sʌ́dnli] 부 갑자기

☐ **though** [ðou] 접 비록 ～일지라도, ～이지만

☐ **value** [vǽljuː] 동 ～을 높이 평가하다, 중시하다

Key Expressions

☐ **a bottle of** ～ ～ 한 병

☐ **fill A with B** B로 A를 채우다

☐ **out of** ～ 밖으로, ～로부터

☐ **pick up** ～을 집어올리다

☐ **pour A into B** A를 B에 붓다

☐ **spend A on B** A를 B하는 데 소비하다[쓰다]

☐ **take care of** ～ ～을 돌보다, ～에 신경을 쓰다

☐ **take out** ～을 꺼내다

☐ **watch+목적어+동사원형(ing)** 목적어가 ～하는 것을 보다

Word Power

※ 다의어

□ **matter**

(명사)

1. 문제, 일, 사건

It's an extremely important **matter**. (그건 매우 중요한 문제이다.)

2. 어려움, 곤란, 걱정

You look sad. What's the **matter**? (너 슬퍼 보인다. 무슨 어려운 일이 있니?)

(동사) 중요하다

Money is the only thing that **matters** to them. (돈은 그들에게 중요한 유일한 것이다.)

□ **value**

(명사) 가치, 값어치

The **value** of the painting is not known. (그 그림의 값어치는 알려지지 않았다.)

(동사) ～을 높이 평가하다, 중시하다

You must **value** your health. (넌 건강을 중요시해야 한다.)

English Dictionary

□ **fill** 채우다, 메우다
→ to make something full
무언가를 가득 차게 만들다

□ **full** 가득 찬
→ having or containing a lot of something
어떤 것을 많이 가지고 있거나 보유하고 있는

□ **jar** 병, 항아리
→ a glass container with a lid and a wide top, especially one in which food is sold or kept
특히 그 안에 음식을 담아 팔거나 보관하는, 뚜껑과 넓은 윗부분을 가진 유리 용기

□ **lose** 잃어버리다
→ to fail to keep or to maintain; cease to have, either physically or in an abstract sense
유지하거나 간직하지 못하다; 물리적으로나 추상적인 의미에서 가지는 것을 중단하다

□ **reply** 대답하다
→ to say or write something as an answer to someone or something
누군가 또는 어떤 것에 대한 대답으로 무언가를 말하거나 쓰다

□ **shake** 흔들다
→ to hold it and move it quickly backwards and forwards or up and down.
어떤 것을 잡고 앞뒤로 또는 위아래로 빠르게 움직이다

□ **space** (비어 있는) 공간
→ an empty area
비어 있는 공간

□ **spend** 소비하다
→ to pay money for things that you want
원하는 것들을 위해 돈을 지불하다

□ **suddenly** 갑자기
→ quickly and without any warning
빠르고 경고 없이

□ **take care of** ～ ～을 돌보다, ～에 신경을 쓰다
→ to make sure that you are/somebody is safe, well, healthy, etc.; look after yourself/somebody
당신이나 누군가가 확실히 안전하고, 건강하도록 하게 하다; 당신 자신이나 다른 사람을 돌보다

Reading

The Full Jar

Mr. Jenkins stood before his class. He had a large jar and a big bag
            ~ 앞에
on the teacher's desk. When the class began, he picked up the jar and
                              = picked the jar up
started to fill it with **golf balls** from the bag. He asked the students, "Is
      = the jar
the jar full?" They all said, "Yes."

The teacher took a box of **small stones** out of the bag and poured
                               ~ 밖으로
them into the jar. He shook the jar a little, and the stones rolled into the
= small stones   shake의 과거   a few(×)
open areas between the golf balls. He asked the same question and got
                                    = "Is the jar full?"
the same answer from his students.
      = "Yes."
Next, the teacher took out a bottle of **sand** and poured it into the jar.
                                the sand
After he watched the sand fill the spaces between the stones, he asked
      지각동사(watched)+목적어+원형부정사
once more, "Is the jar full?" All the students replied, "Yes."

Suddenly Mr. Jenkins took a can of **apple juice** out of the bag. He
poured the apple juice into the jar, and his students watched it fill the
  └ pour A into B: B 안으로 A를 붓다 ┘   지각동사(watched)+목적어+원형부정사
spaces in the sand.

full 가득한

teacher's desk 교탁

pick up 집어 들다

pour 붓다

shake 흔들다

roll into 굴러 들어가다

take out ~을 꺼내다

fill 채우다, 메우다

space 공간

suddenly 갑자기

확인문제

● 다음 문장이 본문의 내용과 일치하면 T, 일치하지 않으면 F를 쓰시오.

1 Mr. Jenkins had a large jar and a big bag on the teacher's desk. ☐

2 Mr. Jenkins picked up the jar and started to put small stones into it first. ☐

3 Mr. Jenkins shook the jar a little to let the stones roll into the open areas between
    the golf balls. ☐

4 Mr. Jenkins put the sand into the jar before putting small stones. ☐

5 Lastly, Mr. Jenkins poured the apple juice into the jar. ☐

6 Mr. Jenkins and his students watched the apple juice spill over the jar. ☐

"Now," the teacher said, "I want you to understand that your life
<u>want</u> you to <u>understand</u>
want+목적어+to부정사

is just <u>like</u> the jar. The golf balls are <u>what is</u> most important in life:
be like: ~와 같다   = the thing that[which]

your family, your friends, your health, and your dreams. Even when

everything else <u>is lost</u>, your life can <u>still</u> be full. The stones are the
be lost: 사라지다, 없어지다   be동사, 조동사 뒤, 일반동사 앞에 위치

other things <u>valued</u> by people, <u>like</u> your job, your house, and your car.
= that[which] are valued   = such as: ~와 같은

The sand is all the small things."

"If you put the sand into the jar first," he said, "there's no <u>room</u>
공간, 여지

for the stones or the golf balls. <u>The same goes for</u> life. If you
~도 마찬가지이다

<u>spend</u> all your time and energy <u>on</u> the small things, you will never have
spend+시간, 돈+on+명사

<u>room</u> for <u>what is</u> really important to you. Take care of the balls first —
공간, 여지   = the thing which[that] really matters

<u>the things that really matter</u>."
= the things that are really important

One student <u>sitting</u> in the back <u>raised</u> her hand and asked, "What
= who is sitting   rose(×)

does the apple juice mean?" Mr. Jenkins smiled, "I'm glad you asked.

<u>It</u> just shows that <u>though</u> your life <u>may</u> seem full, there's always <u>room</u>
= The apple juice   비록 ~이지만   ~할지도 모른다   공간, 여지

for a cool drink with a friend."

health 건강

value 소중하게[가치 있게] 생각하다[여기다]

small 사소한, 대수롭지 않은

room 여지

take care of ~을 신경 쓰다

raise 들다, 올리다

though 비록 ~이지만

확인문제

● 다음 문장이 본문의 내용과 일치하면 T, 일치하지 <u>않으면</u> F를 쓰시오.

1 Mr. Jenkins said, "The golf balls are what is most important in life." [ ]

2 Mr. Jenkins said, "When everything else is lost, your life can't be full." [ ]

3 Mr. Jenkins said, "The stones are the other things valued by people." [ ]

4 Though you spend all your time and energy on the small things, you will have room

   for what is really important to you. [ ]

5 Mr. Jenkins told the students to take care of the balls first, not the sand. [ ]

6 A friend with whom you can have some apple juice is most important in life. [ ]

● 우리말을 참고하여 빈칸에 알맞은 말을 쓰시오.

1 The _____ Jar

2 Mr. Jenkins stood _____ _____ _____.

3 He had _____ _____ _____ and a big bag on the teacher's desk.

4 When the class began, he picked up the jar and started to _____ it _____ **golf balls** _____ _____ _____.

5 He asked the students, "_____ _____ _____ _____?"

6 _____ _____ said, "Yes."

7 The teacher took a box of **small stones** _____ _____ _____ _____ and _____ _____ into the jar.

8 He shook the jar _____ _____, and the stones _____ _____ the open areas between the golf balls.

9 He asked _____ _____ _____ and got _____ _____ _____ from his students.

10 Next, the teacher _____ _____ a bottle of **sand** and _____ it _____ the jar.

11 After he watched the sand _____ the spaces between the stones, he asked _____ _____, "Is the jar full?"

12 All the students _____, "Yes."

13 Suddenly Mr. Jenkins took a can of **apple juice** _____ _____ _____ _____.

1	가득 찬 병
2	Jenkins 선생님이 교실 앞에 섰다.
3	교탁 위에는 큰 병과 커다란 가방이 놓여 있었다.
4	수업이 시작하자, 선생님은 병을 집어 들고 가방에서 꺼낸 골프공으로 채우기 시작했다.
5	그는 학생들에게 "병이 가득 찼나요?"라고 질문했다.
6	학생들은 모두 "예."라고 대답했다.
7	선생님은 가방에서 작은 돌 한 상자를 끄집어내어 병 안에 부었다.
8	그가 병을 살짝 흔들자, 돌들이 골프공 사이의 틈새로 굴러 들어갔다.
9	그는 같은 질문을 했고 학생들에게서 같은 대답을 들었다.
10	그런 다음, 선생님은 모래 병을 꺼내 병 안에 부었다.
11	모래가 돌 사이의 공간을 채우는 것을 지켜보고 나서 그는 "이 병이 가득 찼나요?"라고 한 번 더 물었다.
12	모든 학생들이 "예."라고 답했다.
13	갑자기 Jenkins 선생님은 가방에서 사과 주스 한 캔을 꺼냈다.

14 He poured the apple juice into the jar, and his students watched it _____ _____ _____ in the sand.

15 "Now," the teacher said, "I want you to understand that your life _____ _____ _____ the jar.

16 The golf balls are _____ _____ _____ _____ in life: your family, your friends, your health, and your dreams.

17 Even when everything else _____ _____, your life can still be full.

18 The stones are the other things _____ by people, like your job, your house, and your car.

19 The sand is _____ _____ _____ _____."

20 "If you put the sand into the jar first," he said, "_____ _____ _____ _____ the stones or the golf balls.

21 _____ _____ _____ _____ life.

22 If you _____ all your time and energy _____ the small things, you will never have room for _____ _____ _____ _____ to you.

23 _____ _____ _____ the balls first — the things that really _____."

24 One student _____ in the back _____ her hand and asked, "What does the apple juice mean?"

25 Mr. Jenkins smiled, "I'm glad _____ _____.

26 It just shows that though your life may _____ _____, there's always _____ _____ a cool drink with a friend."

---

14 그는 사과 주스를 병 안에 부었고, 학생들은 주스가 모래 사이의 빈틈을 채우는 것을 지켜보았다.

15 "자, 이제," 선생님이 말했다. "여러분의 인생이 병과 같다는 것을 이해하기 바랍니다.

16 골프공은 여러분의 가족, 친구, 건강, 꿈과 같이 인생에서 가장 중요한 것이랍니다.

17 다른 모든 것을 잃게 될 때라도 여러분의 인생은 여전히 가득 차 있을 수 있습니다.

18 돌은 여러분의 직업, 집, 자동차처럼 사람들이 소중하게 여기는 다른 것들에 해당합니다.

19 모래는 온갖 사소한 것들이랍니다."

20 "만약 병에 모래를 먼저 채우면, 돌이나 골프공을 채울 공간이 없게 됩니다.

21 인생도 똑같습니다.

22 여러분의 시간과 에너지를 사소한 것에 모두 허비한다면 여러분에게 진정으로 중요한 것을 채울 공간은 절대로 없을 겁니다.

23 골프공, 즉 정말로 중요한 것들을 먼저 챙기기 바랍니다."라고 선생님이 말했다.

24 뒤에 앉아 있던 학생 하나가 손을 들고 질문했다. "사과 주스는 무슨 뜻입니까?"

25 Jenkins 선생님은 미소 지었다. "질문을 해줘서 기뻐요.

26 그것은, 여러분의 인생이 가득 차 보일지라도 친구와 시원한 음료수를 나눌 여유는 늘 있다는 점을 보여 줍니다."

● 우리말을 참고하여 본문을 영작하시오.

1 가득 찬 병

➡ _____

2 Jenkins 선생님이 교실 앞에 섰다.

➡ _____

3 교탁 위에는 큰 병과 커다란 가방이 놓여 있었다.

➡ _____

4 수업이 시작하자, 선생님은 병을 집어 들고 가방에서 꺼낸 골프공으로 채우기 시작했다.

➡ _____

5 그는 학생들에게 "병이 가득 찼나요?"라고 질문했다.

➡ _____

6 학생들은 모두 "예."라고 대답했다.

➡ _____

7 선생님은 가방에서 작은 돌 한 상자를 끄집어내어 병 안에 부었다.

➡ _____

8 그가 병을 살짝 흔들자, 돌들이 골프공 사이의 틈새로 굴러 들어갔다.

➡ _____

9 그는 같은 질문을 했고 학생들에게서 같은 대답을 들었다.

➡ _____

10 그런 다음, 선생님은 모래 병을 꺼내 병 안에 부었다.

➡ _____

11 모래가 돌 사이의 공간을 채우는 것을 지켜보고 나서 그는 "이 병이 가득 찼나요?"라고 한 번 더 물었다.

➡ _____

12 모든 학생들이 "예."라고 답했다.

➡ _____

13 갑자기 Jenkins 선생님은 가방에서 사과 주스 한 캔을 꺼냈다.

➡ _____

14 그는 사과 주스를 병 안에 부었고, 학생들은 주스가 모래 사이의 빈틈을 채우는 것을 지켜보았다.

➡ _____

15 "자, 이제," 선생님이 말했다. "여러분의 인생이 병과 같다는 것을 이해하기 바랍니다.

➡ _____

16 골프공은 여러분의 가족, 친구, 건강, 꿈과 같이 인생에서 가장 중요한 것이랍니다.

➡ _____

17 다른 모든 것을 잃게 될 때라도 여러분의 인생은 여전히 가득 차 있을 수 있습니다.

➡ _____

18 돌은 여러분의 직업, 집, 자동차처럼 사람들이 소중하게 여기는 다른 것들에 해당합니다.

➡ _____

19 모래는 온갖 사소한 것들이랍니다."

➡ _____

20 "만약 병에 모래를 먼저 채우면, 돌이나 골프공을 채울 공간이 없게 됩니다.

➡ _____

21 인생도 똑같습니다.

➡ _____

22 여러분의 시간과 에너지를 사소한 것에 모두 허비한다면 여러분에게 진정으로 중요한 것을 채울 공간은 절대로 없을 겁니다.

➡ _____

_____

23 골프공, 즉 정말로 중요한 것들을 먼저 챙기기 바랍니다."라고 선생님이 말했다.

➡ _____

24 뒤에 앉아 있던 학생 하나가 손을 들고 질문했다. "사과 주스는 무슨 뜻입니까?"

➡ _____

25 Jenkins 선생님은 미소 지었다. "질문을 해줘서 기뻐요.

➡ _____

26 그것은, 여러분의 인생이 가득 차 보일지라도 친구와 시원한 음료수를 나눌 여유는 늘 있다는 점을 보여 줍니다."

➡ _____

01 다음 빈칸에 공통으로 들어갈 말을 쓰시오.

> • Who's _____ care of the dog while you're away?
> • The officer started _____ her notebook out.

02 다음 밑줄 친 부분과 바꿔 쓸 수 있는 말을 쓰시오. (v로 시작할 것)

> The more we study the document, the more we appreciate the wisdom of the men who wrote it.

➡ _____

03 다음 빈칸에 알맞은 단어를 〈보기〉에서 골라 쓰시오.

> ┌─ 보기 ─┐
> full   same   suddenly

(1) He sits in the _____ chair every night.
(2) I _____ realized that there was someone following me.
(3) Don't talk with your mouth _____.

04 다음 영영풀이에 해당하는 말을 주어진 철자로 시작하여 쓰시오.

> an empty area

➡ s_____

05 다음 밑줄 친 부분의 쓰임이 자연스럽지 <u>않은</u> 것을 찾아 고치시오.

> ⓐ We're spending a lot more on food than we used to.
> ⓑ She filled the bowl with warm water.
> ⓒ Jill watched the children to build sandcastles.

_____ ➡ _____

06 다음 우리말에 맞도록 빈칸에 알맞은 말을 쓰시오. (철자가 주어진 경우 주어진 철자로 시작할 것.)

(1) 교수가 이름을 불렀을 때 그 학생은 얼굴을 들었다.
　➡ The student _____ her head when the professor called her name.
(2) 나는 뭐라고 대답해야 할지 몰랐다.
　➡ I did not know what to r_____.

07 우리말 해석에 맞게 주어진 단어를 알맞게 배열하시오.

(1) 그들은 이미 많은 시간과 돈을 이 프로젝트에 쏟아부었다. (poured, and, project, already, a, money, this, they've, of, into, time, lot)
　➡ _____
　_____

(2) 공기가 장미의 향기로 채워졌다. (scent, filled, air, the, the, was, roses, of, with)
　➡ _____
　_____

(3) 네가 그걸 어떻게 하든 중요하지 않다. (it, it, you, how, matter, not, does, do)
　➡ _____
　_____

08 다음 문장을 어법에 맞게 고쳐 쓰시오.

(1) I can play the piano a few.

➡ _____

_____

(2) I often watch him to play tennis.

➡ _____

_____

(3) The symbols stand for that we all want: beauty, fame, and wealth.

➡ _____

_____

(4) Can you make yourself understand in French?

➡ _____

_____

(5) She is not the one wears sunglasses indoors to avoid eye contact.

➡ _____

_____

09 다음 두 문장을 같은 뜻을 갖는 한 문장으로 바꿔 쓰시오.

(1) • Herold is the boy.
  • He is dancing to the music.
  ➡ _____

(2) • There were many soldiers.
  • They were injured in the war.
  ➡ _____

(3) • We had a special dish.
  • It was made with milk and ice.
  ➡ _____

10 다음 우리말을 괄호 안에 주어진 어휘를 이용하여 영작하시오.

(1) 그녀는 안경을 쓴 소녀와 이야기를 나누고 있다. (talk, wear, glasses, 8단어)

➡ _____

(2) 그녀는 그가 창문을 여는 소리를 들었다. (open, hear, 6단어)

➡ _____

11 다음 두 문장을 〈보기〉와 같이 지각동사를 이용하여 한 문장으로 완성하시오.

┌─ 보기 ├─────────────────────
• He saw his dog.
• She was sleeping under the table.
→ He saw his dog sleeping under the table.
└──────────────────────────

(1) • Robert watched a thief.
  • He stole a lady's bag.
  ➡ _____

(2) • Theresa heard her dog.
  • He was barking loudly.
  ➡ _____

[12~14] 다음 글을 읽고 물음에 답하시오.

Mr. Jenkins stood before his class. He had a large jar and a big bag on the teacher's desk. When the class began, he picked up the jar and started to fill it with **golf balls** from the bag. He asked the students, "Is the jar full?" They all said, "Yes."

The teacher took a box of **small stones** out of the bag and poured them into the jar. He shook the jar a little, and the stones rolled into the open areas between the golf balls. He asked ⓐthe same question and got ⓑthe same answer from his students.

12 다음 문장에서 위 글의 내용과 다른 부분을 찾아서 고치시오. (두 군데)

> Mr. Jenkins picked up a jar and put small stones into it first, and then put golf balls into it, too.

_____ ➡ _____

_____ ➡ _____

13 위 글의 밑줄 친 ⓐthe same question과 ⓑthe same answer가 가리키는 것을 각각 본문에서 찾아 쓰시오.

➡ ⓐ _____ ⓑ _____

14 Why did Mr. Jenkins shake the jar a little after he poured small stones into the jar? Fill in the blanks with suitable words.

➡ He shook the jar a little to let the stones _____ the open areas between _____ _____.

[15~17] 다음 글을 읽고 물음에 답하시오.

"Now," the teacher said, "I want you to understand that your life is just like the jar. The golf balls are ___ⓐ___ is most important in life: your family, your friends, your health, and your dreams. Even when everything else is lost, your life can still be full. The stones are the other things valued by people, ⓑlike your job, your house, and your car. The sand is all the small things."

15 Fill in the blank ⓐ with a suitable word.

➡ _____

16 위 글의 밑줄 친 ⓑlike와 바꿔 쓸 수 있는 두 단어를 쓰시오.

➡ _____

17 위 글의 골프공, 돌들, 모래가 상징하는 것을 각각 우리말로 쓰시오.

➡ (1) _____
(2) _____
(3) _____

[18~20] 다음 글을 읽고 물음에 답하시오.

"If you put ⓐthe sand into the jar first," he said, "there's no room for ⓑthe stones or the golf balls. ⓒThe same goes for life. ⓓIf you spend all your time and energy on the small things, you will never have a room for what is really important to you. Take care of the balls first — the things that really matter."

18 위 글의 밑줄 친 ⓐ와 ⓑ가 상징하는 것을 본문에서 찾아 각각 쓰시오.

➡ ⓐ _____
ⓑ _____
_____

19 밑줄 친 ⓒ의 의미를 우리말로 자세히 설명하시오.

➡ _____
_____
_____

20 위 글의 밑줄 친 ⓓ에서 어법상 틀린 부분을 찾아 고치시오.

➡ _____ ➡ _____

01 빈칸에 들어갈 말이 나머지 넷과 <u>다른</u> 하나를 고르시오.

① There is an important _____ we need to discuss.
② Stacey _____ all her free time painting.
③ Does it _____ what I think?
④ It was clear that she wanted to discuss the _____.
⑤ It doesn't _____ what you wear, as long as you look neat and tidy.

02 빈칸 (A)와 (B)에 들어갈 말로 알맞은 것끼리 짝지어진 것을 고르시오.

• We stood at the counter, filling our bowls __(A)__ salad.
• They spend quite a lot of money __(B)__ eating out each week.

   (A)   (B)`   (A)   (B)
① to   – on   ② to   – in
③ with – on   ④ with– with
⑤ out – in

03 다음 영영풀이가 나타내는 말을 고르시오.

to make sure that you are/somebody is safe, well, healthy, etc.; look after yourself/somebody

① put down   ② take out
③ take care of   ④ come across
⑤ turn down

04 밑줄 친 부분과 바꿔 쓸 수 있는 말을 쓰시오.

My suitcase was so full that I didn't have <u>room</u> for anything else.

➡ _____

05 다음 우리말에 맞도록 빈칸에 알맞은 말을 쓰시오. (철자가 주어진 경우 주어진 철자로 시작할 것)

(1) 냉장고에서 맥주 한 병 갖다 주시겠어요?
➡ Would you get _____ beer from the refrigerator for me?
(2) 만약에 신용카드를 잃어버린다면, 이 번호로 즉시 전화하세요.
➡ If you _____ your credit card, phone this number immediately.
(3) 내일은 오후 내내 그의 스케줄이 비어 있다.
➡ His schedule is o_____ all afternoon tomorrow.
(4) 그들은 아주 가난할지라도 함께 행복해 보인다.
➡ T_____ they are so poor, they seem happy together.

06 다음 중 어법상 <u>어색한</u> 것은?

① I just felt the building shaking.
② How you play the game is that really counts.
③ She noticed her husband injured during the game.
④ Though he often talks big, I love him so much.
⑤ It is a full year since I left home.

07 다음 문장을 어법에 맞게 고쳐 쓰시오.

(1) He quickly gets bored with his toys and wants them replacing with new ones.

➡ _____

_____

(2) The ball went over the fence and they looked at it flew through the air.

➡ _____

_____

(3) I cannot find the book what I just put on the table.

➡ _____

_____

(4) He addressed himself to her despite he was shy.

➡ _____

_____

08 다음 빈칸에 들어갈 괄호 안에 주어진 동사의 형태가 <u>다른</u> 하나는?

① They watched him _____ the bank. (enter)

② We saw her _____ the heavy box. (carry)

③ He didn't hear them _____ that night. (fight)

④ She wanted me _____ her with her homework. (help)

⑤ Do you want to know what made me _____ mad? (get)

09 다음 중 어법상 적절한 것은?

① The golf balls are that is most important in life.

② There's no rooms for the stones or the golf balls.

③ She watched him carry out his duties, always with a smile.

④ They were seating on each side of the upper platform.

⑤ Because summer is a fun season, I can't stand the heat!

10 다음을 같은 뜻을 갖는 문장으로 바꿔 쓰시오.

(1) The pen is something that I wanted to buy.

➡ _____

(2) The student sitting in the back raised her hand.

➡ _____

_____

[11~13] 다음 글을 읽고 물음에 답하시오.

Mr. Jenkins stood before his class. He had a large jar and a big bag on the teacher's desk. When the class began, he picked up the jar and started to fill (A)it with **golf balls** from the bag. He asked the students, "Is the jar full?" They all said, "Yes."

The teacher took a box of **small stones** ⓐ the bag and poured (B)them into the jar. He shook the jar a little, and the stones rolled ⓑ the open areas between the golf balls. He asked the same question and got the same answer from his students.

11 위 글의 밑줄 친 (A)it과 (B)them이 가리키는 것을 각각 본문에서 찾아 쓰시오.

➡ (A) _____ (B) _____

12 위 글의 빈칸 ⓐ와 ⓑ에 들어갈 전치사가 바르게 짝지어진 것은?

	ⓐ	ⓑ		ⓐ	ⓑ
①	from	– on	②	on	– into
③	out of	– on	④	from	– by
⑤	out of	– into			

13 According to the passage, which is NOT true?

① Mr. Jenkins had a large jar and a big bag on the teacher's desk.

② Mr. Jenkins asked the students if the jar was full after he filled the jar with golf balls.

③ The students answered that the jar was full.

④ Mr. Jenkins couldn't pour the small stones into the jar as it was full.

⑤ Mr. Jenkins shook the jar a little to let the small stones enter the open areas between the golf balls.

[14~15] 다음 글을 읽고 물음에 답하시오.

Next, the teacher took out a bottle of **sand** and poured ⓐit into the jar. After he watched the sand fill the spaces between the stones, he asked once more, "Is the jar full?" All the students replied, "Yes."

Suddenly Mr. Jenkins took a can of **apple juice** out of the bag. He poured the apple juice into the jar, and his students watched ⓑit fill the spaces in the sand.

14 위 글의 내용과 일치하도록 다음 빈칸 (A)와 (B)에 알맞은 단어를 쓰시오. 단, (B)에는 주어진 영영풀이를 참고하여 철자 r로 시작하는 단어를 쓰시오.

> Though the jar seemingly looked (A)_____, there was (B)_____ for the sand and the apple juice to enter.
>
> *seemingly: 외견상으로, 겉보기에는
>
> • (B)에 들어갈 단어의 영영풀이: enough empty space for people or things to be fitted in

15 위 글의 밑줄 친 ⓐit과 ⓑit이 가리키는 것을 각각 본문에서 찾아 쓰시오.

➡ ⓐ _____

　 ⓑ _____

[16~18] 다음 글을 읽고 물음에 답하시오.

"Now," the teacher said, "I want you to understand that your life is just (A)like the jar. The golf balls are what is most important in life: your family, your friends, your health, and your dreams. Even when everything else is lost, your life can still be full. The stones are the other things ____ⓐ____ by people, like your job, your house, and your car. The sand is all the small things."

golf balls, small stones, sand

16 위 글의 빈칸 ⓐ에 value를 알맞은 형태로 쓰시오.

➡ _____

17 위 글의 밑줄 친 (A)like와 같은 의미로 쓰인 것을 고르시오.

① Would you like a drink?
② She responded in like manner.
③ He doesn't like asking his parents for help.
④ He's very like his father.
⑤ You should do it like this.

18 다음 중 위 글의 내용을 올바르게 이해하지 못한 사람을 고르시오.

┌─── 보기 ───┐

① 정호: 셋 중에서 크기가 가장 큰 골프공은 인생에서 가장 중요한 것을 상징하는 거야.
② 상준: 그렇지 않아. 골프공은 가장 크기 때문에, 집과 같은 큰 물체를 상징하는 거야.
③ 지윤: 아니야. 사람들이 소중하게 여기는 집과 같은 것들을 상징하는 것은, 크기가 두 번째인 돌이야.
④ 민규: 그래. 그리고 돌은 직업이나 차를 상징하는 것이기도 해.
⑤ 은희: 그리고 온갖 사소한 것들을 상징하는 것은 모래야.

└──────────┘

① 정호   ② 상준   ③ 지윤
④ 민규   ⑤ 은희

[19~21] 다음 글을 읽고 물음에 답하시오.

"If you put the sand into the jar first," he said, "there's no room for the stones or the golf balls. ⓐ인생도 똑같습니다. If you spend all your time and energy on the small things, you will never have ⓑroom for what is really important to you. Take care of the balls first — ⓒthe things that really matter."

19 위 글의 밑줄 친 ⓐ의 우리말에 맞게 5단어로 영작하시오.

➡ _____

20 위 글의 밑줄 친 ⓑroom과 같은 의미로 쓰인 것을 모두 고르시오.

① I think Simon is in his room.
② This table takes up too much room.
③ He walked out of the room and slammed the door.
④ They had to sit in the waiting room for an hour.
⑤ There could be no room for doubt.

21 위 글의 밑줄 친 ⓒ를 다음과 같이 바꿔 쓸 때 빈칸에 들어갈 알맞은 단어를 쓰시오.

➡ the things that _____ really _____

[22~24] 다음 글을 읽고 물음에 답하시오.

One student (A)[sitting / to sit] in the back ⓐraised her hand and asked, "What does ⓑthe apple juice mean?" Mr. Jenkins smiled, "I'm glad you asked. It just (B)[sees / shows] that though your life may seem (C)[empty / full], there's always room for a cool drink with a friend."

22 위 글의 괄호 (A)~(C)에서 문맥이나 어법상 알맞은 낱말을 골라 쓰시오.

➡ (A) _____ (B) _____ (C) _____

23 위 글의 밑줄 친 ⓐraised와 같은 의미로 쓰인 것을 고르시오.

① The book raised many important questions.
② I was raised as a city boy.
③ She raised her eyes from her work.
④ We raised money for charity.
⑤ They raised an income tax.

24 위 글의 밑줄 친 ⓑthe apple juice가 상징하는 것을 우리말로 쓰시오.

➡ _____

Lesson 3

Be Positive, Be Happy

 의사소통 기능

- 주제 소개하기
  A: I'd like to talk about Frida Kahlo.

- 이유 묻고 답하기
  A: I want to spend more time on social media.
  B: What makes you say that?
  A: I can make more friends from around the world.

 언어 형식

- 현재완료진행형
  Jake **has been sleeping** all afternoon.

- so ～ that ... 구문
  It was **so** cold **that** I put on my coat.

Words & Expressions

Key Words

- □ **appearance** [əpíərəns] 명 외모, 출현
- □ **argue** [ά:rgju:] 동 주장하다
- □ **artificial** [à:rtəfíʃəl] 형 인공적인
- □ **as** [əz] 접 ~처럼
- □ **besides** [bisáidz] 부 그 외에도
- □ **boring** [bɔ́:riŋ] 형 지루한
- □ **bother** [báðər] 동 성가시게 하다
- □ **cause** [kɔ:z] 명 원인
- □ **chemical** [kémikəl] 명 화학물질
- □ **common** [kámən] 형 흔한
- □ **effect** [ifékt] 명 효과
- □ **focus** [fóukəs] 동 집중하다
- □ **friendship** [fréndʃip] 명 우정
- □ **gloomy** [glú:mi] 형 우울한
- □ **grade** [greid] 명 성적
- □ **helpful** [hélpfəl] 형 도움이 되는
- □ **improve** [imprú:v] 동 개선하다
- □ **leave** [li:v] 동 남겨두다
- □ **left-handed hitter** 좌타자
- □ **matter** [mǽtər] 동 문제가 되다, 중요하다
- □ **media** [mí:diə] 명 매체
- □ **method** [méθəd] 명 방법
- □ **nervous** [nɔ́:rvəs] 형 불안한
- □ **patient** [péiʃənt] 형 인내하는
- □ **positive** [pázətiv] 형 긍정적인
- □ **produce** [prədjú:s] 동 생산하다
- □ **relieve** [rilí:v] 동 덜다
- □ **relieved** [rilí:vd] 형 안심이 되는
- □ **salty** [sɔ́:lti] 형 짠
- □ **scary** [skɛ́əri] 형 무서운
- □ **schoolwork** [skúlwərk] 명 학교 공부
- □ **scream** [skri:m] 동 소리를 지르다
- □ **sleepy** [slí:pi] 형 졸리는
- □ **spend** [spend] 동 쓰다, 소비하다
- □ **stressed** [strest] 형 스트레스 받은
- □ **tidy** [táidi] 형 깔끔한
- □ **well-known** 형 유명한
- □ **work** [wə:rk] 동 효과가 있다

Key Expressions

- □ **according to** ~에 따르면
- □ **as long as** ~하는 한
- □ **at bat** 타석에
- □ **at the same time** 동시에
- □ **at the top of my lungs** 있는 힘껏
- □ **break a promise** 약속을 어기다
- □ **deal with** ~을 다루다, 처리하다
- □ **decide on** ~에 대하여 결정하다
- □ **feel like** ~ ~하고 싶은 기분이 들다
- □ **feel low** 우울하게 느끼다
- □ **forget to** ~할 것을 잊어버리다
- □ **get stressed** 스트레스 받다
- □ **get upset** 속이 상하다
- □ **have difficulty -ing** ~에 어려움이 있다
- □ **in other ways** 다른 방식으로
- □ **instead of** ~ ~ 대신에
- □ **make sense** 의미가 통하다
- □ **put down** 내려놓다
- □ **put on** 입다
- □ **something else** 다른 어떤 것
- □ **stress ~ out** 스트레스를 받아 지치게 하다
- □ **take a deep breath** 심호흡을 하다
- □ **take time out** 시간을 내다, 쉬다
- □ **thanks to** ~ 덕택에
- □ **that way** 그런 식으로
- □ **the next time** 다음 번 ~할 때
- □ **used to** ~하곤 했다
- □ **work on a team** 한 팀으로 일하다

Word Power

※ 서로 비슷한 뜻을 가진 어휘

☐ **artificial** 인공적인 : **manufactured** 제조된
☐ **bother** 성가시게 하다 : **disturb** 방해하다
☐ **common** 흔한 : **normal** 보통의
☐ **gloomy** 우울한 : **cheerless** 활기 없는
☐ **nervous** 불안한 : **unstable** 불안한
☐ **relieve** 덜다 : **ease** 편하게 하다
☐ **scream** 소리를 지르다 : **shout** 소리치다
☐ **tidy** 깔끔한 : **neat** 깨끗한

☐ **boring** 지루한 : **dull** 지루한
☐ **cause** 원인 : **reason** 이유
☐ **effect** 결과 : **outcome** 결과
☐ **improve** 개선하다 : **develop** 개발하다
☐ **patient** 인내하는 : **tolerant** 참을성 있는
☐ **matter** 중요하다 : **count** 중요하다
☐ **sleepy** 졸리는 : **drowsy** 졸리는
☐ **produce** 생산하다 : **manufacture** 제작하다

※ 서로 반대의 뜻을 가진 어휘

☐ **agree** 동의하다 ↔ **disagree** 동의하지 않다
☐ **cause** 원인 ↔ **effect** 결과
☐ **gloomy** 우울한 ↔ **cheerful** 활발한
☐ **positive** 긍정적인 ↔ **negative** 부정적인
☐ **relieved** 안심이 되는 ↔ **worried** 걱정되는
☐ **tidy** 깔끔한 ↔ **messy** 어질러진

☐ **artificial** 인공적인 ↔ **natural** 자연적인
☐ **common** 흔한 ↔ **rare** 흔하지 않은
☐ **nervous** 불안한 ↔ **calm** 차분한
☐ **produce** 생산하다 ↔ **consume** 소모하다
☐ **patient** 인내하는 ↔ **impatient** 조바심을 내는

English Dictionary

☐ **appearance** 외모
→ the way someone or something looks to other people
어떤 사람 또는 어떤 것이 다른 사람에게 보여지는 방식

☐ **argue** 주장하다
→ to disagree with someone in words, often in an angry way
말로 또는 종종 화가 나서 다른 사람의 의견에 반박하다

☐ **artificial** 인공적인
→ not made of natural things
자연적인 것들로 만들어지지 않은

☐ **bother** 성가시게 하다
→ to make someone feel slightly worried, upset, or concerned
다른 사람이 좀 걱정되거나 불편하게 느끼도록 만들다

☐ **cause** 원인
→ a person, event, or thing that makes something happen
무엇인가가 일어나도록 만드는 사람, 사건 또는 사물

☐ **effect** 효과
→ a change that is caused by an event, action, etc.
사건이나 행위 등에 의해서 생겨난 변화

☐ **gloomy** 우울한
→ sad because you think the situation will not improve
상황이 나아지지 않을 것이라고 생각해서 슬픈

☐ **improve** 개선하다
→ to make something better, or to become better
어떤 것을 더 좋게 만들거나 더 좋아지다

☐ **positive** 긍정적인
→ expressing support, agreement, or approval
지지, 동의, 찬성을 표현하는

☐ **tidy** 깔끔한
→ neatly arranged with everything in the right place
모든 것이 제자리에 단정하게 정돈된

서답형

[01~02] 다음 짝지어진 단어의 관계가 같도록 빈칸에 알맞은 말을 쓰시오. (주어진 철자로 시작할 것)

01

> cause : effect = a_____ : natural

02 중요

> patient : impatient = n_____ : calm

03 다음 영영풀이에 해당하는 단어를 고르시오.

> to disagree with someone in words, often in an angry way

① argue ② grow
③ destroy ④ support
⑤ produce

04 중요 다음 중 밑줄 친 부분의 뜻풀이가 바르지 <u>않은</u> 것은?

① I'd like to talk about true <u>friendship</u>. (우정)
② I think it's going to be a <u>boring</u> talk show. (지루한)
③ What makes you feel the most <u>stressed</u>? (스트레스를 받은)
④ Problems with friends <u>took</u> second place with 15.3%. (차지했다)
⑤ I understand. I <u>used to</u> feel that way, too. (사용했다)

05 다음 대화의 빈칸에 들어갈 말로 적절한 것을 고르시오.

> A: I'd like to talk about the effects of artificial light.
> B: Oh, I have _____ problems at night.

① eating ② reading
③ running ④ driving
⑤ sleeping

06 중요 문장의 빈칸에 알맞은 것으로 짝지어진 것은?

> • Jane put _____ a new skirt.
> • This book deals _____ educational problems.

① on – with ② on – to
③ in – with ④ to – for
⑤ for – from

07 중요 다음 중 〈보기〉에 있는 단어를 사용하여 자연스러운 문장을 만들 수 <u>없는</u> 것은?

> ┤ 보기 ├
> scary spend bothering gloomy

① What's _____ you the most these days?
② We have _____ to eat.
③ Good horror movies are so _____ that I scream a lot.
④ Some people _____ time with friends when they feel low.
⑤ This is a very _____ situation.

01 다음 빈칸에 공통으로 들어갈 단어를 쓰시오.

> • I'm studying for the math test, Mom. Grades stress me _____.
> • "Me Time" on her calendar. This means she takes some time _____ for herself.

➡ _____

02 다음 밑줄 친 단어와 의미상 반대가 되는 단어를 주어진 철자로 시작하여 쓰시오.

> His brother has a <u>rare</u> disease.

➡ c_____

03 다음 주어진 단어를 이용해 빈칸을 완성하시오.

> What makes you feel the most _____?

➡ _____ (stress)

04 다음 우리말에 맞게 빈칸에 알맞은 말을 쓰시오.

(1) 오늘 학급 티셔츠에 대하여 이야기합시다. 우리는 디자인을 정해야 합니다.
➡ Today, let's talk about the class T-shirt. We have to _____ on the design.

(2) 나는 인공조명의 효과에 대하여 이야기하고 싶습니다.
➡ I'd like to talk about the effects of _____ light.

(3) 시험 공부가 나를 졸리게 만들어.
➡ Studying for tests makes me _____.

05 다음 영영풀이에 해당하는 단어를 쓰시오. (주어진 철자로 시작할 것)

> not real or not made of natural things but made to be like something that is real or natural

➡ a_____

06 다음 빈칸에 공통으로 들어가기에 적절한 한 단어를 쓰시오.

> • I try to forget about problems. It is a good way to deal _____ my feelings.
> • Some people spend time _____ friends when they feel low.

➡ _____

07 다음 중 〈보기〉의 적절한 단어를 넣어 의미상 자연스러운 문장을 완성하시오.

> ┤ 보기 ├
> drinking relax happy deep counting

(1) I'd like to talk about some good ways to _____ when you get upset.

(2) First, it's good to take _____ breaths.

(3) Second, _____ to ten is a great idea.

(4) Also, _____ cold water helps.

(5) Lastly, thinking _____ thoughts can help.

Conversation

1 주제 소개하기

A I'd like to talk about Frida Kahlo. Frida Kahlo에 대하여 이야기하겠습니다.

■ 무엇인가를 하려고 할 때 'I'd like to ~'라고 한다. 지금부터 상대에게 새로운 주제를 소개하려고 할 때 '~에 대하여 말씀드리겠습니다.'라는 의미로 'I'd like to talk about ~'라고 한다.

  • I'd like to talk about true friendship. 진정한 우정에 관하여 말씀드리겠습니다.
  • Today, I'd like to talk to you about teen stress. 오늘 청소년의 스트레스에 관하여 말씀드리겠습니다.

■ 주제를 소개할 때 'I'd like to talk about ~'라고 할 수도 있지만 'Let's talk about ~'라고 하거나 'would like to' 대신 will, want to를 사용하여 'Today, I will talk about ~' 또는 'I want to talk about ~'라고 할 수도 있다.

■ 격식을 차려서 소개할 때는 'I'd like to give a presentation about ~'나 'I'd like to give you an introduction about ~'라고 할 수도 있다.

주제 소개하는 여러 가지 표현

  • I'd like to talk about ~. ~에 대하여 말씀드리겠습니다.
  • I want to talk about ~. ~에 대하여 말씀드리고 싶습니다.
  • I will talk about ~. ~에 대하여 말씀드리겠습니다.
  • Let's talk about ~. ~에 대하여 이야기해 봅시다.

핵심 Check

1. 다음 우리말과 일치하도록 빈칸에 알맞은 말을 쓰시오.

(1) **A:** I'd like to _____ about Spanish art. (스페인 예술에 대하여 말씀드리겠습니다.)

   B: Okay, I'm ready. You may start. (좋아요. 준비됐습니다. 시작하세요.)

(2) **B1:** Today, _____ talk about the class T-shirt. We have to decide on the design.

   (오늘 학급 티셔츠에 대하여 이야기해 보자. 우리는 디자인을 정해야 해.)

   G: Let me show you some designs on the screen. (화면으로 디자인을 몇 개 보여줄게.)

   B2: We have to choose a T-shirt with short sleeves. (우리는 반팔 티셔츠를 골라야 해.)

   B1: What makes you say that? (무슨 이유로 그렇게 말하는 거야?)

   B2: _____ we'll wear the T-shirt on Sports Day. It's in June.

   (우리가 체육대회 때 티셔츠를 입기 때문이야. 그건 6월에 열려.)

   G: That makes _____. What about this green one?

   (그 말이 맞아. 이 초록색 티셔츠는 어때?)

---

② 이유 묻고 답하기

> **A** I want to spend more time on social media. 나는 소셜 미디어에 시간을 더 쓰고 싶어.
> **B** What makes you say that? 왜 그런 말을 하니?
> **A** I can make more friends from around the world.
> 나는 전 세계로부터 더 많은 친구를 사귈 수 있어.

■ 상대방의 말을 듣고 그 이유를 묻는 표현은 'What makes you say that?'이나 'What makes you say so?'이다. '무엇 때문에 그런 말을 하니?'의 의미로 상대방이 한 말의 이유를 확인하기 위하여 묻는 표현이다.

  • M: I'd like to talk about true friendship. 진정한 우정에 대하여 말씀드리겠습니다.

  • B: I think it's going to be a boring talk show. 지루한 토크쇼가 되겠군.

  • G: What makes you say so? 왜 그런 말을 하니?

■ 이유를 물어볼 때는 'What makes you say that?'/ 'What makes you say so?'/ 'What makes you think so?' 등으로 물어볼 수 있다. 대답할 때는 단순히 자기 생각이나 이유를 말하면 되고, Because를 붙여서 말해도 된다.

이유 묻고 답하기

이유 묻기 • What makes you say that? 무엇 때문에 그런 말을 하니?

  • What makes you say so?

  • What makes you think so? 무엇 때문에 그렇게 생각하니?

  • I wonder what makes you say that. 무엇 때문에 그런 말을 하는지 궁금해.

대답 • Because ~

핵심 Check

2. 다음 우리말과 일치하도록 빈칸에 알맞은 말을 쓰시오.

W: What are you doing, Oliver?

B: I'm studying for the math test, Mom. Grades stress me (A)_____.

(성적 때문에 스트레스를 받아 지쳐요.)

W: I understand. I (B)_____ to feel that way, too. (나도 또한 그렇게 느꼈지.)

B: Really? I didn't know that.

W: Yeah, but a little stress was helpful for me.

B: (C)_____ makes you say that? (무엇 때문에 그렇게 말씀하세요?)

W: I got stressed when I had an exam, but at the same time it made me (D)_____

and try harder. (동시에 그것이 집중하고 더 열심히 공부하도록 만들었지.)

Listen & Answer Dialog 1

W: Today, ❶I'd like to talk to you about teen stress. ❷What makes you feel the most stressed? ❸About 9,000 teens answered this question. ❹As you can see, schoolwork was the most common cause of stress. Over half of the students said schoolwork stresses them the most. Problems with friends ❺took second place with 15.3%. ❻Next came family and worries about the future. 8.2% of the students said they ❼get stressed because of their appearance.

W: 오늘, 저는 여러분에게 십 대들의 스트레스에 관해 말 씀드리려고 합니다. 여러분 에게 가장 많이 스트레스를 주는 것은 무엇인가요? 약 9,000명의 십 대들이 이 질 문에 답했습니다. 보시다시 피, 학업이 스트레스의 가장 흔한 원인이었습니다. 절반 이 넘는 학생들은 학업이 스 트레스를 가장 많이 준다고 말했습니다. 친구들과의 문 제는 15.3%로 2위를 차지했 습니다. 다음은 가족, 그리고 장래에 대한 걱정 순이었습 니다. 8.2%의 학생들은 외모 때문에 스트레스를 받는다고 말했습니다.

❶ would like to ~ = ~하고 싶다. ~하겠다
❷ 'What makes you ~?'는 '무엇이 ~하도록 만들었느냐?'의 의미로 이유를 물어보는 표현이다. Why를 사용할 수도 있지만 직설적인 느낌을 주어서 대화가 어색한 느낌을 줄 수도 있을 때는 'What ~?'으로 물어보는 것이 자연스럽다.
❸ about ~ = 약 ~
❹ As ~ (접속사) = ~다시피
❺ take ~ place = ~째 자리를 차지하다
❻ 부사 Next로 시작하는 문장에서 '부사+동사+주어'의 순서로 도치되어 있다. 주어는 'family and worries about the future'이다.
❼ 'get stressed'는 be동사 대신 get을 사용하여 수동의 의미로 사용하고 있다.

Check(√) True or False

(1) Schoolwork was the most common cause of stress. T ☐ F ☐

(2) Problems with friends were the second common cause of stress. T ☐ F ☐

 Listen & Answer Dialog 2

W: What are you doing, Oliver?

B: I'm studying for the math test, Mom. Grades stress me out.

W: I understand. I used to feel that way, too.

B: Really? I didn't know that.

W: Yeah, but a little stress was helpful for me.

B: What makes you say that?

W: I got stressed when I had an exam, but at the same time it made me ❶focus and try harder.

B: I see. Did stress help you in other ways?

W: Yes, ❷it helped improve my memory.

W: 뭐 하고 있니, Oliver?
B: 수학 시험이 있어서 공부하고 있어요, 엄마. 성적이 제게 스 트레스를 줘요.
W: 이해한단다. 나도 그렇게 느 끼곤 했거든.
B: 정말요? 그러신 줄 몰랐어요.
W: 그래, 하지만 약간의 스트레 스는 내게 도움이 되기도 했 단다.
B: 왜 그렇게 말씀하세요?
W: 나는 시험이 있을 때 스트레 스를 받았지만, 동시에 그 스 트레스가 나를 집중하고 더 열심히 노력하게 했거든.
B: 그렇군요. 스트레스가 다른 방식으로 엄마에게 도움이 된 적이 있나요?
W: 그럼. 내 기억력을 높이는 데 도움을 주었단다.

❶ 사역동사 made의 목적격보어로 focus와 try는 원형부정사로 사용되었다.
❷ = it helped (me) (to) improve my memory.

Check(√) True or False

(3) The boy is studying for the math test. T ☐ F ☐

(4) Mom didn't get stressed when she had an exam. T ☐ F ☐

Listen More

B1: Today, let's talk about the class T-shirt. We have to ❶decide on the design.

G: ❷Let me show you some designs on the screen.

B2: We have to choose a T-shirt with short sleeves.

B1: ❸What makes you say that?

B2: Because we'll wear the T-shirt on Sports Day. It's in June.

G: That ❹makes sense. ❺What about this green one?

B2: I like it. The bee on the T-shirt is so cute.

G: And it's not expensive.

B1: Yes. I think it's the best one.

❶ decide on ~ = ~에 대하여 결정하다
❷ Let me ~. = ~하겠습니다.
❸ 'What makes you ~?'는 이유를 묻는 질문이기 때문에 대답에 Because를 사용해서 대답할 수 있다.
❹ make sense = 의미가 통하다, 말이 되다
❺ 'What about ~?'는 '~은 어때?'의 의미로 상대의 의견을 묻거나 권유할 때 쓰는 표현이다.

 Speak – Talk in groups.

Hi. Today, I'd like to talk about Frida Kahlo. She was a Mexican painter. ❶One of her most ❷well-known paintings is *Viva la Vida*.

❶ 'one of the[소유격]+최상급 복수명사'의 형태로 '가장 ~한 것 중 하나'의 의미이다.
❷ well-known은 '잘 알려진'의 의미로 famous와 동의어이다.

 Speak – Talk in pairs.

A: I want to ❶spend more time on social media.

B: What makes you say that?

A: I can ❷make more friends from around the world.

B: That makes sense.

❶ 보통 'spend 시간 -ing'의 구문으로 쓰지만 명사와 함께 사용할 때는 'spend 시간 on 명사'의 형태로 쓰기도 한다.
❷ make friends = 친구를 사귀다

 My Speaking Portfolio Step 3

I'd like to talk about some good ways ❶to relax when you ❷get upset. First, ❸it's good to take deep breaths. Second, ❹counting to ten is a great idea. Also, drinking cold water helps. Lastly, thinking happy thoughts can help.

❶ to relax는 명사 ways를 수식하는 부정사의 형용사적 용법이다.
❷ get upset = 화가 나다, 속상하다
❸ 'it is ~ to부정사'의 형태로 가주어, 진주어의 구문이다.
❹ 'counting to ten', 'drinking cold water', 'thinking happy thoughts'는 모두 동명사가 주어로 사용되었다.

 Wrap Up – Listening & Speaking 1

W: Hello, teens. I'm Dr. Broccoli. Last time, I talked about different foods ❶that are good for your health. Today, I'd like to talk about healthy eating habits. First, ❷try to eat slowly. Second, ❸it's important to ❹stop eating when you're full.

❶ that은 주격 관계대명사로 선행사는 different foods로 복수이다.
❷ try to ~ = ~하려고 노력하다, 애쓰다
❸ it is ~ to부정사의 가주어, 진주어 구문이다.
❹ stop -ing = ~하기를 중단하다

 Wrap Up – Listen & Speaking 2

G: ❶Why don't we make a sport club?

B: ❷Sounds good. Let's make a baseball club.

G: Well, I think a basketball club is a better idea.

B: ❸What makes you say that?

G: ❹All we need is a ball to play basketball.

❶ Why don't we ~? = 우리 ~하는 게 어때? (권유나 제안의 표현이다.)
❷ '(It) sounds good.'에서 It을 생략한 말이다.
❸ 상대방의 말에 대하여 이유를 물어보고 있다.
❹ 'All we need'는 'all that we need'에서 목적격 관계대명사 that을 생략하고 쓴 단수 주어이다. '우리가 필요한 것이라고는 ~뿐이다.'의 의미로 쓴다.

● 다음 우리말과 일치하도록 빈칸에 알맞은 말을 쓰시오.

Listen and Answer – Dialog 1

W: Today, I'd like to _____ to you _____ teen stress. _____ makes you _____ the most _____? _____ 9,000 teens _____ this question. _____ you can _____, schoolwork was the most _____ _____ of stress. _____ half of the students said schoolwork _____ them the most. _____ with friends _____ second place _____ 15.3%. _____ came family and _____ about the future. 8.2% of the students said they _____ _____ because of their _____.

W: 오늘, 저는 여러분에게 십 대들의 스트레스에 관해 말씀드리려고 합니다. 여러분에게 가장 많이 스트레스를 주는 것은 무엇인가요? 약 9,000명의 십 대들이 이 질문에 답했습니다. 보시다시피, 학업이 스트레스의 가장 흔한 원인이었습니다. 절반이 넘는 학생들은 학업이 스트레스를 가장 많이 준다고 말했습니다. 친구들과의 문제는 15.3%로 2위를 차지했습니다. 다음은 가족, 그리고 장래에 대한 걱정 순이었습니다. 8.2%의 학생들은 외모 때문에 스트레스를 받는다고 말했습니다.

Listen and Answer – Dialog 2

W: _____ are you doing, Oliver?

B: I'm _____ _____ the math test, Mom. _____ stress me out.

W: I understand. I _____ _____ feel that _____, too.

B: Really? I didn't _____ that.

W: Yeah, but a little _____ was _____ for me.

B: _____ makes you say that?

W: I _____ _____ when I had an exam, but _____ the same time it made me _____ and try harder.

B: I see. Did stress _____ you in other ways?

W: Yes, it helped _____ my memory.

W: 뭐 하고 있니, Oliver?
B: 수학 시험이 있어서 공부하고 있어요, 엄마. 성적이 제게 스트레스를 줘요.
W: 이해한단다. 나도 그렇게 느끼곤 했거든.
B: 정말요? 그러신 줄 몰랐어요.
W: 그래, 하지만 약간의 스트레스는 내게 도움이 되기도 했단다.
B: 왜 그렇게 말씀하세요?
W: 나는 시험이 있을 때 스트레스를 받았지만, 동시에 그 스트레스가 나를 집중하고 더 열심히 노력하게 했거든.
B: 그렇군요. 스트레스가 다른 방식으로 엄마에게 도움이 된 적이 있나요?
W: 그럼. 내 기억력을 높이는 데 도움을 주었단다.

Listen More – Listen and choose.

B1: Today, let's _____ about the class T-shirt. We have to _____ on the design.

G: _____ me show you some _____ on the screen.

B2: We have to _____ a T-shirt with _____ sleeves.

B1: What makes you _____ that?

B2: _____ we'll _____ the T-shirt on Sports Day. It's in June.

G: That _____ _____. What _____ this green one?

B2: I like it. The bee on the T-shirt is so _____.

G: And it's not _____.

B1: Yes. I think it's the best one.

B1: 오늘은 학급 티셔츠에 관해 이야기해 보자. 우리는 디자인을 정해야 해.
G: 화면으로 몇 가지 디자인을 보여 줄게.
B2: 우리는 반팔 티셔츠를 골라야 해.
B1: 무슨 이유로 그렇게 말하는 거야?
B2: 우리가 체육대회 때 티셔츠를 입기 때문이야. 그건 6월에 열려.
G: 그 말이 맞아. 이 초록색 티셔츠는 어때?
B2: 나는 마음에 들어. 티셔츠 위의 벌 그림이 정말 귀여워.
G: 그리고 비싸지 않아.
B1: 맞아. 그게 제일 좋겠어.

Speak – Talk in groups.

Hi. Today, I'd like to _____ about Frida Kahlo. She was a Mexican painter. _____ of her most _____ paintings is *Viva la Vida*.

Speak – Talk in pairs.

A: I want to _____ more time on social media.
B: What _____ you say that?
A: I can _____ more friends from around the world.
B: That _____ sense.

My Speaking Portfolio Step 3

I'd _____ to talk about some good ways to _____ when you get _____. First, it's good to _____ _____ breaths. Second, _____ to ten is a great idea. Also, _____ cold water helps. _____, thinking happy thoughts can help.

Wrap Up – Listening & Peaking 1

W: Hello, teens. I'm Dr. Broccoli. Last time, I _____ about different _____ that _____ _____ for your health. Today, I'd _____ _____ talk about _____ _____ habits. First, try to eat _____. Second, it's important to stop _____ when you're full.

Wrap Up – Listening & Speaking 2

G: Why _____ we _____ a sport club?
B: Sounds good. Let's _____ a baseball club.
G: Well, I think a _____ club is a better idea.
B: What makes you _____ that?
G: All _____ _____ is a ball to play basketball.

안녕하세요. 오늘은 Frida Kahlo에 대하여 이야기하겠습니다. 그녀는 멕시코인 화가입니다. 그녀의 가장 유명한 그림 중 하나는 Viva la Vida입니다.

A: 나는 소셜 미디어에 더 많은 시간을 쓰고 싶어.
B: 왜 그렇게 생각하니?
A: 나는 전 세계로부터 더 많은 친구를 사귈 수 있어.
B: 옳은 말이야.

여러분이 화가 났을 때 긴장을 풀 수 있는 방법에 관하여 이야기하겠습니다. 첫째, 심호흡을 하는 것이 좋습니다. 둘째, 열까지 세는 것은 좋은 생각입니다. 또한 차가운 물을 마시는 것도 도움이 됩니다. 마지막으로 행복한 생각을 하는 것이 도움이 됩니다.

여: 안녕하세요, 십 대 여러분. 저는 Broccoli 박사입니다. 지난 시간에, 건강에 좋은 다양한 음식에 관해 이야기했죠. 오늘은 건강한 식습관에 관해 이야기하고자 합니다. 먼저, 천천히 먹으려고 노력하세요. 둘째, 배가 부르면 그만 먹는 것이 중요합니다.

G: 우리 운동 동아리를 만드는 게 어때?
B: 좋아. 야구 동아리를 만들자.
G: 글쎄, 농구 동아리가 더 좋은 생각인 것 같아.
B: 왜 그렇게 말하는 거야?
G: 농구를 하기 위해 우리에게 필요한 건 농구공뿐이잖아.

[01~02] 다음 대화의 빈칸에 들어갈 말을 고르시오.

01

> M: I'd like to talk _____ true friendship.
> A: I think it's going to be a boring talk show.
> B: What makes you say so?

① to   ② with   ③ for
④ about   ⑤ by

02

> A: I want to spend more time on social media.
> B: _____ makes you say that?
> A: I can make more friends from around the world.
> B: That makes sense.

① Why   ② What   ③ When
④ Who   ⑤ Which

[03~04] 다음 글을 읽고 물음에 답하시오.

> Hello, teens. I'm Dr. Broccoli. Last time, I ___(A)___ about different foods that are good for your health. Today, I'd like to talk about healthy eating habits. First, try to eat slowly. Second, it's important to stop eating when you're full.

03 빈칸 (A)에 들어갈 알맞은 말을 고르시오.

① studied   ② talked   ③ chose
④ took   ⑤ thought

04 위 글의 내용과 일치하지 <u>않는</u> 것은?

① The speaker's name is Broccoli.
② The speaker is a doctor.
③ He will talk about different foods.
④ We should eat slowly for our health.
⑤ When we feel full, we had better stop eating.

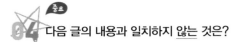

[01~03] 다음 대화를 읽고 물음에 답하시오.

W: What are you doing, Oliver?
B: I'm studying for the math test, Mom. Grades stress me out.
W: I understand. I used to feel (A)that way, too.
B: Really? I didn't know that.
W: Yeah, but a little stress was helpful for me.
B: (B)왜 그렇게 말씀을 하세요? (what, say, that)
W: I got stressed when I had an exam, but at the same time it made me focus and try harder.
B: I see. Did stress help you in other ways?
W: Yes, it helped improve my memory.

01 밑줄 친 (A)가 가리키는 것을 우리말로 쓰시오.

➡ _____

02 (B)의 주어진 우리말을 영어 문장으로 쓰시오. (주어진 단어 반드시 포함)

➡ _____

03 According to the dialogue, which one is NOT true?

① Oliver is studying for the math test.
② Oliver's mom also felt stressed about grades.
③ Oliver knew a little stress was helpful.
④ Stress helped Oliver's mom try harder.
⑤ Oliver's mom got stressed when she had an exam.

04 다음 글의 내용과 일치하지 <u>않는</u> 것은?

W: Today, I'd like to talk to you about teen stress. What makes you feel the most stressed? About 9,000 teens answered this question. As you can see, schoolwork was the most common cause of stress. Over half of the students said schoolwork stresses them the most. Problems with friends took second place with 15.3%. Next came family and worries about the future. 8.2% of the students said they get stressed because of their appearance.

① The topic of this talk is 'teen stress.'
② The largest number of students feel stressed about schoolwork.
③ Problems with friends are the most common cause of stress.
④ Over half of the students get stressed because of schoolwork.
⑤ 8.2% of the students get stressed because of their appearance.

05 다음 대화의 순서가 바르게 배열된 것을 고르시오.

(A) I can make more friends from around the world.
(B) I want to spend more time on social media.
(C) What makes you say that?

① (A) – (C) – (B)　　② (B) – (A) – (C)
③ (B) – (C) – (A)　　④ (C) – (A) – (B)
⑤ (C) – (B) – (A)

[06~07] 다음 대화를 읽고 물음에 답하시오.

G: Why don't we make a sport club?
B: _____(A)_____ Let's make a baseball club.
G: Well, I think a basketball club is a better idea.
B: What makes you say that?
G: All we need is a ball to play basketball.

06 빈칸 (A)에 들어가기에 적절하지 않은 것은?

① That's a good idea.
② Sounds good.
③ Yes, I agree.
④ I can't agree with you more.
⑤ I'm not with you.

07 Which one is true about the dialogue?

① The girl suggests making a sport club.
② The girl wants to make a baseball club.
③ The boy suggests making a basketball club.
④ The girl agrees with the boy's idea.
⑤ Just a ball is needed to play baseball.

[08~09] 다음 대화의 빈칸에 들어갈 말을 고르시오.

08

W: What are you doing, Oliver?
B: I'm studying for the math test, Mom. Grades _____ me out.
W: I understand. I used to feel that way, too.

① stress   ② take
③ get   ④ work
⑤ bring

09

W: A little stress was _____ for me.
B: What makes you say that?
W: I got stressed when I had an exam, but at the same time it made me focus and try harder.
B: I see. Did stress help you in other ways?
W: Yes, it helped improve my memory.

① hopeful   ② helpful   ③ careful
④ stressful   ⑤ tiring

서답형

10 다음 대화의 빈칸에 들어갈 말을 〈보기〉에서 골라 순서대로 배열하시오.

B1: Today, let's talk about the class T-shirt. We have to decide on the design.
G: Let me show you some designs on the screen.
B2: _____
B1: _____
B2: Because we'll wear the T-shirt on Sports Day. It's in June.
G: That makes sense.
_____
B2: I like it. The bee on the T-shirt is so cute.
G: _____
B1: Yes. I think it's the best one.

┤ 보기 ├
(A) What makes you say that?
(B) We have to choose a T-shirt with short sleeves.
(C) And it's not expensive.
(D) What about this green one?

➡ _____

[01~03] 다음 글을 읽고 물음에 답하시오.

W: Today, I'd like to talk to you about teen stress. (A)여러분에게 가장 많이 스트레스를 주는 것은 무엇인가요? About 9,000 teens answered this question. As you can see, schoolwork was the most common cause of stress. Over half of the students said schoolwork stresses them the most. Problems with friends took second place with 15.3%. (B)다음은 가족, 그리고 장래에 관한 걱정 순이었습니다. 8.2% of the students said they get stressed because of their appearance.

01 (A)에 주어진 우리말에 해당하는 영어 문장을 완성하시오. 〈보기〉의 단어를 포함할 것) (7 words)

┌─ 보기 ┐
stressed   make   feel
└──────────────┘

➡ _____

02 다음 단어를 배열하여 (B)의 의미에 해당하는 영어 문장을 완성하시오.

┌────────────────────────────┐
(1) Next로 시작할 것.
(2) family, the future, about, worries, came, and를 배열할 것.
└────────────────────────────┘

➡ _____

03 위 글을 읽고 다음 질문에 대한 답을 완성하시오.

┌────────────────────────────┐
What is the most common cause of stress for teens?
└────────────────────────────┘

➡ The most common cause of stress for teens is _____.

[04~05] 다음 대화를 읽고 물음에 답하시오.

W: What are you doing, Oliver?
B: I'm studying for the math test, Mom. Grades stress me out.
W: I understand. I used to feel that way, too.
B: Really? I didn't know ⓐthat.
W: Yeah, but a little stress was helpful for me.
B: What makes you say that?
W: I got stressed when I had an exam, but ___ⓑ___ the same time it made me focus and try harder.
B: I see. Did stress help you in other ways?
W: Yes, it helped improve my memory.

04 위 대화의 밑줄 친 ⓐ가 가리키는 것을 우리말로 쓰시오.

➡ _____

05 위 대화의 빈칸 ⓑ에 알맞은 전치사를 쓰시오.

➡ _____

06 다음 밑줄 친 우리말을 영어로 쓰시오. (it으로 시작하고 breaths를 포함할 것)

┌────────────────────────────┐
I'd like to talk about some good ways to relax when you get upset. First, 심호흡을 하는 것이 좋습니다. Second, counting to ten is a great idea. Also, drinking cold water helps. Lastly, thinking happy thoughts can help.
└────────────────────────────┘

➡ _____

Grammar

① 현재완료진행형

> • Jake **has been sleeping** all afternoon. Jake는 오후 내내 자고 있다.

■ 형태: have/has been -ing
  의미: ~하고 있다

■ 현재완료진행형은 과거에서 지금까지 계속된 현재완료의 상황과 지금도 지속되고 있는 진행형을 결합한 것으로 '과거에 시작해서 지금까지 계속되었고, 지금도 진행하고 있는 동작'을 나타낸다. 현재완료진행형에서 '~ 이래로'는 since로 나타내고, '~ 동안'은 for로 나타낸다.

  • I**'ve been using** this method for the past several months. 나는 지난 몇 달 동안 이 방법을 사용하고 있다.

  • She **has been waiting** for his call for two hours. 그녀는 두 시간 동안 그의 전화를 기다리고 있다.

■ 현재완료진행형은 현재까지 계속되고 있는 동작을 나타낼 때 사용한다. 상태 동사는 진행 시제를 쓸 수 없기 때문에 현재완료진행형으로 나타내지 않는다. 현재완료진행형은 현재완료와 마찬가지로 명백한 과거 표현과는 같이 쓸 수 없다.

  • I **have been learning** English since I was 10. 나는 10살 이후로 영어를 배우고 있다.

  • Ann **has been living** in this city since she was born. Ann은 태어난 이래로 이 도시에 살고 있다.

핵심 Check

1. 다음 주어진 단어를 적절한 형태로 쓰시오.

   (1) He's been _____ for a job since last month. (look)

   (2) I've been _____ 'Me Time' on my calendar for two months. (write)

   (3) Plum has been _____ with us since last winter. (live)

2. 다음 주어진 문장을 한 문장으로 적절하게 완성하시오.

   (1) They have waited for him to arrive and they are still waiting.

   ➡ They _____ for him to arrive.
   (그들은 그가 도착하기를 기다리고 있다.)

   (2) He started to read the book two hours ago. He is still reading the book.

   ➡ He _____ the book for two hours.
   (그는 두 시간 동안 그 책을 읽고 있다.)

② so ~ that ... 구문

> • It was **so** cold **that** I put on my coat. 날씨가 너무 추워서 나는 코트를 입었다.

■ 형태: so 형용사/부사 that 주어+동사

의미: 너무 ~해서 …하다

■ 'so ~ that …' 구문은 '너무 ~해서 …하다'의 의미로 원인과 결과를 나타내는 표현이다. so와 that 사이에는 형용사나 부사를 써야 한다.

- Good horror movies are **so** scary **that** I scream a lot.
  좋은 공포 영화는 너무 무서워서 나는 소리를 많이 지른다.

- While I fish, I'm **so** focused **that** I can leave all my worries behind.
  낚시를 하는 동안 나는 너무 집중하여 걱정을 뒤로 미뤄놓을 수 있다.

- When she's **so** stressed **that** her life looks gloomy, she cleans her room.
  그녀가 너무 스트레스를 받아 삶이 우울해 보일 때, 그녀는 방청소를 한다.

■ so와 that 사이에는 형용사나 부사를 써야 하지만, 명사구를 써야 할 때는 so가 아니라 such를 써서 'such (a)+형용사+명사 that ~'의 형태가 된다.

- It was **such** an interesting novel **that** I finished reading it last night.
  그것은 너무 재미있는 소설이어서 나는 어젯밤에 그것을 다 읽었다.

- It was **such** a delicious cake **that** he wanted to have some more.
  그것은 너무 맛있는 케이크여서 그는 좀 더 먹기를 원했다.

■ 'so that'은 '그래서 ~'의 의미로 결과를 나타내는 부사절을 유도한다. 'so that 주어 can/will ~'은 '~하기 위하여'의 의미로 목적을 나타내는 부사절을 유도한다.

핵심 Check

3. 다음 주어진 문장에서 적절한 것을 고르시오.

(1) The book was (so / such) interesting that he read it again.

(2) It was (so / such) a heavy bag that I couldn't move it.

4. 다음 주어진 문장을 'so ~ that'을 이용하여 한 문장으로 다시 쓰시오.

(1) Because it was too cold, we didn't go out.

= It was ＿＿＿＿ ＿＿＿＿ ＿＿＿＿ ＿＿＿＿ ＿＿＿＿ go out.

(2) Since the jacket was very expensive, he didn't buy it.

= The jacket was ＿＿＿＿ ＿＿＿＿ ＿＿＿＿ ＿＿＿＿ ＿＿＿＿ buy it.

(3) Because the wind was very strong, they stopped fishing.

= The wind was ＿＿＿＿ ＿＿＿＿ ＿＿＿＿ ＿＿＿＿ ＿＿＿＿ fishing.

01 다음 빈칸에 어법상 적절한 것은?

> I have been _____ in this city since I was born.

① lived   ② lives   ③ live
④ to live   ⑤ living

02 다음 중 어법상 어색한 것은?

① Today, I'd like to talk to you about teen stress.
② What makes you feel the most stressed?
③ Let me show you some designs on the screen.
④ It's so noisy that she wants to shut the window.
⑤ French fries are so salty that I won't eat.

03 다음 〈보기〉의 두 문장을 현재완료진행형을 사용하여 한 문장으로 연결하시오. (단, 숫자는 한 단어로 취급하며, 총 12단어로 주어진 문장을 완성하시오.)

> ┌─ 보기 ─┐
> • James started teaching English 20 years ago.
> • He is still teaching at this middle school.

➡ James _____.

04 다음 문장의 빈칸에 들어갈 알맞은 말을 차례대로 쓰시오.

> I was _____ tired _____ I fell asleep on the bus.

05 다음 빈칸에 어법상 적절한 것은?

> It was so _____ that they stopped sailing.

① windy   ② fog   ③ wind
④ rain   ⑤ rained

서답형

01 〈보기〉를 참고하여 주어진 단어를 이용하여 두 문장을 한 문장으로 쓰시오.

┤ 보기 ├
- They started to play basketball two hours ago.
- They are still playing basketball. (for)
➡ They have been playing basketball for two hours.

(1) • She sat on the bench an hour ago.
   • She is still sitting on the bench. (for)
   ➡ _____
     _____

(2) • She began to work at the store in 2010.
   • She is still working at the store. (since)
   ➡ _____
     _____

(3) • Tom started cleaning the room this morning.
   • He is still cleaning the room. (since)
   ➡ _____
     _____

02 다음 중 빈칸에 들어갈 be동사의 형태가 다른 하나는?

① I have _____ living in this city since I was born.
② The house _____ painted red yesterday.
③ She has _____ reading a book for two hours.
④ They have _____ playing soccer for forty minutes.
⑤ We have _____ running along the river for an hour.

03 다음 빈칸에 어법상 적절한 것은?

Sam has _____ sleeping all afternoon.

① be   ② being
③ been   ④ was
⑤ are

서답형

04 다음 괄호 안에 주어진 어구들을 바르게 배열하여 문장을 완성하시오.

(I've / 'Me Time' / my calendar / been / for / writing / on / two months)

➡ _____
  _____

중요

05 다음 〈보기〉에서 어법상 어색한 문장의 개수는?

┤ 보기 ├
ⓐ My sister is old enough to ride a bike.
ⓑ My fathet was too sleepy to drive.
ⓒ It was such fine that we went outside.
ⓓ Thinking happy thoughts can help.
ⓔ She has been lived here for 5 years.

① 1개   ② 2개   ③ 3개   ④ 4개   ⑤ 5개

06 다음 밑줄 친 부분의 쓰임이 나머지와 다른 하나는?

① It's so noisy that he closed the door.
② The food is so salty that I don't want it.
③ I am so hungry that I will eat a whole pizza.
④ I know the boy that is walking to me.
⑤ The line is so long that I won't wait in line.

07 다음 중 밑줄 친 부분이 어법상 어색한 것은?

① It's good to take deep breaths.
② She has been running for an hour.
③ Counting to ten is a great idea.
④ Drink cold water helps.
⑤ Some people spend time with friends when they feel low.

서답형
08 〈보기〉를 참고하여 주어진 두 문장을 한 문장으로 연결하여 쓰시오.

┌─ 보기 ├─
• She bought the flowers.
• The flowers were very beautiful.
➡ The flowers were so beautiful that she bought them.
└────────────

(1) • She went to bed early.
　• She was very tired.
➡ _____
　_____

(2) • The cake looked very delicious.
　• He decided to buy it.
➡ _____
　_____

(3) • The story was very interesting.
　• He read it in a day.
➡ _____
　_____

서답형
09 다음 우리말을 영어로 옮길 때 빈칸에 알맞은 말을 쓰시오.

┌────────────────────────┐
│ 방이 너무 더워서 그는 창문을 열었다. │
└────────────────────────┘

➡ It was so hot in the room _____ he opened the window.

10 다음 우리말을 영어로 옮긴 것 중 어색한 것은?

① 청소년들의 스트레스에 관하여 말씀드리겠습니다.
➡ I'd like to talk to you about teen stress.
② 무엇이 가장 스트레스를 받게 했습니까?
➡ What makes you feel the most stressed?
③ 그는 한 시간 동안 방에서 음악을 듣고 있다.
➡ He was been listening to music in the room for an hour.
④ 약 9천 명의 청소년이 이 질문에 대답을 했다.
➡ About 9,000 teens answered this question.
⑤ 날씨가 너무 추워서 나는 두꺼운 코트를 입었다.
➡ It was so cold that I wore a thick coat.

11 다음 중 밑줄 친 부분의 쓰임이 어색한 것을 고르시오.

① It was so a nice day that he went out for a walk.
② He felt so tired that he went home early.
③ The cake was so delicious that I wanted to have some more.
④ It was so hot that I drank some cold water.
⑤ The mountain was so high that we couldn't climb it.

서답형
12 다음 괄호 안에서 알맞은 말을 고르시오.

(1) They have [being / been] eating lunch.
(2) He has been [cleaned / cleaning] the room.
(3) The bag was [so / such] heavy that he couldn't move it.
(4) He was [so / such] busy that he couldn't help her.

13 다음 중 어법상 어색한 것을 고르시오.

① She has been watching TV for an hour.
② He has been living here since 2010.
③ They have known each other since 20 years.
④ The weather was so hot that we went to the lake.
⑤ She spoke so fast that we couldn't understand her.

14 다음 우리말을 영어로 바르게 옮긴 것은?

> 그는 너무 고통스러워 잠을 잘 수가 없었다.

① He was very painful that could sleep.
② He was so painful that he couldn't sleep.
③ It was so painful that he can't sleep.
④ He was such painful that he couldn't sleep.
⑤ He couldn't sleep so that he was painful.

15 다음 중 밑줄 친 부분의 쓰임이 어색한 것을 고르시오.

① They have been married for 2005.
② We have been waiting for him since last January.
③ They have been eating lunch for 30 minutes.
④ She has been living here since 2011.
⑤ She has been doing the dishes since she finished dinner.

16 다음 우리말을 영어로 바르게 옮긴 것은?

> 그 차는 너무 오래 되어서 빨리 달릴 수 없었다.

① It was such an old car that it couldn't run fast.
② It was so old car that it could run fast.
③ It was such old a car that it couldn't run fast.
④ It ran so fast that it was very old car.
⑤ It was so an old car that it couldn't run fast.

17 다음 중 어법상 어색한 것은?

① I've been using this method for a long time.
② I know that he hasn't finished the work yet.
③ My uncle graduated from college two years ago.
④ He has been looking for a job since last year.
⑤ She has finished reading a book yesterday.

18 다음 두 문장을 한 문장으로 쓸 때 빈칸에 알맞은 말을 쓰시오.

> • He began watching TV five hours ago.
> • He is still watching TV now.
> ➡ He _____ _____ _____ TV for five hours.

01 다음 우리말에 맞게 괄호 안에 주어진 어휘를 바르게 배열하시오.

(1) 그녀는 이 학교에서 10년 동안 영어를 가르치고 있다.

(teaching, she, been, 10 years, has, English, for, at this school)

➡ _____

_____

(2) 어젯밤부터 비가 내리고 있다.

(it, raining, since, has, last, been, night)

➡ _____

_____

(3) 그가 차를 너무 빠르게 몰아서 그의 아버지가 그에게 차를 천천히 운전하라고 말했다.

(he, his father, drove the car, so, told, that, him, fast, slowly, to drive)

➡ _____

_____

02 다음 주어진 문장을 아래와 같이 바꾸어 쓸 때 적절한 말을 쓰시오.

The mountain was so high that they couldn't climb it.

= It was such _____ _____ _____

that they couldn't climb it.

03 다음 문장의 빈칸에 우리말의 의미에 맞게 채우시오.

(1) Mike has been doing his homework all day.

➡ _____ his homework all day?

(Mike는 하루 종일 그의 숙제를 하고 있는 중이니?)

(2) Jack has been playing the computer game since last night.

➡ _____ the computer game since last night.

(Jack은 지난밤부터 지금까지 계속해서 컴퓨터 게임을 해오고 있지는 않다.)

04 다음 빈칸에 주어진 단어를 적절한 형태로 쓰시오.

(1) She has been _____ on the phone for an hour. (talk)

(2) He has _____ lying on the bed since this morning. (be)

05 다음 두 문장을 한 문장으로 만들 때 빈칸을 완성하시오. (단, 반드시 been을 사용할 것)

• Chris started playing tennis two hours ago.

• He is still playing tennis.

➡ Chris _____

_____.

06 다음 주어진 두 문장을 한 문장으로 연결할 때 빈칸에 알맞은 말을 쓰시오.

He is very rich. He can buy anything

= He is _____ _____ that he can buy anything.

07 다음 우리말을 〈조건〉에 맞게 영작하시오.

> 그녀는 매우 친절해서 모두가 그녀를 좋아한다.

┤ 조건 ├
1. 'so ... that' 구문을 활용할 것.
2. 8단어의 완전한 문장으로 쓸 것.

➡ _____

08 다음 괄호 안에서 알맞은 단어를 골라 〈보기〉와 같이 두 문장을 한 문장으로 바꿔 쓰시오.

┤ 보기 ├
- My father started repairing his car two hours ago.
- He is still repairing it now. (for/since)
➡ <u>My father has been repairing his car for two hours.</u>

- Ann and I started studying Chinese last week.
- We are still studying it now. (for/since)

➡ _____

_____

09 다음 빈칸에 알맞은 말을 넣어 문장을 완성하시오.

(1) He felt too tired. He stopped working.
  ➡ He felt _____ _____ that he stopped working.
(2) Because the box was too heavy, the child couldn't move it.
  ➡ The box was so _____ _____ the child couldn't move it.
(3) Since the pizza was very delicious, they wanted more.
  ➡ The pizza was so delicious _____ _____ _____ _____.

10 다음 두 문장을 한 문장으로 만들 때 빈칸에 들어갈 알맞은 말을 쓰시오.

- My brother started using a computer two hours ago.
- He is still using it.
➡ My brother _____ a computer for two hours.

11 다음 괄호 안에 주어진 단어들을 바르게 배열하여 문장을 다시 쓰시오.

> Some people (with / spend / when / time / feel / they / friends / low).

➡ _____

_____

12 다음 주어진 문장이 같은 의미가 되도록 so, that을 사용하여 다시 쓰시오.

(1) She is too hungry. She can't swim any more.
  ➡ _____
  _____
(2) Because the car was very old, it couldn't run fast.
  ➡ _____
  _____
(3) Since it was very cold, he put on his coat.
  ➡ _____
  _____

Say Goodbye to Stress

Some people spend time with friends when they feel low. Others
eat special foods to feel better. Still others simply sleep for a while.
How do you deal with stress? Here are some stories about people who
suggest different ways.

Mina (15, Daejeon)

Sometimes my friends give me stress by saying bad things about me,
breaking promises, or arguing over small things. When this happens, I
watch horror movies! Good horror movies are so scary that I scream a
lot. I guess that screaming at the top of my lungs helps me feel better.
Also, thanks to scary scenes and sound effects, I can forget about what
bothers me. I've been using this method for the past several months,
and it really works.

Junho (14, Yeosu)

My uncle graduated from college two years ago. He lives with my
family, and he's been looking for a job for some time. I know that
he's stressed out, but he always tries to be positive by going fishing.
He never gets upset when he doesn't catch any fish. He says, "While I
fish, I'm so focused that I can leave all my worries behind. Besides, it
teaches me to be patient." I'm sure that focusing on one thing helps us
forget about something else.

확인문제

● 다음 문장이 본문의 내용과 일치하면 T, 일치하지 않으면 F를 쓰시오.

1 When Mina's friends give her stress, she watches horror movies. ☐

2 Screaming at the top of her lungs prevents Mina from feeling better. ☐

3 Junho's uncle has been looking for a job for some time. ☐

4 Junho's uncle gets upset when he doesn't catch any fish. ☐

---

feel low 기운이 없다, 무기력하다
for a while 잠깐, 잠시 동안
suggest 제안하다, 제시하다
break (약속 등을) 어기다
argue over ~을 두고 논쟁하다
scream 비명을 지르다
thanks to ~덕분에
scene 장면
effect 효과
bother 괴롭히다
method 방법
work 효과가 나다[있다]
graduate 졸업하다
stress out 스트레스를 받다
focused 집중한, 집중적인
worry 걱정거리, 걱정(되는 일)
patient 참을성[인내심] 있는

Dobin (16, Seoul)

My sister, a second-year student in high school, has a wonderful way
to stay free from stress. She feels a lot of stress from schoolwork, but
my mother seems to like the situation for a good reason. It is because
cleaning is my sister's number-one way to make life better! When
she's so stressed that her life looks gloomy, she cleans her room. She
says, "As I clean my room, I feel like I'm also relieving stress. When
my room looks tidy, my life looks brighter."

Yulia (14, Ansan)

Let me tell you what my mother does about her stress. She feels
stressed by all the things she has to do at work and at home. When
she's under stress, she writes "Me Time" on her calendar. This means
she takes some time out for herself. She reads a book, watches a
movie, or talks with her friends. She says, "It doesn't really matter
what I do, as long as it's something I like. I've been writing 'Me Time'
on my calendar for two months, and I feel much better."

Which methods will work for you? Try some of these ideas yourself,
and find your best way to say goodbye to stress.

way 방법
stay free from ~으로부터 벗어나다
schoolwork 학교 공부
situation 상황
reason 이유
gloomy 우울한
relieve 없애[덜어]주다
tidy 깔끔한
bright 밝은
feel stressed 스트레스를 받다
take some time out 잠깐 시간을 갖다
matter 중요하다
method 방법

🔖 **확인문제**

- 다음 문장이 본문의 내용과 일치하면 T, 일치하지 않으면 F를 쓰시오.

1 Dobin's sister is a second-year student in high school. ☐

2 Dobin's sister doesn't have any ways to stay free from stress. ☐

3 When Dobin's mother is so stressed, she cleans her room. ☐

4 Yulia's mother feels stressed by all the things she must do at work and at home. ☐

5 When Yulia's mother is under stress, she writes "Me Time" on her calendar. ☐

6 It really matters what Yulia's mother should do as it's something she doesn't like. ☐

● 우리말을 참고하여 빈칸에 알맞은 말을 쓰시오.

1 Say _____ to Stress

2 Some people spend time with friends when they _____ _____.

3 _____ eat special foods _____ _____ _____.

4 _____ _____ simply sleep for a while.

5 How do you _____ _____ stress?

6 Here are some stories about people who _____ _____ _____.

Mina (15, Daejeon)

7 Sometimes my friends give me stress by _____ bad things about me, _____ promises, or _____ over small things.

8 _____ _____ _____, I watch horror movies!

9 Good horror movies are _____ scary _____ I scream a lot.

10 I guess that screaming _____ _____ _____ _____ _____ _____ helps me feel better.

11 Also, _____ _____ scary scenes and sound effects, I can forget about _____ _____ _____.

12 _____ _____ _____ this method for the past several months, and it really _____.

Junho (14, Yeosu)

13 My uncle _____ _____ college two years ago.

14 He lives with my family, and _____ _____ _____ _____ a job for some time.

15 I know that _____ _____ _____, but he always tries to be positive _____ _____ _____.

16 He never _____ _____ when he doesn't catch any fish.

17 He says, "While I fish, I'm _____ focused _____ I _____ _____ all my worries _____.

18 _____, it teaches me _____ _____ patient."

1	스트레스와 이별하라
2	어떤 사람들은 울적할 때 친구들과 시간을 보낸다.
3	다른 사람들은 기분이 좋아지도록 특별한 음식을 먹는다.
4	또 다른 사람들은 그저 잠시 잠을 자기도 한다.
5	여러분은 스트레스를 어떻게 다루는가?
6	여기 다양한 방법을 제안하는 사람들의 이야기가 있다.

미나 (15살, 대전)

7 때때로 내 친구들은 나에 관해 나쁜 말을 하거나, 약속을 어기거나, 혹은 사소한 일을 두고 언쟁을 하며 내게 스트레스를 준다.

8 이럴 때, 나는 공포 영화를 본다!

9 훌륭한 공포 영화는 너무 무서워서 나는 소리를 많이 지르게 된다.

10 있는 힘껏 소리 지르는 것은 내 기분이 나아지는 데 도움이 된다고 생각한다.

11 또한, 무서운 장면과 음향 효과 덕분에 나를 괴롭히는 것들을 잊을 수 있다.

12 나는 지난 몇 달간 이 방법을 써오고 있는데, 효과가 아주 좋다.

준호 (14살, 여수)

13 우리 삼촌은 2년 전에 대학을 졸업했다.

14 삼촌은 우리 가족과 함께 살고 있고, 얼마 전부터 직장을 구하고 있다.

15 나는 삼촌이 스트레스를 받고 있지만 낚시를 다니며 긍정적으로 지내려고 항상 노력한다는 것을 안다.

16 물고기를 한 마리도 잡지 못했을 때에도 삼촌은 절대 속상해하지 않는다.

17 삼촌은 "낚시하는 동안, 나는 아주 몰입해서 모든 걱정을 잊을 수 있어.

18 게다가 낚시는 나에게 인내를 가르쳐 준단다."라고 말한다

19 I'm sure that _____ _____ one thing helps us _____ about something else.

Dobin (16, Seoul)

20 My sister, a _____ student in high school, has a wonderful way to stay _____ _____ stress.

21 She feels a lot of stress from schoolwork, but my mother _____ _____ _____ the situation _____ _____ _____ _____.

22 It is because cleaning is my sister's _____ _____ to make life better!

23 When she's _____ stressed _____ her life looks gloomy, she cleans her room.

24 She says, "As I clean my room, I _____ _____ I'm also _____ stress.

25 When my room _____ _____, my life _____ _____."

Yulia (14, Ansan)

26 Let me tell you _____ my mother does about her stress.

27 She feels stressed by _____ _____ _____ _____ _____ _____ _____ at work and at home.

28 When _____ _____ _____, she writes "Me Time" on her calendar.

29 This means she _____ _____ _____ _____ for herself.

30 She _____ a book, _____ a movie, or _____ with her friends.

31 She says, "It doesn't really _____ what I do, _____ _____ _____ it's something I like.

32 _____ _____ _____ 'Me Time' on my calendar for two months, and I feel much better."

33 Which methods will _____ _____ _____?

34 Try some of these ideas yourself, and find your best way _____ _____ _____ _____.

19 한 가지 일에 집중하는 것이 다른 무언가를 잊는 데 도움이 된다고 나는 확신한다.

도빈 (16살, 서울)

20 고등학교 2학년인 우리 누나에게는 스트레스에서 벗어나는 훌륭한 방법이 있다.

21 누나가 학업 때문에 많은 스트레스를 받지만, 그럴 만한 이유로 우리 어머니는 그 상황을 좋아하시는 것 같다.

22 그것은 바로, 청소가 누나의 삶을 향상하는 최고의 방법이기 때문이다.

23 스트레스를 너무 많이 받아서 인생이 우울해 보일 때, 누나는 방을 청소한다.

24 누나는 "방을 청소하면서 스트레스도 해소되는 것 같아.

25 내 방이 깔끔해 보이면 내 삶도 더 밝아 보여."라고 말한다.

Yulia (14살, 안산)

26 우리 어머니께서 스트레스를 어떻게 다루시는지 소개하려고 한다.

27 어머니는 직장과 집에서 해야 하는 온갖 일로 인해 스트레스를 받으신다.

28 스트레스를 받을 때면 어머니는 달력에 '나만의 시간'이라고 적으신다.

29 이것은 어머니 자신을 위해 잠깐 시간을 낸다는 의미이다.

30 어머니는 책을 읽거나, 영화를 보거나, 친구들과 이야기를 나누신다.

31 어머니는 "내가 좋아하는 것이라면, 무엇을 하는지는 별로 중요하지 않아.

32 나는 두 달째 달력에 '나만의 시간'을 적어 왔고, 기분이 훨씬 좋아졌어."라고 말씀하신다.

33 어떤 방법이 여러분에게 효과가 있을까?

34 이 아이디어 중 몇 개를 직접 해 보고, 스트레스와 이별하는 자신만의 최고의 방법을 찾아라.

● 우리말을 참고하여 본문을 영작하시오.

1 스트레스와 이별하라
➡ _____

2 어떤 사람들은 울적할 때 친구들과 시간을 보낸다.
➡ _____

3 다른 사람들은 기분이 좋아지도록 특별한 음식을 먹는다.
➡ _____

4 또 다른 사람들은 그저 잠시 잠을 자기도 한다.
➡ _____

5 여러분은 스트레스를 어떻게 다루는가?
➡ _____

6 여기 다양한 방법을 제안하는 사람들의 이야기가 있다.
➡ _____

미나 (15살, 대전) Mina (15, Daejeon)

7 때때로 내 친구들은 나에 관해 나쁜 말을 하거나, 약속을 어기거나, 혹은 사소한 일을 두고 언쟁을 하며 내게 스트레스를 준다.
➡ _____
_____

8 이럴 때, 나는 공포 영화를 본다!
➡ _____

9 훌륭한 공포 영화는 너무 무서워서 나는 소리를 많이 지르게 된다.
➡ _____

10 있는 힘껏 소리 지르는 것은 내 기분이 나아지는 데 도움이 된다고 생각한다.
➡ _____

11 또한, 무서운 장면과 음향 효과 덕분에 나를 괴롭히는 것들을 잊을 수 있다.
➡ _____

12 나는 지난 몇 달간 이 방법을 써 오고 있는데, 효과가 아주 좋다.
➡ _____

준호 (14살, 여수) Junho (14, Yeosu)

13 우리 삼촌은 2년 전에 대학을 졸업했다.
➡ _____

14 삼촌은 우리 가족과 함께 살고 있고, 얼마 전부터 직장을 구하고 있다.
➡ _____

15 나는 삼촌이 스트레스를 받고 있지만 낚시를 다니며 긍정적으로 지내려고 항상 노력한다는 것을 안다.
➡ _____

16 물고기를 한 마리도 잡지 못했을 때에도 삼촌은 절대 속상해 하지 않는다.
➡ _____

17 삼촌은 "낚시하는 동안, 나는 아주 몰입해서 모든 걱정을 잊을 수 있어.

➡ _____

18 게다가 낚시는 나에게 인내를 가르쳐 준단다."라고 말한다.

➡ _____

19 한 가지 일에 집중하는 것이 다른 무언가를 잊는 데 도움이 된다고 나는 확신한다.

➡ _____

도빈 (16살, 서울) Dobin (16, Seoul)

20 고등학교 2학년인 우리 누나에게는 스트레스에서 벗어나는 훌륭한 방법이 있다.

➡ _____

21 누나가 학업 때문에 많은 스트레스를 받지만, 그럴 만한 이유로 우리 어머니는 그 상황을 좋아하시는 것 같다.

➡ _____

22 그것은 바로, 청소가 누나의 삶을 향상하는 최고의 방법이기 때문이다.

➡ _____

23 스트레스를 너무 많이 받아서 인생이 우울해 보일 때, 누나는 방을 청소한다.

➡ _____

24 누나는 "방을 청소하면서 스트레스도 해소되는 것 같아.

➡ _____

25 내 방이 깔끔해 보이면 내 삶도 더 밝아 보여."라고 말한다.

➡ _____

Yulia (14살, 안산) Yulia (14, Ansan)

26 우리 어머니께서 스트레스를 어떻게 다루시는지 소개하려고 한다.

➡ _____

27 어머니는 직장과 집에서 해야 하는 온갖 일로 인해 스트레스를 받으신다.

➡ _____

28 스트레스를 받을 때면 어머니는 달력에 '나만의 시간'이라고 적으신다.

➡ _____

29 이것은 어머니 자신을 위해 잠깐 시간을 낸다는 의미이다.

➡ _____

30 어머니는 책을 읽거나, 영화를 보거나, 친구들과 이야기를 나누신다.

➡ _____

31 어머니는 "내가 좋아하는 것이라면, 무엇을 하는지는 별로 중요하지 않아.

➡ _____

32 나는 두 달째 달력에 '나만의 시간'을 적어 왔고, 기분이 훨씬 좋아졌어."라고 말씀하신다.

➡ _____

33 어떤 방법이 여러분에게 효과가 있을까?

➡ _____

34 이 아이디어 중 몇 개를 직접 해 보고, 스트레스와 이별하는 자신만의 최고의 방법을 찾아라.

➡ _____

[01~03] 다음 글을 읽고 물음에 답하시오.

Mina (15, Daejeon)

  Sometimes my friends give me stress by ①saying bad things about me, ②breaking promises, or ③arguing over small things. When this happens, I watch horror movies! Good horror movies are so scary that I scream a lot. I guess that ④screaming at the top of my lungs helps me feel better. Also, thanks to scary scenes and sound effects, I can forget about what bothers me. I've been ⑤using this method for the past several months, and it really ⓐworks.

01 위 글의 밑줄 친 ①~⑤ 중에서 문법적 쓰임이 나머지 넷과 다른 것은?

①　　　②　　　③　　　④　　　⑤

02 위 글의 밑줄 친 ⓐworks와 같은 의미로 쓰인 것을 고르시오.

① He works for an engineering company.
② This medicine works pretty well.
③ I like the works of Tolstoy.
④ They didn't finish the public works.
⑤ This machine works by electricity.

03 According to the passage, which is NOT true?

① Sometimes Mina feels stressed when her friends say bad things about her.
② When Mina feels stressed, she watches horror movies.
③ Good horror movies are too scary to make Mina scream a lot.
④ Screaming at the top of her lungs helps Mina feel better.
⑤ Scary scenes and sound effects in horror movies help Mina forget about what bothers her.

[04~06] 다음 글을 읽고 물음에 답하시오.

Junho (14, Yeosu)

  My uncle graduated ___ⓐ___ college two years ago. He lives with my family, and (A)he's been looking for a job for some time. I know that he's stressed out, but he always tries to be positive by going fishing. He never gets upset when he doesn't catch any fish. He says, "While I fish, I'm so focused that I can leave all my worries behind. Besides, it teaches me to be patient." I'm sure that focusing ___ⓑ___ one thing helps us forget about something else.

04 위 글의 빈칸 ⓐ와 ⓑ에 들어갈 전치사가 바르게 짝지어진 것은?

　　ⓐ　　ⓑ　　　　　　　ⓐ　　ⓑ
① at – for　　　　② from – on
③ in – on　　　　④ at – to
⑤ from – for

05 위 글에서 알 수 있는 준호의 삼촌 성격으로 가장 알맞은 것을 고르시오.

① passive　　　　② impatient
③ optimistic　　　④ generous
⑤ negative

06 위 글의 밑줄 친 (A)에 쓰인 것과 같은 용법의 현재완료가 쓰인 문장을 모두 고르시오.

① How many times have you considered moving to New York?
② She has been studying English for five years.

③ It has just stopped snowing.

④ Have you ever practiced playing the piano?

⑤ I have been cleaning the house since this morning.

[07~10] 다음 글을 읽고 물음에 답하시오.

Dobin (16, Seoul)

My sister, a second-year student in high school, has (a)a wonderful way to stay free from stress. She feels a lot of stress from schoolwork, but my mother seems to like the situation for a good reason. It is (A)[because / why] cleaning is my sister's number-one way to make life better! When she's so stressed that her life (B)[looks / looks like] gloomy, she cleans her room. She says, "(b)As I clean my room, I feel like I'm also (C)[increasing / relieving] stress. When my room looks ____ⓐ____, my life looks brighter."

서답형

07 주어진 영영풀이를 참고하여 빈칸 ⓐ에 철자 t로 시작하는 단어를 쓰시오.

> neat and arranged in an organized way

➡ _____

서답형

08 위 글의 밑줄 친 (a)a wonderful way가 가리키는 것을 본문에서 찾아 쓰시오.

➡ _____

서답형

09 위 글의 괄호 (A)~(C)에서 문맥이나 어법상 알맞은 낱말을 골라 쓰시오.

➡ (A) _____ (B) _____ (C) _____

10 위 글의 밑줄 친 (b)As와 같은 의미로 쓰인 것을 고르시오.

① Do in Rome as the Romans do.

② He runs as fast as you.

③ As he entered the room, he cried.

④ As I was tired, I soon fell asleep.

⑤ It can be used as a knife.

[11~13] 다음 글을 읽고 물음에 답하시오.

Yulia (14, Ansan)

Let me tell you what my mother does about her stress. She feels stressed by all the things she has to do at work and at home. When she's under stress, she writes "Me Time" on her calendar. This means she takes some time out for herself. She reads a book, watches a movie, or talks with her friends. She says, "ⓐIt doesn't really matter what I do, as long as ⓑit's something I like. I've been writing 'Me Time' on my calendar for two months, and I feel much better."

서답형

11 위 글의 밑줄 친 ⓐIt과 ⓑit이 공통으로 가리키는 것을 본문에서 찾아 쓰시오.

➡ _____

중요

12 위 글의 제목으로 알맞은 것을 고르시오.

① Causes of Yulia's Mom's Stress

② Yulia's Mom's Ways to Deal with Stress

③ How to Write "Me Time" on the Calendar

④ What Really Matters When You Feel Stressed?

⑤ How to Spend "Me Time" Effectively

13 Which question CANNOT be answered after reading the passage?

① By what does Yulia's mother feel stressed?

② When Yulia's mother is under stress, what does she do?

③ What's the meaning of writing "Me Time" on the calendar?

④ How often does Yulia's mother have "Me Time"?

⑤ How long has Yulia been writing 'Me Time' on her calendar?

[14~17] 다음 글을 읽고 물음에 답하시오.

Mina (15, Daejeon)

Sometimes my friends give me stress by saying bad things about me, breaking promises, or arguing over small things. (①) Good horror movies are so scary that I scream a lot. (②) I guess that ⓐ있는 힘껏 소리 지르는 것은 helps me feel better. (③) Also, thanks to scary scenes and sound effects, I can forget about ⓑwhat bothers me. (④) I've been using this method for the past several months, and it really works. (⑤)

14 위 글의 흐름으로 보아, 주어진 문장이 들어가기에 가장 적절한 곳은?

When this happens, I watch horror movies!

①   ②   ③   ④   ⑤

15 위 글의 밑줄 친 ⓐ의 우리말에 맞게 주어진 어휘를 이용하여 7단어로 영작하시오.

top, lungs

➡ _____

16 위 글의 밑줄 친 ⓑwhat과 문법적 쓰임이 같은 것을 모두 고르시오.

① What kind of music do you like?

② He knows what it is to be in debt.

③ What you need is a good meal.

④ He is not what he was.

⑤ What are you looking at?

17 위 글의 주제로 알맞은 것을 고르시오.

① many causes of stress

② friends saying bad things

③ how to deal with stress

④ the benefit of horror movies

⑤ scary sound effects in horror movies

[18~20] 다음 글을 읽고 물음에 답하시오.

Junho (14, Yeosu)

My uncle graduated from college two years ago. He lives with my family, and he's been looking for a job for some time. I know that he's stressed out, but he always tries to be positive by going ___ⓐ___. He never gets upset when he doesn't catch any fish. He says, "While I fish, I'm so focused that I can leave all my worries behind. ___ⓑ___, it teaches me to be patient." I'm sure that focusing on one thing helps us forget about something else.

18 위 글의 빈칸 ⓐ에 fish를 알맞은 형태로 쓰시오.

➡ _____

19 위 글의 빈칸 ⓑ에 들어갈 알맞은 말을 고르시오.

① Instead   ② Besides

③ However   ④ For example

⑤ By contrast

서답형

20 다음 빈칸 (A)~(C)에 알맞은 단어를 넣어 준호의 삼촌에 대한 소개를 완성하시오.

> Junho's uncle has been looking for (A)_____ _____ for some time. Though he is stressed out, he always tries to be optimistic by (B)_____ _____, and he never (C)_____ _____ when he catches no fish.

[21~23] 다음 글을 읽고 물음에 답하시오.

Dobin (16, Seoul)

My sister, a second-year student in high school, has a wonderful way ⓐto stay free from stress. She feels ⓑa lot of stress from schoolwork, but ⓒmy mother seems to like the situation for a good reason. It is because cleaning is my sister's number-one way to make life better! When she's so stressed that her life looks gloomy, she cleans her room. She says, "As I clean my room, I feel like I'm also relieving stress. When my room looks tidy, my life looks brighter."

21 아래 〈보기〉에서 위 글의 밑줄 친 ⓐto stay와 to부정사의 용법이 다른 것의 개수를 고르시오.

> ┤ 보기 ├
> ① His mother lived to be ninety years old.
> ② I don't have any friends to talk with.
> ③ My dream is to travel around the world.
> ④ It is important to use your time well.
> ⑤ She came here to meet Jake.

① 1개   ② 2개   ③ 3개   ④ 4개   ⑤ 5개

22 위 글의 밑줄 친 ⓑa lot of와 바꿔 쓸 수 없는 말을 모두 고르시오.

① many   ② much
③ a number of   ④ lots of
⑤ a great deal of

서답형

23 다음 빈칸 (A)와 (B)에 알맞은 단어를 넣어 밑줄 친 ⓒ의 이유를 완성하시오.

> It's because when Dobin's sister is so stressed that her life looks gloomy, she (A)_____ _____ _____. Cleaning is her number-one way to (B)_____ _____ _____.

[24~25] 다음 글을 읽고 물음에 답하시오.

> Which methods will ⓐwork for you? ⓑTry some of these ideas yourself, and find your best way to say hello to stress.

24 위 글의 밑줄 친 ⓐwork와 의미가 같은 것을 모두 고르시오.

① Taking care of a baby is hard work.
② Do you know how to work the coffee machine?
③ The pills the doctor gave me don't work on me.
④ She had been out of work for a year.
⑤ My plan didn't work well in practice.

서답형

25 위 글의 밑줄 친 ⓑ에서 흐름상 어색한 부분을 찾아 고치시오.

_____ ➡ _____

[01~03] 다음 글을 읽고 물음에 답하시오.

Mina (15, Daejeon)

Sometimes my friends give me stress by _____ⓐ_____ bad things about me, _____ⓑ_____ promises, or _____ⓒ_____ over small things. When this happens, I watch horror movies! ⓓ훌륭한 공포 영화는 너무 무서워서 나는 소리를 많이 지르게 된다. I guess that screaming at the top of my lungs helps me feel better. Also, thanks to scary scenes and sound effects, I can forget about what bothers me. I've been using this method for the past several months, and it really works.

01 위 글의 빈칸 ⓐ~ⓒ에 say, break, argue를 각각 알맞은 형태로 쓰시오.

➡ ⓐ _____ ⓑ _____ ⓒ _____

02 위 글의 밑줄 친 ⓓ의 우리말에 맞게 주어진 어휘를 알맞게 배열하시오.

I / so / are / a lot / scary / scream / good horror movies / that

➡ _____

03 다음 빈칸 (A)와 (B)에 알맞은 단어를 넣어 미나의 스트레스 해소 방법에 대한 소개를 완성하시오.

When Mina feels stressed, she watches (A)_____ _____ and screams at the top of (B)_____ _____.

[04~06] 다음 글을 읽고 물음에 답하시오.

Junho (14, Yeosu)

My uncle graduated from college two years ago. He lives with my family, and he's been looking for a job (A)[for / since] some time.

I know that he's stressed out, but he always tries to be (B)[positive / negative] by going fishing. He never gets upset when he doesn't catch any fish. He says, "While I fish, I'm (C)[so / such] focused that I can leave all my worries behind. ⓐBesides, it teaches me being patient." I'm sure that focusing on one thing helps us forget about something else.

04 위 글의 괄호 (A)~(C)에서 문맥이나 어법상 알맞은 낱말을 골라 쓰시오.

➡ (A) _____ (B) _____ (C) _____

05 위 글의 밑줄 친 ⓐ에서 어법상 틀린 부분을 찾아 고치시오.

_____ ➡ _____

06 다음 문장에서 위 글의 내용과 다른 부분을 찾아서 고치시오.

Junho's uncle has no difficulty finding a job.

_____ ➡ _____

[07~09] 다음 글을 읽고 물음에 답하시오.

Yulia (14, Ansan)

Let me tell you _____ⓐ_____ my mother does about her stress. She feels stressed by all the things she has to do at work and at home. When she's under stress, she writes "Me Time" on her calendar. This means she takes some time out for herself. She reads a book, watches a movie, or talks with her friends. She says, "It doesn't really matter _____ⓑ_____ I do, ⓒas long as it's something I like. ⓓI've been writing 'Me Time' on my calendar for two months, and I feel much better."

07 위 글의 빈칸 ⓐ와 ⓑ에 공통으로 들어갈 알맞은 단어를 쓰시오.

➡ _____

08 위 글의 밑줄 친 ⓒas long as와 바꿔 쓸 수 있는 말을 쓰시오.

➡ _____

09 위 글의 밑줄 친 ⓓ를 다음과 같이 바꿔 쓸 때 빈칸에 들어갈 알맞은 단어를 쓰시오.

➡ I started to write 'Me Time' on my calendar _____ _____ ago, and I am still _____ it on my calendar.

[10~12] 다음 글을 읽고 물음에 답하시오.

Dobin (16, Seoul)

My sister, a second-year student in high school, has a wonderful way to stay ⓐ<u>free from</u> stress. She feels a lot of stress from schoolwork, but my mother seems to like ⓑ <u>the situation</u> for a good reason. It is because cleaning is my sister's number-one way to make life better! When she's so stressed that her life looks gloomy, she cleans her room. She says, "As I clean my room, I feel like I'm also relieving stress. When my room looks tidy, my life looks brighter."

10 위 글의 밑줄 친 ⓐfree from과 바꿔 쓸 수 있는 한 단어를 쓰시오.

➡ _____

11 위 글의 밑줄 친 ⓑ가 가리키는 상황을 우리말로 쓰시오.

➡ _____

12 본문의 내용과 일치하도록 다음 빈칸 (A)와 (B)에 알맞은 단어를 쓰시오.

> • Cause of Dobin's Sister's Stress:
>   (A) _____
> • Dobin's Sister's Method to Relieve Stress:
>   (B) _____ _____

[13~15] 다음 글을 읽고 물음에 답하시오.

Yulia (14, Ansan)

Let me (A)[tell / telling] you what my mother does about her stress. She feels stressed by all the things she has to do at work and at home. When she's (B)[over / under] stress, she writes "ⓐ<u>Me Time</u>" on her calendar. This means she takes some time out for (C)[her / herself]. She reads a book, watches a movie, or talks with her friends. She says, "It doesn't really matter what I do, as long as it's something I like. I've been writing 'Me Time' on my calendar for two months, and I feel ⓑ<u>much</u> better."

13 위 글의 괄호 (A)~(C)에서 문맥이나 어법상 알맞은 낱말을 골라 쓰시오.

➡ (A) _____ (B) _____ (C) _____

14 위 글의 밑줄 친 ⓐMe Time의 의미를 우리말로 쓰시오.

➡ _____

15 위 글의 밑줄 친 ⓑmuch와 바꿔 쓸 수 있는 말을 쓰시오. (두 개)

➡ _____

교과서

구석구석

해석

Words in Action

1. Tests stress me out. Grades give me more stress.
   stress ~ out (스트레스로) ~을 지치게 하다
2. Worry less, smile more. Worry never helps.
   worry (동사) 걱정하다   (명사) 걱정
3. I work hard. I have a lot of work to do.
   work (동사) 일하다   (명사) 일
4. I need a change. I will change my hairstyle.
       change (명사) 변화   기분전환 (동사) 바꾸다
5. I caught just a few fish. I want to fish some more.
              fish (명사) 물고기   (동사) 낚시하다

구문해설 • need a change 기분 전환이 필요하다

1. 시험은 나를 지치게 해. 성적은 나에게 더 많은 스트레스를 준다.
2. 걱정은 줄이고 더 많이 웃어라. 걱정은 전혀 도움이 되지 않아.
3. 나는 열심히 일한다. 나는 할 일이 많다.
4. 나는 기분 전환이 필요하다. 나는 헤어스타일을 바꿀 것이다.
5. 나는 겨우 물고기 몇 마리를 잡았다. 나는 몇 마리 더 낚고 싶다.

Speak – Get ready.

1. I want to spend more/less time on social media.
   spend time on ~ = ~에 시간을 쓰다
2. Working on a team can be difficult/helpful.
                   difficult/helpful 어려운/유익한
3. I like watching/playing sports better.
4. Having a part-time job as a teen can be good/bad.
                      십대일 때   좋은/나쁜

구문해설 • working on a team 팀을 이루어 일하는 것

1. 나는 소셜미디어에 더 많은/적은 시간을 보내기를 원한다.
2. 팀을 이루어 일하는 것은 어려울 수 있다/도움이 될 수 있다.
3. 나는 스포츠 보는 것을/하는 것을 더 좋아한다.
4. 십대일 때 아르바이트를 하는 것은 좋다/나쁘다.

Wrap Up – Reading

Are you stressed or feeling low? Then here is some good news for you. A
few simple steps can help you! First, go outdoors and get plenty of sunlight.
              = measures   = much
According to scientists, this helps produce a special chemical in your brain,
                                    = to produce
and the chemical makes you feel happy! Another thing you can do is exercise.
          사역동사 make+목적어+동사원형   = to exercise
This helps produce even more of the "happiness chemical." Try these simple
        = to produce   비교급 강조(훨씬)
tips the next time you feel low. Instead of sitting in front of a screen, go
    다음에 ~할 때에는   Instead of+동명사
outdoors and run around in the sun!

구문해설 • low: 기분이 저조한 • step: 조치 • outdoors: 옥외[야외]에서
         • according to: ~에 따르면 • chemical: 화학 물질 • instead of: ~ 대신에

스트레스를 받았거나 기분이 우울한가? 그렇다면 여기 당신에게 좋은 소식이 있다. 간단한 몇 가지 절차가 도움이 될 것이다! 첫째, 밖에 나가서 충분한 양의 햇볕을 쬐라. 과학자들에 따르면 이것이 뇌 속에 특별한 화학물질을 만드는 데 도움을 주고, 이 화학물질은 당신을 행복하게 만든다고 한다! 당신이 할 수 있는 또 다른 일은 운동이다. 이것은 훨씬 더 많은 '행복 화학물질'을 만드는 데 도움을 준다. 다음에 당신이 우울하다면 이 간단한 조언을 시도해 보라. 화면 앞에 앉아 있는 대신, 밖에 나가 태양 아래에서 뛰어다녀라!

164 Lesson 3. Be Positive, Be Happy

01 다음 영영풀이에 해당하는 단어를 고르시오.

> the way someone or something looks to other people

① appearance   ② program
③ patient   ④ view
⑤ scene

02 다음 짝지어진 단어의 관계가 같도록 빈칸에 알맞은 말을 쓰시오. (주어진 철자로 시작할 것)

> agree : disagree = a_____ : natural

03 다음 대화의 빈칸에 들어갈 말로 적절한 것을 고르시오.

> A: I want to spend more time on social media.
> B: What makes you say that?
> A: I can _____ more friends from around the world.

① invite   ② make
③ help   ④ visit
⑤ call

04 다음 밑줄 친 단어와 의미가 가장 가까운 것을 고르시오.

> He looked quite cheerless.

> A: This is a very ①gloomy situation.
> B: What's ②bothering you?
> A: We ③have nothing to eat.
> B: Don't ④worry. We can have ⑤free pizza.

05 다음 대화의 순서가 바르게 배열된 것을 고르시오.

> G: Why don't we make a sport club?
> B: Sounds good. Let's make a baseball club.
> (A) What makes you say that?
> (B) Well, I think a basketball club is a better idea.
> (C) All we need is a ball to play basketball.

① (A) – (C) – (B)   ② (B) – (A) – (C)
③ (B) – (C) – (A)   ④ (C) – (A) – (B)
⑤ (C) – (B) – (A)

06 다음 글의 내용과 일치하는 것은?

> I'd like to talk about some good ways to relax when you get upset. First, it's good to take deep breaths. Second, counting to ten is a great idea. Also, drinking cold water helps. Lastly, thinking happy thoughts can help.

① 글의 주제는 화를 푸는 방법이다.
② 심호흡을 하는 것은 건강에 좋다.
③ 열까지 세는 것은 소화를 도와준다.
④ 화가 났을 때는 말을 하지 마라.
⑤ 행복한 생각은 명상에 도움이 된다.

07

다음 대화의 빈칸에 들어가기에 적절한 단어를 주어진 철자로 시작하여 쓰시오.

A: I want to spend more time on social media.

B: What makes you say that?

A: I can make more friends from around the world.

B: That m_____ sense.

08

다음 빈칸 ⓐ~ⓔ에 들어갈 말로 가장 <u>어색한</u> 것은?

B1: Today, let's talk about the class T-shirt. We have to decide on the design.

G: _____ ⓐ _____

B2: We have to choose a T-shirt with short sleeves.

B1: _____ ⓑ _____

B2: Because we'll wear the T-shirt on Sports Day. _____ ⓒ _____

G: _____ ⓓ _____ What about this green one?

B2: I like it. The bee on the T-shirt is so cute.

G: And _____ ⓔ _____

B1: Yes. I think it's the best one.

① ⓐ Let me show you some designs on the screen.

② ⓑ What makes you say that?

③ ⓒ It's in November.

④ ⓓ That makes sense.

⑤ ⓔ it's not expensive.

[09~11] 다음 대화를 읽고 물음에 답하시오.

W: What are you doing, Oliver?

B: I'm studying for the math test, Mom. __(A)__ stress me out.

W: I understand. I used to feel that way, too.

B: Really? I didn't know that.

W: Yeah, but a little stress was helpful for me.

B: (B)What makes you say that?

W: I got stressed when I had an exam, but at the same time it made me focus and try harder.

B: I see. Did stress ___(C)___ you in other ways?

W: Yes, it helped improve my memory.

09

빈칸 (A)에 들어갈 가장 알맞은 말을 고르시오.

① Homework　　② Grades

③ Clothes　　④ Friends

⑤ Foods

10

밑줄 친 (B)와 바꿔 쓸 수 있는 것을 고르시오.

① What makes you think so?

② Why do you study so hard?

③ What is the cause of your stress?

④ How can you avoid this stress?

⑤ When will the stress be away?

11

빈칸 (C)에 알맞은 말을 쓰시오.

➡ _____

Grammar

12

다음 빈칸에 어법상 적절한 것은?

I am _____ hungry that I want to eat *ramyeon*.

① such　　② very

③ too　　④ so

⑤ quite

[13~14] 다음 괄호 안에 주어진 단어들을 바르게 배열하여 문장을 완성하시오.

13

[I guess / screaming / that / of my lungs / at the top / me / helps / feel better].

➡ _____

_____

14

Let me [what / you / my mother / tell / about / does / her stress].

➡ Let me _____

_____.

15 다음 〈보기〉에서 어법상 <u>어색한</u> 문장의 개수는?

┌─ 보기 ─┐

ⓐ My sister has a wonderful way to stay free from stress.
ⓑ She feels a lot of stress from schoolwork.
ⓒ My mother seems to like the situation for a good reason.
ⓓ She has been using this method when she was a child.
ⓔ She was so happy that she sang out.

① 1개 ② 2개 ③ 3개 ④ 4개 ⑤ 5개

[16~17] 다음 빈칸에 들어가기에 적절한 것은?

16

Tom has been living with us _____ last winter.

① after ② before ③ while
④ since ⑤ for

17

It was so cloudy _____ he took his umbrella.

① that ② what ③ which
④ while ⑤ when

18 다음 우리말을 영어로 바르게 옮긴 것은?

그는 너무 기뻐서 마음껏 소리를 질렀다.

① She was so happy what she screamed loudly.
② She felt so pleased that she screamed at the top of her lungs.
③ She was such happy that she screamed at the top of her lungs.
④ She screamed at the top of her lungs that she was so happy.
⑤ She was happy so that she screamed at the top of her lungs.

19 다음 대화에서 어법상 <u>어색한</u> 것을 2개 찾아 고치시오.

W: Little stress was helpful for me.
B: What makes you say that?
W: I got stressed when I had an exam, but at the same time it made me focus and try harder.
B: I see. Did stress help you in other ways?
W: Yes, it helped improving my memory.

(1) _____ ➡ _____
(2) _____ ➡ _____

20 다음 중 어법상 어색한 것은?

① Problems with friends took second place with 15.3%.
② Next family and worries about the future came.
③ My mother takes some time out for herself.
④ They eat special foods to feel better.
⑤ I'd like to talk about some good ways to relax when you get upset.

21 다음 우리말을 영어로 옮긴 것 중 어색한 것은?

① 또 다른 사람들은 단지 잠시 잠을 잔다.
→ Still others simply sleep for a while.
② 집이 너무 조용해서 그는 TV를 켰다.
→ The house was so quiet that he turned on the TV.
③ 왜 그런 생각을 하십니까?
→ Why makes you think so?
④ 당신은 스트레스를 어떻게 처리합니까?
→ How do you deal with stress?
⑤ 이 녹색은 어떻습니까?
→ What about this green one?

22 다음 중 문장의 의미가 나머지와 다른 하나는?

① She was so honest that she couldn't tell a lie.
② She was too honest to tell a lie.
③ She couldn't tell a lie because she was very honest.
④ She was very honest, so she couldn't tell a lie.
⑤ She was very honest though she told a lie.

Reading

[23~26] 다음 글을 읽고 물음에 답하시오.

_____ ⓐ _____ people spend time with friends when they feel low. Others eat special foods (A)to feel better. _____ ⓑ _____ others simply sleep for a while. (B)What do you deal with stress? Here are some stories about people _____ ⓒ _____ suggest different ways.

23 위 글의 빈칸 ⓐ~ⓒ에 들어갈 알맞은 단어를 각각 쓰시오.

➡ ⓐ _____ ⓑ _____ ⓒ _____

24 위 글의 밑줄 친 (A)to feel과 to부정사의 용법이 같은 것을 모두 고르시오.

① I worked hard to pass the test.
② There are many books to read.
③ It is hard for me to study English.
④ She must be mad to say so.
⑤ I don't know where to go.

25 위 글의 밑줄 친 (B)에서 어법상 틀린 부분을 찾아 고치시오.

_____ ➡ _____

26 위 글의 뒤에 올 내용으로 가장 알맞은 것을 고르시오.

① 스트레스의 주된 원인들
② 스트레스를 다루는 방법들 소개
③ 친구들과 즐거운 시간을 보내는 방법들
④ 스트레스를 없애는 음식들 소개
⑤ 효과적인 수면 방법들

[27~28] 다음 글을 읽고 물음에 답하시오.

Junho (14, Yeosu)
My uncle graduated from college two years ago. He lives with my family, and he's been looking for a job for some time. I know that

he's stressed out, but he always tries to be positive by going fishing. He never gets upset when he doesn't catch any fish. He says, "While I fish, I'm so focused that I can leave all my worries behind. Besides, it teaches me to be patient." I'm sure that ⓐ한 가지 일에 집중하는 것이 다른 무엇인가를 잊는 데 도움이 된다.

27 위 글의 밑줄 친 ⓐ의 우리말에 맞게 한 단어를 보충하여, 주어진 어휘를 알맞게 배열하시오.

helps / thing / about / focusing / us / else / something / one / forget

➡ _____

28 According to the passage, which is NOT true?

① Junho's uncle lives with Junho's family.
② Junho's uncle has not found a job yet.
③ Junho's uncle is stressed out and has a negative attitude.
④ While Junho's uncle fishes, he's so focused that he can leave all his worries behind.
⑤ Fishing teaches Junho's uncle to be patient.

[29~30] 다음 글을 읽고 물음에 답하시오.

Dobin (16, Seoul)

My sister, a second-year student in high school, has a wonderful way to stay free _____ⓐ_____ stress. She feels a lot of stress from schoolwork, but my mother seems to like the situation for a good reason. It is because cleaning is my sister's number-one way to make life better! When she's so stressed that her life looks gloomy, she cleans her room.

She says, "As I clean my room, I feel like I'm also relieving stress. ⓑ내 방이 깔끔해 보이면 내 삶도 더 밝아 보여."

29 위 글의 빈칸 ⓐ에 알맞은 것은?

① from ② to ③ over
④ with ⑤ along

30 위 글의 밑줄 친 ⓑ의 우리말에 맞게 주어진 어휘를 이용하여 9단어로 영작하시오.

When, tidy, brighter

➡ _____

[31~32] 다음 글을 읽고 물음에 답하시오.

**Use Your Five Senses
and Stay Free from Stress**

Eye	Look at the sky when you are outdoors.
ⓐ	Drink some tea.
Hand	Give your friend a high-five.
ⓑ	Smell fresh flowers.
Ear	Listen to your favorite song.

31 Fill in the blanks ⓐ and ⓑ with suitable words.

➡ ⓐ _____ ⓑ _____

32 위 글의 '오감을 사용한 스트레스 해소법'에 해당하지 않는 것은?

① 야외에 있을 때는 식물들을 보아라.
② 약간의 차를 마셔라.
③ 친구에게 하이 파이브를 해주어라.
④ 신선한 꽃 냄새를 맡아라.
⑤ 좋아하는 노래를 들어라.

단원별 예상문제

01 출제율 90%
다음 짝지어진 단어의 관계가 같도록 빈칸에 알맞은 말을 쓰시오. (주어진 철자로 시작할 것)

> bright : clever = b_____ : dull

02 출제율 90%
다음 영영풀이에 해당하는 단어를 고르시오.

> to make someone feel slightly worried, upset, or concerned

① bother　　　② produce
③ please　　　④ depress
⑤ frighten

03 출제율 95%
다음 문장의 빈칸에 알맞은 것으로 짝지어진 것은?

> • Did you decide _____ the menu?
> • I met a lot of nice people, thanks _____ you.

① to – on　② for – at　③ to – from
④ on – to　⑤ on – with

04 출제율 100%
다음 중 <보기>에 있는 단어를 사용하여 자연스러운 문장을 만들 수 없는 것은?

> ─┤ 보기 ├─
> positive　graduated　forget　focused

① My uncle _____ from college two years ago.
② I know that he's _____ out by the work.
③ He always tries to be _____ by going fishing.
④ While I fish, I'm so _____ that I can leave all my worries behind.
⑤ I'm sure that focusing on one thing helps us _____ about something else.

[05~06] 다음 빈칸에 들어갈 말로 적절한 것을 고르시오.

05 출제율 95%

> Good horror movies are so _____ that I scream a lot.

① boring　　　② scary
③ gloomy　　　④ patient
⑤ difficult

06 출제율 95%

> I guess that screaming at the top of my _____ helps me feel better. Also, thanks to scary scenes and sound effects, I can forget about what bothers me.

① nose　　② height　　③ sizes
④ fingers　⑤ lungs

07 출제율 95%
다음 짝지어진 단어의 관계가 같도록 빈칸에 알맞은 말을 쓰시오. (주어진 철자로 시작할 것)

> cause : effect = tidy : m_____

08 출제율 95%
다음 중 밑줄 친 부분의 뜻풀이가 바르지 않은 것은?

① Grades stress me out. (학년)
② Yeah, but a little stress was helpful for me. (유익한)
③ At the same time it made me focus and try harder. (집중하다)
④ I see. Did stress help you in other ways? (이해하다)
⑤ Yes, it helped improve my memory. (향상하다)

다음 영영풀이에 해당하는 단어를 고르시오.

> able to wait calmly for a long time or to accept difficulties without becoming angry

① patient
② stressed
③ sleepy
④ gloomy
⑤ positive

10 다음 우리말에 맞게 빈칸에 알맞은 말을 쓰시오.

(1) 고등학교 2학년인 누나는 스트레스를 없애는 좋은 방법을 가지고 있다.
➡ My sister, a second-year student in high school, has a wonderful way to stay _____ from stress.

(2) 엄마는 그 상황을 정당한 이유로 좋아하는 것 같다.
➡ My mother seems to like the situation for a good _____.

(3) 그녀는 너무 스트레스를 받아서 삶이 우울해 보일 때 방을 청소한다.
➡ When she's so stressed that her life looks _____, she cleans her room.

11 다음 대화의 내용과 일치하는 것은?

> G: Why don't we make a sport club?
> B: Sounds good. Let's make a baseball club.
> G: Well, I think a basketball club is a better idea.
> B: What makes you say that?
> G: All we need is a ball to play basketball.

① The girl wants to make a sport club.
② The boy doesn't like to make a sport club.
③ The girl wants to make a baseball club.
④ The girl agrees with the boy about a baseball club.
⑤ The girl and the boy like baseball a lot.

[12~14] 다음 대화를 읽고 물음에 답하시오.

> B1: Today, let's talk about the class T-shirt. We have to decide on the design.
> G: Let me show you some designs on the screen.
> B2: We have to choose a T-shirt ___(A)___ short sleeves.
> B1: What makes you say that?
> B2: Because we'll wear the T-shirt on Sports Day. It's in June.
> G: That makes sense. What about this green one?
> B2: I like it. The bee on the T-shirt is so cute.
> G: _____(B)_____
> B1: Yes. I think it's the best one.

12 위 대화의 빈칸 (A)에 알맞은 것은?

① on
② with
③ for
④ from
⑤ over

13 위 대화의 흐름으로 보아 (B)에 들어가기에 적절한 것은?

① And it's so large.
② But it's too colorful.
③ But how about this one?
④ And it's very dark.
⑤ And it's not expensive

14 위 대화의 내용과 일치하지 <u>않는</u> 것은? 출제율 95%

① They are talking about the T-shirt.

② They are choosing the design.

③ They chose a T-shirt which has short sleeves.

④ They will wear the T-shirt in spring.

⑤ They may choose a green T-shirt.

15 다음 빈칸에 어법상 적절한 것은? 출제율 90%

> He lives with my family, and he's been _____ for a job for some time.

① looked
② looks
③ to look
④ being looked
⑤ looking

16 다음 중 어법상 <u>어색한</u> 것은? 출제율 90%

① How do you deal with stress?

② Here are some stories about people who suggest different ways.

③ The girl has been playing the piano since an hour.

④ As you can see, schoolwork was the most common cause of stress.

⑤ About 9,000 teens answered this question.

17 다음 〈보기〉에서 어법상 <u>어색한</u> 문장의 개수는? 출제율 90%

> ┌─ 보기 ─┐
>
> ⓐ I was so busy that I didn't eat lunch.
>
> ⓑ She has been running around the playground for an hour.
>
> ⓒ The bag was so expensive that she couldn't buy.
>
> ⓓ He was such tired that he stopped working.
>
> ⓔ He was reading a book since this morning.

① 1개 ② 2개 ③ 3개 ④ 4개 ⑤ 5개

[18~20] 다음 글을 읽고 물음에 답하시오.

Mina (15, Daejeon)

Sometimes my friends give me stress by saying bad things about me, breaking promises, or arguing over small things. When (A)this happens, I watch horror movies! Good horror movies are so scary that I scream a lot. I guess that screaming at the top of my lungs helps me feel better. Also, thanks to scary scenes and sound effects, I can forget about what bothers me. I've been ___(B)___ this method for the past several months, and it really works.

18 위 글의 밑줄 친 (A)this가 가리키는 내용을 우리말로 쓰시오. 출제율 95%

➡ _____

_____

19 위 글의 빈칸 (B)에 use를 알맞은 형태로 쓰시오. 출제율 95%

➡ _____

20 What TWO things in horror movies help Mina forget about the thing which bothers her? Answer in English. 출제율 95%

➡ ① _____ ② _____

[21~22] 다음 글을 읽고 물음에 답하시오.

Junho (14, Yeosu)

My uncle (A)[graduated / graduated from] college two years ago. He lives with my family, and he's been looking for a job for some time. I know that he's stressed out, but he always tries to be positive by going fishing. He never gets (B)[relaxed / upset] when he doesn't catch any fish. He says, "While I fish, I'm so focused that I can leave all my worries behind. ⓐBesides, it teaches me to be (C) [patient / impatient]." I'm sure that focusing on one thing helps us forget about something else.

21 위 글의 괄호 (A)~(C)에서 문맥이나 어법상 알맞은 낱말을 골라 쓰시오.

➡ (A) _____ (B) _____ (C) _____

22 위 글의 밑줄 친 ⓐBesides와 바꿔 쓸 수 없는 말을 모두 고르시오.

① Therefore　　　② In addition to
③ Moreover　　　④ What's more
⑤ Furthermore

[23~25] 다음 글을 읽고 물음에 답하시오.

Yulia (14, Ansan)

Let me tell you what my mother does about her stress. She feels stressed by all the things she has to do at work and at home. When she's under stress, she writes "Me Time" on her calendar. (A)This means she takes some time out for her. She reads a book, watches a movie, or talks with her friends. She says, "(B)It doesn't really matter what I do, as long as it's something I like. I've been writing 'Me Time' on my calendar for two months, and I feel much better."

23 위 글의 밑줄 친 (A)에서 어색한 것을 고치시오.

_____ ➡ _____

24 위 글의 밑줄 친 (B)를 다음과 같이 바꿔 쓸 때 빈칸에 들어갈 알맞은 단어를 쓰시오.

➡ It isn't really _____

25 위 글의 내용과 일치하도록 다음 빈칸 (A)와 (B)에 알맞은 단어를 쓰시오.

- Cause of Yulia's Mother's Stress:
(A) _____ _____ _____ _____ _____ _____ _____ at work and at home
- Yulia's Mother's Method to Relieve Stress:
(B) having "_____ _____"

[26~27] 다음 글을 읽고 물음에 답하시오.

Are you stressed or feeling low? Then here is some good news for you. A few simple steps can help you! First, go outdoors and get plenty of sunlight. According to scientists, (A)this helps produce a special chemical in your brain, and the chemical makes you feel happy! Another thing you can do is exercise. (B)This helps produce even more of the "happiness chemical." Try these simple tips the next time you feel low. ____ⓐ____ sitting in front of a screen, go outdoors and run around in the sun!

26 위 글의 빈칸 ⓐ에 들어갈 알맞은 말을 고르시오.

① Besides　　　② Instead of
③ Along with　　④ In spite of
⑤ In addition

27 위 글의 밑줄 친 (A)this와 (B)This가 가리키는 것을 각각 본문에서 찾아 쓰시오. ((A)는 동명사를 사용하여 답하시오.)

➡ (A) _____
　　(B) _____

[01~02] 다음 짝지어진 단어의 관계가 같도록 빈칸에 알맞은 말을 쓰시오. (주어진 철자로 시작할 것)

01
bother : disturb = cause : r_____

02
cheap : expensive = relieved : w_____

03 다음 영영풀이에 해당하는 단어를 주어진 철자로 시작하여 쓰시오.

a change that is caused by an event, action, etc.

➡ e_____

[04~06] 다음 대화를 읽고 물음에 답하시오.

W: What are you doing, Oliver?
B: I'm studying for the math test, Mom. Grades stress me out.
W: I understand. I used to feel ⓐthat way, too.
B: Really? I didn't know that.
W: Yeah, but a little stress was ⓑhelp for me.
B: What ___ⓒ___ you say that?
W: I got stressed when I had an exam, but at the same time it made me focus and try harder.
B: I see. Did stress help you in other ways?
W: Yes, it helped improve my memory.

04 위 대화의 밑줄 친 ⓐ를 본문에 나오는 한 단어로 바꿔 쓰시오.

➡ _____

05 위 대화의 밑줄 친 ⓑ를 알맞은 형으로 고치시오.

➡ _____

06 위 대화의 빈칸 ⓒ에 알맞은 말을 쓰시오.

➡ _____

[07~08] 다음 글을 읽고 물음에 답하시오.

W: Today, I'd like to talk to you about teen stress. What makes you feel the most stressed? About 9,000 teens answered ⓐthis question. As you can see, schoolwork was the most common cause of stress. Over half of the students said schoolwork stresses them the most. Problems with friends took second place with 15.3%. Next came family and worries about the future. 8.2% of the students said they get stressed because of their ⓑappear.

07 위 글의 밑줄 친 ⓐthis question의 내용을 우리말로 구체적으로 쓰시오.

➡ _____

08 밑줄 친 ⓑappear를 알맞은 형으로 고치시오.

➡ _____

09 다음 〈보기〉의 두 문장을 현재완료진행시제를 사용하여 한 문장으로 연결하시오.

┌─ 보기 ─┐
• My mother started cooking dinner at 6:00.
• My mother is still cooking dinner.
└────────┘

➡ _____

10 다음 〈보기〉의 두 문장을 적절한 단어를 사용하여 한 문장으로 쓰시오.

> ┤ 보기 ├
>
> • He was very excited.
> • He shouted for the team.

➡ He was _____ excited _____ he shouted for the team.

[11~13] 다음 글을 읽고 물음에 답하시오.

Mina (15, Daejeon)

Sometimes my friends give me stress by saying bad things about me, breaking promises, or arguing over small things. When this (A)[happens / is happened], I watch horror movies! Good horror movies are ___ⓐ___ scary ___ⓑ___ I scream a lot. I guess that screaming at the top of my lungs (B)[help / helps] me feel better. Also, thanks to scary scenes and sound effects, I can forget about (C)[that / what] bothers me. I've been using this method for the past several months, and ⓒit really works.

11 Fill in the blanks ⓐ and ⓑ with the suitable words.

➡ ⓐ _____ ⓑ _____

12 위 글의 괄호 (A)~(C)에서 어법상 알맞은 낱말을 골라 쓰시오.

➡ (A) _____ (B) _____ (C) _____

13 위 글의 밑줄 친 ⓒit이 가리키는 것을 본문에서 찾아 쓰시오.

➡ _____

[14~16] 다음 글을 읽고 물음에 답하시오.

Junho (14, Yeosu)

My uncle graduated from college two years ago. He lives with my family, and ⓐhe's been looking for a job for some time. I know that he's stressed out, but he always tries to be positive by going fishing. He never gets upset when he doesn't catch any fish. He says, "While I fish, ⓑI'm so focused that I can leave all my worries behind. Besides, it teaches me to be patient." I'm sure that focusing on one thing helps us forget about something else.

14 위 글의 밑줄 친 ⓐ를 다음과 같이 바꿔 쓸 때 빈칸에 들어갈 알맞은 단어를 쓰시오.

➡ he started to look for a job some time _____, and he _____ still _____ for a job

15 위 글의 밑줄 친 ⓑ를 단문으로 고칠 때, 빈칸에 들어갈 알맞은 단어를 쓰시오.

➡ I'm focused _____ _____ leave all my worries behind.

16 다음 빈칸 (A)와 (B)에 알맞은 단어를 넣어 준호 삼촌의 구직 활동으로 인한 스트레스 해소 방법을 완성하시오.

> Junho's uncle goes (A)_____, which enables him to have a (B)_____ attitude though he has a hard time finding a job.
>
> *attitude: 태도

창의사고력 서술형 문제

01 다음 대화의 빈칸에 알맞은 말을 넣어 대화를 완성해 봅시다.

A: What's the matter?
B: I've been _____ all day.
A: You need a _____. Why don't you go to the river and fish?
B: That's a good idea.
   ……
A: What's the matter this time?
B: I haven't caught a _____. It _____ me out.
A: Don't _____. You'll catch one soon.

02 다음 항목들을 'have been -ing'를 사용하여 말해 봅시다.

since I was ten -　　　• live in this city
　　　　　　　　　　• hang out with my best friend
　　　　　　　　　　• learn English
　　　　　　　　　　• play the guitar
　　　　　　　　　　• use this computer

➡ I _____ since I was ten.

03 다음 그림을 바탕으로 오감을 사용한 스트레스 해소법을 소개하는 포스터를 완성하시오.

Use Your Five Senses and Stay Free from Stress
(A)_____ : Look at the sky when you are outdoors.
(B)_____ : Drink some tea.
(C)_____ : Give your friend a high-five.
(D)_____ : Smell fresh flowers.
(E)_____ : Listen to your favorite song.

단원별 모의고사

01 다음 짝지어진 단어의 관계가 같도록 빈칸에 알맞은 것은?

> tidy : neat = _____ : shout

① affect   ② scream   ③ laugh
④ sense   ⑤ weep

02 다음 영영풀이에 해당하는 단어를 고르시오.

> to make something better, or to become better

① produce   ② present   ③ stress
④ improve   ⑤ decide

03 다음 중 밑줄 친 부분의 뜻풀이가 바르지 <u>않은</u> 것은?

① This is a very <u>gloomy</u> situation. (우울한)
② What's <u>bothering</u> you? (괴롭히는)
③ We can have <u>free</u> pizza here. (공짜의)
④ I'm so <u>relieved</u>. (안심이 되는)
⑤ Let's be <u>patient</u> and wait for our food. (조바심이 나는)

04 다음 대화의 순서가 바르게 배열된 것을 고르시오.

> **A:** I want to spend more time on social media.
> (A) I can make more friends from around the world.
> (B) What makes you say that?
> (C) That makes sense.

① (A) − (C) − (B)   ② (B) − (A) − (C)
③ (B) − (C) − (A)   ④ (C) − (A) − (B)
⑤ (C) − (B) − (A)

05 다음 대화의 문맥상 또는 어법상 <u>어색한</u> 것을 찾아 고치시오.

> **W:** What are you doing, Oliver?
> **B:** I'm ①<u>studying</u> for the math test, Mom. Grades stress me out.
> **W:** I understand. I ②<u>used to</u> feel that way, too.
> **B:** Really? I didn't know that.
> **W:** Yeah, but a little stress was ③<u>helpful</u> for me.
> **B:** What makes you ④<u>say</u> that?
> **W:** I got ⑤<u>stress</u> when I had an exam, but at the same time it made me focus and try harder.
> **B:** I see. Did stress help you in other ways?
> **W:** Yes, it helped improve my memory.

_____ ➡ _____

06 다음 대화의 내용과 일치하지 <u>않는</u> 것은?

> **B1:** Today, let's talk about the class T-shirt. We have to decide on the design.
> **G:** Let me show you some designs on the screen.
> **B2:** We have to choose a T-shirt with short sleeves.
> **B1:** What makes you say that?
> **B2:** Because we'll wear the T-shirt on Sports Day. It's in June.
> **G:** That makes sense. What about this green one?
> **B2:** I like it. The bee on the T-shirt is so cute.
> **G:** And it's not expensive.
> **B1:** Yes. I think it's the best one.

① 오늘의 주제는 티셔츠 디자인 결정이다.
② 그들은 안내책자를 보고 디자인을 결정할 것이다.
③ 소매가 짧은 셔츠 디자인을 결정할 것이다.
④ 고르려고 하는 셔츠는 비싸지 않다.
⑤ 티셔츠에는 꿀벌 그림이 있다.

07 다음 중 어법상 <u>어색한</u> 문장은?

① He has been working for two hours.
② It was so cold that we stayed home.
③ He is a such kind boy that I like him.
④ He has been singing for two hours.
⑤ She has lived here for ten years.

08 다음 〈보기〉와 같이 주어진 두 문장을 한 문장으로 바꾸어 쓰시오.

┌─── 보기 ───┐

• I started working at the Chinese restaurant six months ago.
• I am still working there.
➡ I have been working at the Chinese restaurant for six months.

• My father started repairing his car this morning.
• He is still repairing it now.

➡ _____

_____

09 다음 빈칸에 어법상 적절한 것은?

I've been using this method _____ the past several months, and it really works.

① for   ② since
③ before   ④ after
⑤ during

10 다음 문장에 들어가기에 적절한 것은?

Because the soup was too hot, he decided to eat it later.
= The soup was _____ _____ _____ he decided to eat it later.

11 다음 괄호 안에 주어진 어구를 바르게 배열하여 문장을 완성하시오.

(1) I'd (to / some / talk / ways / like / about / you / good / when / relax / upset / to / get).
➡ I'd _____
_____.

(2) While I (focused / fish, / I / I'm / so / that / all my worries / can leave / behind).
➡ While I _____
_____.

12 다음 중 어법상 <u>어색한</u> 문장은?

① She has been doing the dishes since half an hour.
② He has been playing the piano for two hours.
③ We have been waiting for him since this morning.
④ He has been living in the house for three years.
⑤ They have been studying for the test for three hours.

13 다음 〈보기〉에서 어법상 어색한 문장의 개수는?

> ┌─── 보기 ───
> ⓐ Last time, I talked about different foods that are good for your health.
> ⓑ Ann was such hungry that she wanted to eat *ramyeon*.
> ⓒ Today, I'd like to talk about healthy eating habits.
> ⓓ First, it's important to stop eating when you're full.
> ⓔ The weather is so fine which I can go to the park today.
> ⓕ I have been read this novel for three hours.

① 1개 ② 2개 ③ 3개 ④ 4개 ⑤ 5개

[14~15] 다음 글을 읽고 물음에 답하시오.

Mina (15, Daejeon)

ⓐSometimes my friends give me stress by saying bad things about me, keeping promises, or arguing over small things. When this happens, I watch horror movies! Good horror movies are so scary that I scream a lot. I guess that screaming at the top of my lungs helps me feel better. Also, thanks to scary scenes and sound effects, I can forget about ⓑwhat bothers me. I've been using this method for the past several months, and it really works.

14 위 글의 밑줄 친 ⓐ에서 흐름상 어색한 부분을 찾아 고치시오.

_____ ➡ _____

15 위 글의 밑줄 친 ⓑwhat을 3 단어로 바꿔 쓰시오.

➡ _____

[16~17] 다음 글을 읽고 물음에 답하시오.

Junho (14, Yeosu)

My uncle graduated from college two years ago. He lives with my family, and he's been looking for a job for some time. I know that he's stressed out, but he always tries to be positive by going fishing. He never gets upset when he doesn't catch any fish. He says, "ⓐWhile I fish, I'm so focused that I can leave all my worries behind. Besides, ⓑit teaches me to be patient." I'm sure that focusing on one thing helps us forget about something else.

16 위 글의 밑줄 친 ⓐWhile과 같은 의미로 쓰인 것을 모두 고르시오.

① I fell asleep while I was reading.
② Where have you been all this while?
③ The walls are green, while the ceiling is white.
④ Did anyone call while I was away?
⑤ Some are rich, while others are poor.

17 위 글의 밑줄 친 ⓑ가 가리키는 것을 한 단어로 쓰시오.

➡ _____

[18~19] 다음 글을 읽고 물음에 답하시오.

Dobin (16, Seoul)

My sister, a second-year student in high school, has a wonderful way to stay free _____ⓐ_____ stress. She feels a lot of stress _____ⓑ_____ schoolwork, but my mother seems to like the situation for a good reason.

It is because cleaning is my sister's number-one way to make life better! When she's so stressed that her life looks gloomy, she cleans her room. She says, "As I clean my room, I feel like I'm also relieving stress. When my room looks tidy, my life looks brighter."

18 위 글의 빈칸 ⓐ와 ⓑ에 공통으로 들어갈 알맞은 전치사를 쓰시오.

➡ _____

19 According to the passage, which is NOT true?

① Dobin's sister is a second-year student in high school.
② When Dobin's sister feels much stress, Dobin's mother doesn't like it.
③ Cleaning is Dobin's sister's number-one way to make life better.
④ When Dobin's sister is so stressed that her life looks gloomy, she cleans her room.
⑤ As Dobin's sister cleans her room, she feels like she's also relieving stress.

[20~22] 다음 글을 읽고 물음에 답하시오.

Yulia (14, Ansan)

Let me tell you what my mother does about her stress. She feels stressed by all the things she has to do at work and at home. When she's under stress, she writes "Me Time" on her calendar. This means she takes some time out for herself. She reads a book, watches a movie, or talks with her friends. She says,

ⓐThis doesn't really matter what I do, as long as it's something I like. ⓑI've been writing 'Me Time' on my calendar for two months, and I feel much better."

20 위 글의 밑줄 친 ⓐ에서 어법상 틀린 부분을 찾아 고치시오.

_____ ➡ _____

21 위 글의 밑줄 친 ⓑ에 쓰인 것과 같은 용법의 현재완료가 쓰인 문장의 개수를 고르시오.

┌─ 보기 ─┐
① Have you ever seen it before?
② She has gone to Paris.
③ I have just solved the problem.
④ How long have you known each other?
⑤ He hasn't finished it yet.
└─────────┘

① 1개 ② 2개 ③ 3개 ④ 4개 ⑤ 5개

22 위 글의 내용으로 보아 대답할 수 없는 질문은?

① What does Yulia tell you about?
② What kind of job does Yulia's mother have?
③ What does Yulia's mother do when she is stressed?
④ What does Yulia's mother write on her calendar?
⑤ How long has Yulia been writing 'Me Time' on her calendar?

Lesson

4

Opening a Window to the World

 의사소통 기능

- 궁금한 점 표현하기

  A: I wonder if there's a bank around here.

  B: I'm sorry, but we don't have one near here.

- 도움 제안하기

  A: Do you want me to play *baduk* with you?

  B: That'd be great. Thank you.

 언어 형식

- 관계부사

  Friday evening is the time **when** my family likes to go for a walk.

- 접속사 if/whether

  I wonder **if** they are angry.

Words & Expressions

Key Words

- **add** [æd] 동 더하다
- **alive** [əláiv] 형 살아 있는
- **architect** [á:rkətèkt] 명 건축가
- **attract** [ətrǽkt] 동 끌어들이다, 끌어당기다, 매혹하다
- **bill** [bil] 명 계산서
- **carry** [kǽri] 동 운반하다
- **cart** [kɑ:rt] 명 수레
- **covered** [kʌ́vərd] 형 지붕이 덮인
- **culture** [kʌ́ltʃər] 명 문화
- **design** [dizáin] 동 설계하다
- **digest** [didʒést] 동 소화하다
- **directly** [diréktli] 부 곧장, 바로, 직접적으로
- **disappear** [dìsəpíər] 동 사라지다
- **discover** [diskʌ́vər] 동 발견하다, 알아내다
- **effective** [iféktiv] 형 효과적인, 실질적인
- **electric-powered** 형 전기로 동력이 주어지는
- **environment** [inváiərənmənt] 명 환경
- **experience** [ikspíəriəns] 명 경험
- **fishing pole** 낚싯대
- **float** [flout] 동 뜨다
- **follow** [fálou] 동 따르다
- **gardening** [gá:rdniŋ] 명 원예
- **house** [hauz] 동 살 곳을 주다, 거처를 제공하다
- **imaginable** [imǽdʒənəbl] 형 상상할 수 있는
- **insect** [ínsekt] 명 곤충
- **last** [læst] 동 지속하다, 오래가다
- **local** [lóukəl] 형 현지의, 지역의
- **mostly** [móustli] 부 주로, 대부분

- **natural** [nǽtʃərəl] 형 천연의, 자연스러운
- **notice** [nóutis] 동 주목하다
- **pick** [pik] 동 고르다, 뽑다, 수확하다
- **planet** [plǽnit] 명 지구, 행성
- **plant** [plænt] 명 식물
- **popular** [pɑ́pjulər] 형 인기 있는
- **present** [préznt] 명 선물
- **producer** [prədjú:sər] 명 생산자
- **recipe** [résəpi] 명 조리법
- **relax** [rilǽks] 동 쉬다
- **send** [send] 동 보내다
- **share** [ʃɛər] 동 공유하다
- **ship** [ʃip] 동 운송하다, 실어 나르다
- **spider** [spáidər] 명 거미
- **suggest** [səgdʒést] 동 제안하다
- **taste** [teist] 동 맛보다
- **therefore** [ðɛ́ərfɔ̀:r] 부 그러므로, 따라서
- **tourist** [túərist] 명 관광객
- **trade** [treid] 명 무역
- **tradition** [trədíʃən] 명 전통
- **translate** [trænsléit] 동 번역하다
- **transportation** [trænspərtéiʃən] 명 운송, 교통
- **try** [trai] 동 맛보다
- **way** [wei] 명 방식
- **whether** [hwéðər] 접 ~인지 아닌지
- **wholesale** [hóulseil] 형 도매의
- **wonder** [wʌ́ndər] 동 궁금하다
- **work** [wə:rk] 동 작동하다, 효과가 있다

Key Expressions

- **all corners of the world** 세계의 곳곳
- **be crowded with** ~로 붐비다, 꽉 차다
- **be good for** ~에 유익하다
- **be rich in** ~이 풍부하다
- **chat with** ~와 잡담하다
- **floating market** 수상 시장

- **have ~ in common** ~한 공통점이 있다
- **Here you are.** 여기 있습니다.
- **make an appointment** 약속하다
- **make sure to** 반드시 ~하다
- **take a nap** 낮잠을 자다
- **best-before date** 유효 기한, 유통 기한

Word Power

※ 서로 비슷한 뜻을 가진 어휘

□ **attract** 끌어들이다, 끌어당기다 : **draw** 끌다

□ **disappear** 사라지다 : **vanish** 사라지다

□ **mostly** 주로, 대부분 : **largely** 주로

□ **suggest** 제안하다 : **propose** 제안하다

□ **carry** 운반하다 : **transport** 운반하다

□ **local** 현지의, 지역의 : **regional** 지역의

□ **pick** 수확하다 : **harvest** 수확하다

□ **tourist** 관광객 : **traveler** 여행자

※ 서로 반대의 뜻을 가진 어휘

□ **add** 더하다 ↔ **subtract** 빼다

□ **directly** 직접적으로 ↔ **indirectly** 간접적으로

□ **effective** 효과적인 ↔ **ineffective** 효과가 없는

□ **alive** 살아 있는 ↔ **dead** 죽은

□ **disappear** 사라지다 ↔ **appear** 나타나다

□ **float** 뜨다 ↔ **sink** 가라앉다

※ 동사 → 형용사

□ **select** 고르다 → **selective** 선택적인

□ **impress** 인상을 주다 → **impressive** 인상적인

□ **create** 창조하다 → **creative** 창조적인

□ **invent** 발명하다 → **inventive** 독창적인

□ **defense** 방어하다 → **defensive** 방어적인

□ **attract** 끌다 → **attractive** 매력적인

※ 명사 → 형용사

□ **emotion** 감정 → **emotional** 감정적인

□ **person** 개인 → **personal** 개인적인

□ **cost** 비용 → **costly** 많은 돈이 드는

□ **time** 시간 → **timely** 시기적절한

□ **courage** 용기 → **courageous** 용감한

□ **fame** 명성 → **famous** 유명한

□ **magic** 마법 → **magical** 마법 같은

□ **season** 계절 → **seasonal** 계절적인

□ **friend** 친구 → **friendly** 친한

□ **adventure** 모험 → **adventurous** 모험적인

□ **danger** 위험 → **dangerous** 위험한

□ **humor** 유머 → **humorous** 유머가 있는

English Dictionary

□ **disappear** 사라지다
→ to see no longer 더 이상 보이지 않다

□ **discover** 발견하다
→ to find out 찾아내다

□ **imaginable** 상상할 수 있는
→ possible to think of in your mind
마음 속에서 생각해 내는 것이 가능한

□ **tourist** 여행자
→ a person who is traveling for pleasure
즐거움을 위해 여행하는 사람

□ **attract** 끌다, 매혹하다
→ to make someone interested in something and cause them to come to it
누군가가 어떤 것에 관심을 갖게 하고 그것에게 오도록 하다

□ **tradition** 전통
→ cultural beliefs and customs passed down through generations 세대에 걸쳐 전해지는 문화적 신념과 관습

□ **wholesale** 도매의
→ the action of selling things in large amounts and at low prices 대량으로 그리고 낮은 가격으로 물건을 판매하는 행위

□ **ship** 운송하다
→ to send people or things somewhere by ship, truck, and so on 선박, 트럭 등으로 사람이나 물건을 보내다

□ **floating market** 수상 시장
→ the market which buys and sells things directly on a boat 보트 위에서 물건을 직접 사고파는 시장

□ **directly** 직접적으로
→ without stopping; with nothing in between
멈추지 않고; 중간에 개입하는 것 없이

01 다음 짝지어진 단어의 관계가 같도록 빈칸에 알맞은 말을 쓰시오.

> float : sink = alive : _____

02 다음 영영풀이가 가리키는 것을 고르시오.

> the action of selling things in large amounts and at low prices

① wholesale ② retail
③ buyer ④ store
⑤ seller

03 다음 중 밑줄 친 부분의 뜻풀이가 바르지 <u>않은</u> 것은?

① He loves to visit the <u>local</u> markets and eat food there. (현지의, 지역의)
② Did you eat something before the <u>meal</u>? (식사)
③ Milk is <u>rich</u> in calcium. (부자인)
④ Babies cannot <u>digest</u> meat well. (소화하다)
⑤ Let me write a <u>recipe</u> for you. (조리법)

04 다음 문장에 공통으로 들어갈 말을 고르시오.

> • The school is _____d in two buildings.
> • My _____ looks south, so it is warm.
> • Most of _____s are built of woods.

① share ② house
③ trade ④ taste
⑤ notice

05 다음 짝지어진 단어의 관계가 나머지와 <u>다른</u> 것은?

① person – personal
② friend – friendly
③ humor – humorous
④ advent – adventure
⑤ cost – costly

06 다음 주어진 문장의 밑줄 친 covered와 같은 의미로 쓰인 것은?

> It is the largest <u>covered</u> market in the world.

① Did you remember the <u>covered</u> area of the stadium with seats?
② The survey <u>covers</u> all aspects of the business.
③ I think $100 can <u>cover</u> your expenses.
④ The lecture <u>covered</u> a lot of strategy in the game.
⑤ My grandparents didn't <u>cover</u> my father's tuition fees.

서답형

07 다음 우리말에 맞게 빈칸을 완성하시오.

(1) 몇몇 앱들은 효과적인 가르침의 도구들로서 사랑받는다.
➡ Some apps are loved as _____ teaching tools.

(2) 내 친구들과 나는 대부분 시험 후에 영화관에 간다.
➡ My friends and I _____ go to the movies after exams.

(3) 서울의 대중교통 시스템은 깨끗하고, 빠르고 안전하다.
➡ The public _____ system in Seoul is clean, fast and safe.

01 다음 짝지어진 단어의 관계가 같도록 빈칸에 알맞은 말을 쓰시오.

> appear : disappear = add : _____

02 다음 영영풀이가 가리키는 것을 쓰시오.

> the market which buys and sells things directly on a boat

➡ _____

03 주어진 단어에 -al이나 -ive를 붙여 형용사를 완성하시오.

(1) select → _____
(2) invent → _____
(3) magic → _____
(4) impress → _____
(5) person → _____
(6) collect → _____
(7) emotion → _____
(8) season → _____

04 다음 우리말을 주어진 단어를 이용하여 영작하시오.

(1) 영화가 다소 길다. 그것은 두 시간 반 동안 지속된다. (two and a half)
   ➡ The movie is a bit long. It _____
   _____.

(2) 나는 몇 시에 가게 문을 닫는지 궁금합니다. (to, going)
   ➡ I wonder _____
   _____.

(3) 만약 당신이 비로부터 상품들을 보호하고 싶다면, 당신은 반드시 지붕이 덮인 트럭을 사용해야 합니다. (must)
   ➡ If you want to protect your goods from the rain, _____
   _____.

05 다음 우리말에 맞게 빈칸에 알맞은 말을 쓰시오.

(1) 모든 초콜릿은 최소 6개월의 유통 기한이 있다.
   ➡ All chocolate has a _____
   of at least 6 months.

(2) 여러분은 여기서 세계 곳곳의 음식을 맛볼 수 있다.
   ➡ You can taste food from _____
   _____ here.

(3) 대부분의 고양이는 우유를 잘 소화하지 못한다는 것을 유념해라.
   ➡ Remember most cats cannot _____
   milk very well.

(4) 과학자들은 암에 대한 약을 발견하기 위해 연구하고 있다.
   ➡ Scientists are working to _____
   medicine for cancers.

(5) 그랜드 캐니언은 세계 자연 경관 중의 하나이다.
   ➡ The Grand Canyon is one of the
   _____ wonders of the world.

06 다음 〈보기〉의 단어들을 이용하여 빈칸을 완성하시오.

> ┌ 보기 ┐
> local   transportation   last   tourist   discover

Are you a _____ in a new city? Do you want to _____ its beauty? Then, use public _____. Your memory of the new place will _____ longer. You should visit local market too. If you try some food there, you can enjoy the _____ culture.

Conversation

1 궁금한 점 표현하기

> **A** I wonder if there's a bank around here. 이 근방에 은행이 있는지 궁금해요.
>
> **B** I'm sorry, but we don't have one near here. 유감스럽게도 이 근방에 은행이 없어요.

■ 자신의 궁금함을 상대방에게 나타내는 표현은 wonder(궁금하다), curious(궁금한, 호기심이 많은), want to know(알고 싶다) 등의 표현을 이용하여 나타낼 수 있다. 궁금함을 나타낼 때, 궁금한 내용이 '주어+동사'의 절의 형태이면 접속사 if[wether]를 사용하여 'I wonder if[wether] 주어+동사 ~.'(~ 인지 궁금하다) 또는 'I wonder+의문사+주어+동사 ~.'로 나타내고, 궁금한 내용이 명사구이면 'I wonder+명사구'의 구문을 이용한다.

■ 궁금함을 나타낼 때 'I wonder ~.' 대신에 쓸 수 있는 표현으로는 'I'm curious ~.' 또는 'I want to know ~.' 등이 있다. 'I'm curious'와 명사구를 같이 쓸 때는 'I'm curious about+명사구'이고, 명사절과 함께 쓸 때는 'I'm curious if/whether ~.' 또는 'I'm curious+의문사+주어+동사'이다.

■ 'I want to know'를 명사구와 함께 사용할 때는 'I want to know+명사구'이고, 명사절과 함께 사용할 때는 'I want to know+명사절'이다. 그 외에 궁금증을 나타낼 때는 'Do you know ~?' 또는 'Can you tell me ~?' 등을 사용할 수도 있다.

궁금한 점 표현하기

- I wonder if/whether+주어+동사. ~인지 궁금하다
- I wonder+의문사절.
- I wonder+명사구.
- I'm curious if/whether+주어+동사. ~가 궁금하다
- I'm curious about+명사구.
- I want to know+명사구/명사절. ~을 알고 싶다
- I'd be very interested to ~. 나는 ~이 알고 싶다.
- Can you tell me about ~? ~에 대해 말해 줄 수 있니?

핵심 Check

1. 다음 우리말과 일치하도록 주어진 표현을 포함하여 빈칸에 알맞은 말을 쓰시오.

M: Welcome to the Tourist Information Office! How may I help you?

W: Hi, _____. (a tourist map of the town)
(여행자가 이용할 수 있는 마을 지도가 있는지 궁금해요.)

M: Is there a special place you're looking for?

W: Yes. I'd like to try some local food.

M: Then go to Jeongseon Market. It opens every five days, and it's open today.

2 도움 제안하기

A Do you want me to play *baduk* with you? 제가 바둑을 같이 두기를 원하세요?

B That'd be great. Thank you. 그거 좋지. 고마워.

■ 일반적으로 도움을 제안하는 표현은 help(도움을 주다), give a hand(도움을 주다) 등을 사용하여 'May I help you?', 'How may I help you?', 'Do you need any help?' 등으로 나타낸다. 'give ~ a hand'는 '~를 돕다'라는 관용적 표현이다. 도움을 제공하고자 할 때는 'Can I give you a hand?'라고 물어볼 수 있다. 이는 레스토랑, 호텔, 기내 등과 같이 서비스를 제공받을 수 있는 공간에서 흔히 쓸 수 있는 표현이다.

■ 상대방이 지루해 하거나 힘들어 하는 등, 현재 처해 있는 상황을 보고 구체적인 도움을 제안할 때는 'Do you want me to ~?'(제가 ~해드리기를 원하세요?)라고 물어본다. 상대방에게 닥친 어려움이나 힘든 일을 도와준다고 제안할 때 'Let me help you with ~.'(내가 너에게 ~하도록 도와줄게.)와 같은 표현을 쓸 수 있다. 도와 달라는 표현은 'Can you help me with ~?'(~ 좀 도와주시겠어요?)이다.

도움 제안하기

- Do you want me to+동사원형? 당신은 내가 ~해 주기를 원합니까?
- May/Can I help you? 도와 드릴까요?
- How may I help you? 어떻게 도와드릴까요?
- What can I do for you? 무엇을 도와 드릴까요?
- Do you need any help? 도움이 필요하세요?
- Let me give you a hand. 제가 도와드리겠습니다.
- Can I give you a hand? 도와 드릴까요?
- Is there anything that I can help you? 도와드릴 일이 있을까요?
- Let me help you. 내가 도와줄게.

핵심 Check

2. 다음 우리말과 일치하도록 빈칸에 알맞은 말을 쓰시오.

W: Excuse me. Can _____? (with this milk)
　　(이 우유 (사는 것) 좀 도와주겠니?)

B: Sure. What is it?

W: Read me the date, please.

B: Oh, _____? (want, the best-before date)
　　(유통 기한을 말씀드리길 원하세요?)

W: Yes, I forgot my glasses.

Listen – Listen & Answer Dialog 1

M: Welcome to the Tourist Information Office! ❶How may I help you?

W: Hi, ❷I wonder ❸if there's a tourist map of the town.

M: Sure. Is there a special place you're ❹looking for?

W: Yes. I'd like to try some local food.

M: Then go to Jeongseon Market. It opens every five days, and it's open today.

W: I'm so lucky. How can I get ❺there?

M: You can walk there. It takes about 10 minutes.

W: Great. Will you mark the way on the map, please?

M: Sure. Try *gondrebap* when you get ❺there.

남: 관광 안내소에 오신 것을 환영합니다! 무엇을 도와드릴까요?
여: 안녕하세요. 저는 마을 관광 지도가 있는지 궁금합니다.
남: 물론이죠. 특별히 찾으시는 곳이 있나요?
여: 네. 이 지역 음식을 먹어 보고 싶어요.
남: 그렇다면 정선 시장에 가 보세요. 시장이 5일마다 열리는데, 오늘 열렸네요.
여: 제가 정말 운이 좋군요. 그곳에 어떻게 가나요?
남: 거기까지 걸어갈 수 있어요. 10분 정도 걸려요.
여: 잘됐군요. 지도에 길을 표시해 주시겠어요?
남: 물론이죠. 거기에 가면 곤드레밥을 드셔 보세요.

❶ 도움을 제안하는 표현으로 'May I help you?', 'Can I give you a hand?' 또는 'Do you need any help?' 등으로 바꾸어 쓸 수 있다.
❷ 궁금함을 나타내는 표현으로 'I wonder ～' 대신에 쓸 수 있는 표현으로는 'I'm curious ～.' 또는 'I want to know ～.' 등이 있다.
❸ if는 '～인지 아닌지'를 뜻하며 whether와 바꾸어 쓸 수 있다.
❹ look for: ～을 찾다
❺ there = to Jeongseon Market

Check(√) True or False

(1) The woman wants to try some local food.　　　　T ☐ F ☐

(2) Jeongseon Market opens once a week.　　　　T ☐ F ☐

 Listen – Listen & Answer Dialog 2

W: Can I have the ❶bill, please?

M: Here you are. Did you enjoy the meal?

W: It was great. I liked the *gondrebap* very much.

M: Thanks. ❷It's also good for your health.

W: Oh, really?

M: Yes. *Gondre* ❸is rich in vitamins A and C. It also ❹digests well.

W: Good. I wonder if I could buy some *gondre* here.

M: Sure. Do you want me to give you the recipe for *gondrebap*?

W: Yes, that'd be great.

여: 계산서 좀 주시겠어요?
남: 여기 있습니다. 식사는 맛있게 하셨나요?
여: 아주 훌륭했어요. 저는 곤드레밥이 정말 좋았어요.
남: 고맙습니다. 그것은 건강에도 좋답니다.
여: 오. 정말이요?
남: 네. 곤드레는 비타민 A와 C가 풍부합니다. 그리고 소화도 잘돼요.
여: 그렇군요. 여기서 곤드레를 좀 살 수 있을까요?
남: 물론이죠. 제가 곤드레밥 조리법을 드릴까요?
여: 네. 그러면 정말 좋겠어요.

❶ bill: 계산서　　❷ be good for: ～에 좋다, 유익하다　　❸ be rich in: ～이 풍부하다　　❹ digest: 소화하다

Check(√) True or False

(3) The woman is satisfied with *gondrebap*.　　　　T ☐ F ☐

(4) The man knows how to make *gondrebap*.　　　　T ☐ F ☐

Listen More – Listen and complete

W: Excuse me. ❶Can you help me with this milk?

B: Sure. What is it?

W: Read me the date, please.

B: Oh, do you want me to tell you ❷the best-before date?

W: Yes, I forgot my glasses.

B: Let me see. You should drink ❸it by June 7.

W: That's too soon. I wonder ❹if there's one that ❺lasts longer.

B: Wait. I found one. This one is good until June 11.

W: Oh, I'll take that one. Thank you very much.

B: You're welcome.

❶ 도움을 요청하는 표현으로 'Would you do me a favor?' 또는 'Could you give me a hand?'로 바꾸어 쓸 수 있다.

❷ the best-before date: 유효 기한

❸ it은 the milk를 가리킨다.

❹ if는 '~인지 아닌지'를 뜻하며 'whether'로 바꾸어 쓸 수 있다.

❺ last: 지속하다, 오래가다

 Speak – Talk in pairs. 1

A: Excuse me. ❶I wonder if there's a bank around here.

B: I'm sorry, but we don't have ❷one near here.

A: That's all right. Thanks.

❶ 궁금함을 나타내는 표현으로 'I'm curious if there's a bank around here.' 또는 'I want to know if there's a bank around here.'로 바꾸어 쓸 수 있다.

❷ one은 a bank를 가리킨다.

 Speak – Talk in pairs. 2

A: ❶What's wrong, Grandpa?

B: I'm ❷bored.

A: Do you want me to play *baduk* with you?

B: That'd be great. Thank you.

❶ 'What's the matter?', 'What's the problem?' 등으로 바꾸어 쓸 수 있다.

❷ 감정을 나타내므로 과거분사 형태이다.

 Wrap Up 1

G: I feel hungry.

B: I'll make *ramyeon* for you.

G: ❶How nice!

B: Do you want me to ❷add an egg?

G: ❸That'd be great.

❶ 'How nice you are!'의 줄임말이다.

❷ add: 더하다

❸ That's good! 또는 'Sounds great.' 등으로 바꾸어 말할 수 있다.

 Wrap Up 2

G: Dad, look at ❶that cute bag. I wonder ❷how much it is.

M: ❸Why don't we go in and check?

G: Really? Thanks, Dad.

M: I didn't say I will buy ❹it for you. We're just asking the price.

G: Of course.

❶ 지시형용사로 사용되었다.

❷ 간접의문문 어순으로 '의문사+주어+동사' 순서로 이어진다.

❸ 들어가서 확인해 볼 것을 제안하는 표현으로 'How[What] about going in and checking?' 또는 'Let's go in and check.'로 바꾸어 쓸 수 있다.

❹ it은 the cute bag을 가리킨다.

● 다음 우리말과 일치하도록 빈칸에 알맞은 말을 쓰시오.

Listen – Listen & Answer Dialog 1

M: _____ _____ the Tourist Information Office! How may I _____ you?

W: Hi, I wonder _____ there's a _____ _____ of the town.

M: Sure. _____ _____ a special place you're _____ _____?

W: Yes. I'd _____ _____ _____ some _____ food.

M: Then go to Jeongseon Market. It opens every _____ _____, and it's _____ today.

W: I'm so _____. _____ _____ _____ _____ _____?

M: You can walk there. It _____ _____ 10 _____.

W: Great. Will you _____ the way on the map, please?

M: Sure. _____ *gondrebap* _____ you _____ there.

남: 관광 안내소에 오신 것을 환영합니다! 무엇을 도와드릴까요?

여: 안녕하세요, 저는 마을 관광 지도가 있는지 궁금합니다.

남: 물론이죠. 특별히 찾으시는 곳이 있나요?

여: 네. 이 지역 음식을 먹어 보고 싶어요.

남: 그렇다면 정선 시장에 가 보세요. 시장이 5일마다 열리는데, 오늘 열렸네요.

여: 제가 정말 운이 좋군요. 그곳에 어떻게 가나요?

남: 거기까지 걸어갈 수 있어요. 10분 정도 걸려요.

여: 잘됐군요. 지도에 길을 표시해 주시겠어요?

남: 물론이죠. 거기에 가면 곤드레밥을 드셔 보세요.

Listen – Listen & Answer Dialog 2

W: Can I have the _____, please?

M: _____ you are. Did you enjoy the _____?

W: It was great. I liked the *gondrebap* very much.

M: Thanks. It's also _____ _____ your health.

W: Oh, really?

M: Yes. *Gondre* is _____ in vitamins A and C. It also _____ well.

W: Good. I _____ _____ I could buy some *gondre* here.

M: Sure. Do you want me _____ _____ you the _____ for *gondrebap*?

W: Yes, that'd be great.

여: 계산서 좀 주시겠어요?

남: 여기 있습니다. 식사는 맛있게 하셨나요?

여: 아주 훌륭했어요. 저는 곤드레밥이 정말 좋았어요.

남: 고맙습니다. 그것은 건강에도 좋답니다.

여: 오, 정말이요?

남: 네. 곤드레는 비타민 A와 C가 풍부합니다. 그리고 소화도 잘돼요.

여: 그렇군요. 여기서 곤드레를 좀 살 수 있을까요?

남: 물론이죠. 제가 곤드레밥 조리법을 드릴까요?

여: 네, 그러면 정말 좋겠어요.

Listen More – Listen and complete

W: Excuse me. Can you _____ _____ _____ this _____?

B: Sure. What is it?

W: _____ me the date, please.

B: Oh, do you want me to tell you _____ _____ _____?

W: Yes, I forgot my _____.

B: _____ me _____. You should drink it _____ June 7.

여: 미안하지만, 이 우유 (사는 것) 좀 도와주겠니?

남: 그럼요. 뭔데요?

여: 날짜를 좀 읽어 주렴.

남: 아, 유통 기한을 말씀드리길 원하세요?

여: 그래, 내가 안경을 두고 왔단다.

남: 잠깐만요. 6월 7일까지 드셔야 해요.

W: That's too soon. _____ _____ _____ there's one that _____ _____.

B: Wait. I found one. This _____ is good _____ _____ _____.

W: Oh, I'll take that _____. Thank you very much.

B: You're _____.

Speak – Talk in pairs. 1

A: _____ me. I _____ if there's a bank _____ _____.

B: I'm sorry, _____ we _____ _____ _____ near here.

A: That's _____ _____. Thanks.

Speak – Talk in pairs. 2

A: What's _____, Grandpa?

B: I'm _____.

A: Do you _____ _____ _____ play *baduk* _____ you?

B: That'd _____ _____. Thank you.

Wrap Up 1

G: I feel _____.

B: I'll make *ramyeon* for you.

G: _____ nice!

B: Do you _____ me _____ _____ an egg?

G: That'd be great.

Wrap Up 2

G: Dad, _____ _____ that cute bag. _____ _____ _____ _____ _____ _____ _____.

M: _____ _____ we _____ _____ and _____?

G: Really? Thanks, Dad.

M: I didn't say I will _____ _____ _____ _____. We're just _____ the _____.

G: Of _____.

해석

여: 그건 너무 짧네. 기한이 더 긴 게 있는지 궁금하구나.
남: 잠깐만요. 하나 찾았어요. 이것은 6월 11일까지 드실 수 있어요.
여: 오, 그걸로 사야겠다. 정말 고맙구나.
남: 천만에요.

A: 실례합니다. 이 근처에 은행이 있는지 궁금합니다.
B: 미안하지만 이 근처에는 없어요.
A: 괜찮아요. 고맙습니다.

A: 무슨 일이세요, 할아버지?
B: 지루하구나.
A: 제가 함께 바둑을 두길 원하세요?
B: 그러면 좋겠구나. 고맙구나.

여: 나 배고파.
남: 내가 널 위해 라면을 끓여 줄게.
여: 좋아!
남: 달걀을 넣길 원하니?
여: 그러면 정말 좋겠어.

여: 아빠, 저 귀여운 가방을 보세요. 얼마인지 궁금해요.
남: 들어가서 확인해 보는 게 어떻겠니?
여: 정말요? 고마워요, 아빠.
남: 사 주겠다고는 말하지 않았단다. 그냥 가격만 물어보는 거야.
여: 물론이죠.

01 다음 대화의 빈칸에 주어진 단어를 사용하여 대답을 완성하시오.

> A: How do you want to travel? I wonder if you want to travel with friends or family.
>
> B: Well, _____. (friends)

➡ _____

02 다음 대화가 자연스럽게 이어지도록 순서대로 배열하시오.

> (A) Do you want me to add an egg?
> (B) How nice!
> (C) I'll make *ramyeon* for you.
> (D) I feel hungry.

> That'd be great.

➡ _____

[03~04] 다음 대화를 읽고 물음에 답하시오.

> Jane: Dad, look at ⓐthat cute bag. I wonder ⓑhow much it is.
> Dad: Why don't we go in and ⓒchecking?
> Jane: Really? Thanks, Dad.
> Dad: I didn't say I ⓓwill buy it for you. We're just ⓔasking the price.
> Jane: Of course.

03 위 대화의 밑줄 친 ⓐ~ⓔ 중 어법상 어색한 것을 찾아 바르게 고치시오.

_____ ➡ _____

04 위 대화를 읽고 대답할 수 없는 것은?

① What is Jane looking at?
② What does Jane want to know?
③ What does Dad suggest doing?
④ Where are Dad and Jane going to go?
⑤ How much is the cute bag?

[01~03] 다음 대화를 읽고 물음에 답하시오.

M: Welcome to the Tourist Information Office! How may I help you?

W: Hi, (a)I wonder if there's a tourist map of the town.

M: Sure. Is there a special place you're looking for?

W: Yes. I'd like to try some local food.

M: Then go to Jeongseon Market. It opens every five days, and it's open today.

W: I'm so lucky. How can I get there?

M: You can walk there. It takes about 10 minutes.

W: Great. _____ (A) _____, please?

M: Sure. Try *gondrebap* when you get there.

서답형

01 위 대화의 빈칸 (A)에 들어갈 말을 주어진 어구를 배열하여 영작하시오.

> the way / the map / you / will / on / mark

➡ _____

서답형

02 위 대화에서 주어진 영영풀이가 나타내는 말을 찾아 쓰시오.

> a person who is traveling for pleasure

➡ _____

03 위 대화의 밑줄 친 (a)와 바꾸어 쓸 수 있는 것을 모두 고르시오.

① I'm curious whether there's a tourist map of the town.

② I believe there's a tourist map of the town.

③ I want to know if there's a tourist map of the town.

④ I doubt if there's a tourist map of the town.

⑤ I'm sure there's a tourist map of the town.

[04~05] 다음 대화를 읽고 물음에 답하시오.

W: Can I have the ___(A)___, please?

M: Here you are. Did you enjoy the meal?

W: It was great. I liked the *gondrebap* very much.

M: Thanks. It's also good for your health.

W: Oh, really?

M: Yes. *Gondre* is rich in vitamins A and C. It also digests well.

W: Good. I wonder if I could buy some *gondre* here.

M: Sure. Do you want me to give you the recipe for *gondrebap*?

W: Yes, that'd be great.

서답형

04 위 대화의 빈칸 (A)에 다음 영영풀이가 나타내는 말을 쓰시오.

> a document that shows how much you owe somebody for goods or services

➡ _____

05 위 대화의 내용과 일치하지 <u>않는</u> 것은?

① The woman asked the bill after having *gondrebap*.

② The woman was satisfied with her meal.

③ *Gondrebap* is good for the health.

④ It is easy to digest *gondre*.

⑤ The woman wants to know where to buy some *gondre*.

[06~08] 다음 대화를 읽고 물음에 답하시오.

> Grandma: Excuse me. Can you help me with this milk?
> Brian: Sure. What is it?
> Grandma: Read me the date, please.
> Brian: Oh, do you want me to tell you the best-before date?
> Grandma: Yes, I forgot my glasses. ⓐ
> Brian: Let me see. ⓑ
> Grandma: That's too soon. I wonder if there's one that lasts longer. ⓒ
> Brian: Wait. I found one. This one is good until June 11. ⓓ
> Grandma: Oh, I'll take that one. Thank you very much. ⓔ
> Brian: You're welcome.

06 위 대화의 ⓐ~ⓔ 중 주어진 문장이 들어가기에 적절한 곳을 고르시오.

> You should drink it by June 7.

① ⓐ ② ⓑ ③ ⓒ ④ ⓓ ⑤ ⓔ

07 위 대화가 이루어지는 곳을 고르시오.

① Airport
② Tourist information office
③ Post office
④ Restaurant
⑤ Grocery store

08 위 대화를 읽고 대답할 수 <u>없는</u> 것은?

① What's the matter with the grandma?
② What does the grandma want Brian to do?
③ What did the grandma forget?
④ Which milk is the grandma going to take?
⑤ What date is it today?

[09~11] 다음 대화를 읽고 물음에 답하시오.

> Jane: Dad, look at that cute bag. (A)<u>I wonder how much is it.</u>
> Dad: (B)<u>Why don't we go in and check?</u> (let)
> Jane: Really? Thanks, Dad.
> Dad: I didn't say I will buy it for you. We're just asking the price.
> Jane: Of course.

서답형

09 위 대화의 밑줄 친 (A)를 어법에 맞게 고치시오.

➡ _____

서답형

10 위 대화의 밑줄 친 (B)와 의도가 같도록 주어진 어휘를 사용하여 다시 쓰시오.

➡ _____

서답형

11 What are Jane and Dad going to do together?

➡ _____

12 다음 대화가 자연스럽게 이어지도록 순서대로 배열하시오.

> W: Can I have the bill, please?
> (A) Oh, really?
> (B) It was great. I liked the *gondrebap* very much.
> (C) Here you are. Did you enjoy the meal?
> (D) Thanks. It's also good for your health.
> (E) Yes. *Gondre* is rich in vitamins A and C. It also digests well.
> W: Good. I wonder if I could buy some *gondre* here.

➡ _____

01 다음 대화의 밑줄 친 우리말을 주어진 단어를 사용하여 영작하시오.

> A: Excuse me. 저는 이 근처에 은행이 있는지 궁금합니다. (if, wonder, around)
>
> B: I'm sorry, but we don't have one near here.

➡ _____

02 다음 대화를 읽고 Brian이 박물관을 방문하고 싶은 이유를 서술하시오.

> Amy: Do you want to visit museums or markets?
>
> Brian: I want to visit museums. It's a great way to learn about the local culture.

➡ _____

_____

[03~04] 다음 대화를 읽고 물음에 답하시오.

> Grandma: Excuse me. Can you help me with this milk?
>
> Brian: Sure. What is it?
>
> Grandma: Read me the date, please.
>
> Brian: Oh, do you want me to tell you the best-before date?
>
> Grandma: Yes, I forgot my glasses.
>
> Brian: Let me see. You should drink it by June 7.
>
> Grandma: That's too soon. (A)기한이 더 긴 게 있는지 궁금하구나.
>
> Brian: Wait. I found one. This one is good until June 11.
>
> Grandma: Oh, I'll take that one. Thank you very much.
>
> Brian: You're welcome.

03 위 대화의 밑줄 친 (A)의 우리말을 주어진 단어를 모두 배열하여 영작하시오.

> if / longer / that / there's / I / lasts / wonder / one

➡ _____

04 위 대화의 내용과 일치하도록 할머니가 쓴 일기의 빈칸을 완성하시오.

> Friday, June 5th, 2020.
> Today, I didn't bring (A)_____ to the grocery store. It was hard for me to read (B)_____ because it was too small. I asked a boy to tell it to me. I didn't buy the first milk that I picked up because its best-before date was too soon. Fortunately, the boy found the one that its best-before date (C)_____. I think I can finish it until (D)_____. I really appreciate him.

05 다음 대화가 자연스럽게 이어지도록 순서대로 배열하시오.

> (A) Of course.
> (B) I didn't say I will buy it for you. We're just asking the price.
> (C) Really? Thanks, Dad.
> (D) Dad, look at that cute bag. I wonder how much it is.
> (E) Why don't we go in and check?

➡ _____

Grammar

교과서

① 관계부사

- Friday evening is the time **when** my family likes to go for a walk. 금요일 저녁은 우리 가족이 산책하기를 좋아하는 시간이다.

- Lake Park is the place **where** my family likes to go for a walk. 호수 공원은 우리 가족이 산책하기를 좋아하는 장소이다.

■ 관계부사는 두 문장을 연결하는 접속사의 역할과 부사의 역할을 동시에 한다. 관계부사 앞에 오는 수식을 받는 명사를 선행사라 하고, 그 선행사에 따라 관계부사 when(시간), where(장소), why(이유), how(방법)를 쓴다.

- Summer is a time **when** a lot of rain comes down. 여름은 비가 많이 내리는 시기이다.
- Is this the place **where** it happened? 여기가 그 일이 일어난 장소인가요?

■ 관계부사 how는 선행사 the way와 함께 쓰지 않고 둘 중의 하나만 써야 하며 how 대신 the way that이나 the way in[by] which를 쓸 수 있다. 다른 관계부사의 경우 the time, the place, the reason과 같은 선행사가 나올 경우 선행사나 관계부사 중 하나를 생략할 수 있다.

- He loved **the way**[또는 **how**] she smiled. (○) 그는 그녀가 미소 짓는 모습이 너무 좋았다.

  He loved the way how she smiled. (×)

■ 관계부사는 '전치사+관계대명사(which)'로 바꿔 쓸 수 있으며, which를 쓸 때는 전치사를 which 바로 앞에 쓰거나 관계사절의 끝에 쓴다.

- This is the house **where** I was born. 이곳이 내가 태어난 집이다.
  = This is the house **in which** I was born. = This is the house **which** I was born **in**.

■ 선행사에 따른 관계부사

	선행사	관계부사	전치사+관계대명사
때	the time	when	in/on/at which
장소	the place	where	in/on/at which
이유	the reason	why	for which
방법	the way	how	in/by which

■ 주의: 관계대명사는 관계사절에서 주어나 목적어의 역할을 하므로 주어나 목적어가 빠진 불완전한 절이 나오지만 관계부사는 부사 역할을 하므로 완전한 절이 나온다.

핵심 Check

1. 다음 괄호 안에서 알맞은 말을 고르시오.

(1) There are days (when / where) I can't do my homework.

(2) I remember the house (when / where) I was born.

(3) I cannot think of one reason (why / how) we should accept his proposal.

2 접속사 if/whether

• I wonder **if** they are angry. 나는 그들이 화가 났는지 궁금하다.

• Can you tell me **whether** they speak Chinese? 그들이 중국어를 할 수 있는지 내게 말해 줄래?

■ if나 whether는 '~인지 (아닌지)'라는 의미의 접속사로 어떠한 사실의 여부를 확인하거나 불확실함을 나타낼 때 쓰이며, 주로 ask, be not sure, find out, know, see, tell, wonder 등의 동사의 목적어 역할을 하는 명사절을 이끈다. if[whether] 뒤에 오는 절은 의문사가 없는 간접의문문으로 'if[whether]+주어+동사'의 어순으로 쓴다.

• I'm not sure **if** I can do it. 내가 그것을 할 수 있을지 모르겠어. 〈목적어〉

• **Whether** Jack will come or not is another matter. Jack이 올지 안 올지는 다른 문제이다. 〈주어〉

• My chief concern is **whether** or not they are alive. 나의 주요 관심사는 그들의 생사 여부다. 〈보어〉

• I wonder. + Can you help me?
→ I wonder **if** you can help me. 나를 도와주실 수 있는지 궁금하네요.

■ if가 명사절을 이끄는 접속사로 그 명사절이 문장 내에서 동사의 목적어로 쓰일 때는 whether로 바꿔 쓸 수 있다. whether가 이끄는 절이 주어 역할을 할 경우에는 if로 바꿔 쓸 수 없으며, whether 다음에는 or not을 바로 붙여 쓸 수 있지만, if는 바로 붙여 쓸 수 없다.

• I can't tell **if** he is happy or not. 그가 행복한지 아닌지 모르겠다.
= I can't tell **whether** he is happy or not.

• **Whether** he will come or not is doubtful. 그가 올지 안 올지 의심스럽다.
= If he will come or not is doubtful. (×)

• I was anxious about **whether** or not I would fail the exam. 나는 시험에 떨어질까봐 마음을 졸였다.
= I was anxious about if or not I would fail the exam. (×)

cf. 보통 if가 조건의 부사절을 이끌 때는 '만약 ~라면'이라는 의미로 쓰이며, whether가 부사절을 이끌 경우에는 '~이든 (아니든)'이라는 '양보'의 의미로 쓰인다.

• Is it OK **if** I leave now? 제가 지금 떠나도 될까요? 〈조건〉

• **Whether** or not we're successful, we will do our best. 우리가 성공을 하든 못 하든, 우리는 최선을 다할 것이다. 〈양보〉

핵심 Check

2. 다음 빈칸에 들어갈 말을 〈보기〉에서 골라 쓰시오.

> ┤ 보기 ├
> whether   if   that

(1) She asked me _____ I was alright.

(2) I wasn't sure _____ I could handle such a powerful car.

(3) It's questionable _____ or not the news is true.

01 다음 빈칸에 들어갈 말로 알맞은 것은?

> I remember the day _____ I got my first cell phone.

① when   ② where   ③ why
④ how   ⑤ which

02 다음 괄호 안에서 알맞은 말을 고르시오.

(1) This is the library (when / where) I met her for the first time.
(2) The day (when / where) I start for my journey is drawing near.
(3) Nick wonders (if / that) she likes roses.
(4) The question arises as to (if / whether) or not he knew about the situation.

03 다음 빈칸에 들어갈 말로 알맞은 것은?

> Tell us _____ you know the answer.

① that   ② what   ③ which
④ if   ⑤ unless

04 다음 우리말에 맞게 주어진 어휘를 바르게 배열하시오.

(1) 네가 늦은 이유를 내게 말해.
   (the reason, you, me, late, tell, were, why)
   ➡ _____

(2) 그는 자신이 도울 수 있는지를 물었다.
   (he, he, could, asked, help, whether)
   ➡ _____

(3) 그분이 지금 시간이 있는지 알아봐 주시겠어요?
   (he, you, available, find, can, is, now, if, out)
   ➡ _____

01 다음 중 어법상 <u>어색한</u> 것은?

① This is the town where I was born.
② Can you tell me the reason how he got angry?
③ He cares for the children on the days when he's not working.
④ I remember the restaurant where I met her first.
⑤ Winter is the season when it snows.

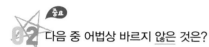

02 다음 중 어법상 바르지 <u>않은</u> 것은?

① Thanks for your suggestion, but I'm not sure if it's realistic.
② Food will last longer if it is kept in an airtight container.
③ I asked her if she wanted to join my birthday party.
④ I asked her that she wanted to marry me, but she wouldn't answer.
⑤ Every child needs to know that he is loved.

03 다음 빈칸에 알맞은 말이 바르게 짝지어진 것은?

> • I wonder _____ he can help me.
> • May 5 is the day _____ I visit the children's home in my neighborhood with my parents.

① if – when
② that – when
③ if – where
④ that – where
⑤ whether – how

04 다음 괄호 안에서 알맞은 말을 고르시오.

(1) Penguin Snack is the place (when / where) I like to go with my friends.
(2) Do you know the reason (how / why) she didn't come?
(3) Shirley will go to the restaurant (which / where) she can have delicious *samgyupsal* with her friends.
(4) I asked her (whether / that) she was ready to go.
(5) She asked me (if / that) I would be able to finish my work.
(6) Decide (whether / if) or not you're going to continue the job.

05 주어진 두 문장을 한 문장으로 바꿀 때 옳지 <u>않은</u> 것은?

> • This is the way.
> • I solved the math problem in the way.

① This is how I solved the math problem.
② This is the way I solved the math problem.
③ This is the way in which I solved the math problem.
④ This is the way that I solved the math problem.
⑤ This is the way how I solved the math problem.

06 빈칸 (A)와 (B)에 알맞은 것으로 바르게 짝지어진 것은?

> • I wonder _____(A)_____ Jane can come to the party.
> • I want you to tell me _____(B)_____ or not he is a good person.

	(A)	(B)
①	whether	if
②	that	if
③	if	whether
④	that	whether
⑤	if	that

07 다음 문장의 밑줄 친 부분 중 어법상 어색한 것은?

> I ⓐhave been ⓑto ⓒthe house ⓓwhen Mozart ⓔwas born.

① ⓐ ② ⓑ ③ ⓒ ④ ⓓ ⑤ ⓔ

08 다음 밑줄 친 부분과 바꿔 쓸 수 있는 것은?

> She asked me _if_ I would give her English lessons.

① unless   ② that
③ what   ④ which
⑤ whether

서답형

09 다음 두 문장을 한 문장으로 바꿔 쓸 때 빈칸에 들어갈 알맞은 말을 쓰시오.

> • This is a country.
> • Trading on boats has a long history in this country.
> ➡ This is a country _____ trading on boats has a long history.

중요

10 밑줄 친 부분의 쓰임이 주어진 문장과 같은 것은?

> Apr. 26 is the day when I confessed my love to her.

① When did you last see him?
② Do you remember the moment when you decided to become a singer?
③ I loved history when I was a student.
④ I was standing there lost in thought when I was called from behind.
⑤ I will contact you later to advise you when to come.

11 다음 우리말을 바르게 영작한 것을 고르시오.

> 오늘 밤에 비가 올지 안 올지 확실하지 않다.

① It is not certain whether it will rain tonight or not.
② It is certain whether it will not rain tonight or not.
③ It is not certain that it will rain tonight or not.
④ It is certain because it will not rain tonight.
⑤ It is not certain if or not it will rain tonight.

서답형

12 다음 문장에서 생략할 수 있는 것을 찾아 쓰시오.

(1) This is the time when the government should take action.
    ➡ _____

(2) I'd like to know the reason why you're so late.
    ➡ _____

13 주어진 문장의 틀린 부분을 찾아, 올바르게 고치지 <u>않은</u> 것을 고르시오.

> He didn't know that he could win the race or not.

① He didn't know whether he could win the race or not.
② He didn't know whether or not he could win the race.
③ He didn't know if he could win the race or not.
④ He didn't know if or not he could win the race.
⑤ He didn't know whether he could win the race.

서답형

14 다음 문장에서 어법상 <u>어색한</u> 것을 바르게 고쳐 다시 쓰시오.

(1) Sandra wonders if it is fine tomorrow.

➡ _____

(2) If he stays or goes doesn't matter that much.

➡ _____

(3) That is the place when I buy food for the coming week.

➡ _____

(4) The reason which he did it is complicated.

➡ _____

(5) The way how it was done was the best they could do at the time.

➡ _____

15 다음 우리말을 바르게 영작한 것을 고르시오.

> 우리는 작년에 갔던 해변에 다시는 가지 않을 것이다.

① We will never go back to the beach when we went last year.
② We will never go back to the beach why we went last year.
③ We will never go back to the beach which we went last year.
④ We will never go back to the beach which we went last year for.
⑤ We will never go back to the beach to which we went last year.

16 다음 중 어법상 <u>어색한</u> 것을 고르시오. (2개)

① I'm not sure if I'm qualified enough or not.
② They are arguing about if they should begin the project.
③ It is a place which you can experience the traditional type of house in Korea.
④ I don't understand the reason why he's gone.
⑤ The time when we can drive flying cars will come soon.

17 다음 두 문장을 한 문장으로 바꿔 쓰시오.

> • Will you tell me?
> • Do I still have a place in your heart?

➡ _____

01 다음 두 문장을 관계부사를 써서 한 문장으로 바꿔 쓰시오.

(1) • March 14 is the day.
 • People around the world celebrate Pi Day on the day.

➡ _____
_____

(2) • School is the place.
 • I learn, eat, and have fun with my friends at the place.

➡ _____
_____

(3) • Tell me the reason.
 • You were late for the reason.

➡ _____
_____

(4) • This is the way.
 • He killed the big bear in the way.

➡ _____
_____

02 if를 이용하여 다음 두 문장을 한 문장으로 바꿔 쓰시오.

(1) • Please let me know.
 • Is the movie fun?

➡ _____

(2) • Ask him.
 • Is it true?

➡ _____

(3) • I'm not sure.
 • Can I do this?

➡ _____

03 다음 우리말에 맞게 주어진 어구를 바르게 배열하시오.

(1) 내가 시험에 통과할 수 있을지 나는 잘 모르겠다. (I, I'm, the exam, if, can, sure, pass, not)

➡ _____

(2) 비가 곧 올 것인지는 농부들에게 중요하다. (farmers, it, whether, rain, is, will, important, soon, to)

➡ _____

(3) 펭귄 분식은 우리 학교 학생들이 가기 좋아하는 장소이다. (Penguin Snack, students, the place, my school, like, go, is, where, to, in)

➡ _____

(4) 네가 기차를 타러 가야 할 시간을 잊지 마라. (the time, the train, you, forget, leave, don't, should, when, for)

➡ _____
_____

04 다음 문장에서 잘못된 것을 알맞게 고치시오.

(1) If you win the fight or not is important.
_____ ➡ _____

(2) Decide if or not you're going to continue the job.
_____ ➡ _____

(3) You'll have to choose if to buy it or not.
_____ ➡ _____

05 그림을 보고 주어진 어휘를 이용하여 빈칸을 알맞게 채우시오.

(1) She wonders _____

_____. (he, help, that milk)

(2) The hair dresser asked my brother

_____.

(he, like, done)

06 알맞은 단어 하나를 추가하여 주어진 두 문장을 하나의 문장으로 쓰시오.

(1) • I'm not sure.

• I should tell you the news.

➡ _____

_____

(2) • I don't know.

• He will get better.

➡ _____

_____

(3) • Turkey is a country.

• East meets West in Turkey.

➡ _____

_____

07 다음 우리말을 괄호 안의 지시대로 영작하시오.

(1) 이곳은 Ben 삼촌이 매주 토요일에 빵을 사는 빵집이다.

➡ _____

_____ (관계부사를 써서)

➡ _____

_____ (관계대명사를 써서)

(2) 그의 행동 방식은 나를 화나게 만든다.

➡ _____

(관계부사를 생략해서)

➡ _____

(선행사를 생략해서)

➡ _____

(that을 써서)

08 다음 문장에서 어법상 어색한 것을 바르게 고쳐 다시 쓰시오.

(1) I am just considering if to go or not.

➡ _____

_____

(2) Please let me know if you are late tonight.

➡ _____

_____

(3) The way how he worked has left much to be desired.

➡ _____

_____

(4) This is the hospital which I was born.

➡ _____

_____

Leah's Travel Story

I am Leah. I have been writing a travel blog since I was 18. I go
places and share my experiences with my readers.

Must-Visit Markets Around the World   July 15, 20**

Visiting markets is a good way to learn about the culture of a country.
Markets are places where you can meet people, learn history, and
taste local food. I wonder whether there is any better way to discover
another culture.

1 Grand Bazaar, Turkey

Turkey is a country where East meets West, so it has a long tradition
of trade. It is a natural place for large markets like the Grand Bazaar.
The market was built in 1455 in Istanbul. Back then, the market had
two big buildings, and people traded goods like cloth and gold there.

Today the Grand Bazaar is much bigger, and it is the largest covered
market in the world. It has 64 streets and more than 4,000 shops under
one roof. The market attracts over 250,000 visitors every day. You can
buy almost any imaginable item there.

whether ~인지 아닌지
discover 발견하다, 알아내다
attract 끌어들이다, 끌어당기다
imaginable 상상할 수 있는

확인문제

- 다음 문장이 본문의 내용과 일치하면 T, 일치하지 않으면 F를 쓰시오.

1 Leah has been writing a travel blog since she was 18. ☐

2 Visiting museums is a good way to learn about the culture of the country. ☐

3 Markets are places where you can meet people, learn history, and taste local food. ☐

4 Turkey is a country where East meets West, so it has a long tradition of art. ☐

5 The Grand Bazaar was built in 1455 in Istanbul. ☐

6 Today the Grand Bazaar is much bigger, and it is the largest outdoor market in the
world. ☐

Extra Tip Ask shop owners if they carry *nazar boncuğu*, a traditional

if는 명사절을 이끄는 접속사로 '~인지 아닌지'라는 의미   nazar boncuğu와 이어지는 명사구는 동격 관계

Turkish symbol for good luck. Also, if you want a nice snack,

make sure to try *lokum*, a traditional Turkish candy.

반드시 (…하도록) 하래[(…을) 확실히 하라]

2 Damnoen Saduak Floating Market, Thailand

In the past, Thai people traded goods on rivers. This was the

This는 앞 문장 전체 내용(과거에, 태국인들은 강 위에서 물건을 사고팔았다)을 받는 대명사

beginning of floating markets in Thailand. With better road

transportation, many floating markets disappeared. Since the late

were disappeared(×)

1960s, however, some of them have come back and kept the tradition

앞 문장에 언급된 '도로 교통 개선으로   have come back: 재기했다. kept the tradition

alive.

인해 사라진 많은 수상 시장 중 몇 개'   alive: (물 위에서 무역하던) 전통을 사라지지 않게 살려왔다

O.C. living(×)

Today, one of the most popular floating markets is Damnoen Saduak

Floating Market. It is always crowded with tourists from all over the

Damnoen Saduak Floating Market

world. You can buy local foods and traditional gift items directly from

boats.

if not: '그렇지 않다면'(If you haven't had a meal on water). if: 조건의 부사절을 이끄는 접속사

Extra Tip I wonder if you have ever had a meal on water. If not, try

'~인지 아닌지'(접속사)   경험을 나타내는 현재완료

noodles like *pad thai*. The sellers will cook them on their boats and

noodles like *pad thai*

pass them to you with a long fishing pole.

noodles like *pad thai*

carry (가게에서 물품을) 팔다
transportation 운송. 교통
disappear 사라지다
keep ~ alive ~을 존속시키다. 살려두다
crowded with ~으로 붐비는
directly 직접
fishing pole 낚싯대

확인문제

● 다음 문장이 본문의 내용과 일치하면 T, 일치하지 않으면 F를 쓰시오.

1 *Nazar boncuğu* is a traditional Turkish symbol for good luck. ☐

2 In the past, Thai people usually traded goods on lands. ☐

3 As the road transportation got better, many floating markets disappeared. ☐

4 Since the late 1960s, some of the floating markets have come back but lost their tradition. ☐

5 Damnoen Saduak Floating Market is always crowded with tourists from all over the world. ☐

6 The sellers of noodles will cook them on their boats and pass them to you with their hands. ☐

3 Aalsmeer Flower Market, The Netherlands

The Netherlands means "low lands." As the name suggests, about
'~하듯이'라는 의미로 부사절을 이끄는 접속사

70% of the country sits below sea level. Thus, the Dutch built up the
문장의 주어(나라의 약 70%)가 단수이므로 3인칭 단수형 동사인 sits 사용

land, and one effective way to use it was to grow flowers and sell
형용사적 용법의 to부정사   명사적 용법의 to부정사(보어)

them. It is, therefore, no surprise that the country has the largest flower
It: 가주어   that이 이끄는 절: 진주어
It is no surprise that: '~라는 것은 놀라운 일이 아니다'

market in the world: the Aalsmeer Flower Market.

The building where the market is housed is bigger than 120 soccer
주어   선행사 The building을 수식하는 관계부사

fields. The market is busy with thousands of flower-filled carts.
명사와 과거분사가 하이픈(-)으로 연결되어 하나의 의미를 나타내는 복합 형용사

They are moved mostly by electric-powered trucks. Every day, around
flower-filled carts

20 million flowers are traded and shipped to all corners of the world.
수동태 are traded와 (are) shipped가 접속사 and로 연결되어 있음.

Extra Tip You may wonder whether you can buy just a few flowers
'~인지 아닌지'(접속사), 동사 wonder의 목적어가 되는 명사절을 이끌고 있음.

at the market. Sadly, you cannot, but you can see how wholesale
간접의문문으로 동사 see의 목적어 역할을 함.

flower trading works.
'의문사(how)+주어(wholesale flower trading)+동사(works)'의 어순에 주의한다.

suggest 시사하다, 암시하다
effective 효과적인, 유효한
house 거처를 제공하다
be busy with ~으로 바쁘다
mostly 대부분
wholesale 도매의

확인문제

● 다음 문장이 본문의 내용과 일치하면 T, 일치하지 <u>않으면</u> F를 쓰시오.

1   About 70% of the Netherlands is situated below sea level. ☐

2   It is surprising that the Netherlands has the largest flower market in the world. ☐

3   The building where the Aalsmeer Flower Market is housed is bigger than 120 soccer fields. ☐

4   The Aalsmeer Flower Market is busy with hundreds of flower-filled carts. ☐

5   Every day, around 20 million flowers are traded and shipped to all corners of the world at the Aalsmeer Flower Market. ☐

6   You can buy only a few flowers at the Aalsmeer Flower Market. ☐

● 우리말을 참고하여 빈칸에 알맞은 말을 쓰시오.

1　Leah's _____ Story

2　_____ _____ Leah.

3　I _____ _____ _____ a travel blog since I was 18.

4　I go places and _____ my experiences _____ my readers.

5　_____ Markets Around the World

6　_____ 15, 20**

7　_____ _____ is a good way to learn about the culture of a country.

8　Markets are _____ _____ you can meet people, learn history, and taste local food.

9　I _____ _____ there is any better way _____ _____ another culture.

10　1 _____ _____, Turkey

11　Turkey is a country _____ East meets West, so it has a _____ _____ _____ _____.

12　It is _____ _____ _____ _____ large markets _____ the Grand Bazaar.

13　The market _____ _____ in 1455 in Istanbul.

14　Back then, the market had two big buildings, and people _____ _____ like cloth and gold there.

1	Leah의 여행 이야기
2	저는 Leah입니다.
3	18세 때부터 여행 블로그를 써 왔습니다.
4	저는 여기저기 다니며 제 경험을 독자들과 공유하고 있습니다.
5	꼭 방문해야 할 세계의 시장들
6	20**년 7월 15일
7	시장 방문은 한 나라의 문화에 대해 배우는 좋은 방법입니다.
8	시장은 사람들을 만나고, 역사를 배우고, 또 지역 음식을 맛볼 수 있는 장소입니다.
9	다른 문화를 발견하는 데에 더 좋은 방법이 있을지 모르겠습니다.
10	1 터키의 Grand Bazaar(그랜드 바자)
11	터키는 동양과 서양이 만나는 나라이고, 그래서 오랜 교역의 전통을 가지고 있습니다.
12	터키는 Grand Bazaar 같은 대형 시장이 생겨나기에 자연스러운 곳입니다.
13	Grand Bazaar는 1455년 이스탄불에 지어졌습니다.
14	그 당시에 이 시장에는 큰 건물이 두 개 있었고, 거기서 사람들은 직물이나 금 같은 물건을 교환했습니다.

15 Today the Grand Bazaar is _____ bigger, and it is the _____ _____ _____ in the world.

16 It has 64 streets and more than 4,000 shops _____ _____ _____.

17 The market _____ over 250,000 visitors every day.

18 You can buy _____ _____ _____ item there.

19 **Extra Tip** Ask shop owners _____ they carry *nazar boncuğu*, a _____ _____ _____ for good luck.

20 Also, if you want a nice snack, make sure to try *lokum*, a _____ _____ _____.

21 **2 Damnoen Saduak _____ Market, Thailand**

22 In the past, Thai people _____ _____ on rivers.

23 This was the _____ _____ _____ _____ in Thailand.

24 _____ _____ _____ _____, many floating markets disappeared.

25 Since the late 1960s, however, some of them _____ _____ _____ and kept the tradition _____.

26 Today, one of the most popular floating _____ _____ Damnoen Saduak Floating Market.

27 It is always _____ _____ tourists from all over the world.

28 You can buy local foods and traditional gift items _____ _____ _____.

---

15 오늘날 Grand Bazaar는 훨씬 크고, 세계에서 가장 큰 지붕이 덮인 시장입니다.

16 64개의 거리와 4,000개 이상의 상점이 한 지붕 아래에 있습니다.

17 그 시장은 매일 25만 명 이상의 방문객을 불러 모읍니다.

18 그곳에서는 상상할 수 있는 거의 모든 물건을 살 수 있습니다.

19 추가 정보 가게 주인에게 행운을 기원하는 터키 전통 상징인 'nazar boncuğu(나자르 본주)'를 파는지 물어보세요.

20 또한, 만약 맛있는 간식을 원한다면, 터키 전통 사탕인 'lokum(로쿰)'을 꼭 드셔 보세요.

21 2 태국의 Damnoen Saduak(담는 사두악) 수상 시장

22 과거에 태국 사람들은 강에서 물건을 교환했습니다.

23 이것이 태국 수상 시장의 시작이었습니다.

24 도로 교통이 개선되면서, 많은 수상 시장이 사라졌습니다.

25 그러나 1960년대 후반부터 일부가 다시 생겨나 전통을 이어가고 있습니다.

26 오늘날, 가장 인기 있는 수상 시장 중 하나는 Damnoen Saduak 수상 시장입니다.

27 그곳은 전 세계에서 온 관광객들로 항상 붐빕니다.

28 배에서 직접 현지 음식과 전통 선물을 살 수 있습니다.

29 Extra Tip I _____ _____ you have ever had a meal on water.

30 _____ _____, try noodles like *pad thai*.

31 The sellers will cook them on their boats and pass them to you _____ _____ _____ _____ _____.

32 3 Aalsmeer Flower Market, _____ _____

33 The Netherlands means "_____ _____."

34 _____ the name _____, about 70% of the country sits _____ _____ _____.

35 _____, the Dutch built up the land, and one effective way to use it was _____ _____ flowers and sell them.

36 It is, _____, _____ _____ that the country has the largest flower market in the world: the Aalsmeer Flower Market.

37 The building _____ the market _____ _____ is bigger than 120 soccer fields.

38 The market is busy with thousands of _____ carts.

39 They are _____ mostly by electric-powered trucks.

40 Every day, _____ _____ _____ flowers are traded and shipped to all _____ of the world.

41 Extra Tip You may wonder _____ you can buy _____ _____ _____ flowers at the market.

42 Sadly, you cannot, but you can see _____ _____ _____ _____ _____.

29 추가 정보 여러분이 물 위에서 식사해 본 적이 있는지 궁금하네요.

30 만약 그렇지 않다면, 'pad thai(팟 타이)' 같은 면 요리를 드셔 보세요.

31 상인들이 배에서 음식을 만들어 긴 낚싯대로 건네줄 겁니다.

32 3 네덜란드 Aalsmeer(알스메이르) 꽃 시장

33 네덜란드는 '저지대'라는 뜻입니다.

34 이름에서 알 수 있듯이, 이 나라의 약 70%가 해수면보다 낮습니다.

35 그래서 네덜란드 사람들은 땅을 지어 올렸고, 그것을 사용하는 효과적인 방법은 꽃을 재배하고 파는 것이었습니다.

36 그러므로 네덜란드에 세계에서 가장 큰 꽃 시장인 Aalsmeer 꽃 시장이 있다는 것은 놀라운 일이 아닙니다.

37 시장이 들어선 건물은 축구장 120개보다 큽니다.

38 시장은 꽃이 가득 든 수천 개의 수레로 분주합니다.

39 수레는 대부분 전동 트럭에 의해 움직입니다.

40 매일, 약 2천만 송이의 꽃이 거래되어 세계 각지로 운송됩니다.

41 추가 정보 시장에서 꽃을 조금 살 수 있는지 궁금할 겁니다.

42 애석하게도 안 되지만, 꽃이 도매로 어떻게 거래되는지를 볼 수 있습니다.

● 우리말을 참고하여 본문을 영작하시오.

1 Leah의 여행 이야기

➡ _____

2 저는 Leah입니다.

➡ _____

3 18세 때부터 여행 블로그를 써 왔습니다.

➡ _____

4 저는 여기저기 다니며 제 경험을 독자들과 공유하고 있습니다.

➡ _____

5 꼭 방문해야 할 세계의 시장들

➡ _____

6 20**년 7월 15일

➡ _____

7 시장 방문은 한 나라의 문화에 대해 배우는 좋은 방법입니다.

➡ _____

8 시장은 사람들을 만나고, 역사를 배우고, 또 지역 음식을 맛볼 수 있는 장소입니다.

➡ _____

9 다른 문화를 발견하는 데에 더 좋은 방법이 있을지 모르겠습니다.

➡ _____

10 1 터키의 Grand Bazaar(그랜드 바자)

➡ _____

11 터키는 동양과 서양이 만나는 나라이고, 그래서 오랜 교역의 전통을 가지고 있습니다.

➡ _____

12 터키는 Grand Bazaar 같은 대형 시장이 생겨나기에 자연스러운 곳입니다.

➡ _____

13 Grand Bazaar는 1455년 이스탄불에 지어졌습니다.

➡ _____

14 그 당시에 이 시장에는 큰 건물이 두 개 있었고, 거기서 사람들은 직물이나 금 같은 물건을 교환했습니다.

➡ _____

15 오늘날 Grand Bazaar는 훨씬 크고, 세계에서 가장 큰 지붕이 덮인 시장입니다.

➡ _____

16 64개의 거리와 4,000개 이상의 상점이 한 지붕 아래에 있습니다.

➡ _____

17 그 시장은 매일 25만 명 이상의 방문객을 불러 모읍니다.

➡ _____

18 그곳에서는 상상할 수 있는 거의 모든 물건을 살 수 있습니다.

➡ _____

19 추가 정보: 가게 주인에게 행운을 기원하는 터키 전통 상징인 'nazar boncuğu(나자르 본주)'를 파는지 물어보세요.

➡ _____

20 또한, 만약 맛있는 간식을 원한다면, 터키 전통 사탕인 'lokum(로쿰)'을 꼭 드셔 보세요.

➡ _____

21 2 태국의 Damnoen Saduak(담는 사두악) 수상 시장

➡ _____

22 과거에 태국 사람들은 강에서 물건을 교환했습니다.

➡ _____

23 이것이 태국 수상 시장의 시작이었습니다.

➡ _____

24 도로 교통이 개선되면서, 많은 수상 시장이 사라졌습니다.

➡ _____

25 그러나 1960년대 후반부터 일부가 다시 생겨나 전통을 이어 가고 있습니다.

➡ _____

26 오늘날, 가장 인기 있는 수상 시장 중 하나는 Damnoen Saduak 수상 시장입니다.

➡ _____

27 그곳은 전 세계에서 온 관광객들로 항상 붐빕니다.

➡ _____

28 배에서 직접 현지 음식과 전통 선물을 살 수 있습니다.

➡ _____

29 추가 정보: 여러분이 물 위에서 식사해 본 적이 있는지 궁금하네요.

➡ _____

30 만약 그렇지 않다면, 'pad thai(팟 타이)' 같은 면 요리를 드셔 보세요.

➡ _____

31 상인들이 배에서 음식을 만들어 긴 낚싯대로 건네줄 겁니다.

➡ _____

32 3 네덜란드 Aalsmeer(알스메이르) 꽃 시장

➡ _____

33 네덜란드는 '저지대'라는 뜻입니다.

➡ _____

34 이름에서 알 수 있듯이, 이 나라의 약 70%가 해수면보다 낮습니다.

➡ _____

35 그래서 네덜란드 사람들은 땅을 지어 올렸고, 그것을 사용하는 효과적인 방법은 꽃을 재배하고 파는 것이었습니다.

➡ _____

_____

36 그러므로 네덜란드에 세계에서 가장 큰 꽃 시장인 Aalsmeer 꽃 시장이 있다는 것은 놀라운 일이 아닙니다.

➡ _____

_____

37 시장이 들어선 건물은 축구장 120개보다 큽니다.

➡ _____

38 시장은 꽃이 가득 든 수천 개의 수레로 분주합니다.

➡ _____

39 수레는 대부분 전동 트럭에 의해 움직입니다.

➡ _____

40 매일, 약 2천만 송이의 꽃이 거래되어 세계 각지로 운송됩니다.

➡ _____

41 추가 정보: 시장에서 꽃을 조금 살 수 있는지 궁금할 겁니다.

➡ _____

42 애석하게도 안 되지만, 꽃이 도매로 어떻게 거래되는지를 볼 수 있습니다.

➡ _____

[01~03] 다음 글을 읽고 물음에 답하시오.

Must-Visit Markets Around the World

July 15, 20**

Visiting markets (A)[is / are] a good way ⓐto learn about the culture of a country. Markets are places where you can meet people, learn history, and taste local food. I wonder (B)[that / whether] there is any better way to discover (C)[another / the other] culture.

 서답형

01 위 글의 괄호 (A)~(C)에서 문맥이나 어법상 알맞은 낱말을 골라 쓰시오.

➡ (A) _____ (B) _____ (C) _____

중요

02 위 글의 종류로 알맞은 것을 고르시오.

① review　　　　② travel blog
③ biography　　　④ summary
⑤ book report

03 위 글의 밑줄 친 ⓐto learn과 to부정사의 용법이 같은 것을 모두 고르시오.

① It is about time for you to learn English.
② Can you tell me how to learn English?
③ She is old enough to learn ballet.
④ He is not a man to learn from his mistakes.
⑤ English is hard to learn.

[04~06] 다음 글을 읽고 물음에 답하시오.

1 Grand Bazaar, Turkey

Turkey is a country where East meets West, so it has a long tradition of trade. (①) The market was built in 1455 in Istanbul. (②) Back then, the market had two big buildings, and people traded goods like cloth and gold there. (③)

Today the Grand Bazaar is ⓐmuch bigger, and it is the largest covered market in the world. (④) It has 64 streets and more than 4,000 shops under one roof. (⑤) The market attracts over 250,000 visitors every day. You can buy almost any imaginable item there.

04 위 글의 밑줄 친 ⓐmuch와 바꿔 쓸 수 없는 말을 고르시오.

① still　　　　② more　　　　③ even
④ a lot　　　　⑤ far

05 위 글의 흐름으로 보아, 주어진 문장이 들어가기에 가장 적절한 곳은?

> It is a natural place for large markets like the Grand Bazaar.

①　　　②　　　③　　　④　　　⑤

중요

 According to the passage, which is NOT true?

① Turkey has a long tradition of trade because it is a country in which East meets West.
② The Grand Bazaar was built in 1455 in Istanbul.
③ At that time when it was built, the Grand Bazaar had two big buildings.
④ Today the Grand Bazaar is the largest outdoor market in the world.
⑤ The Grand Bazaar attracts over 250,000 visitors every day.

[07~09] 다음 글을 읽고 물음에 답하시오.

2 Damnoen Saduak Floating Market, Thailand

In the past, Thai people traded goods on rivers. This was the beginning of floating markets in Thailand. With better road transportation, many floating markets disappeared. Since the late 1960s, however, some of (A)them have come back and kept the tradition alive.

Today, one of the most popular floating markets is Damnoen Saduak Floating Market. It is always crowded _____ⓐ_____ tourists from all over the world. You can buy local foods and traditional gift items directly _____ⓑ_____ boats.

07 위 글의 빈칸 ⓐ와 ⓑ에 들어갈 전치사가 바르게 짝지어진 것은?

ⓐ	ⓑ		ⓐ	ⓑ
① at – in			② with – from	
③ at – from			④ by – for	
⑤ with – for				

08 다음 빈칸에 위 글의 밑줄 친 (A)them이 가리키는 것을 쓰시오.

➡ the _____ _____ that disappeared

09 위 글의 주제로 알맞은 것을 고르시오.

① the beginning of floating markets in Thailand

② the disappearance of many floating markets

③ the comeback of some floating markets in Thailand and the revival of the tradition

④ the most famous tourist attraction in Thailand

⑤ how to buy local foods and traditional gift items in Thailand

[10~13] 다음 글을 읽고 물음에 답하시오.

3 Aalsmeer Flower Market, The Netherlands

The Netherlands means "low lands." (A)As the name suggests, about 70% of the country sits below sea level. (①) Thus, the _____ⓐ_____ built up the land, and one effective way to use it was to grow flowers and sell them. (②)

The building where the market is housed is bigger than 120 soccer fields. (③) The market is busy with thousands of flower-filled carts. (④) They are moved mostly by electric-powered trucks. (⑤) Every day, around 20 million flowers are traded and shipped to all corners of the world.

10 위 글의 빈칸 ⓐ에 d로 시작하는 말을 쓰시오.

➡ _____

11 위 글의 밑줄 친 (A)As와 같은 의미로 쓰인 것을 고르시오.

① As one grows older, one becomes more silent.

② As the door was open, I could see the inside.

③ Her anger grew as she talked.

④ As he is honest, he is trusted by everyone.

⑤ As the proverb says, a little learning is a dangerous thing.

12 위 글의 흐름으로 보아, 주어진 문장이 들어가기에 가장 적절한 곳은?

> It is, therefore, no surprise that the country has the largest flower market in the world: the Aalsmeer Flower Market.

①	②	③	④	⑤

13 위 글의 네덜란드의 사례에 어울리는 속담으로 가장 알맞은 것을 고르시오.

① Prevention is better than cure.

② Haste makes waste.

③ If life gives you a lemon, make lemonade.

④ It never rains but it pours.

⑤ Many hands make light work.

[14~17] 다음 글을 읽고 물음에 답하시오.

1 Grand Bazaar, Turkey

Turkey is a country ___ⓐ___ East meets West, so it has a long tradition of trade. ⓑIt is a natural place for large markets like the Grand Bazaar. The market was built in ① 1455 in Istanbul. Back then, the market had two big buildings, and people traded goods ②like cloth and gold there.

Today the Grand Bazaar is much bigger, and it is the largest covered market in the world. It has ③64 streets and more than ④4,000 shops under one roof. The market attracts over ⑤250,000 visitors every day. You can buy almost any imaginable item there.

14 위 글의 빈칸 ⓐ에 들어갈 알맞은 말을 모두 고르시오.

① for which　　② where　　③ when

④ which　　⑤ in which

15 위 글의 밑줄 친 ⓑIt이 가리키는 것을 본문에서 찾아 쓰시오.

➡ _____

16 다음 중 위 글의 밑줄 친 ①~⑤에 대한 설명이 옳지 않은 것을 고르시오.

① fourteen fifty-five로 읽는다.

② such as로 바꿔 쓸 수 있다.

③ sixty-four로 읽는다.

④ four thousands로 읽는다.

⑤ two hundred and fifty thousand로 읽는다.

17 위 글의 주제로 알맞은 것을 고르시오.

① Thanks to its location, Turkey has various cultures.

② People built the Grand Bazaar in Istanbul.

③ The location of Turkey led to the birth of the Grand Bazaar.

④ Today the Grand Bazaar is much bigger than before.

⑤ The Grand Bazaar is an ideal place for shopping.

[18~19] 다음 글을 읽고 물음에 답하시오.

2 Damnoen Saduak Floating Market, Thailand

In the past, Thai people traded goods on rivers. This was the beginning of floating markets in Thailand. With better road transportation, many floating markets disappeared. Since the late 1960s, ___ⓐ___, some of them have come back and kept the tradition alive.

18 위 글의 빈칸 ⓐ에 들어갈 알맞은 말을 고르시오.

① for example　　② in addition

③ however　　④ as a result

⑤ that is

서답형

19 Why did many floating markets disappear? Fill in the blanks with suitable words.

> As the _____ _____ got better, many of them disappeared.

[20~22] 다음 글을 읽고 물음에 답하시오.

2 Damnoen Saduak Floating Market, Thailand
  Today, ⓐ가장 인기 있는 수상 시장 중 하나는 Damnoen Saduak 수상 시장입니다. It is always crowded with tourists from all over the world. You can buy local foods and traditional gift items directly from boats.

Extra Tip I wonder if you ⓑhave ever had a meal on water. If not, try noodles like *pad thai*. The sellers will cook them on their boats and pass them to you with a long fishing pole.

서답형

20 위 글의 밑줄 친 ⓐ의 우리말에 맞게 주어진 어휘를 이용하여 12 단어로 영작하시오.

> floating, Damnoen Saduak Floating Market

➡ _____

_____

21 위 글의 밑줄 친 ⓑ의 현재완료와 용법이 같은 것을 모두 고르시오.

① How many times <u>has</u> she <u>eaten</u> *pad thai*?
② I <u>have</u> just <u>finished</u> reading the book.
③ How long <u>have</u> you <u>studied</u> English?
④ I <u>have</u> never <u>visited</u> New York.
⑤ We <u>have</u> lived in this house for 10 years.

중요

22 Which question CANNOT be answered after reading the passage?

① What is Damnoen Saduak Floating Market?
② When was Damnoen Saduak Floating Market developed?
③ What can you buy at Damnoen Saduak Floating Market?
④ What kind of dish is *pad thai*?
⑤ Can you buy *pad thai* without getting off your boats?

[23~25] 다음 글을 읽고 물음에 답하시오.

3 Aalsmeer Flower Market, The Netherlands
  (A)The building which the market is housed is bigger than 120 soccer fields. The market is busy with thousands of flower-filled carts. They are moved mostly by electric-powered trucks. Every day, (B)약 2천만 송이의 꽃이 거래되어 세계 각지로 운송됩니다.

Extra Tip You may wonder whether you can buy just a few flowers at the market. Sadly, you cannot, but you can see how ⓐ_____ flower trading works.

서답형

23 주어진 영영풀이를 참고하여 빈칸 ⓐ에 철자 w로 시작하는 단어를 쓰시오.

> the selling of goods to merchants, usually in large quantities for resale to consumers

➡ _____

서답형

24 위 글의 밑줄 친 (A)에서 어법상 틀린 부분을 찾아 고치시오.

_____ ➡ _____ 또는

_____ ➡ _____

서답형

25 위 글의 밑줄 친 (B)의 우리말에 맞게 주어진 어휘를 알맞게 배열하시오.

> shipped / around / the world / and / of / are / 20 million flowers / corners / to / traded / all

➡ _____

_____

[26~28] 다음 글을 읽고 물음에 답하시오.

2 Damnoen Saduak Floating Market, Thailand

(A)Today, one of the most popular floating markets are Damnoen Saduak Floating Market. It is always crowded with tourists ____ⓐ____ all over the world. You can buy local foods and traditional gift items directly from boats.

Extra Tip I wonder if you have ever had a meal on water. If not, try noodles like *pad thai*. The sellers will cook (B)them on their boats and pass them to you ____ⓑ____ a long fishing pole.

26 위 글의 빈칸 ⓐ와 ⓑ에 들어갈 전치사가 바르게 짝지어진 것은?

　　　ⓐ　　ⓑ　　　　　ⓐ　　ⓑ
① from – with　② at – on
③ on – by　④ from – on
⑤ at – with

서답형

27 위 글의 밑줄 친 (A)에서 어법상 틀린 부분을 찾아 고치시오.

_____ ➡ _____

서답형

28 위 글의 밑줄 친 (B)them이 가리키는 것을 본문에서 찾아 쓰시오.

➡ _____

[29~30] 다음 글을 읽고 물음에 답하시오.

3 Aalsmeer Flower Market, The Netherlands

The Netherlands means "low lands." As the name suggests, about 70% of the country sits (A)[above / below] sea level. Thus, the Dutch built up the land, and one effective way to use it was to grow flowers and sell them. It is, therefore, no surprise that the country has the largest flower market in the world: the Aalsmeer Flower Market.

The building where the market is housed is bigger than 120 soccer fields. The market is busy with (B)[thousand / thousands] of flower-filled carts. They are moved mostly by electric-powered trucks. Every day, around 20 (C)[million / millions] flowers are traded and shipped to all corners of the world.

서답형

29 위 글의 괄호 (A)~(C)에서 문맥이나 어법상 알맞은 낱말을 골라 쓰시오.

➡ (A) _____ (B) _____ (C) _____

30 위 글의 제목으로 알맞은 것을 고르시오.

① The Reason the Netherlands Means "Low Lands"
② How to Utilize Low Lands
③ Could It Be Possible? A Flower Market Bigger than 120 Soccer Fields?
④ The Netherlands Has the Largest Flower Market in the World? No Wonder!
⑤ Thousands of Carts! Don't Worry, They're Electric-powered Trucks!

[01~03] 다음 글을 읽고 물음에 답하시오.

> I am Leah. I ___ⓐ___ a travel blog since I was 18. I go places and share my experiences ___ⓑ___ my readers.
>
> **Must-Visit Markets Around the World**
>
> July 15, 20**
>
> Visiting markets is a good way to learn about the culture of a country. Markets are places where you can meet people, learn history, and taste local food. I wonder whether there is any better way to discover another culture.

01 다음 문장과 같은 뜻이 되도록 위 글의 빈칸 ⓐ에 write를 알맞은 형태로 쓰시오.

> I started to write a travel blog when I was 18, and I am still writing it.

➡ _____

02 위 글의 빈칸 ⓑ에 들어갈 알맞은 전치사를 쓰시오.

➡ _____

03 본문의 내용과 일치하도록 다음 빈칸 (A)와 (B)에 알맞은 단어를 쓰시오.

> Leah thinks it wouldn't be easy to find any better way to discover another culture than _____ _____.

[04~06] 다음 글을 읽고 물음에 답하시오.

> **1 Grand Bazaar, Turkey**
>
> Turkey is a country where East meets West, so it has a long tradition of trade. It is a natural place for large markets like the Grand Bazaar. The market was built in 1455 in Istanbul. Back then, the market had two big buildings, and people traded goods like cloth and gold there.
>
> Today the Grand Bazaar is much bigger, and it is the largest covered market in the world. It has 64 streets and ⓐmore than 4,000 shops under one roof. The market attracts over 250,000 visitors every day. You can buy almost any imaginable item there.

04 Why is Turkey a natural place for large markets like the Grand Bazaar? Write two reasons in English beginning with "Because".

➡ (1) _____
   (2) _____

05 위 글의 밑줄 친 ⓐmore than과 바꿔 쓸 수 있는 말을 본문에서 찾아 쓰시오.

➡ _____

06 다음 빈칸 (A)와 (B)에 알맞은 단어를 넣어 처음 지어질 당시의 Grand Bazaar에 대한 소개를 완성하시오.

> It was built in the mid 15th century in Istanbul and *consisted of (A)_____ big buildings. People bought, sold, or exchanged (B)_____ such as cloth and gold at the market.
>
> *consist of: ~으로 이루어지다[구성되다]

[07~09] 다음 글을 읽고 물음에 답하시오.

2 Damnoen Saduak Floating Market, Thailand

In the past, Thai people traded goods on rivers. This was the beginning of floating markets in Thailand. With better road transportation, many floating markets (A)[disappeared / were disappeared]. Since the late 1960s, however, some of them have come back and ⓐ the tradition (B)[live / alive].

Today, one of the most popular floating markets is Damnoen Saduak Floating Market. It is always crowded with tourists from all over the world. You can buy local foods and traditional gift items (C)[directly / indirectly] from boats.

07 위 글의 빈칸 ⓐ에 keep을 알맞은 형태로 쓰시오. (한 단어)

➡ _____

08 위 글의 괄호 (A)~(C)에서 문맥이나 어법상 알맞은 낱말을 골라 쓰시오.

➡ (A) _____ (B) _____ (C) _____

09 본문의 내용과 일치하도록 다음 빈칸 (A)와 (B)에 알맞은 단어를 쓰시오.

> The (A)_____ _____ in Thailand began from the tradition that people traded goods (B)_____ _____ and today, one of the most popular floating markets is Damnoen Saduak Floating Market.

[10~11] 다음 글을 읽고 물음에 답하시오.

3 Aalsmeer Flower Market, The Netherlands

The Netherlands means "low lands." As the name suggests, about 70% of the country sits below sea level. Thus, the Dutch built up the land, and one effective way to use it was to grow flowers and sell them. It is, therefore, no surprise that the country has the largest flower market in the world: the Aalsmeer Flower Market.

The building where the market ⓐ is bigger than 120 soccer fields. The market is busy with thousands of flower-filled carts. They are moved mostly by electric-powered trucks. Every day, around 20 million flowers are traded and shipped to all corners of the world.

10 위 글의 빈칸 ⓐ에 house를 알맞은 형태로 쓰시오.

➡ _____

11 Why is it no surprise that the Netherlands has the largest flower market in the world: the Aalsmeer Flower Market? Fill in the blanks (A) and (B) with suitable words.

> Because about 70% of the Netherlands is situated (A)_____ _____ _____, the Dutch built up the land. One effective way to use it was (B)_____ _____ _____ and sell them, which resulted in the largest flower market in the world.

구석구석

My Speaking Portfolio – Step 2

A: How do you want to travel? I wonder <u>if you want to travel with friends or</u>
    if = whether   간접의문문
<u>family.</u>

B: Well, I want to travel with my friends.

                ......

A: Okay. Do you want to visit museums or markets?

B: I want to visit museums. It's a great way <u>to learn</u> about the local culture.
        앞 문장의 내용(= To visit museums)   to부정사의 형용사적 용법

구문해설 • local: 지역의, 현지의

A: 어떻게 여행하는 것을 원하니? 나는 네가 친구들이나 가족들과 여행하는 것을 좋아하는지 궁금해.

B: 음, 나는 내 친구들과 여행하고 싶어.

A: 알겠어. 너는 박물관 또는 시장을 방문하고 싶니?

B: 나는 박물관을 가보고 싶어. 그것은 지역 문화에 대해 배우는 데 좋은 방법이야.

After You Read

This country is a place <u>where</u> East meets West and has a long tradition of
        관계부사
trade.

This is a country <u>where</u> trading on boats has a long history.
        관계부사
<u>More than two-thirds of</u> the country <u>is</u> below sea level.
부분을 나타내는 말이 주어일 경우 뒤에 나오는 명사의 수에 동사를 일치시킨다.

구문해설 • tradition: 전통 • sea level: 해수면

이 나라는 동양과 서양이 만나는 장소이고, 오랜 교역의 전통을 가지고 있다.

이곳은 배에서 거래하는 오랜 역사가 있는 나라이다.

그 나라의 3분의 2 이상이 해수면보다 낮다.

Wrap Up READING

Every Saturday, I go to Oakville Farmers' Market. That is the place <u>where</u>
            선행사가 장소일 때 관계부사 where
I buy food for the coming week. <u>There</u> I find all kinds of fresh vegetables.
            = At Oakville Farmers' Market
<u>They</u> are usually picked only a few hours before I buy <u>them</u>. I also find
= All kinds of fresh vegetables that I find there   = all kinds of fresh vegetables
bread, meat, and home-made jam. Because I can buy the items directly from

the producers, <u>they</u> are usually <u>much</u> cheaper than at other stores. The local
        = the items   = even/still/far/a lot
farmers are always kind and ready to <u>share</u> gardening tips and recipes with
                share A with B: A를 B와 공유하다
visitors, too. I love <u>going</u> to the farmers' market.
        = to go

구문해설 • pick: (꽃을) 꺾다, (과일 등을) 따다 • directly: 직접적으로 • producer: 생산자
       • gardening: 원예 • recipe: 조리법

토요일마다 나는 **Oakville** 농산물 직거래 시장에 간다. 그곳은 내가 다음 주에 먹을 음식을 사는 곳이다. 그곳에서 나는 온갖 종류의 신선한 채소를 구한다. 채소들은 대개 내가 사기 불과 몇 시간 전에 수확된 것이다. 나는 또한 빵, 고기, 그리고 집에서 만든 잼도 구한다. 물건을 생산자에게서 직접 살 수 있어서 그것들은 대개 다른 가게에서보다 훨씬 저렴하다. 지역 농부들은 항상 친절하고, 원예 정보나 조리법을 방문객들과 공유할 준비가 되어 있다. 나는 농산물 직거래 시장에 가는 것을 좋아한다.

영역별 핵심문제

Words & Expressions

01 다음 짝지어진 단어의 관계가 같도록 빈칸에 알맞은 말을 쓰시오.

> effective: ineffective = directly: _____

02 다음 영영풀이가 가리키는 것을 고르시오.

> cultural beliefs and customs passed down through generations

① tradition   ② civilization
③ taste   ④ transportation
⑤ cart

03 다음 주어진 문장의 밑줄 친 last와 같은 의미로 쓰인 것은?

> I wonder if there's milk that lasts longer.

① Who wants the last piece of pizza?
② It hardly snowed last winter.
③ I voted Tom in the last election.
④ With his last jump, he won the game.
⑤ While my strength lasts, I'll work for my students.

04 다음 문장에 공통으로 들어갈 말을 고르시오.

> • Did you _____ how your brother was in a bad mood?
> • Prices can be changed without any _____.
> • Did you _____ any changes on her face?

① pick   ② notice   ③ carry
④ discover   ⑤ suggest

05 다음 중 밑줄 친 부분의 뜻풀이가 바르지 않은 것은?

① Most teenagers think youth will last forever. (지속하다, 오래가다)
② Can you discover the secret of his magic trick? (발견하다)
③ In order to save his dog, he tried every means imaginable. (상상할 수 있는)
④ Fruit attracts flies and bugs. (끌어들이다)
⑤ The art museum is housed in an old school. (집)

06 다음 주어진 우리말과 일치하도록 주어진 어구를 알맞게 배열하시오.

(1) 우리는 마을에 두 개의 지역 신문을 갖고 있다.
(have / our / local / we / newspapers / town / two / in)
➡ _____

(2) 박물관은 관광객들로 늘 붐빈다.
(with / is / always / the museum / tourists / crowded)
➡ _____

(3) 교육을 위해 학생들이 소셜 미디어를 사용할 수 있는 약간의 효과적인 방법들이 있다.
(effective / can / use / for / social media / there / education / are / ways / some / students)
➡ _____

07 다음 우리말에 맞게 빈칸에 알맞은 말을 쓰시오.

(1) 공원은 좋은 날씨를 즐기러 나온 사람들로 붐빈다.

➡ The park _____ people who come out to enjoy the good weather.

(2) 나의 오빠는 요즘 구직으로 바쁘다.

➡ My brother _____ his job search these days.

(3) 당근에는 비타민과 미네랄이 풍부하다.

➡ Carrots _____ vitamins and minerals.

Conversation

[08~10] 다음 대화를 읽고 물음에 답하시오.

W: Can I have the bill, please?

M: Here you are. Did you enjoy the meal? ⓐ

W: It was great. I liked the *gondrebap* very much. ⓑ

M: Thanks. It's also good for your health. ⓒ

W: Oh, really? ⓓ

M: Yes. *Gondre* is rich in vitamins A and C. ⓔ

W: Good. _____ (A)

M: Sure. Do you want me to give you the recipe for *gondrebap*?

W: Yes, that'd be great.

08 위 대화의 ⓐ~ⓔ 중 주어진 문장이 들어가기에 적절한 곳은?

> It also digests well.

① ⓐ   ② ⓑ   ③ ⓒ   ④ ⓓ   ⑤ ⓔ

09 위 대화의 빈칸 (A)에 들어갈 말로 나머지와 의도가 <u>다른</u> 것은?

① I'm curious whether I could buy some *gondre* here.

② Can you tell me if I could buy some *gondre* here?

③ I wonder if I could buy some *gondre* here.

④ I want to know if I could buy some *gondre* here.

⑤ I don't have any doubt that I could buy some *gondre* here.

10 위 대화의 내용과 일치하도록 빈칸을 완성하시오.

> The woman liked the *gondrebap* very much. She heard that it is good for the health, because (A)_____ _____. In addition, she found that (B)_____. So, she decided to buy some *gondre*.

[11~13] 다음 대화를 읽고 물음에 답하시오.

Grandma: Excuse me. Can you help me with this milk?

Brian: Sure. What is it?

Grandma: Read me the date, please.

Brian: Oh, do you want me to tell you the best-before date?

Grandma: Yes, I forgot my glasses.

Brian: Let me see. You should drink it by June 7.

Grandma: That's too soon. I wonder if there's one that lasts longer.

Brian: Wait. I found one. This one is good until June 11.

Grandma: Oh, I'll take that one. Thank you very much.

Brian: You're welcome.

11 What does the grandma want Brian to do for her?

➡ _____
_____

12 Why doesn't the grandma take the first milk?

➡ _____

13 Until when should the grandma drink the milk that she took?

➡ _____

14 다음 대화가 자연스럽게 이어지도록 순서대로 배열하시오.

> M: Welcome to the Tourist Information Office! How may I help you?
> (A) I'm so lucky. Thank you.
> (B) Is there a special place you're looking for?
> (C) Yes. I'd like to try some local food.
> (D) Hi, I wonder if there's a tourist map of the town.
> (E) Then go to Jeongseon Market. It opens every five days, and it's open today.

➡ _____

Grammar

15 다음 문장 중에서 어법상 어색한 문장을 고르시오.

① Markets are places where you can meet people, learn history, and taste local food.
② Do you know the year in which the next Olympic Games take place?
③ I remember the summer when I learned water skiing.
④ This was the way I made *bibimbab*.
⑤ Do you know the reason which she left the party so early?

16 다음 밑줄 친 부분과 바꿔 쓸 수 있는 것은?

> We want to know <u>if</u> she is safe.

① why   ② that   ③ what
④ which   ⑤ whether

17 다음 그림을 보고 주어진 어휘를 활용하여 빈칸을 알맞게 채우시오.

Justin asked her _____.
(with him, hiking, will)

➡ _____

18 두 문장을 관계부사를 사용하여 한 문장으로 썼을 때, 빈칸의 문장을 쓰시오.

(1) May is the month.
  + _____
  → May is the month when I take the mid-term exam.
(2) Is this the store?
  + _____
  → Is this the store where you bought the shoes yesterday?
(3) Tell me the reason.
  + _____
  → Tell me the reason why she was so upset last night.

19 다음 @~⑨ 중 어법상 옳은 것을 <u>모두</u> 고르시오.

> @ The building when the market is housed is bigger than 120 soccer fields.
>
> ⓑ Do you remember the date where our school festival will take place?
>
> ⓒ Computers have changed the way how people work.
>
> ⓓ This is actually one of the reasons which I am applying to your company.
>
> ⓔ Tell me whether ants lay eggs.
>
> ⓕ He thought deeply if to change jobs.
>
> ⓖ Do you want to know whether your axe is in this pond?

➡ _____

Reading

[20~22] 다음 글을 읽고 물음에 답하시오.

1 Grand Bazaar, Turkey
Extra Tip Ask shop owners @if they ⓑcarry *nazar boncuğu*, a traditional Turkish symbol for good luck. Also, ⓒif you want a nice snack, ⓓ꼭 드셔 보세요 *lokum*, a traditional Turkish candy.

20 아래 〈보기〉에서 위 글의 밑줄 친 @if, ⓒif와 문법적 쓰임이 같은 것을 각각 고르시오.

> ┌ 보기 ┐
> ① He couldn't tell if she was laughing or crying.
> ② I can come at once if necessary.
> ③ Give him this note if you see him.
> ④ Do you know if he's married?
> ⑤ You can stay for the weekend if you like.

➡ @와 같은 것: _____, ⓒ와 같은 것: _____

21 위 글의 밑줄 친 ⓑcarry와 같은 의미로 쓰인 것을 고르시오.

① This elevator cannot <u>carry</u> more than twelve persons.
② I always <u>carry</u> a camera.
③ Newspapers <u>carry</u> weather reports.
④ This shop doesn't <u>carry</u> clothing for men.
⑤ Metals <u>carry</u> heat easily.

22 위 글의 밑줄 친 ⓓ의 우리말에 맞게 주어진 어휘를 이용하여 4 단어로 영작하시오.

> make, try

➡ _____

[23~24] 다음 글을 읽고 물음에 답하시오.

JJIMJILBANG Do you want to experience the real Korea? Then try a *jjimjilbang*. It is a place where you can experience a traditional Korean way to relax. It can easily be found in any big city. You can rest on a hot floor or take a nap. Also, you can read a book or chat with friends as you lie on the floor. The best food you can try here is boiled eggs. The place is easy on your wallet because it only costs about 13,000 won. It is usually open 24 hours a day.

23 위 글의 종류로 알맞은 것을 고르시오.

① essay ② travel brochure
③ manual ④ book report
⑤ article

24 위 글을 읽고 알 수 <u>없는</u> 것을 고르시오.

① 추천하는 장소 ② 추천 음식
③ 부대시설들 ④ 입장료
⑤ 운영 시간

[25~27] 다음 글을 읽고 물음에 답하시오.

2 Damnoen Saduak Floating Market, Thailand

In the past, _____ⓐ_____ people traded goods on rivers. This was the beginning of floating markets in Thailand. ⓑ도로 교통이 개선되면서, 많은 수상 시장이 사라졌습니다. Since the late 1960s, however, some of them have come back and kept the tradition alive.

Today, one of the most popular floating markets is Damnoen Saduak Floating Market. It is always crowded with tourists from all over the world. You can buy local foods and traditional gift items directly from boats.

25 위 글의 빈칸 ⓐ에 Thailand를 알맞은 형태로 쓰시오.

➡ _____

26 위 글의 밑줄 친 ⓑ의 우리말에 맞게 주어진 어휘를 이용하여 8 단어로 영작하시오.

> with, road transportation

➡ _____

_____

27 According to the passage, which is NOT true?

① In the past, people traded goods on rivers in Thailand.

② As the road transportation becomes better, many of the floating markets have come back in Thailand.

③ Since the late 1960s, some of the floating markets have kept the tradition of trading goods on rivers alive.

④ Damnoen Saduak Floating Market is always crowded with tourists from all over the world.

⑤ It is possible to buy local foods and traditional gift items directly from boats at Damnoen Saduak Floating Market.

[28~29] 다음 글을 읽고 물음에 답하시오.

3 Aalsmeer Flower Market, The Netherlands

The Netherlands means "low lands." As the name suggests, about 70% of the country sits below sea level. _____ⓐ_____, the Dutch built up the land, and one effective way to use it was to grow flowers and sell them. It is, therefore, no surprise that the country has the largest flower market in the world: the Aalsmeer Flower Market.

The building where the market is housed is bigger than 120 soccer fields. The market is busy with thousands of flower-filled carts. They are moved mostly by electric-powered trucks. Every day, around 20 million flowers are traded and shipped to all corners of the world.

28 위 글의 빈칸 ⓐ에 알맞은 것은?

① In other words   ② Thus

③ That is   ④ However

⑤ For example

29 According to the passage, which is NOT true?

① About 70% of the Netherlands is located below sea level.

② One effective way to use the built-up land was to grow flowers and sell them.

③ It is natural that the Netherlands should have the largest flower market in the world.

④ 120 soccer fields are bigger than the building where the market is housed.

⑤ Thousands of flower-filled carts are moved mostly by electric-powered trucks.

[01~03] 다음 대화를 읽고 물음에 답하시오.

M: Welcome to the Tourist Information Office! How may I help you?

W: Hi, I wonder if there's a tourist map of the town.

M: Sure. Is there a special place you're looking for?

W: (A) Yes. I'd like to try some local food.

M: (B) Then go to Jeongseon Market. It opens every five days, and it's open today.

W: (C) I'm so lucky. How can I get there?

M: (D) It takes about 10 minutes.

W: (E) Great. Will you mark the way on the map, please?

M: Sure. Try *gondrebap* when you get there.

✏️ 출제율 95%

01 위 대화의 (A)~(E) 중 주어진 문장이 들어가기에 적절한 곳은?

> You can walk there.

① (A) ② (B) ③ (C) ④ (D) ⑤ (E)

✏️ 출제율 90%

02 위 대화에서 남자와 여자의 관계로 적절한 것은?

① doctor – nurse
② attendant – tourist
③ teacher – student
④ librarian – student
⑤ interviewer – reporter

✏️ 출제율 100%

03 위 대화를 읽고 대답할 수 없는 것은?

① What is the woman looking for at the Tourist Information Office?
② What does the woman want to do?
③ Where does the man recommend to the woman?

④ How long does it take for the woman to get to Jeongseon Market?
⑤ Until what time is Jeongseon Market open?

[04~06] 다음 대화를 읽고 물음에 답하시오.

Grandma: Excuse me. Can you help me with this milk?

Brian: Sure. What is it?

Grandma: Read me the date, please.

Brian: Oh, do you want me to tell you the _____(A)_____ ?

Grandma: Yes, I forgot my glasses.

Brian: Let me see. You should drink it by June 7.

Grandma: That's too soon. I wonder if there's one that (B)lasts longer.

Brian: Wait. I found one. This one is good until June 11.

Grandma: Oh, I'll take that one. Thank you very much.

Brian: You're welcome.

✏️ 출제율 90%

04 위 대화의 빈칸 (A)에 '유통 기한'을 뜻하는 표현을 2 단어로 쓰시오.

➡ _____

✏️ 출제율 95%

05 위 대화의 내용과 일치하지 <u>않는</u> 것은?

① 할머니는 Brian에게 도움을 요청하였다.
② 할머니는 안경을 잃어버리셔서 그것을 계속 찾고 계신다.
③ 할머니는 Brian이 우유의 유통 기한을 읽어주길 원한다.
④ 할머니는 유통 기한이 6월 7일보다 더 긴 게 있는지 궁금해 하신다.
⑤ 할머니는 유통 기한이 6월 11일까지인 우유를 사기로 하셨다.

06 위 대화의 밑줄 친 (B)와 같은 의미로 쓰인 것은?

① Last night, I saw the movie with my friend.
② I caught the last bus home.
③ This is our last bottle of water.
④ She came last in the race.
⑤ The storm lasted three days.

[07~08] 다음 대화를 읽고 물음에 답하시오.

W: Can I have the ⓐbill, please?
M: Here you are. Did you enjoy the meal?
W: It was great. I liked the *gondrebap* very much.
M: Thanks. It's also good for your ⓑhealth.
W: Oh, really?
M: Yes. *Gondre* is rich in vitamins A and C. It also ⓒdigests well.
W: Good. I ⓓwander if I could buy some *gondre* here.
M: Sure. Do you want me to give you the ⓔ recipe for *gondrebap*?
W: Yes, that'd be great.

07 위 대화의 밑줄 친 ⓐ~ⓔ 중 문맥상 어색한 것을 찾아 바르게 고치시오.

➡ _____

08 위 대화를 읽고 대답할 수 없는 것은?

① Where is the woman now?
② What is *gondrebap* good for?
③ Where can the woman buy *gondre*?
④ Who is going to give the recipe for *gondrebap*?
⑤ How much is the woman going to pay for *gondrebap*?

[09~10] 다음 대화를 읽고 물음에 답하시오.

Jane: Dad, look at that cute bag. I wonder how much it is.
Dad: (A)Why don't we go in and check?
Jane: Really? Thanks, Dad.
Dad: I didn't say I will buy it for you. We're just asking the price.
Jane: Of course.

09 위 대화의 밑줄 친 (A)와 바꾸어 쓰기 어색한 것은?

① How about going in and checking?
② I think we can go in and check.
③ It's not fair to go in and check.
④ Let's go in and check.
⑤ What about going in and checking?

10 위 대화의 내용과 일치하지 않는 것은?

① Jane looks at the cute bag.
② Jane wants to know the price of the bag.
③ Jane's dad suggests checking the price of the bag.
④ Jane's dad promises her to buy the bag.
⑤ Jane wants to go into the store with her dad.

11 다음 중 밑줄 친 if의 쓰임이 다른 하나는?

① I'm not sure *if* you're aware of that.
② I wonder *if* my robot can choose the best clothes for me.
③ Put your hand up *if* you know the answer.
④ I asked him *if* he wanted a watch.
⑤ Please tell me *if* you're coming to my show or not.

12 다음 그림을 보고 주어진 어휘를 이용하여 빈칸을 알맞게 채우시오.

Do you know _____?
(this morning, jog, or not)

➡ _____

13 다음 중 어법상 올바른 문장은?

① That's the way how the system works.
② I still remember the evening where we watched the sun go down.
③ The reason when she quit her job is not clear.
④ This is the moment at which the thing begins to move.
⑤ I'm not sure that this will be enough food for the party.

14 다음 두 문장을 관계부사를 이용하여 한 문장으로 쓰시오.

(1) • I often go to the gallery.
   • My mother works at the gallery.

   ➡ _____
   _____

(2) • May I ask you the reason?
   • You made that decision for the reason.

   ➡ _____
   _____

(3) • The pictures were taken on a holiday.
   • We had a picnic together on the holiday.

   ➡ _____
   _____

[15~17] 다음 글을 읽고 물음에 답하시오.

1 Grand Bazaar, Turkey

Turkey is a country where East meets West, so it has a long tradition of trade. It is a natural place for large markets like the Grand Bazaar. The market was built in 1455 in Istanbul. Back then, the market had two big buildings, and people traded goods like cloth and gold there.

Today the Grand Bazaar is much bigger, and it is the largest covered market in the world. It has 64 streets and more than 4,000 shops under one roof. The market attracts over 250,000 visitors every day. You can buy almost any imaginable item there.

15 위 글의 제목으로 알맞은 것을 고르시오.

① In Turkey, East meets West!
② The Effect of Geographical Feature on History
③ The Culture and Economy of Turkey
④ The Grand Bazaar, a Natural Product of the Location of Turkey
⑤ The Effect of Markets on Tourism

16 What's the difference between the old Grand Bazaar and the modern Grand Bazaar? Fill in the blanks (A) and (B) with suitable words.

> The number of the buildings has decreased from (A)_____ to one and the size of the market has become (B)_____ than before.

17 위 글을 읽고 예전의 Grand Bazaar에 대해 알 수 없는 것을 고르시오.

① 탄생 배경   ② 건설 연도
③ 위치   ④ 취급 품목의 예
⑤ 교역 규모

[18~19] 다음 글을 읽고 물음에 답하시오.

2 Damnoen Saduak Floating Market, Thailand
Today, one of the most popular floating markets is Damnoen Saduak Floating Market. It is always crowded with tourists from all over the world. You can buy local foods and traditional gift items directly from boats.

Extra Tip I wonder if you have ever had a meal on water. ⓐIf not, try noodles like *pad thai*. The sellers will cook them on their boats and pass them to you with a long ⓑfishing pole.

18 위 글의 밑줄 친 ⓐIf not에 생략된 말을 넣어 문장을 다시 쓰시오.

➡ _____

19 위 글의 밑줄 친 ⓑfishing과 문법적 쓰임이 같은 것을 <u>모두</u> 고르시오.

① Please smoke in the <u>smoking</u> room.
② Who is the man <u>fishing</u> over there?
③ He needed a <u>walking</u> stick.
④ She is wearing her <u>dancing</u> shoes.
⑤ I saw him <u>fishing</u> in the river yesterday.

[20~22] 다음 글을 읽고 물음에 답하시오.

3 Aalsmeer Flower Market, The Netherlands
The building where the market is housed is bigger than 120 soccer fields. The market is busy with (A)thousands of flower-filled carts. (B)They are moved mostly by electric-powered trucks. Every day, around 20 million flowers are traded and shipped to all corners of the world.

Extra Tip You may wonder whether you can buy just a few flowers at the market. Sadly, you cannot, but you can see _____ⓐ_____ .

20 위 글의 빈칸 ⓐ에 다음 주어진 문장과 같은 의미가 되도록 쓰시오.

How does wholesale flower trading work?

➡ _____

21 위 글의 밑줄 친 (A)를 다음과 같이 바꿔 쓸 때 빈칸에 들어갈 알맞은 말을 두 단어로 쓰시오.

➡ thousands of carts _____ _____ flowers

22 위 글의 밑줄 친 (B)They가 가리키는 것을 본문에서 찾아 쓰시오.

➡ _____

[23~24] 다음 글을 읽고 물음에 답하시오.

Every Saturday, I go to Oakville Farmers' Market. That is the place where I buy food for the coming week. There I find all kinds of fresh vegetables. They are usually picked only a few hours before I buy them. I also find bread, meat, and home-made jam. Because I can buy the items directly from the producers, they are usually much cheaper than at other stores. The local farmers are always kind and ready to share gardening tips and recipes with visitors, too. I love going to the farmers' market.

23 다음 중 글쓴이가 Oakville 농산물 직거래 시장에서 구입하는 것이 <u>아닌</u> 것을 고르시오.

① 신선한 채소　　② 빵　　③ 고기
④ 꽃　　　　　　⑤ 집에서 만든 잼

24 Why can the writer buy the items at a much cheaper price at Oakville Farmers' Market than at other stores? Answer in English beginning with "Because".

➡ _____

_____

[01~03] 다음 대화를 읽고 물음에 답하시오.

M: Welcome to the Tourist Information Office! How may I help you?

W: Hi, I wonder if there's a tourist map of the town.

M: Sure. Is there a special place you're looking for?

W: Yes. I'd like to try some local food.

M: Then go to Jeongseon Market. It opens every five days, and it's open today.

W: I'm so lucky. How can I get there?

M: You can walk there. It takes about 10 minutes.

W: Great. Will you mark the way on the map, please?

M: Sure. Try *gondrebap* when you get there.

01 Why does the woman visit the Tourist Information Office?

➡ _____

02 How often does the market open?

➡ _____

03 What would the woman like to do?

➡ _____

04 다음 문장의 빈칸에 알맞은 말을 쓰시오.

(1) This is the park _____ I played basketball with my friends.

= This is the park _____ _____ I played basketball with my friends.

= This is the park _____ I played basketball with my friends _____.

(2) 1955 was the year _____ my grandpa was born.

= 1955 was the year _____ _____ my grandpa was born.

= 1955 was the year _____ my grandpa was born _____.

(3) That is the reason _____ he visited the tax office again.

= That is the reason _____ _____ he visited the tax office again.

= That is the reason _____ he visited the tax office _____ again.

05 다음 두 문장을 관계부사나 적절한 접속사를 이용하여 한 문장으로 쓰시오.

(1) • The valley was in the national park.
   • Lots of people came to the national park in summer.

➡ _____

(2) • Do you want to know the reason?
   • Why is he so happy?

➡ _____
_____

(3) • I'm curious.
   • Will he tell the truth?

➡ _____
_____

06 다음 우리말을 주어진 어휘를 이용하여 영작하시오.

(1) 경찰관은 그에게 도둑을 봤는지 묻고 있다.
(the police officer, the thief, see, asking, 11 단어)

➡ _____
_____

(2) 어린이날은 내가 많은 선물을 받았던 공휴일이다. (presents, Children's Day, the holiday, lots, got, 11 단어)

➡ _____

_____

[07~09] 다음 글을 읽고 물음에 답하시오.

1 Grand Bazaar, Turkey

Today the Grand Bazaar is much bigger, and it is the largest (A)[covering / covered] market in the world. It has 64 streets and more than 4,000 shops under one roof. The market (B)[attacks / attracts] over 250,000 visitors every day. You can buy almost any (C)[imaginable / imaginary] item there.

Extra Tip Ask shop owners if they carry *nazar boncuğu*, a traditional Turkish symbol for good luck. Also, if you want a nice snack, make sure to try *lokum*, a traditional Turkish candy.

07 위 글의 괄호 (A)~(C)에서 문맥이나 어법상 알맞은 낱말을 골라 쓰시오.

➡ (A) _____ (B) _____ (C) _____

08 다음 빈칸 (A)와 (B)에 알맞은 단어를 넣어 *nazar boncuğu* 와 *lokum*에 대한 소개를 완성하시오.

> *Nazar boncuğu* is a (A)_____ _____
> _____ for good luck and *lokum* is a
> (B)_____ _____ _____.

09 다음 빈칸 (A)와 (B)에 알맞은 단어를 넣어 오늘날의 Grand Bazaar에 대한 소개를 완성하시오.

> It is the (A)_____ market with a roof in the world and there are 64 streets and over 4,000 shops (B)_____ _____ _____. More than 250,000 visitors visit it every day.

[10~11] 다음 글을 읽고 물음에 답하시오.

2 Damnoen Saduak Floating Market, Thailand

In the past, Thai people traded goods on rivers. This was the beginning of floating markets in Thailand. With better road transportation, many floating markets disappeared. Since the late 1960s, however, some of them have come back and kept ⓐthe tradition alive.

Today, one of the most popular floating markets is Damnoen Saduak Floating Market. It is always crowded with tourists from all over the world. You can buy local foods and traditional gift items directly from boats.

Extra Tip I wonder if you have ever had a meal on water. If not, try noodles like *pad thai*. The sellers will cook them on their boats and pass them to you with a long fishing pole.

10 위 글의 밑줄 친 ⓐthe tradition이 가리키는 것을 본문에서 찾아 쓰시오.

➡ _____

11 How do the sellers on floating boats pass the food they cook to the customers? Answer in English beginning with "By using".

➡ _____

창의사고력 서술형 문제

01 다음 대화의 내용과 일치하도록 여자의 일기를 완성하시오.

> M: Welcome to the Tourist Information Office! How may I help you?
>
> W: Hi, I wonder if there's a tourist map of the town.
>
> M: Sure. Is there a special place you're looking for?
>
> W: Yes. I'd like to try some local food.
>
> M: Then go to Jeongseon Market. It opens every five days, and it's open today.
>
> W: I'm so lucky. How can I get there?
>
> M: You can walk there. It takes about 10 minutes.
>
> W: Great. Will you mark the way on the map, please?
>
> M: Sure. Try *gondrebap* when you get there.

> It was my first time to visit Jeongseon. I needed (A)_____ because I liked to try some local food, so I dropped by (B)_____. The officer was so kind that he recommended visiting (C)_____. He said it opens every five days and it was open today. Fortunately, it wasn't far from the office. It took about 10 minutes on (D)_____. I tried *gondrebap* and had wonderful time there.

02 다음 내용을 바탕으로 찜질방을 소개하는 안내문을 쓰시오.

> What is the name of the place? Describe the place.
> • *Jjimjilbang*: a place where you can experience a traditional Korean way to relax
> What can people do there?
> • rest on a hot floor or take a nap   • read a book or chat with friends as you lie on the floor
> What kind of food can people try there?
> • boiled eggs
> Are there any extra tips?
> • about 13,000 won   • open 24 hours

> *JJIMJILBANG*__Do you want to experience the real Korea? Then try a *jjimjilbang*. It is a place where you can experience (A)_____. It can easily be found in any big city. You can (B)_____. Also, you can read a book or (C)_____. The best food you can try here is (D)_____. The place is easy on your wallet because it only costs (E)_____. It is usually open (F)_____ a day.

단원별 모의고사

01 다음 문장의 빈칸에 들어갈 말을 〈보기〉에서 골라 알맞게 쓰시오.

┌─ 보기 ─┐

be good for / be crowded with / take a nap / make sure to / make an appointment

(1) Please _____ clean up after using these cups.

(2) The hospital _____ patients.

(3) Vegetables _____ your health.

(4) If you don't _____, you may wait to see a doctor for a long time.

(5) Sleepy drivers need to stop along a road to _____.

02 다음 문장의 빈칸에 들어갈 말을 〈보기〉에서 골라 쓰시오.

┌─ 보기 ─┐

attract   translate   producers
pick   coming   suggest

(1) The _____ always listen to the weather forecast.

(2) It will turn colder in the _____ months.

(3) Don't _____ flowers. We should protect nature.

(4) I _____ that you should replace your old computers.

(5) Can you _____ this page for me?

(6) The flowers in the garden _____ bees.

03 다음 대화의 우리말을 주어진 단어를 사용하여 영작하시오.

┌─────┐

A: I'm thirsty.

B: 제가 물을 좀 가져다드리길 원하세요? (me, get)

└─────┘

➡ _____

04 다음 짝지어진 대화가 어색한 것을 고르시오.

① A: I'm hungry
   B: Do you want me to give you some food?

② A: Could you give me a hand?
   B: How nice! Thank you so much.

③ A: I wonder whether I can make an appointment with him at eleven.
   B: No problem. You can see him anytime after seven.

④ A: My cow is sick. I wonder if you can visit my farm now.
   B: No problem. I can go and see your cow.

⑤ A: Do you want me to give you something to drink, Jake?
   B: Sure. I'd love a milkshake.

05 다음 주어진 단어를 이용하여 영작하시오.

(1) 나는 친구들과 잡담하기 위해 SNS를 사용한다. (chat)

   ➡ _____

(2) 피곤해 보이는구나. 낮잠을 자는 게 어떠니? (why, take)

   ➡ You look tired. _____

(3) 여행과 관련하여 나와 아빠는 몇 가지 공통점을 갖고 있다. (things / in)

   ➡ When it comes to traveling, _____
   _____.

06 다음 대화의 밑줄 친 (A)를 주어진 단어를 사용하여 의미가 통하도록 다시 쓰시오.

┌─────┐

A: My cow is sick. (A)I wonder if you can visit my farm now. (curious)

B: No problem. I can go and see your cow.

└─────┘

➡ _____

[07~09] 다음 대화를 읽고 물음에 답하시오.

W: Can I have the bill, please?

M: Here you are. Did you enjoy the meal?

W: It was great. I liked the *gondrebap* very much.

M: Thanks. It's also good for your health.

W: Oh, really?

M: Yes. *Gondre* is rich in vitamins A and C. It also digests well.

W: Good. I wonder if I could buy some *gondre* here.

M: Sure. Do you want me to give you the recipe for *gondrebap*?

W: Yes, that'd be great.

07 How did the woman like the *gondrebap*?

➡ _____

08 What does the woman want to buy?

➡ _____

09 What does *gondre* have plentifully?

➡ _____

[10~12] 다음 대화를 읽고 물음에 답하시오.

M: Welcome to the Tourist Information Office! How may I help you?

W: Hi, (A)저는 마을 관광 지도가 있는지 궁금합니다. (the town / wonder / I / there's / of / a tourist map / if)

M: Sure. Is there a special place you're looking for?

W: Yes. I'd like to try some local food.

M: Then go to Jeongseon Market. It opens every five days, and it's open today.

W: I'm so lucky. How can I get there?

M: You can walk there. It takes about 10 minutes.

W: Great. Will you (B)mark the way on the map, please?

M: Sure. Try *gondrebap* when you get there.

10 위 대화의 밑줄 친 (A)의 우리말을 주어진 어구를 모두 배열하여 영작하시오.

➡ _____

11 위 대화의 밑줄 친 (B)와 같은 의미로 쓰인 것은?

① My dog had a black mark on its head.

② I was sad when my teacher gave me a low mark.

③ Can you mark the message after you read it?

④ Mark is a smart and wise student in my class.

⑤ It is considered as a mark of respect.

12 위 대화의 내용과 일치하지 않는 것은?

① 여자는 관광 안내소를 방문하였다.

② 여자는 지역 음식을 먹고 싶어한다.

③ 정선 시장은 매달 5일에 열린다.

④ 정선 시장은 관광 안내소에서 걸어서 약 10분 정도 걸린다.

⑤ 남자는 정선 시장에서 곤드레밥을 먹어 볼 것을 추천하였다.

13 Which is grammatically WRONG?

① I want to know if there are ghosts.

② The question is whether I should go abroad or stay here.

③ Go outside and see if or not it's raining.

④ I wonder if I can find my axe.

⑤ Jack asks the waiter if he can have a milkshake.

14 다음 두 문장을 한 문장으로 바르게 바꿔 쓴 것을 고르시오.

① It is a place. + You can experience a traditional Korean way to relax there.
　→ It is a place how you can experience a traditional Korean way to relax.

② I can't forget the week. + I had so many projects to do that week.
　→ I can't forget the week where I had so many projects to do.

③ I don't like the way. + She laughs in the way.
　→ I don't like the way how she laughs.

④ She refused to tell the reason. + She left her school for the reason.
　→ She refused to tell the reason why she left her school.

⑤ My dad doesn't like the restaurant. + The service is very slow at that restaurant.
　→ My dad doesn't like the restaurant which the service is very slow.

15 다음 두 문장을 한 문장으로 바꿔 쓸 때 빈칸에 알맞은 말을 쓰시오.

(1) • I am not sure.
　• Is it open on Sundays?
　→ I am not sure ＿＿＿＿＿＿＿＿＿＿＿ ＿＿＿＿＿＿＿＿＿＿＿.

(2) • I wonder.
　• Is there any better way to discover another culture?
　→ I wonder ＿＿＿＿＿＿＿＿＿ ＿＿＿＿＿＿＿＿＿＿＿.

(3) • This is the restaurant.
　• My parents met for the first time.
　→ This is the restaurant ＿＿＿＿＿＿ ＿＿＿＿＿＿＿＿＿＿＿.

16 다음 문장에서 어법상 어색한 것을 바르게 고쳐 다시 쓰시오.

(1) It is not certain if they apologize when we meet again.
　➡ ＿＿＿＿＿＿＿＿＿＿＿＿＿＿＿
　＿＿＿＿＿＿＿＿＿＿＿＿＿＿＿

(2) Can you tell me do they speak Chinese?
　➡ ＿＿＿＿＿＿＿＿＿＿＿＿＿＿＿
　＿＿＿＿＿＿＿＿＿＿＿＿＿＿＿

(3) Please ask shop owners that they carry *nazar boncuğu*, a traditional Turkish symbol for good luck.
　➡ ＿＿＿＿＿＿＿＿＿＿＿＿＿＿＿
　＿＿＿＿＿＿＿＿＿＿＿＿＿＿＿

(4) I know a country which people speak Portuguese.
　➡ ＿＿＿＿＿＿＿＿＿＿＿＿＿＿＿
　＿＿＿＿＿＿＿＿＿＿＿＿＿＿＿

(5) I still remember the evening in when we watched the sun go down.
　➡ ＿＿＿＿＿＿＿＿＿＿＿＿＿＿＿
　＿＿＿＿＿＿＿＿＿＿＿＿＿＿＿

17 어법상 올바른 문장을 모두 고르시오.

① Seollal is the holiday when I get lots of money.

② I saw my friend at the convenience store which my sister works.

③ May 5 is the day when I go hiking with my family.

④ You may wonder whether you can buy just a few flowers at the market.

⑤ I wonder if or not spiders are insects, too.

⑥ I want to know if my robot does my homework tomorrow.

⑦ The question is whether he will return on time.

[18~21] 다음 글을 읽고 물음에 답하시오.

2 Damnoen Saduak Floating Market, Thailand

In the past, Thai people traded goods on rivers. ⓐThis was the beginning of floating markets in Thailand. (①) With better road transportation, many floating markets disappeared. (②) Since the late 1960s, however, some of them ⓑhave come back and kept the tradition alive. (③)

Today, one of the most popular floating markets is Damnoen Saduak Floating Market. (④) You can buy local foods and traditional gift items directly from boats. (⑤)

18 위 글의 흐름으로 보아, 주어진 문장이 들어가기에 가장 적절한 곳은?

> It is always crowded with tourists from all over the world.

①   ②   ③   ④   ⑤

19 위 글의 밑줄 친 ⓐThis가 가리키는 내용을 우리말로 쓰시오.

➡ _____

20 아래 〈보기〉에서 위 글의 밑줄 친 ⓑhave come과 현재완료의 용법이 다른 것의 개수를 고르시오.

> ┌── 보기 ──┐
> ① Tom <u>has</u> just <u>finished</u> his homework.
> ② I <u>haven't eaten</u> anything since breakfast.
> ③ They <u>have been</u> married for 10 years.
> ④ She <u>has lost</u> her key.
> ⑤ I <u>have learned</u> French for a long time.

① 1개   ② 2개   ③ 3개   ④ 4개   ⑤ 5개

21 What is special about the Damnoen Saduak Floating Market? Fill in the blanks (A) and (B) with suitable words.

> You can not only buy local foods and traditional gift items (A)_____ _____ _____ but also eat noodles like *pad thai* without getting off your (B)_____ at the Damnoen Saduak Floating Market.

[22~24] 다음 글을 읽고 물음에 답하시오.

3 Aalsmeer Flower Market, The Netherlands

(A)[Netherlands / The Netherlands] means "low lands." As the name suggests, about 70% of the country sits below sea level. Thus, the Dutch built up the land, and one effective way to use it was ⓐto grow flowers and sell them. It is, therefore, no surprise that the country has the largest flower market in the world: the Aalsmeer Flower Market.

The building where the market is housed is bigger than 120 soccer fields. The market is busy with thousands of flower-filled carts. They are moved (B)[most / mostly] by electric-powered trucks. Every day, around 20 million flowers are traded and shipped to all corners of the world.

Extra Tip You may wonder whether you can buy just a few flowers at the market. Sadly, you cannot, but you can see how (C)[retail / wholesale] flower trading works.

22 위 글의 괄호 (A)~(C)에서 문맥이나 어법상 알맞은 낱말을 골라 쓰시오.

➡ (A) _____ (B) _____
(C) _____

23 위 글의 밑줄 친 ⓐto grow와 to부정사의 용법이 <u>다른</u> 것을 <u>모두</u> 고르시오.

① Who is the right person <u>to grow</u> flowers well?
② My hobby is <u>to grow</u> flowers.
③ I was pleased <u>to grow</u> flowers well.
④ It's not easy <u>to grow</u> flowers well.
⑤ I tried <u>to grow</u> flowers in the garden.

24 위 글의 주제로 알맞은 것을 고르시오.

① the difficulty the Dutch had while building up the land
② the reason why the Aalsmeer Flower Market is the largest flower market in the world
③ the success story of changing the geographical weakness into strong point
④ the amazing size of the building where the Aalsmeer Flower Market is housed
⑤ the amount of flowers traded and shipped to all corners of the world at the Aalsmeer Flower Market every day

[25~26] 다음 글을 읽고 물음에 답하시오.

Bukchon Hanok Village

Do you want to experience the real Korea? Then, try Bukchon Hanok Village, (A)[that / which] means north village. It is a place (B)[where / which] you can experience the traditional type of house in Korea. You can rent *hanbok*, the traditional Korean clothing,

for a day and take photos at 8 photo spots. It costs about 15,000 won to rent *hanbok* (C)[during / for] 4 hours. Also, you can experience a one-day traditional arts workshop or various cultural events. The best foods you can try here are *mandu* and noodles. People actually live in the neighborhood, so respect their privacy and be careful not to make noise.

25 위 글의 괄호 (A)~(C)에서 문맥이나 어법상 알맞은 낱말을 골라 쓰시오.

➡ (A) _____ (B) _____ (C) _____

26 Which question CANNOT be answered after reading the passage?

① What can you experience in Bukchon Hanok Village?
② How much does it cost to rent *hanbok* for 4 hours?
③ What's the price of experiencing a one-day traditional arts workshop or various cultural events?
④ What are the best foods you can try in Bukchon Hanok Village?
⑤ Do people actually live in the neighborhood?

MEMO

Reading for Fun 2(1)

A Slice of History

Words & Expressions

Key Words

- **agree** [əgríː] 동 동의하다
- **almost** [ɔ́ːlmoust] 부 거의
- **as** [æz] 접 ~할 때, ~하면서
- **bake** [beik] 동 (음식을) 굽다
- **bread** [bred] 명 빵
- **bring** [briŋ] 동 가지고 오다
- **busy** [bízi] 형 분주한, 바쁜
- **century** [séntʃəri] 명 세기
- **cheap** [tʃiːp] 형 값싼
- **cook** [kuk] 명 요리사
- **delicious** [dilíʃəs] 형 맛있는
- **differ** [dífər] 동 다르다
- **disagree** [dìsəgríː] 동 의견이 다르다
- **everywhere** [évriweər] 부 모든 곳에서
- **far** [fɑːr] 형 멀리 떨어진
- **fast-food** [fǽstfùːd] 명 패스트푸드
- **favorite** [féivərit] 형 아주 좋아하는
- **flat** [flæt] 형 납작한, 평평한
- **global** [glóubəl] 형 전 세계적인
- **healthy** [hélθi] 형 건강한
- **however** [hauévər] 부 그러나
- **introduce** [ìntrədjúːs] 동 소개하다
- **learn** [ləːrn] 동 알다, 배우다
- **meat** [miːt] 명 고기
- **move** [muːv] 동 이동하다, 움직이다

- **name** [neim] 동 이름 붙이다
- **national** [nǽʃənl] 형 국가의
- **national flag** 국기
- **onion** [ʌ́njən] 명 양파
- **quickly** [kwíkli] 부 빠르게
- **record** [rékɔːrd] 명 기록
- **restaurant** [réstərənt] 명 식당
- **share** [ʃɛər] 동 공유하다
- **shop** [ʃɑp] 명 상점
- **sick** [sik] 형 아픈
- **since** [sins] 접 ~ 이후로
- **slice** [slais] 명 (얇은) 조각
- **sell** [sel] 동 팔다
- **such** [sʌtʃ] 형 그런, ~와 같은
- **the Greeks** 그리스인들
- **the New World** 신세계
- **the Romans** 로마인들
- **the Stone Age** 석기시대
- **topping** [tápiŋ] 명 고명, 토핑
- **try** [trai] 동 맛보다
- **type** [taip] 명 유형
- **vegetable** [védʒətəbl] 명 채소
- **visit** [vízit] 동 방문하다
- **while** [hwail] 접 ~인 반면에, ~하는 동안에
- **widely** [wáidli] 부 폭넓게

Key Expressions

- **around the world** 전 세계에 걸친
- **at any time** 어느 때이든지
- **at the same time** 동시에
- **be born** 태어나다
- **be used to + 동사원형** ~하기 위하여 사용되다
- **go on to ~** (다음으로) 넘어가다
- **in most parts of** ~의 대부분 지역에서
- **in one form or another** 여러 가지 형태로
- **in time** 이윽고

- **It is believed that ~** ~라고들 믿고 있다
- **near and far** 사방, 천지
- **not ~ until** …까지 ~하지 않다
- **of course** 물론
- **on the street** 거리에서
- **outside of** ~의 바깥쪽에
- **put ~ on** ~에 올려놓다
- **so ~ that** 너무 ~해서 …한
- **topped with** ~로 덮여 있는

Word Power

※ 서로 비슷한 뜻을 가진 어휘

☐ **agree** 동의하다 : **consent** 동의하다

☐ **delicious** 맛있는 : **tasty** 맛있는

☐ **global** 전 세계적인 : **worldwide** 세계적인

☐ **almost** 거의 : **nearly** 거의

☐ **differ** 다르다 : **vary** 다르다

☐ **widely** 폭넓게 : **broadly** 폭넓게

※ 서로 반대의 뜻을 가진 어휘

☐ **agree** 동의하다 ↔ **disagree** 의견이 다르다

☐ **busy** 분주한, 바쁜 ↔ **idle** 한가한

☐ **far** 멀리 떨어진 ↔ **near** 가까운

☐ **healthy** 건강한 ↔ **ill, sick** 아픈, 병이 든

☐ **sell** 팔다 ↔ **buy** 사다

☐ **bring** 가지고 오다 ↔ **take** 가지고 가다

☐ **cheap** 값싼 ↔ **expensive** 값비싼

☐ **favorite** 좋아하는 ↔ **dislikable** 싫어하는

☐ **quickly** 빠르게 ↔ **slowly** 느리게

☐ **widely** 폭넓게 ↔ **narrowly** 협소하게

※ 동사 → 명사

☐ **agree** 동의하다 → **agreement** 동의

☐ **introduce** 소개하다 → **introduction** 소개

☐ **differ** 다르다 → **difference** 차이점

☐ **move** 이동하다 → **movement** 이동, 움직임

※ 명사 → 형용사

☐ **difference** 차이 → **different** 다른

☐ **health** 건강 → **healthy** 건강한

☐ **nation** 국가 → **national** 국가의

☐ **globe** 지구 → **global** 전 세계적인

☐ **introduction** 소개 → **introductive** 소개하는

☐ **type** 유형 → **typical** 전형적인

English Dictionary

☐ **agree** 동의하다
→ to have or express the same opinion
같은 의견을 가지거나 표현하다

☐ **bake** (음식을) 굽다
→ to cook something using dry heat, in an oven
오븐에서 열을 이용하여 음식을 조리하다

☐ **bread** 빵
→ a type of food made from flour and water that is mixed together and then baked
물과 밀가루를 섞어서 구워 만든 음식의 한 종류

☐ **century** 세기
→ a period of 100 years
100년의 기간

☐ **flag** 깃발
→ a piece of cloth with a coloured pattern or picture on it that represents a country or organization
어떤 국가나 조직을 나타내는 무늬나 그림이 있는 천 조각

☐ **global** 전 세계적인
→ affecting or including the whole world
세계 전체에 영향을 주거나 포함하는

☐ **introduce** 소개하다
→ to bring a plan, system, or product into use for the first time
처음으로 어떤 계획, 시스템 혹은 상품을 사용하다

☐ **onion** 양파
→ a round white vegetable with a brown, red, or white skin and many layers
여러 겹으로 되어 있으면서 갈색, 빨간색 또는 흰색의 껍질을 가진 둥글고 하얀 채소

☐ **slice** (얇은) 조각
→ a thin flat piece of food cut from a larger piece
큰 덩어리에서 잘라낸 얇고 납작한 음식의 한 조각

☐ **topping** 고명, 토핑
→ something you put on top of food to make it look nicer or taste better
보기 좋거나 맛을 좋게 하기 위하여 음식의 꼭대기에 올리는 것

A Slice of History

What do you like on your pizza? Though you may <u>disagree</u> on the
_{What toppings}   '~에 대해 의견을 달리하다'
best toppings, you will agree that <u>it</u> is now a global food. <u>It</u> is sold in
        = pizza   = pizza
fast-food restaurants or on the street in most parts of the world. How
has pizza become <u>such a favorite food</u> around the world?
          such+a+형용사+명사

Since the Stone Age, people <u>have been eating</u> pizza in one form or
'~ 이래로'   현재완료진행형: 과거에서부터 현재까지 계속 이어지는 동작을 나타낸다.
another. Stone Age people baked flat bread on hot rocks. Records show
that the Greeks and the Romans started <u>to put</u> meat and vegetables on
          = putting
flat bread. <u>It</u> is believed <u>that</u> the word "pizza" was first used in Italy
    가주어   명사절(진주어)을 이끄는 접속사
<u>to name</u> the food over 1,000 years ago.
목적을 나타내는 부사적 용법의 to부정사

However, pizza with tomato toppings was <u>not</u> born <u>until</u> the 16th
            'not ~ until ...': '...까지는 ~하지 않다' '...이 되어서야 비로소 ~하다'
century. There were no tomatoes in Italy before Christopher Columbus
and other Europeans brought <u>them</u> from the New World. When <u>they</u>
        = tomatoes   = tomatoes
were first introduced to Europe, people thought that tomatoes would
make <u>them</u> sick. In time, people learned that tomatoes were delicious
    = people
and healthy.

📎 **확인문제**

● 다음 문장이 본문의 내용과 일치하면 T, 일치하지 <u>않으면</u> F를 쓰시오.

1   Pizza is sold in fast-food restaurants or on the street in most parts of the world. ☐

2   Since the Stone Age, people have been eating pizza in one form. ☐

3   The Greeks and the Romans started to put meat and vegetables on flat bread. ☐

4   It is believed that the word "pizza" was first used in Greece. ☐

5   Pizza with tomato toppings was born only after the 16th century. ☐

6   When tomatoes were first introduced to Europe, people thought that tomatoes were delicious and healthy. ☐

In the 18th century, Naples was a large city where there were many jobs. Workers from near and far came to the city, and what they needed in their busy lives was food they could eat quickly at any time. Cooks in Naples began to put tomato and other toppings on flat bread and sold slices of pizza on the street. The street food was so cheap and delicious that workers ate it for breakfast, lunch, and dinner. They could buy slices of pizza and eat them as they walked on the street. In 1830, the world's first pizza shop opened in Naples.

In 1889, Queen Margherita of Italy visited Naples and tried pizza. The type of pizza that she loved most had tomato, cheese, and green leaf toppings that showed the three colors on Italy's national flag—red, white, and green. After the queen's visit, pizza went on to become a truly national dish.

Pizza became known outside of Italy in the late 19th century, when many Italians moved to the United States. Italians brought pizza with them, and Americans loved the flat bread topped with meat and vegetables because they could eat bread, meat, and vegetables at the same time. The first pizza restaurant in the United States opened its doors in 1905.

Pizza is now enjoyed almost everywhere. Of course, toppings differ widely from place to place. Koreans love *bulgogi* on their pizza, while Russians like to have fish and onion toppings on their pizza. However, all types of pizza share two things. Each begins with flat bread, and each is a slice of history.

near and far 도처에서, 사방에서
national 국가의
top (다른 것 위에) 얹다
at the same time 동시에
differ 다르다
widely 널리, 크게

확인문제

● 다음 문장이 본문의 내용과 일치하면 T, 일치하지 <u>않으면</u> F를 쓰시오.

1 Cooks in Naples began to put tomato and other toppings on flat bread and sold slices of pizza on the street. ☐

2 In 1830, the world's first pizza shop opened in Naples. ☐

3 Queen Margherita of Italy visited Naples and cooked pizza in 1889. ☐

4 Pizza was introduced to England by Italian immigrants. ☐

5 In 1905, the first pizza restaurant in the United States opened its doors. ☐

6 Russians like to have meat and onion toppings on their pizza. ☐

● 우리말을 참고하여 빈칸에 알맞은 말을 쓰시오.

1 A _____ of History

2 _____ _____ _____ _____ on your pizza?

3 _____ you may _____ _____ the best toppings, you will agree that it is now a global food.

4 _____ _____ _____ in fast-food restaurants or on the street in most parts of the world.

5 How has pizza become _____ _____ _____ _____ around the world?

6 Since the Stone Age, people _____ _____ _____ pizza in one form or another.

7 Stone Age people baked flat bread _____ _____ _____.

8 _____ _____ that the Greeks and the Romans started to put meat and vegetables on flat bread.

9 _____ _____ _____ that the word "pizza" was first used in Italy _____ _____ the food over 1,000 years ago.

10 However, pizza with tomato toppings _____ _____ _____ _____ the 16th century.

11 There were no tomatoes in Italy _____ Christopher Columbus and other Europeans _____ them _____ the New World.

12 When they were first introduced to Europe, people thought that tomatoes would _____ _____ _____.

13 _____ _____, people learned that tomatoes were delicious and healthy.

14 In the 18th century, Naples was a large city _____ there were many jobs.

15 Workers _____ _____ _____ _____ came to the city, and what they needed in their busy lives was food they could eat quickly _____ _____ _____.

1 한 조각의 역사

2 여러분은 어떤 피자 토핑을 좋아하는가?

3 비록 제일 좋아하는 피자 토핑에 대해 의견이 다를 수 있지만, 피자가 오늘날 세계적인 음식이라는 데에는 모두 동의할 것이다.

4 피자는 세계 대부분 지역의 패스트푸드 식당이나 길거리에서 팔리고 있다.

5 어떻게 해서 피자가 세계적으로 이토록 사랑받는 음식이 되었을까?

6 석기시대부터 사람들은 여러 가지 형태로 피자를 먹어 왔다.

7 석기시대 사람들은 납작한 빵을 뜨거운 돌에 구워 먹었다.

8 기록에 의하면 그리스와 로마 사람들이 납작한 빵에 고기와 채소를 얹기 시작했다.

9 '피자'라는 단어는 이러한 음식을 지칭하기 위해 약 천 년 전에 이탈리아에서 처음 사용되었다고 알려져 있다.

10 하지만 토마토 토핑을 얹은 피자는 16세기까지는 존재하지 않았다.

11 크리스토퍼 콜럼버스와 다른 유럽인들이 신세계에서 가져오기 전까지 이탈리아에는 토마토가 없었다.

12 유럽에 처음 소개되었을 때 사람들은 토마토가 사람들을 아프게 할 거라고 여겼다.

13 시간이 지나며 사람들은 토마토가 맛있고 건강에도 좋다는 것을 알게 되었다.

14 18세기에 나폴리는 다양한 직업이 존재하는 대도시였다.

15 사방에서 노동자들이 이 도시로 모여들었고, 바쁜 생활 중 그들에게 필요했던 것은 언제든지 빨리 먹을 수 있는 음식이었다.

16 Cooks in Naples began to put tomato and other toppings on flat bread and sold _____ _____ _____ on the street.

17 The street food was _____ cheap and delicious _____ workers ate it _____ breakfast, lunch, and dinner.

18 They could buy slices of pizza and eat them _____ they walked _____ _____ _____.

19 In 1830, the _____ _____ _____ _____ opened in Naples.

20 In 1889, Queen Margherita of Italy visited Naples and _____ pizza.

21 The type of pizza _____ _____ _____ _____ had tomato, cheese, and green leaf toppings _____ _____ the three colors _____ Italy's national flag–red, white, and green.

22 After the queen's visit, pizza _____ _____ a truly national dish.

23 Pizza _____ _____ outside of Italy in the late 19th century, when many Italians _____ _____ the United States.

24 Italians _____ _____ _____ _____, and Americans loved the flat bread topped with meat and vegetables because they could eat bread, meat, and vegetables _____ _____ _____.

25 The first pizza restaurant in the United States _____ _____ _____ in 1905.

26 Pizza is now enjoyed _____ _____.

27 Of course, toppings differ widely _____ _____.

28 Koreans love *bulgogi* on their pizza, _____ Russians like to have fish and onion toppings on their pizza.

29 However, all types of pizza _____ _____ _____.

30 Each _____ _____ flat bread, and each is _____ _____ _____.

16 나폴리의 요리사들이 납작한 빵에 토마토와 다른 토핑을 얹기 시작해 길거리에서 피자 조각을 팔았다.

17 이 길거리 음식은 무척 저렴하고 맛이 좋아서, 노동자들은 이것을 아침, 점심, 저녁으로 먹었다.

18 그들은 피자 조각을 사서 길을 걸어가며 먹을 수 있었다.

19 1830년에는 세계 최초의 피자 가게가 나폴리에서 문을 열었다.

20 1889년에 이탈리아의 마르게리타 왕비가 나폴리를 방문하여 피자를 맛보았다.

21 그녀가 가장 좋아했던 피자는 이탈리아 국기의 세 가지 색깔인 빨강, 하양, 초록을 나타낸 토마토, 치즈, 녹색 잎 채소 토핑으로 된 것이었다.

22 왕비의 방문 이후로 피자는 진정한 이탈리아의 국가 음식이 되었다.

23 19세기 후반에는 피자가 이탈리아 밖으로 알려지게 되었는데, 이 시기에 많은 이탈리아 사람들이 미국으로 이주를 하였다.

24 이탈리아인들은 피자도 함께 가져갔고, 빵, 고기, 채소를 한꺼번에 먹을 수 있어서 미국인들은 고기와 채소를 얹은 이 납작한 빵을 좋아했다.

25 미국 최초의 피자 가게가 1905년에 문을 열었다.

26 오늘날 피자는 거의 어디에서나 즐길 수 있다.

27 물론, 토핑은 지역에 따라 매우 다양하다.

28 한국인은 불고기를 피자에 얹어 먹기를 좋아하고, 러시아 사람들은 생선과 양파 토핑을 좋아한다.

29 그러나 모든 종류의 피자가 두 가지 사실만큼은 똑같다.

30 모든 피자는 납작한 빵에서 시작하고, 각각은 역사의 한 조각이다.

● 우리말을 참고하여 본문을 영작하시오.

1 한 조각의 역사

➡ _____

2 여러분은 어떤 피자 토핑을 좋아하는가?

➡ _____

3 비록 제일 좋아하는 피자 토핑에 대해 의견이 다를 수 있지만, 피자가 오늘날 세계적인 음식이라는 데에는 모두 동의할 것이다.

➡ _____

4 피자는 세계 대부분 지역의 패스트푸드 식당이나 길거리에서 팔리고 있다.

➡ _____

5 어떻게 해서 피자가 세계적으로 이토록 사랑받는 음식이 되었을까?

➡ _____

6 석기시대부터 사람들은 여러 가지 형태로 피자를 먹어 왔다.

➡ _____

7 석기시대 사람들은 납작한 빵을 뜨거운 돌에 구워 먹었다.

➡ _____

8 기록에 의하면 그리스와 로마 사람들이 납작한 빵에 고기와 채소를 얹기 시작했다.

➡ _____

9 '피자'라는 단어는 이러한 음식을 지칭하기 위해 약 천 년 전에 이탈리아에서 처음 사용되었다고 알려져 있다.

➡ _____

10 하지만 토마토 토핑을 얹은 피자는 16세기까지는 존재하지 않았다.

➡ _____

11 크리스토퍼 콜럼버스와 다른 유럽인들이 신세계에서 가져오기 전까지 이탈리아에는 토마토가 없었다.

➡ _____

12 유럽에 처음 소개되었을 때 사람들은 토마토가 사람들을 아프게 할 거라고 여겼다.

➡ _____

13 시간이 지나며 사람들은 토마토가 맛있고 건강에도 좋다는 것을 알게 되었다.

➡ _____

14 18세기에 나폴리는 다양한 직업이 존재하는 대도시였다.

➡ _____

15 사방에서 노동자들이 이 도시로 모여들었고, 바쁜 생활 중 그들에게 필요했던 것은 언제든지 빨리 먹을 수 있는 음식이었다.

➡ _____

_____

16 나폴리의 요리사들이 납작한 빵에 토마토와 다른 토핑을 얹기 시작해 길거리에서 피자 조각을 팔았다.

➡ _____

17 이 길거리 음식은 무척 저렴하고 맛이 좋아서, 노동자들은 이것을 아침, 점심, 저녁으로 먹었다.

➡ _____

18 그들은 피자 조각을 사서 길을 걸어가며 먹을 수 있었다.

➡ _____

19 1830년에는 세계 최초의 피자 가게가 나폴리에서 문을 열었다.

➡ _____

20 1889년에 이탈리아의 마르게리타 왕비가 나폴리를 방문하여 피자를 맛보았다.

➡ _____

21 그녀가 가장 좋아했던 피자는 이탈리아 국기의 세 가지 색깔인 빨강, 하양, 초록을 나타낸 토마토, 치즈, 녹색 잎 채소 토핑으로 된 것이었다.

➡ _____

_____

22 왕비의 방문 이후로 피자는 진정한 이탈리아의 국가 음식이 되었다.

➡ _____

23 19세기 후반에는 피자가 이탈리아 밖으로 알려지게 되었는데, 이 시기에 많은 이탈리아 사람들이 미국으로 이주를 하였다.

➡ _____

_____

24 이탈리아인들은 피자도 함께 가져갔고, 빵, 고기, 채소를 한꺼번에 먹을 수 있어서 미국인들은 고기와 채소를 얹은 이 납작한 빵을 좋아했다.

➡ _____

_____

25 미국 최초의 피자 가게가 1905년에 문을 열었다.

➡ _____

26 오늘날 피자는 거의 어디에서나 즐길 수 있다.

➡ _____

27 물론, 토핑은 지역에 따라 매우 다양하다.

➡ _____

28 한국인은 불고기를 피자에 얹어 먹기를 좋아하고, 러시아 사람들은 생선과 양파 토핑을 좋아한다.

➡ _____

29 그러나 모든 종류의 피자가 두 가지 사실만큼은 똑같다.

➡ _____

30 모든 피자는 납작한 빵에서 시작하고, 각각은 역사의 한 조각이다.

➡ _____

01 다음 짝지어진 단어의 관계가 같도록 빈칸에 알맞은 말을 쓰시오.

> appear : disappear = agree : _____

02 다음 문장의 빈칸에 들어갈 말을 〈보기〉에서 골라 쓰시오.

> ┌── 보기 ──┐
> at the same time / Stone Age /
> near and far / a slice of

(1) I want to use _____ lemon for my tea.
(2) People in the _____ survived by hunting.
(3) People from _____ came to the singer's last concert.
(4) They left the room _____.

03 다음 우리말에 맞게 빈칸에 알맞은 말을 쓰시오.

(1) 그 여성은 자기 아이가 크고 납작한 빵을 먹고 있는 것을 보았다.
➡ The woman saw her child eating a large _____ bread.
(2) 양파는 강한 맛과 냄새를 갖고 있다.
➡ An _____ has a strong taste and smell.
(3) 그녀는 자기 남편이 결백하다고 진정으로 믿었다.
➡ She _____ believed that her husband was innocent.

04 다음 우리말을 주어진 단어를 이용하여 영작하시오.

(1) 나는 여가 시간에 보통 케이크를 굽는다. (free)
➡ _____
(2) 당신은 국기를 그리고 있나요? (draw, national)
➡ _____
(3) 우리는 여기저기서 사진을 찍었다. (place)
➡ _____

05 다음 두 문장을 한 문장으로 바꿔 쓰시오.

> • People started to eat pizza in the Stone Age.
> • People still are eating pizza.

➡ _____
_____

06 다음 빈칸에 알맞은 말을 쓰시오.

> As the street food was very cheap and delicious, workers ate it for breakfast.
> = The street food was _____ cheap and delicious _____ workers ate it for breakfast

[07~08] 다음 글을 읽고 물음에 답하시오.

What do you like on your pizza? ⓐAs you may disagree on the best toppings, you will agree that it is now a global food. It is sold in fast-food restaurants or on the street in most parts of the world. How has pizza become ⓑ그토록 좋아하는 음식 around the world?

07 위 글의 밑줄 친 ⓐ에서 흐름상 어색한 부분을 찾아 고치시오.

➡ _____ ➡ _____

08 위 글의 밑줄 친 ⓑ의 우리말에 맞게 주어진 어휘를 알맞게 배열하시오.

> favorite / a / food / such

➡ _____

[09~10] 다음 글을 읽고 물음에 답하시오.

However, ⓐpizza with tomato toppings was not born until the 16th century. There were no tomatoes in Italy before Christopher Columbus and other Europeans brought them from the New World. When they were first introduced to Europe, people thought that tomatoes would make them sick. In time, people learned that tomatoes were delicious and healthy.

09 위 글의 밑줄 친 ⓐ를 다음과 같이 바꿔 쓸 때 빈칸에 들어갈 알맞은 말을 두 단어로 쓰시오.

➡ _____ _____ the 16th century was pizza with tomato toppings born

10 In Italy, why was there no pizza with tomato toppings until the 16th century? Answer in Korean.

➡ _____
 _____

[11~12] 다음 글을 읽고 물음에 답하시오.

In 1889, Queen Margherita of Italy visited Naples and tried pizza. The type of pizza ___ⓐ___ she loved most had (A)tomato, cheese, and green leaf toppings ___ⓑ___ showed the three colors on Italy's national flag–red, white, and green. After the queen's visit, pizza went on to become a truly national dish.

11 위 글의 빈칸 ⓐ와 ⓑ에 공통으로 들어갈 알맞은 말을 쓰시오.

➡ _____

12 위 글의 밑줄 친 (A)의 토핑이 상징하는 이탈리아 국기의 색을 각각 영어로 쓰시오.

(1) tomato topping이 상징하는 색: _____
(2) cheese topping이 상징하는 색: _____
(3) green leaf topping이 상징하는 색: _____

[13~14] 다음 글을 읽고 물음에 답하시오.

Pizza became known outside of Italy in the late 19th century, when many Italians moved to the United States. Italians brought pizza with them, and Americans loved the flat bread ___ⓐ___ with meat and vegetables because they could eat bread, meat, and vegetables at the same time. The first pizza restaurant in the United States opened its doors in 1905.

Pizza is now enjoyed almost everywhere. Of course, toppings differ widely from place to place. Koreans love *bulgogi* on their pizza, while Russians like to have fish and onion toppings on their pizza. However, all types of pizza share ⓑtwo things. Each begins with flat bread, and each is a slice of history.

13 위 글의 빈칸 ⓐ에 top을 알맞은 형태로 쓰시오.

➡ _____

14 위 글의 밑줄 친 ⓑtwo things가 가리키는 것을 우리말로 쓰시오.

➡ (1) _____
 (2) _____

01 다음 문장의 빈칸에 들어갈 말을 <보기>에서 골라 쓰시오. 출제율 100%

┌─ 보기 ─────────────────────┐
flag   flat   differ   national   top
└───────────────────────────┘

(1) Do you want to _____ your dessert with chocolate and strawberries?

(2) Chuseok is a _____ holiday in Korea.

(3) The two sisters look alike, but they _____ in personality.

(4) The _____ is waving in the breeze.

(5) It is a wide and _____ type of Italian pasta.

02 다음 영영풀이가 가리키는 것을 고르시오. 출제율 95%

┌───────────────────────────┐
to put on the surface of something
└───────────────────────────┘

① top   ② down
③ left   ④ right
⑤ turn

03 다음 문장의 빈칸에 공통으로 들어갈 말을 고르시오. 출제율 90%

┌───────────────────────────┐
• In old times people believed that the earth was _____.
• The woman is changing a _____ tire.
• There is a house with a _____ roof.
└───────────────────────────┘

① flat   ② round
③ smooth   ④ sharp
⑤ global

04 다음 중 밑줄 친 부분의 뜻풀이가 바르지 않은 것은? 출제율 95%

① It is widely known that she will be the next president. 널리, 크게

② The school keeps a record of its students dating back 30 years. 기록(물)

③ Trash is one of the global issues. 세계적인

④ What toppings did you put on your ice cream? 최고, 정상

⑤ I'm afraid I have to disagree with you on that issue. 의견이 다르다

05 다음 주어진 문장의 밑줄 친 record와 같은 의미로 쓰인 것은? 출제율 95%

┌───────────────────────────┐
The records show that this movie is one of the popular genres in Korea.
└───────────────────────────┘

① Did you remember to record the performance in the afternoon?

② The band will record their new album.

③ You should keep a record of your expenses.

④ His speech has been recorded by the tape recorder.

⑤ From now on, we'll record what you say.

06 다음 우리말과 일치하도록 주어진 단어를 올바르게 배열하시오. 출제율 85%

(1) 지금 사람들은 전 세계의 다른 토핑들을 가진 피자를 즐긴다.

(around / the / world / all / with / toppings / pizza / now / enjoy / people / different)

➡ _____

_____

(2) 방문객들이 지역 문화를 즐기기 위해 사방에서 모여들었다.

(near / to / far / came / culture / the / enjoy / from / visitors / and / local)

➡ _____

_____

출제율 90%

07 다음 빈칸에 들어갈 말의 의미가 <u>다른</u> 하나는?

① I doubt _____ he has ever given the matter a thought.

② Try this pizza and see _____ you like it.

③ Only time will tell _____ the treatment has been successful.

④ The judge must decide _____ the DNA evidence is enough.

⑤ Please let me know _____ you cannot come to the party.

출제율 100%

08 다음 중 어법상 <u>어색한</u> 것은?

① Naples was a large city where there were many jobs.

② It was in the days when medical services were rare.

③ You could tell she was foreign by the way how she dressed.

④ May I ask you the reason why you made that decision?

⑤ I always remember the moments when I was at my mother's knees.

출제율 95%

09 다음 우리말을 주어진 어휘를 활용하여 영작하시오.

(1) 그것이 내가 네게 화난 이유이다. (that, angry, the reason)

➡ _____

(2) 수요일은 내가 가장 못생겨 보이는 날이다. (look, ugly, when)

➡ _____

(3) 나는 그녀가 이 시끄러운 곳에서 잘 수 있을지 알고 싶다. (know, this noisy place)

➡ _____

_____

(4) 그는 지난 금요일 이후로 춤 연습을 하지 않고 있다. (since, practice, dance)

➡ _____

_____

(5) 그녀는 너무 배가 고파서 계속 걸을 수 없었다. (feel, keep, to)

➡ _____

(6) 그는 춤을 무척 잘 춰서 1등상을 받았다. (well, win, so)

➡ _____

출제율 95%

10 다음 중 어법상 <u>어색한</u> 것은?

① I was so hungry that I ate all the food.

② She was very kind that everyone likes her.

③ How has pizza become such a favorite food around the world?

④ It was too noisy to talk and too dark to see.

⑤ Dave said, "You are good enough to win a national championship."

출제율 95%

11 다음 빈칸에 알맞은 말을 쓰시오.

> That is the reason _____ she got angry.

➡ _____

12 다음 중 어법상 바르게 쓰인 문장은?

① This is one of the toy cars what are displayed at a toy exhibition.

② She loved the toppings that they showed the three colors on Italy's national flag.

③ She will have to take the things what he gave to her.

④ Is the new position what he is looking for in the company?

⑤ The report showed that I wanted to know.

13 다음 두 문장을 한 문장으로 바꿔 쓰시오. (관계대명사나 that 사용 금지)

(1) • I know a country.
• People speak Portuguese in the country.

➡ _____

_____

(2) • Scientists studied the way.
• Those birds could fly so high up in the sky in the way.

➡ _____

_____

(3) • We all know the reason.
• He failed for the reason.

➡ _____

_____

(4) • Do you remember the moment?
• You decided to become a singer at the moment.

➡ _____

_____

14 다음 빈칸에 들어갈 말이 바르게 짝지어진 것을 고르시오.

Linda felt _____ nervous _____ she could barely stand on her own two feet.

① so – that

② that – so

③ very – that

④ enough – to

⑤ too – to

[15~16] 다음 글을 읽고 물음에 답하시오.

In 1889, Queen Margherita of Italy visited Naples and tried pizza. The type of pizza that she loved most had tomato, cheese, and green leaf toppings that showed the three colors on Italy's national flag — red, white, and green. ⓐAfter the queen's visit, pizza went on to become a truly national dish.

15 위 글의 밑줄 친 ⓐ를 다음과 같이 바꿔 쓸 때 빈칸에 들어갈 알맞은 한 단어를 쓰시오.

➡ Pizza _____ become a truly national dish until the queen's visit.

16 본문의 내용과 일치하도록 다음 빈칸에 알맞은 단어를 쓰시오. (세 단어)

The type of pizza that Queen Margherita loved most was the pizza with tomato, cheese, and green leaf toppings that showed the three colors on _____ _____ _____ — red, white, and green.

[17~19] 다음 글을 읽고 물음에 답하시오.

What do you like on your pizza? Though you may disagree on the best toppings, you will agree that it is now a global food. It is sold in fast-food restaurants or on the street in most parts of the world. (A)[How / What] has pizza become such a favorite food around the world?

(B)[For / Since] the Stone Age, people have been eating pizza in one form or another. Stone Age people baked flat bread on hot rocks. Records show that the Greeks and the Romans started to put meat and vegetables on flat bread. It (C)[believes / is believed] that the word "pizza" was first used in Italy ⓐto name the food over 1,000 years ago.

17 위 글의 괄호 (A)~(C)에서 어법상 알맞은 낱말을 골라 쓰시오.

➡ (A) _____ (B) _____ (C) _____

18 아래 〈보기〉에서 위 글의 밑줄 친 ⓐto name과 to부정사의 용법이 같은 것의 개수를 고르시오.

┌── 보기 ├──
① I don't know how to name the food.
② She was clever enough to name the food.
③ We met yesterday to name the food.
④ It won't be easy to name the food.
⑤ He was eager to name the food.

① 1개 ② 2개 ③ 3개 ④ 4개 ⑤ 5개

19 According to the passage, which is NOT true?

① People sell pizza in fast-food restaurants or on the street in most parts of the world.

② People have been eating pizza in one form since the Stone Age.

③ In the Stone Age, people baked flat bread on hot rocks.

④ According to the records, it was the Greeks and the Romans that started to put meat and vegetables on flat bread.

⑤ People first used the word "pizza" in Italy over 1,000 years ago.

[20~22] 다음 글을 읽고 물음에 답하시오.

However, ⓐ토마토 토핑을 얹은 피자는 16세기까지는 존재하지 않았다. There were no tomatoes in Italy before Christopher Columbus and other Europeans brought them from the New World. When ⓑthey were first introduced to Europe, people thought that tomatoes would make ⓒthem sick. In time, people learned that tomatoes were delicious and healthy.

20 위 글의 밑줄 친 ⓐ의 우리말에 맞게 주어진 어휘를 이용하여 11 단어로 영작하시오.

┌─────────────────────────────┐
│ with tomato toppings, not born │
└─────────────────────────────┘

➡ _____

_____

21 위 글의 밑줄 친 ⓑthey와 ⓒthem이 가리키는 것을 각각 본문에서 찾아 쓰시오.

➡ ⓑthey가 가리키는 것: _____ ,
ⓒthem이 가리키는 것: _____

22 본문의 내용과 일치하도록 다음 빈칸에 알맞은 접속사를 쓰시오.

┌─────────────────────────────┐
│ There were tomatoes in Italy only │
│ _____ Christopher Columbus and │
│ other Europeans brought them from the │
│ New World. │
└─────────────────────────────┘

[23~25] 다음 글을 읽고 물음에 답하시오.

In the 18th century, Naples was a large city (A)[where / which] there were many jobs. (①) Workers from near and far came to the city, and (B)[that / what] they needed in their busy lives was food they could eat quickly at any time. (②) Cooks in Naples began to put tomato and other toppings on flat bread and sold slices of pizza on the street. (③) The street food was (C)[so / such] cheap and delicious that workers ate it for breakfast, lunch, and dinner. (④) In 1830, the world's first pizza shop opened in Naples. (⑤)

출제율 90%

23 위 글의 괄호 (A)~(C)에서 어법상 알맞은 낱말을 골라 쓰시오.

➡ (A) _____ (B) _____ (C) _____

출제율 95%

24 위 글의 흐름으로 보아, 주어진 문장이 들어가기에 가장 적절한 곳은?

> They could buy slices of pizza and eat them as they walked on the street.

①   ②   ③   ④   ⑤

출제율 100%

25 위 글의 제목으로 알맞은 것을 고르시오.

① Pizza Becomes a National Dish
② What Do You Know About Pizza?
③ Naples, the Home of Pizza
④ Pizza as a Global Dish
⑤ The Birth of the Word "Pizza"

[26~28] 다음 글을 읽고 물음에 답하시오.

Pizza is now enjoyed almost everywhere. Of course, toppings differ widely from place to place. Koreans love *bulgogi* on their pizza, (A)while Russians like to have fish and onion toppings on their pizza. ____ⓐ____, all types of pizza share two things. Each begins with flat bread, and each is a slice of history.

출제율 95%

26 위 글의 빈칸 ⓐ에 들어갈 알맞은 말을 고르시오.

① As a result   ② However
③ For example   ④ Therefore
⑤ In other words

출제율 90%

27 위 글의 밑줄 친 (A)while과 같은 의미로 쓰인 것을 고르시오.

① Strike while the iron is hot.
② While there is life, there is hope.
③ Please wait for a while.
④ While eating, you shouldn't speak.
⑤ The walls are green, while the ceiling is white.

출제율 100%

28 위 글의 주제로 알맞은 것을 고르시오.

① pizza toppings different from place to place
② the difference between the toppings of ancient times and those of today
③ the way pizza became a global dish
④ pizza as a global dish and a slice of history
⑤ the way pizza became known outside of Italy

MEMO

1학기 전과정

적중100 plus

영어 기출문제집

영어 중 3

천재 | 이재영

Best Collection

내용문의 중등영어발전소 적중100 편집부 TEL 070-7707-0457

INSIGHT
on the textbook

교과서 파헤치기

영어 기출 문제집

적중 100 plus
1학기 전과정

영어 중 3

천재 | 이재영

INSIGHT
on the textbook

교과서 파헤치기

※ 다음 영어를 우리말로 쓰시오.

01	pack		22	present
02	appear		23	merchant
03	priceless		24	subject
04	chase		25	tool
05	realize		26	delighted
06	prepare		27	spice
07	chew		28	puzzled
08	serve		29	trade
09	jealous		30	valuable
10	relax		31	whisper
11	repay		32	pleased
12	hurry		33	kitten
13	chest		34	wonder
14	allowance		35	after a while
15	include		36	thanks to ~
16	speechless		37	chase A away
17	palace		38	take care of ~
18	invention		39	get over
19	faraway		40	all day long
20	worthless		41	have two left feet
21	servant		42	take ~ hard
			43	be sure that ~

※ 다음 우리말을 영어로 쓰시오.

01 추적하다

02 기쁜

03 비옷

04 상품

05 서두르다

06 나타나다

07 말문이 막힌

08 하인

09 용돈

10 멀리 떨어진

11 새끼 고양이

12 도구, 연장

13 보물, 보석

14 무역하다, 교역하다

15 갚다

16 상인

17 짐을 꾸리다, 가득 채우다

18 상자, 가슴

19 향료

20 쉬다

21 궁전

22 주다, 선사하다

23 속삭이다

24 포함하다

25 소중한

26 당황스러운

27 씹다

28 깨닫다

29 준비하다

30 발명, 발명품

31 질투하는

32 음식을 날라 주다

33 가치 없는

34 소중한

35 극복하다

36 하루 종일

37 ~을 돌보다

38 동작이 어색하다, 몸치이다

39 행운을 빌어!

40 ~ 덕택에

41 A를 쫓아내다

42 ~을 확신하다

43 시간을 알아보다

※ 다음 영영풀이에 알맞은 단어를 <보기>에서 골라 쓴 후, 우리말 뜻을 쓰시오.

1 _____ : a young cat: _____

2 _____ : extremely valuable or important: _____

3 _____ : the official home of a king, queen, president, etc.: _____

4 _____ : to make someone or something part of a larger group: _____

5 _____ : someone who buys and sells goods in large quantities: _____

6 _____ : to pay back the money that you have borrowed from somebody: _____

7 _____ : a precious stone such as a diamond, ruby, etc.: _____

8 _____ : to put things into cases, bags etc ready for a trip somewhere: _____

9 _____ : to quickly follow someone or something in order to catch them: _____

10 _____ : an amount of money that you are given regularly or for a special purpose: _____

11 _____ : to speak very quietly to somebody so that other people cannot hear what you are saying: _____

12 _____ : a film, television programme, computer game etc that has pictures, clay models etc that seem to be really moving: _____

13 _____ : a large strong box that you use to store things in or to move your personal possessions from one place to another: _____

14 _____ : someone, especially in the past, who was paid to clean someone's house, cook for them, answer the door etc.: _____

15 _____ : something such as a hammer, saw, shovel, etc. that you hold in your hand and use for a particular task: _____

16 _____ : to bite food into small pieces in your mouth with your teeth to make it easier to swallow: _____

보기			
chase	servant	jewel	chew
include	kitten	tool	priceless
repay	merchant	palace	pack
whisper	animation	allowance	chest

※ 다음 우리말과 일치하도록 빈칸에 알맞은 말을 쓰시오.

Listen – Listen and Answer – Dialog 1

G: Hey, Minjun. _____ a _____!

B: Hi, Sora. I'm _____ we're in the _____ _____.

G: I _____, _____. We're now in our _____ _____ in middle school. _____ do you _____?

B: I'm _____ _____ _____ that there'll be more schoolwork.

G: Me, too. We also _____ _____ think about our _____ school.

B: _____ _____ of school do you _____ in _____?

G: I'm _____ of an animation high school. I love _____.

Listen – Listen and Answer – Dialog 2

G: Oliver, _____ _____ are you _____ to _____?

B: I'm not _____. _____ _____ you, Sora?

G: I want _____ _____ the school dance club.

B: Really? But I _____ you're _____ _____ an animation high school.

G: Right, but I _____ some time _____ _____. We all _____ to do something _____ _____ _____ stress.

B: _____ _____ _____ that again.

G: _____ _____ you join me? It'll be fun.

B: No, _____. Dancing is not _____ _____. I have _____ _____ _____.

Listen More – Listen and say

B: Jimin, look! That red phone _____ _____ _____!

G: You can _____ _____ again! Mom would love it _____ a _____ _____.

B: I _____ _____ _____ it _____.

G: _____ me _____. It _____ 40,000 won.

B: Really? That's so _____.

G: I don't _____. Look! It _____ _____ a wallet, _____.

B: Oh, I didn't see that. Then _____ _____ it for Mom.

G: Okay. I'm _____ _____ _____ something _____ for Mom.

B: _____ _____ I.

G: 야, 민준아. 정말 놀랍다!

B: 안녕, 소라야. 우리가 같은 반에 있어서 기뻐.

G: 나도 그래. 우리 이제 중학교의 마지막 학년이야. 기분이 어떠니?

B: 공부할 게 더 많을 것 같아서 조금 걱정이야.

G: 나도 그래. 고등학교에 대해서도 생각해야 하지.

B: 너는 어떤 학교를 마음에 두고 있니?

G: 나는 애니메이션 고등학교를 생각하고 있어. 내가 그림 그리는 걸 좋아하거든.

G: Oliver, 넌 어느 동아리에 들어갈 거니?

B: 잘 모르겠어. 소라, 너는?

G: 난 학교 춤 동아리에 가입하고 싶어.

B: 정말? 하지만 네가 애니메이션 고등학교를 준비하고 있다고 들었는데.

G: 그렇긴 한데, 좀 쉴 시간이 필요해. 우리 모두 스트레스를 극복하려면 뭔가를 할 필요가 있잖아.

B: 전적으로 동의해.

G: 너 나랑 함께하는 게 어때? 재미있을 거야.

B: 고맙지만 사양할게. 춤은 내게 맞지 않아. 난 몸치야.

B: 지민아, 봐! 저 빨간 전화기 케이스 멋지다!

G: 정말 그렇다! 생신 선물로 어머니께서 좋아하실 거야.

B: 난 가격이 얼마인지 궁금해.

G: 어디 보자. 가격은 40,000원이야.

B: 정말? 그거 너무 비싸다!

G: 난 동의하지 않아. 봐! 이건 지갑 역할도 해.

B: 아, 그건 못 봤어. 그럼 어머니를 위해 그걸 사자.

G: 알았어. 어머니께 뭔가 특별한 것을 사 드리게 되어 기뻐.

B: 나도 그래.

Speak - Talk in pairs.

A: Did you _____ the _____ _____?

B: Yes. It's _____ _____ _____ all day _____.

A: Really? I'm _____ I can _____ my new _____.

B: _____ _____ you.

Speak - Talk in groups.

A: I think _____ _____ _____ day of the _____ is Monday.

B: You _____ _____ that _____.

C: I _____ _____ so. Thursday is the _____ _____.

D: I _____. We have all the _____ _____ on Thursday.

My Speaking Portfolio

1. B1: _____ do you do in your _____ time? I _____ to music.
   I think it's the _____ _____. I can't _____ _____ it.

2. G: I think chocolate is the _____ _____. It makes me _____
   _____. It also helps me _____ _____ when I study.

3. B2: Many people will _____ that paper is the greatest invention.
   _____ _____ paper, we all can _____ books and
   _____ things _____.

Wrap up - Listening & Speaking ⑤

B: You _____ so _____. What's _____ _____?

G: Oh, I'm just _____ for the school play tomorrow.

B: _____ do you _____ _____ it?

G: I'm _____ I may _____ a _____.

B: I'm _____ you'll do well. _____ a _____!

G: Thanks.

Wrap up - Listening & Speaking ⑥

G: _____ you _____ about Mr. Oh?

B: No. _____ _____ him?

G: He _____ first _____ in the TV quiz show.

B: It's not _____. He _____ _____ know about everything.

G: You can say that again! He's a _____ _____.

A: 일기예보 들었니?
B: 들었어. 하루 종일 비가 올 거야.
A: 정말! 새 비옷을 입을 수 있어 기뻐.
B: 좋겠다.

A: 나는 가장 지루한 날이 월요일이라고 생각해.
B: 네 말이 맞아.
C: 나는 그렇게 생각하지 않아. 목요일이 가장 지루해.
D: 나도 동의해. 우리는 목요일에 어려운 과목이 모두 있어.

1. B1: 여러분은 여가 시간에 무엇을 하나요? 나는 음악을 듣습니다. 나는 음악이 가장 위대한 발명품이라고 생각합니다. 나는 음악 없이는 살 수 없습니다.

2. G: 나는 초콜릿이 가장 위대한 발명품이라고 생각합니다. 초콜릿은 내가 기분이 좋아지도록 해 줍니다. 그것은 또한 내가 공부할 때 더 잘 집중하도록 도와줍니다.

3. B2: 종이가 가장 위대한 발명품이라는 데 많은 사람이 동의할 것입니다. 종이 덕분에 우리는 모두 책을 읽고 무언가를 적을 수 있습니다.

B: 너 진지해 보인다. 무슨 일이니?
G: 아, 그냥 내일 있을 학교 연극을 연습하는 중이야.
B: 기분이 어때?
G: 실수할까 봐 걱정돼.
B: 너는 틀림없이 잘할 거야. 행운을 빌어!
G: 고마워.

G: 오 선생님에 관해 들었니?
B: 아니. 선생님에 관해 뭘?
G: 선생님이 TV 퀴즈 쇼에서 우승하셨대.
B: 놀랄 일도 아니지. 선생님은 모든 것에 관해 알고 계신 것 같아.
G: 맞아! 걸어 다니는 사전이시지.

※ 다음 우리말에 맞도록 대화를 영어로 쓰시오.

Listen – Listen and Answer – Dialog 1

G: _____

B: _____

G: _____

B: _____

G: _____

B: _____

G: _____

G: 야, 민준아. 정말 놀랍다!
B: 안녕, 소라야. 우리가 같은 반에 있어서 기뻐.
G: 나도 그래. 우리 이제 중학교의 마지막 학년이야. 기분이 어떠니?
B: 공부할 게 더 많을 것 같아서 조금 걱정이야.
G: 나도 그래. 고등학교에 대해서도 생각해야 하지.
B: 너는 어떤 학교를 마음에 두고 있니?
G: 나는 애니메이션 고등학교를 생각하고 있어. 내가 그림 그리는 걸 좋아하거든.

Listen – Listen and Answer – Dialog 2

G: _____

B: _____

G: _____

B: _____

G: _____

B: _____

G: _____

B: _____

G: Oliver, 넌 어느 동아리에 들어갈 거니?
B: 잘 모르겠어. 소라, 너는?
G: 난 학교 춤 동아리에 가입하고 싶어.
B: 정말? 하지만 네가 애니메이션 고등학교를 준비하고 있다고 들었는데.
G: 그렇긴 한데, 좀 쉴 시간이 필요해. 우리 모두 스트레스를 극복하려면 뭔가를 할 필요가 있잖아.
B: 전적으로 동의해.
G: 너 나랑 함께하는 게 어때? 재미있을 거야.
B: 고맙지만 사양할게. 춤은 내게 맞지 않아. 난 몸치야.

Listen More – Listen and say

B: _____

G: _____

B: _____

G: _____

B: _____

G: _____

B: _____

G: _____

B: _____

B: 지민아, 봐! 저 빨간 전화기 케이스 멋지다!
G: 정말 그렇다! 생신 선물로 어머니께서 좋아하실 거야.
B: 난 가격이 얼마인지 궁금해.
G: 어디 보자. 가격은 40,000원이야.
B: 정말? 그거 너무 비싸다!
G: 난 동의하지 않아. 봐! 이건 지갑 역할도 해.
B: 아, 그건 못 봤어. 그럼 어머니를 위해 그걸 사자.
G: 알았어. 어머니께 뭔가 특별한 것을 사 드리게 되어 기뻐.
B: 나도 그래.

Speak - Talk in pairs.

A: _____

B: _____

A: _____

B: _____

A: 일기예보 들었니?
B: 들었어. 하루 종일 비가 올 거야.
A: 정말! 새 비옷을 입을 수 있어 기뻐.
B: 좋겠다.

Speak - Talk in groups.

A: _____

B: _____

C: _____

D: _____

A: 나는 가장 지루한 날이 월요일이라고 생각해.
B: 네 말이 맞아.
C: 나는 그렇게 생각하지 않아. 목요일 이 가장 지루해.
D: 나도 동의해. 우리는 목요일에 어려 운 과목이 모두 있어.

My Speaking Portfolio

1. B1: _____

_____

2. G: _____

_____

3. B2: _____

_____

1. B1: 여러분은 여가 시간에 무엇을 하나요? 나는 음악을 듣습니다. 나는 음악이 가장 위대한 발명 품이라고 생각합니다. 나는 음 악 없이는 살 수 없습니다.
2. G: 나는 초콜릿이 가장 위대한 발명 품이라고 생각합니다. 초콜릿은 내가 기분이 좋아지도록 해 줍니 다. 그것은 또한 내가 공부할 때 더 잘 집중하도록 도와줍니다.
3. B2: 종이가 가장 위대한 발명품이라 는 데 많은 사람이 동의할 것입 니다. 종이 덕분에 우리는 모두 책을 읽고 무언가를 적을 수 있 습니다.

Wrap up - Listening & Speaking ⑤

B: _____

G: _____

B: _____

G: _____

B: _____

G: _____

B: 너 진지해 보인다. 무슨 일이니?
G: 아, 그냥 내일 있을 학교 연극을 연 습하는 중이야.
B: 기분이 어때?
G: 실수할까 봐 걱정돼.
B: 너는 틀림없이 잘할 거야. 행운을 빌 어!
G: 고마워.

Wrap up - Listening & Speaking ⑥

G: _____

B: _____

G: _____

B: _____

G: _____

G: 오 선생님에 관해 들었니?
B: 아니. 선생님에 관해 뭘?
G: 선생님이 TV 퀴즈 쇼에서 우승하셨 대.
B: 놀랄 일도 아니지. 선생님은 모든 것 에 관해 알고 계신 것 같아.
G: 맞아! 걸어 다니는 사전이시지.

※ 다음 우리말과 일치하도록 빈칸에 알맞은 것을 골라 쓰시오.

1 A _____ _____

A. Gift   B. Priceless

2 Long _____, an _____ _____ lived _____ Genoa, Italy.

A. in   B. merchant   C. ago   D. honest

3 His name was Antonio, and he went to different _____ to _____ his family _____ _____.

A. support   B. trading   C. by   D. places

4 One day, he _____ his ship _____ _____ and visited a _____ island.

A. faraway   B. filled   C. goods   D. with

5 There he _____ tools for _____ and books _____ _____.

A. nuts   B. traded   C. spices   D. for

6 _____ _____ Antonio, the islanders could get _____ they _____.

A. to   B. needed   C. thanks   D. what

7 One night, Antonio had _____ _____ the island's _____ at her _____.

A. palace   B. dinner   C. queen   D. with

8 When dinner was _____, rats _____, and some servants _____ them _____ with sticks.

A. chased   B. served   C. away   D. appeared

9 Antonio was _____ _____ that _____ were rats in the _____.

A. surprised   B. palace   C. greatly   D. there

10 He asked, "_____ _____ _____ _____ on this island?"

A. cats   B. are   C. no   D. there

11 The queen _____ _____.

A. puzzled   B. looked

12 "What is a _____?" _____ _____.

A. she   B. cat   C. asked

13 The merchant _____ to _____, "What the islanders here need is _____ tools or books, _____ cats."

A. not   B. himself   C. said   D. but

14 He _____ two cats _____ his ship and _____ them _____ free.

A. let   B. brought   C. run   D. from

1 소중한 선물

2 먼 옛날 이탈리아 제노바에 정직한 상인 한 명이 살았다.

3 그의 이름은 Antonio로, 그는 교역으로 가족을 부양하기 위해 여러 곳을 다녔다.

4 어느 날 그는 배에 상품을 가득 싣고 머나먼 섬으로 갔다.

5 거기서 그는 공구를 향신료와 바꾸었고, 책을 견과류와 바꾸었다.

6 Antonio 덕에 섬사람들은 필요한 것을 얻을 수 있었다.

7 어느 날 밤, Antonio는 궁전에서 그 섬의 여왕과 저녁 식사를 했다.

8 식사가 나왔을 때 쥐들이 나타났고, 하인 몇 명이 막대기로 쥐를 쫓아내었다.

9 Antonio는 궁전에 쥐가 있다는 사실에 무척 놀랐다.

10 그는 "이 섬에는 고양이가 없습니까?"라고 물었다.

11 여왕은 어리둥절한 것처럼 보였다.

12 "고양이가 뭔가요?"라고 그녀가 물었다.

13 상인은 "여기 섬사람들이 필요로 하는 것은 공구나 책이 아니라 고양이야."라고 혼자 중얼거렸다.

14 그는 배에서 고양이 두 마리를 데리고 와서, 자유롭게 돌아다니도록 풀어놓았다.

15 "_____ amazing animals!" cried the queen _____ she saw all the rats _____ _____.

    A. run   B. what   C. when   D. away

16 She gave Antonio a _____ that was _____ _____ _____.

    A. filled   B. chest   C. jewels   D. with

17 _____ in Italy, Antonio _____ his friends about his _____ _____.

    A. good   B. back   C. told   D. fortune

18 Luigi, the _____ _____ in Genoa, _____ the story and was _____.

    A. heard   B. merchant   C. jealous   D. richest

19 "Cats _____ _____," Luigi _____.

    A. thought   B. worthless   C. are

20 "I'll _____ the queen _____ is really _____.

    A. what   B. bring   C. valuable

21 I'm _____ that the _____ will give _____ more _____."

    A. me   B. sure   C. jewels   D. queen

22 Luigi _____ his ship _____ wonderful paintings and _____ _____ of art.

    A. with   B. works   C. packed   D. other

23 He _____ the _____ to the _____.

    A. gifts   B. took   C. island

24 To get a _____ to meet the queen, he told the _____ a _____ that he was a _____ friend of Antonio's.

    A. lie   B. chance   C. islanders   D. good

25 When the queen _____ about Luigi, she _____ him to her _____ for _____.

    A. invited   B. heard   C. dinner   D. palace

26 Before _____ down at the table, Luigi _____ the queen _____ all his gifts, and the queen thanked him _____ and again.

    A. with   B. sitting   C. again   D. presented

27 "I'll _____ you _____ a _____ gift," said the queen.

    A. with   B. repay   C. priceless

28 Luigi _____ the queen _____ in a servant's _____.

    A. whisper   B. watched   C. ear

---

15 "정말 놀라운 동물이네요!" 쥐가 모두 도망가는 것을 보자 여왕이 감탄하였다.

16 그녀는 Antonio에게 보석이 가득한 상자를 주었다.

17 이탈리아로 돌아와서, Antonio는 자신에게 일어난 행운을 친구들에게 이야기했다.

18 제노바에서 가장 부유한 상인인 Luigi는 그 이야기를 듣고 시샘이 일었다.

19 "고양이는 쓸모없어." Luigi가 생각했다.

20 "난 여왕에게 정말로 귀중한 것을 가지고 갈 거야.

21 틀림없이 여왕이 내게 더 많은 보석을 줄 거야."

22 Luigi는 멋진 그림들과 다른 예술 작품을 배에 실었다.

23 그는 선물을 섬으로 가지고 갔다.

24 여왕을 만날 기회를 얻기 위해서, 그는 자신이 Antonio의 친한 친구라고 섬사람들에게 거짓말을 했다.

25 Luigi에 관해 듣고, 여왕은 그를 궁전으로 저녁 식사에 초대했다.

26 식탁에 앉기 전에 Luigi는 여왕에게 자신이 가져온 온갖 선물을 전했고, 여왕은 그에게 여러 차례 감사하다고 했다.

27 "당신께 값진 선물로 보답하겠습니다."라고 여왕이 말했다.

28 Luigi는 여왕이 하인의 귀에 대고 속삭이는 것을 지켜보았다.

29 He _____ _____ and _____.

A. excited   B. became   C. hopeful

30 He was sure that he would _____ _____ _____ _____ Antonio.

A. more   B. receive   C. than   D. jewels

31 After a _____, the servant _____ with a box, and the queen _____ it _____ Luigi.

A. returned   B. while   C. presented   D. to

32 _____ Luigi _____ the box, he was _____.

A. opened   B. when   C. speechless

33 _____ was a _____ in the _____.

A. box   B. there   C. kitten

34 "Antonio _____ us the _____ cats, and we now have some _____," said the _____.

A. kittens   B. priceless   C. queen   D. gave

35 "In _____ for the wonderful gifts you gave us, we want to give you _____ is _____ _____ to us."

A. what   B. return   C. valuable   D. most

36 Luigi _____ that, in the queen's _____, the kitten was _____ _____ more than all the jewels in the world.

A. mind   B. far   C. realized   D. worth

37 He _____ to _____ _____ with the gift.

A. look   B. tried   C. pleased

38 He knew that was the _____ _____ _____ _____.

A. to   B. right   C. do   D. thing

39 Luigi did not _____ _____ a _____ _____.

A. home   B. man   C. richer   D. return

40 But he was _____ a _____.

A. wiser   B. surely   C. one

---

29 그는 흥분되고 기대에 부풀었다.

30 그는 Antonio보다 많은 보석을 받게 될 거라고 확신했다.

31 잠시 후에 하인이 상자 하나를 가지고 돌아왔고, 여왕은 그것을 Luigi에게 주었다.

32 상자를 열어본 Luigi는 말문이 막혔다.

33 상자 안에는 새끼 고양이 한 마리가 들어 있었다.

34 "Antonio가 우리에게 매우 귀한 고양이들을 줬는데, 이제 새끼 고양이 몇 마리가 생겼어요."라고 여왕이 말했다.

35 "당신이 우리에게 준 멋진 선물에 보답하는 뜻에서, 우리에게 가장 값진 것을 당신에게 드리고 싶어요."

36 여왕의 생각에는 세상의 온갖 보석보다 새끼 고양이가 훨씬 더 가치 있다는 것을 Luigi는 깨달았다.

37 그는 선물에 대해 기뻐하는 표정을 지으려고 애썼다.

38 그게 올바른 행동이라는 것을 그는 알았다.

39 Luigi는 더 부유한 사람이 되어 집으로 돌아오지는 않았다.

40 하지만 그는 분명히 더 현명한 사람이 되었다.

※ 다음 우리말과 일치하도록 빈칸에 알맞은 것을 골라 쓰시오.

1 A _____ _____

2 Long ago, _____ _____ _____ _____ in Genoa, Italy.

3 His name was Antonio, and he went to different places _____ _____ _____ _____ _____ _____ _____ .

4 One day, he _____ his ship _____ goods and visited a _____ _____ .

5 There he _____ tools _____ spices and books _____ nuts.

6 _____ _____ Antonio, the islanders could get _____ they _____ .

7 One night, Antonio _____ _____ _____ the island's queen at her palace.

8 When dinner _____ _____ , rats _____ , and some servants _____ _____ _____ _____ _____ .

9 Antonio was _____ _____ that _____ _____ rats in the palace.

10 He asked, " _____ _____ _____ _____ _____ on this island?"

11 The queen _____ _____ .

12 "What is a cat?" _____ _____ .

13 The merchant _____ _____ _____ , " _____ the islanders here need is _____ tools or books, _____ cats."

14 He _____ two cats _____ his ship and _____ _____ _____ _____ .

1	소중한 선물
2	먼 옛날 이탈리아 제노바에 정직한 상인 한 명이 살았다.
3	그의 이름은 Antonio로, 그는 교역으로 가족을 부양하기 위해 여러 곳을 다녔다.
4	어느 날 그는 배에 상품을 가득 싣고 머나먼 섬으로 갔다.
5	거기서 그는 공구를 향신료와 바꾸었고, 책을 견과류와 바꾸었다.
6	Antonio 덕에 섬사람들은 필요한 것을 얻을 수 있었다.
7	어느 날 밤, Antonio는 궁전에서 그 섬의 여왕과 저녁 식사를 했다.
8	식사가 나왔을 때 쥐들이 나타났고, 하인 몇 명이 막대기로 쥐를 쫓아내었다.
9	Antonio는 궁전에 쥐가 있다는 사실에 무척 놀랐다.
10	그는 "이 섬에는 고양이가 없습니까?"라고 물었다.
11	여왕은 어리둥절한 것처럼 보였다.
12	"고양이가 뭔가요?"라고 그녀가 물었다.
13	상인은 "여기 섬사람들이 필요로 하는 것은 공구나 책이 아니라 고양이야."라고 혼자 중얼거렸다.
14	그는 배에서 고양이 두 마리를 데리고 와서, 자유롭게 돌아다니도록 풀어놓았다.

15 "_____ _____ animals!" cried the queen when she saw all the rats _____ _____.

16 She gave Antonio a chest that _____ _____ _____ jewels.

17 _____ _____ Italy, Antonio told his friends about his _____ _____.

18 Luigi, _____ _____ _____ in Genoa, _____ the story and was _____.

19 "Cats are _____," Luigi _____.

20 "I'll bring the queen _____ is really _____.

21 _____ _____ that the queen will give me _____ _____."

22 Luigi _____ his ship _____ wonderful paintings and other _____ _____ _____.

23 He _____ the gifts _____ the island.

24 _____ _____ a chance to meet the queen, he told the islanders a lie that he was _____ _____ _____ _____ _____.

25 When the queen _____ _____ Luigi, she _____ him _____ her palace for dinner.

26 Before _____ down at the table, Luigi _____ the queen _____ all his gifts, and the queen _____ him _____ _____ _____.

27 "I'll _____ you _____ a _____ gift," said the queen.

28 Luigi _____ the queen _____ in a servant's ear.

---

15 "정말 놀라운 동물이네요!" 쥐가 모두 도망가는 것을 보자 여왕이 감탄하였다.

16 그녀는 Antonio에게 보석이 가득한 상자를 주었다.

17 이탈리아로 돌아와서, Antonio는 자신에게 일어난 행운을 친구들에게 이야기했다.

18 제노바에서 가장 부유한 상인인 Luigi는 그 이야기를 듣고 시샘이 일었다.

19 "고양이는 쓸모없어." Luigi가 생각했다.

20 "난 여왕에게 정말로 귀중한 것을 가지고 갈 거야.

21 틀림없이 여왕이 내게 더 많은 보석을 줄 거야."

22 Luigi는 멋진 그림들과 다른 예술 작품을 배에 실었다.

23 그는 선물을 섬으로 가지고 갔다.

24 여왕을 만날 기회를 얻기 위해서, 그는 자신이 Antonio의 친한 친구라고 섬사람들에게 거짓말을 했다.

25 Luigi에 관해 듣고, 여왕은 그를 궁전으로 저녁 식사에 초대했다.

26 식탁에 앉기 전에 Luigi는 여왕에게 자신이 가져온 온갖 선물을 전했고, 여왕은 그에게 여러 차례 감사하다고 했다.

27 "당신께 값진 선물로 보답하겠습니다."라고 여왕이 말했다.

28 Luigi는 여왕이 하인의 귀에 대고 속삭이는 것을 지켜보았다.

29 He became _____ and _____.

30 He _____ _____ that he would receive _____ _____ _____ Antonio.

31 _____ _____ _____, the servant returned with a box, and the queen _____ it _____ Luigi.

32 When Luigi _____ the box, he was _____.

33 There was a _____ in the box.

34 "Antonio gave us the _____ cats, and we now have some kittens," said the queen.

35 "_____ _____ _____ the wonderful gifts you gave us, we want to give you _____ _____ _____ _____ to us."

36 Luigi _____ that, in the queen's _____, the kitten was _____ _____ _____ _____ all the jewels in the world.

37 He tried to _____ _____ _____ the gift.

38 He knew that was the _____ _____ _____ _____.

39 Luigi did not _____ _____ a _____ man.

40 But he was _____ _____ _____ _____.

29 그는 흥분되고 기대에 부풀었다.

30 그는 Antonio보다 많은 보석을 받게 될 거라고 확신했다.

31 잠시 후에 하인이 상자 하나를 가지고 돌아왔고, 여왕은 그것을 Luigi에게 주었다.

32 상자를 열어본 Luigi는 말문이 막혔다.

33 상자 안에는 새끼 고양이 한 마리가 들어 있었다.

34 "Antonio가 우리에게 매우 귀한 고양이들을 줬는데, 이제 새끼 고양이 몇 마리가 생겼어요."라고 여왕이 말했다.

35 "당신이 우리에게 준 멋진 선물에 보답하는 뜻에서, 우리에게 가장 값진 것을 당신에게 드리고 싶어요."

36 여왕의 생각에는 세상의 온갖 보석보다 새끼 고양이가 훨씬 더 가치 있다는 것을 Luigi는 깨달았다.

37 그는 선물에 대해 기뻐하는 표정을 지으려고 애썼다.

38 그게 올바른 행동이라는 것을 그는 알았다.

39 Luigi는 더 부유한 사람이 되어 집으로 돌아오지는 않았다.

40 하지만 그는 분명히 더 현명한 사람이 되었다.

※ 다음 문장을 우리말로 쓰시오.

1 ▶ A Priceless Gift

➡ _____

2 ▶ Long ago, an honest merchant lived in Genoa, Italy.

➡ _____

3 ▶ His name was Antonio, and he went to different places to support his family by trading.

➡ _____

4 ▶ One day, he filled his ship with goods and visited a faraway island.

➡ _____

5 ▶ There he traded tools for spices and books for nuts.

➡ _____

6 ▶ Thanks to Antonio, the islanders could get what they needed.

➡ _____

7 ▶ One night, Antonio had dinner with the island's queen at her palace.

➡ _____

8 ▶ When dinner was served, rats appeared, and some servants chased them away with sticks.

➡ _____

9 ▶ Antonio was greatly surprised that there were rats in the palace.

➡ _____

10 ▶ He asked, "Are there no cats on this island?"

➡ _____

11 ▶ The queen looked puzzled.

➡ _____

12 ▶ "What is a cat?" she asked.

➡ _____

13 ▶ The merchant said to himself, "What the islanders here need is not tools or books, but cats."

➡ _____

14 ▶ He brought two cats from his ship and let them run free.

➡ _____

15 "What amazing animals!" cried the queen when she saw all the rats run away.

➡ _____

16 She gave Antonio a chest that was filled with jewels.

➡ _____

17 Back in Italy, Antonio told his friends about his good fortune.

➡ _____

18 Luigi, the richest merchant in Genoa, heard the story and was jealous.

➡ _____

19 "Cats are worthless," Luigi thought.

➡ _____

20 "I'll bring the queen what is really valuable.

➡ _____

21 I'm sure that the queen will give me more jewels."

➡ _____

22 Luigi packed his ship with wonderful paintings and other works of art.

➡ _____

23 He took the gifts to the island.

➡ _____

24 To get a chance to meet the queen, he told the islanders a lie that he was a good friend of Antonio's.

➡ _____

25 When the queen heard about Luigi, she invited him to her palace for dinner.

➡ _____

26 Before sitting down at the table, Luigi presented the queen with all his gifts, and the queen thanked him again and again.

➡ _____

27 "I'll repay you with a priceless gift," said the queen.

➡ _____

28 Luigi watched the queen whisper in a servant's ear.

➡ _____

29▶ He became excited and hopeful.

➡ _____

30▶ He was sure that he would receive more jewels than Antonio.

➡ _____

31▶ After a while, the servant returned with a box, and the queen presented it to Luigi.

➡ _____

32▶ When Luigi opened the box, he was speechless.

➡ _____

33▶ There was a kitten in the box.

➡ _____

34▶ "Antonio gave us the priceless cats, and we now have some kittens," said the queen.

➡ _____

35▶ "In return for the wonderful gifts you gave us, we want to give you what is most valuable to us."

➡ _____

36▶ Luigi realized that, in the queen's mind, the kitten was worth far more than all the jewels in the world.

➡ _____

37▶ He tried to look pleased with the gift.

➡ _____

38▶ He knew that was the right thing to do.

➡ _____

39▶ Luigi did not return home a richer man.

➡ _____

40▶ But he was surely a wiser one.

➡ _____

※ 다음 괄호 안의 단어들을 우리말에 맞도록 바르게 배열하시오.

1 (Priceless / Gift / A)
➡ _____

2 (ago, / long / honest / an / lived / merchant / Genoa, / in / Italy.)
➡ _____

3 (name / his / Antonio, / was / he / and / to / went / places / different / support / to / family / his / trading. / by)
➡ _____
_____

4 (day, / one / filled / he / ship / his / goods / with / and / a / visited / island. / faraway)
➡ _____

5 (he / there / tools / traded / spices / for / and / nuts. / for / books)
➡ _____

6 (to / thanks / Antonio, / islanders / the / get / could / what / needed. / they)
➡ _____

7 (night, / one / had / Antonio / with / dinner / the / queen / island's / at / palace. / her)
➡ _____

8 (dinner / when / served, / was / appeared, / rats / and / servants / some / them / chased / with / away / sticks.)
➡ _____

9 (was / Antonio / surprised / greatly / there / that / rats / were / the / palace. / in)
➡ _____

10 (asked, / he / there / "are / cats / no / this / on / island?")
➡ _____

11 (queen / the / puzzled. / looked)
➡ _____

12 (is / "what / cat?" / a / asked. / she)
➡ _____

13 (merchant / the / to / said / himself, / the / "what / here / islanders / is / need / tools / not / books, / or / cats." / but)
➡ _____

14 (brought / he / cats / two / his / from / ship / and / them / let / free. / run)
➡ _____

1 소중한 선물

2 먼 옛날 이탈리아 제노바에 정직한 상인 한 명이 살았다.

3 그의 이름은 Antonio로, 그는 교역으로 가족을 부양하기 위해 여러 곳을 다녔다.

4 어느 날 그는 배에 상품을 가득 싣고 머나먼 섬으로 갔다.

5 거기서 그는 공구를 향신료와 바꾸었고, 책을 견과류와 바꾸었다.

6 Antonio 덕에 섬사람들은 필요한 것을 얻을 수 있었다.

7 어느 날 밤, Antonio는 궁전에서 그 섬의 여왕과 저녁 식사를 했다.

8 식사가 나왔을 때 쥐들이 나났고, 하인 몇 명이 막대기로 쥐를 쫓아내었다.

9 Antonio는 궁전에 쥐가 있다는 사실에 무척 놀랐다.

10 그는 "이 섬에는 고양이가 없습니까?"라고 물었다.

11 여왕은 어리둥절한 것처럼 보였다.

12 "고양이가 뭔가요?"라고 그녀가 물었다.

13 상인은 "여기 섬사람들이 필요로 하는 것은 공구나 책이 아니라 고양이야."라고 혼자 중얼거렸다.

14 그는 배에서 고양이 두 마리를 데리고 와서, 자유롭게 돌아다니도록 풀어놓았다.

15 (amazing / "what / animals!" / the / cried / queen / she / when / all / saw / rats / the / away. / run)

➡ _____

_____

16 (gave / she / a / Antonio / chest / was / that / with / filled / jewels.)

➡ _____

17 (in / back / Italy, / told / Antonio / friends / his / about / good / fortune. / his)

➡ _____

18 (the / Luigi / merchant / richest / Genoa, / in / the / heard / story / and / jealous. / was)

➡ _____

19 (are / "cats / worthless," / thought. / Luigi)

➡ _____

20 (bring / "I'll / queen / the / is / what / valuable. / really)

➡ _____

21 (sure / I'm / the / that / will / queen / me / give / jewels." / more)

➡ _____

22 (packed / Luigi / ship / his / wonderful / with / and / paintings / works / other / art. / of)

➡ _____

23 (took / he / gifts / the / to / island. / the)

➡ _____

24 (get / to / chance / a / meet / to / queen, / the / told / he / islanders / the / lie / a / that / was / he / a / friend / good / Antonio's. / of)

➡ _____

_____

25 (the / when / heard / queen / Luigi, / about / invited / she / to / him / her / dinner. / for / palace)

➡ _____

_____

26 (sitting / before / at / down / table, / the / presented / Luigi / queen / the / with / his / all / gifts, / and / queen / the / him / thanked / and / again / again.)

➡ _____

_____

27 (repay / "I'll / with / you / priceless / a / gift," / the / said / queen.)

➡ _____

28 (watched / Luigi / the / whisper / queen / a / in / ear. / servant's)

➡ _____

15 "정말 놀라운 동물이네요!" 쥐가 모두 도망가는 것을 보자 여왕이 감탄하였다.

16 그녀는 Antonio에게 보석이 가득한 상자를 주었다.

17 이탈리아로 돌아와서, Antonio는 자신에게 일어난 행운을 친구들에게 이야기했다.

18 제노바에서 가장 부유한 상인인 Luigi는 그 이야기를 듣고 시샘이 일었다.

19 "고양이는 쓸모없어." Luigi가 생각했다.

20 "난 여왕에게 정말로 귀중한 것을 가지고 갈 거야.

21 틀림없이 여왕이 내게 더 많은 보석을 줄 거야."

22 Luigi는 멋진 그림들과 다른 예술 작품을 배에 실었다.

23 그는 선물을 섬으로 가지고 갔다.

24 여왕을 만날 기회를 얻기 위해서, 그는 자신이 Antonio의 친한 친구라고 섬사람들에게 거짓말을 했다.

25 Luigi에 관해 듣고, 여왕은 그를 궁전으로 저녁 식사에 초대했다.

26 식탁에 앉기 전에 Luigi는 여왕에게 자신이 가져온 온갖 선물을 전했고, 여왕은 그에게 여러 차례 감사하다고 했다.

27 "당신께 값진 선물로 보답하겠습니다."라고 여왕이 말했다.

28 Luigi는 여왕이 하인의 귀에 대고 속삭이는 것을 지켜보았다.

29 (became / he / hopeful. / and / excited)

➡ _____

30 (was / he / that / sure / would / he / more / receive / than / jewels / Antonio.)

➡ _____

31 (a / after / while, / servant / the / with / returned / box, / a / and / queen / the / it / presented / Luigi. / to)

➡ _____

_____

32 (Luigi / when / the / opened / box, / was / he / speechless.)

➡ _____

33 (was / there / kitten / a / the / box. / in)

➡ _____

34 (gave / us / "Antonio / the / cats, / priceless / and / now / we / some / have / kittens," / the / said / queen.)

➡ _____

_____

35 (return / "in / the / for / gifts / wonderful / gave / you / us, / want / we / give / to / what / you / valuable / most / us." / to)

➡ _____

_____

36 (realized / Luigi / that, / the / in / queen's / mind, / kitten / the / worth / was / more / far / than / the / all / jewels / the / world. / in)

➡ _____

_____

37 (tried / he / look / to / with / pleased / gift. / the)

➡ _____

38 (knew / he / was / that / the / thing / right / do. / to)

➡ _____

39 (did / Luigi / return / not / a / home / man. / richer)

➡ _____

40 (he / but / surely / was / one. / wiser / a)

➡ _____

29 그는 흥분되고 기대에 부풀었다.

30 그는 Antonio보다 많은 보석을 받게 될 거라고 확신했다.

31 잠시 후에 하인이 상자 하나를 가지고 돌아왔고, 여왕은 그것을 Luigi에게 주었다.

32 상자를 열어본 Luigi는 말문이 막혔다.

33 상자 안에는 새끼 고양이 한 마리가 들어 있었다.

34 "Antonio가 우리에게 매우 귀한 고양이들을 줬는데, 이제 새끼 고양이 몇 마리가 생겼어요."라고 여왕이 말했다.

35 "당신이 우리에게 준 멋진 선물에 보답하는 뜻에서, 우리에게 가장 값진 것을 당신에게 드리고 싶어요."

36 여왕의 생각에는 세상의 온갖 보석보다 새끼 고양이가 훨씬 더 가치 있다는 것을 Luigi는 깨달았다.

37 그는 선물에 대해 기뻐하는 표정을 지으려고 애썼다.

38 그게 올바른 행동이라는 것을 그는 알았다.

39 Luigi는 더 부유한 사람이 되어 집으로 돌아오지는 않았다.

40 하지만 그는 분명히 더 현명한 사람이 되었다.

※ 다음 우리말을 영어로 쓰시오.

1 소중한 선물

➡ _____

2 먼 옛날 이탈리아 제노바에 정직한 상인 한 명이 살았다.

➡ _____

3 그의 이름은 Antonio로, 그는 교역으로 가족을 부양하기 위해 여러 곳을 다녔다.

➡ _____

4 어느 날 그는 배에 상품을 가득 싣고 머나먼 섬으로 갔다.

➡ _____

5 거기서 그는 공구를 향신료와 바꾸었고, 책을 견과류와 바꾸었다.

➡ _____

6 Antonio 덕에 섬사람들은 필요한 것을 얻을 수 있었다.

➡ _____

7 어느 날 밤, Antonio는 궁전에서 그 섬의 여왕과 저녁 식사를 했다.

➡ _____

8 식사가 나왔을 때 쥐들이 나타났고, 하인 몇 명이 막대기로 쥐를 쫓아내었다.

➡ _____

9 Antonio는 궁전에 쥐가 있다는 사실에 무척 놀랐다.

➡ _____

10 그는 "이 섬에는 고양이가 없습니까?"라고 물었다.

➡ _____

11 여왕은 어리둥절한 것처럼 보였다.

➡ _____

12 "고양이가 뭔가요?"라고 그녀가 물었다.

➡ _____

13 상인은 "여기 섬사람들이 필요로 하는 것은 공구나 책이 아니라 고양이야."라고 혼자 중얼거렸다.

➡ _____

14 그는 배에서 고양이 두 마리를 데리고 와서, 자유롭게 돌아다니도록 풀어놓았다.

➡ _____

15 "정말 놀라운 동물이네요!" 쥐가 모두 도망가는 것을 보자 여왕이 감탄하였다.

➡ _____

16 그녀는 Antonio에게 보석이 가득한 상자를 주었다.

➡ _____

17 이탈리아로 돌아와서, Antonio는 자신에게 일어난 행운을 친구들에게 이야기했다.

➡ _____

18 제노바에서 가장 부유한 상인인 Luigi는 그 이야기를 듣고 시샘이 일었다.

➡ _____

19 "고양이는 쓸모없어." Luigi가 생각했다.

➡ _____

20 "난 여왕에게 정말로 귀중한 것을 가지고 갈 거야.

➡ _____

21 틀림없이 여왕이 내게 더 많은 보석을 줄 거야."

➡ _____

22 Luigi는 멋진 그림들과 다른 예술 작품을 배에 실었다.

➡ _____

23 그는 선물을 섬으로 가지고 갔다.

➡ _____

24 여왕을 만날 기회를 얻기 위해서, 그는 자신이 Antonio의 친한 친구라고 섬사람들에게 거짓말을 했다.

➡ _____

25 Luigi에 관해 듣고, 여왕은 그를 궁전으로 저녁 식사에 초대했다.

➡ _____

26 식탁에 앉기 전에 Luigi는 여왕에게 자신이 가져온 온갖 선물을 전했고, 여왕은 그에게 여러 차례

감사하다고 했다.

➡ _____

27 "당신께 값진 선물로 보답하겠습니다."라고 여왕이 말했다.

➡ _____

28 Luigi는 여왕이 하인의 귀에 대고 속삭이는 것을 지켜보았다.

➡ _____

29 그는 흥분되고 기대에 부풀었다.

➡ _____

30 그는 Antonio보다 많은 보석을 받게 될 거라고 확신했다.

➡ _____

31 잠시 후에 하인이 상자 하나를 가지고 돌아왔고, 여왕은 그것을 Luigi에게 주었다.

➡ _____

32 상자를 열어본 Luigi는 말문이 막혔다.

➡ _____

33 상자 안에는 새끼 고양이 한 마리가 들어 있었다.

➡ _____

34 "Antonio가 우리에게 매우 귀한 고양이들을 줬는데, 이제 새끼 고양이 몇 마리가 생겼어요."라고

여왕이 말했다.

➡ _____

35 "당신이 우리에게 준 멋진 선물에 보답하는 뜻에서, 우리에게 가장 값진 것을 당신에게 드리고 싶어요."

➡ _____

36 여왕의 생각에는 세상의 온갖 보석보다 새끼 고양이가 훨씬 더 가치 있다는 것을 Luigi는 깨달았다.

➡ _____

37 그는 선물에 대해 기뻐하는 표정을 지으려고 애썼다.

➡ _____

38 그게 올바른 행동이라는 것을 그는 알았다.

➡ _____

39 Luigi는 더 부유한 사람이 되어 집으로 돌아오지는 않았다.

➡ _____

40 하지만 그는 분명히 더 현명한 사람이 되었다.

➡ _____

구석구석 지문 Test

※ 다음 우리말과 일치하도록 빈칸에 알맞은 말을 쓰시오.

My Speaking Portfolio

1. A: What is _____ _____ _____ in history?

2. B: _____ _____ the clock. We can't _____ _____ _____ without it.

3. C: I _____ really _____ _____ you. I think the cell phone is _____ _____ _____.

4. D: You can _____ _____ _____.

1. A: 무엇이 역사상 가장 위대한 발명품이니?
2. B: 나는 시계라고 말하겠어. 그것이 없으면 시간을 알 수 없어.
3. C: 나는 동의하지 않아. 나는 휴대전화가 가장 위대한 발명품이라고 생각해.
4. D: 네 말이 맞아.

All Ears

1. M: 1. I _____ _____ _____ you _____ _____ _____.

   2. I _____ _____ you _____ the plan.

2. A: I'm _____ I can _____ _____ _____ _____.

3. B: You're _____ _____ the zoo? _____ _____ you.

4. A: I _____ I have _____ _____ _____ a snack.

5. B: I _____ _____. You must _____ _____ _____.

1. M: 1. 나는 그 문제에 대하여 너에게 동의하지 않아.
       2. 나는 네가 그 계획을 좋아하지 않는 다는 것을 알지 못했어.
2. A: 나는 동물원에 갈 수 있어서 기뻐.
3. B: 동물원에 가니? 좋겠구나.
4. A: 나는 간식을 먹을 시간이 있다고 생각해.
5. B: 나는 동의하지 않아. 너는 서둘러 되돌아가야 해.

Wrap Up - Reading

1. Isabel _____ in a _____ _____ _____ Kakamega, Kenya.

2. In the past, she _____ _____ walk a _____ _____ every day _____ _____ clean water.

3. She sometimes _____ _____ _____ _____ the _____ _____ _____ _____.

4. Three months _____, she _____ a _____ _____ from a _____ _____.

5. It _____ _____ a thick straw.

6. Dirty water _____ _____ _____ _____, and clean water _____ _____ _____ it.

7. Isabel _____ the straw _____.

8. Now, she does _____ _____ _____ _____.

9. She can go to school _____ _____.

10. So, the straw is _____ _____ _____ _____ to Isabel.

1. Isabel은 케냐의 Kakamega 인근 마을에 살고 있다.
2. 예전에 그녀는 깨끗한 물을 구하기 위해 매일 먼 거리를 걸어야 했다.
3. 그녀는 가끔 그녀가 마신 더러운 물로 인해 병에 걸리기도 했다.
4. 석달 전 그녀는 자원봉사자 한 명에게서 귀한 선물을 받았다.
5. 그것은 두꺼운 빨대처럼 생겼다.
6. 더러운 물이 빨대로 들어가면 깨끗한 물이 나온다.
7. Isabel은 그것을 어디나 가지고 다닌다.
8. 이제 그녀는 더 이상 병에 걸리지 않는다.
09 매일 학교에 갈 수 있다.
10. 그래서 그 빨대는 Isabel에게 가장 귀중한 것이다.

※ 다음 우리말을 영어로 쓰시오.

My Speaking Portfolio

1. A: 무엇이 역사상 가장 위대한 발명품이니?
➡ _____

2. B: 나는 시계라고 말하겠어. 그것이 없으면 시간을 알 수 없어.
➡ _____

3. C: 나는 동의하지 않아. 나는 휴대전화가 가장 위대한 발명품이라고 생각해.
➡ _____

4. D: 네 말이 맞아.
➡ _____

All Ears

1. M: 1. 나는 그 문제에 대하여 너에게 동의하지 않아.
➡ _____

   2. 나는 네가 그 계획을 좋아하지 않는 다는 것을 알지 못했어.
➡ _____

2. 2. A: 나는 동물원에 갈 수 있어서 기뻐.
➡ _____

3. 3. B: 동물원에 가니? 좋겠구나.
➡ _____

4. 4. A: 나는 간식을 먹을 시간이 있다고 생각해.
➡ _____

5. 5. B: 나는 동의하지 않아. 너는 서둘러 되돌아가야 해.
➡ _____

Wrap Up - Reading

1. Isabel은 케냐의 Kakamega 인근 마을에 살고 있다.
➡ _____

2. 예전에 그녀는 깨끗한 물을 구하기 위해 매일 먼 거리를 걸어야 했다.
_____

3. 그녀는 가끔 그녀가 마신 더러운 물로 인해 병에 걸리기도 했다.
➡ _____

4. 석달 전 그녀는 자원봉사자 한 명에게서 귀한 선물을 받았다.
➡ _____

5. 그것은 두꺼운 빨대처럼 생겼다.
➡ _____

6. 더러운 물이 빨대로 들어가면 깨끗한 물이 나온다.
➡ _____

7. Isabel은 그것을 어디나 가지고 다닌다.
_____

8. 이제 그녀는 더 이상 병에 걸리지 않는다.
➡ _____

9. 매일 학교에 갈 수 있다.
➡ _____

10. 그래서 그 빨대는 Isabel에게 가장 귀중한 것이다.
➡ _____

※ 다음 영어를 우리말로 쓰시오.

01	rub	22	protect
02	defend	23	female
03	chestnut	24	social
04	beehive	25	appear
05	hold	26	chemical
06	unbelievable	27	except
07	endangered	28	extremely
08	Arctic	29	including
09	skinny	30	billion
10	stripe	31	hardly
11	offer	32	weigh
12	entire	33	colony
13	male	34	resident
14	exchange	35	pass on
15	flesh	36	have a hard time
16	sensitive	37	learn by heart
17	faraway	38	out of nowhere
18	lung	39	cost an arm and a leg
19	breathe	40	one another
20	underwater	41	keep an eye on
21	nap	42	have a long face
		43	be all ears

※ 다음 우리말을 영어로 쓰시오.

01 줄무늬

02 북극의

03 여윈, 두께가 얇은

04 ~에 민감한, 예민한

05 벌집

06 나타나다, (글 속에) 나오다

07 화학물질

08 수용하다, 지니다

09 믿을 수 없는

10 살, 고기

11 낮잠

12 거주자

13 멀리 떨어진

14 밤

15 ~을 제외하고

16 보호하다

17 극심하게

18 ~을 포함하여

19 위험에 처한, 멸종 위기의

20 십억

21 거의 ~않다

22 무게가 나가다

23 군락, 군집

24 전체의

25 남성의, 수컷의

26 방어하다

27 문지르다, 비비다

28 여성의, 암컷의

29 폐

30 호흡하다

31 수중의, 물속의

32 생산하다, 만들어 내다

33 교환하다

34 백만

35 알을 낳다

36 어디선지 모르게, 느닷없이

37 서로

38 ~을 지켜보다, ~을 감시하다

39 암기하다

40 어려움을 겪다

41 ~을 돌보다

42 경청하다

43 표정이 우울하다

※ 다음 영영풀이에 알맞은 단어를 <보기>에서 골라 쓴 후, 우리말 뜻을 쓰시오.

1 _____ : to have a particular weight: _____

2 _____ : to protect somebody/something from attack: _____

3 _____ : relating to the most northern part of the world: _____

4 _____ : a structure where bees are kept for producing honey: _____

5 _____ : a short sleep, especially during the day: _____

6 _____ : very thin, especially in a way that you find unpleasant or ugly: _____

7 _____ : to take air into your lungs and send it out again through your nose or mouth: _____

8 _____ : a long narrow line of colour, that is a different colour from the areas next to it: _____

9 _____ : to decide which one of a number of things or people you want: _____

10 _____ : someone who lives or stays in a particular place: _____

11 _____ : to like someone or something more than someone or something else: _____

12 _____ : a large round fruit with hard green skin, red flesh, and black seeds: _____

13 _____ : a small creature such as a fly or ant, that has six legs, and sometimes wings: _____

14 _____ : a group of animals or plants of the same type that are living or growing together: _____

15 _____ : the act of giving someone something and receiving something else from them: _____

16 _____ : to put someone or something in a situation in which they could be harmed or damaged: _____

보기			
stripe	endangered	insect	colony
weigh	choose	watermelon	prefer
exchange	breathe	nap	skinny
resident	defend	beehive	Arctic

※ 다음 우리말과 일치하도록 빈칸에 알맞은 말을 쓰시오.

Listen – Listen and Answer – Dialog 1

B: Amber, _____ do you _____ the camp?

G: It's _____ . I'm _____ _____ _____ _____ fun.

B: _____ , too. The talent _____ last night was really _____ .

G: Yeah. _____ _____ _____ , did you _____ on the afternoon program?

B: No, I haven't _____ . _____ do you _____ is _____ , hiking or _____ ?

G: I'll go _____ because we can _____ _____ birds and _____ in the woods.

B: I'll _____ you. I like _____ and _____ .

G: Great. I _____ we'll have a hiking _____ .

B: Sounds good.

Listen – Listen and Answer – Dialog 2

W: Everyone, _____ at this _____ tree. This is _____ _____ tree in these _____ .

B: Can you _____ me _____ _____ _____ _____ ?

W: It's _____ 150 years old.

B: Wow! It's _____ _____ my _____ .

G: Ms. Oh, is that a _____ _____ in the tree?

W: Yes. Can you _____ how many _____ _____ there?

G: 500 bees?

W: Good _____ , but it's _____ to _____ _____ 50,000 bees.

B, G: _____ !

Listen More - Listen and choose.

B: Sora, can you _____ a _____ _____ these pictures?

G: _____ are these _____ ?

B: I'm _____ to _____ a picture for my _____ in the school newspaper.

G: _____ your story _____ ?

B: Nature's _____ .

G: Can you _____ me _____ _____ it?

B: It's about _____ _____ in the _____ _____ .

G: That _____ interesting.

B: _____ _____ do you _____ is _____ ?

G: I like the one _____ a _____ polar bear.

B: Amber, 캠프 어때?
G: 좋아. 아주 재미있어.
B: 나도 그래. 어젯밤 장기 자랑은 정말 멋졌어.
G: 맞아. 그런데 너는 오후 프로그램 결정했니?
B: 아니, 아직 못했어. 너는 산행과 수영 중에 뭐가 낫다고 생각해?
G: 숲에서 야생 조류와 곤충을 볼 수 있으니까 난 산행을 할 거야.
B: 나도 같이할게. 나는 새와 곤충을 좋아하거든.
G: 좋아. 산행 가이드가 있을 거라고 들었어.
B: 잘됐다.

W: 여러분, 이 밤나무를 보세요. 이것은 이 숲에서 가장 오래된 나무랍니다.
B: 그 나무가 몇 살인지 알려 주실 수 있나요?
W: 150살쯤 되었어요.
B: 와! 제 나이의 열 배군요.
G: 오 선생님, 나무 위에 있는 저것은 벌집인가요?
W: 맞아요. 벌이 저곳에서 몇 마리나 사는지 짐작할 수 있겠어요?
G: 500마리요?
W: 좋은 추측입니다. 하지만 저것은 5만 마리 이상을 수용할 만큼 커요.
B, G: 믿을 수 없어요!

B: 소라야, 이 사진들을 한번 봐 줄래?
G: 어디에 쓸 건데?
B: 학교 신문에 실을 내 이야기에 넣을 사진을 고르고 있어.
G: 네 이야기가 무엇에 관한 건데?
B: 자연의 미래.
G: 그것에 대해 더 말해 줄 수 있니?
B: 북극 지역에 사는 멸종 위기의 동물들에 관한 거야.
G: 흥미롭다.
B: 네 생각에는 어느 사진이 더 낫니?
G: 나는 여윈 북극곰을 보여 주는 사진이 마음에 들어.

Speak – Talk in groups.

A: _____ do _____ _____, dogs or cats?

B: I _____ dogs _____. They are more _____. _____ _____ you?

C: I _____ cats _____.

D: _____, too. Cats are _____ _____ than dogs.

A: 개와 고양이 중에 어느 것을 더 좋아하니?
B: 개를 더 좋아해. 그들이 더 친절해. 너는 어떠니?
C: 나는 고양이를 더 좋아해.
D: 나도 그래. 고양이가 개보다 훨씬 더 깨끗해.

Speak – Talk in pairs.

A: What _____ you _____?

B: An _____.

A: What's an elephant?

B: It's an _____.

A: Can you _____ _____ _____ _____ it?

B: It's a _____ animal _____ _____ a long nose and big ears.

A: 너는 무엇을 그리고 있니?
B: 코끼리.
A: 코끼리가 뭐니?
B: 그것은 동물이야.
A: 그것에 대하여 더 말해 줄 수 있니?
B: 그것은 긴 코와 큰 귀를 가진 덩치 큰 동물이야.

My Speaking Portfolio Step 1

1. People _____ to the _____ and _____ the forest. Many of my friends have _____ their homes. I don't know _____ to go.

2. I get _____ _____ I have to _____ a big street. This morning I was _____ _____. I don't _____ _____ people are _____ _____ _____ _____.

3. I have a _____ _____. I _____ _____ _____. I think it's _____ someone _____ _____ the sea.

4. Sometimes I _____ _____ not because it's _____ _____ but because it's _____ _____. When lights are too bright, I can't tell _____ _____ _____ _____.

1. 사람들이 숲에 와서 삼림을 파괴해요. 내 친구들 중 많은 수가 집을 잃었어요. 나는 어디로 가야 할지 모르겠어요.
2. 나는 큰 길을 건너야 할 때마다 겁이 나요. 오늘 아침 나는 차에 치일 뻔했다고요. 사람들이 왜 그리 급한지 이해가 안 돼요.
3. 나는 배가 몹시 아파요. 나는 이상한 것을 먹었어요. 내 생각에 그것은 누군가 바다에 버린 것 같아요.
4. 때때로 나는 너무 어두워서가 아니라 너무 밝아서 길을 잃어요. 불빛이 너무 밝으면 나는 어디로 날아가야 할지 분간할 수 없어요.

Wrap Up – Listening & Speaking ⑤

G: What do you _____ in your _____ _____?

B: I _____ _____ music _____ EDM or hip-hop.

G: _____ do you _____ _____?

B: I _____ hip-hop.

G: Why?

B: Well, it _____ _____ _____.

여: 너는 한가한 시간에 뭘 하니?
남: 나는 EDM이나 힙합 같은 음악을 들어.
여: 어떤 것을 더 좋아하는데?
남: 나는 힙합을 더 좋아해.
여: 왜?
남: 글쎄. 그게 더 신나거든.

30 Lesson 2. Animals, Big and Small

※ 다음 우리말에 맞도록 대화를 영어로 쓰시오.

Listen – Listen and Answer – Dialog 1

B: _____

G: _____

B: _____

G: _____

B: _____

G: _____

B: _____

G: _____

B: _____

B: Amber, 캠프 어때?

G: 좋아. 아주 재미있어.

B: 나도 그래. 어젯밤 장기 자랑은 정말 멋졌어.

G: 맞아. 그런데 너는 오후 프로그램 결정했니?

B: 아니, 아직 못했어. 너는 산행과 수영 중에 뭐가 낫다고 생각해?

G: 숲에서 야생 조류와 곤충을 볼 수 있으니까 난 산행을 할 거야.

B: 나도 같이할게. 나는 새와 곤충을 좋아하거든.

G: 좋아. 산행 가이드가 있을 거라고 들었어.

B: 잘됐다.

Listen – Listen and Answer – Dialog 2

W: _____

B: _____

W: _____

B: _____

G: _____

W: _____

G: _____

W: _____

B, G: _____

W: 여러분, 이 밤나무를 보세요. 이것은 이 숲에서 가장 오래된 나무랍니다.

B: 그 나무가 몇 살인지 알려 주실 수 있나요?

W: 150살쯤 되었어요.

B: 와! 제 나이의 열 배군요.

G: 오 선생님, 나무 위에 있는 저것은 벌집인가요?

W: 맞아요. 벌이 저곳에서 몇 마리나 사는지 짐작할 수 있겠어요?

G: 500마리요?

W: 좋은 추측입니다. 하지만 저것은 5만 마리 이상을 수용할 만큼 커요.

B, G: 믿을 수 없어요!

Listen More - Listen and choose.

B: _____

G: _____

B: _____

G: _____

B: _____

G: _____

B: _____

G: _____

B: _____

G: _____

B: 소라야, 이 사진들을 한번 봐 줄래?

G: 어디에 쓸 건데?

B: 학교 신문에 실을 내 이야기에 넣을 사진을 고르고 있어.

G: 네 이야기가 무엇에 관한 건데?

B: 자연의 미래.

G: 그것에 대해 더 말해 줄 수 있니?

B: 북극 지역에 사는 멸종 위기의 동물들에 관한 거야.

G: 흥미롭다.

B: 네 생각에는 어느 사진이 더 낫니?

G: 나는 여윈 북극곰을 보여 주는 사진이 마음에 들어.

Speak – Talk in groups.

A: _____

B: _____

C: _____

D: _____

A: 개와 고양이 중에 어느 것을 더 좋아하니?
B: 개를 더 좋아해. 그들이 더 친절해. 너는 어떠니?
C: 나는 고양이를 더 좋아해.
D: 나도 그래. 고양이가 개보다 훨씬 더 깨끗해.

Speak – Talk in pairs.

A: _____

B: _____

A: _____

B: _____

A: _____

B: _____

A: 너는 무엇을 그리고 있니?
B: 코끼리.
A: 코끼리가 뭐니?
B: 그것은 동물이야.
A: 그것에 대하여 더 말해 줄 수 있니?
B: 그것은 긴 코와 큰 귀를 가진 덩치 큰 동물이야.

My Speaking Portfolio Step 1

1. _____

   _____

2. _____

   _____

3. _____

   _____

4. _____

   _____

1. 사람들이 숲에 와서 삼림을 파괴해요. 내 친구들 중 많은 수가 집을 잃었어요. 나는 어디로 가야 할지 모르겠어요.
2. 나는 큰 길을 건너야 할 때마다 겁이 나요. 오늘 아침 나는 차에 치일 뻔했다고요. 사람들이 왜 그리 급한지 이해가 안 돼요.
3. 나는 배가 몹시 아파요. 나는 이상한 것을 먹었어요. 내 생각에 그것은 누군가 바다에 버린 것 같아요.
4. 때때로 나는 너무 어두워서가 아니라 너무 밝아서 길을 잃어요. 불빛이 너무 밝으면 나는 어디로 날아가야 할지 분간할 수 없어요.

Wrap Up - Listening & Speaking ⑤

G: _____

B: _____

G: _____

B: _____

G: _____

B: _____

여: 너는 한가한 시간에 뭘 하니?
남: 나는 EDM이나 힙합 같은 음악을 들어.
여: 어떤 것을 더 좋아하는데?
남: 나는 힙합을 더 좋아해.
여: 왜?
남: 글쎄. 그게 더 신나거든.

※ 다음 우리말과 일치하도록 빈칸에 알맞은 것을 골라 쓰시오.

1 The _____ _____
A. Ants　　　　　B. Amazing

2 For the science _____, our group _____ _____ very special _____.
A. chosen　　　B. project　　　C. has　　　D. insects

3 They are _____ _____.
A. social　　　B. very

4 They are _____ _____ as the T-Rex.
A. old　　　B. as

5 They _____ in Aesop's _____.
A. stories　　　B. appear

6 They _____ a special _____ to _____.
A. communicate　　B. use　　C. chemical

7 Can you _____ _____ they _____?
A. are　　　B. what　　　C. guess

8 Yes, the _____ is _____.
A. ants　　　B. answer

9 We want to _____ _____ you _____ we have _____ about these insects.
A. what　　B. share　　C. learned　　D. with

10 _____ _____ Ants Are _____ Earth?
A. on　　　B. Many　　　C. How

11 We often see ants come _____ _____ _____.
A. out　　　B. nowhere　　　C. of

12 _____ humans, they live almost everywhere in the world, _____ a few _____ cold places _____ Antarctica.
A. except　　B. like　　C. including　　D. extremely

13 _____ 2018, there were _____ 7 _____ people on Earth.
A. over　　B. as　　C. billion　　D. of

14 Then, _____ _____ ants?
A. about　　　B. how

15 _____ _____ scientists, there are _____ one million ants for _____ human in the world.
A. every　　B. according　　C. about　　D. to

16 Though each ant _____ weighs _____, one million ants are as _____ as a human being _____ about 62 kilograms.
A. weighing　　B. heavy　　C. hardly　　D. anything

17 What _____ the Ant Society _____?
A. Like　　　B. Is

18 Ants live in _____ which have _____ of _____ together.
A. residents　　B. colonies　　C. living　　D. lots

19 _____ a colony, there are usually _____ _____ of ants.
A. three　　B. types　　C. within　　D. different

---

1 놀라운 개미

2 과학 프로젝트를 위해, 우리 모둠은 매우 특별한 곤충을 선택했습니다.

3 그들은 매우 사회적입니다.

4 그들은 티라노사우루스만큼 오래되었습니다.

5 그들은 이솝 이야기에 등장합니다.

6 그들은 의사소통하기 위해 특별한 화학물질을 사용합니다.

7 그들이 어떤 곤충인지 추측할 수 있나요?

8 네, 정답은 개미입니다.

9 저희들은 이 곤충에 관해 알게 된 것을 여러분과 함께 나누고 싶습니다.

10 지구상에는 얼마나 많은 개미가 있을까?

11 우리는 종종 난데없이 나타나는 개미들을 본다.

12 인간처럼, 개미도 남극을 포함한 일부 극도로 추운 곳을 제외한 전 세계 거의 모든 곳에 살고 있다.

13 2018년 현재, 지구상에 70억이 넘는 인구가 있었다.

14 그렇다면, 개미는 어떨까?

15 과학자들에 의하면, 세상에는 사람 한 명당 약 백만 마리의 개미가 있다.

16 개미 한 마리는 거의 무게가 나가지 않지만 백만 마리의 개미는 체중이 약 62kg인 사람 한 명과 무게가 같다.

17 개미 사회는 어떠할까?

18 개미는 많은 거주자가 함께 사는 군집을 이루어 산다.

19 군집 안에는 보통 세 가지 다른 종류의 개미가 있다.

20 There is the queen, and _____ she does her _____ life is _____ eggs.
A. entire　　　B. what　　　C. lay

21 The second _____ of ant is the _____ that helps the queen _____ these eggs.
A. male　　　B. produce　　　C. type

22 The _____ _____ of ant is the _____.
A. type　　　B. worker　　　C. third

23 Worker ants are all female and do very important jobs, _____ _____ for eggs, _____ the colony, and _____ food.
A. like　　　B. collecting　　　C. defending　　　D. caring

24 _____ Do Ants _____?
A. Communicate　　　B. How

25 _____ ants do not speak _____ _____, they _____ have a "language."
A. like　　　B. though　　　C. actually　　　D. humans

26 Ants produce a chemical _____ a pheromone to _____ _____ one _____.
A. another　　　B. called　　　C. with　　　D. communicate

27 _____ _____ the chemical, they can _____ _____ about food or danger.
A. using　　　B. information　　　C. by　　　D. exchange

28 Ants also use _____ _____ _____.
A. for　　　B. touch　　　C. communication

29 _____ example, if an ant finds food, it passes on the good news _____ _____ its body _____ its neighbor.
A. on　　　B. rubbing　　　C. for　　　D. by

30 _____ an ant has legs _____ _____ very sensitive hairs, it can sense even the _____ touch.
A. with　　　B. smallest　　　C. covered　　　D. since

31 _____ _____ ABOUT _____
A. ANTS　　　B. FACTS　　　C. FUN

32 01 Some Queen ants _____ _____ _____ 30 years.
A. up　　　B. live　　　C. to

33 02 Some ants can _____ things that are 50 _____ their own _____.
A. weight　　　B. carry　　　C. times　　　D. body

34 03 Ants do not have _____ but _____ _____ small holes in their bodies.
A. through　　　B. lungs　　　C. breathe

35 04 An _____ has two _____.
A. stomachs　　　B. ant

36 _____ stomach holds food for _____, and the _____ holds food to share _____ others.
A. other　　　B. itself　　　C. one　　　D. with

37 05 _____ _____ can swim and _____ 24 hours _____.
A. underwater　　　B. ants　　　C. live　　　D. most

20 여왕개미가 있고, 그녀가 평생 하는 일은 알을 낳는 것이다.

21 두 번째 종류는 여왕이 알을 낳는 것을 돕는 수개미이다.

22 세 번째 종류는 일개미이다.

23 일개미는 모두 암컷인데, 알을 돌보고, 군집을 방어하며, 먹이를 모으는 것과 같은 매우 중요한 일을 한다.

24 개미는 어떻게 의사소통할까?

25 개미들이 인간처럼 말을 하는 것은 아니지만, 그들은 실제로 '언어'를 가지고 있다.

26 개미는 서로 소통하기 위해 '페로몬'이라고 불리는 화학물질을 분비한다.

27 그 화학물질을 사용하여 그들은 먹이나 위험에 관한 정보를 교환할 수 있다.

28 개미는 또한 의사소통을 위해 접촉을 이용한다.

29 예를 들어, 먹이를 발견할 경우 개미는 자기 몸을 이웃의 개미에게 문질러서 좋은 소식을 전달한다.

30 개미는 (자극에) 매우 민감한 털로 덮인 다리가 있기 때문에, 아주 미세한 접촉도 감지할 수 있다.

31 개미에 관한 재미있는 사실

32 01 어떤 여왕개미는 30년까지 살 수 있다.

33 02 어떤 개미들은 자기 몸무게의 50배에 달하는 것을 들 수 있다.

34 03 개미는 폐가 없지만, 몸에 있는 작은 구멍을 통해 호흡한다.

35 04 개미는 위가 두 개 있다.

36 하나에는 자신의 먹이를 저장하고 다른 하나에는 다른 개미들과 함께 나눌 먹이를 저장한다.

37 05 대부분의 개미는 수영할 수 있고 물속에서 24시간 동안 살 수 있다.

※ 다음 우리말과 일치하도록 빈칸에 알맞은 말을 쓰시오.

1 The _____ _____

2 _____ _____ _____ _____ , our group _____ _____ very _____ _____.

3 They are very _____.

4 They are _____ _____ _____ the T-Rex.

5 They _____ in _____ _____.

6 They use _____ _____ _____ to _____.

7 Can you _____ _____ _____ _____?

8 Yes, _____ _____ is _____.

9 We want to _____ _____ you _____ we _____ _____ about these insects.

10 _____ _____ _____ Are _____ Earth?

11 We often see ants come _____ _____ _____.

12 _____ _____, they live almost everywhere in the world, _____ a few _____ cold places _____ _____.

13 _____ _____ _____, there were _____ 7 _____ _____ on Earth.

14 Then, _____ _____ ants?

15 _____ _____ _____, there are about one million ants _____ _____ _____ in the world.

16 Though each ant _____ _____ _____, one million ants are _____ _____ a human _____ _____ about 62 kilograms.

17 What _____ the Ant Society _____?

18 Ants live in colonies _____ _____ lots of _____ together.

19 _____ a _____, there are usually _____ of ants.

20 There is the queen, and _____ _____ _____ her entire life is _____ _____.

21 The _____ _____ of ant is the _____ that helps the queen _____ _____ _____ _____.

22 _____ _____ _____ of ant is the _____.

23 Worker ants are all female and do very important jobs, _____ _____ _____ eggs, _____ the colony, and _____ food.

24 _____ Do Ants _____?

25 _____ ants do not speak _____ _____, they _____ _____ a "language."

26 Ants produce a chemical _____ a pheromone _____ _____ _____ _____ _____.

27 _____ _____ the chemical, they can _____ _____ about food or _____.

28 Ants also use _____ _____ _____.

29 _____ _____, if an ant finds food, it passes on the good news _____ _____ its body _____ _____ _____.

30 Since an ant has legs _____ _____ very sensitive hairs, it can sense _____ _____ _____ _____.

31 _____ _____ ABOUT ANTS

32 01 Some Queen ants _____ _____ _____ 30 years.

33 02 Some ants can _____ _____ that are _____ _____ _____ _____ _____.

34 03 Ants do not have lungs but _____ _____ _____ in their bodies.

35 04 An ant has _____ _____.

36 _____ stomach holds food _____, and _____ holds food to _____ _____ others.

37 05 _____ _____ can swim and live 24 hours _____.

20 여왕개미가 있고, 그녀가 평생 하는 일은 알을 낳는 것이다.
21 두 번째 종류는 여왕이 알을 낳는 것을 돕는 수개미이다.
22 세 번째 종류는 일개미이다.
23 일개미는 모두 암컷인데, 알을 돌보고, 군집을 방어하며, 먹이를 모으는 것과 같은 매우 중요한 일을 한다.
24 개미는 어떻게 의사소통할까?
25 개미들이 인간처럼 말을 하는 것은 아니지만, 그들은 실제로 '언어'를 가지고 있다.
26 개미는 서로 소통하기 위해 '페로몬'이라고 불리는 화학물질을 분비한다.
27 그 화학물질을 사용하여 그들은 먹이나 위험에 관한 정보를 교환할 수 있다.
28 개미는 또한 의사소통을 위해 접촉을 이용한다.
29 예를 들어, 먹이를 발견할 경우 개미는 자기 몸을 이웃의 개미에게 문질러서 좋은 소식을 전달한다.
30 개미는 (자극에) 매우 민감한 털로 덮인 다리가 있기 때문에, 아주 미세한 접촉도 감지할 수 있다.
31 개미에 관한 재미있는 사실
32 01 어떤 여왕개미는 30년까지 살 수 있다.
33 02 어떤 개미들은 자기 몸무게의 50배에 달하는 것을 들 수 있다.
34 03 개미는 폐가 없지만, 몸에 있는 작은 구멍을 통해 호흡한다.
35 04 개미는 위가 두 개 있다.
36 하나에는 자신의 먹이를 저장하고 다른 하나에는 다른 개미들과 함께 나눌 먹이를 저장한다.
37 05 대부분의 개미는 수영할 수 있고 물속에서 24시간 동안 살 수 있다.

※ 다음 문장을 우리말로 쓰시오.

1 The Amazing Ants
➡ _____

2 For the science project, our group has chosen very special insects.
➡ _____

3 They are very social.
➡ _____

4 They are as old as the T-Rex.
➡ _____

5 They appear in Aesop's stories.
➡ _____

6 They use a special chemical to communicate.
➡ _____

7 Can you guess what they are?
➡ _____

8 Yes, the answer is ants.
➡ _____

9 We want to share with you what we have learned about these insects.
➡ _____

10 How Many Ants Are on Earth?
➡ _____

11 We often see ants come out of nowhere.
➡ _____

12 Like humans, they live almost everywhere in the world, except a few extremely cold places including Antarctica.
➡ _____

13 As of 2018, there were over 7 billion people on Earth.
➡ _____

14 Then, how about ants?
➡ _____

15 According to scientists, there are about one million ants for every human in the world..
➡ _____

16 Though each ant hardly weighs anything, one million ants are as heavy as a human being weighing about 62 kilograms.
➡ _____

17 What Is the Ant Society Like?
➡ _____

18 Ants live in colonies which have lots of residents living together.
➡ _____

19 Within a colony, there are usually three different types of ants.
➡ _____

20 There is the queen, and what she does her entire life is lay eggs.
➡ _____

21 The second type of ant is the male that helps the queen produce these eggs.
➡ _____

22 The third type of ant is the worker.
➡ _____

23 Worker ants are all female and do very important jobs, like caring for eggs, defending the colony, and collecting food.
➡ _____

24 How Do Ants Communicate?
➡ _____

25 Though ants do not speak like humans, they actually have a "language."
➡ _____

26 Ants produce a chemical called a pheromone to communicate with one another.
➡ _____

27 By using the chemical, they can exchange information about food or danger.
➡ _____

28 Ants also use touch for communication.
➡ _____

29 For example, if an ant finds food, it passes on the good news by rubbing its body on its neighbor.
➡ _____

30 Since an ant has legs covered with very sensitive hairs, it can sense even the smallest touch.
➡ _____

31 FUN FACTS ABOUT ANTS
➡ _____

32 01 Some Queen ants live up to 30 years.
➡ _____

33 02 Some ants can carry things that are 50 times their own body weight.
➡ _____

34 03 Ants do not have lungs but breathe through small holes in their bodies.
➡ _____

35 04 An ant has two stomachs.
➡ _____

36 One stomach holds food for itself, and the other holds food to share with others.
➡ _____

37 05 Most ants can swim and live 24 hours underwater.
➡ _____

Step4

※ 다음 괄호 안의 단어들을 우리말에 맞도록 바르게 배열하시오.

1 (Amazing / The / Ants)
➡ _____

2 (the / for / project, / science / group / our / chosen / has / special / very / insects.)
➡ _____

3 (are / they / social. / very)
➡ _____

4 (are / they / old / as / the / as / T-Rex.)
➡ _____

5 (appear / they / Aesop's / in / stories.)
➡ _____

6 (use / they / special / a / to / communicate. / chemical)
➡ _____

7 (you / can / what / guess / are? / they)
➡ _____

8 (yes, / answer / the / ants. / is)
➡ _____

9 (want / we / share / to / you / with / we / what / learned / have / these / insects. / about)
➡ _____

10 (Many / How / Are / Ants / Earth? / on)
➡ _____

11 (often / we / ants / see / out / come / nowhere. / of)
➡ _____

12 (humans, / like / live / they / everywhere / almost / the / in / world, / a / except / extremely / few / places / cold / Antarctica. / including)
➡ _____
_____

13 (of / as / 2018, / were / there / 7 / over / people / billion / Earth. / on)
➡ _____

14 (how / then, / ants? / about)
➡ _____

1 놀라운 개미

2 과학 프로젝트를 위해, 우리 모둠은 매우 특별한 곤충을 선택했습니다.

3 그들은 매우 사회적입니다.

4 그들은 티라노사우루스만큼 오래되었습니다.

5 그들은 이솝 이야기에 등장합니다.

6 그들은 의사소통하기 위해 특별한 화학물질을 사용합니다.

7 그들이 어떤 곤충인지 추측할 수 있나요?

8 네. 정답은 개미입니다.

9 저희들은 이 곤충에 관해 알게 된 것을 여러분과 함께 나누고 싶습니다.

10 지구상에는 얼마나 많은 개미가 있을까?

11 우리는 종종 난데없이 나타나는 개미들을 본다.

12 인간처럼, 개미도 남극을 포함한 일부 극도로 추운 곳을 제외한 전 세계 거의 모든 곳에 살고 있다.

13 2018년 현재, 지구상에 70억이 넘는 인구가 있었다.

14 그렇다면, 개미는 어떨까?

15 (to / according / scientists, / are / there / one / about / million / for / ants / human / every / the / world. / in)

➡ _____

_____

16 (each / though / hardly / ant / anything, / weighs / million / one / ants / as / are / heavy / a / as / being / human / about / weighing / kilograms. / 62)

➡ _____

_____

17 (Is / What / Ant / the / Like? / Society)

➡ _____

18 (live / ants / colonies / in / have / which / of / lots / residents / together. / living)

➡ _____

19 (a / within / colony, / are / there / three / usually / types / different / ants. / of)

➡ _____

20 (is / there / queen, / the / what / and / does / she / entire / her / is / life / eggs. / lay)

➡ _____

21 (second / the / of / type / is / ant / male / the / that / the / helps / queen / these / produce / eggs.)

➡ _____

_____

22 (third / the / of / type / ant / the / is / worker.)

➡ _____

23 (ants / worker / all / are / and / female / very / do / important / jobs, / caring / like / eggs, / for / the / defending / colony, / collecting / and / food.)

➡ _____

_____

24 (Do / How / Communicate? / Ants)

➡ _____

25 (ants / though / not / do / speak / humans, / like / actually / they / a / "language." / have)

➡ _____

26 (produce / ants / chemical / a / called / pheromone / a / communicate / to / one / with / another.)

➡ _____

27 (using / by / chemical, / the / can / they / information / exchange / about / danger. / or / food)

➡ _____

_____

15 과학자들에 의하면, 세상에는 사람 한 명당 약 백만 마리의 개미가 있다.

16 개미 한 마리는 거의 무게가 나가지 않지만 백만 마리의 개미는 체중이 약 62kg인 사람 한 명과 무게가 같다.

17 개미 사회는 어떠할까?

18 개미는 많은 거주자가 함께 사는 군집을 이루어 산다.

19 군집 안에는 보통 세 가지 다른 종류의 개미가 있다.

20 여왕개미가 있고, 그녀가 평생 하는 일은 알을 낳는 것이다.

21 두 번째 종류는 여왕이 알을 낳는 것을 돕는 수개미이다.

22 세 번째 종류는 일개미이다.

23 일개미는 모두 암컷인데, 알을 돌보고, 군집을 방어하며, 먹이를 모으는 것과 같은 매우 중요한 일을 한다.

24 개미는 어떻게 의사소통할까?

25 개미들이 인간처럼 말을 하는 것은 아니지만, 그들은 실제로 '언어'를 가지고 있다.

26 개미는 서로 소통하기 위해 '페로몬'이라고 불리는 화학물질을 분비한다.

27 그 화학물질을 사용하여 그들은 먹이나 위험에 관한 정보를 교환할 수 있다.

28 (also / ants / touch / use / communication. / for)

➡ _____

29 (example, / for / an / if / finds / ant / food, / passes / it / the / on / good / by / news / rubbing / body / its / its / on / neighbor.)

➡ _____
_____

30 (an / since / has / ant / legs / with / covered / sensitive / very / hairs, / can / it / even / sense / smallest / the / touch.)

➡ _____
_____

31 (FACTS / FUN / ANTS / ABOUT)

➡ _____

32 (01 / Queen / Some / live / ants / up / 30 / to / years.)

➡ _____

33 (02 / ants / some / carry / can / that / things / are / times / 50 / own / their / weight. / body)

➡ _____

34 (03 / do / ants / have / not / but / lungs / through / breathe / holes / small / their / bodies. / in)

➡ _____
_____

35 (04 / ant / an / two / has / stomachs.)

➡ _____

36 (stomach / one / food / holds / itself, / for / and / other / the / food / holds / to / with / share / others.)

➡ _____
_____

37 (05 / ants / most / swim / can / and / 24 / live / underwater. / hours)

➡ _____

28 개미는 또한 의사소통을 위해 접촉을 이용한다.

29 예를 들어, 먹이를 발견할 경우 개미는 자기 몸을 이웃의 개미에게 문질러서 좋은 소식을 전달한다.

30 개미는 (자극에) 매우 민감한 털로 덮인 다리가 있기 때문에, 아주 미세한 접촉도 감지할 수 있다.

31 개미에 관한 재미있는 사실

32 01 어떤 여왕개미는 30년까지 살 수 있다.

33 02 어떤 개미들은 자기 몸무게의 50배에 달하는 것을 들 수 있다.

34 03 개미는 폐가 없지만, 몸에 있는 작은 구멍을 통해 호흡한다.

35 04 개미는 위가 두 개 있다.

36 하나에는 자신의 먹이를 저장하고 다른 하나에는 다른 개미들과 함께 나눌 먹이를 저장한다.

37 05 대부분의 개미는 수영할 수 있고 물속에서 24시간 동안 살 수 있다.

※ 다음 우리말을 영어로 쓰시오.

1 놀라운 개미
➡ _____

2 과학 프로젝트를 위해, 우리 모둠은 매우 특별한 곤충을 선택했습니다.
➡ _____

3 그들은 매우 사회적입니다.
➡ _____

4 그들은 티라노사우루스만큼 오래되었습니다.
➡ _____

5 그들은 이솝 이야기에 등장합니다.
➡ _____

6 그들은 의사소통하기 위해 특별한 화학물질을 사용합니다.
➡ _____

7 그들이 어떤 곤충인지 추측할 수 있나요?
➡ _____

8 네. 정답은 개미입니다.
➡ _____

9 저희들은 이 곤충에 관해 알게 된 것을 여러분과 함께 나누고 싶습니다.
➡ _____

10 지구상에는 얼마나 많은 개미가 있을까?
➡ _____

11 우리는 종종 난데없이 나타나는 개미들을 본다.
➡ _____

12 인간처럼, 개미도 남극을 포함한 일부 극도로 추운 곳을 제외한 전 세계 거의 모든 곳에 살고 있다.
➡ _____

13 2018년 현재, 지구상에 70억이 넘는 인구가 있었다.
➡ _____

14 그렇다면. 개미는 어떨까?
➡ _____

15 과학자들에 의하면, 세상에는 사람 한 명당 약 백만 마리의 개미가 있다.
➡ _____

16 개미 한 마리는 거의 무게가 나가지 않지만 백만 마리의 개미는 체중이 약 62kg인 사람 한 명과 무게가 같다.
➡ _____
_____

17 개미 사회는 어떠할까?
➡ _____

18 개미는 많은 거주자가 함께 사는 군집을 이루어 산다.
➡ _____

19 군집 안에는 보통 세 가지 다른 종류의 개미가 있다.
➡ _____

20 여왕개미가 있고, 그녀가 평생 하는 일은 알을 낳는 것이다.
➡ _____

21 두 번째 종류는 여왕이 알을 낳는 것을 돕는 수개미이다.
➡ _____

22 세 번째 종류는 일개미이다.
➡ _____

23 일개미는 모두 암컷인데, 알을 돌보고, 군집을 방어하며, 먹이를 모으는 것과 같은 매우 중요한 일을 한다.
➡ _____
_____

24 개미는 어떻게 의사소통할까?
➡ _____

25 개미들이 인간처럼 말을 하는 것은 아니지만, 그들은 실제로 '언어'를 가지고 있다.
➡ _____

26 개미는 서로 소통하기 위해 '페로몬'이라고 불리는 화학물질을 분비한다.
➡ _____

27 그 화학물질을 사용하여 그들은 먹이나 위험에 관한 정보를 교환할 수 있다.
➡ _____

28 개미는 또한 의사소통을 위해 접촉을 이용한다.
➡ _____

29 예를 들어, 먹이를 발견할 경우 개미는 자기 몸을 이웃의 개미에게 문질러서 좋은 소식을 전달한다.
➡ _____

30 개미는 (자극에) 매우 민감한 털로 덮인 다리가 있기 때문에, 아주 미세한 접촉도 감지할 수 있다.
➡ _____

31 개미에 관한 재미있는 사실
➡ _____

32 01 어떤 여왕개미는 30년까지 살 수 있다.
➡ _____

33 02 어떤 개미들은 자기 몸무게의 50배에 달하는 것을 들 수 있다.
➡ _____

34 03 개미는 폐가 없지만, 몸에 있는 작은 구멍을 통해 호흡한다.
➡ _____

35 04 개미는 위가 두 개 있다.
➡ _____

36 하나에는 자신의 먹이를 저장하고 다른 하나에는 다른 개미들과 함께 나눌 먹이를 저장한다.
➡ _____

37 05 대부분의 개미는 수영할 수 있고 물속에서 24시간 동안 살 수 있다.
➡ _____

※ 다음 우리말과 일치하도록 빈칸에 알맞은 말을 쓰시오.

Communicate: Speak

1. A: _____ do you _____, pizza or fried chicken?
2. B: I like pizza better. I can _____ _____ _____ _____
   _____. _____ _____ you?
3. A: I _____ fried chicken _____.
4. C: _____, _____. I'm a _____ _____.

1. A: 피자와 치킨 중 어느 것을 좋아하니?
2. B: 피자를 더 좋아해. 나는 내가 좋아하는 토핑을 고를 수 있어. 너는 어떠니?
3. A: 나는 프라이드 치킨을 더 좋아해.
4. C: 나도 그래. 나는 고기를 좋아해.

My Speaking Portfolio

1. M: Honeybees _____ _____ _____ in warm places which
   _____ _____ _____ and flowers.
2. A queen _____ _____ _____ five years, but worker bees
   _____ _____ _____ about seven weeks.
3. Honeybees go _____ flower _____ flower _____ _____
   _____.
4. A worker bee makes _____ _____ trips to produce _____
   _____ _____ _____ honey.
5. _____ _____ _____, honeybees _____ plants _____.

1. 남: 꿀벌은 식물과 꽃이 많은 따뜻한 곳에서 쉽게 발견된다.
2. 여왕벌은 5년까지 살지만, 일벌은 겨우 7주 정도만 산다.
3. 꿀벌은 먹이를 모으기 위해 꽃에서 꽃으로 옮겨 다닌다.
4. 일벌은 적은 양의 꿀을 만들기 위해 수백 번의 이동을 한다.
5. 여기저기 옮겨 다니면서 꿀벌은 식물이 성장하는 것을 돕는다.

Wrap Up - Reading

1. Ants _____ _____ be busy _____ _____ _____ and
   never rest.
2. But this is _____ _____.
3. Worker ants _____ _____ _____ _____ very short naps _____
   250 times _____ _____.
4. _____ _____ these naps _____ only _____ _____
   _____.
5. This means that the worker ants sleep _____ _____ _____
   _____ _____ _____.
6. _____ _____ _____ _____, queen ants _____ _____
   90 times a day, and they sleep for about six minutes _____
   _____ _____.
7. This means _____ they sleep _____ _____ _____
   _____ _____.
8. _____ _____, ants sleep and rest just _____ us _____
   they do so _____ _____ _____ _____.

1. 개미는 항상 바쁘고 전혀 휴식을 취하지 않는 것처럼 보인다.
2. 하지만 이것은 사실이 아니다.
3. 일개미는 하루에 약 250번의 짧은 잠을 자며 휴식을 취한다.
4. 이 잠은 불과 1분 정도 이어진다.
5. 이것은 일개미가 하루에 4시간 정도 잠을 잔다는 의미이다.
6. 반면에, 여왕개미는 하루에 90번 잠을 자고, 한 번에 약 6분 동안 잠을 잔다.
7. 이것은 여왕개미가 하루에 약 9시간 동안 잠을 잔다는 것을 의미한다.
8. 즉, 방식이 다르기는 하지만 개미도 우리처럼 잠을 자고 휴식을 취한다.

※ 다음 우리말을 영어로 쓰시오.

Communicate: Speak

1. A: 피자와 치킨 중 어느 것을 좋아하니?
   ➡ _____

2. B: 피자를 더 좋아해. 나는 내가 좋아하는 토핑을 고를 수 있어. 너는 어떠니?
   ➡ _____

3. A: 나는 프라이드 치킨을 더 좋아해.
   ➡ _____

4. C: 나도 그래. 나는 고기를 좋아해.
   ➡ _____

My Speaking Portfolio

1. 남: 꿀벌은 식물과 꽃이 많은 따뜻한 곳에서 쉽게 발견된다.
   ➡ _____

2. 여왕벌은 5년까지 살지만, 일벌은 겨우 7주 정도만 산다.
   ➡ _____

3. 꿀벌은 먹이를 모으기 위해 꽃에서 꽃으로 옮겨 다닌다.
   ➡ _____

4. 일벌은 적은 양의 꿀을 만들기 위해 수백 번의 이동을 한다.
   ➡ _____

5. 여기저기 옮겨 다니면서 꿀벌은 식물이 성장하는 것을 돕는다.
   ➡ _____

Wrap Up - Reading

1. 개미는 항상 바쁘고 전혀 휴식을 취하지 않는 것처럼 보인다.
   ➡ _____

2. 하지만 이것은 사실이 아니다.
   ➡ _____

3. 일개미는 하루에 약 250번의 짧은 잠을 자며 휴식을 취한다.
   ➡ _____

4. 이 잠은 불과 1분 정도 이어진다.
   ➡ _____

5. 이것은 일개미가 하루에 4시간 정도 잠을 잔다는 의미이다.
   ➡ _____

6. 반면에, 여왕개미는 하루에 90번 잠을 자고, 한 번에 약 6분 동안 잠을 잔다.
   ➡ _____

7. 이것은 여왕개미가 하루에 약 9시간 동안 잠을 잔다는 것을 의미한다.
   ➡ _____

8. 즉, 방식이 다르기는 하지만 개미도 우리처럼 잠을 자고 휴식을 취한다.
   ➡ _____

※ 다음 영어를 우리말로 쓰시오.

01 raise	16 seem	
02 golf ball	17 room	
03 same	18 shake	
04 health	19 though	
05 reply	20 value	
06 matter	21 spend	
07 fill	22 suddenly	
08 roll	23 take out	
09 open	24 pick up	
10 space	25 a bottle of ~	
11 jar	26 out of	
12 lose	27 take care of ~	
13 stand	28 pour A into B	
14 full	29 spend A on B	
15 pour	30 watch+목적어+동사원형(ing)	
	31 fill A with B	

※ 다음 우리말을 영어로 쓰시오.

01	골프공	_____
02	건강	_____
03	중요하다	_____
04	열려 있는, 막혀 있지 않은	_____
05	~을 들어 올리다	_____
06	채우다, 메우다	_____
07	흔들다	_____
08	붓다, 따르다	_____
09	가득 찬	_____
10	(비어 있는) 공간	_____
11	대답하다	_____
12	~을 높이 평가하다, 중시하다	_____
13	같은	_____
14	서 있다	_____
15	병, 항아리	_____

16	~으로 보이다, ~(인 것) 같다	_____
17	잃어버리다	_____
18	비록 ~일지라도, ~이지만	_____
19	갑자기	_____
20	굴러가다	_____
21	소비하다, 쓰다	_____
22	공간, 여지	_____
23	~ 밖으로, ~ 로부터	_____
24	~을 집어올리다	_____
25	~ 한 병	_____
26	~을 꺼내다	_____
27	A를 B에 붓다	_____
28	목적어가 ~하는 것을 보다	_____
29	A를 B하는 데 소비하다	_____
30	~에 신경을 쓰다, ~을 돌보다	_____
31	B로 A를 채우다	_____

※ 다음 영영풀이에 알맞은 단어를 <보기>에서 골라 쓴 후, 우리말 뜻을 쓰시오.

1 _____ : to be important: _____

2 _____ : an empty area: _____

3 _____ : to make something full: _____

4 _____ : quickly and without any warning: _____

5 _____ : having or containing a lot of something: _____

6 _____ : to pay money for things that you want: _____

7 _____ : to say or write something as an answer to someone or something:
　　　　　_____

8 _____ : to hold it and move it quickly backwards and forwards or up and down:
　　　　　_____

9 _____ : a glass container with a lid and a wide top, especially one in which food
　　　　　is sold or kept: _____

10 _____ : to fail to keep or to maintain; cease to have, either physically or in an
　　　　　abstract sense: _____

11 _____ : to evaluate or estimate the nature, quality, ability, extent, or significance
　　　　　of: _____

12 _____ : to make sure that you are/somebody is safe, well, healthy, etc.; look after
　　　　　yourself/somebody: _____

보기			
value	space	lose	take care of
fill	full	spend	reply
shake	suddenly	jar	matter

※ 다음 우리말과 일치하도록 빈칸에 알맞은 것을 골라 쓰시오.

1 The _____ _____

A. Jar   B. Full

2 Mr. Jenkins _____ _____ his _____.

A. before   B. stood   C. class

3 He had a large _____ and a big bag _____ the teacher's _____.

A. jar   B. desk   C. on

4 When the class began, he _____ _____ the jar and started to _____ it _____ **golf balls** from the bag.

A. up   B. fill   C. picked   D. with

5 He _____ the students, "Is the _____ _____?"

A. full   B. asked   C. jar

6 _____ _____ _____, "Yes."

A. said   B. they   C. all

7 The teacher took a box of **small stones** _____ _____ the bag and _____ them _____ the jar.

A. poured   B. out   C. into   D. of

8 He shook the jar a _____, and the stones _____ _____ the open areas _____ the golf balls.

A. little   B. into   C. between   D. rolled

9 He asked the _____ _____ and got the same _____ _____ his students.

A. question   B. answer   C. same   D. from

10 Next, the teacher _____ _____ a bottle of **sand** and _____ it _____ the jar.

A. out   B. poured   C. took   D. into

11 After he watched the sand _____ the spaces between the stones, he asked _____ _____, "Is the jar _____?"

A. once   B. full   C. fill   D. more

12 _____ _____ students _____, "Yes."

A. the   B. all   C. replied

13 _____ Mr. Jenkins _____ a can of **apple juice** _____ _____ the bag.

A. took   B. of   C. suddenly   D. out

1 가득 찬 병

2 Jenkins 선생님이 교실 앞에 섰다.

3 교탁 위에는 큰 병과 커다란 가방이 놓여 있었다.

4 수업이 시작하자, 선생님은 병을 집어 들고 가방에서 꺼낸 골프공으로 채우기 시작했다.

5 그는 학생들에게 "병이 가득 찼나요?"라고 질문했다.

6 학생들은 모두 "예."라고 대답했다.

7 선생님은 가방에서 작은 돌 한 상자를 끄집어내어 병 안에 부었다.

8 그가 병을 살짝 흔들자, 돌들이 골프공 사이의 틈새로 굴러 들어갔다.

9 그는 같은 질문을 했고 학생들에게서 같은 대답을 들었다.

10 그런 다음, 선생님은 모래 병을 꺼내 병 안에 부었다.

11 모래가 돌 사이의 공간을 채우는 것을 지켜보고 나서 그는 "이 병이 가득 찼나요?"라고 한 번 더 물었다.

12 모든 학생들이 "예."라고 답했다.

13 갑자기 Jenkins 선생님은 가방에서 사과 주스 한 캔을 꺼냈다.

14 He _____ the apple juice into the jar, and his students _____ it _____ the _____ in the sand.

A. watched   B. spaces   C. poured   D. fill

15 "Now," the teacher said, "I want you to _____ _____ your life is _____ _____ the jar.

A. like   B. that   C. just   D. understand

16 The golf balls are _____ _____ _____ _____ in life: your family, your friends, your health, and your dreams.

A. most   B. what   C. important   D. is

17 _____ when everything else _____ _____, your life can still be _____.

A. lost   B. full   C. even   D. is

18 The _____ are the _____ things _____ by people, _____ your job, your house, and your car.

A. vauled   B. like   C. other   D. stones

19 The sand is _____ _____ _____ _____."

A. the   B. all   C. things   D. small

20 "If you put the sand into the jar first," he said, "_____ _____ _____ the stones or the golf balls.

A. no   B. for   C. there's   D. room

21 The _____ _____ _____ life.

A. goes   B. same   C. for

22 If you _____ all your time and energy _____ the small things, you will never have _____ for _____ is really important to you.

A. what   B. on   C. room   D. spend

23 _____ _____ of the balls first — the _____ that really _____."

A. care   B. things   C. take   D. matter

24 One student _____ in the back _____ her hand and asked, "What does the apple juice _____?"

A. mean   B. raised   C. sitting

25 Mr. Jenkins _____, "I'm glad _____ _____.

A. asked   B. smiled   C. you

26 It just shows that though your life may _____ _____, there's always _____ _____ a cool drink with a friend."

A. full   B. for   C. room   D. seem

---

14 그는 사과 주스를 병 안에 부었고, 학생들은 주스가 모래 사이의 빈틈을 채우는 것을 지켜보았다.

15 "자, 이제," 선생님이 말했다. "여러분의 인생이 병과 같다는 것을 이해하기 바랍니다.

16 골프공은 여러분의 가족, 친구, 건강, 꿈과 같이 인생에서 가장 중요한 것이랍니다.

17 다른 모든 것을 잃게 될 때라도 여러분의 인생은 여전히 가득 차 있을 수 있습니다.

18 돌은 여러분의 직업, 집, 자동차처럼 사람들이 소중하게 여기는 다른 것들에 해당합니다.

19 모래는 온갖 사소한 것들이랍니다."

20 "만약 병에 모래를 먼저 채우면, 돌이나 골프공을 채울 공간이 없게 됩니다.

21 인생도 똑같습니다.

22 여러분의 시간과 에너지를 사소한 것에 모두 허비한다면 여러분에게 진정으로 중요한 것을 채울 공간은 절대로 없을 겁니다.

23 골프공, 즉 정말로 중요한 것들을 먼저 챙기기 바랍니다."라고 선생님이 말했다.

24 뒤에 앉아 있던 학생 하나가 손을 들고 질문했다. "사과 주스는 무슨 뜻입니까?"

25 Jenkins 선생님은 미소 지었다. "질문을 해줘서 기뻐요.

26 그것은, 여러분의 인생이 가득 차 보일지라도 친구와 시원한 음료수를 나눌 여유는 늘 있다는 점을 보여 줍니다."

※ 다음 우리말과 일치하도록 빈칸에 알맞은 것을 골라 쓰시오.

1 The _____ _____

2 Mr. Jenkins stood _____ _____ _____.

3 He had _____ _____ _____ and a big bag on the _____ _____.

4 When the class began, he _____ _____ the jar and started to _____ it _____ **golf balls** _____ _____ _____.

5 He asked the students, "_____ _____ _____ _____?"

6 _____ _____ said, "Yes."

7 The teacher took _____ _____ _____ **small stones** _____ _____ _____ and _____ _____ _____ the jar.

8 He shook the jar _____ _____, and the stones _____ _____ the _____ _____ between the golf balls.

9 He asked _____ _____ _____ and got _____ _____ _____ from his students.

10 Next, the teacher _____ _____ a bottle of **sand** and _____ it _____ the jar.

11 After he _____ the sand _____ the spaces between the stones, he asked _____ _____, "Is the jar _____?"

12 _____ _____ _____ _____, "Yes."

13 _____ Mr. Jenkins took a can of **apple juice** _____ _____ _____.

1 가득 찬 병

2 Jenkins 선생님이 교실 앞에 섰다.

3 교탁 위에는 큰 병과 커다란 가방이 놓여 있었다.

4 수업이 시작하자, 선생님은 병을 집어 들고 가방에서 꺼낸 골프공으로 채우기 시작했다.

5 그는 학생들에게 "병이 가득 찼나요?"라고 질문했다.

6 학생들은 모두 "예."라고 대답했다.

7 선생님은 가방에서 작은 돌 한 상자를 끄집어내어 병 안에 부었다.

8 그가 병을 살짝 흔들자, 돌들이 골프공 사이의 틈새로 굴러 들어갔다.

9 그는 같은 질문을 했고 학생들에게서 같은 대답을 들었다.

10 그런 다음, 선생님은 모래 병을 꺼내 병 안에 부었다.

11 모래가 돌 사이의 공간을 채우는 것을 지켜보고 나서 그는 "이 병이 가득 찼나요?"라고 한 번 더 물었다.

12 모든 학생들이 "예."라고 답했다.

13 갑자기 Jenkins 선생님은 가방에서 사과 주스 한 캔을 꺼냈다.

14 He _____ the apple juice _____ the jar, and his students watched it _____ _____ _____ in the sand.

14 그는 사과 주스를 병 안에 부었고, 학생들은 주스가 모래 사이의 빈틈을 채우는 것을 지켜보았다.

15 "Now," the teacher said, "I _____ you to _____ that your life _____ _____ _____ the jar.

15 "자. 이제." 선생님이 말했다. "여러분의 인생이 병과 같다는 것을 이해하기 바랍니다.

16 The golf balls are _____ _____ _____ _____ in life: your family, your friends, your _____, and your _____.

16 골프공은 여러분의 가족, 친구, 건강, 꿈과 같이 인생에서 가장 중요한 것이랍니다.

17 _____ _____ everything else _____ _____, your life can still be full.

17 다른 모든 것을 잃게 될 때라도 여러분의 인생은 여전히 가득 차 있을 수 있습니다.

18 The stones are the other things _____ by people, _____ your job, your house, and your car.

18 돌은 여러분의 직업, 집, 자동차처럼 사람들이 소중하게 여기는 다른 것들에 해당합니다.

19 The sand is _____ _____ _____ _____."

19 모래는 온갖 사소한 것들이랍니다."

20 "If you _____ the sand _____ the jar first," he said, "_____ _____ _____ _____ the stones or the golf balls.

20 "만약 병에 모래를 먼저 채우면, 돌이나 골프공을 채울 공간이 없게 됩니다.

21 _____ _____ _____ _____ _____ life.

21 인생도 똑같습니다.

22 If you _____ all your time and energy _____ the small things, you will never have _____ for _____ _____ _____ _____ to you.

22 여러분의 시간과 에너지를 사소한 것에 모두 허비한다면 여러분에게 진정으로 중요한 것을 채울 공간은 절대로 없을 겁니다.

23 _____ _____ _____ the balls first — the things that really _____."

23 골프공, 즉 정말로 중요한 것들을 먼저 챙기기 바랍니다."라고 선생님이 말했다.

24 One student _____ in the back _____ her hand and asked, "_____ does the apple juice _____?"

24 뒤에 앉아 있던 학생 하나가 손을 들고 질문했다. "사과 주스는 무슨 뜻입니까?"

25 Mr. Jenkins _____, "I'm glad _____ _____.

25 Jenkins 선생님은 미소 지었다. "질문을 해줘서 기뻐요.

26 It just shows that though your life may _____ _____, there's always _____ _____ a cool drink with a friend."

26 그것은, 여러분의 인생이 가득 차 보일지라도 친구와 시원한 음료수를 나눌 여유는 늘 있다는 점을 보여 줍니다."

Step3

※ 다음 문장을 우리말로 쓰시오.

1 ▶ The Full Jar

➡ _____

2 ▶ Mr. Jenkins stood before his class.

➡ _____

3 ▶ He had a large jar and a big bag on the teacher's desk.

➡ _____

4 ▶ When the class began, he picked up the jar and started to fill it with golf balls from the bag.

➡ _____

5 ▶ He asked the students, "Is the jar full?"

➡ _____

6 ▶ They all said, "Yes."

➡ _____

7 ▶ The teacher took a box of small stones out of the bag and poured them into the jar.

➡ _____

8 ▶ He shook the jar a little, and the stones rolled into the open areas between the golf balls.

➡ _____

9 ▶ He asked the same question and got the same answer from his students.

➡ _____

10 ▶ Next, the teacher took out a bottle of and poured it into the jar.

➡ _____

11 ▶ After he watched the sand fill the spaces between the stones, he asked once more, "Is the jar full?"

➡ _____

12 ▶ All the students replied, "Yes."

➡ _____

13 ▶ Suddenly Mr. Jenkins took a can of apple juice out of the bag.

➡ _____

14 ▶ He poured the apple juice into the jar, and his students watched it fill the spaces in the sand.

➡ _____

15 ▶ "Now," the teacher said, "I want you to understand that your life is just like the jar.

➡ _____

16 ▶ The golf balls are what is most important in life: your family, your friends, your health, and your dreams.

➡ _____

17 ▶ Even when everything else is lost, your life can still be full.

➡ _____

18 ▶ The stones are the other things valued by people, like your job, your house, and your car.

➡ _____

19 ▶ The sand is all the small things."

➡ _____

20 ▶ "If you put the sand into the jar first," he said, "there's no room for the stones or the golf balls.

➡ _____

21 ▶ The same goes for life.

➡ _____

22 ▶ If you spend all your time and energy on the small things, you will never have room for what is really important to you.

➡ _____

_____

23 ▶ Take care of the balls first — the things that really matter."

➡ _____

24 ▶ One student sitting in the back raised her hand and asked, "What does the apple juice mean?"

➡ _____

25 ▶ Mr. Jenkins smiled, "I'm glad you asked.

➡ _____

26 ▶ It just shows that though your life may seem full, there's always room for a cool drink with a friend."

➡ _____

※ 다음 괄호 안의 단어들을 우리말에 맞도록 바르게 배열하시오.

1 (Full / The / Jar)
➡ _____

2 (Jenkins / Mr. / before / stood / class. / his)
➡ _____

3 (had / he / large / a / jar / a / and / big / on / bag / the / desk. / teacher's)
➡ _____

4 (the / when / began, / class / he / up / picked / jar / the / and / to / started / fill / with / it / balls / golf / the / from / bag.)
➡ _____

5 (asked / he / students, / the / "is / full?" / jar / the)
➡ _____

6 (all / they / "yes." / said,)
➡ _____

7 (teacher / the / a / took / box / small / of / out / stones / of / bag / the / and / them / poured / into / jar. / the)
➡ _____
_____

8 (shook / he / jar / the / little, / a / and / stones / the / into / rolled / open / the / areas / the / between / balls. / golf)
➡ _____
_____

9 (asked / he / same / the / question / and / the / got / answer / same / from / students. / his)
➡ _____

10 (the / next, / teacher / out / took / bottle / a / of / and / sand / it / poured / into / jar. / the)
➡ _____

11 (he / after / the / watched / sand / the / fill / spaces / the / between / stones, / asked / he / more, / once / "is / jar / the / full?")
➡ _____
_____

12 (the / all / replied, / students / "yes.")
➡ _____

13 (Mr. / suddenly / Jenkins / took / can / a / apple / of / juice / of / out / bag. / the)
➡ _____

14 (poured / he / apple / the / juice / the / into / jar, / his / and / watched / students / fill / it / spaces / the / the / sand. / in)
➡ _____
_____

1 가득 찬 병

2 Jenkins 선생님이 교실 앞에 섰다.

3 교탁 위에는 큰 병과 커다란 가방이 놓여 있었다.

4 수업이 시작하자, 선생님은 병을 집어 들고 가방에서 꺼낸 골프공으로 채우기 시작했다.

5 그는 학생들에게 "병이 가득 찼나요?"라고 질문했다.

6 학생들은 모두 "예."라고 대답했다.

7 선생님은 가방에서 작은 돌 한 상자를 끄집어내어 병 안에 부었다.

8 그가 병을 살짝 흔들자, 돌들이 골프공 사이의 틈새로 굴러 들어갔다.

9 그는 같은 질문을 했고 학생들에게서 같은 대답을 들었다.

10 그런 다음, 선생님은 모래 병을 꺼내 병 안에 부었다.

11 모래가 돌 사이의 공간을 채우는 것을 지켜보고 나서 그는 "이 병이 가득 찼나요?"라고 한 번 더 물었다.

12 모든 학생들이 "예."라고 답했다.

13 갑자기 Jenkins 선생님은 가방에서 사과 주스 한 캔을 꺼냈다.

14 그는 사과 주스를 병 안에 부었고, 학생들은 주스가 모래 사이의 빈틈을 채우는 것을 지켜보았다.

15 (the / "now," / said, / teacher / want / "I / to / want / you / understand / that / life / your / just / is / like / the / jar.)

➡ _____

_____

16 (golf / the / are / balls / what / most / is / important / life: / in / family, / your / friends, / your / and / health, / your / dreams. / your)

➡ _____

_____

17 (even / everything / when / is / else / lost, / life / your / can / be / still / full.)

➡ _____

18 (stones / the / the / are / things / other / valued / people, / by / your / like / job, / house, / your / and / car. / your)

➡ _____

_____

19 (sand / the / all / is / small / the / things.")

➡ _____

20 ("if / put / you / the / into / sand / jar / the / first," / said, / he / no / "there's / room / the / for / stones / the / or / balls. / golf)

➡ _____

_____

21 (same / the / for / goes / life.)

➡ _____

22 (you / if / spend / time / your / all / energy / and / the / on / thiings, / small / will / you / have / never / room / what / for / is / important / really / you. / to)

➡ _____

_____

23 (care / of / take / first / the / balls / – / things / the / really / that / matter.")

➡ _____

_____

24 (student / one / in / sitting / the / back / her / raised / hand / and / asked, / does / "what / apple / the / mean?" / juice)

➡ _____

_____

25 (Jenins / Mr. / smiled, / glad / "I'm / asked. / you)

➡ _____

26 (just / it / that / shows / your / though / life / seem / may / full, / always / there's / for / room / a / cool / with / drink / friend." / a)

➡ _____

_____

---

15 "자, 이제." 선생님이 말했다. "여러분의 인생이 병과 같다는 것을 이해하기 바랍니다.

16 골프공은 여러분의 가족, 친구, 건강, 꿈과 같이 인생에서 가장 중요한 것이랍니다.

17 다른 모든 것을 잃게 될 때라도 여러분의 인생은 여전히 가득 차 있을 수 있습니다.

18 돌은 여러분의 직업, 집, 자동차 처럼 사람들이 소중하게 여기는 다른 것들에 해당합니다.

19 모래는 온갖 사소한 것들이랍니다."

20 "만약 병에 모래를 먼저 채우면, 돌이나 골프공을 채울 공간이 없게 됩니다.

21 인생도 똑같습니다.

22 여러분의 시간과 에너지를 사소한 것에 모두 허비한다면 여러분에게 진정으로 중요한 것을 채울 공간은 절대로 없을 겁니다.

23 골프공, 즉 정말로 중요한 것들을 먼저 챙기기 바랍니다."라고 선생님이 말했다.

24 뒤에 앉아 있던 학생 하나가 손을 들고 질문했다. "사과 주스는 무슨 뜻입니까?"

25 Jenkins 선생님은 미소 지었다. "질문을 해줘서 기뻐요.

26 그것은, 여러분의 인생이 가득 차 보일지라도 친구와 시원한 음료수를 나눌 여유는 늘 있다는 점을 보여 줍니다."

※ 다음 우리말을 영어로 쓰시오.

1 가득 찬 병

➡ _____

2 Jenkins 선생님이 교실 앞에 섰다.

➡ _____

3 교탁 위에는 큰 병과 커다란 가방이 놓여 있었다.

➡ _____

4 수업이 시작하자, 선생님은 병을 집어 들고 가방에서 꺼낸 골프공으로 채우기 시작했다.

➡ _____

5 그는 학생들에게 "병이 가득 찼나요?"라고 질문했다.

➡ _____

6 학생들은 모두 "예."라고 대답했다.

➡ _____

7 선생님은 가방에서 작은 돌 한 상자를 끄집어내어 병 안에 부었다.

➡ _____

8 그가 병을 살짝 흔들자, 돌들이 골프공 사이의 틈새로 굴러 들어갔다.

➡ _____

9 그는 같은 질문을 했고 학생들에게서 같은 대답을 들었다.

➡ _____

10 그런 다음, 선생님은 모래 병을 꺼내 병 안에 부었다.

➡ _____

11 모래가 돌 사이의 공간을 채우는 것을 지켜보고 나서 그는 "이 병이 가득 찼나요?"라고 한 번 더 물었다.

➡ _____

12 모든 학생들이 "예."라고 답했다.

➡ _____

13 갑자기 Jenkins 선생님은 가방에서 사과 주스 한 캔을 꺼냈다.

➡ _____

14 그는 사과 주스를 병 안에 부었고, 학생들은 주스가 모래 사이의 빈틈을 채우는 것을 지켜보았다.

➡ _____

15 "자, 이제," 선생님이 말했다. "여러분의 인생이 병과 같다는 것을 이해하기 바랍니다.

➡ _____

16 골프공은 여러분의 가족, 친구, 건강, 꿈과 같이 인생에서 가장 중요한 것이랍니다.

➡ _____

17 다른 모든 것을 잃게 될 때라도 여러분의 인생은 여전히 가득 차 있을 수 있습니다.

➡ _____

18 돌은 여러분의 직업, 집, 자동차처럼 사람들이 소중하게 여기는 다른 것들에 해당합니다.

➡ _____

19 모래는 온갖 사소한 것들이랍니다."

➡ _____

20 "만약 병에 모래를 먼저 채우면, 돌이나 골프공을 채울 공간이 없게 됩니다.

➡ _____

21 인생도 똑같습니다.

➡ _____

22 여러분의 시간과 에너지를 사소한 것에 모두 허비한다면 여러분에게 진정으로 중요한 것을 채울 공간은 절대로 없을 겁니다.

➡ _____

_____

23 골프공, 즉 정말로 중요한 것들을 먼저 챙기기 바랍니다."라고 선생님이 말했다.

➡ _____

24 뒤에 앉아 있던 학생 하나가 손을 들고 질문했다. "사과 주스는 무슨 뜻입니까?"

➡ _____

25 Jenkins 선생님은 미소 지었다. "질문을 해줘서 기뻐요.

➡ _____

26 그것은, 여러분의 인생이 가득 차 보일지라도 친구와 시원한 음료수를 나눌 여유는 늘 있다는 점을 보여 줍니다."

➡ _____

※ 다음 영어를 우리말로 쓰시오.

01	artificial	
02	bother	
03	cause	
04	relieved	
05	gloomy	
06	friendship	
07	helpful	
08	positive	
09	stressed	
10	improve	
11	appearance	
12	scream	
13	well-known	
14	relieve	
15	argue	
16	patient	
17	chemical	
18	besides	
19	method	
20	common	
21	nervous	

22	boring	
23	matter	
24	scary	
25	produce	
26	effect	
27	focus	
28	salty	
29	sleepy	
30	tidy	
31	work	
32	schoolwork	
33	media	
34	leave	
35	used to	
36	thanks to	
37	at the same time	
38	feel low	
39	according to	
40	make sense	
41	deal with	
42	as long as	
43	have difficulty -ing	

※ 다음 우리말을 영어로 쓰시오.

01	매체	
02	안심이 되는	
03	생산하다	
04	주장하다	
05	도움이 되는	
06	졸리는	
07	그 외에도	
08	집중하다	
09	개선하다	
10	소리를 지르다	
11	외모	
12	문제가 되다, 중요하다	
13	화학물질	
14	무서운	
15	흔한	
16	남겨두다	
17	불안한	
18	스트레스 받은	
19	인내하는	
20	방법	
21	유명한	
22	덜다	
23	지루한	
24	짠	
25	깔끔한	
26	효과가 있다	
27	우울한	
28	인공적인	
29	성가시게 하다	
30	원인	
31	긍정적인	
32	효과	
33	학교 공부	
34	우정	
35	~에 따르면	
36	다른 방식으로	
37	~하는 한	
38	~할 것을 잊어버리다	
39	동시에	
40	~ 대신에	
41	~을 다루다, 처리하다	
42	약속을 어기다	
43	~하곤 했다	

※ 다음 영영풀이에 알맞은 단어를 <보기>에서 골라 쓴 후, 우리말 뜻을 쓰시오.

1 _____ : a relationship between friends: _____

2 _____ : a particular way of doing something: _____

3 _____ : known about by a lot of people: _____

4 _____ : not real or not made of natural things: _____

5 _____ : a person, event, or thing that makes something happen: _____

6 _____ : a change that is caused by an event, action, etc.: _____

7 _____ : sad because you think the situation will not improve: _____

8 _____ : to make something better, or to become better: _____

9 _____ : expressing support, agreement, or approval: _____

10 _____ : to disagree with someone in words, often in an angry way: _____

11 _____ : neatly arranged with everything in the right place: _____

12 _____ : happening often; existing in large numbers or in many places: _____

13 _____ : the way someone or something looks to other people: _____

14 _____ : to make someone feel slightly worried, upset, or concerned: _____

15 _____ : to shout something in a loud, high voice because of fear, anger, etc.: _____

16 _____ : to give attention, effort, etc. to one particular subject, situation or person rather than another: _____

보기			
cause	scream	artificial	bother
gloomy	appearance	method	focus
common	well-known	tidy	effect
argue	friendship	positive	improve

※ 다음 우리말과 일치하도록 빈칸에 알맞은 말을 쓰시오.

Listen and Answer – Dialog 1

W: Today, I'd like to _____ to you _____ teen stress. _____ _____ you _____ the most _____? _____ 9,000 teens _____ this question. _____ you can _____, schoolwork was the most _____ _____ of stress. _____ _____ _____ the students said schoolwork _____ them the most. _____ with friends _____ second place _____ 15.3%. _____ came family and _____ about the future. 8.2% of the students said they _____ _____ _____ _____ their _____.

W: 오늘, 저는 여러분에게 십 대들의 스트레스에 관해 말씀드리려고 합니다. 여러분에게 가장 많이 스트레스를 주는 것은 무엇인가요? 약 9,000명의 십 대들이 이 질문에 답했습니다. 보시다시피, 학업이 스트레스의 가장 흔한 원인이었습니다. 절반이 넘는 학생들은 학업이 스트레스를 가장 많이 준다고 말했습니다. 친구들과의 문제는 15.3%로 2위를 차지했습니다. 다음은 가족, 그리고 장래에 대한 걱정 순이었습니다. 8.2%의 학생들은 외모 때문에 스트레스를 받는다고 말했습니다.

Listen and Answer – Dialog 2

W: _____ are you _____, Oliver?

B: I'm _____ _____ the math test, Mom. _____ stress me out.

W: I understand. I _____ _____ feel that _____, _____.

B: Really? I didn't _____ that.

W: Yeah, but _____ _____ _____ was _____ for me.

B: _____ _____ you _____ that?

W: I _____ _____ when I had an exam, but _____ _____ _____ _____ it made me _____ and _____ _____.

B: I see. Did stress _____ you _____ _____ _____?

W: Yes, it helped _____ my _____.

W: 뭐 하고 있니, Oliver?
B: 수학 시험이 있어서 공부하고 있어요, 엄마. 성적이 제게 스트레스를 줘요.
W: 이해한단다. 나도 그렇게 느끼곤 했거든.
B: 정말요? 그러신 줄 몰랐어요.
W: 그래, 하지만 약간의 스트레스는 내게 도움이 되기도 했단다.
B: 왜 그렇게 말씀하세요?
W: 나는 시험이 있을 때 스트레스를 받았지만, 동시에 그 스트레스가 나를 집중하고 더 열심히 노력하게 했거든.
B: 그렇군요. 스트레스가 다른 방식으로 엄마에게 도움이 된 적이 있나요?
W: 그럼, 내 기억력을 높이는 데 도움을 주었단다.

Listen More – Listen and choose.

B1: Today, let's _____ about the class T-shirt. We _____ _____ _____ on the design.

G: _____ me _____ you some _____ on the screen.

B2: We have to _____ a T-shirt with _____ _____.

B1: _____ _____ you _____ that?

B2: _____ we'll _____ the T-shirt on Sports Day. It's in June.

G: That _____. What _____ this green one?

B2: I like it. The bee on the T-shirt is so _____.

G: And it's not _____.

B1: Yes. I think it's the _____ _____.

B1: 오늘은 학급 티셔츠에 관해 이야기해 보자. 우리는 디자인을 정해야 해.
G: 화면으로 몇 가지 디자인을 보여 줄게.
B2: 우리는 반팔 티셔츠를 골라야 해.
B1: 무슨 이유로 그렇게 말하는 거야?
B2: 우리가 체육대회 때 티셔츠를 입기 때문이야. 그건 6월에 열려.
G: 그 말이 맞아. 이 초록색 티셔츠는 어때?
B2: 나는 마음에 들어. 티셔츠 위의 벌 그림이 정말 귀여워.
G: 그리고 비싸지 않아.
B1: 맞아. 그게 제일 좋겠어.

Speak – Talk in groups.

Hi. Today, I'd _____ _____ _____ about Frida Kahlo. She was a Mexican painter. _____ of her _____ _____ _____ is *Viva la Vida*.

안녕하세요. 오늘은 Frida Kahlo에 대하여 이야기하겠습니다. 그녀는 멕시코인 화가입니다. 그녀의 가장 유명한 그림 중 하나는 Viva la Vida입니다.

Speak – Talk in pairs.

A: I want to _____ more time on social media.

B: What _____ you _____ that?

A: I can _____ more friends from _____ _____ _____.

B: That _____ _____.

A: 나는 소셜 미디어에 더 많은 시간을 쓰고 싶어.
B: 왜 그렇게 생각하니?
A: 나는 전 세계로부터 더 많은 친구를 사귈 수 있어.
B: 옳은 말이야.

My Speaking Portfolio Step 3

I'd _____ to talk about some _____ _____ _____ when you get _____. First, it's good to _____ _____ _____. Second, _____ to ten is a great idea. Also, _____ cold water helps. _____, _____ happy _____ can help.

여러분이 화가 났을 때 긴장을 풀 수 있는 방법에 관하여 이야기하겠습니다. 첫째, 심호흡을 하는 것이 좋습니다. 둘째, 열까지 세는 것은 좋은 생각입니다. 또한 차가운 물을 마시는 것도 도움이 됩니다. 마지막으로 행복한 생각을 하는 것이 도움이 됩니다.

Wrap Up – Listening & Speaking 1

W: Hello, teens. I'm Dr. Broccoli. Last time, I _____ about different _____ that _____ _____ for your health. Today, I'd _____ _____ talk about _____ _____ habits. First, try to eat _____. Second, it's important _____ _____ _____ when you're _____.

여: 안녕하세요, 십 대 여러분. 저는 Broccoli 박사입니다. 지난 시간에, 건강에 좋은 다양한 음식에 관해 이야기했죠. 오늘은 건강한 식습관에 관해 이야기하고자 합니다. 먼저, 천천히 먹으려고 노력하세요. 둘째, 배가 부르면 그만 먹는 것이 중요합니다.

Wrap Up – Listening & Speaking 2

G: Why _____ we _____ a sport club?

B: Sounds good. Let's _____ a baseball club.

G: Well, I think a _____ club is a _____ _____.

B: What _____ you _____ that?

G: All _____ _____ is a ball to play basketball.

G: 우리 운동 동아리를 만드는 게 어때?
B: 좋아. 야구 동아리를 만들자.
G: 글쎄, 농구 동아리가 더 좋은 생각인 것 같아.
B: 왜 그렇게 말하는 거야?
G: 농구를 하기 위해 우리에게 필요한 건 농구공뿐이잖아.

※ 다음 우리말에 맞도록 대화를 영어로 쓰시오.

Listen and Answer – Dialog 1

W: _____
_____
_____
_____
_____

W: 오늘, 저는 여러분에게 십 대들의 스트레스에 관해 말씀드리려고 합니다. 여러분에게 가장 많이 스트레스를 주는 것은 무엇인가요? 약 9,000명의 십 대들이 이 질문에 답했습니다. 보시다시피, 학업이 스트레스의 가장 흔한 원인이었습니다. 절반이 넘는 학생들은 학업이 스트레스를 가장 많이 준다고 말했습니다. 친구들과의 문제는 15.3%로 2위를 차지했습니다. 다음은 가족, 그리고 장래에 대한 걱정 순이었습니다. 8.2%의 학생들은 외모 때문에 스트레스를 받는다고 말했습니다.

Listen and Answer – Dialog 2

W: _____
B: _____
W: _____
B: _____
W: _____
B: _____
W: _____
B: _____
W: _____

W: 뭐 하고 있니, Oliver?
B: 수학 시험이 있어서 공부하고 있어요, 엄마. 성적이 제게 스트레스를 줘요.
W: 이해한단다. 나도 그렇게 느끼곤 했거든.
B: 정말요? 그러신 줄 몰랐어요.
W: 그래, 하지만 약간의 스트레스는 내게 도움이 되기도 했단다.
B: 왜 그렇게 말씀하세요?
W: 나는 시험이 있을 때 스트레스를 받았지만, 동시에 그 스트레스가 나를 집중하고 더 열심히 노력하게 했거든.
B: 그렇군요. 스트레스가 다른 방식으로 엄마에게 도움이 된 적이 있나요?
W: 그럼, 내 기억력을 높이는 데 도움을 주었단다.

Listen More – Listen and choose.

B1: _____
G: _____
B2: _____
B1: _____
B2: _____
G: _____
B2: _____
G: _____
B1: _____

B1: 오늘은 학급 티셔츠에 관해 이야기해 보자. 우리는 디자인을 정해야 해.
G: 화면으로 몇 가지 디자인을 보여 줄게.
B2: 우리는 반팔 티셔츠를 골라야 해.
B1: 무슨 이유로 그렇게 말하는 거야?
B2: 우리가 체육대회 때 티셔츠를 입기 때문이야. 그건 6월에 열려.
G: 그 말이 맞아. 이 초록색 티셔츠는 어때?
B2: 나는 마음에 들어. 티셔츠 위의 벌 그림이 정말 귀엽다.
G: 그리고 비싸지 않아.
B1: 맞아. 그게 제일 좋겠어.

Speak – Talk in groups.

_____

_____

안녕하세요. 오늘은 Frida Kahlo에 대하여 이야기하겠습니다. 그녀는 멕시코인 화가입니다. 그녀의 가장 유명한 그림 중 하나는 Viva la Vida입니다.

Speak – Talk in pairs.

A: _____

B: _____

A: _____

B: _____

A: 나는 소셜 미디어에 더 많은 시간을 쓰고 싶어.
B: 왜 그렇게 생각하니?
A: 나는 전 세계로부터 더 많은 친구를 사귈 수 있어.
B: 옳은 말이야.

My Speaking Portfolio Step 3

_____

_____

여러분이 화가 났을 때 긴장을 풀 수 있는 방법에 관하여 이야기하겠습니다. 첫째, 심호흡을 하는 것이 좋습니다. 둘째, 열까지 세는 것은 좋은 생각입니다. 또한 차가운 물을 마시는 것도 도움이 됩니다. 마지막으로 행복한 생각을 하는 것이 도움이 됩니다.

Wrap Up – Listening & Speaking 1

W: _____

_____

_____

여: 안녕하세요, 십 대 여러분. 저는 Broccoli 박사입니다. 지난 시간에, 건강에 좋은 다양한 음식에 관해 이야기했죠. 오늘은 건강한 식습관에 관해 이야기하고자 합니다. 먼저, 천천히 먹으려고 노력하세요. 둘째, 배가 부르면 그만 먹는 것이 중요합니다.

Wrap Up – Listening & Speaking 2

G: _____

B: _____

G: _____

B: _____

G: _____

G: 우리 운동 동아리를 만드는 게 어때?
B: 좋아. 야구 동아리를 만들자.
G: 글쎄, 농구 동아리가 더 좋은 생각인 것 같아.
B: 왜 그렇게 말하는 거야?
G: 농구를 하기 위해 우리에게 필요한 건 농구공뿐이잖아.

※ 다음 우리말과 일치하도록 빈칸에 알맞은 것을 골라 쓰시오.

1 Say _____ to _____
A. Stress   B. Goodbye

2 Some people _____ time _____ friends when they _____
_____.
A. feel   B. with   C. low   D. spend

3 _____ eat special foods to _____ _____.
A. feel   B. others   C. better

4 _____ _____ simply sleep for a _____.
A. while   B. others   C. still

5 _____ do you _____ _____ stress?
A. deal   B. how   C. with

6 _____ are some stories about people who _____ _____
_____.
A. different   B. suggest   C. ways   D. here

Mina (15, Daejeon)

7 Sometimes my friends give me stress _____ _____ bad things
about me, _____ promises, or _____ over small things.
A. breaking   B. saying   C. arguing   D. by

8 _____ this _____, I watch _____ movies!
A. happens   B. horror   C. when

9 Good horror movies are _____ scary _____ I scream a _____.
A. that   B. so   C. lot

10 I guess that _____ at the _____ of my _____ helps
me _____ better.
A. lungs   B. feel   C. top   D. screaming

11 Also, _____ to scary _____ and sound _____, I can forget
about what _____ me.
A. bothers   B. scenes   C. effects   D. thanks

12 I've _____ _____ this _____ for the past several months,
and it really _____.
A. method   B. usinig   C. works   D. been

Junho (14, Yeosu)

13 My uncle _____ _____ college two years _____.
A. from   B. ago   C. graduated

14 He lives _____ my family, and he's _____
_____ a job for some time.
A. looking   B. with   C. for   D. been

15 I know that he's _____ _____, but he always tries to be
positive by _____ _____.
A. out   B. fishing   C. stressed   D. going

16 He never _____ when he doesn't _____ any _____.
A. catch   B. gets   C. fish   D. upset

17 He says, "_____ I fish, I'm _____ focused _____ I can
leave all my worries _____.
A. behind   B. that   C. so   D. while

18 _____, it teaches me to _____."
A. besides   B. patient   C. be

---

1 스트레스와 이별하라

2 어떤 사람들은 울적할 때 친구들과 시간을 보낸다.

3 다른 사람들은 기분이 좋아지도록 특별한 음식을 먹는다.

4 또 다른 사람들은 그저 잠시 잠을 자기도 한다.

5 여러분은 스트레스를 어떻게 다루는가?

6 여기 다양한 방법을 제안하는 사람들의 이야기가 있다.

미나 (15살, 대전)

7 때때로 내 친구들은 나에 관해 나쁜 말을 하거나, 약속을 어기거나, 혹은 사소한 일을 두고 언쟁을 하며 내게 스트레스를 준다.

8 이럴 때, 나는 공포 영화를 본다!

9 훌륭한 공포 영화는 너무 무서워서 나는 소리를 많이 지르게 된다.

10 있는 힘껏 소리 지르는 것은 내 기분이 나아지는 데 도움이 된다고 생각한다.

11 또한, 무서운 장면과 음향 효과 덕분에 나를 괴롭히는 것들을 잊을 수 있다.

12 나는 지난 몇 달간 이 방법을 써 오고 있는데, 효과가 아주 좋다.

준호 (14살, 여수)

13 우리 삼촌은 2년 전에 대학을 졸업했다.

14 삼촌은 우리 가족과 함께 살고 있고, 얼마 전부터 직장을 구하고 있다.

15 나는 삼촌이 스트레스를 받고 있지만 낚시를 다니며 긍정적으로 지내려고 항상 노력한다는 것을 안다.

16 물고기를 한 마리도 잡지 못했을 때에도 삼촌은 절대 속상해 하지 않는다.

17 삼촌은 "낚시하는 동안, 나는 아주 몰입해서 모든 걱정을 잊을 수 있어.

18 게다가 낚시는 나에게 인내를 가르쳐 준단다."라고 말한다

---

19 I'm _____ that _____ _____ one thing helps us _____ about something else.

　A. forget　　　　　B. on　　　　　C. sure　　　　　D. focusing

Dobin (16, Seoul)

20 My sister, a _____ student in high school, has a wonderful _____ to stay _____ _____ stress.

　A. free　　　　　B. second-year　　C. from　　　　D. way

21 She feels a lot of stress from schoolwork, but my mother _____ to _____ the situation _____ a good _____.

　A. seems　　　　B. reason　　　　C. for　　　　D. like

22 It is _____ cleaning is my sister's _____ _____ to make life _____!

　A. because　　　B. way　　　　　C. number-one　　D. better

23 When she's _____ stressed _____ her life _____ _____, she cleans her room.

　A. gloomy　　　　B. that　　　　　C. so　　　　　D. looks

24 She says, "_____ I clean my room, I _____ _____ I'm also _____ stress.

　A. relieving　　　B. as　　　　　C. like　　　　D. feel

25 _____ my room looks _____, my life _____ _____."

　A. tidy　　　　　B. when　　　　C. brighter　　　D. looks

Yulia (14, Ansan)

26 _____ me _____ you _____ my mother does about her stress.

　A. tell　　　　　B. what　　　　C. let

27 She feels _____ by all the _____ she _____ to do at _____ and at home.

　A. has　　　　　B. stressed　　　C. work　　　　D. things

28 When she's _____ _____, she _____ "Me Time" on her _____.

　A. writes　　　　B. under　　　　C. calendar　　　D. stress

29 This means she _____ some time _____ for _____.

　A. herself　　　B. takes　　　　C. out

30 She _____ a book, _____ a movie, or _____ with her friends.

　A. watches　　　B. reads　　　　C. talks

31 She says, "It doesn't really _____ what I do, _____ _____ it's something I like.

　A. as　　　　　B. matter　　　　C. as　　　　　D. long

32 I've _____ _____ 'Me Time' _____ my calendar for two months, and I feel _____ better."

　A. writing　　　B. much　　　　C. on　　　　　D. been

33 _____ _____ will _____ _____ you?

　A. work　　　　B. methods　　　C. which　　　D. for

34 _____ some of these ideas _____, and find your best _____ to say goodbye to _____.

　A. way　　　　　B. yourself　　　C. stress　　　D. try

---

19 한 가지 일에 집중하는 것이 다른 무언가를 잊는 데 도움이 된다고 나는 확신한다.

도빈 (16살, 서울)

20 고등학교 2학년인 우리 누나에게는 스트레스에서 벗어나는 훌륭한 방법이 있다.

21 누나가 학업 때문에 많은 스트레스를 받지만, 그럴 만한 이유로 우리 어머니는 그 상황을 좋아하시는 것 같다.

22 그것은 바로, 청소가 누나의 삶을 향상하는 최고의 방법이기 때문이다.

23 스트레스를 너무 많이 받아서 인생이 우울해 보일 때, 누나는 방을 청소한다.

24 누나는 "방을 청소하면서 스트레스도 해소되는 것 같아.

25 내 방이 깔끔해 보이면 내 삶도 더 밝아 보여."라고 말한다.

Yulia (14살, 안산)

26 우리 어머니께서 스트레스를 어떻게 다루시는지 소개하려고 한다.

27 어머니는 직장과 집에서 해야 하는 온갖 일로 인해 스트레스를 받으신다.

28 스트레스를 받을 때면 어머니는 달력에 '나만의 시간'이라고 적으신다.

29 이것은 어머니 자신을 위해 잠깐 시간을 낸다는 의미이다.

30 어머니는 책을 읽거나, 영화를 보거나, 친구들과 이야기를 나누신다.

31 어머니는 "내가 좋아하는 것이라면, 무엇을 하는지는 별로 중요하지 않아.

32 나는 두 달째 달력에 '나만의 시간'을 적어 왔고, 기분이 훨씬 좋아졌어."라고 말씀하신다.

33 어떤 방법이 여러분에게 효과가 있을까?

34 이 아이디어 중 몇 개를 직접 해 보고, 스트레스와 이별하는 자신만의 최고의 방법을 찾아라.

※ 다음 우리말과 일치하도록 빈칸에 알맞은 말을 쓰시오.

1 _____ _____ to Stress

2 Some people _____ _____ _____ friends when they _____ _____.

3 _____ eat special foods _____ _____ _____.

4 _____ simply sleep _____ _____ _____.

5 How do you _____ _____ stress?

6 Here are some stories about people who _____ _____ _____.

Mina (15, Daejeon)

7 Sometimes my friends give me stress by _____ bad things about me, _____ promises, or _____ _____ small things.

8 _____ _____ _____, I watch horror movies!

9 Good horror movies are _____ scary _____ I scream a lot.

10 I guess that screaming _____ _____ _____ _____ _____ _____ me _____ better.

11 Also, _____ _____ scary _____ and sound _____, I can forget about _____ _____ _____.

12 _____ _____ _____ this method for the past _____ _____, and it really _____.

Junho (14, Yeosu)

13 My uncle _____ _____ college two years _____.

14 He lives with my family, and _____ _____ _____ a job for some time.

15 I know that _____ _____, but he _____ _____ to be positive _____ _____ _____.

16 He never _____ _____ when he doesn't catch any fish.

17 He says, "While I fish, I'm _____ focused _____ I _____ all my _____ _____.

18 _____, it teaches me _____ _____ _____."

1 스트레스와 이별하라

2 어떤 사람들은 울적할 때 친구들과 시간을 보낸다.

3 다른 사람들은 기분이 좋아지도록 특별한 음식을 먹는다.

4 또 다른 사람들은 그저 잠시 잠을 자기도 한다.

5 여러분은 스트레스를 어떻게 다루는가?

6 여기 다양한 방법을 제안하는 사람들의 이야기가 있다.

미나 (15살, 대전)

7 때때로 내 친구들은 나에 관해 나쁜 말을 하거나, 약속을 어기거나, 혹은 사소한 일을 두고 언쟁을 하며 내게 스트레스를 준다.

8 이럴 때, 나는 공포 영화를 본다!

9 훌륭한 공포 영화는 너무 무서워서 나는 소리를 많이 지르게 된다.

10 있는 힘껏 소리 지르는 것은 내 기분이 나아지는 데 도움이 된다고 생각한다.

11 또한, 무서운 장면과 음향 효과 덕분에 나를 괴롭히는 것들을 잊을 수 있다.

12 나는 지난 몇 달간 이 방법을 써 오고 있는데, 효과가 아주 좋다.

준호 (14살, 여수)

13 우리 삼촌은 2년 전에 대학을 졸업했다.

14 삼촌은 우리 가족과 함께 살고 있고, 얼마 전부터 직장을 구하고 있다.

15 나는 삼촌이 스트레스를 받고 있지만 낚시를 다니며 긍정적으로 지내려고 항상 노력한다는 것을 안다.

16 물고기를 한 마리도 잡지 못했을 때에도 삼촌은 절대 속상해 하지 않는다.

17 삼촌은 "낚시하는 동안, 나는 아주 몰입해서 모든 걱정을 잊을 수 있어.

18 게다가 낚시는 나에게 인내를 가르쳐 준단다."라고 말한다

19 I'm sure that _____ _____ one thing helps us _____ about _____ _____.

Dobin (16, Seoul)

20 My sister, a _____ student in high school, has a wonderful way _____ _____ _____ _____ stress.

21 She feels a lot of stress from schoolwork, but my mother _____ _____ _____ the situation _____ _____ _____ _____.

22 It is because cleaning is my sister's _____ _____ life better!

23 When she's _____ stressed _____ her life _____ _____, she cleans her room.

24 She says, " _____ I clean my room, I _____ _____ _____ I'm also _____ stress.

25 When my room _____ _____, my life _____ _____."

Yulia (14, Ansan)

26 _____ me tell you _____ my mother does about her stress.

27 She feels stressed by _____ _____ _____ _____ _____ _____ _____ _____ and at home.

28 When _____ _____ _____, she writes "Me Time" on her calendar.

29 This means she _____ _____ _____ _____ for herself.

30 She _____ a book, _____ a movie, or _____ with her friends.

31 She says, "It doesn't really _____ _____ I do, _____ _____ it's something I like.

32 _____ _____ _____ 'Me Time' on my calendar for two months, and I _____ _____ _____."

33 _____ methods will _____ _____ _____ _____ ?

34 Try some of these ideas yourself, and find your best way _____ _____ _____ _____ _____.

---

19 한 가지 일에 집중하는 것이 다른 무언가를 잊는 데 도움이 된다고 나는 확신한다.

도빈 (16살, 서울)

20 고등학교 2학년인 우리 누나에게는 스트레스에서 벗어나는 훌륭한 방법이 있다.

21 누나가 학업 때문에 많은 스트레스를 받지만, 그럴 만한 이유로 우리 어머니는 그 상황을 좋아하시는 것 같다.

22 그것은 바로, 청소가 누나의 삶을 향상하는 최고의 방법이기 때문이다.

23 스트레스를 너무 많이 받아서 인생이 우울해 보일 때, 누나는 방을 청소한다.

24 누나는 "방을 청소하면서 스트레스도 해소되는 것 같아.

25 내 방이 깔끔해 보이면 내 삶도 더 밝아 보여."라고 말한다.

Yulia (14살, 안산)

26 우리 어머니께서 스트레스를 어떻게 다루시는지 소개하려고 한다.

27 어머니는 직장과 집에서 해야 하는 온갖 일로 인해 스트레스를 받으신다.

28 스트레스를 받을 때면 어머니는 달력에 '나만의 시간'이라고 적으신다.

29 이것은 어머니 자신을 위해 잠깐 시간을 낸다는 의미이다.

30 어머니는 책을 읽거나, 영화를 보거나, 친구들과 이야기를 나누신다.

31 어머니는 "내가 좋아하는 것이라면, 무엇을 하는지는 별로 중요하지 않아.

32 나는 두 달째 달력에 '나만의 시간'을 적어 왔고, 기분이 훨씬 좋아졌어."라고 말씀하신다.

33 어떤 방법이 여러분에게 효과가 있을까?

34 이 아이디어 중 몇 개를 직접 해보고, 스트레스와 이별하는 자신만의 최고의 방법을 찾아라.

※ 다음 문장을 우리말로 쓰시오.

1 Say Goodbye to Stress

➡ _____

2 Some people spend time with friends when they feel low.

➡ _____

3 Others eat special foods to feel better.

➡ _____

4 Still others simply sleep for a while.

➡ _____

5 How do you deal with stress?

➡ _____

6 Here are some stories about people who suggest different ways.

➡ _____

미나 (15살, 대전) Mina (15, Daejeon)

7 Sometimes my friends give me stress by saying bad things about me, breaking promises, or arguing over small things.

➡ _____

8 When this happens, I watch horror movies!

➡ _____

9 Good horror movies are so scary that I scream a lot.

➡ _____

10 I guess that screaming at the top of my lungs helps me feel better.

➡ _____

11 Also, thanks to scary scenes and sound effects, I can forget about what bothers me.

➡ _____

12 I've been using this method for the past several months, and it really works.

➡ _____

준호 (14살, 여수) Junho (14, Yeosu)

13 My uncle graduated from college two years ago.

➡ _____

14 He lives with my family, and he's been looking for a job for some time.

➡ _____

15 I know that he's stressed out, but he always tries to be positive by going fishing.

➡ _____

16 He never gets upset when he doesn't catch any fish.

➡ _____

17 He says, "While I fish, I'm so focused that I can leave all my worries behind.

➡ _____

18 Besides, it teaches me to be patient."

➡ _____

19 I'm sure that focusing on one thing helps us forget about something else.

➡ _____

도빈 (16살, 서울) Dobin (16, Seoul)

20 My sister, a second-year student in high school, has a wonderful way to stay free from stress.

➡ _____

21 She feels a lot of stress from schoolwork, but my mother seems to like the situation for a good reason.

➡ _____

22 It is because cleaning is my sister's number-one way to make life better!

➡ _____

23 When she's so stressed that her life looks gloomy, she cleans her room.

➡ _____

24 She says, "As I clean my room, I feel like I'm also relieving stress.

➡ _____

25 When my room looks tidy, my life looks brighter."

➡ _____

Yulia (14살, 안산) Yulia (14, Ansan)

26 Let me tell you what my mother does about her stress.

➡ _____

27 She feels stressed by all the things she has to do at work and at home.

➡ _____

28 When she's under stress, she writes "Me Time" on her calendar.

➡ _____

29 This means she takes some time out for herself.

➡ _____

30 She reads a book, watches a movie, or talks with her friends.

➡ _____

31 She says, "It doesn't really matter what I do, as long as it's something I like.

➡ _____

32 I've been writing 'Me Time' on my calendar for two months, and I feel much better."

➡ _____

33 Which methods will work for you?

➡ _____

34 Try some of these ideas yourself, and find your best way to say goodbye to stress.

➡ _____

※ 다음 괄호 안의 단어들을 우리말에 맞도록 바르게 배열하시오.

1 (to / Say / Stress / Goodbye)
➡ _____

2 (people / some / time / spend / friends / with / they / when / low. / feel)
➡ _____

3 (eat / others / foods / special / feel / better. / to)
➡ _____

4 (others / still / sleep / simply / for / while. / a)
➡ _____

5 (do / how / you / with / stress? / deal)
➡ _____

6 (are / here / stories / some / people / about / suggest / who / ways. / different)
➡ _____

Mina (15, Daejeon)

7 (my / sometimes / friends / me / give / stress / saying / by / things / bad / me, / about / promises, / breaking / or / over / arguing / things. / small)
➡ _____

8 (this / when / happens, / watch / I / movies! / horror)
➡ _____

9 (horror / good / are / movies / scary / so / I / that / a / scream / lot.)
➡ _____

10 (guess / I / screaming / that / the / at / of / top / lungs / my / me / helps / better. / feel)
➡ _____

11 (thanks / also, / scary / to / scenes / and / effects, / sound / can / I / forget / what / about / me / bothers)
➡ _____

12 (been / I've / this / using / method / the / for / several / past / months, / and / really / it / works.)
➡ _____

Junho (14, Yeosu)

13 (uncle / my / from / graduated / college / ago. / years / two)
➡ _____

14 (lives / he / my / with / family, / he's / and / looking / been / for / job / a / for / time. / some)
➡ _____

15 (know / I / that / stressed / he's / out, / but / always / he / to / tries / be / positive / going / by / fishing.)
➡ _____

16 (never / he / upset / gets / he / when / catch / doesn't / fish. / any)
➡ _____

17 (says, / he / I / "while / fish, / so / I'm / that / focused / can / I / leave / all / worries / my / behind.)
➡ _____

18 (it / besides, / teaches / to / me / patient." / be)
➡ _____

---

1 스트레스와 이별하라

2 어떤 사람들은 울적할 때 친구들과 시간을 보낸다.

3 다른 사람들은 기분이 좋아지도록 특별한 음식을 먹는다.

4 또 다른 사람들은 그저 잠시 잠을 자기도 한다.

5 여러분은 스트레스를 어떻게 다루는가?

6 여기 다양한 방법을 제안하는 사람들의 이야기가 있다.

미나 (15살, 대전)

7 때때로 내 친구들은 나에 관해 나쁜 말을 하거나, 약속을 어기거나, 혹은 사소한 일을 두고 언쟁을 하며 내게 스트레스를 준다.

8 이럴 때, 나는 공포 영화를 본다!

9 훌륭한 공포 영화는 너무 무서워서 나는 소리를 많이 지르게 된다.

10 있는 힘껏 소리 지르는 것은 내 기분이 나아지는 데 도움이 된다고 생각한다.

11 또한, 무서운 장면과 음향 효과 덕분에 나를 괴롭히는 것들을 잊을 수 있다.

12 나는 지난 몇 달간 이 방법을 써 오고 있는데, 효과가 아주 좋다.

준호 (14살, 여수)

13 우리 삼촌은 2년 전에 대학을 졸업했다.

14 삼촌은 우리 가족과 함께 살고 있고, 얼마 전부터 직장을 구하고 있다.

15 나는 삼촌이 스트레스를 받고 있지만 낚시를 다니며 긍정적으로 지내려고 항상 노력한다는 것을 안다.

16 물고기를 한 마리도 잡지 못했을 때에도 삼촌은 절대 속상해 하지 않는다.

17 삼촌은 "낚시하는 동안, 나는 아주 몰입해서 모든 걱정을 잊을 수 있어.

18 게다가 낚시는 나에게 인내를 가르쳐 준단다."라고 말한다

19 (sure / I'm / focusing / that / one / on / helps / thing / forget / us / something / about / else.)

➡ _____

Dobin (16, Seoul)

20 (sister, / my / second-year / a / in / student / school, / high / a / has / wonderful / to / way / free / stay / stress. / from)

➡ _____

21 (feels / she / lot / a / of / from / stress / schoolwork, / my / but / mother / to / seems / like / to / the / situation / for / good / a / reason.)

➡ _____

22 (is / it / cleaning / because / my / is / sister's / way / number-one / make / to / better! / life)

➡ _____

23 (she's / when / stressed / so / that / life / her / gloomy, / looks / cleans / she / room. / her)

➡ _____

24 (says, / she / "as / clean / I / room, / my / feel / I / like / I'm / releiving / stress. / also)

➡ _____

25 (my / when / room / tidy, / looks / life / my / brighter." / looks)

➡ _____

Yulia (14, Ansan)

26 (me / let / you / tell / what / mother / my / about / does / stress. / her)

➡ _____

27 (feels / she / by / stressed / all / things / the / has / she / to / at / do / work / and / home. / at)

➡ _____

28 (she's / when / stress, / under / writes / she / Time" / "Me / her / on / calender.)

➡ _____

29 (means / this / takes / she / time / some / for / out / herself.)

➡ _____

30 (reads / she / book, / a / watches / movie, / a / talks / or / her / with / friends.)

➡ _____

31 (says / she / "it / really / doesn't / what / matter / do, / I / long / as / it's / as / something / like. / I)

➡ _____

32 (been / I've / writing / Time' / 'Me / my / on / calender / two / for / months, / I / and / much / feel / better.")

➡ _____

33 (methods / which / work / will / you? / for)

➡ _____

34 (some / try / these / of / yourself, / ideas / and / your / find / way / best / say / to / goodbye / stress. / to)

➡ _____

19 한 가지 일에 집중하는 것이 다른 무언가를 잊는 데 도움이 된다고 나는 확신한다.

도빈 (16살, 서울)

20 고등학교 2학년인 우리 누나에게는 스트레스에서 벗어나는 훌륭한 방법이 있다.

21 누나가 학업 때문에 많은 스트레스를 받지만, 그럴 만한 이유로 우리 어머니는 그 상황을 좋아하시는 것 같다.

22 그것은 바로, 청소가 누나의 삶을 향상하는 최고의 방법이기 때문이다.

23 스트레스를 너무 많이 받아서 인생이 우울해 보일 때, 누나는 방을 청소한다.

24 누나는 "방을 청소하면서 스트레스도 해소되는 것 같아.

25 내 방이 깔끔해 보이면 내 삶도 더 밝아 보여."라고 말한다.

Yulia (14살, 안산)

26 우리 어머니께서 스트레스를 어떻게 다루시는지 소개하려고 한다.

27 어머니는 직장과 집에서 해야하는 온갖 일로 인해 스트레스를 받으신다.

28 스트레스를 받을 때면 어머니는 달력에 '나만의 시간'이라고 적으신다.

29 이것은 어머니 자신을 위해 잠깐 시간을 낸다는 의미이다.

30 어머니는 책을 읽거나, 영화를 보거나, 친구들과 이야기를 나누신다.

31 어머니는 "내가 좋아하는 것이라면, 무엇을 하는지는 별로 중요하지 않아.

32 나는 두 달째 달력에 '나만의 시간'을 적어 왔고, 기분이 훨씬 좋아졌어."라고 말씀하신다.

33 어떤 방법이 여러분에게 효과가 있을까?

34 이 아이디어 중 몇 개를 직접 해보고, 스트레스와 이별하는 자신만의 최고의 방법을 찾아라.

※ 다음 우리말을 영어로 쓰시오.

1 스트레스와 이별하라

➡ _____

2 어떤 사람들은 울적할 때 친구들과 시간을 보낸다.

➡ _____

3 다른 사람들은 기분이 좋아지도록 특별한 음식을 먹는다.

➡ _____

4 또 다른 사람들은 그저 잠시 잠을 자기도 한다.

➡ _____

5 여러분은 스트레스를 어떻게 다루는가?

➡ _____

6 여기 다양한 방법을 제안하는 사람들의 이야기가 있다.

➡ _____

미나 (15살, 대전) Mina (15, Daejeon)

7 때때로 내 친구들은 나에 관해 나쁜 말을 하거나, 약속을 어기거나, 혹은 사소한 일을 두고 언쟁을 하며 내게 스트레스를 준다.

➡ _____

_____

8 이럴 때, 나는 공포 영화를 본다!

➡ _____

9 훌륭한 공포 영화는 너무 무서워서 나는 소리를 많이 지르게 된다.

➡ _____

10 있는 힘껏 소리 지르는 것은 내 기분이 나아지는 데 도움이 된다고 생각한다.

➡ _____

11 또한, 무서운 장면과 음향 효과 덕분에 나를 괴롭히는 것들을 잊을 수 있다.

➡ _____

12 나는 지난 몇 달간 이 방법을 써 오고 있는데, 효과가 아주 좋다.

➡ _____

준호 (14살, 여수) Junho (14, Yeosu)

13 우리 삼촌은 2년 전에 대학을 졸업했다.

➡ _____

14 삼촌은 우리 가족과 함께 살고 있고, 얼마 전부터 직장을 구하고 있다.

➡ _____

15 나는 삼촌이 스트레스를 받고 있지만 낚시를 다니며 긍정적으로 지내려고 항상 노력한다는 것을 안다.

➡ _____

16 물고기를 한 마리도 잡지 못했을 때에도 삼촌은 절대 속상해 하지 않는다.

➡ _____

17 삼촌은 "낚시하는 동안, 나는 아주 몰입해서 모든 걱정을 잊을 수 있어.

➡ _____

18 게다가 낚시는 나에게 인내를 가르쳐 준단다."라고 말한다.

➡ _____

19 한 가지 일에 집중하는 것이 다른 무언가를 잊는 데 도움이 된다고 나는 확신한다.

➡ _____

도빈 (16살, 서울) Dobin (16, Seoul)

20 고등학교 2학년인 우리 누나에게는 스트레스에서 벗어나는 훌륭한 방법이 있다.

➡ _____

21 누나가 학업 때문에 많은 스트레스를 받지만, 그럴 만한 이유로 우리 어머니는 그 상황을 좋아하시는 것 같다.

➡ _____

22 그것은 바로, 청소가 누나의 삶을 향상하는 최고의 방법이기 때문이다.

➡ _____

23 스트레스를 너무 많이 받아서 인생이 우울해 보일 때, 누나는 방을 청소한다.

➡ _____

24 누나는 "방을 청소하면서 스트레스도 해소되는 것 같아.

➡ _____

25 내 방이 깔끔해 보이면 내 삶도 더 밝아 보여."라고 말한다.

➡ _____

Yulia (14살, 안산) Yulia (14, Ansan)

26 우리 어머니께서 스트레스를 어떻게 다루시는지 소개하려고 한다.

➡ _____

27 어머니는 직장과 집에서 해야 하는 온갖 일로 인해 스트레스를 받으신다.

➡ _____

28 스트레스를 받을 때면 어머니는 달력에 '나만의 시간'이라고 적으신다.

➡ _____

29 이것은 어머니 자신을 위해 잠깐 시간을 낸다는 의미이다.

➡ _____

30 어머니는 책을 읽거나, 영화를 보거나, 친구들과 이야기를 나누신다.

➡ _____

31 어머니는 "내가 좋아하는 것이라면, 무엇을 하는지는 별로 중요하지 않아.

➡ _____

32 나는 두 달째 달력에 '나만의 시간'을 적어 왔고, 기분이 훨씬 좋아졌어."라고 말씀하신다.

➡ _____

33 어떤 방법이 여러분에게 효과가 있을까?

➡ _____

34 이 아이디어 중 몇 개를 직접 해 보고, 스트레스와 이별하는 자신만의 최고의 방법을 찾아라.

➡ _____

※ 다음 우리말과 일치하도록 빈칸에 알맞은 말을 쓰시오.

Words in Action

1. Tests _____ me _____. Grades give _____ _____
   _____.

2. _____ _____, smile more. Worry _____ _____.

3. I work hard. I have _____ _____ _____ _____
   _____.

4. I need a _____. I will _____ _____ _____.

5. I _____ just _____ _____ fish. I want _____ _____
   some more.

1. 시험은 나를 지치게 해. 성적은 나에게 더 많은 스트레스를 준다.
2. 걱정은 줄이고 더 많이 웃어라. 걱정은 전혀 도움이 되지 않아.
3. 나는 열심히 일한다. 나는 할 일이 많다.
4. 나는 기분 전환이 필요하다. 나는 헤어스타일을 바꿀 것이다.
5. 나는 겨우 물고기 몇 마리를 잡았다. 나는 몇 마리 더 낚고 싶다.

Speak – Get ready.

1. I want to _____ more/_____ _____ on social media.

2. _____ _____ a team _____ _____ difficult/_____.

3. I like _____/playing sports _____.

4. _____ a _____ _____ as a teen can be good/_____.

1. 나는 소셜미디어에 더 많은/적은 시간을 보내기를 원한다.
2. 팀을 이루어 일하는 것은 어려울 수 있다/도움이 될 수 있다.
3. 나는 스포츠 보는 것을/하는 것을 더 좋아한다.
4. 십대일 때 아르바이트를 하는 것은 좋다/나쁘다.

Wrap Up - Reading

1. Are you _____ or _____ _____?

2. Then here is _____ _____ _____ for you.

3. _____ _____ simple _____ can _____ you!

4. First, go _____ and get _____ _____ sunlight.

5. _____ _____ scientists, this helps _____ a special chemical
   _____ _____ _____, and the chemical _____ _____
   _____ happy!

6. _____ _____ _____ _____ _____ _____ is exercise.

7. This helps _____ _____ of the "_____ _____."

8. _____ these _____ _____ the next time you
   _____.

9. _____ _____ _____ in _____ of a screen, go outdoors
   and _____ _____ in the sun!

1. 스트레스를 받았거나 기분이 우울한가?
2. 그렇다면 여기 당신에게 좋은 소식이 있다.
3. 간단한 몇 가지 절차가 도움이 될 것이다!
4. 첫째, 밖에 나가서 충분한 양의 햇볕을 쬐라.
5. 과학자들에 따르면 이것이 뇌 속에 특별한 화학물질을 만드는 데 도움을 주고, 이 화학물질은 당신을 행복하게 만든다고 한다!
6. 당신이 할 수 있는 또 다른 일은 운동이다.
7. 이것은 훨씬 더 많은 '행복 화학물질'을 만드는 데 도움을 준다.
8. 다음에 당신이 우울하다면 이 간단한 조언을 시도해 보라.
9. 화면 앞에 앉아 있는 대신, 밖에 나가 태양 아래에서 뛰어 다녀라!

※ 다음 우리말을 영어로 쓰시오.

Words in Action

1. 시험은 나를 지치게 해. 성적은 나에게 더 많은 스트레스를 준다.
   ➡ _____

2. 걱정은 줄이고 더 많이 웃어라. 걱정은 전혀 도움이 되지 않아.
   ➡ _____

3. 나는 열심히 일한다. 나는 할 일이 많다.
   ➡ _____

4. 나는 기분 전환이 필요하다. 나는 헤어스타일을 바꿀 것이다.
   ➡ _____

5. 나는 겨우 물고기 몇 마리를 잡았다. 나는 몇 마리 더 낚고 싶다.
   ➡ _____

Speak – Get ready.

1. 나는 소셜미디어에 더 많은/적은 시간을 보내기를 원한다.
   ➡ _____

2. 팀을 이루어 일하는 것은 어려울 수 있다/도움이 될 수 있다.
   ➡ _____

3. 나는 스포츠 보는 것을/하는 것을 더 좋아한다.
   ➡ _____

4. 십대일 때 아르바이트를 하는 것은 좋다/나쁘다.
   ➡ _____

Wrap Up - Reading

1. 스트레스를 받았거나 기분이 우울한가?
   ➡ _____

2. 그렇다면, 여기 당신에게 좋은 소식이 있다.
   ➡ _____

3. 간단한 몇 가지 절차가 도움이 될 것이다!
   ➡ _____

4. 첫째, 밖에 나가서 충분한 양의 햇볕을 쬐라.
   ➡ _____

5. 과학자들에 따르면 이것이 뇌 속에 특별한 화학물질을 만드는 데 도움을 주고, 이 화학물질은 당신을 행복하게 만든다고 한다.
   ➡ _____

6. 당신이 할 수 있는 또 다른 일은 운동이다.
   ➡ _____

7. 이것은 훨씬 더 많은 "행복 화학물질"을 만드는 데 도움을 준다.
   ➡ _____

8. 다음에 당신이 우울하다면 이 간단한 조언을 시도해 보라.
   ➡ _____

9. 화면 앞에 앉아 있는 대신, 밖에 나가 태양 아래에서 뛰어 다녀라!
   ➡ _____

※ 다음 영어를 우리말로 쓰시오.

01 alive	_____	
02 popular	_____	
03 relax	_____	
04 directly	_____	
05 present	_____	
06 effective	_____	
07 gardening	_____	
08 whether	_____	
09 producer	_____	
10 electric-powered	_____	
11 wholesale	_____	
12 imaginable	_____	
13 digest	_____	
14 recipe	_____	
15 architect	_____	
16 translate	_____	
17 bill	_____	
18 insect	_____	
19 last	_____	
20 ship	_____	
21 attract	_____	

22 transportation	_____	
23 local	_____	
24 environment	_____	
25 mostly	_____	
26 suggest	_____	
27 discover	_____	
28 notice	_____	
29 float	_____	
30 therefore	_____	
31 disappear	_____	
32 trade	_____	
33 way	_____	
34 work	_____	
35 chat with	_____	
36 take a nap	_____	
37 be crowded with	_____	
38 have ~ in common	_____	
39 be good for	_____	
40 make an appointment	_____	
41 be rich in	_____	
42 best-before date	_____	
43 make sure to	_____	

Step2

※ 다음 우리말을 영어로 쓰시오.

01 번역하다 _____

02 상상할 수 있는 _____

03 지속하다, 오래가다 _____

04 살아 있는 _____

05 뜨다 _____

06 건축가 _____

07 ~인지 아닌지 _____

08 곤충 _____

09 끌어들이다, 끌어당기다 _____

10 운반하다 _____

11 운송, 교통 _____

12 계산서 _____

13 사라지다 _____

14 도매의 _____

15 지붕이 덮인 _____

16 작동하다, 효과가 있다 _____

17 제안하다 _____

18 발견하다, 알아내다 _____

19 그러므로, 따라서 _____

20 효과적인, 실질적인 _____

21 환경 _____

22 현지의, 지역의 _____

23 천연의, 자연스러운 _____

24 주로, 대부분 _____

25 경험 _____

26 무역 _____

27 원예 _____

28 주목하다 _____

29 운송하다, 실어 나르다 _____

30 곧장, 바로, 직접적으로 _____

31 조리법 _____

32 쉬다 _____

33 소화하다 _____

34 선물 _____

35 낮잠을 자다 _____

36 ~이 풍부하다 _____

37 ~와 잡담하다 _____

38 ~로 붐비다, 꽉 차다 _____

39 약속하다 _____

40 ~에 유익하다 _____

41 반드시 ~하다 _____

42 ~한 공통점아 있다 _____

43 유효 기한, 유통 기한 _____

※ 다음 영영풀이에 알맞은 단어를 <보기>에서 골라 쓴 후, 우리말 뜻을 쓰시오.

1 _____ : to find out: _____

2 _____ : to see no longer: _____

3 _____ : a person who designs buildings: _____

4 _____ : a set of instructions for making food: _____

5 _____ : possible to think of in your mind: _____

6 _____ : a person who is traveling for pleasure: _____

7 _____ : without stopping; with nothing in between: _____

8 _____ : cultural beliefs and customs passed down through generations: _____

9 _____ : the activity or process of buying, selling, or exchanging goods or services: _____

10 _____ : the action of selling things in large amounts and at low prices: _____

11 _____ : to send people or things somewhere by ship, truck, and so on: _____

12 _____ : the market which buys and sells things directly on a boat: _____

13 _____ : a small animal that has six legs and a body formed of three parts and that may have wings: _____

14 _____ : something that you give to someone especially as a way of showing affection or thanks: _____

15 _____ : to make someone interested in something and cause them to come to it: _____

16 _____ : a system for carrying people or goods from one place to another using vehicles, roads, etc.: _____

보기			
attract	wholesale	directly	tradition
trade	ship	disappear	architect
present	transportation	tourist	imaginable
floating market	insect	discover	recipe

※ 다음 우리말과 일치하도록 빈칸에 알맞은 말을 쓰시오.

Listen – Listen & Answer Dialog 1

M: _____ _____ the Tourist Information Office! _____ may I _____ you?

W: Hi, I _____ _____ there's a _____ _____ of the town.

M: Sure. _____ a special place you're _____ _____?

W: Yes. I'd _____ _____ _____ some _____ food.

M: Then go to Jeongseon Market. It _____ every _____ _____, and it's _____ today.

W: I'm so _____. _____ _____ _____ _____ _____?

M: You _____ _____ there. It _____ _____ 10 _____.

W: Great. Will you _____ the _____ on the map, please?

M: Sure. _____ gondrebap _____ you _____ there.

Listen – Listen & Answer Dialog 2

W: Can I _____ the _____, please?

M: _____ you are. Did you enjoy the _____?

W: It was great. I liked the gondrebap very much.

M: Thanks. It's also _____ _____ _____ _____.

W: Oh, really?

M: Yes. Gondre _____ _____ _____ vitamins A and C. It also _____ well.

W: Good. I _____ _____ I could buy some gondre here.

M: Sure. Do you _____ _____ _____ _____ you the _____ _____ gondrebap?

W: Yes, that'd _____ _____.

Listen More – Listen and complete

W: _____ me. Can you _____ _____ _____ this _____?

B: Sure. What is it?

W: _____ _____ the _____, please.

B: Oh, do you _____ _____ _____ _____ you _____ _____ _____?

W: Yes, I _____ my _____.

B: _____ me _____. You should drink it _____ June 7.

남: 관광 안내소에 오신 것을 환영합니다! 무엇을 도와드릴까요?
여: 안녕하세요, 저는 마을 관광 지도가 있는지 궁금합니다.
남: 물론이죠. 특별히 찾으시는 곳이 있나요?
여: 네. 이 지역 음식을 먹어 보고 싶어요.
남: 그렇다면 정선 시장에 가 보세요. 시장이 5일마다 열리는데, 오늘 열렸네요.
여: 제가 정말 운이 좋군요. 그곳에 어떻게 가나요?
남: 거기까지 걸어갈 수 있어요. 10분 정도 걸려요.
여: 잘됐군요. 지도에 길을 표시해 주시겠어요?
남: 물론이죠. 거기에 가면 곤드레밥을 드셔 보세요.

여: 계산서 좀 주시겠어요?
남: 여기 있습니다. 식사는 맛있게 하셨나요?
여: 아주 훌륭했어요. 저는 곤드레밥이 정말 좋았어요.
남: 고맙습니다. 그것은 건강에도 좋답니다.
여: 오, 정말이요?
남: 네. 곤드레는 비타민 A와 C가 풍부합니다. 그리고 소화도 잘돼요.
여: 그렇군요. 여기서 곤드레를 좀 살 수 있을까요?
남: 물론이죠. 제가 곤드레밥 조리법을 드릴까요?
여: 네, 그러면 정말 좋겠어요.

여: 미안하지만, 이 우유 (사는 것) 좀 도와주겠니?
남: 그럼요. 뭔데요?
여: 날짜를 좀 읽어 주렴.
남: 아, 유통 기한을 말씀드리길 원하세요?
여: 그래, 내가 안경을 두고 왔단다.
남: 잠깐만요. 6월 7일까지 드셔야 해요.

W: That's too soon. _____ _____ _____ there's one that
_____ _____.

B: Wait. I _____ one. This _____ is good _____ _____
_____.

W: Oh, I'll take that _____. Thank you very much.

B: You're _____.

여: 그건 너무 짧네. 기한이 더 긴 게 있는지 궁금하구나.
남: 잠깐만요. 하나 찾았어요. 이것은 6월 11일까지 드실 수 있어요.
여: 오, 그걸로 사야겠다. 정말 고맙구나.
남: 천만에요.

Speak – Talk in pairs. 1

A: _____ me. I _____ if there's a bank _____ _____.

B: I'm sorry, _____ we _____ _____ _____ _____ here.

A: That's _____ _____. Thanks.

A: 실례합니다. 이 근처에 은행이 있는지 궁금합니다.
B: 미안하지만 이 근처에는 없어요.
A: 괜찮아요. 고맙습니다.

Speak – Talk in pairs. 2

A: What's _____, Grandpa?

B: I'm _____.

A: Do you _____ _____ _____ play baduk _____ you?

B: That'd _____ _____. Thank you.

A: 무슨 일이세요, 할아버지?
B: 지루하구나.
A: 제가 함께 바둑을 두길 원하세요?
B: 그러면 좋겠구나. 고맙구나.

Wrap Up 1

G: I _____ _____.

B: I'll make ramyeon for you.

G: _____ nice!

B: Do you _____ me _____ _____ an egg?

G: That'd be great.

여: 나 배고파.
남: 내가 널 위해 라면을 끓여 줄게.
여: 좋아!
남: 달걀을 넣길 원하니?
여: 그러면 정말 좋겠어.

Wrap Up 2

G: Dad, _____ _____ that cute bag. _____ _____ _____
_____ _____ _____.

M: _____ _____ we _____ _____ and _____?

G: Really? Thanks, Dad.

M: I _____ _____ I will _____ _____ _____ _____.
We're just _____ the _____.

G: Of _____.

여: 아빠, 저 귀여운 가방을 보세요. 얼마인지 궁금해요.
남: 들어가서 확인해 보는 게 어떻겠니?
여: 정말요? 고마워요, 아빠.
남: 사 주겠다고는 말하지 않았단다. 그냥 가격만 물어보는 거야.
여: 물론이죠.

※ 다음 우리말에 맞도록 대화를 영어로 쓰시오.

Listen – Listen & Answer Dialog 1

M: _____

W: _____

M: _____

W: _____

M: _____

W: _____

M: _____

W: _____

M: _____

남: 관광 안내소에 오신 것을 환영합니다! 무엇을 도와드릴까요?

여: 안녕하세요, 저는 마을 관광 지도가 있는지 궁금합니다.

남: 물론이죠. 특별히 찾으시는 곳이 있나요?

여: 네. 이 지역 음식을 먹어 보고 싶어요.

남: 그렇다면 정선 시장에 가 보세요. 시장이 5일마다 열리는데, 오늘 열렸네요.

여: 제가 정말 운이 좋군요. 그곳에 어떻게 가나요?

남: 거기까지 걸어갈 수 있어요. 10분 정도 걸려요.

여: 잘됐군요. 지도에 길을 표시해 주시겠어요?

남: 물론이죠. 거기에 가면 곤드레밥을 드셔 보세요.

Listen – Listen & Answer Dialog 2

W: _____

M: _____

W: _____

M: _____

W: _____

M: _____

W: _____

M: _____

W: _____

여: 계산서 좀 주시겠어요?

남: 여기 있습니다. 식사는 맛있게 하셨나요?

여: 아주 훌륭했어요. 저는 곤드레밥이 정말 좋았어요.

남: 고맙습니다. 그것은 건강에도 좋답니다.

여: 오, 정말이요?

남: 네. 곤드레는 비타민 A와 C가 풍부합니다. 그리고 소화도 잘돼요.

여: 그렇군요. 여기서 곤드레를 좀 살 수 있을까요?

남: 물론이죠. 제가 곤드레밥 조리법을 드릴까요?

여: 네, 그러면 정말 좋겠어요.

Listen More – Listen and complete

W: _____

B: _____

W: _____

B: _____

W: _____

B: _____

여: 미안하지만, 이 우유 (사는 것) 좀 도와주겠니?

남: 그럼요. 뭔데요?

여: 날짜를 좀 읽어 주렴.

남: 아, 유통 기한을 말씀드리길 원하세요?

여: 그래, 내가 안경을 두고 왔단다.

남: 잠깐만요. 6월 7일까지 드셔야 해요.

W: _____

B: _____

W: _____

B: _____

여: 그건 너무 짧네. 기한이 더 긴 게 있는지 궁금하구나.
남: 잠깐만요. 하나 찾았어요. 이것은 6월 11일까지 드실 수 있어요.
여: 오, 그걸로 사야겠다. 정말 고맙구나.
남: 천만에요.

Speak – Talk in pairs. 1

A: _____

B: _____

A: _____

A: 실례합니다. 이 근처에 은행이 있는지 궁금합니다.
B: 미안하지만 이 근처에는 없어요.
A: 괜찮아요. 고맙습니다.

Speak – Talk in pairs. 2

A: _____

B: _____

A: _____

B: _____

A: 무슨 일이세요, 할아버지?
B: 지루하구나.
A: 제가 함께 바둑을 두길 원하세요?
B: 그러면 좋겠구나. 고맙구나.

Wrap Up 1

G: _____

B: _____

G: _____

B: _____

G: _____

여: 나 배고파.
남: 내가 널 위해 라면을 끓여 줄게.
여: 좋아!
남: 달걀을 넣길 원하니?
여: 그러면 정말 좋겠어.

Wrap Up 2

G: _____

M: _____

G: _____

M: _____

G: _____

여: 아빠, 저 귀여운 가방을 보세요. 얼마인지 궁금해요.
남: 들어가서 확인해 보는 게 어떻겠니?
여: 정말요? 고마워요, 아빠.
남: 사 주겠다고는 말하지 않았단다. 그냥 가격만 물어보는 거야.
여: 물론이죠.

※ 다음 우리말과 일치하도록 빈칸에 알맞은 것을 골라 쓰시오.

1 **Leah's** _____ _____
   A. Travel   B. Story

2 _____ _____ Leah.
   A. am   B. I

3 I _____ _____ _____ a travel blog _____ I was 18.
   A. since   B. writing   C. been   D. have

4 I go _____ and _____ my _____ _____ my readers.
   A. with   B. places   C. experiences   D. share

5 _____ **Markets** _____ **the World**
   A. Around   B. Must-Visit

6 _____ _____, 20**
   A. 15   B. July

7 _____ markets is a good _____ to learn about the _____ of a _____.
   A. culture   B. visiting   C. country   D. way

8 Markets are _____ _____ you can meet people, learn history, and _____ _____ food.
   A. where   B. taste   C. places   D. local

9 I _____ _____ there is any better _____ to discover _____ culture.
   A. whether   B. another   C. wonder   D. way

10 **1** _____ Bazaar, _____
   A. Turkey   B. Grand

11 Turkey is a country _____ East meets West, so it has a _____ _____ of _____.
   A. trade   B. where   C. tradition   D. long

12 It is a _____ _____ for large _____ _____ the Grand Bazaar.
   A. like   B. natural   C. markets   D. place

13 The market _____ _____ in 1455 _____ Istanbul.
   A. built   B. was   C. in

14 _____ then, the market had two big buildings, and people _____ _____ like _____ and gold there.
   A. traded   B. back   C. cloth   D. goods

1 Leah의 여행 이야기

2 저는 Leah입니다.

3 18세 때부터 여행 블로그를 써 왔습니다.

4 저는 여기저기 다니며 제 경험을 독자들과 공유하고 있습니다.

5 꼭 방문해야 할 세계의 시장들

6 20**년 7월 15일

7 시장 방문은 한 나라의 문화에 대해 배우는 좋은 방법입니다.

8 시장은 사람들을 만나고, 역사를 배우고, 또 지역 음식을 맛볼 수 있는 장소입니다.

9 다른 문화를 발견하는 데에 더 좋은 방법이 있을지 모르겠습니다.

10 1 터키의 Grand Bazaar(그랜드 바자)

11 터키는 동양과 서양이 만나는 나라이고, 그래서 오랜 교역의 전통을 가지고 있습니다.

12 터키는 Grand Bazaar 같은 대형 시장이 생겨나기에 자연스러운 곳입니다.

13 Grand Bazaar는 1455년 이스탄불에 지어졌습니다.

14 그 당시에 이 시장에는 큰 건물이 두 개 있었고, 거기서 사람들은 직물이나 금 같은 물건을 교환했습니다.

15 Today the Grand Bazaar is _____ bigger, and it is the _____ _____ _____ in the world.

A. covered   B. much   C. largest   D. market

16 It has 64 _____ and more than 4,000 _____ _____ one _____.

A. roof   B. streets   C. under   D. shops

17 The market _____ _____ 250,000 visitors _____ day.

A. every   B. over   C. attracts

18 You can buy _____ any _____ _____ there.

A. imaginable   B. almost   C. item

19 **Extra Tip** Ask shop _____ if they _____ *nazar boncuğu*, a _____ Turkish symbol for good _____.

A. traditional   B. owners   C. carry   D. luck

20 Also, if you want a nice snack, _____ _____ to _____ *lokum*, a _____ Turkish candy.

A. sure   B. try   C. traditional   D. make

21 **2 Damnoen Saduak** _____ _____, _____

A. Market   B. Floating   C. Thailand

22 In the _____, Thai people _____ goods _____ rivers.

A. on   B. past   C. traded

23 This was the _____ of _____ _____ in Thailand.

A. floating   B. beginning   C. markets

24 _____ better road _____, many _____ markets _____.

A. disappeared   B. transportation   C. floating   D. with

25 _____ the late 1960s, _____, some of them have come _____ and kept the tradition _____.

A. alive   B. however   C. back   D. since

26 Today, _____ of the _____ _____ floating _____ is Damnoen Saduak Floating Market.

A. popular   B. most   C. one   D. markets

27 It is always _____ _____ tourists _____ all _____ the world.

A. from   B. crowded   C. over   D. with

28 You can buy _____ foods and _____ gift _____ directly from _____.

A. items   B. local   C. boats   D. traditional

---

15 오늘날 Grand Bazaar는 훨씬 크고, 세계에서 가장 큰 지붕이 덮인 시장입니다.

16 64개의 거리와 4,000개 이상의 상점이 한 지붕 아래에 있습니다.

17 그 시장은 매일 25만 명 이상의 방문객을 불러 모읍니다.

18 그곳에서는 상상할 수 있는 거의 모든 물건을 살 수 있습니다.

19 추가 정보 가게 주인에게 행운을 기원하는 터키 전통 상징인 'nazar boncuğu(나자르 본주)'를 파는지 물어보세요.

20 또한, 만약 맛있는 간식을 원한다면, 터키 전통 사탕인 'lokum(로쿰)'을 꼭 드셔 보세요.

21 2 태국의 Damnoen Saduak(담는 사두악) 수상 시장

22 과거에 태국 사람들은 강에서 물건을 교환했습니다.

23 이것이 태국 수상 시장의 시작이었습니다.

24 도로 교통이 개선되면서, 많은 수상 시장이 사라졌습니다.

25 그러나 1960년대 후반부터 일부가 다시 생겨나 전통을 이어가고 있습니다.

26 오늘날, 가장 인기 있는 수상 시장 중 하나는 Damnoen Saduak 수상 시장입니다.

27 그곳은 전 세계에서 온 관광객들로 항상 붐빕니다.

28 배에서 직접 현지 음식과 전통 선물을 살 수 있습니다.

29 **Extra Tip** I _____ if you have ever _____ a _____ on water.

    A. meal   B. wonder   C. had

30 _____ not, _____ noodles _____ *pad thai*.

    A. try   B. like   C. if

31 The sellers will _____ them on their boats and _____ them to you _____ a long fishing _____ .

    A. with   B. cook   C. pole   D. pass

32 **3 Aalsmeer** _____ _____ , The _____

    A. Netherlands   B. Market   C. Flower

33 The Netherlands _____ " _____ _____ ."

    A. lands   B. means   C. low

34 _____ the name _____ , about 70% of the country sits _____ sea _____ .

    A. suggests   B. level   C. as   D. below

35 Thus, the Dutch _____ _____ the land, and one _____ way to use it was to _____ flowers and sell them.

    A. effective   B. built   C. grow   D. up

36 It is, _____ , no _____ _____ the country has the _____ flower market in the world: the Aalsmeer Flower Market.

    A. surprise   B. largest   C. therefore   D. that

37 The building _____ the market is _____ is _____ _____ 120 soccer fields.

    A. housed   B. than   C. bigger   D. where

38 The market is _____ _____ thousands of _____ carts.

    A. with   B. flower-filled   C. busy

39 They are _____ _____ _____ electric-powered trucks.

    A. mostly   B. moved   C. by

40 Every day, _____ 20 million flowers are _____ and _____ to all _____ of the world.

    A. corners   B. traded   C. around   D. shipped

41 **Extra Tip** You may _____ _____ you can _____ just a _____ flowers at the market.

    A. few   B. wonder   C. buy   D. whether

42 Sadly, you cannot, but you can see _____ _____ flower _____ .

    A. wholesale   B. works   C. how   D. trading

---

29 추가 정보 여러분이 물 위에서 식사해 본 적이 있는지 궁금하네요.

30 만약 그렇지 않다면, 'pad thai(팟 타이)' 같은 면 요리를 드셔 보세요.

31 상인들이 배에서 음식을 만들어 긴 낚싯대로 건네줄 겁니다.

32 3 네덜란드 Aalsmeer(알스메이르) 꽃 시장

33 네덜란드는 '저지대'라는 뜻입니다.

34 이름에서 알 수 있듯이, 이 나라의 약 70%가 해수면보다 낮습니다.

35 그래서 네덜란드 사람들은 땅을 지어 올렸고, 그것을 사용하는 효과적인 방법은 꽃을 재배하고 파는 것이었습니다.

36 그러므로 네덜란드에 세계에서 가장 큰 꽃 시장인 Aalsmeer 꽃 시장이 있다는 것은 놀라운 일이 아닙니다.

37 시장이 들어선 건물은 축구장 120개보다 큽니다.

38 시장은 꽃이 가득 든 수천 개의 수레로 분주합니다.

39 수레는 대부분 전동 트럭에 의해 움직입니다.

40 매일, 약 2천만 송이의 꽃이 거래되어 세계 각지로 운송됩니다.

41 추가 정보 시장에서 꽃을 조금 살 수 있는지 궁금할 겁니다.

42 애석하게도 안 되지만, 꽃이 도매로 어떻게 거래되는지를 볼 수 있습니다.

※ 다음 우리말과 일치하도록 빈칸에 알맞은 것을 골라 쓰시오.

1 Leah's _____ _____

2 _____ _____ Leah.

3 I _____ _____ _____ a travel blog _____ I was 18.

4 I go places and _____ _____ _____ _____ my readers.

5 _____ Markets _____ the World

6 _____ 15, 20**

7 _____ _____ is a _____ _____ _____ _____ _____ about the culture of a country.

8 Markets are _____ _____ you can meet people, learn history, and _____ _____ _____.

9 I _____ _____ there is any better way _____ _____ _____ _____.

10 1 _____ _____, Turkey

11 Turkey is a country _____ East meets West, _____ it has a _____ _____ _____ _____.

12 It is _____ _____ _____ _____ large markets _____ the Grand Bazaar.

13 The market _____ _____ _____ 1455 in Istanbul.

14 Back then, the market had two big buildings, and people _____ _____ _____ _____ and _____ there.

1	Leah의 여행 이야기
2	저는 Leah입니다.
3	18세 때부터 여행 블로그를 써 왔습니다.
4	저는 여기저기 다니며 제 경험을 독자들과 공유하고 있습니다.
5	꼭 방문해야 할 세계의 시장들
6	20**년 7월 15일
7	시장 방문은 한 나라의 문화에 대해 배우는 좋은 방법입니다.
8	시장은 사람들을 만나고, 역사를 배우고, 또 지역 음식을 맛볼 수 있는 장소입니다.
9	다른 문화를 발견하는 데에 더 좋은 방법이 있을지 모르겠습니다.
10	1 터키의 Grand Bazaar(그랜드 바자)
11	터키는 동양과 서양이 만나는 나라이고, 그래서 오랜 교역의 전통을 가지고 있습니다.
12	터키는 Grand Bazaar 같은 대형 시장이 생겨나기에 자연스러운 곳입니다.
13	Grand Bazaar는 1455년 이스탄불에 지어졌습니다.
14	그 당시에 이 시장에는 큰 건물이 두 개 있었고, 거기서 사람들은 직물이나 금 같은 물건을 교환했습니다.

15 Today the Grand Bazaar is _____ _____ , and it is the _____ _____ _____ in the world.

16 It has 64 streets and _____ _____ 4,000 shops _____ _____ _____ .

17 The market _____ _____ 250,000 visitors every day.

18 You can buy _____ _____ _____ _____ there.

19 **Extra Tip** Ask shop owners _____ they carry *nazar boncuğu*, a _____ _____ _____ for _____ _____ .

20 Also, if you want a nice snack, _____ _____ _____ try *lokum*, a _____ _____ _____ .

21 **2 Damnoen Saduak _____ Market, _____**

22 In the past, Thai people _____ _____ _____ rivers.

23 This was the _____ _____ _____ _____ in Thailand.

24 _____ _____ _____ _____ , many _____ _____ _____ .

25 _____ the late 1960s, however, some of them _____ _____ _____ and _____ the tradition _____ .

26 Today, one of _____ _____ _____ floating _____ _____ Damnoen Saduak Floating Market.

27 It is always _____ _____ _____ from all over the world.

28 You can buy local foods and _____ items _____ _____ .

15 오늘날 Grand Bazaar는 훨씬 크고, 세계에서 가장 큰 지붕이 덮인 시장입니다.

16 64개의 거리와 4,000개 이상의 상점이 한 지붕 아래에 있습니다.

17 그 시장은 매일 25만 명 이상의 방문객을 불러 모읍니다.

18 그곳에서는 상상할 수 있는 거의 모든 물건을 살 수 있습니다.

19 추가 정보 가게 주인에게 행운을 기원하는 터키 전통 상징인 'nazar boncuğu(나자르 본주)'를 파는지 물어보세요.

20 또한, 만약 맛있는 간식을 원한다면, 터키 전통 사탕인 'lokum(로쿰)'을 꼭 드셔 보세요.

21 2 태국의 Damnoen Saduak(담는 사두악) 수상 시장

22 과거에 태국 사람들은 강에서 물건을 교환했습니다.

23 이것이 태국 수상 시장의 시작이었습니다.

24 도로 교통이 개선되면서, 많은 수상 시장이 사라졌습니다.

25 그러나 1960년대 후반부터 일부가 다시 생겨나 전통을 이어가고 있습니다.

26 오늘날, 가장 인기 있는 수상 시장 중 하나는 Damnoen Saduak 수상 시장입니다.

27 그곳은 전 세계에서 온 관광객들로 항상 붐빕니다.

28 배에서 직접 현지 음식과 전통 선물을 살 수 있습니다.

29 **Extra Tip** I _____ _____ you _____ ever _____ a meal on water.

30 _____ _____, try noodles _____ *pad thai*.

31 The sellers will cook them on their boats and pass them to you _____ _____ _____ _____ _____.

32 **3 Aalsmeer Flower Market,** _____ _____

33 The Netherlands _____ "_____ _____."

34 _____ the name _____, _____ 70% of the country sits _____ _____ _____.

35 _____, the Dutch _____ _____ the land, and one _____ _____ to use it was _____ _____ flowers and sell them.

36 It is, _____, _____ _____ that the country has _____ _____ _____ _____ in the world: the Aalsmeer Flower Market.

37 The building _____ the market _____ _____ is _____ _____ 120 soccer fields.

38 The market is _____ _____ thousands of _____ carts.

39 They are _____ _____ _____ electric-powered trucks.

40 Every day, _____ _____ _____ flowers are _____ and _____ to all _____ of the world.

41 **Extra Tip** You may wonder _____ you can buy _____ _____ _____ flowers at the market.

42 Sadly, you cannot, but you can see _____ _____ _____ _____ _____.

29 추가 정보 여러분이 물 위에서 식사해 본 적이 있는지 궁금하네요.

30 만약 그렇지 않다면, 'pad thai(팟 타이)' 같은 면 요리를 드셔 보세요.

31 상인들이 배에서 음식을 만들어 긴 낚싯대로 건네줄 겁니다.

32 3 네덜란드 Aalsmeer(알스메이르) 꽃 시장

33 네덜란드는 '저지대'라는 뜻입니다.

34 이름에서 알 수 있듯이, 이 나라의 약 70%가 해수면보다 낮습니다.

35 그래서 네덜란드 사람들은 땅을 지어 올렸고, 그것을 사용하는 효과적인 방법은 꽃을 재배하고 파는 것이었습니다.

36 그러므로 네덜란드에 세계에서 가장 큰 꽃 시장인 Aalsmeer 꽃 시장이 있다는 것은 놀라운 일이 아닙니다.

37 시장이 들어선 건물은 축구장 120개보다 큽니다.

38 시장은 꽃이 가득 든 수천 개의 수레로 분주합니다.

39 수레는 대부분 전동 트럭에 의해 움직입니다.

40 매일, 약 2천만 송이의 꽃이 거래되어 세계 각지로 운송됩니다.

41 추가 정보 시장에서 꽃을 조금 살 수 있는지 궁금할 겁니다.

42 애석하게도 안 되지만, 꽃이 도매로 어떻게 거래되는지를 볼 수 있습니다.

※ 다음 문장을 우리말로 쓰시오.

1   Leah's Travel Story

➡ _____

2   I am Leah.

➡ _____

3   I have been writing a travel blog since I was 18.

➡ _____

4   I go places and share my experiences with my readers.

➡ _____

5   Must-Visit Markets Around the World

➡ _____

6   July 15, 20**

➡ _____

7   Visiting markets is a good way to learn about the culture of a country.

➡ _____

8   Markets are places where you can meet people, learn history, and taste local food.

➡ _____

9   I wonder whether there is any better way to discover another culture.

➡ _____

10   1 Grand Bazaar, Turkey

➡ _____

11   Turkey is a country where East meets West, so it has a long tradition of trade.

➡ _____

12   It is a natural place for large markets like the Grand Bazaar.

➡ _____

13   The market was built in 1455 in Istanbul.

➡ _____

14   Back then, the market had two big buildings, and people traded goods like cloth and gold there.

➡ _____

15 ▶ Today the Grand Bazaar is much bigger, and it is the largest covered market in the world.

➡ _____

16 ▶ It has 64 streets and more than 4,000 shops under one roof.

➡ _____

17 ▶ The market attracts over 250,000 visitors every day.

➡ _____

18 ▶ You can buy almost any imaginable item there.

➡ _____

19 ▶ Extra Tip: Ask shop owners if they carry nazar boncuğu, a traditional Turkish symbol for good luck.

➡ _____

20 ▶ Also, if you want a nice snack, make sure to try lokum, a traditional Turkish candy.

➡ _____

21 ▶ 2 Damnoen Saduak Floating Market, Thailand

➡ _____

22 ▶ In the past, Thai people traded goods on rivers.

➡ _____

23 ▶ This was the beginning of floating markets in Thailand.

➡ _____

24 ▶ With better road transportation, many floating markets disappeared.

➡ _____

25 ▶ Since the late 1960s, however, some of them have come back and kept the tradition alive.

➡ _____

26 ▶ Today, one of the most popular floating markets is Damnoen Saduak Floating Market.

➡ _____

27 ▶ It is always crowded with tourists from all over the world.

➡ _____

28 ▶ You can buy local foods and traditional gift items directly from boats.

➡ _____

29 ▶ Extra Tip: I wonder if you have ever had a meal on water.

➡ _____

30 If not, try noodles like *pad thai*.

➡ _____

31 The sellers will cook them on their boats and pass them to you with a long fishing pole.

➡ _____

32 3 Aalsmeer Flower Market, The Netherlands

➡ _____

33 The Netherlands means "low lands."

➡ _____

34 As the name suggests, about 70% of the country sits below sea level.

➡ _____

35 Thus, the Dutch built up the land, and one effective way to use it was to grow flowers and sell them.

➡ _____

36 It is, therefore, no surprise that the country has the largest flower market in the world: the Aalsmeer Flower Market.

➡ _____

37 The building where the market is housed is bigger than 120 soccer fields.

➡ _____

38 The market is busy with thousands of flower-filled carts.

➡ _____

39 They are moved mostly by electric-powered trucks.

➡ _____

40 Every day, around 20 million flowers are traded and shipped to all corners of the world.

➡ _____

41 Extra Tip: You may wonder whether you can buy just a few flowers at the market.

➡ _____

42 Sadly, you cannot, but you can see how wholesale flower trading works.

➡ _____

※ 다음 괄호 안의 단어들을 우리말에 맞도록 바르게 배열하시오.

1 (Travel / Leah's / Story)
➡ _____

2 (Leah. / am / I)
➡ _____

3 (have / I / writing / been / travel / a / blog / I / since / 18. / was)
➡ _____

4 (go / I / and / places / my / share / expreriences / my / with / readers.)
➡ _____

5 (Markets / Must-Visit / the / World / Around)
➡ _____

6 (20** / 15, / July)
➡ _____

7 (markets / visiting / a / is / good / to / way / about / learn / culture / the / a / of / country.)
➡ _____

8 (are / markets / where / places / can / you / people, / meet / history, / learn / taste / and / food. / local)
➡ _____

9 (wonder / I / there / whether / is / better / any / to / way / discover / culture. / another)
➡ _____

10 (Grand / 1 / Turkey / Bazaar)
➡ _____

11 (is / Turkey / a / where / country / meets / East / West, / it / so / a / has / tradition / long / trade. / of)
➡ _____

12 (is / it / natural / a / for / place / markets / large / the / like / Bazaar. / Grand)
➡ _____

13 (market / the / built / was / 1455 / in / Istanbul. / in)
➡ _____

14 (then, / back / market / the / two / had / buildings / big / and / traded / people / like / goods / cloth / gold / and / there.)
➡ _____

1 Leah의 여행 이야기

2 저는 Leah입니다.

3 18세 때부터 여행 블로그를 써 왔습니다.

4 저는 여기저기 다니며 제 경험을 독자들과 공유하고 있습니다.

5 꼭 방문해야 할 세계의 시장들

6 20**년 7월 15일

7 시장 방문은 한 나라의 문화에 대해 배우는 좋은 방법입니다.

8 시장은 사람들을 만나고, 역사를 배우고, 또 지역 음식을 맛볼 수 있는 장소입니다.

9 다른 문화를 발견하는 데에 더 좋은 방법이 있을지 모르겠습니다.

10 1 터키의 Grand Bazaar(그랜드 바자)

11 터키는 동양과 서양이 만나는 나라이고, 그래서 오랜 교역의 전통을 가지고 있습니다.

12 터키는 Grand Bazaar 같은 대형 시장이 생겨나기에 자연스러운 곳입니다.

13 Grand Bazaar는 1455년 이스탄불에 지어졌습니다.

14 그 당시에 이 시장에는 큰 건물이 두 개 있었고, 거기서 사람들은 직물이나 금 같은 물건을 교환했습니다.

15 (the / today / Grand / is / Bazaar / bigger, / much / it / and / is / largest / the / market / covered / the / world. / in)

➡ _____

_____

16 (has / it / streets / 64 / and / than / more / shops / 4,000 / one / roof. / under)

➡ _____

17 (market / the / over / attracts / visitors / 250,000 / day. / every)

➡ _____

18 (can / you / almost / buy / imaginable / any / there. / item)

➡ _____

19 (Tip / Extra // shop / ask / if / owners / carry / they / *boncuğu*, / *nazar* / a / Turkish / traditional / for / luck. / symbol / good)

➡ _____

_____

20 (if / also, / you / want / nice / a / snack, / sure / make / try / to / *lokum*, / a / Turkish / candy. / traditional)

➡ _____

_____

21 (2 / Saduak / Damnoen / Market, / Floating / Thailand)

➡ _____

22 (the / in / past, / people / Thai / goods / traded / rivers. / on)

➡ _____

23 (was / this / beginning / the / floating / of / in / markets / Thailand.)

➡ _____

24 (better / with / transportation, / road / floating / many / disappeared. / markets)

➡ _____

25 (the / since / 1960s, / late / some / however, / them / of / come / have / back / and / the / kept / alive. / tradition)

➡ _____

_____

26 (one / today, / of / most / the / floating / popular / is / markets / Saduak / Damnoen / Market. / Floating)

➡ _____

_____

27 (is / it / crowded / always / tourists / with / all / from / the / over / world.)

➡ _____

28 (can / you / local / buy / foods / and / gift / traditional / directly / items / boats. / from)

➡ _____

15 오늘날 Grand Bazaar는 훨씬 크고, 세계에서 가장 큰 지붕이 덮인 시장입니다.

16 64개의 거리와 4,000개 이상의 상점이 한 지붕 아래에 있습니다.

17 그 시장은 매일 25만 명 이상의 방문객을 불러 모읍니다.

18 그곳에서는 상상할 수 있는 거의 모든 물건을 살 수 있습니다.

19 추가 정보 가게 주인에게 행운을 기원하는 터키 전통 상징인 'nazar boncuğu(나자르 본주)'를 파는지 물어보세요.

20 또한, 만약 맛있는 간식을 원한다면, 터키 전통 사탕인 'lokum(로쿰)'을 꼭 드셔 보세요.

21 2 태국의 Damnoen Saduak(담는 사두악) 수상 시장

22 과거에 태국 사람들은 강에서 물건을 교환했습니다.

23 이것이 태국 수상 시장의 시작이었습니다.

24 도로 교통이 개선되면서, 많은 수상 시장이 사라졌습니다.

25 그러나 1960년대 후반부터 일부가 다시 생겨나 전통을 이어가고 있습니다.

26 오늘날, 가장 인기 있는 수상 시장 중 하나는 Damnoen Saduak 수상 시장입니다.

27 그곳은 전 세계에서 온 관광객들로 항상 붐빕니다.

28 배에서 직접 현지 음식과 전통 선물을 살 수 있습니다.

29 (Tip / Extra // wonder / I / you / if / ever / have / had / meal / a / water. / on)

➡ _____

30 (not, / if / noodles / try / *pad* / like / *thai*.)

➡ _____

31 (sellers / the / cook / will / them / their / on / boats / and / them / pass / you / to / a / with / long / pole. / fishing)

➡ _____

_____

32 (3 / Flower / Aalsmeer / Market, / Netherlands / The)

➡ _____

33 (Netherlands / The / means / lands." / "low)

➡ _____

34 (the / as / suggests / name / 70% / about / the / of / sits / country / sea / below / level.)

➡ _____

35 (the / thus, / built / Dutch / the / up / land, / one / and / way / effective / use / to / it / to / was / flowers / grow / and / them. / sell)

➡ _____

_____

36 (is, / it / therefore, / surprise / no / the / that / country / the / has / flower / largest / in / market / the / world: / the / Flower / Aalsmeer / Market.)

➡ _____

_____

37 (building / the / the / where / market / housed / is / bigger / is / 120 / than / fields. / soccer)

➡ _____

38 (market / the / busy / is / thousands / with / flower-filled / of / carts.)

➡ _____

39 (are / they / mostly / moved / electric-powered / by / trucks.)

➡ _____

40 (day, / every / 20 / around / flowers / million / traded / are / and / to / shipped / all / corners / the / of / world.)

➡ _____

_____

41 (Tip / Extra // you / wonder / may / you / whether / can / just / buy / few / a / flowers / the / at / market.)

➡ _____

_____

42 (you / sadly, / cannot, / you / but / see / can / wholesale / how / trading / flower / works.)

➡ _____

29 추가 정보 여러분이 물 위에서 식사해 본 적이 있는지 궁금하네요.

30 만약 그렇지 않다면, 'pad thai(팟 타이)' 같은 면 요리를 드셔 보세요.

31 상인들이 배에서 음식을 만들어 긴 낚싯대로 건네줄 겁니다.

32 3 네덜란드 Aalsmeer(알스메이르) 꽃 시장

33 네덜란드는 '저지대'라는 뜻입니다.

34 이름에서 알 수 있듯이, 이 나라의 약 70%가 해수면보다 낮습니다.

35 그래서 네덜란드 사람들은 땅을 지어 올렸고, 그것을 사용하는 효과적인 방법은 꽃을 재배하고 파는 것이었습니다.

36 그러므로 네덜란드에 세계에서 가장 큰 꽃 시장인 Aalsmeer 꽃 시장이 있다는 것은 놀라운 일이 아닙니다.

37 시장이 들어선 건물은 축구장 120개보다 큽니다.

38 시장은 꽃이 가득 든 수천 개의 수레로 분주합니다.

39 수레는 대부분 전동 트럭에 의해 움직입니다.

40 매일, 약 2천만 송이의 꽃이 거래되어 세계 각지로 운송됩니다.

41 추가 정보 시장에서 꽃을 조금 살 수 있는지 궁금할 겁니다.

42 애석하게도 안 되지만, 꽃이 도매로 어떻게 거래되는지를 볼 수 있습니다.

※ 다음 우리말을 영어로 쓰시오.

1 Leah의 여행 이야기

➡ _____

2 저는 Leah입니다.

➡ _____

3 18세 때부터 여행 블로그를 써 왔습니다.

➡ _____

4 저는 여기저기 다니며 제 경험을 독자들과 공유하고 있습니다.

➡ _____

5 꼭 방문해야 할 세계의 시장들

➡ _____

6 20**년 7월 15일

➡ _____

7 시장 방문은 한 나라의 문화에 대해 배우는 좋은 방법입니다.

➡ _____

8 시장은 사람들을 만나고, 역사를 배우고, 또 지역 음식을 맛볼 수 있는 장소입니다.

➡ _____

9 다른 문화를 발견하는 데에 더 좋은 방법이 있을지 모르겠습니다.

➡ _____

10 1 터키의 Grand Bazaar(그랜드 바자)

➡ _____

11 터키는 동양과 서양이 만나는 나라이고, 그래서 오랜 교역의 전통을 가지고 있습니다.

➡ _____

12 터키는 Grand Bazaar 같은 대형 시장이 생겨나기에 자연스러운 곳입니다.

➡ _____

13 Grand Bazaar는 1455년 이스탄불에 지어졌습니다.

➡ _____

14 그 당시에 이 시장에는 큰 건물이 두 개 있었고, 거기서 사람들은 직물이나 금 같은 물건을
교환했습니다.

➡ _____

15 오늘날 Grand Bazaar는 훨씬 크고, 세계에서 가장 큰 지붕이 덮인 시장입니다.

➡ _____

16 64개의 거리와 4,000개 이상의 상점이 한 지붕 아래에 있습니다.

➡ _____

17 그 시장은 매일 25만 명 이상의 방문객을 불러 모읍니다.

➡ _____

18 그곳에서는 상상할 수 있는 거의 모든 물건을 살 수 있습니다.

➡ _____

19 추가 정보: 가게 주인에게 행운을 기원하는 터키 전통 상징인 'nazar boncuğu(나자르 본주)'를 파는지 물어보세요.

➡ _____

20 또한, 만약 맛있는 간식을 원한다면, 터키 전통 사탕인 'lokum(로쿰)'을 꼭 드셔 보세요.

➡ _____

21 2 태국의 Damnoen Saduak(담는 사두악) 수상 시장

➡ _____

22 과거에 태국 사람들은 강에서 물건을 교환했습니다.

➡ _____

23 이것이 태국 수상 시장의 시작이었습니다.

➡ _____

24 도로 교통이 개선되면서, 많은 수상 시장이 사라졌습니다.

➡ _____

25 그러나 1960년대 후반부터 일부가 다시 생겨나 전통을 이어 가고 있습니다.

➡ _____

26 오늘날, 가장 인기 있는 수상 시장 중 하나는 Damnoen Saduak 수상 시장입니다.

➡ _____

27 그곳은 전 세계에서 온 관광객들로 항상 붐빕니다.

➡ _____

28 배에서 직접 현지 음식과 전통 선물을 살 수 있습니다.

➡ _____

29 추가 정보: 여러분이 물 위에서 식사해 본 적이 있는지 궁금하네요.

➡ _____

30 만약 그렇지 않다면, 'pad thai(팟 타이)' 같은 면 요리를 드셔 보세요.

➡ _____

31 상인들이 배에서 음식을 만들어 긴 낚싯대로 건네줄 겁니다.

➡ _____

32 3 네덜란드 Aalsmeer(알스메이르) 꽃 시장

➡ _____

33 네덜란드는 '저지대'라는 뜻입니다.

➡ _____

34 이름에서 알 수 있듯이, 이 나라의 약 70%가 해수면보다 낮습니다.

➡ _____

35 그래서 네덜란드 사람들은 땅을 지어 올렸고, 그것을 사용하는 효과적인 방법은 꽃을 재배하고 파는 것이었습니다.

➡ _____

_____

36 그러므로 네덜란드에 세계에서 가장 큰 꽃 시장인 Aalsmeer 꽃 시장이 있다는 것은 놀라운 일이 아닙니다.

➡ _____

_____

37 시장이 들어선 건물은 축구장 120개보다 큽니다.

➡ _____

38 시장은 꽃이 가득 든 수천 개의 수레로 분주합니다.

➡ _____

39 수레는 대부분 전동 트럭에 의해 움직입니다.

➡ _____

40 매일, 약 2천만 송이의 꽃이 거래되어 세계 각지로 운송됩니다.

➡ _____

41 추가 정보: 시장에서 꽃을 조금 살 수 있는지 궁금할 겁니다.

➡ _____

42 애석하게도 안 되지만, 꽃이 도매로 어떻게 거래되는지를 볼 수 있습니다.

➡ _____

※ 다음 우리말과 일치하도록 빈칸에 알맞은 말을 쓰시오.

My Speaking Portfolio - Step 2

1. A: _____ do you _____ _____ _____? I _____ _____
   you want to travel _____ _____ or _____.

2. B: Well, I _____ _____ _____ _____ _____ my friends.

......

3. A: Okay. Do you want _____ _____ _____ or _____?

4. B: I want to visit museums. _____ a great way _____ _____
   _____ the _____ _____.

1. A: 어떻게 여행하는 것을 원하니? 나는 네가 친구들이나 가족들과 여행하는 것을 좋아하는지 궁금해.
2. B: 음, 나는 내 친구들과 여행하고 싶어.
......
3. A: 알겠어. 너는 박물관 또는 시장을 방문하고 싶니?
4. B: 나는 박물관을 가보고 싶어. 그것은 지역 문화에 대해 배우는 데 좋은 방법이야.

After You Read

1. This country is a _____ _____ _____ _____
   and has a _____ _____ _____ _____.

2. This is a _____ _____ _____ _____ _____ has a _____
   _____.

3. _____ _____ _____ of the country _____ _____ _____
   _____.

1. 이 나라는 동양과 서양이 만나는 장소이고, 오랜 교역의 전통을 가지고 있다.
2. 이곳은 배에서 거래하는 오랜 역사가 있는 나라이다.
3. 그 나라의 3분의 2 이상이 해수면보다 낮다.

Wrap Up READING

1. _____ _____, I _____ _____ _____ Oakville Farmers' Market.

2. That is _____ _____ _____ I buy food for the _____
   _____.

3. There I find _____ _____ _____ _____ _____ _____.

4. They _____ _____ _____ only _____ _____ _____
   before I buy them.

5. I _____ _____ bread, _____, and _____ jam.

6. _____ I can buy _____ _____ _____ _____ _____ the producers,
   they are usually _____ _____ _____ _____ _____.

7. The _____ _____ are always kind and _____ _____ _____
   gardening tips and _____ _____ visitors, too.

8. I _____ _____ _____ _____ the _____ _____.

1. 토요일마다 나는 Oakville 농산물 직거래 시장에 간다.
2. 그곳은 내가 다음 주에 먹을 음식을 사는 곳이다.
3. 그곳에서 나는 온갖 종류의 신선한 채소를 구한다.
4. 채소들은 대개 내가 사기 불과 몇 시간 전에 수확된 것이다.
5. 나는 또한 빵, 고기, 그리고 집에서 만든 잼도 구한다.
6. 물건을 생산자에게서 직접 살 수 있어서 그것들은 대개 다른 가게에서보다 훨씬 저렴하다.
7. 지역 농부들은 항상 친절하고, 원예 정보나 조리법을 방문객들과 공유할 준비가 되어 있다.
8. 나는 농산물 직거래 시장에 가는 것을 좋아한다.

※ 다음 우리말을 영어로 쓰시오.

My Speaking Portfolio - Step 2

1. A: 어떻게 여행하는 것을 원하니? 나는 네가 친구들이나 가족들과 여행하는 것을 좋아하는지 궁금해.
   ➡ _____

2. B: 음, 나는 내 친구들과 여행하고 싶어.
   ➡ _____

......

3. A: 알겠어. 너는 박물관 또는 시장을 방문하고 싶니?
   ➡ _____

4. B: 나는 박물관을 가보고 싶어. 그것은 지역 문화에 대해 배우는 데 좋은 방법이야.
   ➡ _____

After You Read

1. 이 나라는 동양과 서양이 만나는 장소이고, 오랜 교역의 전통을 가지고 있다.
   ➡ _____

2. 이곳은 배에서 거래하는 오랜 역사가 있는 나라이다.
   ➡ _____

3. 그 나라의 3분의 2 이상이 해수면보다 낮다.
   ➡ _____

Wrap Up READING

1. 토요일마다 나는 Oakville 농산물 직거래 시장에 간다.
   ➡ _____

2. 그곳은 내가 다음 주에 먹을 음식을 사는 곳이다.
   ➡ _____

3. 그곳에서 나는 온갖 종류의 신선한 채소를 구한다.
   ➡ _____

4. 채소들은 대개 내가 사기 불과 몇 시간 전에 수확된 것이다.
   ➡ _____

5. 나는 또한 빵, 고기, 그리고 집에서 만든 잼도 구한다.
   ➡ _____

6. 물건을 생산자에게서 직접 살 수 있어서 그것들은 대개 다른 가게에서보다 훨씬 저렴하다.
   ➡ _____

7. 지역 농부들은 항상 친절하고, 원예 정보나 조리법을 방문객들과 공유할 준비가 되어 있다.
   ➡ _____

8. 나는 농산물 직거래 시장에 가는 것을 좋아한다.
   ➡ _____

※ 다음 영어를 우리말로 쓰시오.

01	onion	22	national flag
02	widely	23	topping
03	sick	24	the New World
04	cheap	25	record
05	delicious	26	national
06	century	27	favorite
07	everywhere	28	global
08	sell	29	since
09	healthy	30	type
10	differ	31	such
11	slice	32	busy
12	however	33	the Stone Age
13	flat	34	vegetable
14	introduce	35	outside of
15	learn	36	in time
16	disagree	37	topped with
17	share	38	at the same time
18	far	39	put ~ on
19	bring	40	in one form or another
20	meat	41	at any time
21	almost	42	be used to+동사원형
		43	It is believed that ~

※ 다음 우리말을 영어로 쓰시오.

01 분주한, 바쁜 _____

02 세기 _____

03 맛보다 _____

04 유형 _____

05 거의 _____

06 ～인 반면에,
～하는 동안에 _____

07 ～할 때, ～하면서 _____

08 ～ 이후로 _____

09 맛있는 _____

10 국기 _____

11 양파 _____

12 공유하다 _____

13 다르다 _____

14 폭넓게 _____

15 고기 _____

16 상점 _____

17 멀리 떨어진 _____

18 납작한, 평평한 _____

19 전 세계적인 _____

20 그러나 _____

21 이름 붙이다 _____

22 가지고 오다 _____

23 팔다 _____

24 값싼 _____

25 국가의 _____

26 의견이 다르다 _____

27 건강한 _____

28 모든 곳에서 _____

29 기록 _____

30 이동하다 _____

31 (얇은) 조각 _____

32 그런, ～와 같은 _____

33 고명, 토핑 _____

34 소개하다 _____

35 이윽고 _____

36 어느 때이든지 _____

37 ～로 덮여 있는 _____

38 너무 ～해서 …한 _____

39 (다음으로) 넘어가다 _____

40 동시에 _____

41 ～하기 위하여 사용되다 _____

42 전 세계에 걸친 _____

43 ～라고들 믿고 있다 _____

※ 다음 영영풀이에 알맞은 단어를 <보기>에서 골라 쓴 후, 우리말 뜻을 쓰시오.

1 _____ : where you buy something: _____

2 _____ : to have or express the same opinion: _____

3 _____ : a period of 100 years: _____

4 _____ : affecting or including the whole world: _____

5 _____ : to cook something using dry heat, in an oven: _____

6 _____ : costing little money or less money than you expected: _____

7 _____ : a thin flat piece of food cut from a larger piece: _____

8 _____ : to bring a plan, system, or product into use for the first time: _____

9 _____ : a round white vegetable with a brown, red, or white skin and many
　　　　　　　 layers: _____

10 _____ : something you put on top of food to make it look nicer or taste better:
　　　　　　　 _____

11 _____ : a type of food made from flour and water that is mixed together and then
　　　　　　　 baked: _____

12 _____ : a piece of cloth with a coloured pattern or picture on it that represents a
　　　　　　　 country or organization: _____

보기			
century	agree	shop	global
bread	topping	slice	flag
cheap	bake	onion	introduce

Step1

※ 다음 우리말과 일치하도록 빈칸에 알맞은 것을 골라 쓰시오.

1 A _____ of _____

   A. History   B. Slice

2 _____ do you _____ on _____ pizza?

   A. like   B. what   C. your

3 _____ you may _____ _____ the best toppings, you will agree that it is now a _____ food.

   A. global   B. disagree   C. on   D. though

4 It is _____ in fast-food restaurants or on the _____ in _____ _____ of the world.

   A. parts   B. sold   C. most   D. street

5 How has pizza _____ _____ a _____ food _____ the world?

   A. favorite   B. become   C. around   D. such

6 _____ the Stone Age, people have been _____ pizza in one _____ or _____.

   A. form   B. since   C. another   D. eating

7 Stone Age people _____ _____ bread on _____ _____.

   A. flat   B. rocks   C. baked   D. hot

8 Records _____ that the Greeks and the Romans started to _____ _____ and vegetables _____ flat bread.

   A. put   B. on   C. show   D. meat

9 It is _____ that the word "pizza" was first _____ in Italy to _____ the food _____ 1,000 years ago.

   A. over   B. believed   C. name   D. used

10 However, pizza _____ tomato toppings was not _____ _____ the 16th _____.

   A. until   B. with   C. century   D. born

11 There were no tomatoes in Italy _____ Christopher Columbus and _____ Europeans _____ them _____ the New World.

   A. other   B. from   C. brought   D. before

---

1 한 조각의 역사

2 여러분은 어떤 피자 토핑을 좋아하는가?

3 비록 제일 좋아하는 피자 토핑에 대해 의견이 다를 수 있지만, 피자가 오늘날 세계적인 음식이라는 데에는 모두 동의할 것이다.

4 피자는 세계 대부분 지역의 패스트푸드 식당이나 길거리에서 팔리고 있다.

5 어떻게 해서 피자가 세계적으로 이토록 사랑받는 음식이 되었을까?

6 석기시대부터 사람들은 여러 가지 형태로 피자를 먹어 왔다.

7 석기시대 사람들은 납작한 빵을 뜨거운 돌에 구워 먹었다.

8 기록에 의하면 그리스와 로마 사람들이 납작한 빵에 고기와 채소를 얹기 시작했다.

9 '피자'라는 단어는 이러한 음식을 지칭하기 위해 약 천 년 전에 이탈리아에서 처음 사용되었다고 알려져 있다.

10 하지만 토마토 토핑을 얹은 피자는 16세기까지는 존재하지 않았다.

11 크리스토퍼 콜럼버스와 다른 유럽인들이 신세계에서 가져오기 전까지 이탈리아에는 토마토가 없었다.

12 When they were first _____ to Europe, people _____ that tomatoes would _____ them _____.

A. thought   B. sick   C. make   D. introduced

13 _____ time, people _____ that tomatoes were _____ and _____.

A. learned   B. healthy   C. delicious   D. in

14 In the 18th _____, Naples was a _____ city _____ there were many _____.

A. where   B. century   C. large   D. jobs

15 Workers from _____ and _____ came to the city, and what they needed in their busy _____ was food they could eat quickly at any _____.

A. lives   B. time   C. far   D. near

16 Cooks in Naples began to put tomato and _____ toppings on _____ bread and _____ _____ of pizza on the street.

A. flat   B. slices   C. other   D. sold

17 The _____ food was so _____ and _____ that _____ ate it for breakfast, lunch, and dinner.

A. workers   B. cheap   C. delicious   D. street

18 They could buy _____ _____ pizza and eat them _____ they walked _____ the street.

A. as   B. of   C. on   D. slices

19 In 1830, the _____ _____ pizza _____ _____ in Naples.

A. shop   B. world's   C. opened   D. first

20 _____ 1889, Queen Margherita _____ Italy _____ Naples and _____ pizza.

A. visited   B. tried   C. in   D. of

21 The _____ of pizza that she loved most had tomato, cheese, and green _____ toppings that showed the three _____ on Italy's national _____ –red, white, and green.

A. leaf   B. type   C. flag   D. colors

---

12 유럽에 처음 소개되었을 때 사람들은 토마토가 사람들을 아프게 할 거라고 여겼다.

13 시간이 지나며 사람들은 토마토가 맛있고 건강에도 좋다는 것을 알게 되었다.

14 18세기에 나폴리는 다양한 직업이 존재하는 대도시였다.

15 사방에서 노동자들이 이 도시로 모여들었고, 바쁜 생활 중 그들에게 필요했던 것은 언제든지 빨리 먹을 수 있는 음식이었다.

16 나폴리의 요리사들이 납작한 빵에 토마토와 다른 토핑을 얹기 시작해 길거리에서 피자 조각을 팔았다.

17 이 길거리 음식은 무척 저렴하고 맛이 좋아서, 노동자들은 이것을 아침, 점심, 저녁으로 먹었다.

18 그들은 피자 조각을 사서 길을 걸어가며 먹을 수 있었다.

19 1830년에는 세계 최초의 피자 가게가 나폴리에서 문을 열었다.

20 1889년에 이탈리아의 마르게리타 왕비가 나폴리를 방문하여 피자를 맛보았다.

21 그녀가 가장 좋아했던 피자는 이탈리아 국기의 세 가지 색깔인 빨강, 하양, 초록을 나타낸 토마토, 치즈, 녹색 잎 채소 토핑으로 된 것이었다.

22 After the queen's _____, pizza went _____ to _____ a truly national _____.

    A. on   B. dish   C. become   D. visit

23 Pizza _____ _____ outside of Italy in the _____ 19th century, when many Italians _____ to the United States.

    A. moved   B. known   C. late   D. became

24 Italians _____ pizza with them, and Americans loved the flat bread topped _____ meat and vegetables _____ they could eat bread, meat, and vegetables at the _____ time.

    A. with   B. same   C. brought   D. because

25 The _____ pizza restaurant in the United States _____ _____ _____ in 1905.

    A. opened   B. first   C. doors   D. its

26 Pizza is now _____ _____ _____.

    A. almost   B. enjoyed   C. everywhere

27 Of _____, toppings _____ widely _____ place _____ place.

    A. from   B. differ   C. course   D. to

28 Koreans love _bulgogi_ on their pizza, _____ Russians like to _____ fish and _____ toppings _____ their pizza.

    A. have   B. on   C. while   D. onion

29 _____, all _____ _____ pizza _____ two things.

    A. share   B. types   C. however   D. of

30 _____ begins _____ _____ bread, and each is a _____ of history.

    A. slice   B. with   C. each   D. flat

22 왕비의 방문 이후로 피자는 진정한 이탈리아의 국가 음식이 되었다.

23 19세기 후반에는 피자가 이탈리아 밖으로 알려지게 되었는데, 이 시기에 많은 이탈리아 사람들이 미국으로 이주를 하였다.

24 이탈리아인들은 피자도 함께 가져갔고, 빵, 고기, 채소를 한꺼번에 먹을 수 있어서 미국인들은 고기와 채소를 얹은 이 납작한 빵을 좋아했다.

25 미국 최초의 피자 가게가 1905년에 문을 열었다.

26 오늘날 피자는 거의 어디에서나 즐길 수 있다.

27 물론, 토핑은 지역에 따라 매우 다양하다.

28 한국인은 불고기를 피자에 얹어 먹기를 좋아하고, 러시아 사람들은 생선과 양파 토핑을 좋아한다.

29 그러나 모든 종류의 피자가 두 가지 사실만큼은 똑같다.

30 모든 피자는 납작한 빵에서 시작하고, 각각은 역사의 한 조각이다.

※ 다음 우리말과 일치하도록 빈칸에 알맞은 것을 골라 쓰시오.

1 A _____ _____ _____

2 _____ _____ _____ _____ on your pizza?

3 _____ you may _____ _____ the best toppings, you will agree that it is now a _____ _____.

4 _____ _____ _____ in fast-food restaurants or on the street _____ _____ _____ of the _____.

5 How _____ pizza _____ _____ _____ _____ around the world?

6 _____ the Stone Age, people _____ _____ _____ pizza in one form or _____.

7 Stone Age people baked flat bread _____ _____ _____.

8 _____ _____ that the Greeks and the Romans started _____ _____ meat and vegetables _____ flat bread.

9 _____ _____ _____ that the word "pizza" was first used in Italy _____ _____ the food _____ 1,000 years ago.

10 _____, pizza with tomato toppings _____ _____ _____ _____ the 16th century.

11 There were no tomatoes in Italy _____ Christopher Columbus and other Europeans _____ them _____ the New World.

12 When they _____ first _____ to Europe, people thought that tomatoes would _____ _____ _____.

13 _____ _____, people learned that tomatoes were _____ and _____.

14 _____ the 18th _____, Naples was a large city _____ there were many jobs.

15 Workers _____ _____ _____ _____ came to the city, and what they needed in their _____ _____ was food they could eat quickly _____ _____ _____.

1 한 조각의 역사

2 여러분은 어떤 피자 토핑을 좋아하는가?

3 비록 제일 좋아하는 피자 토핑에 대해 의견이 다를 수 있지만, 피자가 오늘날 세계적인 음식이라는 데에는 모두 동의할 것이다.

4 피자는 세계 대부분 지역의 패스트푸드 식당이나 길거리에서 팔리고 있다.

5 어떻게 해서 피자가 세계적으로 이토록 사랑받는 음식이 되었을까?

6 석기시대부터 사람들은 여러 가지 형태로 피자를 먹어 왔다.

7 석기시대 사람들은 납작한 빵을 뜨거운 돌에 구워 먹었다.

8 기록에 의하면 그리스와 로마 사람들이 납작한 빵에 고기와 채소를 얹기 시작했다.

9 '피자'라는 단어는 이러한 음식을 지칭하기 위해 약 천 년 전에 이탈리아에서 처음 사용되었다고 알려져 있다.

10 하지만 토마토 토핑을 얹은 피자는 16세기까지는 존재하지 않았다.

11 크리스토퍼 콜럼버스와 다른 유럽인들이 신세계에서 가져오기 전까지 이탈리아에는 토마토가 없었다.

12 유럽에 처음 소개되었을 때 사람들은 토마토가 사람들을 아프게 할 거라고 여겼다.

13 시간이 지나며 사람들은 토마토가 맛있고 건강에도 좋다는 것을 알게 되었다.

14 18세기에 나폴리는 다양한 직업이 존재하는 대도시였다.

15 사방에서 노동자들이 이 도시로 모여들었고, 바쁜 생활 중 그들에게 필요했던 것은 언제든지 빨리 먹을 수 있는 음식이었다.

16 Cooks in Naples began to _____ tomato and other toppings _____ flat bread and sold _____ _____ _____ on the street.

17 The street food was _____ _____ and _____ _____ workers ate it _____ breakfast, lunch, and dinner.

18 They could buy _____ _____ pizza and eat them _____ they walked _____ _____ _____.

19 In 1830, the _____ _____ _____ _____ opened in Naples.

20 In 1889, Queen Margherita of Italy visited Naples and _____ pizza.

21 The type of pizza _____ _____ _____ _____ had tomato, cheese, and green leaf toppings _____ _____ the three colors _____ Italy's national flag–red, white, and green.

22 After the queen's visit, pizza _____ _____ _____ _____ a truly _____ _____.

23 Pizza _____ _____ _____ _____ Italy in the late 19th century, when many Italians _____ _____ the United States.

24 Italians _____ _____ _____ _____, and Americans loved the flat bread _____ _____ meat and vegetables because they could eat bread, meat, and vegetables _____ _____ _____ _____.

25 The first pizza restaurant in the United States _____ _____ _____ _____ 1905.

26 Pizza is now enjoyed _____ _____.

27 _____ _____, toppings _____ widely _____ _____ _____ _____.

28 Koreans love *bulgogi* on their pizza, _____ Russians like to have fish and _____ _____ on their pizza.

29 However, all types of pizza _____ _____ _____.

30 Each _____ _____ flat bread, and each is _____ _____ _____ _____.

16 나폴리의 요리사들이 납작한 빵에 토마토와 다른 토핑을 얹기 시작해 길거리에서 피자 조각을 팔았다.

17 이 길거리 음식은 무척 저렴하고 맛이 좋아서, 노동자들은 이것을 아침, 점심, 저녁으로 먹었다.

18 그들은 피자 조각을 사서 길을 걸어가며 먹을 수 있었다.

19 1830년에는 세계 최초의 피자 가게가 나폴리에서 문을 열었다.

20 1889년에 이탈리아의 마르게리타 왕비가 나폴리를 방문하여 피자를 맛보았다.

21 그녀가 가장 좋아했던 피자는 이탈리아 국기의 세 가지 색깔인 빨강, 하양, 초록을 나타낸 토마토, 치즈, 녹색 잎 채소 토핑으로 된 것이었다.

22 왕비의 방문 이후로 피자는 진정한 이탈리아의 국가 음식이 되었다.

23 19세기 후반에는 피자가 이탈리아 밖으로 알려지게 되었는데, 이 시기에 많은 이탈리아 사람들이 미국으로 이주를 하였다.

24 이탈리아인들은 피자도 함께 가져갔고, 빵, 고기, 채소를 한꺼번에 먹을 수 있어서 미국인들은 고기와 채소를 얹은 이 납작한 빵을 좋아했다.

25 미국 최초의 피자 가게가 1905년에 문을 열었다.

26 오늘날 피자는 거의 어디에서나 즐길 수 있다.

27 물론, 토핑은 지역에 따라 매우 다양하다.

28 한국인은 불고기를 피자에 얹어 먹기를 좋아하고, 러시아 사람들은 생선과 양파 토핑을 좋아한다.

29 그러나 모든 종류의 피자가 두 가지 사실만큼은 똑같다.

30 모든 피자는 납작한 빵에서 시작하고, 각각은 역사의 한 조각이다.

※ 다음 문장을 우리말로 쓰시오.

1 A Slice of History
➡ _____

2 What do you like on your pizza?
➡ _____

3 Though you may disagree on the best toppings, you will agree that it is now a global food.
➡ _____
_____

4 It is sold in fast-food restaurants or on the street in most parts of the world.
➡ _____

5 How has pizza become such a favorite food around the world?
➡ _____

6 Since the Stone Age, people have been eating pizza in one form or another.
➡ _____

7 Stone Age people baked flat bread on hot rocks.
➡ _____

8 Records show that the Greeks and the Romans started to put meat and vegetables on flat bread.
➡ _____

9 It is believed that the word "pizza" was first used in Italy to name the food over 1,000 years ago.
➡ _____

10 However, pizza with tomato toppings was not born until the 16th century.
➡ _____

11 There were no tomatoes in Italy before Christopher Columbus and other Europeans brought them from the New World.
➡ _____

12 When they were first introduced to Europe, people thought that tomatoes would make them sick.
➡ _____

13 In time, people learned that tomatoes were delicious and healthy.
➡ _____

14 In the 18th century, Naples was a large city where there were many jobs.
➡ _____

15 Workers from near and far came to the city, and what they needed in their busy lives was food they could eat quickly at any time.
➡ _____

16 Cooks in Naples began to put tomato and other toppings on flat bread and sold slices of pizza on the street.

➡ _____

17 The street food was so cheap and delicious that workers ate it for breakfast, lunch, and dinner.

➡ _____

18 They could buy slices of pizza and eat them as they walked on the street.

➡ _____

19 In 1830, the world's first pizza shop opened in Naples.

➡ _____

20 In 1889, Queen Margherita of Italy visited Naples and tried pizza.

➡ _____

21 The type of pizza that she loved most had tomato, cheese, and green leaf toppings that showed the three colors on Italy's national flag—red, white, and green.

➡ _____

_____

22 After the queen's visit, pizza went on to become a truly national dish.

➡ _____

23 Pizza became known outside of Italy in the late 19th century, when many Italians moved to the United States.

➡ _____

24 Italians brought pizza with them, and Americans loved the flat bread topped with meat and vegetables because they could eat bread, meat, and vegetables at the same time.

➡ _____

_____

25 The first pizza restaurant in the United States opened its doors in 1905.

➡ _____

26 Pizza is now enjoyed almost everywhere.

➡ _____

27 Of course, toppings differ widely from place to place.

➡ _____

28 Koreans love *bulgogi* on their pizza, while Russians like to have fish and onion toppings on their pizza.

➡ _____

29 However, all types of pizza share two things.

➡ _____

30 Each begins with flat bread, and each is a slice of history.

➡ _____

※ 다음 괄호 안의 단어들을 우리말에 맞도록 바르게 배열하시오.

1 (Slice / A / History / of)
➡ _____

2 (do / what / like / you / on / pizza? / your)
➡ _____

3 (you / though / disagree / may / the / on / best / toppings, / will / you / that / agree / is / it / a / now / food. / global)
➡ _____
_____

4 (is / it / in / sold / fast-food / or / restaurants / on / street / the / most / in / of / parts / world. / the)
➡ _____
_____

5 (has / how / become / pizza / a / such / food / favorite / around / world? / the)
➡ _____

6 (the / since / Age, / Stone / have / people / eating / been / in / pizza / form / one / another. / or)
➡ _____
_____

7 (Age / Stone / baked / people / bread / flat / on / rocks. / hot)
➡ _____

8 (show / records / the / that / and / Greeks / the / started / Romans / put / to / meat / and / vegetables / flat / on / bread.)
➡ _____
_____

9 (is / it / believed / the / that / word / was / "pizza" / first / in / used / Italy / name / to / food / the / 1,000 / over / ago. / years)
➡ _____
_____

10 (pizza / however, / tomato / with / was / toppings / born / not / until / 16th / the / century.)
➡ _____

11 (were / there / tomatoes / no / Italy / in / before / Colombus / Christopher / and / Europeans / other / brought / from / them / New / the / World.)
➡ _____
_____

1 한 조각의 역사

2 여러분은 어떤 피자 토핑을 좋아하는가?

3 비록 제일 좋아하는 피자 토핑에 대해 의견이 다를 수 있지만, 피자가 오늘날 세계적인 음식이라는 데에는 모두 동의할 것이다.

4 피자는 세계 대부분 지역의 패스트푸드 식당이나 길거리에서 팔리고 있다.

5 어떻게 해서 피자가 세계적으로 이토록 사랑받는 음식이 되었을까?

6 석기시대부터 사람들은 여러 가지 형태로 피자를 먹어 왔다.

7 석기시대 사람들은 납작한 빵을 뜨거운 돌에 구워 먹었다.

8 기록에 의하면 그리스와 로마 사람들이 납작한 빵에 고기와 채소를 얹기 시작했다.

9 '피자'라는 단어는 이러한 음식을 지칭하기 위해 약 천 년 전에 이탈리아에서 처음 사용되었다고 알려져 있다.

10 하지만 토마토 토핑을 얹은 피자는 16세기까지는 존재하지 않았다.

11 크리스토퍼 콜럼버스와 다른 유럽인들이 신세계에서 가져오기 전까지 이탈리아에는 토마토가 없었다.

12 (they / when / first / were / to / introduced / Europe, / thought / people / tomatoes / that / make / would / sick. / them)

➡ _____

_____

13 (time, / in / learned / people / tomatoes / that / delicious / were / healthy. / and)

➡ _____

14 (the / in / century, / 18th / was / Naples / a / city / large / there / where / were / jobs. / many)

➡ _____

15 (from / workers / near / and / came / far / the / to / city, / what / and / needed / they / in / busy / their / lives / food / was / could / they / quickly / eat / any / time. / at)

➡ _____

_____

16 (in / cooks / began / Naples / put / to / tomato / and / toppings / other / flat / on / bread / and / slices / sold / pizza / of / the / on / street.)

➡ _____

_____

17 (street / the / was / food / cheap / so / and / that / delicious / workers / it / ate / breakfast, / for / and / lunch, / dinner.)

➡ _____

_____

18 (could / they / slices / buy / pizza / of / and / them / eat / as / walked / they / the / on / street.)

➡ _____

19 (1830, / in / world's / the / pizza / first / opened / shop / Naples. / in)

➡ _____

20 (1889, / in / Margherita / Queen / Italy / of / Naples / visited / and / pizza. / tried)

➡ _____

21 (type / the / pizza / of / she / that / most / loved / tomato, / had / and / cheese, / green / toppings / leaf / showed / that / three / the / on / colors / national / Italy's / flag / – / white, / red, / green. / and)

➡ _____

_____

12 유럽에 처음 소개되었을 때 사람들은 토마토가 사람들을 아프게 할 거라고 여겼다.

13 시간이 지나며 사람들은 토마토가 맛있고 건강에도 좋다는 것을 알게 되었다.

14 18세기에 나폴리는 다양한 직업이 존재하는 대도시였다.

15 사방에서 노동자들이 이 도시로 모여들었고, 바쁜 생활 중 그들에게 필요했던 것은 언제든지 빨리 먹을 수 있는 음식이었다.

16 나폴리의 요리사들이 납작한 빵에 토마토와 다른 토핑을 얹기 시작해 길거리에서 피자 조각을 팔았다.

17 이 길거리 음식은 무척 저렴하고 맛이 좋아서, 노동자들은 이것을 아침, 점심, 저녁으로 먹었다.

18 그들은 피자 조각을 사서 길을 걸어가며 먹을 수 있었다.

19 1830년에는 세계 최초의 피자 가게가 나폴리에서 문을 열었다.

20 1889년에 이탈리아의 마르게리타 왕비가 나폴리를 방문하여 피자를 맛보았다.

21 그녀가 가장 좋아했던 피자는 이탈리아 국기의 세 가지 색깔인 빨강, 하양, 초록을 나타낸 토마토, 치즈, 녹색 잎 채소 토핑으로 된 것이었다.

22 (the / after / visit, / queen's / went / pizza / to / on / become / truly / a / dish. / national)

➡ _____

23 (became / pizza / outside / known / Italy / of / the / in / late / century, / 19th / many / when / moved / Italians / to / United / the / States.)

➡ _____
_____

24 (brought / Italians / with / pizza / them, / Americans / and / loved / flat / the / bread / with / topped / meat / and / because / vegetables / could / they / eat / bread, / and / meat, / vegetables / the / at / time. / same)

➡ _____
_____

25 (fist / the / restaurant / pizza / the / in / States / United / its / opened / doors / 1905. / in)

➡ _____

26 (is / pizza / enjoyed / now / everywhere. / almost)

➡ _____

27 (couese, / of / differ / toppings / from / widely / place / place. / to)

➡ _____

28 (love / Koreans / *bulgogi* / their / on /. pizza, / Russians / while / to / like / fish / have / onion / and / on / toppings / pizza. / their)

➡ _____
_____

29 (all / however, / of / types / share / pizza / things. / two)

➡ _____

30 (begins / each / flat / with / bread, / each / and / a / is / slice / history. / of)

➡ _____

22 왕비의 방문 이후로 피자는 진정한 이탈리아의 국가 음식이 되었다.

23 19세기 후반에는 피자가 이탈리아 밖으로 알려지게 되었는데, 이 시기에 많은 이탈리아 사람들이 미국으로 이주를 하였다.

24 이탈리아인들은 피자도 함께 가져갔고, 빵, 고기, 채소를 한꺼번에 먹을 수 있어서 미국인들은 고기와 채소를 얹은 이 납작한 빵을 좋아했다.

25 미국 최초의 피자 가게가 1905년에 문을 열었다.

26 오늘날 피자는 거의 어디에서나 즐길 수 있다.

27 물론, 토핑은 지역에 따라 매우 다양하다.

28 한국인은 불고기를 피자에 얹어 먹기를 좋아하고, 러시아 사람들은 생선과 양파 토핑을 좋아한다.

29 그러나 모든 종류의 피자가 두 가지 사실만큼은 똑같다.

30 모든 피자는 납작한 빵에서 시작하고, 각각은 역사의 한 조각이다.

Step5

※ 다음 우리말을 영어로 쓰시오.

1 한 조각의 역사

➡ _____

2 여러분은 어떤 피자 토핑을 좋아하는가?

➡ _____

3 비록 제일 좋아하는 피자 토핑에 대해 의견이 다를 수 있지만, 피자가 오늘날 세계적인 음식이라는 데에는 모두 동의할 것이다.

➡ _____

4 피자는 세계 대부분 지역의 패스트푸드 식당이나 길거리에서 팔리고 있다.

➡ _____

5 어떻게 해서 피자가 세계적으로 이토록 사랑받는 음식이 되었을까?

➡ _____

6 석기시대부터 사람들은 여러 가지 형태로 피자를 먹어 왔다.

➡ _____

7 석기시대 사람들은 납작한 빵을 뜨거운 돌에 구워 먹었다.

➡ _____

8 기록에 의하면 그리스와 로마 사람들이 납작한 빵에 고기와 채소를 얹기 시작했다.

➡ _____

9 '피자'라는 단어는 이러한 음식을 지칭하기 위해 약 천 년 전에 이탈리아에서 처음 사용되었다고 알려져 있다.

➡ _____

10 하지만 토마토 토핑을 얹은 피자는 16세기까지는 존재하지 않았다.

➡ _____

11 크리스토퍼 콜럼버스와 다른 유럽인들이 신세계에서 가져오기 전까지 이탈리아에는 토마토가 없었다.

➡ _____

12 유럽에 처음 소개되었을 때 사람들은 토마토가 사람들을 아프게 할 거라고 여겼다.

➡ _____

13 시간이 지나며 사람들은 토마토가 맛있고 건강에도 좋다는 것을 알게 되었다.

➡ _____

14 18세기에 나폴리는 다양한 직업이 존재하는 대도시였다.

➡ _____

15 사방에서 노동자들이 이 도시로 모여들었고, 바쁜 생활 중 그들에게 필요했던 것은 언제든지 빨리 먹을 수 있는 음식이었다.

➡ _____

16 나폴리의 요리사들이 납작한 빵에 토마토와 다른 토핑을 얹기 시작해 길거리에서 피자 조각을 팔았다.

➡ _____

_____

17 이 길거리 음식은 무척 저렴하고 맛이 좋아서, 노동자들은 이것을 아침, 점심, 저녁으로 먹었다.

➡ _____

18 그들은 피자 조각을 사서 길을 걸어가며 먹을 수 있었다.

➡ _____

19 1830년에는 세계 최초의 피자 가게가 나폴리에서 문을 열었다.

➡ _____

20 1889년에 이탈리아의 마르게리타 왕비가 나폴리를 방문하여 피자를 맛보았다.

➡ _____

21 그녀가 가장 좋아했던 피자는 이탈리아 국기의 세 가지 색깔인 빨강, 하양, 초록을 나타낸 토마토, 치즈, 녹색 잎 채소 토핑으로 된 것이었다.

➡ _____

_____

22 왕비의 방문 이후로 피자는 진정한 이탈리아의 국가 음식이 되었다.

➡ _____

23 19세기 후반에는 피자가 이탈리아 밖으로 알려지게 되었는데, 이 시기에 많은 이탈리아 사람들이 미국으로 이주를 하였다.

➡ _____

_____

24 이탈리아인들은 피자도 함께 가져갔고, 빵, 고기, 채소를 한꺼번에 먹을 수 있어서 미국인들은 고기와 채소를 얹은 이 납작한 빵을 좋아했다.

➡ _____

_____

25 미국 최초의 피자 가게가 1905년에 문을 열었다.

➡ _____

26 오늘날 피자는 거의 어디에서나 즐길 수 있다.

➡ _____

27 물론, 토핑은 지역에 따라 매우 다양하다.

➡ _____

28 한국인은 불고기를 피자에 얹어 먹기를 좋아하고, 러시아 사람들은 생선과 양파 토핑을 좋아한다.

➡ _____

29 그러나 모든 종류의 피자가 두 가지 사실만큼은 똑같다.

➡ _____

30 모든 피자는 납작한 빵에서 시작하고, 각각은 역사의 한 조각이다.

➡ _____

적중100 plus

1학기 전과정

영어 기출 문제집

적중100

영어 기출 문제집

정답 및 해설

1학기

천재 | 이재영

적중 100

중 3

What Matters to You?

시험대비 실력평가
p.08

01 ④ 02 ② 03 ① 04 ③
05 ⑤ 06 ⑤ 07 ③
08 inventions

01 "온종일 비가 내릴 거야."라는 말에 Really라는 반응은 놀라움을 나타낸다. 자신의 새 비옷을 입을 수 있어 기뻐한다는 것을 알 수 있다.

02 "You can say that again."은 상대의 말에 동의하는 표현이다.

03 "by trading"은 직업을 나타내는 것으로 직업을 통해서 가족을 "부양하다"라고 해야 한다.

04 goods: 상품, 제품

05 ① 동사 rain은 "비가 내리다"의 의미이다. ② "사람을 지루하게 하는"의 의미는 boring이다. ③ delicious는 "맛있는"이라는 뜻이다. ④ agree: 동의하다 ⑤ 동사 like는 "좋아하다"의 뜻이다.

06 chase A away A를 쫓아내다 / take good care of ~ ~을 잘 돌보다

07 "음식을 삼키기 전에 몇 번 물다"는 "음식을 씹다"에 해당한다.

08 many great의 수식을 받는 단어는 명사의 복수형이어야 한다. invent(발명하다)의 명사는 invention(발명, 발명품)이다.

서술형 시험대비
p.09

01 (s)urprising 02 (a)llowance
03 (b)oring 04 (T)hanks to
05 (g)et over / (g)et over / (g)et over
06 (p)uzzled 07 (p)resented 08 (g)ift
08 (1) subjects (2) hurry (3) mind

01 주어진 단어는 동의어 관계이다. boring 지루한 dull 지루한, amazing 놀라운 surprising 놀라운

02 "규칙적이거나 특별한 목적을 위하여 주어지는 상당한 양의 돈"은 "용돈 = allowance"를 가리킨다.

03 주어진 단어는 반의어 관계이다. appear 나타나다, disappear 사라지다 exciting 흥미진진한 boring 지루한

04 paper를 가장 위대한 발명품이라고 생각하는 이유로 "종이 덕택에 우리가 책을 읽을 수 있고, 기록을 남길 수 있는 것"이므로

이유를 나타내는 "~ 덕택에, ~ 때문에"의 의미로 "Thanks to"가 적절하다.

05 • 스트레스를 극복하기 위하여 휴식 기간이 필요하다. • 혼자서 이 어려움을 극복하겠다. • 그가 너의 아픈 마음을 극복하도록 너를 도와 줄 것이다. get over = 극복하다

06 Antonio의 질문에 대하여 the queen이 다시 질문하는 것으로 보아 the queen은 아마 질문의 내용을 몰라서 "어리둥절해하는 =puzzled" 것이라고 할 수 있다.

07 하인이 가지고 온 상자를 "the queen이 Luigi에게 주었다"는 의미로 "present 주다"가 적절하다.

08 present는 "선물"이라는 뜻으로 다른 말로 gift라고 할 수 있다.

09 (1) 과목 = subject (2) 서두르다 = hurry (3) 염두에 두다 = have ~ in mind

Conversation

핵심 Check
p.10~11

1 glad 2 (D) → (B) → (C) → (A)
3 (1) say (2) agree 4 (C) → (A) → (D) → (E) → (B)

04 (C) 감정 표현에 대한 동의, 상대에 대한 질문 → (A) 질문에 대한 대답 → (D) 고등학교 진학에 대한 고민 소개 → (E) 진학할 고등학교에 대한 질문 → (B) 대답으로 진학할 고등학교에 대한 생각 소개'의 순서가 자연스러운 배열이다.

교과서 대화문 익히기

Check(√) True or False
p.12

1 T 2 F 3 T 4 F 5 F

교과서 확인학습
p.14~15

Listen – Listen and Answer – Dialog 1
What, surprise / glad, same / am, last, How / worried / have to, high / Which, have, mind / thinking, painting

Listen – Listen and Answer – Dialog 2
what, going, join / sure, about / join / heard, preparing / need, relax, need / get over / You can say / Why don't / for me, two left

case looks / say that, as / wonder how much / Let,
costs / expensive / agree, works as / buy / delighted,
special / So am

Speak – Talk in pairs.

weather report / going to rain / glad, wear / Good

Speak – Talk in groups.

boring, week / can say / don't think / agree, difficult
subjects

My Speaking Portfolio.

(1) What, free, listen, greatest invention, live
(2) greatest invention, feel good, focus
(3) agree, Thanks to, read, write

Wrap Up - Listening & Speaking ❺

serious, going / practicing / feel about / worried,
make / sure, Break, leg

Wrap Up - Listening & Speaking ❻

heard / What / won, prize / surprising, seems /
walking

시험대비 기본평가   p.16

01 ①　　　　　　　　　　　02 ①
03 You can say that again.　04 ③

01 '비가 올 것이다'라는 말에 '새로운 레인코트'를 입을 수 있다는
　것으로 보아 잘된 상황에서 할 수 있는 대답이 적절하다.

02 말하는 사람이 기쁘다고 감정을 드러내는 것을 보고, 그것에 대
　하여 '좋겠구나.'라고 말하는 것이 자연스럽다.

03 전적으로 동의해. = You can say that again.

04 (B) '연극에 대하여 어떻게 느끼느냐'는 질문에 (C) 실수할까
　봐 걱정이라고 대답하고 (D) 위로가 되는 행운을 빌어준 다음
　(A) 감사를 표시하는 순서가 자연스러운 배열이다.

시험대비 실력평가   p.17~18

01 ③　　02 ③　　03 ②　　04 Me
05 ③　　06 ②　　07 ①　　08 ②
09 ⑤　　10 (C) → (E) → (D) → (A) → (B)

01 대화의 내용으로 보아 소녀는 소년의 말에 동의하는 것으로 연
　결되는 것이 자연스럽다. "Me, neither."는 부정적인 내용에
　동의하여 "나도 마찬가지야."라고 할 때 쓰는 말이다.

02 ③ red phone case가 너무 비싸다고 말한 것은 소년이다. ⑤
　마지막에 "So am I."를 보면 소년도 선물을 사게 된 것을 기뻐
　한다는 것을 알 수 있다.

---

03 두 사람의 대화를 보았을 때, 같은 반에 있게 된 것에 대하여 긍
　정적인 내용이 이어지는 것으로 보아 기뻐하는 것으로 생각할
　수 있다.

04 상대방의 말에 대하여 동의하는 의미로 'Me, too.'가 적절하다.

05 상대의 걱정에 대하여 해결책을 주고, 위로하는 의미로 '너무 심
　각하게 여기지 마.'가 되도록 take가 적절하다.

06 상대의 걱정에 대하여 잘할 것이라고 위로하며 행운을 빌어주는
　말은 'Break a leg.'이다.

07 일기예보를 들었는지 물어보는 질문에 (A) 대답하고, 하루 종
　일 비가 올 것이라고 알려준다. (C) 그 말을 듣고 새 레인코트를
　입을 수 있다고 기뻐하는 것에 대하여 (B) 잘되었다고 대답하는
　것이 자연스러운 순서이다.

08 학교 공부가 많아질 것에 대한 걱정에 (B) 동의하고 고등학교
　진학에 대한 이야기를 한다. (A) 그 이야기를 듣고 어떤 고등학
　교를 갈 것인지 물어보고, (C) 그에 대하여 대답한다.

09 ⑤ 일기예보를 들었는지에 대한 질문을 받고 날씨를 이야기해주
　는 것으로 보아 일기예보를 들었다고 하는 것이 자연스러운 대
　화이다.

10 댄스 동아리 가입을 원한다는 말에 (C) 다른 준비를 한다는 것
　을 들었다는 놀라움을 표시하자 (E) 맞지만 휴식도 필요하다고
　말한다. (D) 그 말에 동의하자 (A) 상대에게도 같이 하자는 권
　유를 하고, (B) 그것에 대한 거부를 표시하는 순서가 되어야 한
　다.

서술형 시험대비   p.19

01 time　　　02 worried　　　03 What
04 (m)istake　05 Break a leg!　06 won
07 He is a walking dictionary.
08 I don't really agree with you.

01 A의 말에 대하여 B가 반대하면서, 서둘러야 한다는 것으로 보
　아 빈칸에는 time이 적절하다.

02 학교 공부가 많아질 것이라는 내용을 원인으로 보았을 때 그 부
　담에 대한 걱정을 나타내는 말이 적절하다.

03 '무슨 일이 있느냐?'의 의미로 주어 역할을 할 수 있는 의문 대명
　사 What이 적절하다.

04 걱정을 한다는 내용에 이어지는 것으로 보아 그 이유가 연극에
　서 실수할까봐 걱정하는 것이라는 것을 알 수 있다.

05 leg를 포함하는 '행운을 빌어!'에 해당하는 표현은 'Break a
　leg!'이다.

06 대화의 내용으로 보아 Mr. Oh는 많은 것을 알고 있으므로 TV
　퀴즈쇼에서 일등상을 수상했다는 것을 알 수 있다.

07 a walking dictionary: 박식한 사람, 만물박사

08 상대의 의견에 동의 여부를 나타낼 때는 agree를 사용한다.

Grammar

p.20~21

핵심 Check

1 (1) what (2) what (3) What (4) that (5) what
2 (1) draw (2) set (3) rising (4) falling (5) making
    (6) to go (7) to take (8) running (9) falling (10) fall

시험대비 기본평가

p.22

01 ③   02 ①
03 (1) He heard many people shout/shouting at the market.
    (2) Yuna saw them play/playing on the ground.
04 ③   05 ③

01 선행사를 포함한 관계대명사 what이 적절하다.
02 동사 ask, allow의 목적격보어는 to부정사이어야 하고, hear, see의 목적격보어는 to가 없는 원형부정사이어야 한다.
03 지각동사 hear, see의 목적격보어는 원형부정사를 쓴다. 진행의 의미를 강조할 때는 목적격보어로 현재분사를 쓸 수 있다.
04 동사 found의 목적어 역할을 하는 명사절, 선행사가 포함된 관계대명사 what이 들어가야 한다.
05 지각동사 listen to의 목적격보어는 동사원형이나 현재분사가 되어야 한다.

시험대비 실력평가

p.23~25

01 ③   02 ③   03 ③   04 ③
05 ④   06 ①   07 ③
08 (1) that (2) what (3) What (4) play (5) running
09 (1) He didn't understand what I explained.
    (2) She didn't like what I had bought for her.
    (3) He showed me what he had painted.
    (4) I heard her cry in the room.
    (5) We expect him to come on time.
10 ③   11 ③, ④, ⑤   12 ③   13 ②
14 ②   15 ⑤   16 ③   17 ①, ③
18 We found what we could enjoy
19 ④   20 ①

01 ③ to meet은 목적을 나타내는 부사적 용법이고, 나머지는 모두 목적격보어로 쓰인 부정사이다.
02 목적격보어에 to부정사가 있는 것으로 보아 지각동사를 쓰기에는 어색하다.
03 동사 told, asked의 목적격보어는 to부정사이어야 하고, saw의 목적격보어는 원형부정사이다.

04 지각동사 hear의 목적격보어는 원형부정사이다.
05 ④ 'she wanted'의 목적어가 필요하므로 목적격 관계대명사이면서 선행사를 포함한 what이 들어가야 한다.
06 ① 지각동사는 목적격보어 자리에 동사원형, 현재분사가 올 수 있다.
07 ③ 지각동사 saw의 목적격보어는 원형부정사이어야 한다.
08 (1) 선행사 the gift가 있으므로 관계대명사 that (2), (3) 선행사가 없을 때는 관계대명사 what이 적절하다. (4), (5) 지각동사의 목적격보어는 원형부정사이다.바
09 (1) '내가 설명해 준 것'은 관계대명사 what을 사용하여 'what I explained'라고 한다. (2) '내가 그녀에게 사 준 것'은 'what I had bought for her'이다. (3) 그가 그린 것 = what he had painted (4) 지각동사의 목적격보어는 원형부정사이다. (5) '기대하다 = expect'는 지각동사가 아니기 때문에 목적격보어로 to있는 부정사를 쓴다.
10 선행사 the building이 있을 때에는 관계대명사 that 또는 which를 쓴다. 선행사가 없을 때는 관계대명사 what을 쓴다.
11 ③ touches → touch[touching] ④ takes → take[taking] ⑤ to sing → sing[singing]
12 중요한 것 = What is important
13 지각동사 listened to의 목적격보어는 원형부정사 또는 현재분사를 쓰고, 일반동사 told의 목적격보어는 to부정사가 적절하다.
14 그가 말하는 것 = what he said
15 ⑤ 동사 order의 목적격보어는 to부정사가 되어야 한다.
16 ③ 선행사가 없는 명사절의 관계대명사는 what이다.
17 ①과 ③은 명사절로 선행사가 포함된 관계대명사 what이 적절하고, ②, ④, ⑤는 사물을 선행사로 하는 관계대명사 which 또는 that이 들어가야 한다.
18 우리가 즐길 수 있는 것 = what we could enjoy
19 지각동사 heard의 목적격보어는 원형부정사가 되어야 한다.
20 선행사를 포함하고 명사절을 유도하는 것은 관계대명사 what이다.

서술형 시험대비

p.26~27

01 (1) What surprised me was his rude answer.
    (2) He told me what he had heard at school.
    (3) You have to be responsible for what you are saying.
    (4) We saw him build/building the house last summer.
    (5) She asked me to open the door.
    (6) She heard us go out of the house.
    (7) We will give you what he brought to us.

02 (1) I heard him talk/talking on the phone.

   (2) She felt the man pull/pulling her by the hand.

   (3) They expected him to be quiet during the class

   (4) What is important is to finish the work before dinner.

03 (1) ③, She heard the child cry[crying].

   (2) ⓔ, They saw him wearing that hat.

04 advised me to be satisfied with what I had

05 She watched them playing[play] soccer.

06 (1) drawing (2) what (3) that (4) to exercise

   (5) walk[walking]

07 (1) I watched him stop at the traffic light.

   (2) I saw him swimming in the pool

   (3) My mother heard him laugh loudly at the table.

   (4) I felt her push me on the back.

   (5) I felt him pulling my hand.

08 (1) watched her brother cook

   (2) eat what she cooked

   (3) heard his mother open the window

   (4) read what she had sent to me

09 what

---

01 (1) 나를 놀라게 한 것 = what surprised me (2) 그가 학교에서 들은 것 = what he had heard at school (3) 네가 말하는 것 = what you are saying (4), (6) 지각동사의 목적격보어는 원형부정사를 쓰고, (5) 동사 ask의 목적격보어는 to부정사를 써야 한다. (7) 그가 우리에게 가지고 온 것 = what he brought to us

02 (1), (2) 지각동사의 목적격보어는 원형부정사나 현재분사이어야 한다. (3) 동사 expect의 목적격보어는 to부정사가 되어야 한다. (4) 선행사를 포함하는 관계대명사는 what이다.

03 ⓒ 지각동사의 목적격보어는 원형부정사 또는 현재분사 ⓔ 지각동사의 인칭대명사 목적어는 목적격을 사용하여야 한다.

04 advise는 'advise+목적어+목적격보어(to부정사)'로 써서 '~에게 …하라고 조언하다'를 나타낸다. '~에 만족하다'는 be satisfied with이므로 to be satisfied with ~가 된다. '내가 가진 것'은 what을 사용하여 what I had라고 영작한다.

05 지각동사의 목적격보어는 동사원형 또는 현재분사가 되도록 한다.

06 (1) 지각동사의 목적격보어로 원형부정사나 현재분사 (2) 선행사를 포함하는 관계대명사는 what (3) the bag을 선행사로 하는 관계대명사는 that (4) 동사 advise의 목적격보어는 to부정사 (5) 지각동사 heard의 목적격보어는 원형부정사나 현재분사

07 (1), (2), (3), (4), (5) 지각동사의 목적격보어를 원형부정사나 현재분사로 하는 문장 형태를 만든다.

08 (1), (3) 지각동사의 목적격보어는 원형부정사가 되고 (2), (4)

명사절을 유도하는 관계대명사로 선행사를 포함하는 것은 what이다.

09 선행사를 포함하고 명사절을 유도하는 관계대명사는 what이다.

Reading

확인문제   p.28

1 T 2 F 3 T 4 F 5 T 6 F

확인문제   p.29

1 F 2 T 3 T 4 F 5 T 6 F

확인문제   p.30

1 T 2 F 3 F 4 T 5 T 6 F

교과서 확인학습 A   p.31~32

01 Priceless

02 an honest merchant

03 to support his family

04 filled, with

05 traded, for, for

06 Thanks to, what

07 had dinner with

08 was served, appeared, chased them away

09 greatly surprised

10 Are there no cats

11 looked puzzled

12 she asked

13 said to himself, What, not, but

14 brought, from, let them run

15 What, run

16 was filled with

17 Back, good fortune

18 the richest merchant, jealous

19 worthless

20 what

21 I'm sure

22 packed, with, works

23 took, to

24 a good friend of Antonio's

25 invited, to

26 sitting, presented, with, again and again

27 repay, with

28 whisper

29 excited, hopeful

30 more jewels than

31 presented, to

32 speechless

33 kitten

34 priceless

35 In return for, what is most valuable

36 far more than

37 look pleased

38 right thing to do

39 richer

40 a wiser one

1 A Priceless Gift

2 Long ago, an honest merchant lived in Genoa, Italy.

3 His name was Antonio, and he went to different places to support his family by trading.

4 One day, he filled his ship with goods and visited a faraway island.

5 There he traded tools for spices and books for nuts.

6 Thanks to Antonio, the islanders could get what they needed.

7 One night, Antonio had dinner with the island's queen at her palace.

8 When dinner was served, rats appeared, and some servants chased them away with sticks.

9 Antonio was greatly surprised that there were rats in the palace.

10 He asked, "Are there no cats on this island?"

11 The queen looked puzzled.

12 "What is a cat?" she asked.

13 The merchant said to himself, "What the islanders here need is not tools or books, but cats."

14 He brought two cats from his ship and let them run free.

15 "What amazing animals!" cried the queen when she saw all the rats run away.

16 She gave Antonio a chest that was filled with jewels.

17 Back in Italy, Antonio told his friends about his good fortune.

18 Luigi, the richest merchant in Genoa, heard the story and was jealous.

19 "Cats are worthless," Luigi thought.

20 "I'll bring the queen what is really valuable.

21 I'm sure that the queen will give me more jewels."

22 Luigi packed his ship with wonderful paintings and other works of art.

23 He took the gifts to the island.

24 To get a chance to meet the queen, he told the islanders a lie that he was a good friend of Antonio's.

25 When the queen heard about Luigi, she invited him to her palace for dinner.

26 Before sitting down at the table, Luigi presented the queen with all his gifts, and the queen thanked him again and again.

27 "I'll repay you with a priceless gift," said the queen.

28 Luigi watched the queen whisper in a servant's ear.

29 He became excited and hopeful.

30 He was sure that he would receive more jewels than Antonio.

31 After a while, the servant returned with a box, and the queen presented it to Luigi.

32 When Luigi opened the box, he was speechless.

33 There was a kitten in the box.

34 "Antonio gave us the priceless cats, and we now have some kittens," said the queen.

35 "In return for the wonderful gifts you gave us, we want to give you what is most valuable to us."

36 Luigi realized that, in the queen's mind, the kitten was worth far more than all the jewels in the world.

37 He tried to look pleased with the gift.

38 He knew that was the right thing to do.

39 Luigi did not return home a richer man.

40 But he was surely a wiser one.

---

01 ③	02 ①	03 ④	04 What
05 ④	06 ①	07 ⑤	
08 a good friend of Antonio's			09 ③
10 what is most valuable to us			11 ④
12 (A) what (B) other (C) Antonio's			13 ④
14 ③		15 ②	
16 there was a kitten in the box			
17 In spite of → In return for			18 one
19 (A) what (B) more (C) pleased			20 ②
21 was served		22 ④	23 rats
24 ③	25 ③ / ①, ④ / ②, ⑤		
26 She gave Antonio a chest filled with jewels.			
27 ④	28 ③	29 ②	

01 ⓐ fill A with B: A를 B로 채우다, ⓑ trade A for B: A와 B를 교환하다

02 (A)와 ①은 부사적 용법, ②와 ⑤는 형용사적 용법, ③과 ④는 명사적 용법

03 Antonio가 여왕과 저녁식사를 한 장소는 '그의 배'가 아니라 '여왕의 궁전'이었다.

04 ⓐ에는 관계대명사 What, ⓑ에는 감탄문을 이끄는 What(단수 가산명사를 이끌 때에는 부정관사를 수반함)이 적절하다.

05 이 글은 '섬사람들이 필요로 하는 것은 고양이라고 생각하고,

Antonio가 고양이를 선물하는' 내용의 글이므로, 제목으로는 ④번 '그들이 정말 필요한 것은 고양이다!'가 적절하다.

06 ①의 his는 Luigi가 아니라 Antonio를 지칭한다.

07 ⓐ와 ⑤: 가치 없는, ① 대단히 귀중한, ②, ③, ④: 귀중한

08 한정사(관사/소유격/지시형용사)끼리 중복해서 쓸 수 없으므로 이중소유격(of+소유대명사/~'s)으로 쓰는 것이 적절하다.

09 present A to B: B에게 A를 주다

10 선행사를 포함하는 관계대명사 what을 써서 영작하면 된다

11 Antonio가 여왕에게 고양이를 몇 마리 줬는지는 알 수 없다. ① More jewels than Antonio received. ② A kitten. ③ He was speechless. ⑤ Because she wanted to give him what was most valuable to them in return for the wonderful gifts he gave them.

12 (A) '나는 여왕에게 정말로 귀중한 것을 가지고 갈 거야'라고 해야 하므로 선행사를 포함한 관계대명사 what이 적절하다. (B) another 뒤에는 단수 명사를 써야 하므로 other가 적절하다. (C) 한정사(관사/소유격/지시형용사)끼리 중복해서 쓸 수 없어서 이중소유격(of+소유대명사/~'s)으로 써야 하므로 Antonio's가 적절하다.

13 ④ invite: 초대하다, visit: 방문하다, ① envious: 부러워하는, 질투하는(= jealous), ② pack A with B: A를 B로 가득[빽빽히] 채우다, fill A with B: A를 B로 채우다, ③ opportunity: 기회, ⑤ again and again = over and over: 몇 번이고, 되풀이해서

14 Luigi는 Antonio의 친한 친구라고 거짓말을 했다.

15 뒤 문장에 '그는 Antonio보다 많은 보물을 받게 될 것이라고 확신했다'는 내용이 이어지므로 빈칸에는 '흥분된'과 '기대에 부푼'이 적절하다. ① nervous: 초조한, upset: 속상한, ③ hopeless: 가망 없는, 절망적인, ⑤ disappointed: 실망한

16 Antonio가 받았던 것보다 더 많은 보석 대신 '상자 안에 새끼 고양이가 들어 있었기' 때문이다.

17 '당신이 우리에게 준 멋진 선물에 보답하는 뜻에서'라고 해야 하므로, In spite of를 In return for로 고쳐야 한다. in spite of: ~에도 불구하고, in return for: ~의 답례로서

18 man을 대신하여 one을 쓰는 것이 적절하다. one은 앞에 이미 언급했거나 상대방이 알고 있는 사람이나 사물을 가리킬 때, 명사의 반복을 피하기 위해 쓸 수 있다.

19 (A) 관계대명사 앞에 선행사가 없으므로 what이 적절하다. (B) 여왕의 생각에는 세상의 온갖 보석보다 새끼 고양이가 훨씬 '더 가치 있다'고 해야 하므로 more가 적절하다. (C) 감정을 나타내는 동사는 사람을 수식할 때 보통 과거분사를 써야 하므로 pleased가 적절하다.

20 원치 않았던 선물을 받았지만 내색하지 않고 새끼 고양이를 선물로 준 여왕의 마음을 헤아린 것으로 보아 thoughtful(사려 깊은)이 알맞다.

21 '식사가 나왔을 때'라고 해야 하므로, 수동태로 쓰는 것이 적절하다.

22 Antonio가 공구를 향신료와, 그리고 책을 견과류와 바꾸어 준 덕분에 섬사람들은 필요한 것을 얻을 수 있었다고 해야 하므로 ④번이 적절하다.

23 '쥐'를 가리킨다.

24 '여기 섬사람들이 필요로 한 것은 공구나 책이 아니라 고양이야'라고 하는 것이 적절하다. ① either A or B: A이거나 B인(A나 B 둘 중 하나), ② neither A nor B: A도 B도 아닌, ③ not A but B: A가 아니라 B, ④ both A and B: A와 B 둘 다, ⑤ at once A and B: A하기도 (하고) B하기도 하다(A이면서 동시에 B)

25 (A)와 ③은 의문대명사 What, (B)와 ①, ④는 관계대명사 What, (C)와 ②, ⑤는 감탄문을 이끄는 What(단수 가산명사를 이끌 때에는 부정관사를 수반함.)

26 주격 관계대명사 that과 be동사인 was를 생략할 수 있다.

27 ④ 'Luigi는 더 부유한 사람이 되어 집으로 돌아오지 않았다. 하지만 그는 분명히 더 현명한 사람이 되었다'고 해야 하므로, ⓐ에는 richer, ⓑ에는 wiser가 적절하다.

28 very는 원급을 강조하는 말이며, 비교급을 강조할 수 없다.

29 (B)와 ②, ⑤는 형용사적 용법, ①, ④는 부사적 용법, ③은 명사적 용법

서술형 시험대비
p.40~41

01 to get **02** were appeared → appeared

03 (A) spices (B) nuts

04 ⓐ I'll bring what is really valuable to the queen.
ⓑ the queen will give more jewels to me

05 he was a good friend of Antonio's

06 he sat **07** (A) greatly (B) puzzled (C) himself

08 What the islanders here need is not tools or books, but cats.

09 How **10** was full of **11** with it

12 worthless → priceless 또는 valuable **13** a kitten

14 (A) wonderful gifts[presents] (B) most valuable

01 enable+목적어+to부정사: ~이 …할 수 있게 하다, 가능하게 하다, A+can+동사+thanks to B = B+enable+A+to부정사

02 appear는 자동사이므로 수동태로 쓸 수 없는 동사이다.

03 섬사람들은 Antonio와 '향신료'를 공구와 '견과류'를 책과 교환함으로써 그들이 필요로 하는 것을 얻을 수 있었다. trade A for

7

B: A와 B를 교환하다

04 bring과 give는 to를 사용하여 3형식으로 고친다.

05 '그는 Antonio의 친한 친구이다'라는 것을 가리킨다.

06 sitting을 '주어+동사'로 바꿔 쓸 수 있다.

07 (A) 형용사 'surprised'를 수식하므로 부사 greatly가 적절하다. (B) 감정을 나타내는 동사는 사람을 수식할 때 보통 과거분사를 써야 하므로 puzzled가 적절하다. (C) 주어와 목적어가 같을 때는 재귀대명사를 써야 하므로 himself가 적절하다.

08 관계대명사 'What'을 보충하여 등위 상관접속사 not A but B(A가 아니라 B)를 사용하여 배열하는 것이 적절하다.

09 What+(a/an)+형용사+명사+주어+동사! = How+형용사/부사+주어+동사!

10 be filled with = be full of: ~로 가득 차다

11 present+사물+to+사람 = present+사람+with+사물.

12 Antonio가 우리에게 '매우 귀한' 고양이들을 주었다고 해야 하므로 priceless 또는 valuable이 적절하다. priceless: 대단히 귀중한, worthless: 가치 없는

13 '새끼 고양이'를 가리킨다.

14 Luigi는 여왕에게 '멋진 선물'을 주고 Antonio보다 더 많은 보석을 받을 것이라고 확신했지만, 여왕은 새끼 고양이가 그들에게 '가장 값지기' 때문에 Luigi에게 보답으로 새끼 고양이를 주었다.

하다.

04 'tell the time'은 '시간을 알다'의 의미이다.

05 월요일이 가장 지루한 요일이라는 주장에 대하여 목요일이 가장 지루한 요일이라고 하는 것으로 보아 동의하지 않는 의미가 되어야 한다.

06 일기예보를 들었는지 물어보는 말에 (B) 들어서 날씨를 알려주고 (A) 비가 올 것이라는 내용을 듣고 기뻐하는 것에 대하여 (C) 좋겠다고 말하는 순서의 배열이 자연스럽다.

07 '살아있는 사전, 만물박사'의 의미는 'a walking dictionary'이다.

08 ④ 일기 예보에서 하루 종일 비가 올 것이라는 내용을 듣고 새로운 레인코트를 입을 기회를 가지게 된 것을 기뻐하는 내용이 자연스럽다.

09 가격에 대한 대답이 이어지는 것으로 보아 가격이 얼마인지 물어본다는 의미로 '궁금해 하다'의 의미인 wonder가 적절하다.

10 '나도 마찬가지야.'에 해당하는 세 단어는 'So am I.'이다.

11 그들의 어머니가 생일 선물로 무엇을 원하는지 알 수 없다.

12 그녀가 만든 것 = what she had made

13 선행사를 포함하는 관계대명사는 what이고, 지각동사의 목적격보어는 원형부정사를 쓰는 것이 적절하다.

14 관계대명사 what은 종속절에서 주어, 목적어 역할을 한다. ③ 'he had some time to rest'는 주어와 목적어가 있는 형태로 관계대명사 what을 쓸 수 없다.

15 ④ 지각동사 saw의 목적격보어는 to 없는 원형부정사가 와야 한다.

16 동사 listened to의 목적격보어는 원형부정사가 와야 한다.다.

17 동사 tell의 목적격보어는 to부정사가 적절하다.

18 (1), (3) 선행사가 없는 관계대명사는 what이고, (2), (5) 지각동사의 목적격보어는 원형부정사 또는 현재분사이다. (4) 동사 ask의 목적격보어는 to부정사이다.

19 ① 지각동사 heard의 목적격보어는 원형부정사이다.

20 선행사가 없는 관계대명사로 '하는 것'의 의미를 가지는 것은 관계대명사 what이다.

영역별 핵심문제   p.43~47

01 ②	02 ⑤	03 ⑤	04 ①
05 ①	06 ②	07 ①	08 ④
09 ①	10 So am I.	11 ④	12 ⑤
13 ③	14 ③	15 ④	16 ③
17 ③	18 (1) what (2) swimming (3) what (4) to take (5) study	19 ①	20 ④
21 ②, ④, ⑤	22 ②, ⑤	23 the things which[that]	
24 ①	25 ③, ⑤ / ①, ②, ④	26 ③	
27 ②	28 ①, ②	29 aren't you	
30 (A)basketball shoes (B) a writer		31 ④	

01 '무엇인가를 붙잡기 위하여 빠르게 따라가다'는 '추적하다 = chase'에 해당한다.

02 B가 애니메이션 고등학교를 생각 중이라고 대답하는 것으로 보아 "어떤 종류의 고등학교에 가기를 원하는지" 묻는 말로 "생각하다, 마음에 두다, 염두에 두다"의 의미로 "have in mind"가 적절하다.

03 상인은 물건을 사고파는 사람이므로 '거래하다 = trade'가 적절

21 ⓐ와 ②, ④, ⑤는 동명사, ①, ③은 현재분사

22 thanks to = because of = owing to = due to: ~ 때문에
② instead of: ~ 대신에, ⑤ in spite of:~에도 불구하고

23 관계대명사 what은 the thing(s) which[that]으로 바꿔 쓸 수 있다. 지금은 교환하는 물건들이 여러 개이므로 선행사를 복수(the things)로 쓰는 것이 적절하다.

24 사역동사 let+목적어+원형부정사, 지각동사 saw+목적어+원형부정사(running도 가능함)

25 (A)와 ③, ⑤: 원인과 이유를 나타내는 부사절을 이끄는 접속사, (B)와 ①, ②, ④: 주격 관계대명사

26 '섬사람들이 공구나 책을 필요로 하지 않은 것'이 아니라, 'Antonio가 섬사람들이 필요로 하는 것은 공구나 책이 아니라 고양이라고' 혼잣말을 한 것이다.

27 ⓐ와 ②: (문학·예술 따위의) 작품, 저작물, 제작품, ① (기계의) 움직이는 부분, 장치, ③ 일하다, ④ 공장, 제작소, ⑤ (약 따위가) 작용하다, 듣다

28 ⓑ와 ①, ②는 형용사적 용법, ③, ⑤는 명사적 용법, ④는 부사적 용법

29 be동사가 있으므로, be동사를 사용하여 부가의문문을 만드는 것이 적절하다.

30 지훈이는 '농구 신발'이 농구 동아리에서 많은 친구들을 사귀도록 도와주었기 때문에, 그리고 그가 좋아하는 책이 '작가'가 되고 싶은 꿈을 그에게 주었기 때문에 그 두 가지를 타임캡슐에 넣었다.

31 (A)의 rats가 (C)의 rats를 가리키므로 (C) 다음에 (A)가 이어지고 (B)의 질문은 (A)의 마지막 질문에 대한 반문이므로 (A) 다음에 (B)가 와야 한다. 그러므로 (C)-(A)-(B)의 순서가 적절하다.

단원별 예상문제
p.48~51

01 ②	02 ④	03 (c)hest	04 (g)oods
05 ②	06 ①	07 (p)riceless	08 ⑤
09 ③	10 ④	11 Dancing is not for me.	
12 ①	13 ②	14 ⑤	15 ⑤
16 ②	17 ③	18 chased	19 ②
20 tools, books		21 ⑤	
22 two cats	23 (A) the rats	(B) jewels	
24 ③, ⑤	25 ②	26 ④	
27 because[as]		28 ④	

01 time capsule에는 원하는 물건을 담아서 보관하는 것이므로 '포함하다 = include'가 적절하다.

02 take good care of ~ = ~을 잘 돌보다

03 '물건을 옮기거나 보관하기 위하여 사용하는 크고 튼튼한 상자'는 chest이다.

04 '팔기 위하여 생산되는 물품'은 '상품=goods'이다.

05 '하루 종일 비가 올 것이다.'는 '일기예보를 듣고 대답하는 말이다.

06 'Don't take it so hard.'는 걱정할 때 위로하는 말이다.

07 delighted와 pleased는 비슷한 뜻이다. valuable과 유사한 의미로 priceless가 적절하다.

08 춤을 잘 추지 못해서 댄스 동아리에 가입하고 싶지 않다는 내용이 적절하다. have two left feet = 동작이 서툴다

09 Mr. Oh에 대하여 무슨 일이 있는지 묻는 질문에 (B) 퀴즈에서 상을 받았다는 소개를 하고, (C) 그가 많은 것을 알기 때문에 놀랄 일이 아니라는 말에 (A) 동의한다는 말을 하는 것이 자연스러운 배열이다.

10 상대방의 의견을 물어보거나 상대방에게 권하거나 제안하는 표현은 'How about ~?'이다.

11 '춤을 추는 것은 나와 어울리지 않아.'는 'Dancing is not for me.'이다.

12 ① 댄스 클럽에 가입하기를 원하는 사람은 소라이다.

13 지각동사 listen to의 목적격보어는 원형부정사 또는 현재분사이다.

14 선행사 the plan이 있는 경우 관계대명사는 that 또는 which이고, 선행사가 없는 경우의 관계대명사는 what이다.

15 지각동사 saw의 목적격보어는 동사원형이 되어야 한다.

16 전치사 with의 목적어 역할을 하는 명사절을 유도하며, 선행사가 없는 관계대명사 what이 들어가야 한다.

17 지각동사 saw의 목적격보어는 원형부정사이다.

18 chase: 쫓다, 쫓아내다, 어떤 것을 잡거나 닿기 위해 빨리 뒤쫓거나 따라가다, chase away: ~을 쫓아내다

19 fill A with B: A를 B로 채우다, pack A with B: A를 B로 가득[빽빽히] 채우다, ③ pick: 고르다, 선택하다, ④ gather: 모으다

20 '공구'와 '책'을 가리킨다.

21 전반부의 The queen looked puzzled.에서 'puzzled'를, 하반부의 What amazing animals!에서 'amazed'를 찾을 수 있다. ① bored: 지루한, ② nervous: 초조한, ③ confused: 혼란스러워 하는, ⑤ puzzled: 어리둥절해하는, amazed: 놀란

22 '고양이 두 마리'를 가리킨다.

23 Antonio가 배에서 가져온 고양이 두 마리가 자유롭게 돌아다니자 모든 '쥐들'이 도망치는 것을 여왕이 보았을 때, 그녀는 Antonio의 도움에 대해 보답하는 뜻으로 '보석'이 가득한 상자를 그에게 주었다. in return for: ~의 답례로서

24 지각동사 watched+목적어+원형부정사 또는 현재분사

25 이 글은 'Luigi가 많은 보석을 선물로 받을 것을 기대했다가 새끼 고양이를 선물로 받았다'는 내용의 글이므로, 제목으로는 '불쌍한 Luigi의 실현되지 못한 기대'가 적절하다.

26 Antonio가 언제 여왕에게 귀중한 고양이들을 주었는지는 대답할 수 없다. ① When he watched the queen whisper in a servant's ear. ② No. ③ No. ⑤ A kitten.

27 because of+명사구, because+주어+동사. because of일 때는 she drank가 수식하니까 dirty water 앞에 the를 붙였지만, because[as]로 고치면 수식하는 말이 없어지므로 dirty water

앞에 the를 생략하는 것이 적절하다.

28 Isabel은 그것을 어디나 가지고 다닌다.

01 (1) left   (2) support   (3) Thanks   (4) servants
02 (s)ervant
03 I'm a little worried that there'll[there will] be more schoolwork.
04 So am I
05 (1) I heard the rain fall[falling] on the window.
    (2) We saw him kicking the ball on the ground.
    (3) She couldn't understand what I told her.
06 (h)urry   07 certain, surely
08 to the queen
09 (A) merchant   (B) to support   (C) goods
10 Thanks to Antonio, the islanders could get what they needed.
11 chased away them → chased them away

01 (1) 동작이 서투르다 = have two left feet (2) 부양하다 = support (3) ~ 덕택에 = thanks to (4) 하인 = servant
02 '집을 청소하기, 요리하기, 손님맞이 등을 위하여 돈을 받는 사람'은 '하인 = servant'이다.
03 좀 = a little, 학교 공부가 더 많을 것이다. = there will be more schoolwork
04 Me, too.: 나도 그래.(=So am I.)
05 지각동사의 목적격보어는 원형부정사 또는 현재분사이고 선행사가 포함된 관계대명사는 what이다.
06 간식을 먹을 시간이 있다는 말에 동의하지 않는 것으로 보아 시간이 없어서 서둘러야 한다는 것을 알 수 있다.
07 I'm sure = It is certain = surely
08 present+사람+with+사물= present+사물+to+사람
09 (A) Antonio는 상품을 교역하는 사람이므로, '상인 (merchant)'이라고 하는 것이 적절하다. merchant: 상인, (특히) 무역상, consumer: 소비자, (B) 가족을 '부양하기 위해서'라고 해야 하므로 to support가 적절하다. (C) '상품'이라고 해야 하므로 goods가 적절하다. goods: 상품, 제품, good: 선(善); 좋은
10 thanks to: ~ 덕분에
11 이어동사에서 목적어가 인칭대명사일 때는 목적어를 동사와 부사 사이에 써야 하므로, chased them away로 고치는 것이 적절하다.

|모범답안|

01 two cats, a chest filled with jewels, queen, presented a kitten to Luigi
02 (1) gimbap   (2) To see[Seeing] movies
    (3) you told me
03 (A) a writer   (B) basketball shoes
    (C) many friends   (D) favorite book
    (E) a writer

01 Antonio는 여왕에게 고양이를 주고 보석 상자를 받았지만, Luigi는 비싼 선물을 주고 새끼 고양이를 받았다.

01 (s)urprising   02 (e)xclude
03 (1) himself   (2) (c)hest   (3) (p)acked
04 ③   05 (m)erchant   06 ①
07 ③   08 ②   09 feet   10 ③
11 ⑤   12 So   13 ③   14 ①
15 ①   16 ④   17 ①   18 ③
19 (1) what   (2) that   (3) talk   (4) taking   20 ②
21 ③   22 ③   23 chest
24 (A) worthless   (B) valuable   (C) priceless
25 ①, ④   26 ②, ⑤

01 주어진 단어는 유사한 의미를 가지는 단어로 amazing과 유사한 의미는 surprising이다.
02 두 단어의 관계는 반의어이다. delighted 기쁜, sorrowful 슬픈 include 포함하다 exclude 제외하다
03 (1) 혼잣말을 하다 = say to oneself (2) 상자 = chest, box (3) 채우다 = pack
04 'Don't take it so hard.'는 '너무 심각하게 여기지 마.'에 해당하는 의미이다.
05 '대량으로 물건을 사고파는 사람'은 '상인 = merchant'이다.
06 valuable 소중한 priceless 매우 가치 있는 valueless 가치 없는 worthless 가치 없는 expensive 비싼 terrible 지독한
07 '너무 비싸다'는 말에 (B) 동의하지 않는 내용과 새로운 기능을 언급하고 (C) 그렇다면 그것을 사자고 동의하고 (A) 거기에 동의하는 내용과 구입 결정의 순서가 자연스러운 배열이다.
08 쉬는 시간을 가지는 것은 스트레스를 극복하는 것이므로 '극복하다'의 의미로 'get over'가 되어야 한다.

09 '움직임이 서툴다'의 의미로 'have two left feet'이 적절하다.

10 소라의 질문에 "I'm not sure."라고 대답하는 것으로 보아 Oliver는 가입할 동아리를 정하지 못했다는 것을 알 수 있다.

11 이어지는 대화에서 가격에 대한 정보가 주어지는 것으로 보아 앞에서 가격에 대한 궁금증을 나타내는 표현이 있었음을 알 수 있다.

12 '~도 마찬가지이다.'의 의미로 동의를 나타낼 때는 'So+동사+주어.'의 표현이 된다.

13 ① Jimin은 전화기 케이스가 좋다고 동의한다. ② 싼 것을 구한다는 내용은 없다. ③ 소년의 말에 동의하지 않는 것으로 보아 소녀는 케이스가 너무 비싸다고 생각하지 않는다. ④, ⑤ 소년은 케이스 구입에 동의한다.

14 동사 told의 직접목적어가 되는 명사절을 유도하는 것은 관계대명사 what이다.

15 선행사 the picture가 있을 때 관계대명사는 that/which이다.

16 동사 expect의 목적격보어는 to부정사이다. arrive를 to arrive라고 해야 한다.

17 지각동사 heard의 목적격보어는 원형부정사가 되어야 한다.

18 ③ the letter라는 선행사가 있을 때는 관계대명사 that 또는 which를 써야 한다.

19 (1) 선행사를 포함하는 관계대명사는 what (2) the money를 선행사로 하는 관계대명사는 that (3), (4) 지각동사 heard, noticed의 목적격보어는 원형부정사

20 선행사를 포함하는 관계대명사 what이 이끄는 절이 '~하는 것'이라는 의미로 쓰여 문장에서 목적어 역할을 하고 있다.

21 Antonio가 머나먼 섬을 방문하는 데 얼마나 오래 걸렸는지는 대답할 수 없다. ① He lived in Genoa, Italy. ② He supported his family by trading. ④ He traded tools for spices and books for nuts. ⑤ They appeared when dinner was served.

22 ③번 다음 문장의 amazing animals에 주목한다. 주어진 문장의 two cats를 가리키므로 ③번이 적절하다.

23 chest: (보통 나무로 만든) 궤[상자], 물건을 보관하기 위해 사용되는 크고 무거운 상자

24 (A) 고양이는 '쓸모없다'고 해야 하므로 worthless가 적절하다. worthless: 가치 없는, priceless: 대단히 귀중한, (B) 나는 여왕에게 '값진' 것을 가져다 줄 것이라고 해야 하므로 valuable이 적절하다. valueless: 가치 없는, (C) '대단히 귀중한' 선물이라고 해야 하므로 priceless가 적절하다.

25 ⓐ와 ②, ③, ⑤는 부사적 용법, ① 명사적 용법, ④ 형용사적 용법

26 ⓑ와 ②, ⑤번: 동격의 접속사, ① 목적격 관계대명사, ③ 지시부사, ④ = the climate, [반복의 대명사로서] (…의) 그것

11

Lesson 2

Animals, Big and Small

01 ④   02 ⑤   03 ②   04 ①
05 ③   06 ④   07 ①
08 difference(s)

01 '꿀을 생산하기 위하여 벌이 길러지는 구조물'은 벌집이다.

02 '꿈에 대하여 말해 주겠니?'에 이어서 꿈에 대한 설명이 이어지는 것으로 보아 긍정적인 대답이 되도록 해야 한다.

03 'It's great.'에 이어지는 긍정적인 내용이 되어야 한다.

04 'Many of my friends have lost their homes.'를 통해서 서식지가 없어지는 파괴의 내용이 되어야 한다는 것을 알 수 있다.

05 'I was almost hit.'을 통해서 길을 건널 때 차량을 피하는 것이 어려움을 알 수 있다. 차량이 서둘러 지나가는 것을 나타내어 '서두르는'의 'in a hurry'가 되는 것이 적절하다.

06 ④ come out of nowhere: 느닷없이 나타나다

07 guess는 '추측하다'의 의미로 estimate와 비슷한 의미이다.

08 소유격에 이어지는 명사가 있어야 하므로 differ의 명사 difference가 적절하다.

서술형 시험대비 p.63

01 (r)egularly   02 (c)ontain
03 (A)rctic
04 (1) (t)errible   (2) lost   (3) (t)ell   (4) (n)owhere
05 (1) (t)breathe   (2) shy   (3) after   (4) common
06 (1) (k)eep, (e)ye, (o)n   (2)(h)as, (l)ong, (f)ace
07 (s)ensitive

01 주어진 단어는 반의어의 관계이다. defend 방어하다 attack 공격하다 irregularly 불규칙적으로 regularly 규칙적으로

02 hold는 '수용하다'의 의미로 '포함하다, 담다'의 의미에 해당하는 contain이 적절하다.

03 '지구의 가장 북쪽과 관련이 있는'은 '북극의'에 해당하는 영어 설명이다.

04 (1) 끔찍한, 지독한 = terrible (2) 길을 잃다 = get lost (3) 분간하다 = tell (4) 느닷없이 나오다 = come out of nowhere

05 (1) 공기가 신선하여 등산하던 사람들이 천천히 숨을 쉬기 시작했다. 숨을 쉬다: breathe (2) 초등학교에 친구가 별로 없었던 이유는 내성적이어서였다. 내성적인: shy (3) 테레사 수녀는 가난한 사람을 돌보며 평생을 보냈다. 돌보다 look after (4) 세탁

기는 집에서 흔히 보는 기계이다. 흔한: common

06 (1) keep an eye on 지켜보다 (2) have a long face 표정이 우울하다

07 내용상 '개는 사람보다 냄새에 예민하다'가 되어야 한다. 예민한 = sensitive

교과서
Conversation

핵심 Check p.64~65

1 (1) Which   (2) prefer   2 (B) → (D) → (C) → (A)
3 tell / tell   4 (C) → (D) → (A) → (E) → (B)

04 (C) 새가 어려움을 겪는 것에 대하여 더 많은 설명을 요청한다. → (D) 새들이 어려움을 겪는 이유를 설명해 준다. → (A) 새들이 어려움을 겪는 것에 대한 설명을 듣고 상황을 이해하고 도움을 줄 방법을 묻는다. → (E) 새들에게 도움을 줄 방법을 설명해 준다. → (B) 도움을 줄 방법들에 대하여 칭찬한다.

교과서 대화문 익히기

Check(√) True or False p.66

1 F   2 T   3 T   4 F   5 F

교과서 확인학습 p.68~69

Listen – Listen and Answer – Dialog 1
how / great, having / Me, show, great / By, decide / yet, Which, think, better / hiking, see wild, insects / join, birds / heard, guide

Listen – Listen and Answer – Dialog 2
look, chestnut, woods / tell, how old / about / ten times / beehive up / guess, bees live / guess, big enough, hold / Unbelievable

Listen More - Listen and choose.
take, look / What, for / trying, choose, story / What's, about / tell, more about / endangered animals, Arctic / sounds / Which picture / showing, skinny

Speak – Talk in groups.
like better / like, friendly, How about / Me, much cleaner

대한 추가적인 설명을 해주고 (A) 마침내 무엇에 대한 설명인지 알아듣는 순서가 되어야 한다.

06 이어지는 대화를 보아 장기 자랑을 재미있어 하는 내용이 되도록 해야 한다. have a lot of fun = 매우 재미있게 보내다.

07 상대방의 말에 동의해서 '나도 그래.'라고 할 때는 'So+동사 + 주어.'를 사용한다. 앞에 나온 문장이 be동사를 사용하고 있어서 so 다음에는 be동사를 써야 한다.

08 그런데 = by the way, ~에 대하여 결정하다 = decide on, 오후 프로그램 = the afternoon program

09 "I'll join you."라고 한 것은 소년이었기 때문에 "소년이 소녀를 따라간다"라고 해야 한다.

10 소년이 수영하러 가는 것을 좋아하는 지는 나오지 않았다.

시험대비 기본평가
p.70

01 ④   02 ③   03 ①   04 ②

01 'Me, too.'라고 동의하는 대답을 했기 때문에 어젯밤의 장기 자랑에 대한 긍정적인 대답이 되도록 하여야 한다.

02 'It's about 150 years old.'라는 대답으로 보아 chestnut tree에 대한 설명 'This is the oldest tree in these woods.'에 대한 추가적인 내용을 묻는 질문이 되어야 한다.

03 상대방의 의견을 물어보는 표현이 되어야 한다.

04 'I like cats better.'에 대하여 동의하는 입장이기 때문에 고양이의 장점에 대한 설명이 이어지는 것이 적절하다.

시험대비 실력평가
p.71~72

01 ①   02 ⑤   03 ②   04 ⑤
05 ③   06 ②   07 ③
08 By the way, did you decide on the afternoon program?
09 ④   10 ⑤

01 이어지는 설명으로 보아 사진의 용도를 물어보는 표현이 되어야 한다. 용도를 물어볼 때는 'What ~ for?'라고 한다.

02 이어지는 고양이에 대한 긍정적인 설명으로 보아 고양이를 좋아한다는 말에 대한 동의의 표현이 적절하다.

03 (A) 음악의 구체적인 종류들이 나오기 때문에 사례를 나타내는 like가 적절하다. (B) 'like better'에 대한 대답이기 때문에 더 좋아한다는 내용이 어울린다. (C) 힙합을 더 좋아하기 때문에 그 이유가 될 만한 긍정적인 내용이 와야 한다.

04 (C) sunglasses가 무엇인지에 대한 질문을 하고 (B) 그 질문에 대하여 sunglasses가 무엇인지 설명을 하고, (A) 그에 대하여 추가적인 질문을 하는 순서가 자연스러운 배열이다.

05 (B) 앞에서 설명한 내용에 추가 설명을 요청하고 (C) 그 설명

서술형 시험대비
p.73

01 wants to choose a picture for his story in the school newspaper
02 nature's future
03 I don't understand why people are in such a hurry.
04 What do you prefer, pizza or fried chicken? → Which do you prefer, pizza or fried chicken?
05 age
06 it's big enough to hold over 50,000 bees.

01 대화에 나온 "What are these for?"는 "이것들은 무엇을 위한 것이냐?"의 의미로 이유를 물어보는 질문이므로 그 대답에 해당하는 것을 써야 한다.

03 이해가 안 돼요 = I don't understand, 왜 사람들이 ~인지 = why people ~, 그토록 서두르다 = be in such a hurry

04 'A or B'처럼 범위가 정해진 것 중에서 어느 것인지를 물어볼 때는 what이 아니라 which로 물어본다.

05 나이를 물어본 질문에 이어지는 대화의 열 배는 자기의 나이를 기준으로 말한 것이다.

06 enough는 big 뒤에 써야 한다. 수용하다 = hold

교과서

Grammar

핵심 Check
p.74~75

1 (1) working   (2) sleeping   (3) walking   (4) is waiting
  (5) are   (6) broken   (7) discussed
2 (1) built   (2) written   (3) allowed   (4) climbing   (5) taken
3 (1) Since   (2) Though   (3) since   (4) Though   (5) though

01 ④   02 ④   03 ①   04 ④

05 (1) wearing   (2) since

01 '서 있는'의 의미를 가지는 현재분사를 써야 한다.

02 ④ 수식을 받는 food가 요리를 하는 것이 아니라 요리되는 것이기 때문에 과거분사를 써야 한다.

03 보기 문장의 밑줄 친 taken은 과거분사이다. 밑줄 친 부분 중 과거분사로 쓰인 것은 ①의 named이고 나머지는 모두 과거형이다.

04 주어진 의미에 맞도록 '날씨가 춥다'는 사실이 양보의 부사절이 되어야 하기 때문에 'it is cold'를 접속사 though가 유도해야 한다.

05 (1) 수식을 받는 the man이 셔츠를 입는 입장이기 때문에 현재분사 wearing이 되어야 한다. (2) 내용상 이유를 나타내기 때문에 since가 적절하다.

01 (1) The man running along the road was asking for help.

   (2) The boy eating lunch was sitting on the floor.

   (3) The man reading a book told us to be quiet.

   (4) The boys allowed to watch TV were eating snacks.

02 ③

03 (1) taken   (2) walking   (3) invited   (4) Since

   (5) Though

04 ⑤   05 ②   06 ③   07 ⑤

08 ④   09 ①

10 (1) There was a boy playing on the beach.

   (2) I sat on the bench made of wood.

   (3) Since I am too young, I can't watch the film.

11 (1) made   (2) built   (3) painted   (4) moving

   (5) washed

12 ④   13 ④   14 ⑤   15 ④

16 ①   17 ④   18 ④

01 (1) 현재분사 running ~이 명사 The man을 수식한다. (2) eating ~이 명사 The boy를 수식한다. (3) 현재분사 reading ~이 명사 The man을 수식한다. (4) 과거분사 allowed ~가 명사 The boys를 수식한다.

02 ③ 집에 머무르는 이유가 피곤하다고 느낀 것이므로 이유를 나타내는 접속사 since, because, as가 적절하다.

03 (1) 사진은 찍히기 때문에 과거분사 taken (2) 아이가 걷고 있는 것이므로 현재분사 walking (3) the man은 파티에 초대

를 받는 입장이기 때문에 invited (4) 이유를 나타내기 때문에 Since (5) 서로 대조적인 내용을 연결하기 때문에 양보의 접속사 Though가 적절하다.

04 ⑤ 주어진 내용은 이유를 나타내기 때문에 접속사를 Though가 아니라 Since, Because, As를 쓰는 것이 옳다.

05 동사는 look이고 sing은 현재분사가 되어서 the man을 수식하여야 한다.

06 ③의 found는 과거형 동사이고 나머지는 모두 과거분사이다.

07 ⑤ picture는 그려지는 것이기 때문에 수동의 의미를 나타내는 과거분사 painted가 되어야 한다.

08 내용상 원인과 결과의 관계가 성립하기 때문에 접속사 since가 적절하다.

09 그녀가 요리한 음식을 나타낼 때는 cook이 the food를 수식하는 과거분사가 되어서 'the food cooked ~'가 되어야 한다.

10 (1) 'There is/was ~'의 구문을 이용하고, '놀고 있는 아이'라는 뜻으로 'a boy playing ~'이라고 한다. (2) '나무로 만들어진 벤치'는 'bench made of wood'라고 한다. (3) 이유를 나타내는 접속사 since를 사용하여 문장을 연결한다.

11 (1) a cake는 만들어지는 것이므로 과거분사 made, (2) a castle은 지어지는 것이므로 과거분사 built (3) 벽은 칠해지는 입장이므로 과거분사 painted (4) the taxi driver는 가방을 운반하는 능동적인 입장이므로 현재분사 (5) a car는 세차되는 수동적인 입장이므로 과거분사가 적절하다.

12 ④ 문장의 주어는 An essay, 동사는 will receive이다. 동사 write는 essay를 수식하는 과거분사 written이 되어야 한다.

13 ④ 동사 enjoyed에 이어지는 talking은 동명사이고 나머지는 모두 현재분사이다.

14 ⑤ gift가 '주어진' 것이므로 수동의 의미를 지닌 과거분사 given이 되어야 한다.

15 수식을 받는 cold places가 Antarctica를 포함하기 때문에 현재분사형 전치사인 including이 적절하다.

16 서로 대조적인 내용의 절을 연결하는 접속사는 양보의 접속사 though, although이다.

17 ④의 since는 전치사로 쓰였고 나머지는 모두 접속사이다.

18 접속사 though를 기준으로 서로 대조되는 내용이 연결되도록 해야 한다.

01 (1) He didn't read the message sent to him.

   (2) The children playing basketball are my friends.

   (3) He was looking at the picture painted by my brother.

    (4) Since the book was so interesting, I finished
       reading the book last night.

    (5) Though I was hungry, I didn't eat the food.

02 Although

03 (1) sitting (2) lying (3) broken (4) showing

    (5) made

04 (1) Since (2) Though (3) Since (4) Though

05 a dog barking

06 The man walking his dogs is a famous singer.

07 becase[as, since]

08 (1) The church built 100 years ago has beautiful
      stained glass.

    (2) The car rolling down the road made a loud
      noise.

    (3) The woman cooking apple pies will give them
      to you.

    (4) The photos taken by Ann show some wild
      birds.

    (5) He was reading the message sent to him.

09 showing

10 (1) send → sent (2) sung → singing

    (3) eaten → eating

---

01 (1) message는 보내지는 수동의 입장이므로 sent로 수식한다.
(2) '농구하고 있는 아이들'은 'children playing basketball'
이다. (3) '~에 의해서 그려진 그림'은 'a picture painted by
~'라고 한다. (4) '~해서'의 의미로 이유를 나타내는 접속사는
since이다. (5) 대조를 나타내는 접속사는 though이다.

02 대조를 나타내는 Though 대신에 쓸 수 있는 것은 Although
이다.

03 (1) The man은 앉아 있는 사람이기 때문에 현재분사 sitting
(2) lie는 자동사로 '놓여 있는'이라고 할 때는 현재분사 lying
(3) 문은 부서지는 것이므로 과거분사 broken (4) 사진이 보여
주고 있기 때문에 현재분사 (5) 수동의 의미이기 때문에 과거분사

04 (1), (3)은 이유를 나타내는 since, (2), (4)는 대조를 나타내는
though가 들어가야 한다.

05 "짖고 있는"이라는 의미로 명사 a dog를 꾸며주는 현재분사
"barking"을 쓰는 것이 적절하다.

06 walk는 '(동물을) 걷게 하다[산책시키다]'라는 뜻으로 현재분사
형태여야 한다.

07 이유를 나타내는 접속사 because[as, since]가 적절하다.

08 주어진 명사를 수식하는 분사구가 명사 뒤에 놓이도록 한다. 현
재분사는 능동이나 진행의 의미로, 과거분사는 수동이나 완료의
의미로 사용한다.

09 '보여주는'에 해당하는 현재분사 showing이 적절하다.

10 (1) 신문이 보내진 것이므로 과거분사 sent (2) the actor는 노
래를 부르기 때문에 현재분사 (3) 동물이 먹기 때문에 현재분사

Reading

확인문제   p.82

1 T 2 F 3 T 4 F 5 T 6 F

확인문제   p.83

1 T 2 F 3 T 4 F 5 T 6 F

확인문제   p.84

1 F 2 T 3 T

교과서 확인학습 A   p.85~86

01 Amazing

02 For the science project, has chosen

03 social   04 as old as

05 appear   06 a special chemical

07 what they are   08 the answer

09 share with, what 10 How Many Ants

11 out of nowhere

12 Like humans, except, including Antarctica

13 As of 2018

14 how about

15 According to scientists, for every human

16 hardly weighs anything, as heavy as

17 Is, Like

18 which have, living

19 Within, three different types

20 what she does

21 produce these eggs

22 The third type

23 like caring, defending, collecting

24 How

25 like humans, actually have

26 called, to communicate with

27 By using, exchange information

28 for communication

29 For example, by rubbing, on

30 covered with, even the smallest touch

31 FUN FACTS   32 up to

33 50 times their own body weight

34 breathe through small holes

35 two stomachs

36 One, for itself, the other

37 Most ants, underwater

1 The Amazing Ants

2 For the science project, our group has chosen very special insects.

3 They are very social.

4 They are as old as the T-Rex.

5 They appear in Aesop's stories.

6 They use a special chemical to communicate.

7 Can you guess what they are?

8 Yes, the answer is ants.

9 We want to share with you what we have learned about these insects.

10 How Many Ants Are on Earth?

11 We often see ants come out of nowhere.

12 Like humans, they live almost everywhere in the world, except a few extremely cold places including Antarctica.

13 As of 2018, there were over 7 billion people on Earth.

14 Then, how about ants?

15 According to scientists, there are about one million ants for every human in the world.

16 Though each ant hardly weighs anything, one million ants are as heavy as a human being weighing about 62 kilograms.

17 What Is the Ant Society Like?

18 Ants live in colonies which have lots of residents living together.

19 Within a colony, there are usually three different types of ants.

20 There is the queen, and what she does her entire life is lay eggs.

21 The second type of ant is the male that helps the queen produce these eggs.

22 The third type of ant is the worker.

23 Worker ants are all female and do very important jobs, like caring for eggs, defending the colony, and collecting food.

24 How Do Ants Communicate?

25 Though ants do not speak like humans, they actually have a "language."

26 Ants produce a chemical called a pheromone to communicate with one another.

27 By using the chemical, they can exchange information about food or danger.

28 Ants also use touch for communication.

29 For example, if an ant finds food, it passes on the good news by rubbing its body on its neighbor.

30 Since an ant has legs covered with very sensitive hairs, it can sense even the smallest touch.

31 FUN FACTS ABOUT ANTS

32 01 Some Queen ants live up to 30 years.

33 02 Some ants can carry things that are 50 times their own body weight.

34 03 Ants do not have lungs but breathe through small holes in their bodies.

35 04 An ant has two stomachs.

36 One stomach holds food for itself, and the other holds food to share with others.

37 05 Most ants can swim and live 24 hours underwater.

01 ③   02 ②   03 ⑤   04 ①, ④

05 has → have   06 colony   07 ②

08 ②, ③, ⑤   09 ①   10 ②   11 ①

12 먹이를 발견한 것   13 weighing   14 ②, ③

15 ④   16 (A) which   (B) produce   (C) third

17 ②, ③   18 ①, ④   19 ③

20 (A) times   (B) the other   (C) others   21 ②

22 ②   23 ②   24 ③   25 ③

26 that are 50 times their own body weight

27 개미는 폐가 없지만, 몸에 있는 작은 구멍을 통해 호흡한다.

28 하나의 위에는 자신의 먹이를 저장하고 다른 하나의 위에는 다른 개미들과 함께 나눌 먹이를 저장한다.

01 개미가 등장한다고 했으므로, Aesop's stories는 인간 이외의 동물 또는 식물에 인간의 생활 감정을 부여하여 사람과 꼭 같이 행동하게 함으로써 그들의 행동 속에 교훈을 나타내려고 하는 '우화'에 속한다고 할 수 있다. ① 시, ② 수필, ③ 우화, ④ 희곡, ⑤ 시나리오

02 ⓑ와 ①, ③, ④: 부사적 용법, ②와 ⑤: 명사적 용법

03 '저희들은 이 곤충에 관해 알게 된 것을 여러분과 함께 나누고 싶습니다.'라고 했으므로, ⑤번이 적절하다.

04 그녀가 평생 하는 일은 '알을 낳는 것'이다. lay eggs는 문장의 보어로서, be동사 뒤에서 to부정사가 보어로 쓰일 때 to가 종종 생략된다. 이 경우 주어가 what이나 the only 등이고 do[does] 동사를 포함해야 한다.

05 which가 이끄는 주격 관계대명사절의 선행사가 colonies이므로 동사를 have로 고쳐야 한다.

06 colony: (동일 지역에 서식하는 동·식물의) 군집, 함께 살거나 자라는 같은 유형의 생물 집단

07 ⓐ 인간처럼 개미도 남극을 포함한 일부 극도로 추운 곳을 '제

외한' 전 세계 거의 모든 곳에 살고 있다고 해야 하므로, except 가 적절하다. except: ~ 제외하고는[외에는], ⓑ for: [each, every, 수사 등의 앞에 쓰여] …마다, …에 대하여

08 ⓒ와 ②, ③, ⑤: 현재분사, ①, ④: 동명사

09 개미는 소수의 아주 추운 곳에서는 살지 않는다고 언급되었다. ③ 개미들의 숫자가 인간들의 숫자보다 약 백만 배 더 많다.

10 (A)의 also에 주목한다. 개미들의 의사소통 방법을 설명한 (B) 에 이어서 또 다른 의사소통 방법을 설명하는 것이므로 (B) 다 음에 (A)가 이어지고 (C)의 touch가 (A)의 첫 부분에 나오는 touch에 이어지므로 (A) 다음에 (C)가 와야 한다. 그러므로 (B)-(A)-(C)의 순서가 적절하다.

11 이 글은 '개미들의 의사소통 방법'에 대한 글이므로, 주제로는 ①번이 적절하다.

12 좋은 소식은 '먹이를 발견한 것'을 가리킨다.

13 a human being을 수식하는 현재분사 weighing이 적절하다.

14 ① In spite of+명사구, ④ Despite+명사구, ⑤ As though: 마치 ~인 것처럼

15 위 글은 개미의 숫자에 관한 글이므로, 제목으로는 '지구상에는 얼마나 많은 개미가 있을까?'가 적절하다.

16 (A) 뒤에 불완전한 절이 이어지므로 관계대명사 which를 쓰는 것이 적절하다. (B) help는 준사역동사로 목적보어로 원형부 정사나 to부정사를 쓰는 것이 적절하다. (C) '세 번째' 종류라고 해야 하므로 서수 third가 옳다.

17 ⓐ와 ②, ③: 선행사를 포함하는 관계대명사(~하는 것), ①, ⑤ 의문대명사(무엇) ④ 의문형용사(감탄문에서)

18 ⓑ와 ①, ④: ~을 돌보다, ② take after: ~을 닮다, ③ make sure: ~을 확실히 하다, ⑤ look for: ~을 찾다

19 ⓐ와 ③: (특정한 수)까지, ① (육체적·정신적으로) ~할 수 있 는, ② (특히 나쁜 짓을) 하고 있는, ④ ~의 의무[책임]인, ⑤ (특정한 기준)만큼

20 (A) 자기 몸무게의 '50배'라고 해야 하므로 times가 옳다. times: ~배, hours: ~ 시간, (B) 둘 중 하나는 one, 다른 하나 는 the other로 나타내므로 the other가 옳다. (C) '다른 개미 들'이라고 해야 하므로 others가 옳다.

21 '개미의 몸무게'는 알 수 없다. ① 30년. ③ 몸에 있는 작은 구멍 을 통해 호흡한다. ④ 두 개. ⑤ 24시간 동안 살 수 있다.

22 앞의 내용의 예가 나오고 있으므로 For example이 가장 적절하 다.

23 (A)와 ②, ③, ⑤: 동명사, ①, ④: 현재분사

24 ⓐ to: 한계, 범위, 기간의 끝을 나타냄, ⓑ feed on: ~을 먹다 [먹고 살다]

25 ③ 암컷이 수컷보다 더 오래 살 수 있는 이유는 대답할 수 없다. ① In places with still water. ② For about five to seven days. ④ No. ⑤ Up to 300 eggs.

26 50 times: 50배

27 03번의 내용을 쓰면 된다.

28 04번의 내용을 쓰면 된다.

01 what   02 in order / so as / in order that, may[can] / so that, may[can]

03 Can you guess what they are?

04 ⓐ out of nowhere   ⓑ As of 2018

05 how many ants

06 Since → Though[Although]

07 who[that] live

08 the queen, the male, the worker

09 such as

10 (A) called   (B) exchange   (C) covered

11 but   12 (A) chemical   (B) touch

01 뒤에 불완전한 절이 이어지므로 관계대명사를 써야 하는데, 선행사가 없으므로 what을 쓰는 것이 적절하다. 관계대명사 what은 선행사를 포함하여 '~하는 것'이라고 해석한다.

02 목적을 나타내는 to부정사는 in order to = so as to = in order that[so that] ~ may[can]로 고칠 수 있다.

03 이 문장은 Yes나 No로 대답할 수 있으므로, '동사가 guess일 때 간접의문문에서 의문사를 맨 앞으로 보내는 경우'에 해당하 지 않는다. what they are가 동사 guess의 목적어 역할을 하 는 간접의문문으로, '의문사+주어+동사'의 어순으로 쓰는 것이 적절하다.

04 ⓐ out of nowhere: 어디선지 모르게, 느닷없이 ⓑ as of: ~ 현재, ~일자로

05 바로 뒤 문장에 'According to scientists, there are about one million ants for every human in the world.'라는 말 이 나오므로, 'how about ants?(개미는 어떨까?)'는 '지구상에 얼마나 많은 개미가 있을까?'라는 의미임을 알 수 있다.

06 개미 한 마리는 거의 무게가 '나가지 않지만' 백만 마리의 개미 는 체중이 약 62kg인 사람 한 명과 무게가 같다고 해야 하므로 Since를 Though(Although)로 고치는 것이 적절하다.

07 living together는 lots of residents를 수식하는 분사구이며, who(that) live together로 바꾸어 쓸 수 있다.

08 '여왕개미', '수개미', '일개미'를 가리킨다.

09 like = such as: …와 같은

10 (A) 페로몬이라고 '불리는' 화학물질이라고 해야 하므로 called 가 옳다. (B) 정보를 '교환할 수 있다'고 해야 하므로 exchange 가 옳다. exchange: 교환하다, change: 변하다, 바꾸다, (C) 털로 '덮인' 다리라고 해야 하므로 covered가 옳다.

11 Though 대신 but을 쓸 수 있다.

12 개미는 페로몬이라고 불리는 '화학물질'과 '접촉'을 사용하여 의 사소통을 할 수 있다.

17

01 ①	02 ④	03 ③	04 ⑤
05 ①	06 ②	07 ③	08 ②
09 ⑤			

10 it's time to get serious about protecting birds.

| 11 ② | 12 ④ | 13 ② | 14 ③ |
| 15 ① | 16 ③ | | |

17 (1) I like every song sung by the singer.
   (2) He tried not to wake up the baby sleeping on the bed.

| 18 ② | 19 endangering → endangered |
| 20 ⑤ | 21 ② |

22 (1) He is carrying a basket filled with cherries.
   (2) Since it is cold, I want to drink something hot.
   (3) I am tired though I slept enough last night.

| 23 ③ | 24 ⑤ | 25 ② | 26 ④ |
| 27 ①, ④ | 28 ⑤ | 29 where → which[that] | |

30 (A) honey   (B) hundreds of trips

01 '정확한지 확실하지 않을 때 질문에 답하거나 의견을 형성하려고 하다'는 '추측하다'에 해당한다.

02 '장기 자랑이 재미있었어.'에 동의하는 입장을 나타낼 수 있는 말이 되어야 한다.

03 'too bright'와 대조적인 의미로 'dark 어두운'가 적절하다.

04 ⑤ 동사 like는 '좋아하다'의 의미이다.

05 사진을 살펴보라는 말에 대하여 사진의 용도를 물어보았기 때문에 사진의 용도를 나타낼 수 있는 말이 되어야 한다.

06 이어지는 'Me, too.'에 따라오는 고양이의 장점을 보았을 때 고양이에 대한 긍정적인 언급이 있었다는 것을 알 수 있다.

07 (B) 앞에 나온 질문에 대답하고 선호를 묻는다. (C) 그 질문에 대하여 hiking이라고 대답하고 이유를 말한다. (D) 그 이유를 듣고 함께 가겠다고 하니까 (A) 잘 되었다고 대답한다.

08 ② 이어지는 설명에 '길을 잃어버린다.'는 내용을 보면 새가 겪는 어려움에 대한 언급이 있었음을 알 수 있다.

09 이어지는 새들에게 도움이 되는 일을 해야 한다는 언급을 보면 새들의 어려움에 안타까움을 나타내는 말이 적절하다.

10 ~할 시간이다 = it's time to ~ 진지해지다 = get serious 조류를 보호하다 = protect birds

11 새들이 길을 잃는 것은 밤에 너무 밝은 도시 때문이다.

12 child를 수식하는 현재분사가 와야 한다.

13 나이가 어리다는 것이 이유이므로 'I am young'을 접속사 since가 유도하여야 한다.

14 ③ 동사 mind는 동명사를 목적어로 가진다. your brother는 의미상의 주어이고, talking은 동명사이다. 나머지는 모두 현재분사이다.

15 서로 대조적인 내용을 연결하는 접속사 though가 적절하다.

16 수동의 의미이므로 과거분사가 적절하다.

18 제시된 문장과 ②의 밑줄 친 부분은 현재분사이고 나머지는 모두 동명사이다.

19 '멸종위기에 처한'이라는 의미는 endangered이다.

20 "매우 조심스럽게 일하는 여자"는 'the woman working very carefully'라고 한다.

21 ② 문맥상 이유를 나타내므로 since, because, as를 쓴다.

22 (1) '~로 가득 찬'이라고 할 때는 과거분사 filled (2) 문맥상 이유를 나타내므로 since, as, because가 알맞다. (3) 서로 대조되는 내용의 연결에서는 접속사 though

23 ③번 다음 문장의 내용에 주목한다. 주어진 문장(개미는 어떨까? 즉, 지구상에 얼마나 많은 개미가 있을까?)의 대답에 해당하므로 ③번이 적절하다.

24 ⓐ와 ⑤ ~처럼(전치사), ① ~와 비슷한(전치사), ② 좋아하다(동사), ③ ~과 같은(such as)(전치사), ④ 비슷한(형용사)

25 백만 마리의 개미는 체중이 약 62kg인 사람 한 명과 무게가 같다고 했으므로, 백만 마리의 개미의 무게는 약 62kg이다. ③ less 원급 than: ~보다 덜 …한, ④ not so 원급 as: ~만큼 …하지 않은

26 화학물질과 접촉을 사용한 개미의 의사소통 방법을 설명하는 글이므로, 개미들은 실제로 '언어'를 가지고 있다고 하는 것이 적절하다. ① 문자, ② 규칙, ③ 상징(물), ⑤ 문화

27 ⓑ와 ①, ④: [이유를 나타내어] …이므로, ②, ③, ⑤ …부터[이후]

28 ⑤ 개미들은 아주 미세한 접촉도 감지할 수 있다.

29 where 뒤에 절의 주어가 없기 때문에, where를 관계대명사 which[that]로 고쳐야 한다.

30 적은 양의 '꿀'을 만들기 위해 일벌은 '수백 번의 이동'을 하고, 그렇게 하면서 식물이 수분(受粉)하는 것을 돕는다.

01 (p)rovide	02 endangered		03 ①
04 ④	05 ③	06 ③	07 ②
08 ③	09 ②	10 ④	11 ④
12 ①	13 ④	14 covered	15 ②
16 ③	17 ②	18 ④	

19 ⓐ caring   ⓑ defending   ⓒ collecting

| 20 ③ | 21 ⑤ | 22 ①, ③ | 23 an ant |
| 24 legs | 25 ② | | |

26 (A) 개미는 항상 바쁘고 전혀 휴식을 취하지 않는 것처럼 보이는 것
   (B) 일개미는 하루에 약 250번의 짧은 잠을 자며 휴식을 취하고, 이 잠은 불과 1분 정도 이어진다는 것
   (C) 여왕개미는 하루에 90번 잠을 자고, 한 번에 약 6분 동안 잠을 자는 것

01 주어진 단어는 비슷한 말의 관계이다. offer 제공하다 provide 제공하다

02 북극에 있는 동물들이 '멸종 위기에 처했다.'는 의미로 '멸종 위기에 처한 = endangered'가 적절하다.

03 unbelievable 믿을 수 없는 – incredible 믿을 수 없는

04 'like better'에 대한 대답이기 때문에 '더 좋아하다'에 해당하는 의미가 되어야 한다.

05 communication은 소식을 전하는 것을 나타낸다. give up 포기하다 get over 극복하다 pass on 전달하다 look after 돌보다 wait for 기다리다

06 '여러 가지 중에서 어느 것을 원하는지 결정하다'는 '선택하다'에 해당한다.

07 동식물이 무리를 이루어 살고 있는 집단을 'colony 군집, 군락'이라고 한다.

08 코끼리 무리에서 새끼를 돌보는 것은 암컷이다.

09 문맥상 캠프가 재미있다는 말에 동의하는 내용이기 때문에 "The talent show last night was good."이 적절하다.

10 오후 프로그램으로 hiking을 선택했기 때문에 수영에 관해서는 위 대화를 통해서 알 수 없다.

11 빈칸 뒤에 이어지는 내용으로 보아 빈칸에는 상대방의 말에 동의하는 표현이 들어가야 한다. 'Me, too.'나 'So do I.'가 적절하다.

12 빈칸 앞에 추가 설명을 요청하는 표현이 주어진 것으로 보아 앞에서 설명한 대상에 대한 추가적인 정보를 제공하는 말이 적절하다.

13 제시된 문장과 ④는 현재분사이고 나머지는 동명사이다.

14 legs는 hairs로 덮이는 수동의 입장이기 때문에 과거분사 covered가 적절하다.

15 ② language는 말해지는 수동의 입장이므로 과거분사 spoken이 되어야 한다.

16 소설은 Albert Camus에 의해서 쓰여진 것이기 때문에 과거분사 written이 되어야 한다.

17 '~ 때문에'에 해당하는 since가 적절하다.

18 (A) 서로 대조되는 내용을 연결하는 접속사 (B) 이유를 나타내는 접속사

19 전치사 like 뒤에 동명사 caring, defending, collecting이 병렬로 연결되는 것이 적절하다.

20 (A)와 ②, ③, ⑤: 관계대명사, ①, ④: 지시대명사

21 일개미는 모두 '암컷'이다.

22 ⓐ와 ①, ③: 부사적 용법, ②, ⑤: 명사적 용법, ④: 형용사적 용법

23 '개미'를 가리킨다.

24 개미는 (자극에) 매우 민감한 털로 덮인 '다리' 덕분에, 아주 미세한 접촉도 감지할 수 있다.

25 ⓐ 일개미가 하루에 4시간 정도 잠을 자는 반면에, 여왕개미는 하루에 90번 잠을 잔다고 해야 하므로 On the other hand가 적절하다. ⓑ 앞 문장에서 개미들의 수면 시간을 설명하고 있으므로, '즉', 방식이 다르기는 하지만 개미도 우리처럼 잠을 자

고 휴식을 취한다고 하는 것이 적절하다. In short = In brief: 즉, 간단히 말해서, ① Thus: 이렇게 하여; 이와 같이, To sum up: 요컨대, 요약해서 말하면, ③ As a result: 그 결과

26 각각 앞문장의 내용을 가리킨다.

01 insect   02 (s)elect

03 (1) decide   (2) hold

04 (1) Ants   (2) language   (3) chemical   (4) information

05 better   06 (1) painting   (2) made   (3) invited

07 (T)hough   08 (A) out of   (B) almost   (C) people

09 Though[Although] each ant hardly weighs anything

10 There are about one million ants.

11 ⓐ using   ⓑ rubbing

12 (A) which[that] is   (C) which[that] are

13 먹이를 발견할 경우 개미는 자기 몸을 이웃의 개미에게 문질러서 좋은 소식을 전달한다.

01 여섯 개의 다리와 때로는 날개를 가진 파리나 개미 같은 작은 생물은 '곤충'이다.

02 '선택하다' choose의 비슷한 말은 select이다.

03 (1) 결정하다 = decide (2) 수용하다 = hold

04 (1) 군집을 이루는 것은 보기에서 개미이다. (2) 소통을 하기 위한 언어가 적절하다. (3) 페르몬이라 불리는 것은 화학물질이다. (4) 화학물질을 통해서 정보를 주고받는다.

05 빈칸 앞에서 더 좋아하는 것을 소개하고 상대방의 경우에는 어떤지 물어 본 것이기 때문에 빈칸에는 더 좋아하는 것에 대한 대답이 되도록 한다.

06 (1) 명사 the man을 꾸며주는 분사가 명사와 능동의 관계이므로 현재분사 (2) 명사 the pizza를 꾸며주는 분사가 명사와 수동의 관계이므로 과거분사 (3) 명사 The people을 꾸며주는 분사가 명사와 수동의 관계이므로 과거분사가 적절하다.

07 '비록 ~해도, ~할지라도'의 의미는 대조를 나타내는 접속사 though가 되어야 한다.

08 (A) '난데없이 나타나는' 개미들이라고 해야 하므로 out of가 옳다. out of nowhere 어디선지 모르게. 느닷없이, into: ~ 안으로, (B) '거의' 모든 곳이라고 해야 하므로 almost가 옳다. almost: 거의, most: 대부분의, (C) 70억이 넘는 '인구(사람들)'라고 해야 하므로 people이 옳다. people: 사람들, peoples: 민족들

09 '비록 ~이지만'이라는 뜻의 양보를 나타내는 접속사 Though[Although]를 사용하는 것이 적절하다.

10 세상에는 사람 한 명당 약 백만 마리의 개미가 있다.

11 전치사 by 다음에 동명사로 쓰는 것이 적절하다.

12 주격 관계대명사와 be동사가 생략되어 있다.

13 For example 다음의 내용을 쓰는 것이 적절하다.

|모범답안|

01 (1) keep an eye on   (2) has a long face
    (3) was all ears   (4) turn my nose up at
    (5) learn by heart   (6) cost an arm and a leg
02 (1) Since   (2) since   (3) Though   (4) though
03 (A) warm places   (B) five years
    (C) about seven weeks   (D) to collect food
    (E) hundreds of trips   (F) grow

01 (1) keep an eye on: ~을 지켜보다 (2) has a long face: 표정이 우울하다 (3) be all ears: 경청하다 (4) turn one's nose up at: ~을 거절하다 (5) learn by heart: ~을 암기하다 (6) cost an arm and a leg: 비싼 값을 치르다

01 (1) 비가 심하게 내려서 축구 경기가 취소되었다. (2) 함께 이야기할 사람이 없기 때문에 나는 파티에 가기를 원하지 않는다. (3) 비록 그가 웃고 있어도, 그는 그리 행복해 보이지 않는다. (4) 비록 추워도 날씨는 맑았다.

01 (f)emale   02 (s)elect   03 ①   04 ④
05 ③   06 (1) weighs   (2) colonies
    (3) exchange   (4) sensitive
07 ⑤   08 ①
09 Is there anything we can do to help them?
10 ⑤   11 ①   12 ③   13 ②
14 ②   15 ④   16 ③   17 ④
18 ⑤   19 ③   20 ②, ⑤
21 (A) billion   (B) how about   (C) hardly   22 ②
23 여왕개미: 평생 알을 낳는다.
    수개미: 여왕이 알을 낳는 것을 돕는다.
    일개미: 알을 돌보고, 군집을 방어하며, 먹이를 모으는 것과 같은 매우 중요한 일을 한다.
24 a pheromone   25 sensible → sensitive

01 주어진 단어의 관계가 반의어이므로 'male 수컷 : female 암컷'이 되어야 한다.
02 주어진 단어의 관계가 비슷한 말이므로 'choose 선택하다 : select 선택하다'의 관계가 되어야 한다.
03 '사람들이 원하는 것을 제공하다' offer 제공하다, 제안하다
04 질문이 선호하는 것이기 때문에 대답도 선호하는 것이 되어야 한다. prefer = like better
05 곤충, 식물, 동물의 집단을 '군집, 군락 = colony'이라고 한다.
06 (1) 무게가 나가다 weigh (2) 군집 colony (3) 교환하다 exchange (4) 예민한 sensitive
07 ⑤의 chemical은 명사로 쓰여서 '화학물질'이라는 뜻이다.

08 hold는 '수용하다'는 뜻으로 '담다 = contain'이 적절하다.
09 ~가 있니? = Is there ~?, 우리가 할 수 있는 어떤 일 = anything (that) we can do, 그들을 돕기 위하여 = to help them
10 새들이 밝은 밤하늘에서 길을 찾는 데 어려움이 있으므로 새들을 돕기 위하여 밤에 불필요한 불은 꺼야 한다. catch on 유행하다 turn around 돌아가다 get over 극복하다 care for 좋아하다 turn off 끄다
11 ① 새들이 어려움에 처해 있는 것은 밤에 길을 찾는 것이다.
12 (B) 앞에 나온 질문에 대답을 하고 벌이 몇 마리 사는지 다시 질문한 것에 (C) 500이라고 대답한다. 그리고 (A) 그 대답에 대한 추가 설명이 이어지는 순서가 자연스러운 배열이다.
13 ② 자신이 선호하는 것을 말하고, 상대방은 어떤지 물어보았기 때문에 선호하는 것에 대한 대답이 나와야 한다.
14 어젯밤 장기 자랑에 대한 이야기에서 다른 화제로 전환할 때는 'by the way = 그런데'가 적절하다.
15 ④ 내용상 함께 하이킹을 가기로 하는 내용이므로 '함께 할게.'에 해당하는 말이 들어가야 한다.
16 ③ 'G: I'll go hiking because we can see wild birds and insects in the woods.'를 보면 소녀는 오후 프로그램을 정했다는 것을 알 수 있다.
17 ④ 동사 enjoy는 동명사를 목적어로 가지기 때문에 jogging은 동명사이고 나머지는 분사이다.
18 ⑤ 대조되는 내용을 연결하는 접속사는 though이다. '시간이 별로 없지만 = Though I don't have much time'
19 ③ 원인을 유도하는 접속사는 since가 적절하다. though는 서로 대조적인 내용을 나타내기 때문에 이 문장에서는 적절하지 않다.
20 '지각동사(see)+목적어+목적보어' 구문으로, 목적보어 자리에 동사원형이나 현재분사가 적절하다.
21 (A) 앞에 숫자가 있을 때는 billion에 s를 붙이지 않는다. (B) '그렇다면. 개미는 어떨까?'라고 해야 하므로 how about이 옳다. (C) 개미 한 마리는 '거의 무게가 나가지 않지만'이라고 해야 하므로 hardly가 옳다. hardly: 거의 ~ 아니다[없다]
22 위 글은 개미 사회에 대한 글이므로, 제목으로는 '개미 사회는 어떠한가?'가 적절하다.
23 ⓐ 뒤에 이어지는 문장들의 내용을 쓰면 된다.
24 '페로몬'을 가리킨다.
25 개미는 (자극에) 매우 '민감한' 털로 덮인 다리가 있기 때문에, 아주 미세한 접촉도 감지할 수 있다고 하는 것이 적절하다. sensitive: 예민한, 민감한, sensible: 분별[양식] 있는

The Full Jar

Reading 교과서

확인문제   p.116

1 T 2 F 3 T 4 F 5 T 6 F

확인문제   p.117

1 T 2 F 3 T 4 F 5 T 6 F

교과서 확인학습 A   p.118~119

01 Full   02 before his class
03 a large jar   04 fill, with, from the bag
05 Is the jar full   06 They all
07 out of the bag, poured them
08 a little, rolled into
09 the same question, the same answer
10 took out, poured, into   11 fill, once more
12 replied   13 out of the bag
14 fill the spaces   15 is just like
16 what is most important   17 is lost
18 valued   19 all the small things
20 there's no room for   21 The same goes for
22 spend, on, what is really important
23 Take care of, matter   24 sitting, raised
25 you asked   26 seem full, room for

교과서 확인학습 B   p.120~121

1 The Full Jar
2 Mr. Jenkins stood before his class.
3 He had a large jar and a big bag on the teacher's desk.
4 When the class began, he picked up the jar and started to fill it with golf balls from the bag.
5 He asked the students, "Is the jar full?"

6 They all said, "Yes."
7 The teacher took a box of small stones out of the bag and poured them into the jar.
8 He shook the jar a little, and the stones rolled into the open areas between the golf balls.
9 He asked the same question and got the same answer from his students.
10 Next, the teacher took out a bottle of sand and poured it into the jar.
11 After he watched the sand fill the spaces between the stones, he asked once more, "Is the jar full?"
12 All the students replied, "Yes."
13 Suddenly Mr. Jenkins took a can of apple juice out of the bag.
14 He poured the apple juice into the jar, and his students watched it fill the spaces in the sand.
15 "Now," the teacher said, "I want you to understand that your life is just like the jar.
16 The golf balls are what is most important in life: your family, your friends, your health, and your dreams.
17 Even when everything else is lost, your life can still be full.
18 The stones are the other things valued by people, like your job, your house, and your car.
19 The sand is all the small things."
20 "If you put the sand into the jar first," he said, "there's no room for the stones or the golf balls.
21 The same goes for life.
22 If you spend all your time and energy on the small things, you will never have room for what is really important to you.
23 Take care of the balls first — the things that really matter."
24 One student sitting in the back raised her hand and asked, "What does the apple juice mean?"
25 Mr. Jenkins smiled, "I'm glad you asked.
26 It just shows that though your life may seem full, there's always room for a cool drink with a friend."

서술형 실전문제   p.122~124

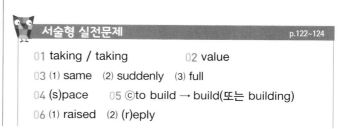

01 taking / taking   02 value
03 (1) same (2) suddenly (3) full
04 (s)pace   05 ⓒto build → build(또는 building)
06 (1) raised (2) (r)eply

21

07 (1) They've already poured a lot of time and money into this project.

(2) The air was filled with the scent of roses.

(3) It does not matter how you do it

08 (1) I can play the piano a little

(2) I often watch him play[playing] tennis.

(3) The symbols stand for what we all want: beauty, fame, and wealth.

(4) Can you make yourself understood in French?

(5) She is not the one wearing sunglasses indoors to avoid eye contact.

09 (1) Herold is the boy dancing to the music.

(2) There were many soldiers injured in the war.

(3) We had a special dish made with milk and ice.

10 (1) She is talking with a girl wearing glasses.

(2) She heard him open[opening] the window.

11 (1) Robert watched a thief steal[stealing] a lady's bag.

(2) Theresa heard her dog barking loudly.

12 small stones → golf balls /
golf balls → small stones

13 ⓐ Is the jar full?　ⓑ Yes.

14 roll into, the golf balls

15 what　　　　　　16 such as

17 (1) 인생에서 가장 중요한 것: 여러분의 가족, 친구, 건강, 꿈

(2) 사람들이 소중하게 여기는 다른 것들: 여러분의 직업, 집, 자동차

(3) 온갖 사소한 것들

18 ⓐ the small things

ⓑ what is really important to you 또는 the things that really matter

19 병에 모래를 먼저 채우면 돌이나 골프공을 채울 공간이 없어지는 것처럼, 사소한 것에 여러분의 시간과 에너지를 모두 허비한다면, 여러분에게 진정으로 중요한 것을 채울 공간은 절대로 없을 것이다.

20 a room → room

01 take care of ~: ~을 돌보다, ~에 신경을 쓰다 / 네가 떠나 있는 동안에 누가 개를 돌봐주니? take out: ~을 꺼내다 / 그 공무원은 그녀의 공책을 꺼내기 시작했다.

02 우리가 그 문헌을 더 많이 연구하면 할수록 저자들의 지혜를 더욱더 높이 평가하게 된다. value: ~을 높이 평가하다, 중시하다 appreciate: ~을 높이 평가하다

03 (1) same: 같은 / 그는 매일 밤 같은 의자에 앉는다. (2) suddenly: 갑자기 / 나를 따라오는 사람이 있다는 것을 갑자기 깨달았다. (3) full: 가득 찬 / 입에 음식을 가득 넣은 채로 말을 하지 마라.

04 space: (비어 있는) 공간 / 비어 있는 공간.

05 watch+목적어+동사원형[현재분사]: 목적어가 ~하는 것을 보다

06 (1) raise: ~을 들다 (2) reply: 대답하다

07 (1) pour A into B: A를 B에 붓다 (2) scent: 향기 fill A with B: A(그릇·장소 등)를 B(물건·사람)로 채우다 (3) matter: 중요하다

08 (1) a little: 조금(은), 다소는, 좀 a few: 조금[약간]은 있는, 조금의, 여기서 little은 부사로 쓰이고 있으나 few에는 부사로서의 용법이 없다. (2) '지각동사(watch)+목적어+원형부정사[현재분사]'이므로 play나 playing이 적절하다. (3) for와 want의 목적어 역할을 할 수 있도록 that을 what으로 고쳐야 한다. (4) yourself가 남에게 이해되는 것이므로 수동의 의미를 나타내는 과거분사가 적절하다. (5) is라는 본동사가 있으므로 wears를 the one을 수식하는 현재분사 wearing으로 고치는 것이 적절하다.

09 분사에 다른 수식어구가 함께 있는 경우 명사를 뒤에서 수식하며 이때 '관계대명사+be동사'를 생략한 형태로 볼 수 있다.

10 (1) 안경을 끼고 있는 것이므로 현재분사가 수식하도록 한다. (2) 지각동사의 목적어가 목적격보어의 행위의 주체이므로 목적격보어로 원형부정사나 현재분사를 쓴다.

11 (1), (2) 지각동사의 목적어가 목적격보어의 행위의 주체이므로 목적격보어로 원형부정사나 현재분사를 쓸 수 있고 진행형의 문장이면 목적격보어로 현재분사가 더 적절하다.

12 Mr. Jenkins는 병에 '골프공'을 먼저 넣고, 그 다음에 '작은 돌들'을 넣었다.

13 ⓐ '병이 가득 찼나요?' ⓑ '네'를 가리킨다.

14 '골프공' 사이의 틈새로 돌이 '굴러 들어가도록' 하기 위해서이다. let+목적어+원형부정사

15 관계대명사 what이 적절하다.

16 like = such as: ~와 같은

17 각각 이어지는 설명을 쓰면 된다.

18 ⓐ는 '사소한 것들'을, ⓑ는 '당신에게 정말 중요한 것' 또는 '정말 중요한 것들'을 상징한다.

19 The same goes for: ~도 마찬가지이다

20 room이 '공간', '여지'의 뜻일 때는 셀 수 없는 명사로 쓰인다.

단원별 예상문제　　　　p.125~128

01 ②　　02 ③　　03 ③　　04 space

05 (1) a bottle of (2) lose (3) (o)pen (4) (T)hough

06 ②

07 (1) He quickly gets bored with his toys and wants them replaced with new ones.

(2) The ball went over the fence and they looked at it fly through the air.

(3) I cannot find the book that I just put on the table.

(4) He addressed himself to her though[although] he was shy.

08 ④　　　　**09** ③

10 (1) The pen is what I wanted to buy.

(2) The student who[that] was sitting in the back raised her hand.

11 (A) the jar (B) small stones　　**12** ⑤

13 ④　　　　**14** (A) full (B) room

15 ⓐ the sand ⓑ the apple juice　**16** valued

17 ④　　　　**18** ②

19 The same goes for life.　　**20** ②, ⑤

21 are, important

22 (A) sitting (B) shows (C) full　　**23** ③

24 친구와 시원한 음료를 나눌 여유

---

01 ②번은 spends가 어울리며 이외의 보기들은 matter가 어울린다. ①, ④ 문제(명사) ② spend: 소비하다, 쓰다 ③, ⑤ 중요하다(동사)

02 (A) fill A with B: A(그릇·장소 등)를 B(물건·사람)로 채우다 / 우리는 카운터에 서서 그릇을 샐러드로 채웠다. (B) spend A on B: A를 B하는 데 소비하다,쓰다 / 그들은 매주 꽤 많은 돈을 외식하는 데 쓴다.

03 take care of ~: ~을 보살피다 / 당신이나 누군가가 확실히 안전하고, 건강하도록 하게 하다; 당신 자신이나 다른 사람을 돌보다

04 space: (비어 있는) 공간 room: 공간 / 내 여행가방은 너무 가득 차서 다른 것을 위한 공간을 가지고 있지 않다.

05 (1) a bottle of ~: ~ 한 병 (2) lose: 잃어버리다 (3) open: 비어 있는 (4) though: 비록 ~일지라도, ~이지만

06 How you play the game is what really counts.

07 (1) 장난감을 교체하는 것이 아니라 교체되는 것이므로 '수동'의 의미를 갖는 replaced가 되어야 한다. (2) 지각동사 다음에 동사원형이나 현재분사가 나와야 한다. (3) the book이 선행사로 나왔으므로 what이 아니라 which나 that을 써야 한다. (4) 뒤에 절이 나오고 있으므로 despite가 아니라 though[although]를 써야 한다.

08 ④번은 목적격보어로 to부정사가 나와야 하며 나머지는 모두 지각동사나 사역동사의 목적격보어로 동사원형이 나와야 한다.

09 ① The golf balls are what is most important in life. ② There's no room for the stones or the golf balls. ④ They were seated on each side of the upper platform. ⑤ Though summer is a fun season, I can't stand the heat!

10 (1) something that = what (2) 명사를 뒤에서 수식하는 분사는 '관계대명사+be동사'가 생략된 것으로 볼 수 있다.

11 (A)는 '병'을, (B)는 '작은 돌들'을 가리킨다.

12 ⓐ 가방에서 작은 돌 한 상자를 끄집어냈다. ⓑ 작은 돌들이 골프공 사이의 '틈새로' '굴러 들어갔다'.

13 Jenkins 선생님은 작은 돌들을 병에 부었다.

14 겉보기에는 병이 꽉 차 보였지만, 모래와 사과 주스가 들어갈 공간이 있었다.

15 ⓐ는 '모래를, ⓑ는 '사과 주스'를 가리킨다.

16 사람들에 의해 '소중하게 여겨지는'이라고 해야 하므로 과거분사로 써야 한다. which[that] are valued에서 주격 관계대명사와 be동사를 생략한 것이다.

17 (A)와 ④: …와 비슷한(전치사), ①, ③: 좋아하다(동사), ② 비슷한(형용사: 명사 앞에만 씀), ⑤ …처럼(전치사)

18 셋 중에서 크기가 가장 큰 골프공은 '인생에서 가장 중요한 것'을 상징하는 것이다.

19 The same goes for: ~도 마찬가지이다

20 ⓑ와 ②, ⑤: 공간, 여지, ①, ③, ④: 방

21 matter = be important: 중요하다

22 (A) '앉아 있는' 학생이라고 해야 하므로 sitting이 적절하다. One student to sit: 앉을 학생, (B) '보여 준다'고 해야 하므로 shows가 적절하다. see: 보다, (C) '여러분의 인생이 '가득 차' 보일지라도'라고 해야 하므로 full이 적절하다.

23 ⓐ와 ③: 들어올리다, ① (안건·문제 등을) 제기[언급]하다, ② (아이·어린 동물을) 키우다[기르다], ④ (자금·사람 등을) 모으다, ⑤ (양·가격·요금·임금 따위를) 끌어올리다

24 room for a cool drink with a friend

23

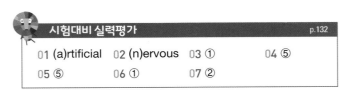

Lesson

3

Be Positive, Be Happy

시험대비 실력평가 　p.132

01 (a)rtificial 　02 (n)ervous 　03 ① 　　04 ⑤

05 ⑤ 　　　06 ① 　　　07 ②

01 주어진 단어는 반의어 관계이다. cause 원인 effect 결과
artificial 인공적인 natural 자연적인

02 주어진 단어는 반의어 관계이다. patient 참을성이 있는
impatient 조바심을 내는 nervous 불안한 calm 차분한

03 '종종 화를 내면서 말로 다른 사람과 의견을 달리하다'는 '주장하
다'에 해당한다.

04 'used to+동사원형'에서 used to는 조동사로 '~하곤 했다'의
의미이다.

05 인공조명 불빛으로 인해서 생기는 문제는 밤에 잠을 자는 것과
관련된 문제이다.

06 put on: ~을 입다 deal with:~을 다루다

07 ① bother 성가시게 하다 ② nothing/something ③ scary
무서운 ④ spend 보내다, 쓰다 ⑤ gloomy 우울한

서술형 시험대비 　p.133

01 out 　　　　02 (c)ommon 　03 stressed

04 (1) decide 　(2) artificial 　(3) sleepy

05 (a)rtificial 　　　　　06 with

07 (1) relax 　(2) deep 　(3) counting 　(4) drinking

　(5) happy

01 stress out 지치게 하다 take some time out 잠시 동안 시간
을 내다

02 "드문, 희귀한"이라는 뜻의 "rare"와 의미상 반대가 되는 단어
는 "common 흔한"이다.

03 '스트레스를 주다'에 해당하는 동사의 과거분사 형용사를 써서
'스트레스를 받은'이라는 의미가 되도록 해야 한다.

05 '진짜처럼 보이도록 만들어졌지만 진짜가 아니거나 자연적인 것
으로 만들어지지 않은'은 '인공적인'에 해당하는 의미이다.

06 deal with 처리하다, 해결하다 spend time with ~와 시간을
보내다

07 (1) 기분이 상했을 때 긴장을 가라앉히는 방법 (2) 깊은 숨을 쉬
다 (3) 열까지 세기 (4) 차가운 물 마시기 (5) 행복한 생각하기'
의 의미가 자연스럽다.

교과서 Conversation

핵심 Check 　p.134~135

1 (1) talk 　(2) let's, Because, sense

2 (A) out 　(B) used 　(C) What 　(D) focus

02 (A) 스트레스로 지치게 하다 = stress out (B) ~하곤 했 다. ~
했었다 = used to (C) ~에 집중하다 = focus, concentrate

교과서 대화문 익히기

Check(√) True or False 　p.136

1 T 　2 T 　3 T 　4 F

교과서 확인학습 　p.138~139

Listen and Answer – Dialog 1

talk, about, What, feel, stressed, About, answered, As,
see, common cause, Over, stresses, Problems, took ,
with, Next, worries, get stressed, appearance

Listen and Answer – Dialog 2

What / studying for, Grades / used to, way / know /
stress, helpful / What / got stressed, at, focus / help
/ improve

Listen More – Listen and choose.

talk, decide / Let, designs / choose, short / say /
Because, wear / makes sense, about / cute /
expensive

Speak – Talk in groups.

talk, One, well-known

Speak – Talk in pairs.

spend / makes / make / makes

My Speaking Portfolio Step 3

like, relax, upset, take deep, counting, drinking, Lastly

Wrap Up – Listening & Speaking 1

talked, foods, are good, like to, healthy eating, slowly,
eating

Wrap Up – Listening & Speaking 2

don't, make / make / basketball / say / we need

시험대비 기본평가 　p.140

01 ④ 　　　02 ② 　　　03 ② 　　　04 ③

01 주제를 소개할 때는 'I'd like to talk about ~'라고 한다.

02 이유를 물어보는 말로 'What makes you say that?'이라고 한다.

03 talk about: ~에 대하여 말하다

04 ③ 'different foods that are good for your health.'는 지난번 소개한 주제이기 때문에 지금부터 소개할 내용은 아니다.

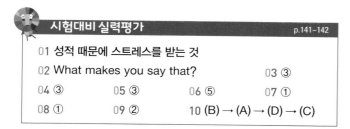

시험대비 실력평가   p.141~142

01 성적 때문에 스트레스를 받는 것
02 What makes you say that?   03 ③
04 ③   05 ③   06 ⑤   07 ①
08 ①   09 ②   10 (B) → (A) → (D) → (C)

01 that way는 앞 문장의 내용을 받는다.

02 "What makes you ~?"는 이유를 묻는 표현이다.

03 약간의 스트레스가 도움이 된다는 엄마의 말에 왜 그런지를 묻는 것으로 보아 Oliver는 그 사실을 모르고 있었다.

04 ③ 스트레스의 가장 흔한 원인은 학교 공부이다.

05 소셜 미디어에 시간을 많이 쓰겠다는 생각을 소개하고 (C) 거기에 대하여 이유를 물어보고, (A) 그 이유에 대한 질문에 대답하는 순서가 자연스러운 배열이다.

06 내용의 흐름상 동의하는 내용이 적절하다. ①~④는 동의하는 의미이고, ⑤는 동의하지 않을 때 쓰는 말이다.

07 소녀가 스포츠 클럽을 만들자는 제안에 대하여 소년은 야구 클럽을 만들고 싶어 하지만, 소녀는 농구가 더 낫다고 서로 다른 의견을 말하고 있다.

08 시험을 앞두고 수학 공부를 할 때 느낄 수 있는 스트레스에 대한 이야기가 적절하다.

09 'Did stress help you in other ways?'를 보면 스트레스가 도움이 되었다는 설명에 이어 또 다른 도움이 된 사실에 대한 설명이라는 것을 파악할 수 있다.

10 (B) 화면에 보여준 티셔츠 중에서 자신이 좋아하는 것을 고른다. (A) 거기에 대하여 이유를 묻는 질문을 하고, 그 뒤에는 그 대답이 이어진다. (D) 또 다른 것에 대한 제안을 하고 그것을 들은 B2는 거기에 대해서 긍정적인 대답을 한다. (C) 앞에 선택된 것에 대한 긍정적인 언급에 이어 또 다른 긍정적인 면에 대한 언급이 이어진다.

서술형 시험대비   p.143

01 What makes you feel the most stressed?
02 Next came family and worries about the future.
03 schoolwork
04 Oliver의 어머니도 스트레스를 느꼈다는 것   05 at
06 it's good to take deep breaths

01 의문대명사 what을 주어로 시작한다.

02 부사 Next로 시작하면 문장은 "부사+동사+주어"의 순서가 되도록 한다.

03 'As you can see, schoolwork was the most common cause of stress.'를 보면 십대의 가장 큰 스트레스 원인은 schoolwork이라는 것을 알 수 있다.

05 at the same time: 동시에

06 심호흡을 하다 = take deep breaths

교과서
Grammar

핵심 Check   p.144~145

1 (1) looking   (2) writing   (3) living
2 (1) have been waiting   (2) has been reading
3 (1) so   (2) such
4 (1) so cold that we didn't
   (2) so expensive that he didn't
   (3) so strong that they stopped

시험대비 기본평가   p.146

01 ⑤   02 ⑤
03 has been teaching English at this middle school for 20 years
04 so, that   05 ①

01 태어난 이후로 현재까지 살았고 지금도 살고 있다는 의미로 현재완료진행이 되어서 'have been living'이 되어야 한다.

02 ⑤ that절에서 eat의 목적어가 필요하다. eat → eat them

04 문맥상 'so ~ that' 구문이 되도록 한다.

05 동사 was의 보어로 형용사가 들어가야 한다.

시험대비 실력평가   p.147~149

01 (1) She has been sitting on the bench for an hour.
   (2) She has been working at the store since 2010.
   (3) Tom has been cleaning the room since this morning.
02 ②   03 ③
04 I've been writing 'Me Time' on my calendar for two months.
05 ②   06 ④   07 ④

25

08 (1) She was so tired that she went to bed early.
  (2) The cake looked so delicious that he decided to buy it.
  (3) The story was so interesting that he read it in a day.
09 that   10 ③   11 ①
12 (1) been   (2) cleaning   (3) so   (4) so   13 ③
14 ②   15 ①   16 ①   17 ⑤
18 has been watching

01 과거에 시작하여 현재에도 계속하고 있는 행위는 현재완료진행으로 나타내고, 형태는 'have/has been -ing'이다.

02 ② 과거형 수동태이므로 was가 들어가야 한다. 나머지는 모두 been이 들어간다.

03 현재완료진행의 동사 형태는 'have/has been -ing'이다.

04 'I've'에 이어지는 것은 과거분사이고 과거분사 been에 이어질 수 있는 것은 -ing 형태인 writing이다. writing의 목적어는 'Me Time'이고 거기에 이어서 장소와 시간의 부사구가 따라온다.

05 ⓒ 'It was such fine that we went outside.'는 'It was so fine that we went outside.'가 되어야 한다. ⓔ 'She has been living here for 5 years.'가 되어야 한다.

06 ④의 that은 관계대명사이고 나머지는 모두 부사절을 유도하는 접속사이다.

07 ④ 문장의 주어는 부정사나 동명사가 되어야 하기 때문에 Drinking이 되어야 한다.

08 '매우 ~해서 …하다'의 의미를 나타낼 때는 'so ~that' 구문을 이용한다. so와 that 사이에 형용사나 부사를 쓴다.

09 '너무 ~해서 …하다'는 내용을 'so ~ that' 구문으로 나타낸 표현이어서 빈칸에는 that이 들어간다.

10 '한 시간 동안 ~하고 있다'는 'have/has been -ing'의 형태로 현재완료진행형을 사용한다. was → has

11 ① so 뒤에는 형용사나 부사를 쓴다. 'a+형용사+명사' 앞에는 such를 쓴다.

12 (1), (2) 현재완료진행 시제는 'have/has been -ing' 형태가 되어야 하고 (3), (4)는 'so 형용사 that'의 구문이다.

13 ③ 현재완료시제와 함께 사용하는 시간의 표현에서 기간을 나타내어 '~ 동안'이라고 할 때는 전치사 for를 사용한다.

14 '너무 고통스러워 ~할 수 없었다'는 'so painful that ~ couldn't …'이다.

15 ① 현재완료 시제에서 '~ 동안'은 전치사 for, '~ 이래로'는 since를 사용하여 나타낸다.

16 '너무 ~해서 ~할 수 없다'는 'so+형용사/부사+that ~'이나 'such a+형용사+명사+that ~'의 형태로 나타낸다.

17 ⑤ 현재완료는 과거의 시간 표시와 함께 쓸 수 없다.

18 5시간 전부터 텔레비전을 보기 시작해서 지금도 보고 있으므로 현재완료진행형을 써서 나타낸다.

01 (1) She has been teaching English at this school for 10 years.
  (2) It has been raining since last night.
  (3) He drove the car so fast that his father told him to drive slowly. .
02 a high mountain
03 (1) Has Mike been doing
  (2) Jack hasn't been playing
04 (1) talking   (2) been
05 has been playing tennis for two hours
06 so rich
07 She is so kind[nice] that everybody likes her.
08 Ann and I have been studying Chinese since last week.
09 (1) so tired   (2) heavy that
  (3) that they wanted more
10 has been using
11 Some people spend time with friends when they feel low.
12 (1) She is so hungry that she can't swim any more.
  (2) The car was so old that it couldn't run fast.
  (3) It was so cold that he put on his coat.

01 전부터 지금까지 하고 있는 일은 현재완료진행 시제로 나타내고, '너무 ~해서 …하다.'는 'so ~ that' 구문으로 나타낸다.

02 '너무 ~해서 ~할 수 없다'는 'such a+형용사+명사+that ~'의 형태로 나타낼 수 있다.

03 (1) 현재완료진행형(have[has] been -ing)의 의문문은 'Have+주어+been -ing ~?'의 어순이다. (2) 현재완료진행형의 부정문은 'have[has] not been -ing'이다.

04 (1), (2) 현재완료진행 시제는 'have[has] been -ing'이다.

05 두 시간 전부터 현재까지 테니스를 치고 있다는 내용의 현재완료진행형(has been playing)을 사용한다.

06 "so ~ that 주어 can" 너무 ~해서 …할 수 있다

07 '매우 ~해서 …하다'는 so ~ that 구문을 이용한다.

08 지난주부터 현재까지 공부하고 있다는 내용은 과거부터 현재까지의 진행을 포함하는 현재완료진행형(have been studying)을 사용한다.

09 '너무 ~해서 …하다'의 의미는 'so 형용사/부사 that'의 구문으로 나타낸다.

10 두 시간 전부터 현재까지 컴퓨터를 사용하고 있다는 내용의 현재완료진행형(has been using)을 사용한다.

11 Some people에 이어지는 동사 spend를 쓰고 종속절은 접속사 when으로 이어지도록 한다.

12 "너무 ~해서 …하다."의 의미로 "so 형용사/부사 that ~"의 구문으로 바꾼다.

확인문제   p.152

1 T   2 F   3 T   4 F

확인문제   p.152

1 T   2 F   3 T   4 F

확인문제   p.153

1 T   2 F   3 F   4 T   5 T   6 F

교과서 확인학습 A   p.154~155

01 Goodbye
02 feel low
03 Others, to feel better
04 Still others
05 deal with
06 suggest different ways
07 saying, breaking, arguing
08 When this happens
09 so, that
10 at the top of my lungs
11 thanks to, what bothers me
12 I've been using, works
13 graduated from
14 he's been looking for
15 he's stressed out, by going fishing
16 gets upset
17 so, that, can leave, behind
18 Besides, to be
19 focusing on, forget
20 second-year, free from
21 seems to like, for a good reason
22 number-one way
23 so, that
24 feel like, relieving
25 looks tidy, looks brighter
26 what
27 all the things she has to do
28 she's under stress
29 takes some time out
30 reads, watches,talks
31 matter, as long as
32 I've been writing
33 work for you
34 to say goodbye to stress

교과서 확인학습 B   p.156~157

1 Say Goodbye to Stress
2 Some people spend time with friends when they feel low.
3 Others eat special foods to feel better.
4 Still others simply sleep for a while.
5 How do you deal with stress?
6 Here are some stories about people who suggest different ways.
7 Sometimes my friends give me stress by saying bad things about me, breaking promises, or arguing over small things.
8 When this happens, I watch horror movies!
9 Good horror movies are so scary that I scream a lot.
10 I guess that screaming at the top of my lungs helps me feel better.
11 Also, thanks to scary scenes and sound effects, I can forget about what bothers me.
12 I've been using this method for the past several months, and it really works.
13 My uncle graduated from college two years ago.
14 He lives with my family, and he's been looking for a job for some time.
15 I know that he's stressed out, but he always tries to be positive by going fishing.
16 He never gets upset when he doesn't catch any fish.
17 He says, "While I fish, I'm so focused that I can leave all my worries behind.
18 Besides, it teaches me to be patient."
19 I'm sure that focusing on one thing helps us forget about something else.
20 My sister, a second-year student in high school, has a wonderful way to stay free from stress.
21 She feels a lot of stress from schoolwork, but my mother seems to like the situation for a good reason.
22 It is because cleaning is my sister's number-one way to make life better!
23 When she's so stressed that her life looks gloomy, she cleans her room.
24 She says, "As I clean my room, I feel like I'm also relieving stress.
25 When my room looks tidy, my life looks brighter."
26 Let me tell you what my mother does about her stress.
27 She feels stressed by all the things she has to do at work and at home.
28 When she's under stress, she writes "Me Time" on her calendar.
29 This means she takes some time out for herself.
30 She reads a book, watches a movie, or talks with her friends.

31 She says, "It doesn't really matter what I do, as long as it's something I like.

32 I've been writing 'Me Time' on my calendar for two months, and I feel much better."

33 Which methods will work for you?

34 Try some of these ideas yourself, and find your best way to say goodbye to stress.

시험대비 실력평가
p.158~161

01 ⑤　　02 ②　　03 ③　　04 ②

05 ③　　06 ②, ⑤　　07 tidy

08 she cleans her room

09 (A) because　(B) looks　(C) relieving

10 ③　　11 what I do　12 ②　　13 ④

14 ①　　15 screaming at the top of my lungs

16 ③, ④　　17 ③　　18 fishing　19 ②

20 (A) a job　(B) going fishing　(C) gets upset

21 ④　　　　　　22 ①, ③

23 (A) cleans her room　(B) make life better

24 ③, ⑤　　25 hello → goodbye

01 ⑤는 현재분사, 나머지는 동명사

02 ⓐ와 ② 효과가 있다, ① 일하다, ③ (문학·예술 따위의) 작품, ④ 토목공사, ⑤ (기계장치 등이) 작동되다

03 ③ too ~ to: 너무 ~해서 …할 수 없다, Good horror movies are scary enough to make Mina scream a lot. 으로 고치는 것이 적절하다.

04 ⓐ graduate from: ~을 졸업하다, ⓑ focus on: ~에 집중하다, 초점을 맞추다

05 ③ 낙관적인, 낙천적인, 준호의 삼촌은 스트레스를 받고 있지만 낚시를 다니며 긍정적으로 지내려고 항상 노력한다고 했으므로, '낙천적인' 성격이라고 할 수 있다. ① 수동적인, 소극적인, ② 짜증난[안달하는], ④ 후한, 관대한, ⑤ 부정적인

06 (A)와 ②, ⑤: 계속 용법, ①, ④: 경험 용법, ③ 완료 용법

07 정돈되고, 조직적인 방식으로 배열된, tidy: 깔끔한, 잘 정돈된

08 '그녀가 방을 청소하는 것'을 가리킨다.

09 (A) 뒤에 '이유'를 설명하는 말이 이어지므로 because가 적절하다. why 뒤에는 앞에서 말하고 있는 내용의 '결과'에 해당하는 말이 이어진다. (B) 뒤에 형용사가 나오므로 looks가 적절하다. look+형용사, look like+명사: ~처럼 보이다, (C) 스트레스도 해소되는 것 같다고 해야 하므로 relieving이 적절하다. relieve: (불쾌감·고통 등을) 없애[덜어] 주다

10 (ⓑ)와 ③: ~할 때, ① …와 같이; …대로, ② …와 같은 정도로 (as … as ~에서, 앞의 as는 지시부사, 뒤의 as는 접속사), ④

[이유] …이기 때문에, ⑤ …으로서(전치사)

11 ⓐ '내가 무엇을 하는지' ⓑ '내가 하는 것'

12 이 글은 '스트레스를 다루는 Yulia의 엄마의 방법'에 관한 글이므로, 제목으로는 ②번이 적절하다.

13 ④ 'Yulia의 어머니가 얼마나 자주 "Me Time"을 가지는지'는 대답할 수 없다. ① By all the things she has to do at work and at home. ② She writes "Me Time" on her calendar. ③ It means she takes some time out for herself. ⑤ For two months.

14 주어진 문장의 this에 주목한다. ①번 앞 문장의 내용을 받고 있으므로 ①번이 적절하다.

15 scream at the top of one's lungs: 있는 힘껏 소리를 지르다

16 ⓑ와 ③, ④: 관계대명사, ① 의문형용사, ②, ⑤ 의문대명사, ② be in debt: 빚이 있다

17 이 글은 '스트레스를 다루는 방법'에 관한 글이므로, 주제로는 ③번이 적절하다. ④ benefit: 이익, 혜택

18 go -ing: ~하러 가다

19 빈칸 앞 문장들에서 '물고기를 한 마리도 잡지 못했을 때에도 삼촌은 절대 속상해 하지 않는다.'고 하면서, '낚시하는 동안, 나는 아주 몰입해서 모든 걱정을 잊을 수 있어.'라고 했고, 빈칸 뒤의 문장에서 낚시는 나에게 인내를 가르쳐 준다.'고 했으므로, 주로 무엇에 대한 또 다른 이유나 주장을 제시할 때 쓰이는 Besides(게다가)가 적절하다. teach+목적어+to부정사: ~하는 법을 가르치다 ① 대신에, ⑤ 그에 반해서, 그와 대조적으로

20 준호의 삼촌은 얼마 전부터 '직장'을 구하고 있다. 그는 스트레스를 받고 있지만 '낚시를 다니며' 긍정적으로 지내려고 항상 노력하고, 물고기를 한 마리도 잡지 못했을 때에도 삼촌은 절대 '속상해 하지' 않는다.

21 ⓐ와 ②: 형용사적 용법, ①, ⑤: 부사적 용법, ③, ④: 명사적 용법

22 뒤에 셀 수 없는 명사가 나오므로, many와 a number of는 바꿔 쓸 수 없다. a lot of와 lots of는 수와 양이 많은 경우에 다 쓸 수 있다.

23 청소가 도빈이 누나의 '삶을 향상하는' 최고의 방법이라서, 스트레스를 너무 많이 받아서 인생이 우울해 보일 때 그녀가 '방을 청소하기' 때문이다.

24 ⓐ와 ③, ⑤: (원하는) 효과가 나다[있다], (계획 따위가) 잘 되어 가다, ① (해야 할) 일(명사), ② (기계나 장치 등을) 작동시키다, ④ 직장(명사)

25 '스트레스와 이별하는 방법'이라고 해야 하므로, hello를 goodbye로 고쳐야 한다. say hello to: ~에게 안부를 전하다, say goodbye to: ~에게 작별인사를 하다

01 ⓐ saying ⓑ breaking ⓒ arguing

02 Good horror movies are so scary that I scream a lot.

03 (A) horror movies (B) her lungs

04 (A) for (B) positive (C) so

05 being → to be

06 no difficulty → difficulty 07 what

08 so long as 09 two months, writing

10 without

11 도빈이의 누나가 학업 때문에 많은 스트레스를 받는 상황

12 (A) schoolwork (B) cleaning her room

13 (A) tell (B) under (C) herself

14 자신을 위해 잠깐 시간을 내는 것

15 even, still, far, a lot 중에서 두 개를 쓰면 된다.

01 전치사 by 다음에 동명사를 쓰는 것이 적절하다.

02 so+형용사/부사+that절: 너무 ~해서 …하다

03 미나는 스트레스를 느낄 때 '공포영화'를 보면서 '있는 힘껏' 소리를 지른다.

04 (A) '얼마 동안'이라고 해야 하므로 for가 적절하다. for: ~ 동안, since: ~ 이후로, (B) '긍정적'으로 지내려고 한다고 해야 하므로 positive가 적절하다. positive: 긍정적인, negative: 부정적인, (C) 뒤에 명사는 없고 형용사만 나오므로 so가 적절하다. so+형용사/부사+that절: 너무 ~해서 …하다, such+a+형용사+명사+that절

05 teach+목적어+to부정사: ~에게 …하기를 가르치다

06 '준호의 삼촌은 얼마 전부터 직장을 구하고 있다'고 했으므로, 일자리를 찾는 데 어려움을 '겪고 있다'로 고치는 것이 적절하다. have difficulty ~ing: ~하는 데 어려움을 겪다

07 ⓐ에는 관계대명사 what, ⓑ에는 의문대명사 what이 적절하다.

08 as long as = so long as: ~이기만[하기만] 하면

09 '두 달째 달력에 '나만의 시간'을 적어 왔다'는 것은 '두 달' 전에 달력에 '나만의 시간'을 쓰기 시작해서 지금도 여전히 '쓰고 있는 중'이라는 뜻이다.

10 free from = without: ~이 없는

11 바로 앞의 내용을 가리킨다.

12 (A) 도빈이 누나의 스트레스의 원인: 학교 공부, (B) 스트레스를 해소하는 도빈이 누나의 방법: 그녀의 방을 청소하는 것

13 (A) '사역동사 let+목적어+동사원형'을 써야 하므로 tell이 적절하다. (B) '스트레스를 받고 있다'고 해야 하므로 under가 적절하다. be under stress: 스트레스를 받고 있다, (C) 주어와 목적어가 같을 때는 재귀대명사를 써야 하므로 herself가 적절

14 뒤 문장(This means she takes some time out for herself.)의 내용을 쓰면 된다.

15 much는 비교급을 강조하는 말이며, '훨씬'으로 해석한다.

01 ① 02 (a)rtificial 03 ② 04 ①

05 ② 06 ① 07 (m)akes 08 ③

09 ② 10 ① 11 help 12 ④

13 I guess that screaming at the top of my lungs helps me feel better.

14 tell you what my mother does about her stress

15 ① 16 ④ 17 ① 18 ②

19 (1) Little → A little (2) improving → (to) improve

20 ② 21 ③ 22 ⑤

23 ⓐ Some ⓑ Still ⓒ who[that] 24 ①, ④

25 What → How 26 ②

27 focusing on one thing helps us forget about something else

28 ③ 29 ①

30 When my room looks tidy, my life looks brighter

31 ⓐ Mouth ⓑ Nose 32 ①

01 '다른 사람에게 보여지는 방식'은 '겉모습, 외모'라는 뜻이다.

02 주어진 단어는 반의의 관계이다. agree 동의하다 disagree 동의하지 않다 artificial 인공적인 natural 자연적인

03 소셜 미디어에 시간을 많이 보내는 이유는 친구를 사귈 수 있다는 장점 때문이다.

04 'cheerless'는 '활기 없는'이라는 뜻으로 gloomy에 해당한다.

05 (B) 상대의 말에 다른 의견을 제시하고 (A) 이에 대한 이유를 묻고 (C) 거기에 대하여 설명하는 순서가 자연스럽다.

06 ① "I'd like to talk about some good ways to relax when you get upset."를 통해서 여기서 소개하는 것은 화를 푸는 방법이라는 것을 알 수 있다.

07 'make sense'는 '의미가 통하다, 말이 되다'의 뜻으로 상대의 말에 동의하는 의미이다.

08 ⓒ 짧은 소매가 좋다는 것으로 보아 여름에 입을 것이라고 생각할 수 있다.

09 시험 공부를 하면서 스트레스를 받는 것으로 보아 성적이 스트레스의 원인이라는 것을 알 수 있다.

10 ① '무엇 때문에 그렇게 말하나요?'는 '무엇 때문에 그렇게 생각하나요?'로 바꿀 수 있다.

11 대답을 통해서 스트레스가 주는 유익함에 대한 질문임을 알 수 있다.

12 '너무 ~해서 …하다'의 의미를 나타내는 'so ~ that …'의 구문이다.

13 '있는 힘껏 소리를 지르는 것이 기분 좋게 느끼도록 도와준다고 생각해'의 의미로 'I guess'를 주절로 하고 종속절의 주어는 'screaming at the top of my lungs'가 되도록 한다.

14 'Let me'에 이어지는 동사원형 tell을 쓰고 직접목적어는 what이 이끄는 명사절이 되도록 한다.

15 ⓓ 명백한 과거를 나타내는 'when she was a child'는 현재완료진행형과 함께 쓸 수 없다.

16 '~ 이후로'의 의미일 때는 since를 쓴다.

17 ① '너무 ~해서 …하다'는 'so 형용사/부사 that ~'의 구문으로 나타낸다.

18 '너무 ~해서 …하다'는 'so 형용사/부사 that ~'의 구문으로 나타낸다.

19 (1) 문맥상 '약간의'라는 긍정의 의미가 되어야 한다. (2) 동사 help의 목적어는 to부정사나 원형부정사이다.

20 ② 부사 Next로 시작하는 문장은 주어와 동사를 도치하도록 한다.

21 ③ makes의 주어가 되어야 하므로 why 대신 what이 와야 한다.

22 '그녀는 아주 정직해서 거짓말을 할 수 없었다.'의 의미인데, ⑤ '그녀는 거짓말을 했지만 '아주 정직했다'라는 뜻이다.

23 Some, Others, Still others: 몇몇은, 다른 사람들은, 또 다른 사람들은, ⓒ 관계대명사 who[that]가 적절하다.

24 (A)와 ①, ④는 부사적 용법, ② 형용사적 용법, ③, ⑤는 명사적 용법

25 What 뒤에 완전한 문장이 이어지므로, What을 부사인 How로 고치는 것이 적절하다.

26 '여기에 다른 방법을 제안하는 사람들에 대한 몇 가지 이야기들이 있다.'고 했으므로, ②번이 적절하다.

27 on을 보충하면 된다. focus on: ~에 집중하다, 초점을 맞추다

28 준호의 삼촌은 스트레스를 받고 있지만 낚시를 다니며 '긍정적'으로 지내려고 항상 노력한다고 했으므로, '부정적인' 태도를 가지고 있다고 한 ③번이 옳지 않다.

29 free from: ~이 없는

30 look+형용사: ~하게 보이다

31 ⓐ '약간의 차를 마셔라.'라고 했으므로, Mouth가 적절하다.
ⓑ '신선한 꽃 냄새를 맡아라.'라고 했으므로, Nose가 적절하다.

32 ① 야외에 있을 때는 '하늘'을 보라고 했다.

단원별 예상문제
p.170~173

| 01 (b)oring | 02 ① | 03 ④ | 04 ② |
| 05 ② | 06 ⑤ | 07 (m)essy | 08 ① |

09 ①	10 (1) free (2) reason (3) gloomy		
11 ①	12 ②	13 ⑤	14 ④
15 ⑤	16 ③	17 ③	

18 친구들이 미나에 관해 나쁜 말을 하거나, 약속을 어기거나, 혹은 사소한 일을 두고 언쟁을 하며 미나에게 스트레스를 주는 것

19 using
20 ① scary scenes ② sound effects
21 (A) graduated from (B) upset (C) patient
22 ①, ②
23 her → herself
24 important
25 (A) all the things she has to do (B) Me Time
26 ②
27 (A) going outdoors and getting plenty of sunlight
(B) Exercise

---

01 주어진 단어는 동의어 관계이다. boring 지루한 dull 지루한

02 '사람이 약간 걱정되거나 속상하게 만들다'는 '성가시게 하다, 괴롭히다'의 의미이다.

03 decide on: ~을 결정하다 thanks to: ~ 덕택에

04 ① graduated 졸업했다 ② '그가 지쳤다'의 의미로 stressed가 들어가는 것이 적절하다. ③ positive 긍정적인 ④ focused 집중한 ⑤ forget 잊어버리다

05 공포영화를 설명할 수 있는 단어는 ② 'scary 무서운'이다.

06 '있는 힘껏'이라는 뜻으로 'at the top of my lungs'가 되어야 한다.

07 주어진 단어는 반의어 관계이다. cause 원인 effect 결과 tidy 깔끔한 messy 어질러진

08 ① 여기에 사용된 grade는 '성적'이라는 뜻이다.

09 '화내지 않고 어려움을 받아들이거나 긴 시간 차분하게 기다릴 수 있는'은 'patient 인내하는'에 해당하는 의미이다.

10 (1) '~가 없는'의 뜻으로 'free from'이 적절하다. (2) ~한 이유로 = for a ~ reason (3) 우울한, 침울한 = gloomy

11 ② 소년은 스포츠 클럽 만드는 것에 동의한다. ③ 소녀는 농구 클럽을 원한다. ④ 소녀는 야구 클럽을 만들고자 하는 소녀와 의견이 다르다. ⑤ 소녀가 야구를 좋아하는지는 알 수 없다.

12 with: ~이 있는, ~을 가지고 있는

13 내용상 앞에서 선택한 것에 대한 장점이 언급되어 있는 것이 적절하다.

14 대화의 내용으로 보아 그들은 티셔츠를 여름에 입을 것이다.

15 현재완료진행시제는 'have/has been –ing'가 되어야 한다.

16 ③ 현재완료진행시제와 함께 사용하는 시간 표현에서 '~동안'은 전치사 for를 쓴다.

17 ⓒ that절에서 buy의 목적어인 it(= the bag)이 필요하다. ⓓ '너무 ~해서 …하다'는 'so 형용사 that'이다. ⓔ since this morning과 함께 쓰는 문장은 현재완료나 현재완료진행시제를 쓴다.

18 앞 문장의 내용을 가리킨다.

19 과거에 시작한 행동을 지금까지 계속하는 것을 강조할 때에는 현재완료진행형(have been -ing)으로 나타낸다.

20 공포영화의 '무서운 장면들'과 '음향 효과' 덕분에 그녀를 괴롭히는 것들을 잊을 수 있다.

21 (A) 대학을 '졸업했다'고 해야 하므로 graduated from이 적절하다. graduate from: ~을 졸업하다, (B) 물고기를 한 마리도 잡지 못했을 때에도 삼촌은 '속상해 하지' 않는다.고 해야 하므로 upset이 적절하다. relaxed: 느긋한, 여유 있는, (C) 낚시는 나에게 '인내'를 가르쳐 준다고 해야 하므로 patient가 적절하다. impatient: 짜증난, 참을성 없는

22 ⓐ와 ③, ④, ⑤: 게다가, 더욱이, ① 그러므로, ② In addition to 뒤에는 목적어가 와야 한다. ⓐ의 경우, In addition과는 바꿔 쓸 수 있다.

23 for 뒤의 목적어가 주어 자신이므로 재귀대명사 herself를 써야 한다.

24 matter = be important: 중요하다

25 (A) Yulia의 어머니의 스트레스의 원인: 직장과 집에서 해야 하는 온갖 일, (B) 스트레스를 해소하는 Yulia의 어머니의 방법: "나만의 시간"을 가지는 것

26 화면 앞에 앉아 있는 '대신' 밖에 나가 태양 아래에서 뛰어다녀라고 해야 하므로 ②번이 적절하다. Instead of: ~ 대신에, ①, ⑤: 게다가, ③ ~에 덧붙여, ④ ~에도 불구하고

27 (A)는 '밖에 나가서 충분한 양의 햇볕을 쬐는 것', (B)는 '운동'을 가리킨다.

서술형 실전문제 p.174~175

01 (r)eason 02 (w)orried 03 (e)ffect
04 stressed 05 helpful 06 makes
07 무엇이 여러분이 가장 스트레스를 느끼도록 만드는가?
08 appearance
09 My mother has been cooking dinner since 6:00.
10 so, that 11 ⓐ so ⓑ that
12 (A) happens (B) helps (C) what
13 this method 14 ago, is, looking
15 enough to 16 (A) fishing (B) positive

01 주어진 단어는 동의어 관계이다. bother 성가시게 하다 – disturb 방해하다 cause 원인 – reason 이유

02 주어진 단어는 반의어 관계이다. cheap 싼 expensive 비싼 – relieved 안심이 되는 worried 걱정되는

03 '어떤 사건이나 행동에 의해서 초래된 변화'는 '결과, 영향'이라는 뜻이다.

04 that way는 '그렇게'의 뜻으로 stressed를 받는다.

05 was의 보어가 되는 형용사로 고친다.

06 이유를 물어보는 말로 'What makes you say that?'이 되어야 한다.

07 this question은 앞 문장을 받는다.

08 appear의 명사형으로 고친다.

09 6시 이후부터 현재까지 요리를 하고 있다는 내용의 현재완료진행형(has been cooking)시제를 사용한다.

10 '너무 ~해서 …하다'의 의미로 'so ~ that …'이 되어야 한다.

11 so+형용사/부사+that절: 너무 ~해서 …하다

12 (A) happen은 자동사로서 수동태로 쓸 수 없으므로 happens가 적절하다. (B) 주어가 동명사 screaming이므로 helps가 적절하다. (C) 뒤에 불완전한 절이 이어지고 선행사가 없으므로 관계대명사 what이 적절하다.

13 '이 방법'을 가리킨다.

14 준호의 삼촌이 '얼마 전부터 직장을 구하고 있다'는 것은 얼마 '전에' 직장을 구하기 시작해서 지금도 여전히 '구하고 있는 중'이라는 뜻이다.

15 so ~ that S can … = ~ enough to 동사원형

16 준호의 삼촌은 낚시를 하러 다니는 덕분에, 직장을 구하는 데 어려움을 겪고 있어도 긍정적인 태도를 가지고 있다.

창의사고력 서술형 문제 p.176

|모범답안|

01 working, change, fish stresses, worry
02 have been living in this city / I have been living in this city since I was ten. I have been hanging out with my best friend since I was ten. I have been learning English since I was ten. I have been playing the guitar since I was ten. I have been using this computer since I was ten.
03 (A) Eye (B) Mouth (C) Hand (D) Nose
  (E) Ear

단원별 모의고사 p.177~180

01 ② 02 ④ 03 ⑤ 04 ②
05 stress → stressed 06 ② 07 ③
08 My father has been repairing his car since this morning.
09 ① 10 so hot that
11 (1) like to talk about some good ways to relax when you get upset
  (2) fish, I'm so focused that I can leave all my worries behind

31

12 ①	13 ③	14 keeping → breaking
15 the thing which[that]	16 ①, ④	17 fishing
18 from	19 ②	20 This → It
21 ①	22 ②	

01 주어진 단어는 동의어 관계이다. tidy 깔끔한 neat 깨끗한 – scream 소리를 지르다 shout 소리치다

02 '더 좋게 만들다 또는 더 좋아지다'의 의미는 improve 이다.

03 patient 참을성이 있는 impatient 조바심이 나는

04 (B) 상대의 말에 이유를 묻고 (A) 그 질문에 대한 이유를 설명하고 (C) 거기에 대하여 동의하는 순서가 자연스럽다.

05 ⑤ '스트레스를 받다'는 'get stressed'로 'get+과거분사'의 형태로 수동의 의미를 나타낸다.

06 'Let me show you some designs on the screen'을 보면 티셔츠 디자인을 화면을 보고 결정할 것이라는 것을 알 수 있다.

07 ③ 'such a+형용사+명사'의 순서가 된다.

08 오늘 아침 이후부터 지금까지 차를 수리하고 있다는 뜻으로 현재완료진행형(has been repairing)을 사용한다.

09 현재완료진행시제와 함께 쓰인 시간 표현에서 '~ 동안'의 의미일 때 전치사 for를 쓴다.

10 '너무 ~하기 때문에 …하다'는 so ~ that ...'으로 바꾸어 쓸 수 있다.

11 (1) ~하고 싶다 = would like to ~ ~하는 좋은 몇 가지 방법 = some good ways to ~ (2) 낚시하는 동안 = While I fish

12 ① 현재완료진행과 함께 쓰인 시간 표현에서 '~ 동안'이라는 의미일 때는 전치사 for로 나타낸다.

13 ⓑ, ⓔ '너무 ~해서 …하다'는 'so ~ that ...'이다. ⓕ 현재완료진행시제는 /have/has been –ing' 형태이다.

14 친구들이 약속을 어김으로써 미나에게 스트레스를 준다고 해야 하므로, keeping을 breaking으로 고쳐야 한다. keep promises: 약속을 지키다, break promises: 약속을 어기다

15 동사가 bothers이므로 선행사를 단수인 the thing으로 쓰는 것이 적절하다.

16 ⓐ와 ①, ④: …하고 있는 동안에(접속사), ② 동안, 시간(명사), ③, ⑤: [주절 뒤에서 반대·비교·대조를 나타내어] 그런데, 한편(으로는)

17 '낚시'를 가리킨다.

18 ⓐ free from: ~이 없는, ⓑ from schoolwork: 학업 때문에

19 도빈이의 어머니는 그 상황을 좋아하는 것 같다고 했다.

20 진주어에 해당하는 간접의문문 what I do를 받은 것이기 때문에, 가주어 It으로 고쳐야 한다.

21 ⓑ와 ④: 계속 용법, ① 경험 용법, ② 결과 용법, ③, ⑤: 완료 용법

22 ② Yulia의 어머니 직업이 무엇인지는 위 글에서 알 수 없다.

Lesson
4

Opening a Window to the World

시험대비 실력평가
p.184

01 dead 02 ① 03 ③ 04 ②
05 ④ 06 ①
07 (1) effective (2) mostly (3) transportation

01 주어진 관계는 반의어 관계이다. alive: 살아 있는, dead: 죽은
02 '대량으로 그리고 낮은 가격으로 물건을 판매하는 행위'를 가리키는 말은 wholesale(도매의)이다.
03 ③번 문장에서 rich는 '풍부한'을 의미한다.
04 house는 명사로는 '집'을 의미하지만 동사로 '살 곳을 주다, 거처를 제공하다'라는 의미를 갖는다.
05 ④번을 제외한 나머지는 모두 명사와 형용사와의 관계를 나타낸다. advent: 출현, 도래, adventure: 모험
06 주어진 문장에서 covered는 '지붕이 덮인'을 뜻하며 이와 같은 의미로 쓰인 것은 ①번이다. ②, ④: '다루다', ③, ⑤: '(비용을) 감당하다' tuition fee: 학비

서술형 시험대비
p.185

01 subtract 02 floating market
03 (1) selective (2) inventive (3) magical
   (4) impressive (5) personal (6) collective
   (7) emotional (8) seasonal
04 (1) lasts for two and a half hours
   (2) what time the store is going to close
   (3) you must use a covered truck
05 (1) best-before date (2) all corners of the world
   (3) digest (4) discover (5) natural
06 tourist, discover, transportation, last, local

01 주어진 관계는 반의어 관계이다. add: 더하다, subtract: 빼다
02 '보트 위에서 물건을 직접 사고파는 시장'을 가리키는 말은 floating market(수상 시장)이다.
04 last: 지속되다, covered: 지붕이 덮인, protect: 보호하다
05 digest: 소화시키다, discover: 발견하다, cancer: 암, natural: 자연의
06 local: 지역의, transportation: 교통, last: 지속되다, tourist: 관광객, discover: 발견하다

교과서
Conversation

핵심 Check
p.186~187

1 I wonder if there's a tourist map of the town
2 you help me with this milk /
   do you want me to tell you the best-before date

01 '~가 있는지 궁금하다.'는 'I wonder if there is ~.'이다.
02 도움을 요청하는 표현은 'Can you help me with ~?'이고 도움을 제안하는 표현은 'Do you want me to ~?'이다.

교과서 대화문 익히기

Check(√) True or False
p.188

1 T 2 F 3 T 4 F

교과서 확인학습
p.190~191

Listen – Listen & Answer Dialog 1

Welcome to, help / if, tourist map / Is there, looking for / like to try, local / five days, open / lucky, How can I get there / takes about, minutes / mark / Try, when, get

Listen – Listen & Answer Dialog 2

bill / Here, meal / good for / rich, digests / wonder if / to give, recipe

Listen More – Listen and complete

help me with, milk / Read / the best-before date / glasses / Let, see, by / I wonder if, lasts longer / one, until June 11 / one / welcome

Speak – Talk in pairs. 1

Excuse, wonder, around here / but, don't have one / all right

Speak – Talk in pairs. 2

wrong / bored / want me to, with / be great

Wrap Up 1

hungry / How / want, to, add

Wrap Up 2

look at, I wonder how much it is / Why don't, go in, check / buy it for you, asking, price / course

시험대비 기본평가   p.192

01 I want to travel with my friends

02 (D) → (C) → (B) → (A)

03 ⓒ → check   04 ⑤

02 (D) 배고픔을 설명 → (C) 제안 → (B) 고마움 표현 → (A) 질문

03 go와 병렬 구조이므로 check가 알맞다.

04 위 대화에서 귀여운 가방이 얼마인지 알 수 없다.

시험대비 실력평가   p.193~194

01 Will you mark the way on the map   02 tourist

03 ①, ③   04 bill   05 ⑤   06 ②

07 ⑤   08 ⑤

09 I wonder how much it is.

10 Let's go in and check.

11 They are going to ask the price of the cute bag.

12 (C) → (B) → (D) → (A) → (E)

02 '즐거움을 위해 여행하는 사람'을 가리키는 말은 tourist(여행자, 여행객)이다.

03 밑줄 친 (a)는 궁금한 점을 나타내고 있으므로 이와 바꾸어 쓸 수 있는 표현은 ①, ③번이다.

04 '상품이나 서비스에 대해 누군가에게 얼마만큼의 빚을 졌는지 보여주는 서류'를 뜻하는 것은 bill(계산서)이다.

05 여자가 어디에서 곤드레를 구매할 수 있는지 알고 싶어 한다는 설명은 대화의 내용과 일치하지 않는다.

06 주어진 문장은 유통 기한을 설명하고 있으므로 ⓑ번이 적절하다.

07 우유를 구매하는 과정에서 이루어지는 대화이므로 식료품점인 것을 알 수 있다.

08 위 대화에서 오늘 날짜는 알 수 없다.

09 간접의문문 어순으로 '의문사+주어+동사' 순서로 이어져야 한다.

10 (B)는 제안을 나타내고 있다.

11 Jane과 아빠는 가방 가격을 물어보려고 한다.

12 (C) 계산서 건네주기 및 식사에 대한 질문 → (B) 식사에 대한 만족 표현 → (D) 감사 표현 및 곤드레에 대한 설명 → (A) 놀라움 표현 → (E) 곤드레에 대한 추가 설명

서술형 시험대비   p.195

01 I wonder if there's a bank around here.

02 박물관은 현지 문화를 배우기에 좋은 장소이므로 Brian은 박물관을 방문하고 싶어 한다.

03 I wonder if there's one that lasts longer.

04 (A) my glasses   (B) the best-before date
   (C) lasts longer   (D) June 11

05 (D) → (E) → (C) → (B) → (A)

01 I wonder if: ~인지 궁금하다

04 오늘 나는 식료품점에 나의 안경을 가져가지 않았다. 너무 작아서 유통 기한을 읽기가 어려웠다. 나는 소년에게 그것을 읽어달라고 부탁했다. 나는 첫 번째로 집었던 우유는 사지 않았다. 왜냐하면 유통 기한이 너무 짧았기 때문이다. 운이 좋게도 소년은 유통 기한이 좀 더 긴 우유를 찾았다. 나는 내가 6월 11일까지 마실 수 있을 것으로 생각한다. 나는 그에게 감사했다.

05 (D) 궁금한 점 묻기 → (E) 제안 → (C) 감사 표현 → (B) 확인 → (A) 대답

교과서
Grammar

핵심 Check   p.196~197

1 (1) when   (2) where   (3) why
2 (1) if[whether]   (2) if[whether]   (3) whether

시험대비 기본평가   p.198

01 ①

02 (1) where   (2) when   (3) if   (4) whether   03 ④

04 (1) Tell me the reason why you were late.

   (2) He asked whether he could help.

   (3) Can you find out if he is available now?

01 선행사가 'the day'이므로 when을 써야 한다.

02 (1) 선행사가 'the library'이므로 where가 적절하다. (2) 선행사가 'The day'이므로 when이 적절하다. (3) '그녀가 장미를 좋아한다는 것을 궁금해 한다'는 말은 어색하다. 사실의 여부를 확인하거나 불확실함을 나타내는 if가 적절하다. (4) 바로 뒤에 'or not'이 이어지고 있으므로 whether가 적절하다.

03 Tell의 직접목적어가 나와야 하는데 '~인지 (아닌지)'라는 의미로 명사절을 이끄는 접속사 if가 적절하다.

04 (1) 선행사가 'the reason'이므로 관계부사 why를 이용한다. (2) '~인지 (아닌지)'라는 의미의 접속사로 어떠한 사실의 여부를 확인하거나 불확실함을 나타낼 때 쓰이는 whether를 이용한다. (3) '~인지 (아닌지)'라는 의미의 접속사 if를 이용한다.

01 ②   02 ④   03 ①

04 (1) where   (2) why   (3) where   (4) whether   (5) if
    (6) whether

05 ⑤   06 ③   07 ④   08 ⑤

09 where   10 ②   11 ①

12 (1) the time 또는 when   (2) the reason 또는 why

13 ④

14 (1) Sandra wonders if it will be fine tomorrow.
   (2) Whether he stays or goes doesn't matter that much.
   (3) That is the place where I buy food for the coming week.
   (4) The reason why he did it is complicated.
   (5) The way it was done was the best they could do at the time.

15 ⑤   16 ②, ③

17 Will you tell me if[whether] I still have a place in your heart?

01 선행사가 'the reason'이므로 관계부사 why가 적절하다.

02 '~인지 (아닌지)'라는 의미의 접속사 if[whether]를 쓰는 것이 적절하다. I asked her if[whether] she wanted to marry me, but she wouldn't answer.

03 첫 번째 빈칸에는 '~인지 (아닌지)'라는 의미의 접속사 if나 whether가 적절하다. 두 번째 빈칸에는 선행사가 the day이므로 관계부사 when이 적절하다.

04 (1) 선행사가 'the place'이므로 where가 적절하다. (2) 선행사가 'the reason'이므로 why가 적절하다. (3) 선행사인 'the restaurant' 다음에 나오는 절이 완전하므로 where가 적절하다. (4) 내용상 '~인지 (아닌지)'라는 의미의 접속사 whether가 적절하다. (5) 내용상 '~인지 (아닌지)'라는 의미의 접속사 if가 적절하다. (6) 뒤에 or not이 바로 이어서 나오고 있으므로 whether가 적절하다.

05 관계부사 how는 선행사 'the way'와 함께 쓸 수 없으므로 'the way'나 how만 써야 하며, 'the way in which'나 'the way that'으로 쓸 수 있다.

06 (A) 내용상 '~인지 (아닌지)'라는 의미가 자연스러우므로 if나 whether가 적절하고, (B) 바로 뒤에 or not이 나오므로 whether가 적절하다.

07 선행사가 'the house'이므로 when을 where로 고쳐야 한다.

08 동사의 목적어로 쓰인 명사절을 이끄는 접속사 if는 whether로 바꿔 쓸 수 있다.

09 'a country'를 선행사로 하는 관계부사 where가 적절하다.

10 시간을 선행사로 하는 관계부사를 고른다. ①, ⑤ 의문사 ③, ④ 접속사

11 '~인지 (아닌지)'라는 의미의 명사절을 이끄는 if나 whether가

적절하며 if는 바로 뒤에 or not을 붙여 쓰지 않는다. It이 가주어이고 whether절이 진주어인 구문이다.

12 선행사가 'the time', 'the place', 'the reason'처럼 일반적인 뜻을 나타낼 때 선행사나 관계부사를 생략할 수 있다.

13 '~인지 (아닌지)'라는 의미의 명사절을 이끄는 if는 바로 뒤에 'or not'을 붙여 쓰지 않는다.

14 (1) if가 wonders의 목적어로 쓰인 명사절을 이끌고 있는데 명사절에서는 미래시제를 현재시제로 쓸 수 없으므로 is를 will be로 고치는 것이 적절하다. (2) if가 이끄는 명사절이 주어 역할을 할 수 없으므로 Whether로 고치는 것이 적절하다. (3) 'coming week'이라고 나오고 있고 'the place'가 선행사이므로 when을 where로 고치는 것이 적절하다. (4) 'The reason'이 선행사이고 which 다음의 절이 완전하므로 which를 why로 고치거나 전치사 for를 which 앞이나 관계사절의 끝에 써 주어야 한다. why를 생략해도 좋다. (5) 'The way how'는 쓸 수 없으므로 how를 생략하거나 that이나 'in which'로 고쳐야 한다.

15 선행사가 'the beach'이므로 관계부사 where를 쓰거나 'to which'로 쓰는 것이 적절하다. We will never go back to the beach. + We went to the beach last year.

16 ② if는 전치사의 목적어로 쓰인 명사절을 이끌지 못한다. ③ 선행사가 'a place'이고 뒤의 절이 완전하므로 which를 where로 고치거나 at을 which 앞이나 관계사절의 끝에 써야 한다.

17 if[whether] 뒤에 오는 절은 의문사가 없는 간접의문문으로 'if[whether]+주어+동사'의 어순으로 쓴다.

01 (1) March 14 is the day when people around the world celebrate Pi Day.
   (2) School is the place where I learn, eat, and have fun with my friends.
   (3) Tell me the reason why you were late.
   (4) This is how he killed the big bear.

02 (1) Please let me know if the movie is fun.
   (2) Ask him if it is true.
   (3) I'm not sure if I can do this.

03 (1) I'm not sure if I can pass the exam.
   (2) Whether it will rain soon is important to farmers.
   (3) Penguin Snack is the place where students in my school like to go.
   (4) Don't forget the time when you should leave for the train.

04 (1) If → Whether   (2) if → whether   (3) if → whether

05 (1) if[whether] he can help her with that milk
   (2) how he would like his hair done

01 (1) 'the day'를 선행사로 하고 관계부사 when을 이용한다.
(2) 'the place'를 선행사로 하고 관계부사 where를 이용한다.
(3) 'the reason'을 선행사로 하고 관계부사 why를 이용한다.
(4) the way how로 쓰면 안 된다. how나 the way 중 어느 하나를 생략해야 한다.

02 '~인지 (아닌지)'라는 의미의 접속사로 쓰이는 if를 이용한다. if 뒤에 오는 절은 의문사가 없는 간접의문문으로 'if+주어+동사'의 어순으로 쓴다.

03 (1) if가 명사절을 이끌도록 한다. (2) Whether가 주어인 명사절을 이끌도록 한다. 주어로 쓰이므로 If를 쓸 수 없음에 유의한다. (3) 선행사가 'the place'이므로 관계부사 where를 쓴다. (4) 선행사가 'the time'이므로 관계부사 when을 이용한다.

04 (1) 문두에서 주어를 이끄는 역할을 하고 있으므로 If를 Whether로 고치는 것이 적절하다. (2) 바로 뒤에 or not이 나오고 있으므로 if를 whether로 고치는 것이 적절하다. (3) whether 다음에 to부정사를 쓸 수 있지만 if는 쓸 수 없다.

05 (1) 명사절을 이끄는 if나 whether를 이용한다. (2) 의문사 how가 있으므로 if나 whether가 아닌 의문사를 이용한다.

06 (1), (2) 명사절을 이끄는 if나 whether를 이용하여 두 문장을 연결한다. (3) 'a country'를 선행사로 하고 관계부사 where를 이용하여 두 문장을 연결한다.

07 (1) 선행사가 '장소'를 나타낼 때 관계부사는 where를 쓰며 여기서 where는 'at which'로 바꿔 쓸 수 있다. at을 관계절 끝에 쓸 수도 있다. (2) 선행사가 '방법'을 나타낼 때 관계부사는 how를 쓰며 이때 how와 함께 the way를 쓰지 않는다는 것을 주의한다. the way나 how 또는 the way that이나 the way in which를 쓴다.

08 (1) whether 다음에 to부정사를 쓸 수 있지만 if는 to부정사와 함께 쓰이지 않는다. (2) if가 이끄는 절이 명사절이므로 미래는 미래시제로 나타내야 한다. (3) The way와 how를 함께 쓰지

않는다. (4) 뒤에 완전한 절이 이어지므로 which를 where로 고치는 것이 적절하다. (which 앞에 in을 넣어도 됨.)

교과서 Reading

확인문제   p.204

1 T   2 F   3 T   4 F   5 T   6 F

확인문제   p.205

1 T   2 F   3 T   4 F   5 T   6 F

확인문제   p.206

1 T   2 F   3 T   4 F   5 T   6 F

교과서 확인학습 A   p.207~209

01 Travel
02 I am
03 have been writing
04 share, with
05 Must-Visit
06 July
07 Visiting markets
08 places where
09 wonder whether, to discover
10 Grand Bazaar
11 where, long tradition of trade
12 a natural place for, like
13 was built
14 traded goods
15 much, largest covered market
16 under one roof
17 attracts
18 almost any imaginable
19 if, traditional Turkish symbol
20 traditional Turkish candy
21 Floating
22 traded goods
23 beginning of floating markets
24 With better road transportation
25 have come back, alive
26 markets is
27 crowded with
28 directly from boats
29 wonder if
30 If not
31 with a long fishing pole
32 The Netherlands
33 low lands
34 As, suggests, below sea level
35 Thus, to grow
36 therefore, no surprise
37 where, is housed
38 flower-filled
39 moved
40 around 20 million, corners
41 whether, just a few
42 how wholesale flower trading works

1 Leah's Travel Story

2 I am Leah.

3 I have been writing a travel blog since I was 18.

4 I go places and share my experiences with my readers.

5 Must-Visit Markets Around the World

6 July 15, 20**

7 Visiting markets is a good way to learn about the culture of a country.

8 Markets are places where you can meet people, learn history, and taste local food.

9 I wonder whether there is any better way to discover another culture.

10 1 Grand Bazaar, Turkey

11 Turkey is a country where East meets West, so it has a long tradition of trade.

12 It is a natural place for large markets like the Grand Bazaar.

13 The market was built in 1455 in Istanbul.

14 Back then, the market had two big buildings, and people traded goods like cloth and gold there.

15 Today the Grand Bazaar is much bigger, and it is the largest covered market in the world.

16 It has 64 streets and more than 4,000 shops under one roof.

17 The market attracts over 250,000 visitors every day.

18 You can buy almost any imaginable item there.

19 Extra Tip: Ask shop owners if they carry nazar boncuğu, a traditional Turkish symbol for good luck.

20 Also, if you want a nice snack, make sure to try lokum, a traditional Turkish candy.

21 2 Damnoen Saduak Floating Market, Thailand

22 In the past, Thai people traded goods on rivers.

23 This was the beginning of floating markets in Thailand.

24 With better road transportation, many floating markets disappeared.

25 Since the late 1960s, however, some of them have come back and kept the tradition alive.

26 Today, one of the most popular floating markets is Damnoen Saduak Floating Market.

27 It is always crowded with tourists from all over the world.

28 You can buy local foods and traditional gift items directly from boats.

29 Extra Tip: I wonder if you have ever had a meal on water.

30 If not, try noodles like *pad thai*.

31 The sellers will cook them on their boats and pass them to you with a long fishing pole.

32 3 Aalsmeer Flower Market, The Netherlands

33 The Netherlands means "low lands."

34 As the name suggests, about 70% of the country sits below sea level.

35 Thus, the Dutch built up the land, and one effective way to use it was to grow flowers and sell them.

36 It is, therefore, no surprise that the country has the largest flower market in the world: the Aalsmeer Flower Market.

37 The building where the market is housed is bigger than 120 soccer fields.

38 The market is busy with thousands of flower-filled carts.

39 They are moved mostly by electric-powered trucks.

40 Every day, around 20 million flowers are traded and shipped to all corners of the world.

41 Extra Tip: You may wonder whether you can buy just a few flowers at the market.

42 Sadly, you cannot, but you can see how wholesale flower trading works.

시험대비 실력평가   p.213~217

01 (A) is   (B) whether   (C) another   02 ②
03 ①, ④   04 ②   05 ①   06 ④
07 ②   08 floating markets   09 ③
10 Dutch   11 ⑤   12 ②   13 ③
14 ②, ⑤   15 Turkey   16 ④   17 ③
18 ③   19 road transportation
20 one of the most popular floating markets is Damnoen Saduak Floating Market.
21 ①, ④   22 ②   23 wholesale
24 which → where나 in which / housed → housed in
25 around 20 million flowers are traded and shipped to all corners of the world
26 ①   27 are → is   28 noodles like *pad thai*
29 (A) below   (B) thousands   (C) million
30 ④

01 (A) 주어가 동명사 Visiting이므로 단수 취급하여 is가 적절하다. (B) '~인지 아닌지' 모르겠다고 해야 하므로 whether가

37

적절하다. **that**: 의미적으로 확정된 사건이나 사실, 의견을 말할 때 쓴다. (C) '더 좋은 방법'이라고 해야 하므로 **another**가 적절하다. **another**: 또 하나(의), 다른, **the other**: 둘 중 다른 하나

02 위 글은 '여행 블로그'이다. ① (책·연극·영화 등에 대한) 논평[비평], 감상문, ③ 전기, ④ 요약, 개요, ⑤ 독후감

03 ⓐ와 ①, ④: 형용사적 용법, ②: 명사적 용법, ③, ⑤: 부사적 용법

04 비교급 강조: much, even, still, far, a lot(훨씬)

05 ①번 다음 문장의 The market에 주목한다. 주어진 문장의 the Grand Bazaar를 받고 있으므로 ①번이 적절하다.

06 Grand Bazaar는 노천 시장이 아니라, 세계에서 가장 큰 '지붕이 덮인' 시장이다. **outdoor market**: 노천 시장

07 ⓐ **be crowded with**: ~로 붐비다, ⓑ **directly from boats**: 배에서 직접

08 '사라진 수상 시장들'을 가리킨다.

09 이 글은 '도로 교통이 개선되면서 사라졌던 많은 수상 시장이 1960년대 후반부터 일부 다시 생겨나 전통을 이어 가고 있다'는 내용의 글이므로, 주제로는 ③번 '태국 수상 시장의 복귀와 전통의 재유행'이 적절하다. **revival**: 부흥, 재유행, ④ **tourist attraction**: 관광 명소

10 **the Dutch**: 네덜란드 사람들

11 (A)와 ⑤: ~하듯이, ①, ③: [비례] ~함에 따라, ~할수록, ②, ④: [이유·원인] ~이므로, ~이기 때문에

12 주어진 문장의 therefore에 주목한다. ②번 앞 문장의 결과에 해당하는 내용을 연결하고 있으므로 ②번이 적절하다.

13 '네덜란드는 국가의 약 70%가 해수면보다 낮기 때문에 네덜란드 사람들은 땅을 지어 올렸고 그것을 사용하는 효과적인 방법으로 꽃을 재배하여 팔았으며, 세계에서 가장 큰 꽃 시장인 Aalsmeer 꽃 시장이 네덜란드에 있다'고 했으므로, 어울리는 속담으로는 '삶이 그대에게 레몬을 준다면, 레모네이드로 만들어라.(살면서 힘든 일이 있다고 해도 그것을 기회로 만들어라)', ① 예방이 치료보다 낫다. ② 급할수록 돌아가라, 급히 먹는 밥이 체한다, ④ 안 좋은 일은 겹쳐서 일어나기 마련이다[불운은 한꺼번에 닥친다], ⑤ 백지장도 맞들면 낫다.

14 'Turkey is a country.'와 'East meets West in the country.'를 합친 문장이므로, 빈칸에는 in which나 where가 적절하다.

15 '터키'를 가리킨다.

16 4,000: four thousand로 읽는다.

17 이 글은 '터키가 동양과 서양이 만나는 나라이고 오랜 교역의 전통을 가지고 있어서 Grand Bazaar 같은 대형 시장이 생겨나기에 자연스러운 곳'이라는 내용의 글이므로, 주제로는 ③번 '터키의 위치가 Grand Bazaar의 탄생을 이끌었다'가 적절하다. ⑤ **ideal**: 이상적인

18 앞에 나오는 내용과 상반되는 내용이 뒤에 이어지므로

however가 가장 적절하다. ② 게다가, 더욱이, ④ 그 결과, ⑤ 즉[말하자면]

19 '도로 교통'이 개선되면서, 많은 수상 시장이 사라졌다.

20 **one of the 복수 명사**: ~ 중의 하나

21 ⓑ와 ①, ④: 경험 용법, ② 완료 용법, ③, ⑤: 계속 용법

22 Damnoen Saduak 수상 시장이 언제 형성되었는지는 대답할 수 없다. ① It is one of the most popular floating markets. ③ Local foods and traditional gift items. ④ It is a noodle dish. ⑤ Yes.

23 **wholesale**: 도매의, 상인들에게 물건을 파는 것, 주로 소비자에게 되팔도록 다량으로

24 which 뒤의 the market is housed가 완전한 문장이므로 관계대명사 which를 관계부사 where 또는 in which로 고치거나, housed 뒤에 전치사 in을 첨가하는 것이 적절하다.

25 **around**: 약, **are traded and shipped**: 거래되어 운송된다n 30%'로 고치는 것이 적절하다. ③ **three-fifths**: 5분의 3

26 ⓐ **from**: ~에서 온, ⓑ **with**: ~로, ~을 써서[이용하여]

27 주어가 'one'이기 때문에, 동사를 is로 고치는 것이 적절하다

28 '*pad thai*와 같은 면 요리'를 가리킨다.

29 (A) 네덜란드는 '저지대'라는 뜻이기 때문에 이 나라의 약 70%가 해수면보다 '낮다'고 하는 것이 적절하므로 below가 적절하다. (B) **thousands of**: 수천의, thousand 앞에 특정한 수가 나오지 않는 경우에 사용 (two 등과 같이 숫자와 함께 thousand를 쓸 때에는 thousand 끝에 s를 붙이지 않음), (C) two, several 등과 함께 million을 쓸 때에는 million 끝에 s를 붙이지 않으므로 million이 적절하다.

30 이 글은 '네덜란드는 국가의 약 70%가 해수면보다 낮기 때문에 네덜란드 사람들은 땅을 지어 올렸고 그것을 사용하는 효과적인 방법으로 꽃을 재배하여 팔았으며, 세계에서 가장 큰 꽃 시장인 Aalsmeer 꽃 시장이 네덜란드에 있다'는 내용의 글이므로, 제목으로는 ④번 '네덜란드에 세계에서 가장 큰 꽃 시장이 있다고? 놀랄 일이 아니야!'가 적절하다. ② **utilize**: 활용[이용]하다

서술형 시험대비 p.218~219

01 have been writing　　**02** with

03 visiting markets

04 (1) Because Turkey[it] is a country where East meets West.
　(2) Because Turkey[it] has a long tradition of trade.

05 over　　**06** (A) two　(B) goods　　**07** kept

08 (A) disappeared　(B) alive　(C) directly

09 (A) floating markets　(B) on rivers

10 is housed

11 (A) below sea level　(B) to grow flowers

01 18세 때에 여행 블로그를 쓰기 시작해서 지금도 쓰고 있는 것이 므로 '현재완료진행시제'로 쓰는 것이 적절하다.

02 share A with B: A를 B와 함께 쓰다, 공유하다

03 Leah는 '시장 방문'이 한 나라의 문화에 대해 배우는 좋은 방법이고 다른 문화를 발견하는 데에 더 좋은 방법이 있을지 모르겠다고 했으므로, 다른 문화를 발견하기에 '시장 방문'보다 더 좋은 방법을 찾는 것이 쉽지 않을 것이라고 생각한다고 하는 것이 적절하다.

04 터키는 동양과 서양이 만나는 나라이고, 그래서 오랜 교역의 전통을 가지고 있기 때문이다.

05 more than = over: ~ 이상

06 그것은 15세기 중엽에 이스탄불에 지어졌고 큰 건물 '두' 개로 이루어져 있었다. 그 시장에서 사람들은 직물이나 금 같은 '물건'을 사거나 팔거나 교환했다..

07 한 단어로 쓰라고 했으므로 have를 생략하고 kept로 써서 have come back과 병렬을 이루도록 하는 것이 적절하다.

08 (A) disappear는 수동태로 쓸 수 없으므로 disappeared가 적절하다. (B) live는 서술적 용법으로 쓸 수 없으므로 alive가 적절하다. (C) 배에서 '직접' 살 수 있다고 해야 하므로 directly가 적절하다. indirectly: 간접적으로

09 태국 '수상 시장'은 태국 사람들이 '강에서' 물건을 교환했던 전통으로부터 시작했고 오늘날, 가장 인기 있는 수상 시장 중 하나는 Damnoen Saduak 수상 시장이다.

10 '시장이 들어선 건물'이라고 해야 하므로 수동태로 쓰는 것이 적절하다.

11 네덜란드의 약 70%가 '해수면보다 낮아서' 네덜란드 사람들은 땅을 지어 올렸다. 그것을 사용하는 효과적인 방법은 '꽃을 재배하고' 파는 것이었고, 그것이 세계에서 가장 큰 꽃 시장의 결과를 가져왔다.

영역별 핵심문제 p.221~225

01 indirectly 02 ① 03 ⑤
04 ② 05 ⑤
06 (1) We have two local newspapers in our town.
  (2) The museum is always crowded with tourists.
  (3) There are some effective ways students can use social media for education.
07 (1) is crowed with (2) is busy with (3) are rich in
08 ⑤ 09 ⑤
10 (A) gondre is rich in vitamins A and C
  (B) it also digests well
11 She wants him to tell her the best-before date of the milk.
12 Because she wants the milk that lasts longer.
13 She should drink it until June 11.

14 (D) → (B) → (C) → (E) → (A)
15 ⑤ 16 ⑤
17 if[whether] she would go hiking with him
18 (1) I take the mid-term exam in the month.
  (2) You bought the shoes at the store yesterday.
  (3) She was so upset for the reason last night.
19 ⓔ, ⓖ 20 ①, ④ / ②, ③, ⑤ 21 ④
22 make sure to try 23 ② 24 ③
25 Thai
26 With better road transportation, many floating markets disappeared.
27 ② 28 ② 29 ④

01 주어진 관계는 반의어 관계이다. directly 곧장, 직접적으로 – indirectly 간접적으로

02 세대에 걸쳐 전해지는 문화적 신념과 관습을 가리키는 말은 tradition(전통)이다.

03 주어진 문장의 last는 '지속하다'라는 의미로 쓰였으며 이와 같은 의미를 나타내는 것은 ⑤번이다. 나머지는 모두 '마지막의' 또는 '지난'의 의미를 나타낸다. election: 선거

04 notice는 동사로는 '알아차리다', 명사로는 '공지'를 뜻한다.

05 ⑤번 문장에서 house는 '거처를 제공하다'라는 의미로 쓰였다.

06 be crowded with: ~로 붐비다, effective: 효과적인, education: 교육

07 be crowded with: ~로 붐비다, 꽉 차다, be busy with: ~으로 바쁘다, be rich in: ~이 풍부하다

08 주어진 문장은 곤드레밥의 장점을 설명하고 있으므로 ⓔ번이 적절하다.

09 ⑤번을 제외한 나머지는 모두 궁금함을 표현하는 표현이다.

10 여자는 곤드레밥이 매우 마음에 들었다. 그녀는 곤드레가 비타민 A와 C가 풍부하여 건강에 좋다는 것을 알았다. 또한 곤드레는 소화가 잘 된다는 것을 알았다. 그래서 그녀는 약간의 곤드레를 사기로 결정했다.

11 할머니는 Brian이 그녀에게 우유의 유통 기한을 말해주길 원하신다.

12 할머니는 유통 기한이 더 긴 우유를 원하시므로 첫 번째 우유를 선택하지 않으셨다.

13 할머니는 우유를 6월 11일까지 마셔야 한다.

14 (D) 인사 및 궁금한 점 묻기 → (B) 특별한 장소를 찾고 있는지 질문 → (C) 대답 → (E) 장소 추천 → (A) 감사 표현

15 뒤에 나오는 절이 완전하므로 which를 why나 'for which'로 고쳐야 한다.

16 동사의 목적어로 쓰인 명사절을 이끄는 접속사 if는 whether로 바꿔 쓸 수 있다.

17 명사절을 이끄는 접속사 if나 whether를 이용하고 주절이 과거 시제이므로 will을 would로 써야 하는 것에 유의한다.

18 (1) when = in the month (2) where = at the store (3)

why = for the reason
19 ⓐ when → where ⓑ where → when ⓒ the way how → the way 또는 how 또는 the way that 또는 the way in which ⓓ which → why ⓕ if → whether
20 ⓐ와 ①, ④: [간접의문문을 이끌어 ~인지 (아닌지) (whether)], ⓒ와 ②, ③, ⑤: [가정·조건을 나타내어] 만약 ~이라면
21 ⓑ와 ④: (가게에서 물품을) 팔다, ① 나르다, 운반하다, ② 휴대하다, 지니다, ③ (신문·TV가) (기사를) 싣다, ⑤ 운반하다, 전하다
22 make sure to: 반드시 (~하도록) 하다[(~을) 확실히 하다]
23 위 글은 '여행 안내서'이다. brochure: (안내·광고용) 책자, ① 수필, ③ (특히 기계 등을 사면 따라 나오는) 설명서, ④ 독후감, ⑤ (신문·잡지의) 글, 기사
24 찜질방의 '부대시설들'은 알 수 없다. ① 찜질방, ② 삶은 달걀, ④ 13,000원, ⑤ 24시간
25 Thai people: 태국 사람들
26 With better road transportation: 도로 교통이 개선되면서
27 도로 교통이 개선되면서, 많은 수상 시장이 '사라졌다.'
28 앞의 내용의 결과가 나오고 있으므로 Thus가 가장 적절하다. ② 그러므로, ① 다시 말해서
29 ④ 시장이 들어선 건물이 축구장 120개보다 크다.

단원별 예상문제

p.226~229

01 ④ 02 ② 03 ⑤
04 best-before date 05 ② 06 ⑤
07 ⓓ → wonder 08 ⑤ 09 ③
10 ④ 11 ③
12 if[whether] he jogged this morning or not
13 ④
14 (1) I often go to the gallery where my mother works.
(2) May I ask you the reason why you made that decision?
(3) The pictures were taken on a holiday when we had a picnic together.
15 ④ 16 (A) two (B) bigger 17 ⑤
18 If you haven't had a meal on water
19 ①, ③, ④
20 how wholesale flower trading works
21 filled[full] with[of]
22 Thousands of flower-filled carts 23 ④
24 Because the writer can buy the items directly from the producers.

01 주어진 문장은 어떻게 갈 수 있는지에 대한 대답으로 적절하므로 (D)가 알맞다.
02 위 대화를 통해 안내원과 관광객의 대화라는 것을 알 수 있다.
03 위 대화를 통해 몇 시까지 정선 시장이 여는지는 알 수 없다.
05 할머니는 안경을 두고 오셨다.
06 (B)는 '지속하다'라는 동사로 쓰였으며 이와 같은 의미를 나타내는 것은 ⑤번이다. 나머지는 '마지막의'를 나타낸다.
07 wonder: 궁금해 하다, wander: 돌아다니다
08 여자가 곤드레밥에 얼마를 지불할지는 대화를 통해 알 수 없다.
09 ③번을 제외한 나머지는 모두 제안하는 표현이다.
10 Jane's dad는 Jane에게 가방을 사주겠다고 약속하지는 않았다.
11 ③번은 '만약 ~한다면'의 의미로 부사절을 이끄는 접속사로 쓰였지만 나머지는 모두 '~인지 아닌지'라는 의미로 명사절을 이끄는 접속사로 쓰였다.
12 명사절을 이끄는 접속사 if나 whether를 이용한다.
13 ① That's the way[how] the system works. ② I still remember the evening when we watched the sun go down. ③ The reason why she quit her job is not clear. ⑤ I'm not sure whether this will be enough food for the party.
14 (1) 'the gallery'를 선행사로 하여 관계부사 where를 쓴다. (2) 'the reason'을 선행사로 하여 관계부사 why를 쓴다. (3) 'a holiday'를 선행사로 하여 관계부사 when을 쓴다.
15 이 글은 '터키가 동양과 서양이 만나는 나라이고 오랜 교역의 전통을 가지고 있어서 Grand Bazaar 같은 대형 시장이 생겨나기에 자연스러운 곳'이라는 내용의 글이므로, 제목으로는 ④번 'Grand Bazaar, 터키의 위치의 자연스러운 산물'이 적절하다. ② feature: 특색, 특징
16 건물의 개수가 '2개'에서 1개로 줄었고, 건물의 규모가 예전보다 더 '커졌다.'
17 '교역 규모'는 알 수 없다. ① 터키는 동양과 서양이 만나는 나라이고 오랜 교역의 전통을 가지고 있어서 Grand Bazaar 같은 대형 시장이 생겨나기에 자연스러운 곳이었다. ② 1455년, ③ 터키의 이스탄불, ④ 직물이나 금
18 If not은 '여러분이 물 위에서 식사해 본 적이 없다면'의 뜻이다.
19 ⓑ와 ①, ③, ④: 동명사, ②, ⑤: 현재분사
20 간접의문문 순서인 '의문사(how)+주어(wholesale flower trading)+동사(works)'의 순서로 쓰는 것이 적절하다.
21 filled with = full of
22 '꽃이 가득 든 수천 개의 수레'를 가리킨다.
23 글쓴이가 '꽃'을 구입한다는 내용은 언급되어 있지 않다.
24 물건을 생산자에게서 직접 살 수 있기 때문이다.

01 She needs a tourist map of the town.

02 It opens every five days.

03 She'd like to try some local food.

04 (1) where / in[at] which / which, in[at]

   (2) when / in which / which, in

   (3) why / for which / which, for

05 (1) The valley was in the national park where lots of people came in summer.

   (2) Do you want to know the reason why he is so happy?

   (3) I'm curious if[whether] he'll tell the truth.

06 (1) The police officer is asking him if[whether] he saw the thief.

   (2) Children's Day is the holiday when I got lots of presents.

07 (A) covered   (B) attracts   (C) imaginable

08 (A) traditional Turkish symbol

   (B) traditional Turkish candy

09 (A) largest   (B) under one roof

10 In the past, Thai people traded goods on rivers.

11 By using a long fishing pole.

01 여자는 마을 관광 지도가 필요하여 관광 안내소에 방문하였다.

02 시장은 5일마다 열린다.

03 여자는 지역 음식을 먹어 보고 싶어한다.

04 관계부사는 '전치사+관계대명사(which)'로 바꿔 쓸 수 있으며, which를 쓸 때는 전치사를 which 바로 앞에 쓰거나 관계사절의 끝에 쓴다. (1) 'the park'가 선행사이므로 관계부사 where가 적절하다. where = in[at] which (2) 'the year'가 선행사이므로 관계부사 when이 적절하다. year에는 전치사 in을 쓰므로 when = in which (3) 'the reason'이 선행사이므로 관계부사 why가 적절하다. why = for which

05 (1) 'the national park'를 선행사로 하여 관계부사 where를 쓴다. (2) 'the reason'을 선행사로 하여 관계부사 why를 쓴다. (3) '~인지 (아닌지)'라는 의미의 명사절을 이끄는 접속사 if[whether]를 이용한다.

06 (1) '~인지 (아닌지)'라는 의미의 명사절을 이끄는 접속사 if[whether]를 이용한다. (2) 'the holiday'를 선행사로 하여 관계부사 when을 쓴다.

07 (A) '지붕이 덮인' 시장이라고 해야 하므로 covered가 적절하다. (B) 방문객을 '불러 모은다'고 해야 하므로 attracts가 적절하다. attack: 공격하다, attract: 끌어들이다, (C) '상상할 수 있는' 거의 모든 물건이라고 해야 하므로 imaginable이 적절하다. imaginable: 상상[생각]할 수 있는, imaginary: 상상에만 존재하는, 가상적인

08 *nazar boncuğu*는 행운을 기원하는 '터키의 전통 상징'이고, *lokum*은 '터키의 전통 사탕'이다.

09 그곳은 세계에서 '가장 큰' 지붕이 덮인 시장이고 64개의 거리와 4,000개 이상의 상점이 '한 지붕 아래에' 있다. 매일 25만 명 이상의 방문객이 그곳을 방문한다.

10 '강에서 무역하던 전통'을 가리킨다.

11 '긴 낚싯대를 사용하여' 건네준다.

|모범답안|

01 (A) a tourist map of the town

   (B) the Tourist Information Office

   (C) Jeongseon Market   (D) foot

02 (A) a traditional Korean way to relax

   (B) rest on a hot floor or take a nap

   (C) chat with friends as you lie on the floor

   (D) boiled eggs   (E) about 13,000 won

   (F) 24 hours

01 (1) make sure to   (2) is crowded with

   (3) are good for   (4) make an appointment

   (5) take a nap

02 (1) producers   (2) coming   (3) pick   (4) suggest

   (5) translate   (6) attract

03 Do you want me to get you some water?

04 ②

05 (1) I use SNS to chat with my friends.

   (2) Why don't you take a nap?

   (3) my father and I have some things in common

06 I'm curious if you can visit my farm now.

07 She liked it very much.

08 She wants to buy some *gondre*.

09 It has vitamins A and C plentifully.

10 I wonder if there's a tourist map of the town.

11 ③   12 ③   13 ③   14 ④

15 (1) if[whether] it is open on Sundays

   (2) if[whether] there is any better way to discover another culture

   (3) where my parents met for the first time

16 (1) It is not certain if they will apologize when we meet again.

   (2) Can you tell me if[whether] they speak Chinese?

   (3) Please ask shop owners if[whether] they carry *nazar boncuğu* , a traditional Turkish symbol for good luck.

(4) I know a country where people speak
    Portuguese.

(5) I still remember the evening when we watched
    the sun go down.

17 ①, ③, ④, ⑦　　　　　　**18** ④

19 과거에 태국 사람들이 강에서 물건을 교환한 것　**20** ③

21 (A) directly from boats　(B) boats

22 (A) The Netherlands　(B) mostly　(C) wholesale

23 ①, ③　　　　　　　　**24** ③

25 (A) which　(B) where　(C) for　　　**26** ③

---

01 be good for: ~에 유익하다, be crowded with: ~으로 붐비다, take a nap: 낮잠을 자다, make sure to: 반드시 ~하다, make an appointment: 약속하다.

02 attract: 끌어들이다, translate: 번역하다, producer: 생산자, pick: 뽑다, coming: 다가오는, suggest: 제안하다

04 도움을 요청하는 말에 감사함을 표하는 것은 어색하다..

05 chat with:~와 잡담하다, take a nap: 낮잠을 자다, have in common: 공통점을 갖다

07 여자는 곤드레밥을 매우 좋아했다.

08 여자는 약간의 곤드레를 사고 싶어한다.

09 곤드레는 비타민 A와 C를 풍부하게 갖고 있다.

11 (B) mark는 동사로 '표시하다'를 뜻하며 이와 같은 의미로 쓰인 것은 ③번이다. ①번은 '점', ②번은 '점수, 등급', ④번은 남자 이름, ⑤번은 '표시'를 뜻한다.

12 정선 시장은 5일마다 열린다.

13 if는 'if or not'의 형태로 쓰이지 않으므로 if만 쓰거나 or not을 '~ or not.'의 형태로 문장의 뒷부분에 써야 한다.

14 ① how → where ② where → when ③ the way how → the way 또는 how ⑤ which → where

15 (1), (2) 의문사가 없는 간접의문문에 쓰인 if[whether]이다. (3) 'the restaurant'을 선행사로 하는 관계부사 where를 쓰는 것이 적절하다.

16 (1) if가 명사절을 이끌고 있으므로 미래는 미래시제로 나타내야 한다. will apologize가 되어야 한다. (2) 의문사가 없는 간접의문문에 쓰인 if[whether]이다. (3) 명사절을 이끄는 접속사 if[whether]를 이용하는 것이 적절하다. (4) 관계사 뒤의 절이 완전하므로 관계부사 where로 쓰는 것이 적절하다. (5) 'the evening'을 선행사로 하여 관계부사 when만 쓰거나 'in which'로 쓰는 것이 적절하다.

17 ② which → where ⑤ or not → 삭제 ⑥ does → will do

18 주어진 문장의 It에 주목한다. ④번 앞 문장의 Damnoen Saduak Floating Market을 받고 있으므로 ④번이 적절하다.

19 앞 문장의 내용을 가리킨다.

20 ⓑ와 ②, ③, ⑤: 계속 용법, ①: 완료 용법, ④: 결과 용법

21 Damnoen Saduak 수상 시장에서 여러분은 '배에서 직접' 현지 음식과 전통 선물을 살 수 있을 뿐 아니라 여러분의 '배'에

서 내리지 않고서도 pad thai 같은 면 요리를 먹을 수 있다.

22 (A) 복수형 국가 이름에는 the를 붙여야 하므로 The Netherlands가 적절하다. (B) '대부분, 주로' 전동 트럭에 의해 움직인다고 해야 하므로 mostly가 적절하다. most: 최대[최고](의), 대부분(의), mostly: 주로, 일반적으로, (C) 꽃이 '도매로' 어떻게 거래되는지를 볼 수 있다고 해야 하므로 wholesale이 적절하다. retail: 소매의, 소매상의, wholesale: 도매의

23 ⓐ와 ②, ④, ⑤: 명사적 용법, ①: 형용사적 용법, ③: 부사적 용법

24 이 글은 '네덜란드는 국가의 약 70%가 해수면보다 낮기 때문에 네덜란드 사람들은 땅을 지어 올렸고 그것을 사용하는 효과적인 방법으로 꽃을 재배하여 팔았으며, 또한 세계에서 가장 큰 꽃 시장인 Aalsmeer 꽃 시장이 네덜란드에 있다'는 내용의 글이므로, 주제로는 ③번 '지리적인 약점을 강점으로 바꾼 성공 이야기'가 적절하다.

25 (A) that은 계속적 용법으로 쓸 수 없으므로 which가 적절하다. (B) 뒤에 완전한 문장이 이어지므로 관계부사 where가 적절하다. (C) 뒤에 숫자가 나오므로 for가 적절하다. during+기간을 나타내는 명사

26 일일 전통 공예 체험 또는 다양한 문화 행사를 경험하는 비용이 얼마인지는 대답할 수 없다. ① We can experience the traditional type of house in Korea. ② It costs about 15,000 won. ④ They are mandu and noodles. ⑤ Yes.

A Slice of History

교과서
Reading

📎 확인문제   p.242

1 T 2 F 3 T 4 F 5 T 6 F

📎 확인문제   p.243

1 T 2 T 3 F 4 F 5 T 6 F

교과서 확인학습 A   p.244~245

01 Slice	02 What do you like
03 Though, disagree on	04 It is sold
05 such a favorite food	06 have been eating
07 on hot rocks	08 Records show
09 It is believed, to name	10 was not born until
11 before, brought, from	12 make them sick
13 In time	14 where
15 from near and far, at any time	
16 slices of pizza	17 so, that, for
18 as, on the street	
19 world's first pizza shop	20 tried
21 that she loved most, that showed, on	
22 went on to become	
23 became known, moved to	
24 brought pizza with them, at the same time	
25 opened its doors	26 almost everywhere
27 from place to place	28 while
29 share two things	
30 begins with, a slice of history	

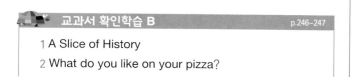

교과서 확인학습 B   p.246~247

1 A Slice of History

2 What do you like on your pizza?

3 Though you may disagree on the best toppings, you will agree that it is now a global food.

4 It is sold in fast-food restaurants or on the street in most parts of the world.

5 How has pizza become such a favorite food around the world?

6 Since the Stone Age, people have been eating pizza in one form or another.

7 Stone Age people baked flat bread on hot rocks.

8 Records show that the Greeks and the Romans started to put meat and vegetables on flat bread.

9 It is believed that the word "pizza" was first used in Italy to name the food over 1,000 years ago.

10 However, pizza with tomato toppings was not born until the 16th century.

11 There were no tomatoes in Italy before Christopher Columbus and other Europeans brought them from the New World.

12 When they were first introduced to Europe, people thought that tomatoes would make them sick.

13 In time, people learned that tomatoes were delicious and healthy.

14 In the 18th century, Naples was a large city where there were many jobs.

15 Workers from near and far came to the city, and what they needed in their busy lives was food they could eat quickly at any time.

16 Cooks in Naples began to put tomato and other toppings on flat bread and sold slices of pizza on the street.

17 The street food was so cheap and delicious that workers ate it for breakfast, lunch, and dinner.

18 They could buy slices of pizza and eat them as they walked on the street.

19 In 1830, the world's first pizza shop opened in Naples.

20 In 1889, Queen Margherita of Italy visited Naples and tried pizza.

21 The type of pizza that she loved most had tomato, cheese, and green leaf toppings that showed the three colors on Italy's national flag—red, white, and green.

22 After the queen's visit, pizza went on to become a truly national dish.

23 Pizza became known outside of Italy in the late 19th century, when many Italians moved to the United States.

43

24 Italians brought pizza with them, and Americans loved the flat bread topped with meat and vegetables because they could eat bread, meat, and vegetables at the same time.

25 The first pizza restaurant in the United States opened its doors in 1905.

26 Pizza is now enjoyed almost everywhere.

27 Of course, toppings differ widely from place to place.

28 Koreans love *bulgogi* on their pizza, while Russians like to have fish and onion toppings on their pizza.

29 However, all types of pizza share two things.

30 Each begins with flat bread, and each is a slice of history.

🦉 서술형 실전문제 p.248~249

01 disagree

02 (1) a slice of (2) Stone Age (3) near and far
   (4) at the same time

03 (1) flat (2) onion (3) truly

04 (1) I usually bake a cake in my free time.
   (2) Are you drawing a national flag?
   (3) We took pictures from place to place.

05 People have been eating pizza since the Stone Age.

06 so, that   07 As → Though[Although]

08 such a favorite food   09 not until

10 크리스토퍼 콜럼버스와 다른 유럽인들이 신세계에서 토마토를 가져오기 전까지 이탈리아에는 토마토가 없었기 때문이다.

11 that 또는 which

12 (1) red (2) white (3) green   13 topped

14 (1) 모든 피자는 납작한 빵에서 시작했다.
   (2) 모든 피자는 역사의 한 조각이다.

01 주어진 관계는 반의어 관계이다. agree: 동의하다, disagree: 의견이 다르다

02 at the same time: 동시에, Stone Age: 석기시대, near and far: 사방, 천지, a slice of: 한 조각의

03 flat: 납작한, 평평한, onion: 양파, truly: 진정으로

05 사람들이 석기시대에 피자를 먹기 시작하여 지금도 먹고 있으므로 현재완료진행시제로 쓸 수 있다. since를 사용함에 주의한다.

06 so ~ that ...: 너무 ~해서 …하다

07 '비록 제일 좋아하는 피자 토핑에 대해 의견이 다를 수 있지만,

피자가 오늘날 세계적인 음식이라는 데에는 모두 동의할 것이다.'라고 해야 하므로, Though[Although]로 고치는 것이 적절하다.

08 such+a+형용사+명사

09 not ~ until[till] ...: …까지는 ~하지 않다, …이 되어서야 비로소 ~하다, 'not until'을 문장 앞으로 도치시키면 'be동사+주어'의 순서로 쓰는 것이 적절하다.

10 'There were no tomatoes in Italy before Christopher Columbus and other Europeans brought them from the New World.'라고 되어 있다.

11 ⓐ에는 목적격 관계대명사 that 또는 which, ⓑ에는 주격 관계대명사 that 또는 which가 적절하다.

12 (1) tomato topping이 상징하는 국기의 색: 빨간색, (2) cheese topping이 상징하는 국기의 색: 하얀색, (3) green leaf topping이 상징하는 국기의 색: 초록색

13 'which was topped with ~'에서 주격 관계대명사와 be동사를 생략한 것이므로, 과거분사 topped로 쓰는 것이 적절하다.

14 마지막 문장의 내용을 쓰는 것이 적절하다.

🦫 단원별 예상문제 p.250~254

01 (1) top (2) national (3) differ (4) flag (5) flat

02 ①   03 ①   04 ④   05 ③

06 (1) Now people enjoy pizza with different toppings all around the world.
   (2) Visitors came from near and far to enjoy the local culture.

07 ⑤   08 ③

09 (1) That is the reason (why) I am angry with you.
   (2) Wednesday is the day when I look ugliest.
   (3) I want to know if[whether] she can sleep in this noisy place.
   (4) He has not been practicing dancing since last Friday.
   (5) She felt too hungry to keep walking.
   (6) He danced so well that he won (the) first prize.

10 ②   11 why   12 ④

13 (1) I know a country where people speak Portuguese.
   (2) Scientists studied the way(또는 how) those birds could fly so high up in the sky.
   (3) We all know the reason why he failed.
   (4) Do you remember the moment when you decided to become a singer?

14 ①   15 didn't   16 Italy's national flag

17 (A) How (B) Since (C) is believed

18 ③ **19** ②

20 pizza with tomato toppings was not born until[till] the 16th century

21 tomatoes, people **22** after

23 (A) where (B) what (C) so **24** ④

25 ③ **26** ② **27** ⑤ **28** ④

채소 토핑으로 된 것이었다.

17 (A) '어떻게 해서 피자가 세계적으로 그토록 사랑받는 음식이 되었을까?'라고 해야 하므로 How가 적절하다. (B) '석기시대부터'라고 해야 하므로 Since가 적절하다. For: ~ 동안, Since: ~부터, (C) '~라고 알려져 있다'고 해야 하므로 is believed가 적절하다.

18 ⓐ와 ②, ③, ⑤: 부사적 용법, ①, ④: 명사적 용법

19 석기시대부터 사람들은 '여러 가지 형태로' 피자를 먹어 왔다.

20 not ~ until[till] ...: …까지는 ~하지 않다, …이 되어서야 비로소 ~하다

21 ⓑ 토마토, ⓒ 사람들

22 '크리스토퍼 콜럼버스와 다른 유럽인들이 신세계에서 가져오기 전까지 이탈리아에는 토마토가 없었다.'는 말은 '크리스토퍼 콜럼버스와 다른 유럽인들이 신세계에서 가져온 뒤에야 이탈리아에 토마토가 있게 되었다'는 뜻이므로 'after'를 쓰는 것이 적절하다.

23 (A) 뒤에 완전한 문장이 나오므로 관계부사 where가 적절하다. (B) 'they needed in their busy lives'가 불완전한 문장이므로 관계대명사를 써야 하는데 앞에 선행사가 없으므로, 선행사를 포함하는 관계대명사 what으로 쓰는 것이 적절하다. (C) 뒤에 명사가 없으므로 so가 적절하다. 'so+형용사+that' 구문: 너무 ~해서 …하다

24 주어진 문장의 They에 주목한다. ④번 앞 문장의 'workers'를 받고 있으므로 ④번이 적절하다.

25 이 글은 '18세기에 다양한 직업이 존재하는 대도시 나폴리로 모여든 노동자들이 빨리 먹을 수 있도록 요리사들이 피자를 만들었다'는 내용의 글이므로, 제목으로는 ③번 '나폴리, 피자의 고향'이 적절하다.

26 앞에 나오는 내용과 상반되는 내용이 뒤에 이어지므로 However가 가장 적절하다. ① 그 결과, ③ 예를 들면, ④ 그러므로, ⑤ 다시 말해서

27 (A)와 ⑤: ~인 반면에 (부사절을 이끄는 접속사, 둘 사이의 대조를 나타냄). ①, ④: ~하는 동안, ② ~하는 한(as long as), ③ (짧은) 동안, 잠깐, 잠시(명사)

28 이 글은 '오늘날 피자는 어디에서나 즐길 수 있고 모든 피자는 역사의 한 조각이다'라는 내용의 글이므로, 주제로는 ④번 '전 세계적인 음식이자 역사의 한 조각으로서의 피자'가 적절하다.

01 flag: 깃발, flat: 납작한, 평평한, differ: 다르다, national: 국가의, top: 얹다

02 무언가를 표면 위에 올려놓다는 'top(얹다)'이다.

03 flat: 평평한, 바람이 빠진, 펑크 난

04 topping: (음식 위에 얹는) 토핑

05 주어진 문장에서 record는 '기록'을 뜻하며 이와 같은 의미로 쓰인 것은 ③번이다. 나머지는 모두 '녹음하다'를 의미한다.

06 topping: (음식 위에 얹는) 토핑, local: 지역의, near and far: 사방, 천지

07 ⑤번은 '조건'을 나타내는 접속사 if가 적절하고 나머지는 모두 '~인지 (아닌지)'라는 의미의 명사절을 이끄는 접속사 if가 적절하다.

08 관계부사 how는 선행사 'the way'와 함께 쓸 수 없으므로 'the way'나 how만 써야 하며, 'the way in which'나 'the way that'으로도 쓸 수 있다.

09 (1) 선행사가 time, place, reason처럼 일반적인 뜻을 나타낼 때 선행사나 관계부사를 생략할 수 있다. (2) 선행사가 the day이므로 관계부사 when을 쓴다. (3) 명사절을 이끄는 접속사 if[whether]를 이용한다. (4) 현재완료진행의 부정문을 이용한다. (5) 'so ~ that 주어 can't ... = too ~ to …: 너무 ~해서 …할 수 없다' 구문을 이용한다. (6) 'so ~ that ...: 너무 ~해서 …하다' 구문을 이용한다.

10 ② She was so kind that everyone likes her.

11 선행사가 the reason이므로 관계부사 why가 적절하다

12 ① what → that[which] ② they 삭제 ③ the things what → the things that 또는 the things 삭제 ⑤ that → what

13 (1) 'a country'를 선행사로 하고 관계부사 where를 쓴다. (2) 'the way'만 쓰거나 'the way' 대신 how를 쓴다. (3) 'the reason'을 선행사로 하고 관계부사 why를 쓴다. (4) 'the moment'를 선행사로 하고 관계부사 when을 쓴다.

14 두 번째 빈칸 다음에 '주어+동사'의 절이 나오고 있으므로 원인과 결과를 나타내는 'so ~ that ...' 구문이 적절하다.

15 '왕비의 방문 이후로 피자는 진정한 이탈리아의 국가 음식이 되었다'는 말은 '왕비가 방문할 때까지는 피자가 진정한 이탈리아의 국가 음식이 되지 못했다'는 것과 같은 의미이다. not ~ until[till] …: …까지는 ~하지 않다, …이 되어서야 비로소 ~하다

16 마르게리타 왕비가 가장 좋아했던 피자는 '이탈리아 국기'의 세 가지 색깔인 빨강, 하양, 초록을 나타낸 토마토, 치즈, 녹색 잎

교과서 파헤치기

Lesson **1**

01 짐을 꾸리다, 가득 채우다		02 나타나다
03 소중한	04 추적하다	05 깨닫다
06 준비하다	07 씹다	08 음식을 날라 주다
09 질투하는	10 쉬다	11 갚다
12 서두르다	13 상자, 가슴	14 용돈
15 포함하다	16 말문이 막힌	17 궁전
18 발명, 발명품	19 멀리 떨어진	20 가치 없는
21 하인	22 주다, 선사하다	23 상인
24 과목	25 도구, 연장	26 기쁜
27 향료	28 당황스러운	
29 무역하다, 교역하다		30 소중한
31 속삭이다	32 기쁜	33 새끼 고양이
34 놀라워하다	35 잠시 후에	36 ~ 덕택에
37 A를 쫓아내다	38 ~을 돌보다	39 극복하다
40 하루 종일	41 동작이 어색하다, 몸치이다	
42 ~을 심각하게 받아들이다		43 ~을 확신하다

01 chase	02 delighted[pleased]	
03 raincoat	04 goods	05 hurry
06 appear	07 speechless	08 servant
09 allowance	10 faraway	11 kitten
12 tool	13 jewel	14 trade
15 repay	16 merchant	17 pack
18 chest	19 spice	20 relax
21 palace	22 present	23 whisper
24 include	25 priceless	26 puzzled
27 chew	28 realize	29 prepare
30 invention	31 jealous	32 serve
33 worthless	34 valuable	35 get over
36 all day long	37 take care of ~	
38 have two left feet		39 Break a leg!
40 thanks to ~	41 chase A away	42 be sure that ~
43 tell the time		

1 kitten, 새끼 고양이   2 priceless, 소중한
3 palace, 궁전   4 include, 포함하다   5 merchant, 상인
6 repay, 갚다   7 jewel, 보석   8 pack, 짐을 꾸리다
9 chase, 추적하다   10 allowance, 용돈
11 whisper, 속삭이다   12 animation, 만화 영화
13 chest, 상자   14 servant, 하인   15 tool, 도구, 연장
16 chew, 씹다

Listen – Listen and Answer – Dialog 1

What, surprise / glad, same class / am, too, last year,
How, feel / a little worried / have to, high / Which
kind, have, mind / thinking, painting

Listen – Listen and Answer – Dialog 2

what club, going, join / sure, How about / to join /
heard, preparing for / need, to relax, need, to get over
/ You can say / Why don't / thanks, for me, two left
feet

Listen More – Listen and say

case looks nice / say that, as, birthday present /
wonder how much, costs / Let, see, costs / expensive
/ agree, works as, too / let's buy / delighted to buy,
special / So am

Speak – Talk in pairs.

hear, weather report / going to rain, long / glad, wear,
raincoat / Good for

Speak – Talk in groups.

the most boring, week / can say, again / don't think,
most boring / agree, difficult subjects

My Speaking Portfolio.

1. What, free, listen, greatest invention, live without
2. greatest invention, feel good, focus better
3. agree, Thanks to, read, write, down

Wrap Up - Listening & Speaking ❺

look, serious, going on / practicing / How, feel about
/ worried, make, mistake / sure, Break, leg

Wrap Up - Listening & Speaking ❻

Have, heard / What about / won, prize / surprising,
seems to / walking dictionary

Listen – Listen and Answer – Dialog 1

G: Hey, Minjun. What a surprise!
B: Hi, Sora. I'm glad we're in the same class.

G: I am, too. We're now in our last year in middle school. How do you feel?

B: I'm a little worried that there'll be more schoolwork.

G: Me, too. We also have to think about our high school.

B: Which kind of school do you have in mind?

G: I'm thinking of an animation high school. I love painting.

Listen – Listen and Answer – Dialog 2

G: Oliver, what club are you going to join?

B: I'm not sure. How about you, Sora?

G: I want to join the school dance club.

B: Really? But I heard you're preparing for an animation high school.

G: Right, but I need some time to relax. We all need to do something to get over stress.

B: You can say that again.

G: Why don't you join me? It'll be fun.

B: No, thanks. Dancing is not for me. I have two left feet.

Listen More – Listen and say

B: Jimin, look! That red phone case looks nice!

G: You can say that again! Mom would love it as a birthday present.

B: I wonder how much it costs.

G: Let me see. It costs 40,000 won.

B: Really? That's so expensive.

G: I don't agree. Look! It works as a wallet, too.

B: Oh, I didn't see that. Then let's buy it for Mom.

G: Okay. I'm delighted to buy something special for Mom.

B: So am I.

Speak – Talk in pairs.

A: Did you hear the weather report?

B: Yes. It's going to rain all day long.

A: Really? I'm glad I can wear my new raincoat.

B: Good for you.

Speak – Talk in groups.

A: I think the most boring day of the week is Monday.

B: You can say that again.

C: I don't think so. Thursday is the most boring.

D: I agree. We have all the difficult subjects on Thursday.

My Speaking Portfolio.

1. B1: What do you do in your free time? I listen to music. I think it's the greatest invention. I can't live without it.

2. G: I think chocolate is the greatest invention. It makes me feel good. It also helps me focus better when I study.

3. B2: Many people will agree that paper is the greatest invention. Thanks to paper, we all can read books and write things down.

Wrap Up - Listening & Speaking ❺

B: You look so serious. What's going on?

G: Oh, I'm just practicing for the school play tomorrow.

B: How do you feel about it?

G: I'm worried I may make a mistake.

B: I'm sure you'll do well. Break a leg!

G: Thanks.

Wrap Up - Listening & Speaking ❻

G: Have you heard about Mr. Oh?

B: No. What about him?

G: He won first prize in the TV quiz show.

B: It's not surprising. He seems to know about everything.

G: You can say that again! He's a walking dictionary.

본문 TEST Step 1   p.09~11

01 Priceless Gift

02 ago, honest merchant, in

03 places, support, by trading

04 filled, with goods, faraway

05 traded, spices, for nuts

06 Thanks to, what, needed

07 dinner with, queen, palace

08 served, appeared, chased, away

09 greatly surprised, there, palace

10 Are there no cats   11 looked puzzled

12 cat, she asked   13 said, himself, not, but

14 brought, from, let, run   15 What, when, run away

16 chest, filled with jewels

17 Back, told, good fortune

18 richest merchant, heard, jealous

19 are worthless, thought   20 bring, what, valuable

21 sure, queen, me, jewels

22 packed, with, other works

23 took, gifts, island

24 chance, islanders, lie, good

25 heard, invited, palace, dinner

26 sitting, presented, with, again

27 repay, with, priceless   28 watched, whisper, ear

29 became excited, hopeful

30 receive more jewels than

31 while, returned, presented, to

32 When, opened, speechless

33 There, kitten, box

34 gave, priceless, kittens, queen

35 return, what, most valuable

36 realized, mind, worth far

37 tried, look pleased　　38 right thing to do

39 return home, richer man

40 surely, wiser one

01 Priceless Gift

02 an honest merchant lived

03 to support his family by trading

04 filled, with, faraway island

05 traded, for, for

06 Thanks to, what, needed

07 had dinner with

08 was served, appeared, chased them away with sticks

09 greatly surprised, there were

10 Are there no cats

11 looked puzzled　　12 she asked

13 said to himself, What, not, but

14 brought, from, let them run free

15 What amazing, run away

16 was filled with　　17 Back in, good fortune

18 the richest merchant, heard, jealous

19 worthless, thought　　20 what, valuable

21 I'm sure, more jewels

22 packed, with, works of art

23 took, to

24 To get, a good friend of Antonio's

25 heard about, invited, to

26 sitting, presented, with, thanked, again and again

27 repay, with, priceless　　28 watched, whisper

29 excited, hopeful

30 was sure, more jewels than

31 After a while, presented, to

32 opened, speechless　　33 kitten

34 priceless

35 In return for, what is most valuable

36 realized, mind, worth far more than

37 look pleased with　　38 right thing to do

39 return home, richer

40 surely a wiser one

1 소중한 선물

2 먼 옛날 이탈리아 제노바에 정직한 상인 한 명이 살았다.

3 그의 이름은 Antonio로, 그는 교역으로 가족을 부양하기 위해 여러 곳을 다녔다.

4 어느 날 그는 배에 상품을 가득 싣고 머나먼 섬으로 갔다.

5 거기서 그는 공구를 향신료와 바꾸었고, 책을 견과류와 바꾸었다.

6 Antonio 덕에 섬사람들은 필요한 것을 얻을 수 있었다.

7 어느 날 밤, Antonio는 궁전에서 그 섬의 여왕과 저녁 식사를 했다.

8 식사가 나왔을 때 쥐들이 나타났고, 하인 몇 명이 막대기로 쥐를 쫓아내었다.

9 Antonio는 궁전에 쥐가 있다는 사실에 무척 놀랐다.

10 그는 "이 섬에는 고양이가 없습니까?"라고 물었다.

11 여왕은 어리둥절한 것처럼 보였다.

12 "고양이가 뭔가요?"라고 그녀가 물었다.

13 상인은 "여기 섬사람들이 필요로 하는 것은 공구나 책이 아니라 고양이야."라고 혼자 중얼거렸다.

14 그는 배에서 고양이 두 마리를 데리고 와서, 자유롭게 돌아다니도록 풀어놓았다.

15 "정말 놀라운 동물이네요!" 쥐가 모두 도망가는 것을 보자 여왕이 감탄하였다.

16 그녀는 Antonio에게 보석이 가득한 상자를 주었다.

17 이탈리아로 돌아와서, Antonio는 자신에게 일어난 행운을 친구들에게 이야기했다.

18 제노바에서 가장 부유한 상인인 Luigi는 그 이야기를 듣고 시샘이 일었다.

19 "고양이는 쓸모없어." Luigi가 생각했다.

20 "난 여왕에게 정말로 귀중한 것을 가지고 갈 거야.

21 틀림없이 여왕이 내게 더 많은 보석을 줄 거야."

22 Luigi는 멋진 그림들과 다른 예술 작품을 배에 실었다.

23 그는 선물을 섬으로 가지고 갔다.

24 여왕을 만날 기회를 얻기 위해서, 그는 자신이 Antonio의 친한 친구라고 섬사람들에게 거짓말을 했다.

25 Luigi에 관해 듣고, 여왕은 그를 궁전으로 저녁 식사에 초대했다.

26 식탁에 앉기 전에 Luigi는 여왕에게 자신이 가져온 온갖 선물을 전했고, 여왕은 그에게 여러 차례 감사하다고 했다.

27 "당신께 값진 선물로 보답하겠습니다."라고 여왕이 말했다.

28 Luigi는 여왕이 하인의 귀에 대고 속삭이는 것을 지켜보았다.

29 그는 흥분되고 기대에 부풀었다.

30 그는 Antonio보다 많은 보석을 받게 될 거라고 확신했다.

31 잠시 후에 하인이 상자 하나를 가지고 돌아왔고, 여왕은 그것을 Luigi에게 주었다.

32 상자를 열어본 Luigi는 말문이 막혔다.

33 상자 안에는 새끼 고양이가 한 마리가 들어 있었다.

34 "Antonio가 우리에게 매우 귀한 고양이들을 줬는데, 이제

35 "당신이 우리에게 준 멋진 선물에 보답하는 뜻에서, 우리에게 가장 값진 것을 당신에게 드리고 싶어요."

36 여왕의 생각에는 세상의 온갖 보석보다 새끼 고양이가 훨씬 더 가치 있다는 것을 Luigi는 깨달았다.

37 그는 선물에 대해 기뻐하는 표정을 지으려고 애썼다.

38 그게 올바른 행동이라는 것을 그는 알았다.

39 Luigi는 더 부유한 사람이 되어 집으로 돌아오지는 않았다.

40 하지만 그는 분명히 더 현명한 사람이 되었다.

본문 TEST Step 4-Step 5   p.18~23

1 A Priceless Gift

2 Long ago, an honest merchant lived in Genoa, Italy.

3 His name was Antonio, and he went to different places to support his family by trading.

4 One day, he filled his ship with goods and visited a faraway island.

5 There he traded tools for spices and books for nuts.

6 Thanks to Antonio, the islanders could get what they needed.

7 One night, Antonio had dinner with the island's queen at her palace.

8 When dinner was served, rats appeared, and some servants chased them away with sticks.

9 Antonio was greatly surprised that there were rats in the palace.

10 He asked, "Are there no cats on this island?"

11 The queen looked puzzled.

12 "What is a cat?" she asked.

13 The merchant said to himself, "What the islanders here need is not tools or books, but cats."

14 He brought two cats from his ship and let them run free.

15 "What amazing animals!" cried the queen when she saw all the rats run away.

16 She gave Antonio a chest that was filled with jewels.

17 Back in Italy, Antonio told his friends about his good fortune.

18 Luigi, the richest merchant in Genoa, heard the story and was jealous.

19 "Cats are worthless," Luigi thought.

20 "I'll bring the queen what is really valuable.

21 I'm sure that the queen will give me more jewels."

22 Luigi packed his ship with wonderful paintings and other works of art.

23 He took the gifts to the island.

24 To get a chance to meet the queen, he told the islanders a lie that he was a good friend of Antonio's.

25 When the queen heard about Luigi, she invited him to her palace for dinner.

26 Before sitting down at the table, Luigi presented the queen with all his gifts, and the queen thanked him again and again.

27 "I'll repay you with a priceless gift," said the queen.

28 Luigi watched the queen whisper in a servant's ear.

29 He became excited and hopeful.

30 He was sure that he would receive more jewels than Antonio.

31 After a while, the servant returned with a box, and the queen presented it to Luigi.

32 When Luigi opened the box, he was speechless.

33 There was a kitten in the box.

34 "Antonio gave us the priceless cats, and we now have some kittens," said the queen.

35 "In return for the wonderful gifts you gave us, we want to give you what is most valuable to us."

36 Luigi realized that, in the queen's mind, the kitten was worth far more than all the jewels in the world.

37 He tried to look pleased with the gift.

38 He knew that was the right thing to do.

39 Luigi did not return home a richer man.

40 But he was surely a wiser one.

구석구석지문 TEST Step 1   p.24

My Speaking Portfolio

1. the greatest invention

2. I'd say, tell the time

3. don't, agree with, the greatest invention

4. say that again

All Ears

1. don't agree with, on that issue / didn't know, didn't like

2. glad, go to the zoo

3. going to, Good for

4. think, time to eat

5. don't agree, hurry to go back

49

Wrap Up - Reading

1. lives, small village near
2. had to, long distance, to get
3. got sick because of, dirty water she drank
4. ago, received, valuable gift, volunteer worker
5. looks like
6. goes into the straw, comes out of
7. carries, everywhere
8. not get sick anymore
9. every day
10. what is most valuable

구석구석지문 TEST Step 2   p.25

My Speaking Portfolio

1. A: What is the greatest invention in history?
2. B: I'd say the clock. We can't tell the time without it.
3. C: I don't really agree with you. I think the cell phone is the greatest invention.
4. D: You can say that again.

All Ears

1. M: 1. I don't agree with you on that issue.
    2. I didn't know you didn't like the plan.
2. A: I'm glad I can go to the zoo.
3. B: You're going to the zoo? Good for you.
4. A: I think I have time to eat a snack.
5. B: I don't agree. You must hurry to go back.

Wrap Up - Reading

1. Isabel lives in a small village near Kakamega, Kenya.
2. In the past, she had to walk a long distance every day to get clean water.
3. She sometimes got sick because of the dirty water she drank.
4. Three months ago, she received a valuable gift from a volunteer worker.
5. It looks like a thick straw.
6. Dirty water goes into the straw, and clean water comes out of it.
7. Isabel carries the straw everywhere.
8. Now, she does not get sick anymore.
9. She can go to school every day.
10. So, the straw is what is most valuable to Isabel.

단어 TEST Step 1   p.26

01 문지르다, 비비다	02 방어하다	03 밤
04 벌집	05 수용하다, 지니다	06 믿을 수 없는
07 위험에 처한, 멸종 위기의		08 북극의
09 여윈, 두께가 얇은	10 줄무늬	11 제공하다
12 전체의	13 남성의, 수컷의	14 교환하다
15 살, 고기	16 ~에 민감한, 예민한	
17 멀리 떨어진	18 폐	19 호흡하다
20 수중의, 물속의	21 낮잠	22 보호하다
23 여성의, 암컷의	24 사회적인, 사교적인	
25 나타나다, (글 속에) 나오다		26 화학물질
27 ~을 제외하고	28 극심하게	29 ~을 포함하여
30 십억	31 거의 ~않다	32 무게가 나가다
33 군락, 군집	34 거주자	35 전달하다
36 어려움을 겪다	37 암기하다	
38 어디선지 모르게, 느닷없이		39 비싼 값을 치르다
40 서로	41 ~을 지켜보다, ~을 감시하다	
42 표정이 우울하다	43 경청하다	

단어 TEST Step 2   p.27

01 stripe	02 Arctic	03 skinny
04 sensitive	05 beehive	06 appear
07 chemical	08 hold	09 unbelievable
10 flesh	11 nap	12 resident
13 faraway	14 chestnut	15 except
16 protect	17 extremely	18 including
19 endangered	20 billion	21 hardly
22 weigh	23 colony	24 entire
25 male	26 defend	27 rub
28 female	29 lung	30 breathe
31 underwater	32 produce	33 exchange
34 million	35 lay eggs	
36 out of nowhere		37 one another
38 keep an eye on		39 learn by heart
40 have a hard time		41 look after
42 be all ears	43 have a long face	

단어 TEST Step 3   p.28

1 weigh, 무게가 나가다   2 defend, 방어하다
3 Arctic, 북극의   4 beehive, 벌집   5 nap, 낮잠
6 skinny, 여윈   7 breathe, 호흡하다   8 stripe, 줄무늬

9 choose, 고르다　10 resident, 거주자

11 prefer, 선호하다　12 watermelon, 수박

13 insect, 곤충　14 colony, 군락, 군집

15 exchange, 교환　16 endangered, 위험에 처한

Listen – Listen and Answer – Dialog 1

how, like / great, having a lot of / Me, show, great / By the way, decide / yet, Which, think, better, swimming / hiking, see wild, insects / join, birds, insects / heard, guide

Listen – Listen and Answer – Dialog 2

look, chestnut, the oldest, woods / tell, how old it is / about / ten times, age / beehive up / guess, bees live / guess, big enough, hold over / Unbelievable

Listen More - Listen and choose.

take, look at / What, for / trying, choose, story / What's, about / future / tell, more about / endangered animals, Arctic areas, / sounds / Which picture, think, better / showing, skinny

Speak – Talk in groups.

Which, like better / like, better, friendly, How about / like, better / Me, much cleaner

Speak – Talk in pairs.

are, drawing / elephant / animal / tell me more about / big, that has

My Speaking Portfolio Step 1

1. come, woods, destroy, lost, where

2. scared whenever, cross, almost hit, understand why, in such a hurry

3. terrible stomachache, ate something strange, what, threw into

4. get lost, too dark, too bright, which way to fly

Wrap Up - Listening & Speaking ❺

do, free time / listen to, like / Which, like better / prefer / sounds more exciting

Listen – Listen and Answer – Dialog 1

B: Amber, how do you like the camp?

G: It's great. I'm having a lot of fun.

B: Me, too. The talent show last night was really great.

G: Yeah. By the way, did you decide on the afternoon program?

B: No, I haven't yet. Which do you think is better, hiking or swimming?

G: I'll go hiking because we can see wild birds and insects in the woods.

B: I'll join you. I like birds and insects.

G: Great. I heard we'll have a hiking guide.

B: Sounds good.

Listen – Listen and Answer – Dialog 2

W: Everyone, look at this chestnut tree. This is the oldest tree in these woods.

B: Can you tell me how old it is?

W: It's about 150 years old.

B: Wow! It's ten times my age.

G: Ms. Oh, is that a beehive up in the tree?

W: Yes. Can you guess how many bees live there?

G: 500 bees?

W: Good guess, but it's big enough to hold over 50,000 bees.

B, G: Unbelievable!

Listen More - Listen and choose.

B: Sora, can you take a look at these pictures?

G: What are these for?

B: I'm trying to choose a picture for my story in the school newspaper.

G: What's your story about?

B: Nature's future.

G: Can you tell me more about it?

B: It's about endangered animals in the Arctic areas.

G: That sounds interesting.

B: Which picture do you think is better?

G: I like the one showing a skinny polar bear.

Speak – Talk in groups.

A: Which do like better, dogs or cats?

B: I like dogs better. They are more friendly. How about you?

C: I like cats better.

D: Me, too. Cats are much cleaner than dogs.

Speak – Talk in pairs.

A: What are you drawing?

B: An elephant.

A: What's an elephant?

B: It's an animal.

A: Can you tell me more about it?

B: It's a big animal that has a long nose and big ears.

My Speaking Portfolio Step 1

1. People come to the woods and destroy the forest. Many of my friends have lost their homes. I don't know where to go.

2. I get scared whenever I have to cross a big street. This morning I was almost hit. I don't understand why people are in such a hurry.

3. I have a terrible stomachache. I ate something strange. I think it's what someone threw into the sea.

4. Sometimes I get lost not because it's too dark but because it's too bright. When lights are too bright, I can't tell which way to fly.

Wrap Up - Listening & Speaking ❺

G: What do you do in your free time?
B: I listen to music like EDM or hip-hop.
G: Which do you like better?
B: I prefer hip-hop.
G: Why?
B: Well, it sounds more exciting.

본문 TEST Step 1 p.33~34

01 Amazing Ants
02 project, has chosen, insects
03 very social   04 as old
05 appear, stories
06 use, chemical, communicate
07 guess what, are   08 answer, ants
09 share with, what, learned
10 How Many, on   11 out of nowhere
12 Like, except, extremely, including
13 As of, over, billion   14 how about
15 According to, about, every
16 hardly, anything, heavy, weighing
17 Is, Like
18 colonies, lots, residents living
19 Within, three different types
20 what, entire, lay
21 type, male, produce
22 third type, worker
23 like caring, defending, collecting
24 How Communicate
25 Though, like humans, actually
26 called, communicate with, another
27 By using, exchange information
28 touch for communication
29 For, by rubbing, on
30 Since, covered with, smallest
31 FUN FACTS, ANTS   32 live up to
33 carry, times, body weight
34 lungs, breathe through 35 ant, stomachs

---

36 One, itself, other, with
37 Most ants, live, underwater

본문 TEST Step 2 p.35~36

01 Amazing Ants
02 For the science project, has chosen, special insects
03 social   04 as old as
05 appear, Aesop's stories
06 a special chemical, communicate
07 guess what they are   08 the answer, ants
09 share with, what, have learned
10 How Many Ants, on
11 out of nowhere
12 Like humans, except, extremely, including Antarctica
13 As of 2018, over, billion people
14 how about
15 According to scientists, for every human
16 hardly weighs anything, as heavy as, being weighing
17 Is, Like
18 which have, residents living
19 Within, colony, three different types
20 what she does, lay eggs
21 second type, male, produce these eggs
22 The third type, worker
23 like caring for, defending, collecting
24 How, Communicate
25 Though, like humans, actually have
26 called, to communicate with one another
27 By using, exchange information, danger
28 touch for communication
29 For example, by rubbing, on its neighbor
30 covered with, even the smallest touch
31 FUN FACTS   32 live up to
33 carry things, 50 times their own body weight
34 breathe through small holes
35 two stomachs
36 One, for itself, the other, share with
37 Most ants, underwater

1 놀라운 개미

2 과학 프로젝트를 위해, 우리 모둠은 매우 특별한 곤충을 선택했습니다.

3 그들은 매우 사회적입니다.

4 그들은 티라노사우루스만큼 오래되었습니다.

5 그들은 이솝 이야기에 등장합니다.

6 그들은 의사소통하기 위해 특별한 화학물질을 사용합니다.

7 그들이 어떤 곤충인지 추측할 수 있나요?

8 네. 정답은 개미입니다.

9 저희들은 이 곤충에 관해 알게 된 것을 여러분과 함께 나누고 싶습니다.

10 지구상에는 얼마나 많은 개미가 있을까?

11 우리는 종종 난데없이 나타나는 개미들을 본다.

12 인간처럼, 개미도 남극을 포함한 일부 극도로 추운 곳을 제외한 전 세계 거의 모든 곳에 살고 있다.

13 2018년 현재, 지구상에 70억이 넘는 인구가 있었다.

14 그렇다면. 개미는 어떨까?

15 과학자들에 의하면, 세상에는 사람 한 명당 약 백만 마리의 개미가 있다.

16 개미 한 마리는 거의 무게가 나가지 않지만 백만 마리의 개미는 체중이 약 62kg인 사람 한 명과 무게가 같다.

17 개미 사회는 어떠할까?

18 개미는 많은 거주자가 함께 사는 군집을 이루어 산다.

19 군집 안에는 보통 세 가지 다른 종류의 개미가 있다.

20 여왕개미가 있고. 그녀가 평생 하는 일은 알을 낳는 것이다.

21 두 번째 종류는 여왕이 알을 낳는 것을 돕는 수개미이다.

22 세 번째 종류는 일개미이다.

23 일개미는 모두 암컷인데, 알을 돌보고, 군집을 방어하며, 먹이를 모으는 것과 같은 매우 중요한 일을 한다.

24 개미는 어떻게 의사소통할까?

25 개미들이 인간처럼 말을 하는 것은 아니지만, 그들은 실제로 '언어'를 가지고 있다.

26 개미는 서로 소통하기 위해 '페로몬'이라고 불리는 화학물질을 분비한다.

27 그 화학물질을 사용하여 그들은 먹이나 위험에 관한 정보를 교환할 수 있다.

28 개미는 또한 의사소통을 위해 접촉을 이용한다.

29 예를 들어, 먹이를 발견할 경우 개미는 자기 몸을 이웃의 개미에게 문질러서 좋은 소식을 전달한다.

30 개미는 (자극에) 매우 민감한 털로 덮인 다리가 있기 때문에, 아주 미세한 접촉도 감지할 수 있다.

31 개미에 관한 재미있는 사실

32 01 어떤 여왕개미는 30년까지 살 수 있다.

33 02 어떤 개미들은 자기 몸무게의 50배에 달하는 것을 들 수 있다.

34 03 개미는 폐가 없지만, 몸에 있는 작은 구멍을 통해 호흡한다.

35 04 개미는 위가 두 개 있다.

36 하나에는 자신의 먹이를 저장하고 다른 하나에는 다른 개미들과 함께 나눌 먹이를 저장한다.

37 05 대부분의 개미는 수영할 수 있고 물속에서 24시간 동안 살 수 있다.

1 The Amazing Ants

2 For the science project, our group has chosen very special insects.

3 They are very social.

4 They are as old as the T-Rex.

5 They appear in Aesop's stories.

6 They use a special chemical to communicate.

7 Can you guess what they are?

8 Yes, the answer is ants.

9 We want to share with you what we have learned about these insects.

10 How Many Ants Are on Earth?

11 We often see ants come out of nowhere.

12 Like humans, they live almost everywhere in the world, except a few extremely cold places including Antarctica.

13 As of 2018, there were over 7 billion people on Earth.

14 Then, how about ants?

15 According to scientists, there are about one million ants for every human in the world.

16 Though each ant hardly weighs anything, one million ants are as heavy as a human being weighing about 62 kilograms.

17 What Is the Ant Society Like?

18 Ants live in colonies which have lots of residents living together.

19 Within a colony, there are usually three different types of ants.

20 There is the queen, and what she does her entire life is lay eggs.

21 The second type of ant is the male that helps the queen produce these eggs.

22 The third type of ant is the worker.

23 Worker ants are all female and do very important jobs, like caring for eggs, defending the colony, and collecting food.

24 How Do Ants Communicate?

25 Though ants do not speak like humans, they actually have a "language."

26 Ants produce a chemical called a pheromone to

communicate with one another.

27 By using the chemical, they can exchange information about food or danger.

28 Ants also use touch for communication.

29 For example, if an ant finds food, it passes on the good news by rubbing its body on its neighbor.

30 Since an ant has legs covered with very sensitive hairs, it can sense even the smallest touch.

31 FUN FACTS ABOUT ANTS

32 01 Some Queen ants live up to 30 years.

33 02 Some ants can carry things that are 50 times their own body weight.

34 03 Ants do not have lungs but breathe through small holes in their bodies.

35 04 An ant has two stomachs.

36 One stomach holds food for itself, and the other holds food to share with others.

37 05 Most ants can swim and live 24 hours underwater.

Communicate: Speak

1. Which, prefer
2. choose the toppings I like, How about
3. like, better
4. Me, too, meat lover

My Speaking Portfolio

1. are easily found, have many plants
2. lives up to, only live for
3. from, to, to collect food
4. hundreds of, a small amount of
5. By moving around, help, grow

Wrap Up - Reading

1. seem to, all the time
2. not true
3. rest by taking, about, a day
4. Each of, lasts, about a minute
5. for about four hours each day
6. On the other hand, fall asleep, at a time
7. that, for about nine hours each day
8. In short, like, though, in a different way

Communicate: Speak

1. A: Which do you prefer, pizza or fried chicken?
2. B: I like pizza better. I can choose the toppings I like. How about you?
3. A: I like fried chicken better.
4. C: Me, too. I'm a meat lover.

My Speaking Portfolio

1. M: Honeybees are easily found in warm places which have many plants and flowers.
2. A queen lives up to five years, but worker bees only live for about seven weeks.
3. Honeybees go from flower to flower to collect food.
4. A worker bee makes hundreds of trips to produce a small amount of honey.
5. By moving around, honeybees help plants grow.

Wrap Up - Reading

1. Ants seem to be busy all the time and never rest.
2. But this is not true.
3. Worker ants rest by taking very short naps about 250 times a day.
4. Each of these naps lasts only about a minute.
5. This means that the worker ants sleep for about four hours each day.
6. On the other hand, queen ants fall asleep 90 times a day, and they sleep for about six minutes at a time.
7. This means that they sleep for about nine hours each day.
8. In short, ants sleep and rest just like us though they do so in a different way.

단어 TEST Step 1
p.46

01 ~을 들어 올리다	02 골프공	03 같은
04 건강	05 대답하다	06 중요하다
07 채우다, 메우다	08 굴러가다	
09 열려 있는, 막혀 있지 않은		10 (비어 있는) 공간
11 병, 항아리	12 잃어버리다	13 서 있다
14 가득 찬	15 붓다, 따르다	
16 ~으로 보이다, ~(인 것) 같다, ~(인 것으)로 생각되다		
17 공간, 여지	18 흔들다	
19 비록 ~일지라도, ~이지만		
20 ~을 높이 평가하다, 중시하다		21 소비하다, 쓰다
22 갑자기	23 ~을 꺼내다	24 ~을 집어올리다
25 ~ 한 병	26 ~ 밖으로, ~로부터	
27 ~에 신경을 쓰다, ~을 돌보다		28 A를 B에 붓다
29 A를 B하는 데 소비하다[쓰다]		
30 목적어가 ~하는 것을 보다		31 B로 A를 채우다

단어 TEST Step 2
p.47

01 golf ball	02 health	03 matter
04 open	05 raise	06 fill
07 shake	08 pour	09 full
10 space	11 reply	12 value
13 same	14 stand	15 jar
16 seem	17 lose	18 though
19 suddenly	20 roll	21 spend
22 room	23 out of	24 pick up
25 a bottle of ~	26 take out	27 pour A into B
28 watch+목적어+동사원형(ing)		29 spend A on B
30 take care of ~	31 fill A with B	

단어 TEST Step 3
p.48

1 matter, 중요하다   2 space, (비어 있는) 공간
3 fill, 채우다, 메우다   4 suddenly, 갑자기   5 full, 가득 찬
6 spend, 소비하다   7 reply, 대답하다   8 shake, 흔들다
9 jar, 병, 항아리   10 lose, 잃어버리다
11 value, ~을 높이 평가하다, 중시하다
12 take care of ~, ~을 돌보다, ~에 신경을 쓰다

본문 TEST Step 1
p.49~50

01 Full Jar	02 stood before, class
03 jar, on, desk	04 picked up, fill, with
05 asked, jar full	06 They all said
07 out of, poured, into	
08 little, rolled into, between	
09 same question, answer, from	
10 took out, poured, into	11 fill, once more, full
12 All the, replied	
13 Suddenly, took, out of	
14 poured, watched, fill, spaces	
15 understand that, just like	
16 what is most important	17 Even, is lost, full
18 stones, other, valued, like	
19 all the small things	
20 there's no room for	21 same goes for
22 spend, on, room, what	
23 Take care, things, matter	
24 sitting, raised, mean	
25 smiled, you asked	26 seem full, room for

본문 TEST Step 2
p.51~52

01 Full Jar	02 before his class
03 a large jar, teacher's desk	
04 picked up, fill, with, from the bag	
05 Is the jar full	06 They all
07 a box of, out of the bag, poured them into	
08 a little, rolled into, open areas	
09 the same question, the same answer	
10 took out, poured, into	
11 watched, fill, once more, full	
12 All the students replied	
13 Suddenly, out of the bag	
14 poured, into, fill the spaces	
15 want, understand, is just like	
16 what is most important, health, dreams	
17 Even when, is lost	18 valued, like
19 all the small things	
20 put, into, there's no room for	
21 The same goes for	
22 spend, on, room, what is really important	
23 Take care of, matter	
24 sitting, raised, What, mean	
25 smiled, you asked	26 seem full, room for

1 가득 찬 병

2 Jenkins 선생님이 교실 앞에 섰다.

3 교탁 위에는 큰 병과 커다란 가방이 놓여 있었다.

4 수업이 시작되자, 선생님은 병을 집어 들고 가방에서 꺼낸 골프공으로 채우기 시작했다.

5 그는 학생들에게 "병이 가득 찼나요?"라고 질문했다.

6 학생들은 모두 "예."라고 대답했다.

7 선생님은 가방에서 작은 돌 한 상자를 끄집어내어 병 안에 부었다.

8 그가 병을 살짝 흔들자, 돌들이 골프공 사이의 틈새로 굴러 들어갔다.

9 그는 같은 질문을 했고 학생들에게서 같은 대답을 들었다.

10 그런 다음, 선생님은 모래 병을 꺼내 병 안에 부었다.

11 모래가 돌 사이의 공간을 채우는 것을 지켜보고 나서 그는 "이 병이 가득 찼나요?"라고 한 번 더 물었다.

12 모든 학생들이 "예."라고 답했다.

13 갑자기 Jenkins 선생님은 가방에서 사과 주스 한 캔을 꺼냈다.

14 그는 사과 주스를 병 안에 부었고, 학생들은 주스가 모래 사이의 빈틈을 채우는 것을 지켜보았다.

15 "자, 이제," 선생님이 말했다. "여러분의 인생이 병과 같다는 것을 이해하기 바랍니다.

16 골프공은 여러분의 가족, 친구, 건강, 꿈과 같이 인생에서 가장 중요한 것이랍니다.

17 다른 모든 것을 잃게 될 때라도 여러분의 인생은 여전히 가득 차 있을 수 있습니다.

18 돌은 여러분의 직업, 집, 자동차처럼 사람들이 소중하게 여기는 다른 것들에 해당합니다.

19 모래는 온갖 사소한 것들이랍니다."

20 "만약 병에 모래를 먼저 채우면, 돌이나 골프공을 채울 공간이 없게 됩니다.

21 인생도 똑같습니다.

22 여러분의 시간과 에너지를 사소한 것에 모두 허비한다면 여러분에게 진정으로 중요한 것을 채울 공간은 절대로 없을 겁니다.

23 골프공, 즉 정말로 중요한 것들을 먼저 챙기기 바랍니다."라고 선생님이 말했다.

24 뒤에 앉아 있던 학생 하나가 손을 들고 질문했다. "사과 주스는 무슨 뜻입니까?"

25 Jenkins 선생님은 미소 지었다. "질문을 해줘서 기뻐요.

26 그것은, 여러분의 인생이 가득 차 보일지라도 친구와 시원한 음료수를 나눌 여유는 늘 있다는 점을 보여 줍니다."

1 The Full Jar

2 Mr. Jenkins stood before his class.

3 He had a large jar and a big bag on the teacher's desk.

4 When the class began, he picked up the jar and started to fill it with golf balls from the bag.

5 He asked the students, "Is the jar full?"

6 They all said, "Yes."

7 The teacher took a box of small stones out of the bag and poured them into the jar.

8 He shook the jar a little, and the stones rolled into the open areas between the golf balls.

9 He asked the same question and got the same answer from his students.

10 Next, the teacher took out a bottle of sand and poured it into the jar.

11 After he watched the sand fill the spaces between the stones, he asked once more, "Is the jar full?"

12 All the students replied, "Yes."

13 Suddenly Mr. Jenkins took a can of apple juice out of the bag.

14 He poured the apple juice into the jar, and his students watched it fill the spaces in the sand.

15 "Now," the teacher said, "I want you to understand that your life is just like the jar.

16 The golf balls are what is most important in life: your family, your friends, your health, and your dreams.

17 Even when everything else is lost, your life can still be full.

18 The stones are the other things valued by people, like your job, your house, and your car.

19 The sand is all the small things."

20 "If you put the sand into the jar first," he said, "there's no room for the stones or the golf balls.

21 The same goes for life.

22 If you spend all your time and energy on the small things, you will never have room for what is really important to you.

23 Take care of the balls first — the things that really matter."

24 One student sitting in the back raised her hand and asked, "What does the apple juice mean?"

25 Mr. Jenkins smiled, "I'm glad you asked.

26 It just shows that though your life may seem full, there's always room for a cool drink with a friend."

단어 TEST Step 1 p.59

01 인공적인	02 성가시게 하다	03 원인
04 안심이 되는	05 우울한	06 우정
07 도움이 되는	08 긍정적인	09 스트레스 받은
10 개선하다	11 외모	12 소리를 지르다
13 유명한	14 덜다	15 주장하다
16 인내하는	17 화학물질	18 그 외에도
19 방법	20 흔한	21 불안한
22 지루한	23 문제가 되다, 중요하다	
24 무서운	25 생산하다	26 효과
27 집중하다	28 짠	29 졸리는
30 깔끔한	31 효과가 있다	32 학교 공부
33 매체	34 남겨두다	35 ~하곤 했다
36 ~ 덕택에	37 동시에	38 우울하게 느끼다
39 ~에 따르면	40 의미가 통하다	
41 ~을 다루다, 처리하다		42 ~하는 한
43 ~에 어려움이 있다		

단어 TEST Step 2 p.60

01 media	02 relieved	03 produce
04 argue	05 helpful	06 sleepy
07 besides	08 focus	09 improve
10 scream	11 appearance	12 matter
13 chemical	14 scary	15 common
16 leave	17 nervous	18 stressed
19 patient	20 method	21 well-known
22 relieve	23 boring	24 salty
25 tidy	26 work	27 gloomy
28 artificial	29 bother	30 cause
31 positive	32 effect	33 schoolwork
34 friendship	35 according to	36 in other ways
37 as long as	38 forget to	
39 at the same time		40 instead of
41 deal with	42 break a promise	
43 used to		

단어 TEST Step 3 p.61

1 friendship, 우정 2 method, 방법
3 well-known, 유명한 4 artificial, 인공적인
5 cause, 원인 6 effect, 효과 7 gloomy, 우울한
8 improve, 개선하다 9 positive, 긍정적인

10 argue, 주장하다 11 tidy, 깔끔한
12 common, 흔한 13 appearance, 외모
14 bother, 성가시게 하다 15 scream, 소리를 지르다
16 focus, 집중하다

대화문 TEST Step 1 p.62~63

Listen and Answer – Dialog 1

talk, about, What makes, feel, stressed, About, answered, As, see, common cause, Over half of, stresses, Problems, took, with, Next, worries, get stressed because of, appearance

Listen and Answer – Dialog 2

What, doing / studying for, Grades / used to, way, too / know / a little stress, helpful / What makes, say / got stressed, at the same time, focus, try harder / help, in other ways / improve, memory

Listen More – Listen and choose.

talk, have to decide / Let, show, designs / choose, short sleeves / What makes, say / Because, wear / makes sense, about / cute / expensive, best one

Speak – Talk in groups.

like to talk, One, most well-known paintings

Speak – Talk in pairs.

spend / makes, say / make, around the world / makes sense

My Speaking Portfolio Step 3

like, good ways to relax, upset, take deep breaths, counting, drinking, Lastly, thinking, thoughts

Wrap Up – Listening & Speaking 1

talked, foods, are good, like to, healthy eating, slowly, to stop eating, full

Wrap Up – Listening & Speaking 2

don't, make / make / basketball, better idea / makes, say / we need

대화문 TEST Step 2 p.64~65

Listen and Answer – Dialog 1

W: Today, I'd like to talk to you about teen stress. What makes you feel the most stressed? About 9,000 teens answered this question. As you can see, schoolwork was the most common cause of stress. Over half of the students said schoolwork stresses them the most. Problems with friends took second place with 15.3%. Next came family and worries about the future. 8.2% of the students said they get stressed because of their appearance.

Listen and Answer – Dialog 2

W: What are you doing, Oliver?

B: I'm studying for the math test, Mom. Grades stress me out.

W: I understand. I used to feel that way, too.

B: Really? I didn't know that.

W: Yeah, but a little stress was helpful for me.

B: What makes you say that?

W: I got stressed when I had an exam, but at the same time it made me focus and try harder.

B: I see. Did stress help you in other ways?

W: Yes, it helped improve my memory.

Listen More – Listen and choose.

B1: Today, let's talk about the class T-shirt. We have to decide on the design.

G: Let me show you some designs on the screen.

B2: We have to choose a T-shirt with short sleeves.

B1: What makes you say that?

B2: Because we'll wear the T-shirt on Sports Day. It's in June.

G: That makes sense. What about this green one?

B2: I like it. The bee on the T-shirt is so cute.

G: And it's not expensive.

B1: Yes, I think it's the best one.

Speak – Talk in groups.

Hi. Today, I'd like to talk about Frida Kahlo. She was a Mexican painter. One of her most well-known paintings is *Viva la Vida*.

Speak – Talk in pairs.

A: I want to spend more time on social media.

B: What makes you say that?

A: I can make more friends from around the world.

B: That makes sense.

My Speaking Portfolio Step 3

I'd like to talk about some good ways to relax when you get upset. First, it's good to take deep breaths. Second, counting to ten is a great idea. Also, drinking cold water helps. Lastly, thinking happy thoughts can help.

Wrap Up – Listening & Speaking 1

W: Hello, teens. I'm Dr. Broccoli. Last time, I talked about different foods that are good for your health. Today, I'd like to talk about healthy eating habits. First, try to eat slowly. Second, it's important to stop eating when you're full.

Wrap Up – Listening & Speaking 2

G: Why don't we make a sport club?

B: Sounds good. Let's make a baseball club.

G: Well, I think a basketball club is a better idea.

B: What makes you say that?

G: All we need is a ball to play basketball.

본문 TEST Step 1 p.66~67

01 Goodbye, Stress

02 spend, with, feel low

03 Others, feel better

04 Still others, while 05 How, deal with

06 Here, suggest different ways

07 by saying, breaking, arguing

08 When, happens, horror 09 so, that, lot

10 screaming, top, lungs, feel

11 thanks, scenes, effects, bothers

12 been using, method, works

13 graduated from, ago

14 with, been looking for

15 stressed out, going fishing

16 gets upset, catch, fish

17 While, so, that, behind

18 Besides, be patient

19 sure, focusing on, forget

20 second-year, way, free from

21 seems, like, for, reason

22 because, number-one way, better

23 so, that, looks glommy

24 As, feel like, relieving

25 When, tidy, looks brighter 26 Let, tell, what

27 stressed, things, has, work

28 under stress, writes, calendar

29 takes, out, herself

30 reads, watches, talks

31 matter, as long as 32 been writing, on

33 Which methods, work for

34 Try, yourself, way, stress

본문 TEST Step 2 p.68~69

01 Say Goodbye

02 spend time with, feel low

03 Others, to feel better

04 Still others, for a while 05 deal with

06 suggest different ways

07 saying, breaking, arguing over

08 When this happens 09 so, that

10 at the top of my lungs helps, feel
11 thanks to, scenes, effects, what bothers me
12 I've been using, several months, works
13 graduated from, ago
14 he's been looking for
15 he's stressed out, always tries, by going fishing
16 gets upset
17 so, that, can leave, worries behind
18 Besides, to be patient
19 focusing on, forget something else
20 second-year, to stay free from
21 seems to like, for a good reason
22 number-one way to make
23 so, that, looks gloomy
24 As, feel like, relieving
25 looks tidy, looks brighter   26 Let, what
27 all the things she has to do at work
28 she's under stress
29 takes some time out
30 reads, watches, talks
31 matter what, as long as
32 I've been writing, feel much better
33 Which, work for you
34 to say goodbye to stress

1 스트레스와 이별하라
2 어떤 사람들은 울적할 때 친구들과 시간을 보낸다.
3 다른 사람들은 기분이 좋아지도록 특별한 음식을 먹는다.
4 또 다른 사람들은 그저 잠시 잠을 자기도 한다.
5 여러분은 스트레스를 어떻게 다루는가?
6 여기 다양한 방법을 제안하는 사람들의 이야기가 있다.
7 때때로 내 친구들은 나에 관해 나쁜 말을 하거나, 약속을 어기거나, 혹은 사소한 일을 두고 언쟁을 하며 내게 스트레스를 준다.
8 이럴 때, 나는 공포 영화를 본다!
9 훌륭한 공포 영화는 너무 무서워서 나는 소리를 많이 지르게 된다.
10 있는 힘껏 소리 지르는 것이 내 기분이 나아지는 데 도움이 된다고 생각한다.
11 또한, 무서운 장면과 음향 효과 덕분에 나를 괴롭히는 것들을 잊을 수 있다.
12 나는 지난 몇 달간 이 방법을 써 오고 있는데, 효과가 아주 좋다.
13 우리 삼촌은 2년 전에 대학을 졸업했다.
14 삼촌은 우리 가족과 함께 살고 있고, 얼마 전부터 직장을 구하고 있다.

15 나는 삼촌이 스트레스를 받고 있지만 낚시를 다니며 긍정적으로 지내려고 항상 노력한다는 것을 안다.
16 물고기를 한 마리도 잡지 못했을 때에도 삼촌은 절대 속상해 하지 않는다.
17 삼촌은 "낚시하는 동안, 나는 아주 몰입해서 모든 걱정을 잊을 수 있어.
18 게다가 낚시는 나에게 인내를 가르쳐 준단다."라고 말한다.
19 한 가지 일에 집중하는 것이 다른 무언가를 잊는 데 도움이 된다고 나는 확신한다.
20 고등학교 2학년인 우리 누나에게는 스트레스에서 벗어나는 훌륭한 방법이 있다.
21 누나가 학업 때문에 많은 스트레스를 받지만, 그럴 만한 이유로 우리 어머니는 그 상황을 좋아하시는 것 같다.
22 그것은 바로, 청소가 누나의 삶을 향상하는 최고의 방법이기 때문이다.
23 스트레스를 너무 많이 받아서 인생이 우울해 보일 때, 누나는 방을 청소한다.
24 누나는 "방을 청소하면서 스트레스도 해소되는 것 같아.
25 내 방이 깔끔해 보이면 내 삶도 더 밝아 보여."라고 말한다.
26 우리 어머니께서 스트레스를 어떻게 다루시는지 소개하려고 한다.
27 어머니는 직장과 집에서 해야 하는 온갖 일로 인해 스트레스를 받으신다.
28 스트레스를 받을 때면 어머니는 달력에 '나만의 시간'이라고 적으신다.
29 이것은 어머니 자신을 위해 잠깐 시간을 낸다는 의미이다.
30 어머니는 책을 읽거나, 영화를 보거나, 친구들과 이야기를 나누신다.
31 어머니는 "내가 좋아하는 것이라면, 무엇을 하는지는 별로 중요하지 않아.
32 나는 두 달째 달력에 '나만의 시간'을 적어 왔고, 기분이 훨씬 좋아졌어."라고 말씀하신다.
33 어떤 방법이 여러분에게 효과가 있을까?
34 이 아이디어 중 몇 개를 직접 해 보고, 스트레스와 이별하는 자신만의 최고의 방법을 찾아라.

1 Say Goodbye to Stress
2 Some people spend time with friends when they feel low.
3 Others eat special foods to feel better.
4 Still others simply sleep for a while.
5 How do you deal with stress?
6 Here are some stories about people who suggest different ways.
7 Sometimes my friends give me stress by saying bad things about me, breaking promises, or

arguing over small things.

8 When this happens, I watch horror movies!

9 Good horror movies are so scary that I scream a lot.

10 I guess that screaming at the top of my lungs helps me feel better.

11 Also, thanks to scary scenes and sound effects, I can forget about what bothers me.

12 I've been using this method for the past several months, and it really works.

13 My uncle graduated from college two years ago.

14 He lives with my family, and he's been looking for a job for some time.

15 I know that he's stressed out, but he always tries to be positive by going fishing.

16 He never gets upset when he doesn't catch any fish.

17 He says, "While I fish, I'm so focused that I can leave all my worries behind.

18 Besides, it teaches me to be patient."

19 I'm sure that focusing on one thing helps us forget about something else.

20 My sister, a second-year student in high school, has a wonderful way to stay free from stress.

21 She feels a lot of stress from schoolwork, but my mother seems to like the situation for a good reason.

22 It is because cleaning is my sister's number-one way to make life better!

23 When she's so stressed that her life looks gloomy, she cleans her room.

24 She says, "As I clean my room, I feel like I'm also relieving stress.

25 When my room looks tidy, my life looks brighter."

26 Let me tell you what my mother does about her stress.

27 She feels stressed by all the things she has to do at work and at home.

28 When she's under stress, she writes "Me Time" on her calendar.

29 This means she takes some time out for herself.

30 She reads a book, watches a movie, or talks with her friends.

31 She says, "It doesn't really matter what I do, as long as it's something I like.

32 I've been writing 'Me Time' on my calendar for two months, and I feel much better."

33 Which methods will work for you?

34 Try some of these ideas yourself, and find your best way to say goodbye to stress.

Words in Action

1. stress, out, me more stress
2. Worry less, never helps
3. a lot of work to do
4. change, change my hairstyle
5. caught, a few, to fish

Speak – Get ready.

1. spend, less time
2. Working on, can be, helpful
3. watching, better
4. Having, part-time job, bad

Wrap Up - Reading

1. stressed, feeling low
2. some good news
3. A few, steps, help
4. outdoors, plenty of
5. According to, produce, in your brain, makes you feel
6. Another thing you can do
7. produce even more, happiness chemical
8. Try, simple tips, feel low
9. Instead of sitting, front, run around

Words in Action

1. Tests stress me out. Grades give me more stress.
2. Worry less, smile more. Worry never helps.
3. I work hard. I have a lot of work to do.
4. I need a change. I will change my hairstyle.
5. I caught just a few fish. I want to fish some more.

Speak – Get ready.

1. I want to spend more/less time on social media.
2. Working on a team can be difficult/helpful.
3. I like watching/playing sports better.
4. Having a part-time job as a teen can be good/bad.

Wrap Up - Reading

1. Are you stressed or feeling low?
2. Then here is some good news for you.
3. A few simple steps can help you!
4. First, go outdoors and get plenty of sunlight.
5. According to scientists, this helps produce a special chemical in your brain, and the chemical makes you feel happy!
6. Another thing you can do is exercise.
7. This helps produce even more of the "happiness chemical."
8. Try these simple tips the next time you feel low.
9. Instead of sitting in front of a screen, go outdoors and run around in the sun!

단어 TEST Step 1 p.78

01 살아 있는	02 인기 있는	03 쉬다
04 곧장, 바로, 직접적으로		05 선물
06 효과적인, 실질적인		07 원예
08 ~인지 아닌지	09 생산자	
10 전기로 동력이 주어지는		11 도매의
12 상상할 수 있는	13 소화하다	14 조리법
15 건축가	16 번역하다	17 계산서
18 곤충	19 지속하다, 오래가다	
20 운송하다, 실어 나르다		
21 끌어들이다, 끌어당기다, 매혹하다		22 운송, 교통
23 현지의, 지역의	24 환경	25 주로, 대부분
26 제안하다	27 발견하다, 알아내다	
28 주목하다	29 뜨다	30 그러므로, 따라서
31 사라지다	32 무역	33 방식
34 작동하다, 효과가 있다		35 ~와 잡담하다
36 낮잠을 자다	37 ~로 붐비다, 꽉 차다	
38 ~한 공통점이 있다		39 ~에 유익하다
40 약속하다	41 ~이 풍부하다	
42 유통 기한, 유효 기간		43 반드시 ~하다

단어 TEST Step 2 p.79

01 translate	02 imaginable	03 last
04 alive	05 float	06 architect
07 whether	08 insect	09 attract
10 carry	11 transportation	12 bill
13 disappear	14 wholesale	15 covered
16 work	17 suggest	18 discover
19 therefore	20 effective	21 environment
22 local	23 natural	24 mostly
25 experience	26 trade	27 gardening
28 notice	29 ship	30 directly
31 recipe	32 relax	33 digest
34 present	35 take a nap	36 be rich in
37 chat with	38 be crowded with	
39 make an appointment		40 be good for
41 make sure to	42 have ~ in common	
43 best-before date		

단어 TEST Step 3 p.80

1 discover, 발견하다   2 disappear, 사라지다
3 architect, 건축가   4 recipe, 조리법
5 imaginable, 상상할 수 있는   6 tourist, 관광객
7 directly, 직접적으로   8 tradition, 전통   9 trade, 무역
10 wholesale, 도매의   11 ship, 운송하다
12 floating market, 수상 시장   13 insect, 곤충
14 present, 선물   15 attract, 끌다, 매혹하다
16 transportation, 운송

대화문 TEST Step 1 p.81~82

Listen – Listen & Answer Dialog 1

Welcome to, How, help / wonder if, tourist map / Is there, looking for / like to try, local / opens, five days, open / lucky. How can I get there / can walk, takes about, minutes / mark, way / Try, when, get

Listen – Listen & Answer Dialog 2

have, bill / Here, meal / good for your health / is rich in, digests / wonder if / want me to give, recipe for / be great

Listen More – Listen and complete

Excuse, help me with, milk / Read me, date / want me to tell, the best-before date / forgot, glasses / Let, see, by / I wonder if, lasts longer / found, one, until June 11 / one / welcome

Speak – Talk in pairs. 1

Excuse, wonder, around here / but, don't have one near / all right

Speak – Talk in pairs. 2

wrong / bored / want me to, with / be great

Wrap Up 1

feel hungry / How / want, to add

Wrap Up 2

look at, I wonder how much it is / Why don't, go in, check / didn't say, buy it for you, asking, price / course

대화문 TEST Step 2 p.83~84

Listen – Listen & Answer Dialog 1

M: Welcome to the Tourist Information Office! How may I help you?
W: Hi, I wonder if there's a tourist map of the town.
M: Sure. Is there a special place you're looking for?
W: Yes. I'd like to try some local food.

M: Then go to Jeongseon Market. It opens every five days, and it's open today.

W: I'm so lucky. How can I get there?

M: You can walk there. It takes about 10 minutes.

W: Great. Will you mark the way on the map, please?

M: Sure. Try gondrebap when you get there.

Listen – Listen & Answer Dialog 2

W: Can I have the bill, please?

M: Here you are. Did you enjoy the meal?

W: It was great. I liked the *gondrebap* very much.

M: Thanks. It's also good for your health.

W: Oh, really?

M: Yes. Gondre is rich in vitamins A and C. It also digests well.

W: Good. I wonder if I could buy some *gondre* here.

M: Sure. Do you want me to give you the recipe for *gondrebap*?

W: Yes, that'd be great.

Listen More – Listen and complete

W: Excuse me. Can you help me with this milk?

B: Sure. What is it?

W: Read me the date, please.

B: Oh, do you want me to tell you the best-before date?

W: Yes, I forgot my glasses.

B: Let me see. You should drink it by June 7.

W: That's too soon. I wonder if there's one that lasts longer.

B: Wait. I found one. This one is good until June 11.

W: Oh, I'll take that one. Thank you very much.

B: You're welcome.

Speak – Talk in pairs. 1

A: Excuse me. I wonder if there's a bank around here.

B: I'm sorry, but we don't have one near here.

A: That's all right. Thanks.

Speak – Talk in pairs. 2

A: What's wrong, Grandpa?

B: I'm bored.

A: Do you want me to play baduk with you?

B: That'd be great. Thank you.

Wrap Up 1

G: I feel hungry.

B: I'll make ramyeon for you.

G: How nice!

B: Do you want me to add an egg?

G: That'd be great.

Wrap Up 2

G: Dad, look at that cute bag. I wonder how much it is.

M: Why don't we go in and check?

G: Really? Thanks, Dad.

M: I didn't say I will buy it for you. We're just asking the price.

G: Of course.

본문 TEST Step 1
p.85~87

01 Travel Story
02 I am
03 have been writing, since
04 places, share, experiences with
05 Must-Visit, Around
06 July 15
07 Visiting, way, culture, country
08 places where, taste local
09 wonder whether, way, another
10 Grand, Turkey
11 where, long tradition, trade
12 natural place, markets like
13 was built, in
14 Back, traded goods, cloth
15 much, largest covered market
16 streets, shops under, roof
17 attracts over, every
18 almost, imaginable item
19 owners, carry, traditional, luck
20 make sure, try, traditional
21 Floating Market, Thailand
22 past, traded, on
23 beginning, floating markets
24 With, transportation, floating, disappeared
25 Since, however, back, alive
26 one, most popular, markets
27 crowded with, from, over
28 local, traditional, items, boats
29 wonder, had, meal
30 If, try, like
31 cook, pass, with, pole
32 Flower Market, Netherlands
33 means, low lands
34 As, suggests, below, level
35 built up, effective, grow
36 therefore, surprise that, largest
37 where, housed, bigger than
38 busy with, flower-filled
39 moved mostly by
40 around, traded, shipped, corners
41 wonder whether, buy, few
42 how wholesale, trading works

01 Travel Story   02 I am

03 have been writing, since

04 share my experiences with

05 Must-Visit, Around   06 July

07 Visiting markets, good way to learn

08 places where, taste local food

09 wonder whether, to discover another culture

10 Grand Bazaar

11 where, so, long tradition of trade

12 a natural place for, like   13 was built in

14 traded goods like cloth, gold

15 much bigger, largest covered market

16 more than, under one roof   17 attracts over

18 almost any imaginable item

19 if, traditional Turkish symbol, good luck

20 make sure to, traditional Turkish candy

21 Floating, Thailand   22 traded goods on

23 beginning of floating markets

24 With better road transportation, floating markets disappeared

25 Since, have come back, kept, alive

26 the most popular, markets is

27 crowded with tourists

28 traditional gift, directly from boats

29 wonder if, have, had   30 If not, like

31 with a long fishing pole   32 The Netherlands

33 means, low lands

34 As, suggests, about, below sea level

35 Thus, built up, effective way, to grow

36 therefore, no surprise, the largest flower market

37 where, is housed, bigger than

38 busy with, flower-filled   39 moved mostly by

40 around 20 million, traded, shipped, corners

41 whether, just a few

42 how wholesale flower trading works

1 Leah의 여행 이야기

2 저는 Leah입니다.

3 18세 때부터 여행 블로그를 써 왔습니다.

4 저는 여기저기 다니며 제 경험을 독자들과 공유하고 있습니다.

5 꼭 방문해야 할 세계의 시장들

6 20**년 7월 15일

7 시장 방문은 한 나라의 문화에 대해 배우는 좋은 방법입니다.

8 시장은 사람들을 만나고, 역사를 배우고, 또 지역 음식을 맛볼 수 있는 장소입니다.

9 다른 문화를 발견하는 데에 더 좋은 방법이 있을지 모르겠습니다.

10 1 터키의 Grand Bazaar(그랜드 바자)

11 터키는 동양과 서양이 만나는 나라이고, 그래서 오랜 교역의 전통을 가지고 있습니다.

12 터키는 Grand Bazaar 같은 대형 시장이 생겨나기에 자연스러운 곳입니다.

13 Grand Bazaar는 1455년 이스탄불에 지어졌습니다.

14 그 당시에 이 시장에는 큰 건물이 두 개 있었고, 거기서 사람들은 직물이나 금 같은 물건을 교환했습니다.

15 오늘날 Grand Bazaar는 훨씬 크고, 세계에서 가장 큰 지붕이 덮인 시장입니다.

16 64개의 거리와 4,000개 이상의 상점이 한 지붕 아래에 있습니다.

17 그 시장은 매일 25만 명 이상의 방문객을 불러 모읍니다.

18 그곳에서는 상상할 수 있는 거의 모든 물건을 살 수 있습니다.

19 추가 정보: 가게 주인에게 행운을 기원하는 터키 전통 상징인 'nazar boncuğu(나자르 본주)'를 파는지 물어보세요.

20 또한, 만약 맛있는 간식을 원한다면, 터키 전통 사탕인 'lokum(로쿰)'을 꼭 드셔 보세요.

21 2 태국의 Damnoen Saduak(담는 사두악) 수상 시장

22 과거에 태국 사람들은 강에서 물건을 교환했습니다.

23 이것이 태국 수상 시장의 시작이었습니다.

24 도로 교통이 개선되면서, 많은 수상 시장이 사라졌습니다.

25 그러나 1960년대 후반부터 일부가 다시 생겨나 전통을 이어 가고 있습니다.

26 오늘날, 가장 인기 있는 수상 시장 중 하나는 Damnoen Saduak 수상 시장입니다.

27 그곳은 전 세계에서 온 관광객들로 항상 붐빕니다.

28 배에서 직접 현지 음식과 전통 선물을 살 수 있습니다.

29 추가 정보: 여러분이 물 위에서 식사해 본 적이 있는지 궁금하네요.

30 만약 그렇지 않다면, 'pad thai(팟 타이)' 같은 면 요리를 드셔 보세요.

31 상인들이 배에서 음식을 만들어 긴 낚싯대로 건네줄 겁니다.

32 3 네덜란드 Aalsmeer(알스메이르) 꽃 시장

33 네덜란드는 '저지대'라는 뜻입니다.

34 이름에서 알 수 있듯이, 이 나라의 약 70%가 해수면보다 낮습니다.

35 그래서 네덜란드 사람들은 땅을 지어 올렸고, 그것을 사용하는 효과적인 방법은 꽃을 재배하고 파는 것이었습니다.

36 그러므로 네덜란드에 세계에서 가장 큰 꽃 시장인 Aalsmeer 꽃 시장이 있다는 것은 놀라운 일이 아닙니다.

37 시장이 들어선 건물은 축구장 120개보다 큽니다.

38 시장은 꽃이 가득 든 수천 개의 수레로 분주합니다.

39 수레는 대부분 전동 트럭에 의해 움직입니다.

40 매일, 약 2천만 송이의 꽃이 거래되어 세계 각지로 운송됩니다.

41 추가 정보: 시장에서 꽃을 조금 살 수 있는지 궁금할 겁니다.

42 애석하게도 안 되지만, 꽃이 도매로 어떻게 거래되는지를 볼 수 있습니다.

1 Leah's Travel Story

2 I am Leah.

3 I have been writing a travel blog since I was 18.

4 I go places and share my experiences with my readers.

5 Must-Visit Markets Around the World

6 July 15, 20**

7 Visiting markets is a good way to learn about the culture of a country.

8 Markets are places where you can meet people, learn history, and taste local food.

9 I wonder whether there is any better way to discover another culture.

10 1 Grand Bazaar, Turkey

11 Turkey is a country where East meets West, so it has a long tradition of trade.

12 It is a natural place for large markets like the Grand Bazaar.

13 The market was built in 1455 in Istanbul.

14 Back then, the market had two big buildings, and people traded goods like cloth and gold there.

15 Today the Grand Bazaar is much bigger, and it is the largest covered market in the world.

16 It has 64 streets and more than 4,000 shops under one roof.

17 The market attracts over 250,000 visitors every day.

18 You can buy almost any imaginable item there.

19 Extra Tip: Ask shop owners if they carry nazar boncuğu, a traditional Turkish symbol for good luck.

20 Also, if you want a nice snack, make sure to try lokum, a traditional Turkish candy.

21 2 Damnoen Saduak Floating Market, Thailand

22 In the past, Thai people traded goods on rivers.

23 This was the beginning of floating markets in Thailand.

24 With better road transportation, many floating markets disappeared.

25 Since the late 1960s, however, some of them have come back and kept the tradition alive.

26 Today, one of the most popular floating markets is Damnoen Saduak Floating Market.

27 It is always crowded with tourists from all over the world.

28 You can buy local foods and traditional gift items directly from boats.

29 Extra Tip: I wonder if you have ever had a meal on water.

30 If not, try noodles like pad thai.

31 The sellers will cook them on their boats and pass them to you with a long fishing pole.

32 3 Aalsmeer Flower Market, The Netherlands

33 The Netherlands means "low lands."

34 As the name suggests, about 70% of the country sits below sea level.

35 Thus, the Dutch built up the land, and one effective way to use it was to grow flowers and sell them.

36 It is, therefore, no surprise that the country has the largest flower market in the world: the Aalsmeer Flower Market.

37 The building where the market is housed is bigger than 120 soccer fields.

38 The market is busy with thousands of flower-filled carts.

39 They are moved mostly by electric-powered trucks.

40 Every day, around 20 million flowers are traded and shipped to all corners of the world.

41 Extra Tip: You may wonder whether you can buy just a few flowers at the market.

42 Sadly, you cannot, but you can see how wholesale flower trading works.

My Speaking Portfolio - Step 2

1. How, want to travel, wonder if, with friends, family

2. want to travel with

3. to visit museums, markets

4. if's, to learn about, local culture

After You Read

1. place where East meets West, long tradition of trade

2. country where trading on boats, long history

3. More than two-thirds, is below sea level

Wrap Up READING

1. Every Saturday, go to

2. the place where, coming week

3. all kinds of fresh vegetables

4. are usually picked, a few hours

5. also find, meet, home-made

6. Because, the items directly from, much cheaper than at other stores

7. local farmers, ready to share, recipes with

8. love going to, farmers' market

구석구석지문 TEST Step 2　　p.101

My Speaking Portfolio - Step 2

1. A: How do you want to travel? I wonder if you want to travel with friends or family.

2. B: Well, I want to travel with my friends.

......

3. A: Okay. Do you want to visit museums or markets?

4. B: I want to visit museums. It's a great way to learn about the local culture.

After You Read

1. This country is a place where East meets West and has a long tradition of trade.

2. This is a country where trading on boats has a long history.

3. More than two-thirds of the country is below sea level.

Wrap Up READING

1. Every Saturday, I go to Oakville Farmers' Market.

2. That is the place where I buy food for the coming week.

3. There I find all kinds of fresh vegetables.

4. They are usually picked only a few hours before I buy them.

5. I also find bread, meet, and home-made jam.

6. Because I can buy the items directly from the producers, they are usually much cheaper than at other stores.

7. The local farmers are always kind and ready to share gardening tips and recipes with visitors, too.

8. I love going to the farmers' market .

단어 TEST Step 1　　p.102

01 양파	02 폭넓게	03 아픈
04 값싼	05 맛있는	06 세기
07 모든 곳에서	08 팔다	09 건강한
10 다르다	11 (얇은) 조각	12 그러나
13 납작한, 평평한	14 소개하다	15 알다, 배우다
16 의견이 다르다	17 공유하다	18 멀리 떨어진
19 가지고 오다	20 고기	21 거의
22 국기	23 고명, 토핑	24 신세계
25 기록	26 국가의	27 아주 좋아하는
28 전 세계적인	29 ~ 이후로	30 유형
31 그런, ~와 같은	32 분주한, 바쁜	33 석기시대
34 채소	35 ~의 바깥쪽에	36 이윽고
37 ~로 덮여 있는	38 동시에	39 ~에 올려놓다
40 여러 가지 형태로	41 어느 때이든지	
42 ~하기 위하여 사용되다		
43 ~라고들 믿고 있다		

단어 TEST Step 2　　p.103

01 busy	02 century	03 try
04 type	05 almost	06 while
07 as	08 since	09 delicious
10 national flag	11 onion	12 share
13 differ	14 widely	15 meat
16 shop	17 far	18 flat
19 global	20 however	21 name
22 bring	23 sell	24 cheap
25 national	26 disagree	27 healthy
28 everywhere	29 record	30 move
31 slice	32 such	33 topping
34 introduce	35 in time	36 at any time
37 topped with	38 so ~ that ...	39 go on to ~
40 at the same time		
41 be used to+동사원형		
42 around the world		
43 It is believed that ~		

1 shop, 상점   2 agree, 동의하다   3 century, 세기
4 global, 전 세계적인   5 bake, (음식을) 굽다
6 cheap, 값싼   7 slice, (얇은) 조각
8 introduce, 소개하다   9 onion, 양파
10 topping, 고명, 토핑   11 bread, 빵   12 flag, 깃발

01 Slice, History   02 What, like, your
03 Though, disagree on, global
04 sold, street, most parts
05 become such, favorite, around
06 Since, eating, form, another
07 baked flat, hot rocks   08 show, put meat, on
09 believed, used, name, over
10 with, born until, century
11 before, other, brought, from
12 introduced, thought, make, sick
13 In, learned, delicious, healthy
14 century, large, where, jobs
15 near, far, lives, time
16 other, flat, sold slices
17 street, cheap, delicious, workers
18 slice of, as, on
19 world's first, shop opened   20 In, of, visited, tried
21 type, leaf, colors, flag
22 visit, on, become, dish
23 became known, late, moved
24 brought, with, because, same
25 first, opened its doors
26 enjoyed almost everywhere
27 course, differ, from, to
28 while, have, onion, on
29 However, types of, share
30 Each, with flat, slice

01 Slice of History   02 What do you like
03 Though, disagree on, global food
04 It is sold, in most parts, world
05 has, become such a favorite food
06 Since, have been eating, another
07 on hot rocks
08 Records show, to put, on
09 It is believed, to name, over
10 However, was not born until
11 before, brought, from
12 were, introduced, make them sick
13 In time, delicious, healthy   14 In, century, where
15 from near and far, busy lives, at any time
16 put, on, slices of pizza
17 so cheap, delicious that, for
18 slices of, as, on the street
19 world's first pizza shop   20 tried
21 that she loved most, that showed, on
22 went on to become, national dish
23 became known outside of, moved to
24 brought pizza with them, topped with, at the same time
25 opened its doors in   26 almost everywhere
27 Of course, differ, from place to place
28 while, onion toppings   29 share two things
30 begins with, a slice of history

1 한 조각의 역사
2 여러분은 어떤 피자 토핑을 좋아하는가?
3 비록 제일 좋아하는 피자 토핑에 대해 의견이 다를 수 있지만, 피자가 오늘날 세계적인 음식이라는 데에는 모두 동의할 것이다.
4 피자는 세계 대부분 지역의 패스트푸드 식당이나 길거리에서 팔리고 있다.
5 어떻게 해서 피자가 세계적으로 이토록 사랑받는 음식이 되었을까?
6 석기시대부터 사람들은 여러 가지 형태로 피자를 먹어 왔다.
7 석기시대 사람들은 납작한 빵을 뜨거운 돌에 구워 먹었다.
8 기록에 의하면 그리스와 로마 사람들이 납작한 빵에 고기와 채소를 얹기 시작했다.
9 '피자'라는 단어는 이러한 음식을 지칭하기 위해 약 천 년 전에 이탈리아에서 처음 사용되었다고 알려져 있다.
10 하지만 토마토 토핑을 얹은 피자는 16세기까지는 존재하지 않았다.
11 크리스토퍼 콜럼버스와 다른 유럽인들이 신세계에서 가져오기 전까지 이탈리아에는 토마토가 없었다.
12 유럽에 처음 소개되었을 때 사람들은 토마토가 사람들을 아프게 할 거라고 여겼다.
13 시간이 지나며 사람들은 토마토가 맛있고 건강에도 좋다는 것을 알게 되었다.
14 18세기에 나폴리는 다양한 직업이 존재하는 대도시였다.
15 사방에서 노동자들이 이 도시로 모여들었고, 바쁜 생활 중그들에게 필요했던 것은 언제든지 빨리 먹을 수 있는

음식이었다.

16 나폴리의 요리사들이 납작한 빵에 토마토와 다른 토핑을 얹기 시작해 길거리에서 피자 조각을 팔았다.

17 이 길거리 음식은 무척 저렴하고 맛이 좋아서, 노동자들은 이것을 아침, 점심, 저녁으로 먹었다.

18 그들은 피자 조각을 사서 길을 걸어가며 먹을 수 있었다.

19 1830년에는 세계 최초의 피자 가게가 나폴리에서 문을 열었다.

20 1889년에 이탈리아의 마르게리타 왕비가 나폴리를 방문하여 피자를 맛보았다.

21 그녀가 가장 좋아했던 피자는 이탈리아 국기의 세 가지 색깔인 빨강, 하양, 초록을 나타낸 토마토, 치즈, 녹색 잎 채소 토핑으로 된 것이었다.

22 왕비의 방문 이후로 피자는 진정한 이탈리아의 국가 음식이 되었다.

23 19세기 후반에는 피자가 이탈리아 밖으로 알려지게 되었는데, 이 시기에 많은 이탈리아 사람들이 미국으로 이주를 하였다.

24 이탈리아인들은 피자도 함께 가져갔고, 빵, 고기, 채소를 한꺼번에 먹을 수 있어서 미국인들은 고기와 채소를 얹은 이 납작한 빵을 좋아했다.

25 미국 최초의 피자 가게가 1905년에 문을 열었다.

26 오늘날 피자는 거의 어디에서나 즐길 수 있다.

27 물론, 토핑은 지역에 따라 매우 다양하다.

28 한국인은 불고기를 피자에 얹어 먹기를 좋아하고, 러시아 사람들은 생선과 양파 토핑을 좋아한다.

29 그러나 모든 종류의 피자가 두 가지 사실만큼은 똑같다.

30 모든 피자는 납작한 빵에서 시작하고, 각각은 역사의 한 조각이다

본문 TEST Step 4~Step 5 p.112~116

1 A Slice of History

2 What do you like on your pizza?

3 Though you may disagree on the best toppings, you will agree that it is now a global food.

4 It is sold in fast-food restaurants or on the street in most parts of the world.

5 How has pizza become such a favorite food around the world?

6 Since the Stone Age, people have been eating pizza in one form or another.

7 Stone Age people baked flat bread on hot rocks.

8 Records show that the Greeks and the Romans started to put meat and vegetables on flat bread.

9 It is believed that the word "pizza" was first used in Italy to name the food over 1,000 years ago.

10 However, pizza with tomato toppings was not born until the 16th century.

11 There were no tomatoes in Italy before Christopher Columbus and other Europeans brought them from the New World.

12 When they were first introduced to Europe, people thought that tomatoes would make them sick.

13 In time, people learned that tomatoes were delicious and healthy.

14 In the 18th century, Naples was a large city where there were many jobs.

15 Workers from near and far came to the city, and what they needed in their busy lives was food they could eat quickly at any time.

16 Cooks in Naples began to put tomato and other toppings on flat bread and sold slices of pizza on the street.

17 The street food was so cheap and delicious that workers ate it for breakfast, lunch, and dinner.

18 They could buy slices of pizza and eat them as they walked on the street.

19 In 1830, the world's first pizza shop opened in Naples.

20 In 1889, Queen Margherita of Italy visited Naples and tried pizza.

21 The type of pizza that she loved most had tomato, cheese, and green leaf toppings that showed the three colors on Italy's national flag—red, white, and green.

22 After the queen's visit, pizza went on to become a truly national dish.

23 Pizza became known outside of Italy in the late 19th century, when many Italians moved to the United States.

24 Italians brought pizza with them, and Americans loved the flat bread topped with meat and vegetables because they could eat bread, meat, and vegetables at the same time.

25 The first pizza restaurant in the United States opened its doors in 1905.

26 Pizza is now enjoyed almost everywhere.

27 Of course, toppings differ widely from place to place.

28 Koreans love *bulgogi* on their pizza, while Russians like to have fish and onion toppings on their pizza.

29 However, all types of pizza share two things.

30 Each begins with flat bread, and each is a slice of history.

MEMO

적중 **100** + 특별부록

Plan B

우리학교 최신기출

천재 · 이재영 교과서를 배우는

학교 시험문제 분석 · 모음 · 해설집

전국단위 학교 시험문제 수집 및 분석
출제 빈도가 높은 문제 위주로 선별
문제 풀이에 필요한 상세한 해설

중3-1
영어

천재 · 이재영

반 이름		점수

문항수 : 선택형(29문항) 서술형(3문항) 　20 ．．．

◎ 선택형 문항의 답안은 컴퓨터용 수정 싸인펜을 사용하여 OMR 답안지에 바르게 표기하시오.
◎ 서술형 문제는 답을 답안지에 반드시 검정 볼펜으로 쓰시오.
◎ 총 32문항 100점 만점입니다. 문항별 배점은 각 문항에 표시되어 있습니다.

[경기 ○○중]

1. 다음 짝지어진 두 단어의 관계가 나머지와 <u>다른</u> 것은?　　(2점)

① use - useless
② little - less
③ end - endless
④ wire - wireless
⑤ care - careless

[인천 ○○중]

2. 다음 단어의 영영 풀이가 바르지 <u>않은</u> 것은?　(3점)

① hardly: almost not at all
② jewel: a precious stone like diamonds
③ repay: to give something in return or pay back
④ insect: a small animal with six legs and usually wings
⑤ jealous: unhappy because someone doesn't have what you have

[인천 ○○중]

3. 다음 밑줄 친 @∼ⓔ 중 대화의 흐름상 <u>어색한</u> 것은?　(2점)

Sora: Oliver, @<u>what club are you going to join</u>?
Oliver: ⓑ<u>I'm not sure.</u> What club are you going to join?
Sora: I want to join the school dance club.
Oliver: Really? ⓒ<u>But I heard you're preparing for an animation high school.</u>
Sora: Right. ⓓ<u>But I don't like dancing.</u> We all need to do something to get over stress.
Oliver: ⓔ<u>You can say that again.</u>

① @　② ⓑ　③ ⓒ　④ ⓓ　⑤ ⓔ

[부산 ○○중]

4. 다음 대화의 빈칸 (가)에 들어갈 말로 가장 알맞은 것은?　　(3점)

B: You look so serious. What's going on?
G: Oh, I'm just practicing for the school play tomorrow.
B: How do you feel about it?
G: I'm worried I may make a mistake.
B: I'm sure you'll do well. (가)_____
G: Thanks.
　　　　　　　　　　　* G: Girl, B: Boy

① Break a leg!
② Come with me!
③ I'll tell you my fortune!
④ Break time will make you feel relieved.
⑤ I'm nervous to practice for the school play.

[경기 ○○중]

5. 다음 대화가 자연스럽도록 @∼ⓓ를 바르게 배열한 것은?　　(3점)

Hey, Minjun. What a surprise!
@ Hi, Sora. I'm glad we're in the same class.
ⓑ I'm a little worried that there'll be more schoolwork.
ⓒ Me, too. We also have to think about our high school.
ⓓ I am, too. We're now in our last year in middle school. How do you feel?

① @-ⓓ-ⓑ-ⓒ
② @-ⓑ-ⓓ-ⓒ
③ ⓑ-ⓒ-ⓓ-@
④ ⓒ-ⓑ-@-ⓓ
⑤ ⓓ-ⓑ-@-ⓒ

[6~7] 다음 대화의 빈칸에 적합한 표현을 〈보기〉에서 찾으시오.

<보기>
ⓐ I'm glad I can wear my new raincoat.
ⓑ You can say that again.
ⓒ Can you tell me more about it?
ⓓ I like dogs better.
ⓔ The pleasure is mine.

6. (2점)

A: Did you hear the weather report?
B: Yes. It's going to rain all day long.
A: Really? _____
B: Good for you.

① ⓐ   ② ⓑ   ③ ⓒ   ④ ⓓ   ⑤ ⓔ

7. (3점)

A: I think the most boring day of the week is Monday.
B: _____

① ⓐ   ② ⓑ   ③ ⓒ   ④ ⓓ   ⑤ ⓔ

8. 다음 주어진 단어를 배열하여 밑줄 친 (A)를 영어 문장으로 쓰시오. (4점)

B: Hi, Sora. (A)같은 반이라서 기쁘다.
G: I am, too. We're now in our last year in middle school. How do you feel?
B: I'm a little worried that there'll be more schoolwork.
G: Me, too. We also have to think about our high school.
B: Which kind of school do you have in mind?
G: I'm thinking of an animation high school. I love painting.

B: Boy G: Girl

• I'm / the same / glad / we're / in / class

<조건>
1. 대·소문자 구분 있음.
2. 구두점 유의 (마침표, 콤마, 물음표 등.)

답: _____

9. 다음 대화의 내용으로 알 수 <u>없는</u> 것은? (4점)

A: Jimin, look! That red phone case looks nice!
B: You can say that again! Mom would love it as a birthday present.
A: I wonder how much it costs.
B: Let me see. It costs 40,000 won.
A: Really? That's so expensive!
B: I don't agree. Look! It works as a wallet, too.
A: Oh, I didn't see that. Then let's buy it for Mom.
B: Okay. I'm delighted to buy something special for Mom.
A: So am I.

① 물건의 색깔   ② 물건을 사려는 이유
③ 물건의 가격   ④ 물건의 기능
⑤ 물건의 상표

10. 다음 빈칸에 들어갈 알맞은 말은? (3점)

• He felt someone _____ his shoulder.

① touch   ② touches   ③ touched
④ to touch   ⑤ to have touched

11. 다음 대화의 빈칸에 공통으로 들어갈 말은? (4점)

A: _____ do you want to do now?
B: _____ I want to do now is to play baseball.

① Why   ② How   ③ What
④ How much   ⑤ Who

12. 다음 문장의 빈칸에 들어갈 수 없는 것은? (2점)

• I saw _____.

① a girl raise her hand
② the woman hug her son
③ someone broke the window
④ my mom coming into my room
⑤ two people argue on the street

13. 다음 중 What/what의 쓰임이 <u>다른</u> 것은? (3점)

① This is <u>what</u> I bought yesterday.
② <u>What</u> I want to have is a nice bike.
③ A sense of humor is <u>what</u> makes her popular.
④ I don't believe <u>what</u> he says.
⑤ <u>What</u> do you think about this?

14. 다음 두 문장을 한 문장으로 바꿔 쓸 때 빈칸에 적절한 말을 쓰시오. (답안지에 빈칸에 들어갈 말만 쓰시오.) (3점)

• Alex told a funny story. Tracy heard this.
→ Tracy heard _____

→ Tracy heard _____.

15. 다음 우리말에 대한 영어 표현의 어순을 바르게 배열하여 쓰시오. (3점)

• 나는 엄마가 내 방에 들어오시는 것을 보았다.
(Mom / I / saw / come / my / into / room)

<조건>
• 주어진 단어들만을 그대로 사용할 것

정답: _____

16. 다음 중 어법상 옳은 것은? (3점)

① John saw the dog bark at him.
② What the girls said are right.
③ I feel the wind to blow.
④ She watched the boys to play the basketball.
⑤ She thinks friendship is that is most important in life.

17. 다음 중 지칭하는 대상이 <u>다른</u> 하나는? (3점)

ⓐThe merchant said to ⓑhimself, "The thing that the islanders here need is not tools or books, but cats." ⓒHe brought two cats from his ship and let them run free. "What amazing animals!" cried ⓓthe queen when she saw all the rats run away. She gave ⓔAntonio a chest that was filled with jewels.

① ⓐ   ② ⓑ   ③ ⓒ   ④ ⓓ   ⑤ ⓔ

[18~20] 다음 글을 읽고 물음에 답하시오.

Long ago, an honest merchant named Antonio lived in Italy. He went to many places to support his family by trading. One day, he ⓐ_____ and visited a faraway island.

(A) He traded tools for spices and books for nuts. Thanks to him, ⓑthe people who live there could get what they needed. The queen of the island heard of Antonio and invited ⓒhim to the palace.

(B) Antonio gave her a cat so that the islanders would not have to chase them away. The queen was greatly pleased with his gift and gave ⓓAntonio a chest that was filled with jewels.

(C) When they were having dinner, ⓔAntonio saw some rats appear and asked, "Are there no cats on this island?" The queen said that they didn't have any cats there.

A greedy merchant named ⓕLuigi heard the story and decided to visit the island to get more jewels than Antonio.

18. 위 글의 빈칸 ⓐ에 들어갈 말로 가장 알맞은 것은? (3점)

① got jealous of his friend
② filled his ship with goods
③ was afraid of travelling
④ saw a lot of jewels outside
⑤ looked puzzled by what he saw

19. 위 글의 (A)~(C)를 앞뒤에 주어진 글과 어울리도록 배열한 것은? (3점)

① (A)-(B)-(C) ② (A)-(C)-(B) ③ (B)-(A)-(C)
④ (B)-(C)-(A) ⑤ (C)-(A)-(B)

20. 위 글의 문맥상 밑줄 친 등장인물들이 느꼈을 심정으로 적절하지 <u>않은</u> 것은? (4점)

① ⓑ: thankful   ② ⓒ: regretful
③ ⓓ: delighted   ④ ⓔ: surprised
⑤ ⓕ: jealous

[21~22] 다음 글을 읽고 물음에 답하시오.

Antonio had dinner with the queen of the island at her palace. When dinner was served, rats appeared, and some servants chased them away with sticks. Antonio was greatly surprised that there were rats in the palace. He asked, "Are there no cats in this island?" The queen looked puzzled. "What is a cat?" she asked. The merchant said to himself, "_____ the islanders here need is not tools or books, but cats." He brought two cats from his ship and let them run free. "What amazing animals!" cried the queen when she saw all the rats run away.

21. 위 글의 Antonia에 관한 내용과 일치하지 <u>않는</u> 것은? (3점)

① Antonio는 그 섬의 여왕과 궁전에서 저녁을 먹었다.
② Antonio는 궁전에 쥐가 나타나자 무서워 도망갔다.
③ Antonio는 여왕에게 섬에 고양이가 있는지 물었다.
④ Antonio는 배에서 고양이를 두 마리 가져왔다.
⑤ Antonio는 고양이를 궁전 안에 자유롭게 풀어두었다.

22. 위 글의 빈칸에 들어갈 말로 알맞은 것은? (3점)

① Who   ② Why   ③ What
④ That   ⑤ Which

[23~26] 다음 글을 읽고 물음에 답하시오.

Back in Italy, Antonio told his friends about his good fortune. Luigi, the richest merchant in Genoa, heard the story and was jealous. "Cats are (A)_____," Luigi thought. "I'll bring the queen (B)_____ is really valuable. I'm sure that the queen will give me more jewels.

Luigi packed his ship with wonderful paintings and other works of art. He took the gifts to the island. (C)To get a change to meet the queen, he told the islanders a lie that he was a good friend of Antonio's. When the queen heard about Luigi, she invited him to her palace for dinner. Before sitting down at the table, Luigi presented the queen with all his gifts, and the queen thanked him again and again. "I'll repay you with a (D)_____ gift," said the queen.

23. 위 글의 내용과 일치하는 것은? (3점)

① Antonio는 제노바에서 가장 부자가 되었다.
② Antonio는 친구들에게 Luigi의 이야기를 들려주었다.
③ Luigi는 Antonio 소개로 여왕을 만났다.
④ 여왕은 Luigi의 배에서 고양이 몇 마리를 샀다.
⑤ Luigi는 섬사람들에게 자신이 Antonio의 친한 친구라고 말했다.

24. 위 글의 내용상 빈칸 (A)와 (D)에 들어갈 가장 알맞은 표현은? (4점)

	(A)	(D)
①	worthless	priceless
②	fearless	priceless
③	worthless	hopeless
④	homeless	hopeless
⑤	fearless	tasteless

25. 위 글의 빈칸 (B)에 들어갈 알맞은 관계대명사는? (4점)

① who   ② whom   ③ which
④ what   ⑤ that

26. 위 글의 밑줄 친 (C)와 to부정사의 쓰임이 같은 것은? (3점)

① Moise studied harder to pass the exam.
② To go to a concert is very exciting.
③ There are a lot of things to buy.
④ I'm sorry to hear the bad news.
⑤ Her hobby is to watch movies.

[27~28] 다음 글을 읽고 물음에 답하시오.

ⓐLong ago, an honest merchant lived in Genoa, Italy. ⓑHis name was Antonio, and he went to different places to support his family by trading. One day, he (A)_____ his ship with goods and visited a faraway island. ⓒHe had dinner with the island's queen. ⓓThere he traded tools for spices and books for nuts. ⓔThanks to Antonio, the islanders could get what they needed.

27. 위 글에서 흐름상 필요 없는 문장은? (4점)

① ⓐ   ② ⓑ   ③ ⓒ   ④ ⓓ   ⑤ ⓔ

28. 위 글의 빈칸 (A)에 들어갈 말로 적절한 것은? (3점)

① filled   ② full   ③ chased
④ traded   ⑤ needed

[29~30] 다음 글을 읽고 물음에 답하시오.

One night, Antonio had dinner with the island's queen at her palace. When dinner ⓐ <u>was served</u>, rats appeared, and some servants chased them away with sticks. Antonio was greatly surprised that there were rats in the palace. He asked, "Are there no cats on this island?" The queen ⓑ<u>looked puzzled</u>. "What is a cat?" she asked. The merchant said to himself, "What the islanders here need is not tools or books, but cats." He brought two cats from his ship and ⓒ<u>let them run free</u>. "What amazing animals!" cried the queen when she saw all the rats ⓓ<u>to run away</u>. She gave Antonio a chest ⓔ<u>that</u> was filled with jewels.

29. 위 글의 밑줄 친 ⓐ~ⓔ 중 어법상 잘못된 것은?

(3점)

① ⓐ　　② ⓑ　　③ ⓒ　　④ ⓓ　　⑤ ⓔ

30. 위 글을 읽고 답할 수 <u>없는</u> 질문은?　(3점)

① Why was Antonio surprised?

② Who did Antonio have dinner with?

③ Why did the queen invite Antonio to dinner?

④ How did the servants chase the rats away?

⑤ How many cats did Antonio bring from his ship?

[31~32] 다음 글을 읽고 물음에 답하시오.

Back in Italy, Antonio told his friends about his good fortune. Luigi, the richest merchant in Genoa, heard the story and was jealous. "Cats are ⓐ<u>worthless</u>," Luigi thought. "I'll bring the queen what is really ⓑ<u>valuable</u>. I'm sure that the queen will give me more jewels."

Luigi packed his ship with ⓒ<u>wonderful</u> paintings and other works of art. He took the gifts to the island. To get a chance to meet the queen, he told the islanders a lie that he was a good friend of Antonio's. When the queen heard about Luigi, she invited him to her palace for dinner. Before sitting down at the table, Luigi presented the queen with all his gifts, and the queen thanked him again and again. "I'll repay you with a ⓓ<u>priceless</u> gift," said the queen. Luigi watched the queen whisper in a servant's ear. He became excited and ⓔ<u>hopeful</u>. He was sure that he would receive more jewels than Antonio.

After a while, the servant returned with a box, and the queen presented it to Luigi. When Luigi opened the box, he was ⓕ<u>speechless</u>.

31. 위 글의 내용과 일치하는 것은?　(4점)

① Luigi was a good friend of Antonio's.

② Luigi thought cats were valuable to the islanders.

③ The queen didn't want to invite Luigi to her palace.

④ Luigi was sure that he would get more jewels than Antonio.

⑤ When Luigi opened the box that the queen gave him, he thanked her again and again.

32. 위 글의 밑줄 친 ⓓ<u>priceless</u>와 바꿔 쓸 수 있는 것은?　(3점)

① ⓐ　　② ⓑ　　③ ⓒ　　④ ⓔ　　⑤ ⓕ

◎ 선택형 문항의 답안은 컴퓨터용 수정 싸인펜을 사용하여 OMR 답안지에 바르게 표기하시오.
◎ 서술형 문제는 답을 답안지에 반드시 검정 볼펜으로 쓰시오.
◎ 총 28문항 100점 만점입니다. 문항별 배점은 각 문항에 표시되어 있습니다.

[경북 ○○중]

1. 다음 중 밑줄 친 부분의 뜻풀이가 <u>잘못된</u> 것은? (3점)

① <u>After a while</u>, the servant returned with a box. (잠시 후에)

② <u>In return for</u> the wonderful gifts he gave me, I made up my mind to help him. (~에 대한 보답으로)

③ In the queen's mind, the kitten was worth <u>far</u> more than all the jewels in the world. (멀리)

④ Luigi packed his ship with wonderful paintings and other <u>works of art</u>. (예술 작품들)

⑤ He <u>was sure that</u> he would receive more jewels than Antonio. (~할 것이라고 확신했다)

[부산 ○○중]

2. 다음 빈칸 (A)~(D)에 들어갈 단어를 아래 표에 순서대로 넣었을 때 표의 흰 사각형 안에 만들어지는 단어는? (4점)

• My uncle is a (A)_____ who sells vegetables at a traditional market.
• The (B)_____ that the prince lived in is huge and beautiful.
• I (C)_____ the organization because it helps children in need, so I donate 50,000 won to it every month.
• A diamond is known to be the most valuable (D)_____.

*donate 기부하다

(A)			r			
		(B)			a	
(C)	s					
		(D)		e		

① care   ② cake   ③ cost
④ make   ⑤ most

[인천 ○○중]

3. 다음 빈칸에 들어갈 말로 가장 알맞은 것은? (3점)

Sujin: _____
Jake: It was fantastic. I had a lot of fun.
Sujin: Me, too. The concert last night was really great.

① Did you like something else?
② Where did you go last night?
③ How did you like the concert?
④ Why didn't you come to school?
⑤ What did you like about the concert?

[부산 ○○중]

4. 다음 대화의 내용과 일치하지 <u>않는</u> 것은? (3점)

G: Oliver, what club are you going to join?
B: I'm not sure. How about you, Sora?
G: I want to join the school dance club.
B: Really? But I heard that you're preparing for an animation high school.
G: Right, but I need some time to relax. We all need to do something to get over stress.
B: You can say that again.
G: Why don't you join me? It'll be fun.
B: No, thanks. Dancing is not for me. I have two left feet.

① Oliver and Sora are talking about joining a school club.
② Oliver made a decision what club he would join.
③ Sora wants to go an animation high school.
④ Sora wants to join a club where she can reduce her stress.
⑤ Oliver cannot dance well, so he doesn't want to join the same club as Sora.

[5～6] 다음 대화를 읽고 물음에 답하시오.

A: Hey, Minjun. What a surprise!
B: Hi, Sora. I'm glad we're in the same class.
A: I am, too. We're now in our last year in middle school. How do you feel?
B: ⓐI'm a little worried that there'll be more schoolwork.
A: Me, too. We also have to think about our high school.
B: Which kind of school do you have in mind?
A: I'm thinking of an animation high school. I love painting.

5. 밑줄 친 ⓐ와 바꿔 쓸 수 있는 말은? (4점)

① I'm happy
② I'm afraid
③ I'm not sure
④ I agree
⑤ I don't know

6. 위 대화의 소라에 관한 내용과 일치하지 않는 것은? (3점)

① 민준이와 같은 반이다.
② 중학교 3학년이다.
③ 진학하고 싶은 고등학교가 있다.
④ 그림 그리는 것을 좋아한다.
⑤ 화가가 되고 싶어 한다.

7. 대화의 빈칸에 들어갈 말로 알맞은 표현 두 개는? (4점)

A: I think teens should sleep eight hours a day.
B: _____ Teens can't sleep that much. They have too many things to do.

① I think so, too.
② I disagree with you.
③ I couldn't agree more.
④ I don't agree with you.
⑤ You can say that again.

8. 다음 대화의 내용과 일치하지 않는 것은? (3점)

Sora: Oliver, what club are you going to join?
Oliver: I'm not sure. How about you, Sora?
Sora: I want to join the school dance club.
Oliver: Really? But I heard you're preparing for an animation high school.
Sora: Right, but I need some time to relax. We all need to do something to get over stress.
Oliver: You can say that again.
Sora: Why don't you join me? It'll be fun.
Oliver: No, thanks. Dancing is not for me. I have two left feet.

① Oliver hasn't decided to join a club yet.
② Sora is interested in the school dance club.
③ Sora wants to enter an animation high school.
④ Sora and Oliver agree to overcome stress by doing something.
⑤ Oliver thinks that dancing isn't for him because he often gets hurt.

9. 다음 표현 중 의미의 연결이 잘못된 것은? (4점)

① Break a leg. - Good luck.
② He has a big mouth. - He often tells people things that are secrets.
③ Can you give me a hand? - Can you help me?
④ He shouted at the top of his lungs. - He shouted very loudly.
⑤ I have butterflies in my stomach. - I have a stomachache.

10. 다음 중 어법상 잘못된 문장은? (3점)

① Did you hear anyone break the window?

② Somi didn't feel a sheep licking her hand.

③ A farmer watched a bird fly away suddenly.

④ What worries my parents most is my personality.

⑤ Last Saturday, one family went to a store to buy things what they wanted.

11. 다음 중 어법상 올바른 문장은? (3점)

① What do I usually do in my free time is hiking.

② I felt Mom whispered something in my ear.

③ She watched him to play an online game.

④ I will never forget that you told me.

⑤ I heard a boy cry loudly.

12. 어법상 옳은 것으로 짝지어진 것은? (4점)

(A) This is the watch what he bought last Sunday.

(B) I saw my brother done his homework.

(C) Jane heard him talk on the phone.

(D) Which makes me happy is my family.

(E) I saw emergency personnel carrying her to a hospital.

① (A), (B)　　② (B), (C)　　③ (C), (E)

④ (C), (D)　　⑤ (D), (E)

13. 다음 중 어법상 옳은 것은? (4점)

① I saw my dog to bark.

② Can you feel the ground shaking?

③ We saw the player caught the ball.

④ Nick felt something moved along his arm.

⑤ We heard somebody to knocking at the door.

14. 다음 주어진 단어를 배열하여 우리말 뜻에 맞게 문장을 다시 쓰시오. (4점)

• Jessie _____ in the kitchen.
(Jessie는 그녀의 오빠가 부엌에서 요리하는 것을 보았다.)

• brother / cook / watch / her

<조 건>
1. 문장을 처음부터 끝까지 쓸 것.
2. 동사의 시제를 알맞게 고쳐 쓸 것.
3. 대·소문자 구분 있음.
4. 구두점 유의. (마침표, 콤마, 물음표 등)

답: _____

15. 밑줄 친 우리말을 영어로 쓰시오. (4점)

• 내가 하고 싶은 것은 is to take a trip to Africa.

<조건>
'want'를 꼭 사용할 것.

정답: _____

- 9 -

[16~19] 다음 글을 읽고 물음에 답하시오.

Luigi watched the queen ⓐwhispering in a servant's ear. He became excited and hopeful. He was sure that he ⓑwould receive ⓒmore jewels than Antonio. After a while, the servant returned with a box, and the queen presented it to Luigi. When Luigi opened the box, he was speechless. There was a kitten in the box. "Antonio gave us the priceless cats, and we now have some kittens," said the queen. (A)"당신이 우리에게 준 멋진 선물에 대한 보답으로, we want to give you ⓓthat is most valuable to us." Luigi realized that, in the queen's mind, the kitten was worth ⓔfar more than all the jewels in the world. He tried to look pleased with the gift. He knew that was the right thing to do.

16. 밑줄 친 ⓐ~ⓔ 중 어법상 어색한 것은? (3점)

① ⓐ   ② ⓑ   ③ ⓒ   ④ ⓓ   ⑤ ⓔ

17. 위 글에 나타난 Luigi의 심경 변화로 가장 적절한 것은? (4점)

① excited → pleased
② upset → delighted
③ hopeful → disappointed
④ nervous → happy
⑤ jealous → satisfied

18. 위 글을 읽고 답할 수 없는 질문은? (3점)

① Why did Luigi become excited?
② What did the queen give to Luigi?
③ What was in the box?
④ What gifts did Luigi give to the queen?
⑤ What was most valuable to the queen?

19. 위 글의 밑줄 친 우리말 (A)를 괄호 안의 단어를 이용하여 영어 문장으로 쓰시오. (5점)

→ _____

[return / wonderful / gifts / in / you / us / gave / for / the]

[20~21] 다음 글을 읽고 물음에 답하시오.

Long ago, an honest merchant lived in Genoa, Italy. His name was Antonio, and he went to different places ⓐto support his family by trading. One day, he ⓑfilled his ship with goods and visited a faraway island. ⓒThere he ⓓtraded tools for spices and books for nuts. ⓔThanks to Antonio, the islanders could get (A)_____ they needed.

20. 위 글의 밑줄 친 ⓐ~ⓔ에 대한 설명으로 알맞지 않은 것은? (3점)

① ⓐ to support: 부양하기 위해
② ⓑ filled his ship with goods: 그의 배에 상품을 가득 실었다
③ ⓒ There는 a faraway island를 말한다.
④ ⓓ traded tools for spices: 향신료를 주고 도구를 얻었다
⑤ ⓔ Thanks to: ~ 덕분에

21. 위 글의 빈칸 (A)에 들어갈 말로 알맞은 것은? (3점)

① what   ② which   ③ that
④ when   ⑤ how

[22~24] 다음 글을 읽고 물음에 답하시오.

A Priceless Gift

Long ago, an honest ⓐmerchant lived in Genoa, Italy. His name was Antonio, and he went to different places to support his family by trading. One day, he filled his ship with goods and visited a faraway island. There he traded tools for spices and books for nuts. Thanks to Antonio, the islanders could get (A)[that / what] they needed.

(a) The merchant said to himself, "What the islanders here need is not tools or books but cats." He brought two cats from his ship and set them loose. "What amazing animals!" cried the queen when she saw all the rats (B)[ran / run] away. She gave Antonio a ⓑchest that was filled with jewels.

(b) Antonio was greatly surprised that there were rats in the palace. He asked, "Are there no cats on this island?" The queen looked (C)[puzzled / puzzling] "What is a cat?" she asked.

(c) One night, Antonio had dinner with the island's queen at her ⓒpalace. When dinner was served, rats appeared, and some servants chased them away with sticks.

Back in Italy, Antonio told his friends about his good fortune. Luigi, the richest merchant in Genoa, heard the story and was ⓓjealous. "Cats are worthless," Luigi thought. "I'll bring the queen what is really ⓔvaluable. I'm sure that the queen will give me more jewels."

---

22. 위 글의 흐름상 (a), (b), (c)의 순서로 가장 적절한 것은? (4점)

① (a)-(b)-(c) ② (a)-(c)-(b)
③ (b)-(a)-(c) ④ (c)-(a)-(b)
⑤ (c)-(b)-(a)

23. 위 글의 밑줄 친 ⓐ~ⓔ의 의미로 옳지 않은 것은? (4점)

① ⓐ: someone who buys and sells products in large amounts

② ⓑ: a wooden box used for storing things

③ ⓒ: the official home of a king or queen

④ ⓓ: unhappy and angry because someone has what you do not have

⑤ ⓔ: lacking in usefulness or value

24. 위 글의 괄호 (A), (B), (C) 안에서 어법에 맞는 표현으로 가장 적절한 것은? (4점)

	(A)	(B)	(C)
①	that	ran	puzzled
②	what	run	puzzled
③	that	ran	puzzling
④	what	ran	puzzled
⑤	what	run	puzzling

25. 다음 글의 Anotonio에 대한 내용과 일치하지 않는 것은? (3점)

Long ago, an honest merchant lived in Genoa, Italy. His name was Antonio, and he went to different places to support his family by trading. One day, he filled his ship with goods and visited a faraway island. There he traded tools for spices and books for nuts. Thanks to Antonio, the islanders could get what they needed.

---

① He gave the islanders some goods for free.

② He was a merchant who traded goods.

③ He had family to support.

④ He was from Italy.

⑤ He was honest.   *for free: 공짜로, 무료로

[26~27] 다음 글을 읽고 물음에 답하시오.

Back in Italy Antonio told his friends about his good fortune. Luigi, the richest merchant in Genoa, heard the story and was jealous. "Cats are worthless," Luigi thought. "I'll bring the queen (A)_____ is really valuable. I'm sure that the queen will give me more jewels."

Luigi packed his ship with wonderful paintings and other works of art. He took the gifts to the island. To get a chance to meet the queen, he told the islanders a lie (B)_____ he was a good friend of Antonio's. When the queen heard about Luigi, she invited him to her palace for dinner. Before sitting down at the table, Luigi presented the queen with all his gifts, and the queen thanked him again and again. "I'll repay you with a priceless gift," said the queen.

Luigi watched the queen whisper in a servant's ear. He was sure (C)_____ he would receive more jewels than Antonio.

After a while, the servant returned with a box, and the queen presented it to Luigi. When Luigi opened the box, he was speechless.

There was a kitten in the box. "In return for the wonderful gifts (D)_____ you gave us, we want to give you what is most valuable to us."

Luigi realized (E)_____, in the queen's mind, the kitten was worth far more than all the jewels in the world. He tried to look pleased with the gift. He knew that was the right thing to do. Luigi did not return home a richer man. But he was surely a wiser one.

26. 위 글의 빈칸 (A)~(E) 중 들어갈 말이 <u>다른</u> 하나는?

(4점)

① (A)   ② (B)   ③ (C)   ④ (D)   ⑤ (E)

27. 다음은 위 글을 읽은 학생들의 감상이다. 글의 교훈과 가장 거리가 <u>먼</u> 것은?   (4점)

① Yuna: 비싼 것이 항상 좋은 선물은 아니야.

② Jimin: 사람들마다 중요하다고 느끼는 가치는 다를 수 있어.

③ Daniel: 선물을 줄 땐 그 사람이 필요한 게 무엇인지를 생각해 봐야 해.

④ Yuri: 내 마음에 드는 값비싼 선물을 주면 상대방은 나에게 더 비싼 선물을 주게 되어 있어.

⑤ Woojin: 선물을 받았을 땐 마음에 들지 않더라도 감사해 하고 기뻐하는 모습을 보이는 게 예의야.

28. 다음 글의 밑줄 친 ⓐ~ⓔ의 해석이 <u>어색한</u> 것은?

(3점)

Antonio was greatly surprised that there were rats in the palace. He asked, "Are there no cats on this island?" The queen ⓐlooked puzzled. "What is a cat?" she asked.

The merchant ⓑsaid to himself, "ⓒWhat the islanders here need is not tools or books, but cats." He brought two cats from his ship and ⓓlet them run free. "What amazing animals!" cried the queen when she saw all the rats run away. She gave Antonio ⓔa chest that was filled with jewels.

① ⓐ looked puzzled: 퍼즐을 보았다.

② ⓑ said to himself: 혼잣말했다.

③ ⓒ What the islanders here need: 이곳 섬사람들이 필요한 것

④ ⓓ let them run free: 그것들을 자유롭게 풀어주었다.

⑤ ⓔ a chest that was filled with jewels: 보석으로 가득 채워져 있던 상자

◎ 선택형 문항의 답안은 컴퓨터용 수정 싸인펜을 사용하여 OMR 답안지에 바르게 표기하시오.
◎ 서술형 문제는 답을 답안지에 반드시 검정 볼펜으로 쓰시오.
◎ 총 28문항 100점 만점입니다. 문항별 배점은 각 문항에 표시되어 있습니다.

[전북 ○○중]

1. 다음 중 단어의 영영풀이로 바르지 못한 것은? (4점)

① except: not including
② colony: a group of plants or animals living or growing in one place
③ repeatedly: very often, again and again
④ female: relating to men or boys
⑤ stomach: the part of your body where food is digested

[경북 ○○중]

2. 다음 단어의 관계를 볼 때 빈칸에 들어갈 알맞은 말은? (3점)

appear : disappear = including : _____

① include   ② contain   ③ extremely
④ except   ⑤ entire

[경기 ○○중]

3. 다음 대화의 내용과 일치하지 않는 것은? (4점)

B: Amber, how do you like the camp?
G: It's great. I'm having a lot of fun.
B: Me, too. The talent show last night was really great.
G: Yeah. By the way, did you decide on the afternoon program?
B: No, I haven't yet. Which do you think is better, hiking or swimming?
G: I'll go hiking because we can see wild birds and insects in the woods.
B: I'll join you. I like birds and insects.
G: Great. I heard we'll have a hiking guide.
B: Sounds good.

B: Boy, G: Amber

① Amber is enjoying herself at the camp.
② Amber prefers swimming to hiking.
③ They are going on a hike with a guide.
④ The boy is interested in birds and insects.
⑤ Amber and the boy will join the same afternoon program.

[경기 ○○중]

4. 자연스러운 대화가 되도록 (A)~(D)를 순서대로 배열한 것은? (4점)

Alex: Sora, can you take a look at these pictures?
Sora: What are these for?
Alex: I'm trying to choose a picture for my story in the school newspaper.
Sora: What's your story about?
Alex: Nature's future.

(A) That sounds interesting
(B) Can you tell me more about it?
(C) Which picture do you think is better?
(D) It's about endangered animals in the Arctic areas.

Sora: I like the one showing a skinny polar bear.

① (A)-(B)-(D)-(C)
② (A)-(C)-(D)-(B)
③ (B)-(C)-(A)-(D)
④ (B)-(D)-(A)-(C)
⑤ (C)-(A)-(D)-(B)

[5~6] 다음 대화를 읽고 물음에 답하시오.

A: I heard (A)_____ are having a hard time these day. Can you tell me more?
B: Sure. There's a lot of trash in the sea. Many (A)_____ eat it and get sick.
A: That's too bad. Is there anything we can do to help them?
B: Yes, first, (B)_____.

5. 위 대화의 내용으로 보아 빈칸 (A)에 들어갈 알맞은 말은? (3점)

① ants ② deer ③ birds
④ monkeys ⑤ whales

6. 위 대화의 빈칸 (B)에 가장 알맞은 말은? (3점)

① we should save water
② we should try to clean up the sea
③ we should turn off unnecessary lights at night
④ we should stop cutting down trees in the forest
⑤ we have to wash our hands after coming back home

7. 다음 대화의 내용과 일치하지 <u>않는</u> 것은? (4점)

W: Everyone, look at this chestnut tree. This is the oldest tree in these woods.
B: Can you tell me how old it is?
W: It's about 150 years old.
B: Wow! It's ten times my age.
G: Ms. Oh, is that a beehive up in the tree?
W: Yes. Can you guess how many bees live there?
G: 500 bees?

W: Good guess, but it's big enough to hold over 50,000 bees.
B, G: Unbelievable!
<W: Woman, B: Boy, G: Girl>

① 이 밤나무는 숲에서 가장 오래된 나무이다.
② 학생들은 벌집에 대한 설명을 듣고 있다.
③ 소년의 나이는 15살 정도이다.
④ 밤나무의 나이는 소년의 나이의 100배이다.
⑤ 벌집은 5만 마리 이상의 벌을 수용할 수 있는 규모이다.

[8~9] 다음 대화의 빈칸에 적합한 표현을 〈보기〉에서 찾으시오.

<보기>
ⓐ I'm glad I can wear my new raincoat.
ⓑ You can say that again.
ⓒ Can you tell me more about it?
ⓓ I like dogs better.
ⓔ The pleasure is mine.

8. 위 〈보기〉에서 다음 대화의 빈칸에 적합한 표현을 찾으면? (4점)

A: Which do you like better, dogs or cats?
B: _____ They are more friendly. How about you?
A: I like cats better.

① ⓐ ② ⓑ ③ ⓒ ④ ⓓ ⑤ ⓔ

9. 위 〈보기〉에서 다음 대화의 빈칸에 적합한 표현을 찾으면? (4점)

A: What are you drawing?
B: An elephant.
A: What is an elephant? _____
B: It's an animal. It's a big animal that has a long nose and big ears.

① ⓐ ② ⓑ ③ ⓒ ④ ⓓ ⑤ ⓔ

10. 다음 대화가 자연스럽게 이어지도록 주어진 단어들을 모두 사용하여, 주어와 동사를 포함한 완전한 한 문장의 영어로 쓰시오.　(3점)

G: Did you decide on the afternoon program?
B: No, I haven't yet. [Which / hiking / swimming / better]?
G: I'll go hiking because we can see wild birds and insects in the woods.
B: I'll join you. I like birds and insects.
G: Great.

정답: _____

11. 다음 글의 밑줄 친 부분 중 어법상 옳지 <u>않은</u> 것은?　(4점)

The old man ⓐ<u>planting</u> some flowers is Mr. Simpson. He has a garden ⓑ<u>filled</u> with beautiful flowers. His granddaughter is drawing ants ⓒ<u>carried</u> a leaf together. His grandsons are talking on a swing ⓓ<u>made</u> of wood. The woman ⓔ<u>taking</u> a picture is Ms. Simpson.

① ⓐ　② ⓑ　③ ⓒ　④ ⓓ　⑤ ⓔ

12. 다음 중 어법상 <u>어색한</u> 것은?　(3점)

① Look at the sun rising over the sea.
② The parrot sat on the tree said "Hi."
③ I visited a pet shop run by my aunt.
④ I like the picture painted by a parrot.
⑤ The kid wearing a cap is my nephew.

13. 다음 대화의 순서를 바르게 배열한 것은?　(4점)

Amber, did you decide on the afternoon program?
ⓐ Sounds good. I'll join you.
ⓑ Not yet. Which do you think is better, soccer or painting?
ⓒ Soccer, of course. I can exercise through the program.
ⓓ Perfect! It will be fun to play soccer together.

① ⓐ-ⓒ-ⓓ-ⓑ　② ⓑ-ⓐ-ⓓ-ⓒ
③ ⓑ-ⓒ-ⓐ-ⓓ　④ ⓒ-ⓑ-ⓐ-ⓓ
⑤ ⓒ-ⓓ-ⓑ-ⓐ

14. 다음 밑줄 친 ⓐ~ⓔ 중 어법상 옳지 <u>않은</u> 것은?　(4점)

This is a picture ⓐ<u>taking</u> last weekend. I visited a pet shop ⓑ<u>run</u> by Aunt Mary. I helped her clean the snake cage ⓒ<u>made</u> of glass. The woman ⓓ<u>moving</u> the snake is Aunt Mary. The parrot ⓔ<u>sitting</u> on the tree said, "Hurry up." The cat watched us from a chair painted green and blue.

① ⓐ　② ⓑ　③ ⓒ　④ ⓓ　⑤ ⓔ

[15~16] 다음 글을 읽고 물음에 답하시오.

How Many Ants Are on Earth?

We often see ants ⓐcome out of nowhere. Like humans, they live almost everywhere in the world, except a few extremely cold ⓑplaces ⓒincluding Antarctica. As of 2018, there were over 7 billion people on Earth. Then, how about ants? ⓓAccording to scientists, there are about one million ants for every human in the world. ⓔSince each ant hardly weighs anything, one million ants are as heavy as a human being weighing about 62 kilograms.

15. 위 글의 밑줄 친 ⓐ~ⓔ 중 올바른 표현이 <u>아닌</u> 것은?　　　　　(4점)

① ⓐ　② ⓑ　③ ⓒ　④ ⓓ　⑤ ⓔ

16. 위 글의 내용과 일치하지 <u>않는</u> 것은? (3점)

① 개미는 남극에서도 살 수 있다.
② 2018년에 70억이 넘는 인구가 있었다.
③ 사람 한 명당 약 백만 마리의 개미가 있다.
④ 개미 한 마리는 거의 무게가 나가지 않는다.
⑤ 백만 마리 개미는 62kg인 사람 한 명 무게와 같다.

17. 다음 글의 개미에 관한 내용과 일치하는 것은?
　　　　　(4점)

FUN FACTS ABOUT ANTS

01 Some queen ants live up to 30 years.
02 Some ants can carry things that are 50 times their own body weight.
03 Ants do not have lungs but breathe through small holes in their bodies.
04 An ant has two stomachs. One stomach holds food for itself, and the other holds foods to share with others.
05 Most ants can swim and live 24 hours underwater.

① 여왕 개미들과 수개미들은 30년까지 살 수 있다.
② 어떤 개미들은 50kg이 넘는 짐을 나를 수 있다.
③ 개미는 폐를 통해 호흡한다.
④ 개미는 하나의 위에는 자신의 먹이를 저장하고, 다른 하나의 위에는 나중에 자신이 먹을 음식을 저장한다.
⑤ 대부분의 개미들은 수영할 수 있고 물속에서 24시간 동안 살 수 있다.

[18~19] 다음 글을 읽고 물음에 답하시오.

What is the Ant Society Like?

Ants live in colonies ⓐwho have lots of residents ⓑlived together. Within a colony, there are usually three different types of ants. There is the queen, and ⓒthat she does her entire life is lay eggs. The second type of ant is the male that helps the queen ⓓproducing these eggs. The third type of ant is the worker. Worker ants are all female and do very important jobs, like caring for eggs, defending the colony, and ⓔcollected food.

18. 위 글의 밑줄 친 ⓐ~ⓔ는 모두 어법상 어색합니다. 바르게 고친 것은? (4점)

① ⓐ who → which
② ⓑ lived → live
③ ⓒ that → which
④ ⓓ producing → producer
⑤ ⓔ collected → collect

19. 위 글의 내용과 일치하지 <u>않는</u> 것은? (3점)

① 글의 주제는 '개미의 종류와 역할'이다.
② 개미는 군집을 이루며 살고 있다.
③ 여왕 개미는 평생 알 낳는 일을 한다.
④ 수컷 개미는 자신의 군집을 방어한다.
⑤ 일개미는 모두 암컷이며 먹이를 모은다.

[20~22] 다음 글을 읽고 물음에 답하시오.

Ants live in colonies which have lots of residents ⓐ<u>living</u> together. There are usually three different types of ants. There is the queen, and ⓑ<u>what</u> she does her entire life is lay eggs. The second type of ant is the male, which helps the queen produce these eggs. The third type of ant is the worker. Worker ants are all female and do very important jobs, like caring for eggs, defending the colony, and collecting food.
Though ants do not speak like humans, they ⓒ<u>actually</u> have a "language." Ants produce a chemical ⓓ<u>calling</u> a pheromone to communicate with one another. By using the chemical, they can exchange information about food or danger. Ants also use touch for communication. For example, if an ant finds food, it passes on the good news by ⓔ<u>rubbing</u> its body on its neighbor. ⓕ_____ an ant has legs covered with very sensitive hairs, it can sense even the smallest touch.

20. 위 글의 밑줄 친 ⓐ~ⓔ 중 문맥상 또는 어법상 맞지 <u>않는</u> 것은? (4점)

① ⓐ ② ⓑ ③ ⓒ ④ ⓓ ⑤ ⓔ

21. 위 글의 빈칸 ⓕ에 들어갈 말로 적절한 것은? (3점)

① Since ② Until ③ While
④ Though ⑤ Therefore

22. 위 글의 내용과 일치하는 것은? (4점)

① 개미의 다리는 아주 민감한 털로 덮여 있다.
② 개미들은 사람처럼 소리를 통해서 의사소통한다.
③ 온갖 중요한 일을 하는 일개미들은 모두 수컷이다.
④ 개미들은 소수의 동료와 작은 군집을 이루어 산다.
⑤ 개미가 음식을 발견하면 동료 개미의 주위를 돌면서 위치를 말해 준다.

[23~24] 다음 글을 읽고 물음에 답하시오.

(A)_____ ants do not speak like humans, they actually have a "language." Ants produce a chemical called a pheromone to communicate with one another. By using the chemical, they can exchange information about food or danger. Ants also use touch for communication. (B)_____, if an ant finds food, it passes on the good news by rubbing its body on its neighbor. Since an ant has legs covered with very sensitive hairs, it can sense even the smallest touch.

23. 위 글의 제목으로 가장 적절한 것은? (3점)

① Why Do Ants Communicate?
② How Do Ants Communicate?
③ Why Do Ants Release Pheromone?
④ How Does the Pheromone Affect the Ants?
⑤ How Do Ants Behave When They Sense Danger?

24. 위 글의 빈칸 (A), (B)에 들어갈 말을 나열한 것으로 옳은 것은? (3점)

	(A)	(B)
①	Because	In addition
②	Since	For example
③	Though	For example
④	Since	In addition
⑤	Though	As a result

[25~28] 다음 글을 읽고 물음에 답하시오.

How Many Ants Are on Earth?

We often see ants come out of nowhere. Like humans, they live almost everywhere in the world, except (A)_____ extremely cold places including Antarctica. As of 2018, there were over 7 billion people on Earth. Then, how about ants? According to scientists, there are about one million ants for every human in the world. Though each ant hardly ⓐ<u>weigh</u> anything, one million ants are as heavy as a human being weighing about 62 kilograms.

(a)_____

Ants live in colonies which have a lot of residents living together. Within a colony, there are usually three different types of ants. There is the queen, and what she does her entire life is ⓑ<u>lay</u> eggs. The second type of ant is the male that helps the queen produce these eggs. The third type of ant is the worker. Worker ants are all female and do very important jobs, like ⓒ<u>taking</u> care of eggs, defending the colony, and collecting food.

How Do Ants Communicate?

Though ants do not speak like humans, they actually have a "language." Ants produce a chemical called a pheromone to communicate with one another. By using the chemical, they can exchange information about food or danger. Ants also use touch for communication. For example, if an ant finds food, it passes on the good news by rubbing its body on its neighbor. (B)_____ an ant has legs covered with very sensitive hairs, it can sense even the smallest touch.

FUN FACTS ABOUT ANTS

1. Some queen ants live ⓓ<u>up to</u> 30 years.
2. Some ants can carry things that are 50 times their own body weight.
3. Ants do not have lungs but breathe through small holes in their bodies.

4. An ant has two stomachs. One stomach holds food for itself, and ⓔ<u>another</u> holds food to share with others.
5. Most ants can swim and live 24 hours underwater.

25. 위 글의 빈칸 (A), (B)에 들어갈 말로 가장 적절한 것은? (3점)

   (A)   (B)
① few   Though
② a few   Since
③ a few   Though
④ a little   Since
⑤ a little   Though

26. 위 글의 ⓐ~ⓔ 중 어법상 어색한 것만을 있는 대로 고른 것은? (4점)

① ⓐ, ⓔ   ② ⓒ, ⓔ   ③ ⓐ, ⓑ, ⓓ
④ ⓐ, ⓒ, ⓔ   ⑤ ⓑ, ⓒ, ⓓ

27. 위 글의 빈칸 (a)에 들어갈 제목으로 가장 적절한 것은? (3점)

① How Do Ants Find Food?
② How Are Male Ants Born?
③ What Is the Ant Society Like?
④ Why Do Ants Work Together?
⑤ What Does the Queen Do All Her Life?

28. 위 글의 내용과 일치하는 것은? (4점)

① Ants live in Antarctica.
② The total weight of all ants on Earth is close to that of a human being.
③ Male ants defend the colony.
④ Ants cannot communicate with each other through the use of pheromones.
⑤ Although ants do not have lungs, they breathe through small holes in their bodies.

문항수 : 선택형(27문항) 서술형(2문항) 　20 ． ． ．

◎ 선택형 문항의 답안은 컴퓨터용 수정 싸인펜을
  사용하여 OMR 답안지에 바르게 표기하시오.
◎ 서술형 문제는 답을 답안지에 반드시 검정
  볼펜으로 쓰시오.
◎ 총 29문항 100점 만점입니다. 문항별 배점
  은 각 문항에 표시되어 있습니다.

[경북 ○○중]

1. 다음 (A)와 (B)의 영어 설명에 알맞은 단어로 연결
   된 것은?　　　　　　　　　　　　　　　(3점)

(A) to put something in a bag or a box
(B) a small animal with six legs and usually
    wings

	(A)	(B)
①	support	female
②	support	resident
③	pack	resident
④	pack	insect
⑤	chase	insect

[경기 ○○중]

2. 다음 빈칸 (A)~(E)에 들어갈 말로 옳지 않은 것은?
   　　　　　　　　　　　　　　　　　(4점)

• How long can whales (A)_____ underwater?
• The library is open every day (B)_____
  national holidays.
• As he gets older, his teeth are becoming
  (C)_____ to cold foods.
• You should not (D)_____ your face with
  a towel after taking a shower.
• The (E)_____ country was excited about
  the victory of its national soccer team.

① (A) - breathe　　　② (B) - except
③ (C) - sensible　　　④ (D) - rub
⑤ (E) - whole

[전북 ○○중]

[3~4] 다음 대화를 읽고 물음에 답하시오.

A: Amber, how do you like the camp?
B: ⓐIt's great. I'm having a lot of fun.
A: ⓑMe, too. The talent show last night
   was really great.
B: Yeah. By the way, did you decide on the
   afternoon program?
A: ⓒNo, I haven't yet. Which do you think
   is better, hiking or swimming?
B: I'll go hiking because we can see wild
   birds and insects in the woods.
A: I'll join you. ⓓI hate birds and insects.
B: Grea. I heard we'll have a hiking guide.
A: ⓔSounds good.

3. 밑줄 친 ⓐ~ⓔ 중 흐름상 어색한 것은?　　(3점)
① ⓐ　② ⓑ　③ ⓒ　④ ⓓ　⑤ ⓔ

4. 위 대화의 내용과 일치하지 않는 것은?　　(2점)
① 두 사람은 캠프에 참가하고 있다.
② 어젯밤에 장기자랑이 있었다.
③ Amber는 오후 프로그램으로 하이킹을 선호한다.
④ 두 사람은 오후에 각각 다른 프로그램에 참여할
   것이다.
⑤ 하이킹 프로그램에는 가이드가 함께 할 것이다.

[인천 ○○중]

5. 다음 빈칸에 들어갈 말로 가장 알맞은 것은?　(2점)

A: Everyone, look. This is the oldest building
   in Seoul.
B: It's beautiful. _____
A: It's 300 years old.
B: Unbelievable! It's twenty times my age!

① Can you tell how old is it?
② Can you tell me how old is it?
③ You can tell me how old is it?
④ Can you tell me how old it is?
⑤ You can tell me how old it is?

[6~7] 다음 대화를 읽고 물음에 답하시오.

Mike: Amber, how do you like the camp?
Amber: It's great, I'm having a lot of fun.
Mike: Me, too. The talent show last night was really great. (A)
Amber: Yeah. By the way, did you decide on the afternoon program? (B)
Mike: No, I haven't yet. (C)
Amber: I'll go hiking because we can see wild birds and insects in the woods. (D)
Mike: I'll join you. I like birds and insects.
Amber: Great. (E) I heard we'll have a hiking guide.
Mike: Sounds good.

6. 위 글에서 아래 문장이 들어가기에 가장 적당한 곳은?　(4점)

Which do you think is better, hiking or swimming?

① (A)　② (B)　③ (C)　④ (D)　⑤ (E)

7. 위 글의 내용과 일치하는 것은?　(3점)
① Amber는 캠프가 지루하다고 생각한다.
② Mike는 이미 오후 프로그램을 결정했다.
③ 그들은 지난밤에 멋진 캠프파이어를 했다.
④ 그들은 동아리 활동에 대해 얘기하고 있다.
⑤ 그들은 오후에 하이킹 프로그램에 참가할 것이다.

8. 다음 빈칸에 공통으로 들어갈 말은? (대·소문자 무시)　(2점)

• I have been writing a travel blog _____ I was 18.
• _____ it rained heavily, the station was closed.

① since　② because　③ for
④ as　⑤ though

9. 다음 밑줄 친 단어의 쓰임이 올바른 것은?　(3점)

This is a picture ⓐtaken last weekend. I visited a pet shop ⓑrunning by Aunt Mary. I helped her clean the snake cage ⓒmaking of glass. The woman ⓓmoved the snake is Aunt Mary. The parrot ⓔsit on the tree said, "Hurry up."

① ⓐ　② ⓑ　③ ⓒ　④ ⓓ　⑤ ⓔ

10. 다음 대화의 밑줄 친 ⓐ~ⓔ 중 가리키는 대상이 나머지 넷과 다른 것은?　(3점)

A: Everyone, look at this ⓐchestnut tree. ⓑThis is the oldest tree in these woods.
B: Can you tell me how old ⓒit is?
A: ⓓIt's about 150 years old.
B: Wow! It's ten times my age.
C: Ms. Oh, is ⓔthat a beehive up in the tree?
A: Yes. Can you guess how many bees live there?
C: 500 bees?
A: Good guess, but it's big enough to hold over 50,000 bees.
B, C: Unbelievable!

① ⓐ　② ⓑ　③ ⓒ　④ ⓓ　⑤ ⓔ

11. 다음 대화의 밑줄 친 ⓐ~ⓔ 중, 어법상 어색한 것은? (3점)

W: Everyone, look at this chestnut tree. ⓐThis is the oldest tree in these woods.
B: ⓑCan you tell me how old is it?
W: It's about 150 years old.
B: Wow! It's ten times my age.
G: Ms. Oh, ⓒis that a beehive up in the tree?
W: Yes. Can you guess? ⓓHow many bees live there?
G: 500 bees?
W: Good guess, ⓔbut it's big enough to hold over 50,000 bees.
B, G: Unbelievable!

W: Woman, B: Boy, G: Girl

① ⓐ ② ⓑ ③ ⓒ ④ ⓓ ⑤ ⓔ

12. 다음 대화의 내용과 일치하는 것은? (4점)

B: Sora, can you take a look at these pictures?
G: What are these for?
B: I'm trying to choose a picture for my story in the school newspaper.
G: What's your story about?
B: Nature's future.
G: Can you tell me more about it?
B: It's about endangered animals in the Arctic areas.
G: Hmm, interesting.
B: Which picture do you think is better?
G: I like the one showing a skinny polar bear. <B: Boy, G: Girl>

① 소년은 학교 신문 기사에 적합한 사진을 고르는 중이다.
② 소년의 기사는 남극 지역의 동물에 관한 것이다.
③ 소년은 소녀에게 신문 기사를 위해 사진 촬영을 요청했다.
④ 소녀는 헤엄치고 있는 곰의 사진을 마음에 들어한다.
⑤ 소녀는 학교 신문인 Nature's future지의 기자이다.

13. 밑줄 친 부분이 어법상 올바른 문장은? (3점)

① I know the woman <u>solved</u> the math problem.
② He gave us some cookies <u>covering</u> with chocolate.
③ The woman <u>waited</u> for the interview looks nervous.
④ Next to the gym, there is a library <u>building</u> in 2019.
⑤ We waved at the boy <u>watering</u> the plants in the garden.

14. 다음 빈칸에 since와 though 중 알맞은 것을 쓰시오. (5점)

(1) I am tired _____ I didn't get enough sleep last night.
(2) I am tired _____ I slept enough last night.

(1) _____ (2) _____

15. 다음 글의 밑줄 친 부분이 내용상 어색한 것은 몇 개인가? (4점)

Jamie is an extraordinary child. <u>Though</u> he is only five years old, he can speak three different languages. <u>Out of</u> the three, he speaks English best <u>while</u> he was born in England. He has one more extraordinary ability. <u>Until</u> he is small now, he climbs big trees very well. He likes to climb up to his tree house <u>since</u> it is his favorite place.

① 1개 ② 2개 ③ 3개 ④ 4개 ⑤ 5개

[16~18] 다음 글을 읽고 물음에 답하시오.

For the science project, our group has chosen very special insects.
• They are very social.
• They appear in Aesop's stories.
• They use a special chemical to communicate.

Can you guess ⓐthat they are? Yes, the answer is ants. We want to share with you ⓑwhat we have learned about these insects.

We often see ants come out of nowhere. Like humans, they live almost everywhere in the world, except a few extremely cold places ⓒincluding Antarctica. As of 2018, there were over 7 billion people on Earth. Then, how about ants? According to scientists, there ⓓare about one million ants for every human in the world. Each ant hardly ⓔweighs anything. However, (가)백만 마리의 개미는 사람 한 명만큼 무겁다.

16. 위 글의 밑줄 친 ⓐ~ⓔ 중, 어법상 어색한 것은?
(3점)

① ⓐ   ② ⓑ   ③ ⓒ   ④ ⓓ   ⑤ ⓔ

17. 위 글의 내용과 일치하는 것은?   (3점)
① 개미는 개인적인 성향을 가진 곤충이다.
② 개미는 의사소통을 하기 위해 화학물질을 사용한다.
③ 개미는 극도로 추운 곳을 포함하여 거의 모든 곳에 살고 있다.
④ 2018년, 지구상에는 70억이 넘는 개미가 있었다.
⑤ 과학자들에 의하면, 세상에는 사람 한 명당 약 1억 마리의 개미가 있다.

18. 위 글의 밑줄 친 우리말 (가)를 <보기> 안에 주어진 단어들을 사용하여 영어로 쓰시오.   (5점)

<보기>
as / a human being / one million ants

정답: _____

[19~20] 다음 글을 읽고 물음에 답하시오.

(A)[Since / Though] ants do not speak like humans, they actually have a "language." Ants produce a chemical called a pheromone to communicate with one another. By using the chemical, they can exchange information about food or danger. Ants also use touch for communication. (B)[In addition / For example], if an ant finds food, it passes on the good news by rubbing its body on its neighbor. (C)[Since / Though] an ant has legs covered with very sensitive hairs, it can sense even the smallest touch.

19. 위 글의 (A)~(C)에서 각각 올바른 것을 골라 짝지은 것은?   (4점)

	(A)	(B)	(C)
①	Since	In addition	Since
②	Since	In addition	Though
③	Since	For example	Though
④	Though	For example	Since
⑤	Though	In addition	Though

20. 위 글의 제목으로 가장 적절한 것은?   (3점)
① How Old Are Ants?
② Three Types of Ants
③ How Do Ants Communicate?
④ How Big Is Ant Society?
⑤ Ways to Communicate Well

21. 다음 글과 표의 내용 중 일치하지 <u>않는</u> 것은? (4점)

Honeybees are easily found in warm places which have many plants and flowers. A queen lives up to five years, but worker bees only live for about seven weeks. Honeybees go from flower to flower to collect food. A worker bee makes hundreds of trips to produce a small amount of honey. By moving around, honeybees help plants grow.

Honeybees	
Home Honeybees are found in ⓐ<u>warm</u> places around the world.	**Food Collection** Honeybees visit ⓓ<u>flowers</u> in the woods to collect food.
Life Span Some queens can live for ⓑ<u>five years</u>, but ⓒ<u>male bees</u> only live for about seven weeks.	**Fun Facts** A worker bee makes ⓔ<u>hundreds</u> of trips to produce a small amount of honey. By moving around, honeybees help plants grow.

① ⓐ ② ⓑ ③ ⓒ ④ ⓓ ⑤ ⓔ

22. 다음 글의 내용과 일치하는 것은? (4점)

For the science project, our group has chosen very special insects.
• They are very social.
• They are as old as the T-Rex.
• They appear in Aesop's stories.
• They use a special chemical to communicate.
Can you guess what they are? Yes, the answer is ants. We want to share with you what we have learned about these insects.

The Amazing Ants
How Many Ants Are on Earth?
We often see ants come out of nowhere. Like humans, they live almost everywhere in the world, except a few extremely cold places including Antarctica. As of 2018, there were over 7 billion people on Earth. Then, how about ants? According to scientists, there are about one million ants for every human in the world. Though each ant hardly weighs anything, one million ants are as heavy as a human being weighing about 62 kilograms.

① The students' project is about T-Rex.
② Ants can live in Antarctica like humans.
③ Ants can communicate by using a chemical.
④ Ten million ants weigh around 62 kilograms.
⑤ In 2018, over 7 billion ants were living on Earth.

23. 다음 글을 읽고 답할 수 있는 질문은? (4점)

FUN FACTS ABOUT ANTS
1. Some queen ants live up to 30 years.
2. Some ants can carry things that are 50 times their own body weight.
3. Ants do not have lungs but breathe through small holes in their bodies.
4. An ant has two stomachs. One stomach holds food for itself, and the other holds food to share with others.
5. Most ants can swim and live 24 hours underwater.

① Do queen ants live longer than worker ants?
② How much does an ant weigh?
③ How many holes do ants have on their bodies?
④ How do ants communicate one another underwater?
⑤ How many stomachs do ants have?

[24~26] 다음 글을 읽고 물음에 답하시오.

Ants live in colonies which ⓐ<u>has</u> lots of residents living together. Within a colony, there are usually three different types of ants. There is the queen, and ⓑ<u>what</u> she does her entire life is ⓒ<u>lay</u> eggs. The second type of ant is the male (A)<u>that</u> helps the queen ⓓ<u>produces</u> these eggs. The third type of ant is the worker. Worker ants are all female and do very important jobs, like ⓔ<u>caring</u> for eggs, defending the colony, and collecting food.

24. 위 글의 제목으로 가장 알맞은 것은?   (4점)

① Strange Facts about Ants
② Difficulty in Studying Ants
③ How Do Ants Communicate?
④ What Is the Ant Society Like?
⑤ How Many Ants Are on Earth?

25. 위 글의 밑줄 친 ⓐ~ⓔ 중 어법상 어색한 것끼리 모은 것은?   (4점)

① ⓐ, ⓒ   ② ⓐ, ⓓ   ③ ⓑ, ⓒ
④ ⓑ, ⓒ, ⓔ   ⑤ ⓒ, ⓓ, ⓔ

26. 위 글의 밑줄 친 (A)that과 아래 보기에서 문법적 쓰임이 같은 것끼리 모은 것은?   (3점)

ⓐ I wonder what <u>that</u> building is?
ⓑ She wants to have a robot <u>that</u> can talk.
ⓒ I know the boy <u>that</u> is singing on the stage.
ⓓ He visited a town <u>that</u> has many beautiful parks.
ⓔ People believe <u>that</u> everyone is equal before the law.

① ⓐ, ⓒ   ② ⓐ, ⓔ   ③ ⓐ, ⓒ, ⓔ
④ ⓑ, ⓒ, ⓓ   ⑤ ⓒ, ⓓ, ⓔ

[27~29] 다음 글을 읽고 물음에 답하시오.

We often see ants come out of nowhere. Like humans, they live almost everywhere in the world, except a few extremely cold places including Antarctica. As of 2018, there were over 7 billion people on Earth. Then, how about ants? According to scientists, there are about one million ants for every human in the world. Though each ant hardly weighs anything, one million ants are as heavy as a human being (A)_____ about 62 kilograms.

27. 위 글의 제목으로 가장 알맞은 것은?   (4점)

① Fun Facts About Ants
② How Many Ants Are on Earth?
③ What Is the Ant Society Like?
④ How Do Ants Communicate?
⑤ How Long Do Ants Live?

28. 위 글의 빈칸 (A)에 들어갈 말로 알맞은 것은?   (3점)

① weighing   ② weighs   ③ weigh
④ is weigh   ⑤ will weight

29. 위 글을 읽고 알 수 있는 것을 <u>두 개</u> 고르면? (4점)

① 개미가 추운 지역에 살지 않는 이유
② 개미의 평균 수명
③ 인구 대비 개미의 개체 수
④ 개미의 천적
⑤ 개미 백만 마리의 무게

◎ 선택형 문항의 답안은 컴퓨터용 수정 싸인펜을 사용하여 OMR 답안지에 바르게 표기하시오.
◎ 서술형 문제는 답을 답안지에 반드시 검정 볼펜으로 쓰시오.
◎ 총 27문항 100점 만점입니다. 문항별 배점은 각 문항에 표시되어 있습니다.

[전북 ○○중]

1. 다음 빈칸에 공통으로 들어갈 말로 알맞은 것은? (3점)

• What's the _____? You look upset.
• It doesn't _____ how much it is.

① point   ② news   ③ matter
④ problem   ⑤ cost

[경북 ○○중]

2. 다음 중 주어진 단어의 영어 설명이 바르게 된 것은? (4점)

① appear: to see no longer
② imaginable: impossible to think of in your mind
③ suggest: to offer an idea or plan to other people to think about
④ positive: thinking about the bad qualities of someone or something
⑤ wholesale: the action of selling things in small amounts and at high prices

[경기 ○○중]

3. 다음 대화의 흐름상 빈칸 ⓐ에 들어갈 말로 가장 적절한 것은? (3점)

A: Why don't we make a sport club?
B: Sounds good. Let's make a baseball club.
A: Well, I think a basketball club is a better idea.
B: ⓐ_____
A: All we need is a ball to play basketball.

① Why do you think so?
② How often do you play basketball?
③ What kind of sports do you like best?
④ Why don't we play basketball together?
⑤ Which sports do you prefer, baseball or basketball?

[경북 ○○중]

4. 자연스러운 대화가 되도록 (A)~(D)를 바르게 배열한 것은? (4점)

(A) What makes you say that?
(B) That makes sense.
(C) Having a part-time job as a teen can be good.
(D) I can learn about money matters from my own experience.

① (C)-(A)-(B)-(D)   ② (C)-(A)-(D)-(B)
③ (C)-(D)-(A)-(B)   ④ (D)-(A)-(B)-(C)
⑤ (D)-(A)-(C)-(B)

[전북 ○○중]

5. 다음 중 두 문장의 의미가 서로 같지 <u>않은</u> 것은? (4점)

① Break a leg.
  = Good luck.
② He has a big mouth.
  = He often tells people things that are secrets.
③ Can you give me a hand?
  = Can you help me?
④ I have butterflies in my stomach.
  = I have a stomachache.
⑤ David shouted at the top of his lungs.
  = David shouted very loudly.

B1: Today, let's talk about the class T-shirt. We have to decide on the design.

G: Let me show you some designs on the screen.

B2: We have to choose a T-shirt with short sleeves.

B1: (A)왜 그렇게 생각하니?

B2: Because we'll wear the T-shirt on Sports Day. It's in June.

G: (B)맞는 말이야.

6. 위 대화의 (A)에 해당하는 표현으로 가장 적절한 것은? (4점)

① What did you do last weekend?
② What are you doing, Oliver?
③ What makes you say that?
④ What's bothering you?
⑤ What comes in second place?

7. 위 대화의 (B)에 해당하는 영어 표현을 쓰시오. (5점)

<조건>
1. "makes"를 포함해야 함.
2. 대·소문자 구분 있음.

답: _____

8. 다음 대화의 순서를 바르게 배열한 것은? (3점)

A: What are you doing, Oliver?
B: I'm studying for the math test, Mom. Grades stress me out.
A: I understand. I used to feel that way, too.
B: Really? I didn't know that.
A: Yeah, but a little stress was helpful for me.
ⓐ Yes, it helped improve my memory.

ⓑ I got stressed when I had an exam, but at the same time it made me focus and try harder.
ⓒ What makes you say that?
ⓓ I see. Did stress help you in other ways?

① ⓐ-ⓑ-ⓓ-ⓒ
② ⓑ-ⓒ-ⓐ-ⓓ
③ ⓒ-ⓑ-ⓓ-ⓐ
④ ⓓ-ⓐ-ⓒ-ⓑ
⑤ ⓓ-ⓒ-ⓑ-ⓐ

[9~10] 다음 글과 대화의 밑줄 친 표현이 의미하는 것을 <보기>에서 찾으시오.

<보기>
ⓐ 주제 소개하기
ⓑ 이유 묻기
ⓒ 궁금한 점 묻기
ⓓ 도움 제안하기
ⓔ 감정 표현하기

9. 위 <보기>에서 다음 글의 밑줄 친 표현이 의미하는 것은? (3점)

Hi. Today, I'd like to talk about Frida Kahlo. She was a Mexican painter. One of her most well-known paintings is Viva la Vida.

① ⓐ　② ⓑ　③ ⓒ　④ ⓓ　⑤ ⓔ

10. 위 <보기>에서 다음 대화의 밑줄 친 표현이 의미하는 것은? (4점)

A: I want to spend more time on social media.
B: What makes you say that?
A: I can make more friends from around the world.
B: That makes sense.

① ⓐ　② ⓑ　③ ⓒ　④ ⓓ　⑤ ⓔ

11. 다음 중 어법상 올바른 문장은? (3점)

① Lily and her aunt has been watching TV for three hours.

② Have Aidan been worked at the bank since 2010?

③ This machine has been not working since last Tuesday.

④ We have preparing a surprise party for John all week.

⑤ I have been studying Chinese for almost seven months.

12. 다음 두 문장을 한 문장으로 바꾸어 쓸 때 적절한 것은? (4점)

> • Sue started volunteering at the library in February.
> • She is still volunteering there.

① Sue is volunteering at the library now.

② Sue volunteered at the library in February.

③ Sue went to the library to volunteer since February.

④ Sue has been volunteering at the library since February.

⑤ Sue went to the library to volunteer in February but she doesn't now.

13. 다음 빈칸에 공통으로 들어갈 말로 알맞은 것은? (4점)

> • Don't _____ a lie.
> • Please _____ me the secret.

① say　　② tell　　③ talk

④ speak　　⑤ mention

14. 다음 중 짝지어진 두 문장의 뜻이 서로 같지 <u>않은</u> 것은? (4점)

① It is so cold that I cannot go out.

= It is too cold for me to go out.

② It was so dark that I couldn't see anything.

= It was dark enough to see anything.

③ He danced so well that he won the first prize.

= He danced well enough to win the first prize.

④ She felt so nervous that she kept biting her nail.

= She felt nervous enough to keep biting her nail.

⑤ She felt so hungry that she could not keep walking.

= She felt too hungry to keep walking.

15. 다음 괄호 안의 표현을 바르게 배열하여 문장을 완성할 때 빈칸의 세 번째와 여섯 번째 올 단어가 순서에 맞게 짝지어진 것은? (4점)

> • My grandfather is _____ _____ (A)_____ _____ _____ (B)_____ _____ _____.
> (can't / so / travel / old / long / that / he / distances)

	(A)	(B)
①	that	travel
②	old	can't
③	he	long
④	so	old
⑤	travel	distances

[16~17] 다음 글을 읽고 물음에 답하시오.

Some people spend time with friends when they ⓐfeel low. Others eat special foods to feel better. Still others simply sleep for a while. How do you deal with stress? Here are some stories about people who suggest different ways.

Mina (15, Daejeon)
Sometimes my friends give me stress by saying bad things about me, breaking promises, or arguing over small things. When this happens, I watch horror movies! Good horror movies are so scary that I scream a lot. I guess that screaming ⓑat the top of my lungs helps me feel better. Also, thanks to scary scenes and sound effects, I can forget about what bothers me. I've been using this method for the past several months, and it really ⓒworks.

Junho (14, Yeosu)
My uncle graduated from college two years ago. He lives with my family, and he's been looking for a job for some time. I know that he's stressed out, but he always tries to be ⓓpositive by going fishing. He never gets upset when he doesn't catch any fish. He says, "While I fish, I'm so focused that I can leave all my worries behind. Besides, it teaches me to be ⓔpatient." I'm sure that focusing on one thing helps us forget about something else.

16. 위 글의 밑줄 친 ⓐ~ⓔ를 다른 표현으로 바꾸어 쓸 때 의미가 맞지 <u>않는</u> 것은? (4점)

① ⓐ: feel depressed
② ⓑ: very loudly
③ ⓒ: has an effect
④ ⓓ: serious and unpleasant
⑤ ⓔ: calm and tolerant

17. 위 글의 내용과 일치하는 것은? (3점)

① 글의 주제는 콤플렉스 해결 방법에 대한 것이다.
② 미나의 스트레스의 원인은 그녀의 가족이다.
③ 미나는 코미디 영화를 보면서 스트레스를 푼다.
④ 준호는 그의 삼촌 때문에 스트레스를 많이 받는다.
⑤ 준호의 삼촌은 낚시하는 동안은 모든 걱정을 잊는다.

18. 다음 도표의 내용과 일치하지 <u>않는</u> 것은? (4점)

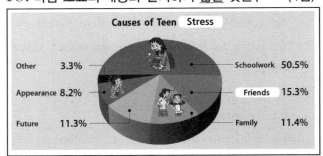

① This graph is about what causes teenagers to get stressed out.
② It shows that schoolwork is the most common cause of stress to the students.
③ Over half of the students said schoolwork stresses them the most.
④ Problems with friends took third place with 15.3%.
⑤ 8.2% of the students said they get stressed because of their appearance.

[19~21] 다음 글을 읽고 물음에 답하시오.

Some people spend time with friends when they feel low. Others eat special foods to feel better. ⓐ_____ others simply sleep for a while. How do you deal with stress? Here are some stories about people who suggest different ways.

Mina (15, Daejeon)

Sometimes my friends give me stress by saying bad things about me, (A)[keeping / breaking] promises, or arguing over small things. When this happens, I watch horror movies! Good horror movies are so scary that I scream a lot. I guess that screaming at the (B)[top / bottom] of my lungs helps me feel better. Also, thanks to scary scenes and sound effects, I can forget about what bothers me. I've been using this method for the past several months, and it really works.

Junho (14, Yeosu)

My uncle graduated from college two years ago. He lives with my family, and he's been looking for a job for some time. I know that he's stressed out, but he always tries to be (C)[positive / negative] by going fishing. He never gets upset when he doesn't catch any fish. He says, "While I fish, I'm so focused that I can leave all my worries behind. ⓑ_____, it teaches me to be patient." I'm sure that focusing on one thing helps us forget about something else.

19. 위 글의 빈칸 ⓐ, ⓑ에 들어갈 말로 가장 적절한 것은? (4점)

	ⓐ	ⓑ
①	And	Thus
②	But	In fact
③	However	On the other hand
④	Still	Besides
⑤	Instead	For example

20. 위 글의 괄호 (A), (B), (C) 안에서 문맥에 맞는 낱말로 가장 적절한 것은? (4점)

	(A)	(B)	(C)
①	keeping	top	positive
②	keeping	bottom	negative
③	breaking	top	positive
④	breaking	top	negative
⑤	breaking	bottom	positive

21. 위 글을 읽고 답할 수 없는 질문은? (3점)

① What kinds of food does Mina like to eat when her friends sometimes give her stress?

② What two things in horror movies help Mina forget about her worries?

③ When did Junho's uncle graduate from college?

④ Who does Junho's uncle live with?

⑤ Does Junho's uncle get upset when he doesn't catch any fish?

22. 다음 글의 전체 흐름과 관계없는 문장은? (3점)

Let me tell you what my mother does about her stress. ⓐShe feels stressed by all the things she has to do at work and at home. ⓑWhen she's under stress, she writes "Me Time" on her calender. ⓒThis means she takes some time out for herself. ⓓShe reads a book, watches a movie, or talks with her friends. ⓔOne of her best friends lives in New York. She says, "It doesn't really matter what I do, as long as it's something I like. I've been writing 'Me Time' on my calendar for two months, and I feel much better."

① ⓐ   ② ⓑ   ③ ⓒ   ④ ⓓ   ⑤ ⓔ

[23~25] 다음 글을 읽고 물음에 답하시오.

Some people spend time with friends when they feel low. Others eat special foods to feel better. Still others simply sleep for a while. How do you deal (A)_____ stress? Here are some stories about people (B)_____ suggest different ways.

Mina(15, Daejeon)
Sometimes my friends give me stress by saying bad things about me, breaking promises, or arguing over small things. When this happens, I watch horror movies! ⓐ훌륭한 공포 영화는 너무 무서워서 나는 소리를 많이 지르게 된다. I guess that screaming at the top of my lungs helps me feel better. Also, thanks to scary scenes and sound effects, I can forget about (C)_____ bothers me. I have used this method of relieving stress for the past several months and it really ⓑworks.

23. 위 글의 (A)~(C)에 들어갈 알맞은 말로 바르게 짝지어진 것은? (4점)

	(A)	(B)	(C)
①	of	who	what
②	with	who	what
③	with	who	that
④	with	which	what
⑤	of	that	which

24. 위 글의 밑줄 친 ⓐ의 우리말과 일치하도록 아래의 단어들을 바르게 배열할 때 ★에 들어갈 말은? (3점)

Good horror movies are _____ _____ _____★_____ _____ _____ _____ _____.

(that / scary / a lot / I / so / scream)

① I   ② that   ③ so
④ scream   ⑤ scary

25. 위 글의 밑줄 친 ⓑwork와 같은 의미로 쓰인 것은? (4점)

① I have a lot of <u>work</u> to do.
② My father <u>works</u> for a company.
③ Look at his <u>works</u> of art. They are truly amazing.
④ The medicine my mother gave me didn't <u>work</u>.
⑤ The other day, the heating system didn't <u>work</u> at night.

[26~27] 다음 글을 읽고 물음에 답하시오.

(A)_____ people spend time with friends when they feel low. (B)_____ eat special foods to feel better. (C)_____ simply sleep for a while. How do you deal with stress? Here are some stories about people who suggest different ways.

26. 위 글의 빈칸 (A), (B), (C)에 차례대로 들어갈 알맞은 표현은? (4점)

	(A)	(B)	(C)
①	Some	Other	The other
②	Some	Others	Still others
③	Some	Another	The others
④	A few	Others	Still others
⑤	A few	Another	The others

27. 위 글의 뒤에 이어질 내용으로 가장 알맞은 것은? (4점)

① 친구와 시간 보내는 방법
② 특별한 음식 만드는 법
③ 스트레스와 음식과의 관계
④ 스트레스와 다양한 수면 형태
⑤ 사람들의 다양한 스트레스 해소법

3학년 영어 1학기 기말고사(3과) 2회

반		점수	
이름			

문항수 : 선택형(23문항) 서술형(1문항)　　20 ．　．　．

◎ 선택형 문항의 답안은 컴퓨터용 수정 싸인펜을
　사용하여 OMR 답안지에 바르게 표기하시오.
◎ 서술형 문제는 답을 답안지에 반드시 검정
　볼펜으로 쓰시오.
◎ 총 24문항 100점 만점입니다. 문항별 배점
　은 각 문항에 표시되어 있습니다.

1. 다음 주어진 단어에 대한 영영풀이 중, (A), (B), (C)
에 들어갈 어휘들을 바르게 짝지은 것은?　　(4점)

> • tidy: arranged (A)_____ and in order
> • patient: able to stay calm or deal with problems without becoming (B)_____
> • relieve: to (C)_____ the pain or to make a problem less serious

	(A)	(B)	(C)
①	dirtily	happy	grow
②	neatly	happy	lessen
③	messily	angry	increase
④	neatly	angry	lessen
⑤	untidily	angry	increase

2. 다음 문장의 의미에 해당하는 것은?　　(4점)

> • He shouted at the top of his lungs.

① He shouted very loudly.
② He often tells people things that are secrets.
③ I'm very nervous.
④ Can you help me?
⑤ Good luck.

3. 다음 단어의 영영풀이가 <u>어색한</u> 것은?　　(4점)

① positive: (adj) full of hope and confidence
② matter: (vi) to be important
③ gloomy: (adj) feeling low and sad
④ beside: (prep) in addition; also
⑤ work: (vi) to be effective

4. 다음 대화의 밑줄 친 부분의 의도로 알맞은 것은?
　　(4점)

> A: Today, let's talk about the class T-shirt. We have to decide on the design.
> B: Let me show you some designs on the screen.
> C: We have to choose a T-shirt with short sleeves.
> B: <u>What makes you say that?</u>
> C: Because we'll wear the T-shirt on Sports Day. It's in June.

① 동의하기　　　　　　② 이유 묻기
③ 조언 구하기　　　　　④ 주제 소개하기
⑤ 감정 표현하기

5. 자연스러운 대화가 되도록 (A)~(D)를 순서대로 배
열한 것은?　　(4점)

> Wendy: What are you doing, Ben?
> Ben: I'm studying for the math test, Mom. Grades stress me out.
> Wendy: I understand. I used to feel that way, too.
> Ben: Really? I didn't know that.
> (A) I got stressed when I had an exam, but at the same time it made me focus and try harder.
> (B) I see. Did stress help you in other ways?
> (C) What makes you say that?
> (D) Yeah, but a little stress was helpful for me.
> Wendy: Yes, it helped improve my memory.

① (A)-(C)-(B)-(D)　　② (B)-(C)-(D)-(A)
③ (C)-(B)-(A)-(D)　　④ (D)-(A)-(B)-(C)
⑤ (D)-(C)-(A)-(B)

6. 다음 두 문장의 의미가 <u>다른</u> 것은? (4점)

① Break a leg!

　= Good luck!

② Can you give me a hand?

　= Can you help me?

③ I have butterflies in my stomach.

　= I have a terrible stomachache.

④ He shouted at the top of his lungs.

　= He shouted very loudly.

⑤ He has a big mouth.

　= He often tells people things that are secrets.

7. 다음 대화의 내용과 일치하는 것은? (5점)

> W: Woman, B: Boy
>
> W: What are you doing, Oliver?
>
> B: I'm studying for the math test, Mom. Grades stress me out.
>
> W: I understand, I used to feel that way too.
>
> B: Really? I didn't know that.
>
> W: Yeah, but a little stress was helpful for me.
>
> B: Why do you think so?
>
> W: I got stressed when I had an exam, but at the same time it made me focus and try harder.
>
> B: I see. Did stress help you in other ways?
>
> W: Yes, it helped improve my memory.

① 남자아이는 영어 점수 때문에 스트레스를 받고 있다.

② 엄마가 아들의 마음을 잘 이해하지 못한다.

③ 엄마는 아들에게 스트레스를 풀지 않으면 우울감이 올 수 있다고 말하고 있다.

④ 엄마는 시험을 칠 때 받은 약간의 스트레스는 시험에 집중하고 더욱 열심히 하게 만든다고 생각한다.

⑤ 아들은 약간의 긴장감과 스트레스가 기억력을 향상시킬 수 있다고 생각한다.

8. 다음 짝지어진 대화 중 <u>어색한</u> 것은? (3점)

① A: How do you like the camp?

　B: It's great. I'm having a lot of fun.

② A: Can you tell me how old the tree is?

　B: It's about 150 years old.

③ A: Dr. Broccoli, what is today's topic?

　B: I'd like to talk about healthy eating habits.

④ A: I want to spend more time on social media.

　B: What makes you say that?

⑤ A: Which do you think is better, hiking or shopping?

　B: I'll go shopping because we can see wild birds and insects in the woods.

9. 다음 대화의 빈칸에 들어갈 말로 알맞은 것은? (4점)

> A: I need some time to relax. We all need to do something to get over stress.
>
> B: You can say that again.
>
> A: Why don't you join me in the dance club? It'll be fun.
>
> B: No, thanks. _____ I have two left feet.

① I was a good dancer.

② My hobby is dancing.

③ Dancing is not for me.

④ I can't use my right foot.

⑤ I'm sorry that you hurt your foot.

10. 다음 중 주어진 두 문장의 의미가 같지 <u>않은</u> 것은? (4점)

① Everybody likes Paul because he is very kind.

= Paul is so kind that everybody likes him.

② He started cleaning the house at 10 o'clock. He is still cleaning the house.

= He had been cleaning the house since 10 o'clock.

③ This is how he solved the problem.

= This is the way he solved the problem.

④ You are too young to watch the movie.

= You are so young that you can't watch the movie.

⑤ This is the thing that he bought yesterday.

= This is what he bought yesterday.

11. 다음 중 어법상 올바른 것은? (4점)

① I have been waited for his call all afternoon.

② They have been playing baseball two hours ago.

③ The Giant Burger is very expensive that I can't buy it.

④ The weather is so nice what I can go to the park today.

⑤ Nancy has been preparing a surprise party for Jason for a week.

12. 다음 중 우리말과 같은 의미가 되도록 어법상 적절하게 영작한 것은? (4점)

① Jake는 오후 내내 잠을 자고 있는 중이다.

→ Jake has been sleeping all afternoon.

② 나는 10년 동안 그를 알고 지내고 있다.

→ I have been knowing him for 10 years.

③ 그녀는 오후 2시부터 영화를 보고 있다.

→ She has been watching a movie for 2 p.m.

④ 나는 세 시간째 이 소설을 읽고 있는 중이다.

→ I have been read this novel for three hours.

⑤ 그는 20분 동안 그녀를 인터뷰하고 있는 중이다.

→ He has been interviewed her for 20 minutes.

13. 다음 글의 목적으로 가장 적절한 것은? (5점)

Today, I'd like to talk to you about teen stress. What makes you feel the most stressed? About 9,000 teens answered this question. As you can see, schoolwork was the most common cause of stress. Over half of the students said schoolwork stresses them the most. Problems with friends took second place with 15.3%. Next came family and worries about the future. 8.2% of the students said they get stressed because of their appearance.

① to warn people not to get stressed

② to advertise the program about teen stress

③ to recommend the way to get over stress

④ to tell teens about how to solve the problem

⑤ to explain the several causes of teen stress

[14~15] 다음 글을 읽고 물음에 답하시오.

Dobin (16, Seoul)
My sister, a second-year student in high school, has a wonderful way to stay free from stress. She feels a lot of stress from schoolwork, but my mother seems to like the situation for a good reason. It is because cleaning is my sister's number-one way to make life better! When she's so stressed that her life looks gloomy, she cleans her room. She says, "As I clean my room, I feel like I'm also relieving stress. When my room looks tidy, my life looks brighter."

Yulia (14, Ansan)
Let me tell you what my mother does about her stress. She feels stressed by all the things she has to do at work and at home. When she's under stress, she writes "Me Time" on her calendar. This means she takes some time out for herself. She reads a book, watches a movie, or talks with her friends. She says, "It doesn't really matter what I do, as long as it's something I like. I've been writing 'Me Time' on my calendar for two months, and I feel much better."

14. 위 글을 읽고 질문에 답할 수 <u>없는</u> 것은? (5점)

① Does Dobin's sister feel much stress?

② What does Dobin's sister do to relieve her stress?

③ How does Dobin feel when his sister gets a lot of stress from schoolwork?

④ Where does Yulia's mother's stress come from?

⑤ How long has Yulia's mother been writing "Me Time" on her calendar?

15. 위 글의 내용을 아래와 같이 요약할 때 빈칸 (A)와 (B)에 들어갈 말이 바르게 짝지어진 것은? (4점)

Dobin's sister gets stressed about schoolwork. She stays free from stress by (A)_____. Yulia's mother feels pressure from her work and family. She relieves stress by (B)_____ and doing something she likes.

	(A)	(B)
①	cleaning her room	taking time for herself
②	doing her school work	watching a movie
③	talking with her friends	doing house chores
④	asking for help to her mother	reading a book
⑤	making her room tidy	having time with her family

16. 다음 중 문장 전환이 바르게 된 것은? (5점)

① He danced so well that he won first prize.
→ He danced well enough to won first prize.

② She felt too hungry to keep walking.
→ She felt so hungry that she could keep walking.

③ Joy was so disappointed that he could not say a word.
→ Joy was too disappointed to say a word.

④ My brother jumps high enough to do a dunk shot.
→ My brother jumps so high that he cannot do a dunk shot.

⑤ Andrew is so strong that he can carry the boxes by himself.
→ Andrew is enough strong to carry the boxes by himself.

[17~19] 다음 글을 읽고 물음에 답하시오.

Say Goodbye to Stress

Mina (15, Daejeon)

Sometimes my friends give me stress by saying bad things about me, breaking promises, or arguing over small things. When this happens, I watch horror movies! Good horror movies are (A)_____ scary that I scream a lot. I guess that ⓐscreaming at the top of my lungs helps me feel better. I've been using this method for the past several months, and it really works.

Junho (14, Yeosu)

My uncle graduated from college two years ago. He lives with my family, and he's been looking for a job for some time. I know that he's stressed out, but he always tries to be positive by going fishing. He never gets upset when he doesn't catch any fish. He says, "While I fish, I'm (A)_____ focused that I can leave all my worries behind. Besides, it teaches me to be patient."

Dobin (16, Seoul)

My sister, a second-year student in high school, feels a lot of stress from schoolwork, but my mother seems to like the situation for a good reason. It is because cleaning is my sister's number-one way to make life better! When she's (A)_____ stressed that her life looks gloomy, she cleans her room. She says, "When my room looks tidy, my life looks brighter."

17. 위 글의 빈칸 (A)에 공통으로 들어갈 가장 적절한 단어를 쓰시오. (4점)

→ _____

18. 위 글을 읽고, 각자의 스트레스의 원인과 스트레스 해소법에 대해 정리한 표이다. 글의 내용과 일치하지 않는 것은? (4점)

who	Causes of Stress	Methods to Relieve Stress
Mina	ⓐtrouble with her friends	ⓒwatching horror movies
Junho's uncle	ⓑpressure from work	ⓓgoing fishing
Dobin's sister	a lot of schoolwork	ⓔcleaning her room

① ⓐ ② ⓑ ③ ⓒ ④ ⓓ ⑤ ⓔ

19. 위 글의 밑줄 친 ⓐ의 의미로 가장 적절한 것은? (4점)

① making a little noise
② shouting on the top of the hill
③ talking very fast without breathing
④ crying out with a loud voice
⑤ speaking very quietly so that other people can't hear

20. 다음 주어진 글의 뒤에 이어질 내용으로 알맞은 것은? (5점)

Some people spend time with friends when they feel low. Others eat special foods to feel better. Still others simply sleep for a while. How do you deal with stress? Here are some stories about people who suggest different ways.

① 스트레스의 다양한 원인
② 스트레스가 건강에 미치는 영향
③ 스트레스를 많이 받는 사람들의 유형
④ 스트레스 받을 때 주로 찾게 되는 음식
⑤ 스트레스를 다양한 방법으로 처리하는 사람들의 이야기

[21~22] 다음 글을 읽고 물음에 답하시오.

Dobin (16, Seoul)

My sister, a second-year student in high school, has a wonderful way to stay free from stress. (A) It is because cleaning is my sister's number-one way to make life better! (B) When she's so stressed that her life looks gloomy, she cleans her room. (C) She says, "As I clean my room, I feel like I'm also relieving stress. (D) When my room looks tidy, my life looks brighter." (E)

21. 위 글의 흐름으로 보아 주어진 문장이 들어가기에
　　가장 적절한 곳은? (4점)

She feels a lot of stress from schoolwork, but my mother seems to like the situation for a good reason.

① (A)　② (B)　③ (C)　④ (D)　⑤ (E)

22. 위 글의 내용과 일치하지 <u>않는</u> 것은? (3점)

① Dobin's sister gets over stress by cleaning her room.
② Dobin's mother gives lots of stress to Dobin.
③ Dobin's sister gets stress from schoolwork.
④ Dobin's sister has her own way of relieving stress.
⑤ Dobin's sister is a high school student.

23. 다음 강연의 내용을 올바르게 이해하지 <u>못한</u> 사람
　　은? (4점)

Today, I'd like to talk to you about teen stress. About 9,000 teens answered this question. As you can see, schoolwork was the most common cause of stress. Over half of the students said schoolwork stresses them the most. Problems with friends took second place with 15.3%. Next came family (11.4%) and worries about the future (11.3%). 8.2% of the students said they get stressed because of their appearance.

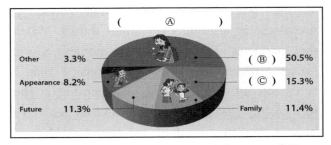

① 지희: Ⓐ에는 강연의 제목으로 'Causes of Teen Stress'라고 하는 것이 좋을 것 같아.
② 근욱: 학업이 주는 스트레스가 가장 높다고 했으니 Ⓑ에 들어갈 알맞은 단어는 'schoolwork'야.
③ 현우: 스트레스 요인 중 두 번째로 높은 것은 각 과목의 숙제하기이므로 Ⓒ에는 'homework'이 와야 해.
④ 자민: 가족과 미래에 대한 스트레스를 받는 십대들은 9000명 중 20%가 넘는구나.
⑤ 정수: 외모에 대한 스트레스도 8.2%나 되는구나.

24. 다음 글의 흐름으로 보아 주어진 문장이 들어가기
　　에 가장 적절한 곳은? (5점)

Then here is some good news for you.

Are you feeling low? (A) A few simple steps can help you! First, go outdoors and get plenty of sunlight. (B) According to scientists, this helps produce a special chemical in your brain, and the chemical makes you feel happy! (C) Another thing you can do is exercise. This helps produce even more of the "happiness chemical." (D) Try these simple tips the next time you feel low. (E) Instead of sitting in front of a screen, go outdoors and run around in the sun!

① (A)　② (B)　③ (C)　④ (D)　⑤ (E)

◎ 선택형 문항의 답안은 컴퓨터용 수정 싸인펜을 사용하여 OMR 답안지에 바르게 표기하시오.

◎ 서술형 문제는 답을 답안지에 반드시 검정 볼펜으로 쓰시오.

◎ 총 26문항 100점 만점입니다. 문항별 배점은 각 문항에 표시되어 있습니다.

[경북 ○○중]

1. 다음 중 주어진 단어의 형용사 형태가 <u>잘못된</u> 것은?

(4점)

① time - timely ② invent - inventive

③ person - personal ④ collect - collection

⑤ danger - dangerous

[경북 ○○중]

2. 다음 글의 밑줄 친 ⓐ~ⓔ 중 쓰임이 바르지 <u>못한</u> 것은?

(4점)

Antoni Gaudi was a Spanish architect. He did not follow the ⓐ<u>traditional</u> ways of designing buildings. He thought in ⓑ<u>creative</u> ways, and for his works he tried things not ⓒ<u>using</u> by other architects. Also, he got his design ideas from plants and other things he could find in the ⓓ<u>natural</u> environment. No wonder his works are still popular and ⓔ<u>attractive</u> to visitors from all over the world.

① ⓐ ② ⓑ ③ ⓒ ④ ⓓ ⑤ ⓔ

[경기 ○○중]

3. 다음 대화에서 문맥상 빈칸에 들어갈 말로 가장 적절한 것은?

(3점)

W: Excuse me. Can you help me with this milk?

B: Sure. What is it?

W: Read me the date, please.

B: Oh, do you want me to tell you the best-before date?

W: Yes, I forgot my glasses.

B: Let me see. You should drink it by June 7.

W: That's too soon. _____

B: Wait. I found one. This one is good until June 11.

W: Oh, I'll take that one. Thank you very much.

B: You're welcome.

① I want to know how I drink it.

② I wonder if there's one that lasts longer.

③ I wonder if there's one that lasts shorter.

④ I wonder whether I can drink anything or not.

⑤ I don't know what the best-before date means.

[경북 ○○중]

4. 다음 〈보기〉의 문장 중, 대화의 내용과 일치하는 문장의 수는 몇 개인가?

(4점)

Lady: Can I have the bill, please?

Man: Here you are. Did you enjoy the meal?

Lady: It was great. I liked the *gondrebap* very much.

Man: Thanks. It's also good for your health.

Lady: Oh, really?

Man: Yes. *Gondre* is rich in vitamins A and C. It also digests well.

Lady: Good. I wonder if I could buy some *gondre* here.

Man: Sure. Do you want me to give you the recipe for *gondrebap*?

Lady: Yes, that'd be great.

<보기>

a. 곤드레밥은 건강에 좋은 음식이다.

b. 두 사람이 식사 전에 나눈 대화이다.

c. 여자는 곤드레밥을 포장해 갈 것이다.

d. 곤드레를 먹으면 부자가 된다는 옛말이 있다.

e. 곤드레밥은 소화가 잘 되지 않는다는 단점이 있다.

f. 위 대화의 두 사람은 식당 주인과 손님의 관계이다.

① 1개 ② 2개 ③ 3개 ④ 4개 ⑤ 5개

[5~8] 다음 대화를 읽고 물음에 답하시오.

W: Can I have the bill, please?
M: Here you are. Did you enjoy the meal?
W: It was great. I liked the *gondrebap* very much.
M: Thanks. It's also good for your health.
W: Oh, really?
M: Yes. *Gondre* is rich in vitamins A and C. It also digests well.
W: Good. (A)여기서 곤드레를 살 수 있는지 궁금하군요.
M: Sure. Do you want me to give you the recipe for *gondrebap*?
W: Yes. (B)_____

* W: A woman, M: A man

5. 위 대화에서 두 사람의 관계는? (4점)

① waiter - customer
② tourist - tour guide
③ employee - employer
④ doctor - patient
⑤ teacher - student

6. 위 대화의 밑줄 친 (A)의 표현을 영어로 가장 바르게 옮긴 것은? (4점)

① I know if I could buy some *gondre* here.
② I wonder if could I buy some *gondre* here.
③ I wonder if I could buy some *gondre* here.
④ If I could buy some *gondre* here, I'll buy.
⑤ I don't know where I could buy some *gondre* here.

7. 위 대화의 빈칸 (B)에 들어갈 말로 알맞은 것은? (4점)

① You can say that again.
② Can you give me a hand?
③ I'd like to stay here.
④ I don't want to.
⑤ That'd be great.

8. 위 대화의 내용과 일치하는 것은? (4점)

① 남자는 여자에게 계산서를 요구했다.
② 여자는 곤드레의 효능을 물었다.
③ 곤드레에는 비타민 A와 D가 풍부하다.
④ 곤드레는 소화가 잘 되는 음식이다.
⑤ 곤드레는 지정된 곳에서만 살 수 있다.

9. 주어진 대화 다음에 이어질 순서로 가장 적절한 것은? (4점)

W: Excuse me. Can you help me with this milk?
B: Sure. What is it?
W: Read me the date, please.
B: Oh, do you want me to tell you the best-before date?
W: Yes, I forgot my glasses.

(A) Oh, I'll take that one. Thank you very much.
(B) Wait. I found one. This one is good until June 11.
(C) That's too soon. I wonder if there's one that lasts longer.
(D) Let me see. You should drink it by June 7.

W: Woman B: Boy

① (B)-(A)-(D)-(C) ② (B)-(D)-(A)-(C)
③ (C)-(A)-(D)-(B) ④ (D)-(A)-(B)-(C)
⑤ (D)-(C)-(B)-(A)

[10~11] 다음 대화를 읽고 물음에 답하시오.

W: Excuse me. Can you help me with this milk?

B: Sure. What is it?

W: Read me the date, please.

B: Oh, do you want me to tell you ⓐ<u>유통기한</u>?

W: Yes, I forgot my glasses.

B: Let me see. You should drink it by June 7.

W: That's too soon. I wonder if there's one that lasts longer.

B: Wait. I found one. This one is good until June 11.

W: Oh, I'll take that one. Thank you very much.

B: You're welcome.

10. 위 대화를 읽고 빈칸에 들어갈 질문으로 가장 알맞은 것은? (4점)

Q: _____

A: Because she wants one that lasts longer.

① Why did the woman forget her glasses?

② Why did the woman pick up the first milk?

③ Why doesn't the woman take the first milk?

④ Why doesn't the woman want to drink milk?

⑤ Why does the woman drink the milk until June 7?

11. 위 대화의 밑줄 친 ⓐ에 해당하는 영어 표현으로 적절한 것은? (4점)

① the last date

② the after-best date

③ the before-best date

④ the best-before date

⑤ the date of deadline

12. 다음 문장의 밑줄 친 부분이 어법상 옳지 <u>않은</u> 것은? (4점)

① I wonder <u>if you will come to my party.</u>

② Nobody knows <u>if she sent him a message.</u>

③ I won't go camping <u>if it will rain tomorrow.</u>

④ It is unclear <u>whether she will pass the exam.</u>

⑤ They don't know <u>whether or not the rumor is true.</u>

13. 다음 중 밑줄 친 if의 쓰임이 <u>다른</u> 하나는? (3점)

① I'm not sure <u>if</u> the library is open on Sundays.

② She wonders <u>if</u> it will be fine tomorrow.

③ He will be late for school <u>if</u> he misses the bus.

④ Tell me <u>if</u> your robot can make delicious *ramyeon*.

⑤ He asked me <u>if</u> I would be able to finish my work.

14. 다음 두 문장을 한 문장으로 표현할 때, 빈칸에 알맞은 말을 쓰시오. (5점)

(1) Do they speak Chinese?

(2) Can you tell me that?

<조건>

(1) 4개 단어로 쓸 것.

(2) 간접의문문.

→ Can you tell me _____?

[15~16] 다음 글을 읽고 물음에 답하시오.

Damnoen Saduak Floating Market, Thailand
(A) In the past, Thai people traded goods on rivers. (B) This was the beginning of floating markets in Thailand. (C) With better road transportation, many floating markets disappeared. (D) Today, one of the most popular floating markets is Damnoen Saduak Floating Market. (E) It is always crowded with tourists from all over the world. You can buy local foods and traditional gift items directly from boats.

Extra Tip I wonder if you have ever had a meal on water. If not, try noodles like *pad thai*. The sellers will cook them on their boats and pass them to you with a long fishing pole.

Aalsmeer Flower Market, The Netherlands
The Netherlands means "low lands." As the name suggests, about 70% of the country sits below sea level. Thus, the Dutch built up the land, and one effective way to use it was to grow flowers and sell them. It is, therefore, no surprise that the country has the largest flower market in the world: the Aalsmeer Flower Market.
The building where the market is housed is bigger than 120 soccer fields. The market is busy with thousands of flower-filled carts. They are moved mostly by electric-powered trucks. Every day, around 20 million flowers are traded and shipped to all corners of the world.

Extra Tip You may wonder whether you can buy just a few flowers at the market. Sadly, you cannot, but you can see how wholesale flower trading works.

15. 위 글의 흐름으로 보아, 주어진 문장이 들어갈 가장 적절한 곳은? (4점)

Since the late 1960s, however, some of them have come back and kept the tradition alive.

① (A)　② (B)　③ (C)　④ (D)　⑤ (E)

16. 위 글의 내용과 일치하는 것은? (4점)
① 네덜란드 국토의 약 70%가 해수면보다 높다.
② Aalsmeer 꽃 시장이 들어선 건물은 축구장 120개보다 더 크다.
③ Aalsmeer 꽃 시장은 꽃이 가득 든 일천 개의 수레로 분주하고 수레의 대부분은 수동으로 움직인다.
④ 매일 약 이백만 송이의 꽃들이 거래되어 세계 각지로 배달된다.
⑤ Aalsmeer 꽃 시장에서는 꽃을 도매로 살 수 없고 소매로만 살 수 있다.

17. 다음 글의 괄호 (A)~(C) 안에서 알맞은 말로 바르게 짝지어진 것은? (4점)

Every Saturday, I go to Oakville Farmers' Market. That is the place (A)[when / where] I buy food for the coming week. There I find all kinds of fresh vegetables. They are usually picked only a few hours (B)[before / after] I buy them. I also find bread, meat, and home-made jam. (C)[Though / Because] I can buy the items directly from the producers, they are usually much cheaper than at other stores.

	(A)	(B)	(C)
①	where	after	Though
②	when	after	Though
③	where	after	Because
④	where	before	Because
⑤	when	before	Though

[18~19] 다음 글을 읽고, 물음에 답하시오.

Aalsmeer Flower Market, The Netherlands

The Netherlands means "low lands." As the name suggests, about 70% of the country sits below sea level. (A) Thus, the Dutch built up the land, and one effective way to use it was to grow flowers and sell them. (B) The building where the market is housed is bigger than 120 soccer fields. (C) The market is busy with thousands of flower-filled carts. (D) They are moved mostly by electric-powered trucks. (E) Every day, around 20 million flowers are traded and shipped to all corners of the world.

Extra Tip You may wonder whether you can buy just a few flowers at the market. Sadly, you cannot, but you can see how wholesale flower trading works.

---

18. 위 글의 흐름상 다음 문장이 들어갈 가장 적절한 곳은? (3점)

It is, therefore, no surprise that the country has the largest flower market in the world: the Aalsmeer Flower Market.

---

① (A) ② (B) ③ (C) ④ (D) ⑤ (E)

19. 위 글에 대한 이해도를 점검하는 평가를 실시할 때, Tom이 받게 될 점수는? (정답을 맞힌 경우 괄호 안의 점수를 획득하며 틀려도 감점은 없음.) (4점)

Comprehension Check-up Test Name: Tom Johnson		
1. Visitors to the market cannot buy flowers in small amounts. (1점)	Ⓣ	F
2. How big is the Aalsmeer Flower Market? (1.5점) → It is bigger than 120 soccer fields.		
3. How many flowers are shipped to the world daily? (2점) → Around 20 million flowers are shipped to the world.		

① 1.5점 ② 2.5점 ③ 3점
④ 3.5점 ⑤ 4.5점

[20~21] 다음 글을 읽고 물음에 답하시오.

I am Leah. I (A)_____ a travel blog since I was 18. I go places and share my experiences with my readers.
(B)_____ markets is a good way to learn about the culture of a country. Markets are places (C)_____ you can meet people, learn history, and taste local food. I wonder (D)_____ there is any better way to discover another culture.

---

20. 위 글의 빈칸 (A)에 write, (B)에 visit를 알맞은 형태로 넣은 것은? (4점)

	(A)	(B)
①	write	Visit
②	wrote	Visiting
③	have written	Visit
④	have been writing	Visiting
⑤	have been written	To visit

21. 위 글의 내용상 빈칸 (C)와 (D)에 들어갈 가장 알맞은 표현은? (4점)

	(C)	(D)
①	where	whether
②	when	what
③	what	why
④	why	how
⑤	how	if

[22~25] 다음 글을 읽고 물음에 답하시오.

The Netherlands means "low lands." As the name suggests, about 70% of the country sits below sea level. Thus, ⓐthe Dutch built up the land, and one effective way to use it was to grow flowers and sell them. It is, (가)_____, no surprise that the country has the largest flower market in the world: the Aalsmeer Flower Market.

The building where the market is housed is bigger than 120 soccer fields. The market is busy with ⓑthousands of flower-filled carts. They are moved mostly by electric-powered trucks. Every day, ⓒaround 20 million flowers are traded and shipped to ⓓall corners of the world.

Extra Tip You may wonder (나)if you can buy ⓔjust a few flowers at the market. Sadly, you cannot, but you can see how wholesale flower trading works.

22. 위 글을 읽고 알 수 없는 것은? (3점)

① '네덜란드'의 뜻
② 해수면보다 낮은 네덜란드 땅의 비율
③ Aalsmeer 꽃 시장의 규모
④ Aalsmeer 꽃 시장에서 거래되는 꽃 종류
⑤ Aalsmeer 꽃 시장에서 소매로 꽃 구매 가능 여부

23. 위 글의 밑줄 친 ⓐ~ⓔ의 우리말 해석이 바른 것은? (4점)

① the Dutch: 독일 사람들
② thousands of: 천 개의
③ around 20 million flowers: 약 2백만 송이의 꽃
④ all corners of the world: 세계의 곳곳
⑤ just a few: 매우 많은

24. 위 글의 빈칸 (가)에 들어갈 가장 알맞은 표현은? (4점)

① besides   ② however   ③ although
④ therefore   ⑤ for example

25. 위 글의 밑줄 친 (나)if와 쓰임이 다른 하나는? (3점)

① I'm not sure if the library is open on Sundays.
② We don't know if the meeting will end soon.
③ He will be late for school if he misses the bus.
④ Tell me if your robot can make delicious *ramyeon*.
⑤ He asked me if I would be able to finish my work.

26. 다음 밑줄 친 ⓐ~ⓔ 중 글의 흐름과 어울리지 않는 것은? (4점)

Damnoen Saduak Floating Market, Thailand
In the past, Thai people traded goods on rivers. This was the beginning of floating markets in Thailand. With better road transportation, many floating markets ⓐdisappeared. Since the late 1960s, however, some of them have come back and kept the tradition ⓑout of Thailand. Today, one of the most ⓒpopular floating markets is Damnoen Saduak Floating Market. It is always ⓓcrowded with tourists from all over the world. You can buy local foods and traditional gift items directly from ⓔboats.

① ⓐ   ② ⓑ   ③ ⓒ   ④ ⓓ   ⑤ ⓔ

◎ 선택형 문항의 답안은 컴퓨터용 수정 싸인펜을 사용하여 OMR 답안지에 바르게 표기하시오.
◎ 서술형 문제는 답을 답안지에 반드시 검정 볼펜으로 쓰시오.
◎ 총 30문항 100점 만점입니다. 문항별 배점은 각 문항에 표시되어 있습니다.

[전북 ○○중]

1. 다음 짝지어진 두 단어의 관계가 나머지와 다른 것은? (3점)

① Canada - Canadian
② The Netherlands - Dutch
③ Turkey - Turkish
④ Portugal - Portuguese
⑤ Thai - Thailand

[경북 ○○중]

2. 다음 문장의 빈칸에 적절한 단어를 넣어서 문장을 완성하려고 할 때 들어갈 수 없는 것은? (3점)

• What is the best _____ to cross the river?
• Taking a nap _____ like a good idea for your health.
• Remember most cats can't _____ milk very well.
• Scientists are working to _____ medicine for cancers.

① digest   ② seems   ③ destroy
④ method   ⑤ discover

[경기 ○○중]

3. 다음 대화에서 문맥상 밑줄 친 표현의 목적으로 옳은 것은? (3점)

W: Can I have the bill, please?
M: Here you are. Did you enjoy the meal?
W: It was great. I liked the *gondrebap* very much.
M: Thanks. It's also good for your health.
W: Oh, really?

M: Yes. *Gondre* is rich in vitamins A and C. It also digests well.
W: Good. I wonder if I could buy some *gondre* here.
M: Sure. <u>Do you want me to give you the recipe for *gondrebap*?</u>
W: Yes, that'd be great.

① to introduce a topic
② to offer help to others
③ to know someone's liking
④ to express agreement or disagreement
⑤ to ask the reason for someone's opinion

[전북 ○○중]

[4~5] 다음 대화의 밑줄 친 표현이 의미하는 것을 〈보기〉에서 찾으시오.

<보기>	
ⓐ 주제 소개하기	ⓑ 이유 묻기
ⓒ 궁금한 점 묻기	ⓓ 도움 제안하기
ⓔ 감정 표현하기	

4. 위 〈보기〉에서 다음 대화의 밑줄 친 표현이 의미하는 것은? (2점)

A: Excuse me. <u>I wonder if there's a bank around here.</u>
B: I'm sorry, but we don't have one near here.
A: That's all right. Thanks.

① ⓐ   ② ⓑ   ③ ⓒ   ④ ⓓ   ⑤ ⓔ

5. 위 〈보기〉에서 다음 대화의 밑줄 친 표현이 의미하는 것은? (4점)

A: What's wrong, Grandpa?
B: I'm bored.
A: <u>Do you want me to play *baduk* with you?</u>
B: That'd be great. Thank you.

① ⓐ   ② ⓑ   ③ ⓒ   ④ ⓓ   ⑤ ⓔ

[6~7] 다음 대화를 읽고, 물음에 답하시오.

Man: Welcome to the Tourist Information Office! ⓐHow may I help you?

Lady: Hi, ⓑI wonder if there's a tourist map of the town.

Man: Sure. ⓒIs there a special place you're looking for?

Lady: Yes. I'd like to try some local food.

Man: Then go to Jeongseon Market. It opens every five days, and it's open today.

Lady: I'm so lucky. ⓓHow can I get there?

Man: You can walk there. It takes about 10 minutes.

Lady: Great. ⓔWill you mark the way on the map, please?

Man: Sure. Try *gondrebap* when you get there.

6. 위 대화에서 간접의문문(Indirect Question)에 해당하는 문장은 무엇인가? (2점)

① ⓐ　　② ⓑ　　③ ⓒ　　④ ⓓ　　⑤ ⓔ

7. 위 대화를 나눈 날짜가 14일이라면, 바로 다음 장이 열리는 날은 언제인지 아래 달력을 참고하여 고르면? (4점)

October

SUN	MON	TUE	WED	THU	FRI	SAT
11	12	13	14 Today	15	16	17
18	19	20	21	22	23	24
25	26	27	28	29	30	31

① 15일　　② 17일　　③ 19일

④ 21일　　⑤ 24일

8. 다음 대화에서 A, B의 관계로 가장 적절한 것은? (3점)

A: Can I have the bill, please?

B: Here you are. Did you enjoy the meal?

A: It was great. I liked the *gondrebap* very much.

B: Thanks. It's also good for your health.

A: Oh, really?

B: Yes. *Gondre* is rich in vitamins A and C. It also digests well.

A: Good. I wonder if I could buy some *gondre* here.

B: Sure. Do you want me to give you the recipe for *gondrebap*?

A: Yes, that'd be great.

① cook – server

② tour guide – tourist

③ food researcher – student

④ flight attendant – passenger

⑤ restaurant staff – customer

9. 다음 우리말을 가장 바르게 영작한 것은? (4점)

① 나는 버스가 언제 떠났는지 궁금하다.
　→ I curious when the bus leaves.

② 너는 덮개가 있는 트럭을 사용해야만 한다.
　→ You must use a crowded truck.

③ 대부분의 고양이는 우유를 잘 소화할 수 없다.
　→ Most cats cannot house milk very well.

④ 과학자들은 암에 대한 약을 발견하기 위해 일하고 있다.
　→ Scientists are working to discover medicine for cancers.

⑤ 그랜드 캐넌은 세계의 자연 경관 중의 하나이다.
　→ The Grand Canyon is one of the national wonders of the world.

10. 다음 중 밑줄 친 부분이 바르게 된 것은? (3점)

① This is the company <u>where</u> my mom works.

② Do you know the town <u>when</u> Taehun was born?

③ I remember the summer <u>why</u> I learned water skiing.

④ Is this the shop <u>which</u> you bought the skirt yesterday?

⑤ I don't know the way <u>how</u> the students came into the room.

11. 다음 두 문장이 같은 의미가 되도록 빈칸에 알맞은 말을 쓰시오. (4점)

- This is the town in which I was born.
= This is the town _____ I was born.

<조건>
(1) 1개 단어로 쓸 것.

정답: _____

12. 다음 문장의 빈칸에 공통으로 들어갈 말로 가장 알맞은 것은? (3점)

- The question is _____ the plan will work.
- We don't know _____ the meeting will end soon.
- _____ the weather will be fine or not is the matter.

① why[Why]   ② how[How]

③ when[When]   ④ where[Where]

⑤ whether[Whether]

13. <보기>에서 ⓐ~ⓕ 중 어법상 옳은 것은? (4점)

<보기>
- This is the place where ⓐ<u>do they keep</u> the food.
- ⓑ<u>Whether it will rain</u> soon is important to farmers.
- My sister wanted to buy a watch ⓒ<u>making in</u> Switzerland.
- ⓓ<u>Collecting old coins and stamps were</u> my sister's hobby.
- Sumin sang ⓔ<u>so well that</u> she won a prize at a music contest.
- Jeremy has been searching for the treasure ⓕ<u>during four months ago.</u>

① ⓐ, ⓑ   ② ⓑ, ⓔ   ③ ⓒ, ⓓ

④ ⓓ, ⓕ   ⑤ ⓔ, ⓕ

14. 다음 중 어법상 옳은 문장은 몇 개인가? (3점)

- Whether Tony will win the game is not certain.
- I wonder whether he knows the way here.
- Tell me whether will you come to the party.
- I am not sure if is it open on Sundays.
- We want to know if he likes the baker.

① 1개   ② 2개   ③ 3개   ④ 4개   ⑤ 5개

15. 우리말에 맞게 영어로 바르게 쓴 것은? (3점)

- 당신은 그것들이 무엇인지 추측할 수 있습니까?

① Can you guess what are they?

② Can you guess what they are?

③ Can you what guess they are?

④ What can you guess they are?

⑤ What can you guess are they?

[16~19] 다음 글을 읽고 물음에 답하시오.

JJIMJILBANG - Do you want to experience the real Korea? Then (A)_____ a *jjimjilbang*. It is a place in which you can experience a traditional Korean way to relax. It can easily be found in any big city. You can rest on a hot floor or take a nap. Also, you can read a book or chat with your friends as you lie on the floor. The best food you can (A)_____ here is boiled eggs. (B)The place is easy on your wallet because it only costs about 13,000 won. It usually open 24 hours a day.

16. 위 글의 제목으로 가장 알맞은 것은? (3점)

① The Most Popular Person in Korea
② A Good Place To Visit in Korea
③ The Best Season To Visit Korea
④ Must-Visit Market in Korea
⑤ How To Travel in Korea

17. 위 글에서 *Jjimjilbang*에 대하여 언급되지 <u>않은</u> 것은? (2점)

① 운영 시간   ② 사용 비용
③ 추천 음식   ④ 가장 인기 있는 찜질방
⑤ 할 수 있는 일

18. 위 글의 밑줄 친 (A)에 공통으로 들어갈 말은? (4점)

① go   ② try   ③ get
④ eat   ⑤ come

19. 위 글의 밑줄 친 (B)의 의미로 가장 적절한 것은? (3점)

① 비용에 대한 부담없이 찜질방을 이용할 수 있다.
② 찜질방에서 지갑을 흔히 볼 수 있다.
③ 찜질방에서 지갑을 잃어버리기 쉽다.
④ 찜질방에서 지갑을 찾기 쉽다.
⑤ 지갑은 항상 휴대해야 한다.

[20~21] 다음 글을 읽고 물음에 답하시오.

In the past, Thai people traded goods on rivers. (A) This was the beginning of floating markets in Thailand. (B) With better road transportation, many floating markets disappeared. (C) Today, one of the most popular floating markets is Damnoen Saduak Floating Market. (D) It is always crowded with tourists from all over the world. (E) You can buy local foods and traditional gift items directly from boats.
Extra Tip
I wonder if you have ever had a meal on water. (A)If not on water, try noodles like *pad thai*. The sellers will cook them on their boats and pass them to you with a long fishing pole.

20. 위 글의 (A)~(E) 중 주어진 문장이 들어가기에 가장 적절한 곳은? (3점)

Since the late 1960s, however, some of them have come back and kept the tradition alive.

① (A)   ② (B)   ③ (C)   ④ (D)   ⑤ (E)

21. 위 글의 문맥상 밑줄 친 (A)를 완전한 절로 바꾼 것은? (4점)

① If they haven't had a meal
② If they would have a meal
③ If you have ever had a meal
④ If they had never had a meal
⑤ If you have never eaten a meal

[22~25] 다음 글을 읽고 물음에 답하시오.

In the past, Thai people traded goods on rivers. ⓐThis was the beginning of floating markets in Thailand. With better road transportation, many floating markets disappeared. Since the late 1960s, (A)_____, some of ⓑthem have come back and kept the (B)tradition alive.

Today, one of the most popular floating markets is Damnoen Saduak Floating Market. ⓒIt is always crowded with tourists from all over the world. You can buy local foods and traditional gift items directly from boats.

Extra Tip Have you ever had a meal on water? If not, try noodles like *pad thai*. The sellers will cook ⓓthem on their boats and pass ⓔthem to you with a long fishing pole.

22. 위 글의 빈칸 (A)에 가장 알맞은 말은? (3점)

① for example
② however
③ in addition
④ besides
⑤ thus

23. 위 글의 밑줄 친 ⓐ~ⓔ의 지칭하는 대상이 바르게 연결된 것은? (4점)

① ⓐ Thailand
② ⓑ road transportations
③ ⓒ Thailand
④ ⓓ sellers
⑤ ⓔ noodles

24. 위 글의 내용과 일치하는 것은? (4점)

① 수상 시장에서 음식을 직접 살 수 있다.
② 과거 태국 사람들은 배에서 상품을 사고 팔지 않았다.
③ 항공교통의 발달로 수상 시장이 사라지기 시작했다.
④ 수상 시장의 전통은 1960년대 초반에 나타나기 시작했다.
⑤ Damnoen Saduak Floating Market는 대만에 있는 시장이다.

25. 위 글의 밑줄 친 (B)를 영어로 가장 잘 설명한 것은? (4점)

① to see no longer
② possible to think of in your mind
③ without stopping; with nothing in between
④ to send people or something somewhere by ship, truck and so on
⑤ cultural beliefs and customs passed down through generations

26. 다음 Grand Bazaar에 관한 설명 중 글의 내용과 일치하는 것은? (3점)

Grand Bazaar, Turkey
Turkey is a country where East meets West, so it has a long tradition of trade. It is a natural place for large markets like the Grand Bazaar. The market was built in 1455 in Istanbul. Back then, the market had two big buildings, and people traded goods like cloth and gold there.
Today the Grand Bazaar is much bigger, and it is the largest covered market in the world. It has 64 streets and more than 4,000 shops under one roof. The market attracts over 250,000 visitors every day. You can buy almost any imaginable item there.

① 터키의 소형 전통 시장이다.
② 매년 약 25만 명이 방문한다.
③ 세계에서 두 번째로 큰 지붕이 덮인 시장이다.
④ 한 지붕 아래에 수백 개의 거리와 상점이 있다.
⑤ 1455년에는 이 시장에 큰 건물이 두 개 있었다.

[27~28] 다음 글을 읽고 물음에 답하시오.

The Netherlands means "low lands." As the name suggests, about 70% of the country sits below sea level. Thus, the Dutch built up the land, and one effective way to use it was to (A)[rise / raise] flowers and sell them. It is, therefore, no surprise that the country has the largest flower market in the world: the Aalsmeer Flower Market.

The building where the market is housed is bigger than 120 soccer fields. The market is busy with thousands of flower-filled carts. They are moved mostly by electric-powered trucks. Every day, around 20 million flowers are traded and (B)[transcribed / transported] to all corners of the world.

Extra Tip

You may wonder whether you can buy just a few flowers at the market. Sadly, you cannot, but you can see how (C)[wholesale / retail] flower trading works.

27. 위 글의 괄호 (A), (B), (C) 안에 들어갈 말을 나열한 것으로 옳은 것은? (4점)

	(A)	(B)	(C)
①	raise	transported	wholesale
②	raise	transcribed	wholesale
③	raise	transported	retail
④	rise	transcribed	wholesale
⑤	rise	transcribed	retail

28. 위 글의 내용과 일치하지 <u>않는</u> 것은? (3점)

① Much of the Netherlands is not above sea level.

② The Dutch figured out the way to use the "low lands".

③ The Aalsmeer flower market is the largest flower market in the world.

④ The Aalsmeer flower market is as big as 120 soccer fields.

⑤ There are lots of carts mostly moved by electricity in the Aalsmeer flower market.

[29~30] 다음 글을 읽고 물음에 답하시오.

Damnoen Saduak Floating Market, Thailand

In the past, Thai people traded goods on rivers. This was the beginning of floating markets in Thailand. ⓐ_____ better road transportation, many floating markets disappeared. Since the late 1960s, however, some of them have come back and kept the tradition alive.

Today, one of the most popular floating markets is Damnoen Saduak Floating Market. It is always crowded ⓐ_____ tourists from all over the world. You can buy local foods and traditional gift items directly from boats.

Extra Tip I wonder if you have ever had a meal on water. If not, try noodles like *pad thai*. The sellers will cook them on their boats and pass them to you with a long fishing pole.

29. 위 글의 빈칸 ⓐ에 공통으로 들어갈 말은? (4점)

① To[to] ② For[for] ③ At[at]

④ With[with] ⑤ From[from]

30. 위 글을 다음과 같이 요약할 때 빈칸에 들어갈 말로 가장 적절한 것은? (4점)

Damnoen Saduak Floating Market in Thailand is a place where visitors can buy goods and order food on (A)_____. It shows Thailand's (B)_____ of trading on rivers.

	(A)	(B)
①	meal	boats
②	boats	tradition
③	pole	items
④	market	gift
⑤	road	transportation

정답 및 해설

Lesson 1 (중간)

01 ② **02** ⑤ **03** ④ **04** ① **05** ① **06** ① **07** ②
08 I'm glad we're in the same class.
09 ⑤ **10** ① **11** ③ **12** ③ **13** ⑤
14 Alex tell a funny story 또는 Alex telling a funny story
15 I saw Mom come into my room.
16 ① **17** ④ **18** ② **19** ② **20** ② **21** ② **22** ③
23 ⑤ **24** ① **25** ④ **26** ① **27** ③ **28** ① **29** ④
30 ③ **31** ④ **32** ②

01 모두 '명사-형용사'의 관계이지만 ②번은 '원급-비교급' 의 관계이다.

02 jealous: unhappy and angry because someone has what you do not have

03 앞에서 'I want to join the school dance club.'이라 고 하고 'But I don't like dancing.'이라고 하는 것은 어색하다.

04 Break a leg! = Good luck!

05 인사하며 놀랍다는 말에 이어 ⓐ 마주 인사하며 같은 반에 있어서 기쁘다고 말하고 ⓓ 자기도 그렇다며 중학교의 마지막 학년인데 기분이 어떤지 묻고 ⓑ 조금 걱정된다고 하자 ⓒ 자기도 그렇다며 고등학교에 대해서도 생각해야 한다고 하는 순서이다.

06 '종일 비가 올 거야.'라는 말에 '새 비옷을 입을 수 있어 기쁘다.'는 말이 어울린다.

07 '월요일이 가장 지루한 요일'이라는 말에 '전적으로 동의한다.'는 말이 어울린다.

08 'I'm glad'를 먼저 쓰고 '같은 반에'를 'in the same class'로 쓴다.

09 물건의 색깔(red), 물건을 사려는 이유(birthday present), 물건의 가격(40,000 won), 물건의 기능 (phone case, wallet) 등은 알 수 있으나 '물건의 상표' 는 알 수 없다.

10 지각동사 felt의 목적격보어로 동사원형이나 현재분사가 적절하다.

11 A에는 의문사 What, B에는 관계대명사 What이 적절하다.

12 지각동사 saw의 목적격보어로 동사원형이나 현재분사가 적절하다.

13 ⑤번은 의문사이지만 나머지는 관계대명사이다.

14 지각동사 heard의 목적격보어로 동사원형이나 현재분사가 적절하다.

15 지각동사 saw의 목적격보어로 동사원형을 쓴다.

16 ② are → is ③ to blow → blow[blowing] ④ to play → play[playing] ⑤ that → what

17 ⓓ는 '여왕'이지만 나머지는 모두 'Antonio'이다.

18 'merchant'라고 했으므로 ②번이 적절하다.

19 배에 상품을 가득 싣고 가서 (A) 공구를 향신료와 책을 견과류와 바꾸고, 여왕의 초대를 받고 (C) 식사할 때 쥐를 보고 고양이가 없다고 하자 (B) 고양이를 한 마리 주고 여왕이 기뻐하고 보석을 주는 순서가 적절하다.

20 ⓒ는 Antonio로 여왕이 초대했으므로 'regretful(후회하는, 불만스러운)'은 적절하지 않다.

21 무서워 도망간 것이 아니다. 'Antonio was greatly surprised that there were rats in the palace.'라고 했다.

22 need의 목적어와 is의 주어 역할을 할 수 있는 What이 적절하다.

23 'he told the islanders a lie that he was a good friend of Antonio's'라고 했다.

24 (A) 뒤에서 'I'll bring the queen what is really valuable'이라고 했으므로 'worthless(가치 없는, 쓸모 없는)'가 적절하다. (D) 앞에서 'the queen thanked him again and again'이라고 했으므로 'priceless(대단히 귀중한)'이 적절하다.

25 bring의 직접목적어와 is의 주어 역할을 할 수 있는 what이 적절하다.

26 (C)와 ①: 부사적 용법 '목적' ② 명사적 용법 ③ 형용사적 용법 ④ 부사적 용법 '원인' ⑤ 명사적 용법

27 Antonio가 상인으로 교역을 하는 글에서 여왕과 식사했다는 언급은 필요 없다.

28 배에 상품을 '가득 실었다'고 하는 것이 적절하다. fill A with B: B로 A를 채우다

29 지각동사 saw의 목적격보어로 동사원형이나 현재분사가 나와야 하므로 'to run away'를 'run away'나 'running away'로 고쳐야 한다.

30 왜 여왕이 Antonio를 만찬에 초대했는지는 알 수 없다.

31 "I'll bring the queen what is really valuable. I'm sure that the queen will give me more jewels."라고 했다.

32 ⓓ priceless: 대단히 귀중한, 돈으로 살 수 없는 ⓐ worthless: 가치 없는, 쓸모없는 ⓑ valuable: 귀중한, 소중한 ⓒ wonderful: 훌륭한, 굉장한 ⓔ hopeful: 희망이 있는 ⓕ speechless: 말을 못 하는, (충격 따위로) 말이 안 나오는

Lesson 1 (중간)

01 ③ **02** ① **03** ③ **04** ② **05** ② **06** ⑤
07 ②, ④ **08** ⑤ **09** ⑤ **10** ⑤ **11** ⑤ **12** ③
13 ②
14 Jessie watched her brother cook(ing) in the kitchen.
15 What I want to do **16** ④ **17** ③ **18** ④
19 In return for the wonderful gifts you gave us
20 ④ **21** ① **22** ⑤ **23** ⑤ **24** ② **25** ① **26** ①
27 ④ **28** ①

01 ③번의 far는 비교급을 강조하는 것으로 '훨씬'의 뜻이다.
02 각각 (A) merchant (B) palace (C) support (D) jewel이다.
03 'It was fantastic. I had a lot of fun.'이라고 답하므로 '콘서트가 어땠는지' 묻는 것이 적절하다.
04 'what club are you going to join?'이라는 질문에 'I'm not sure.'라고 답했다.
05 'I'm worried'는 'I'm afraid'와 비슷한 뜻이다.
06 'I love painting.'이라고 했지만 '화가가 되고 싶다'는 말은 없다.
07 이어지는 말로 보아 '반대하는 표현'이 적절하다.
08 'I have two left feet.'라고 했다.
09 have[get] butterflies in one's stomach: 안절부절 못하다
10 things라는 선행사가 있으므로 선행사를 포함하는 관계대명사 what을 that으로 고쳐야 한다.
11 ① do I → I ② whispered → whisper(ing) ③ to play → play(ing) ④ that → what
12 (A) what → that (B) done → do(ing) (D) Which → What
13 ① to bark → bark(ing) ③ caught → catch(ing) ④ moved → move[moving] ⑤ to knocking → knock(ing)
14 지각동사 watch의 목적격보어로 동사원형이나 현재분사가 적절하다.
15 선행사를 포함하는 관계대명사 what을 이용한다.

16 give의 직접목적어와 is의 주어 역할을 할 수 있는 what이 적절하다.
17 선물로 보물을 받을 생각에 '희망에 찼다가' 고양이를 받고 '실망했을' 것이다.
18 Luigi가 어떤 선물을 주었는지는 알 수 없다.
19 관계대명사절 you gave us가 gifts를 수식하도록 한다. in return for: ~에 대한 보답으로
20 traded tools for spices: 도구를 주고 향신료를 얻었다
21 could get과 needed의 목적어 역할을 할 수 있는 what이 적절하다.
22 교역을 하는 Antonio에 대한 언급에 이어 (c) 여왕과 식사를 하다가 쥐들이 나타나, 하인들이 쥐들을 쫓아내고 (b) Antonio가 놀라 고양이가 없느냐고 묻자 고양이가 뭐냐고 묻고 (a) 고양이 두 마리를 풀어놓자 쥐들이 도망가서 여왕이 보석을 주는 순서가 적절하다.
23 valuable: precious or important to someone
24 (A) could get과 needed의 목적어 역할을 할 수 있는 what이 적절하다. (B) 지각동사 saw의 목적격보어로 동사원형이 적절하다. (C) 사람이 감정을 느끼는 것이므로 과거분사가 적절하다.
25 'There he traded tools for spices and books for nuts.'라고 했으므로 Antonio가 물건을 무료로 준 것은 아니다.
26 (A)에는 what이 들어가야 하지만 나머지는 that이 들어가야 한다.
27 Luigi는 Antonio보다 더 값비싼 선물을 주었지만 상대방으로부터 더 비싼 선물을 받지는 않았다.
28 puzzle: 난처하게 만들다, 어리둥절하게[이해할 수 없게] 만들다

Lesson 2 (중간)

01 ④ **02** ④ **03** ② **04** ④ **05** ⑤ **06** ② **07** ④
08 ④ **09** ③
10 Which do you like better, hiking or swimming?
11 ③ **12** ② **13** ④ **14** ① **15** ⑤ **16** ① **17** ⑤
18 ① **19** ④ **20** ④ **21** ① **22** ① **23** ② **24** ③
25 ② **26** ① **27** ③ **28** ⑤

01 female: relating to women or girls
02 반의어의 관계이다. including: ~을 포함하여 except: ~을 제외하고
03 'I'll go hiking because we can see wild birds and

insects in the woods.'라고 했다.

04 '자연의 미래'에 관한 기사라는 말에 이어 (B) 더 말해달라고 요청하고 (D) 멸종 위기의 동물들에 관한 거라고 답하자 (A) 흥미롭다고 관심을 나타내고 (C) 어느 사진이 더 나은지 묻자, 여윈 북극곰이라고 답하는 순서가 적절하다.

05 'a lot of trash in the sea'라고 했으므로 ⑤번이 적절하다.

06 바다의 쓰레기로 인한 문제이므로 ②번이 적절하다.

07 'It's ten times my age.'라고 했다.

08 'They are more friendly.'라고 했고 상대방은 'I like cats better.'라고 했으므로 ④번이 적절하다.

09 뒤에서 코끼리에 대해 자세히 설명하므로 ③번이 적절하다.

10 'Which do you like better, A or B?'를 이용해 선호하는 것을 묻는다.

11 개미들이(ants) 나뭇잎(a leaf)을 '나르는' 것이므로 carried를 carrying으로 고쳐야 한다.

12 동사 said가 있으므로 sat을 sitting으로 고친다.

13 오후 프로그램 결정했는지 묻자 ⓑ 아직 못했다며 어느 게 더 좋은지 묻고 ⓒ 축구라고 답하며 운동할 수도 있다고 하자 ⓐ 좋다며 함께 하겠고 한다. ⓓ 완벽하다며 같이 축구하면 재미있겠다고 덧붙인다.

14 사진(picture)이 찍힌 것이므로 taken으로 고쳐야 한다.

15 서로 상반되는 내용이 연결되고 있으므로 '양보'의 접속사 Though로 고쳐야 한다.

16 'they live almost everywhere in the world, except a few extremely cold places including Antarctica'라고 했다.

17 'Most ants can swim and live 24 hours underwater.'라고 했다.

18 ⓑ lived → living ⓒ that → what
ⓓ producing → produce 또는 to produce
ⓔ collected → collecting

19 '일개미는 모두 암컷인데 ~ 군집을 방어하며'라고 했다.

20 'a chemical'이 'a pheromone'을 부르는 것이 아니라 'a pheromone'이라고 불리는 것이므로 calling을 called로 고쳐야 한다.

21 뒤에 결과가 이어지므로, '이유'를 나타내는 Since가 적절하다.

22 'an ant has legs covered with very sensitive hairs'라고 했다.

23 개미들이 화학물질과 접촉을 이용해 의사소통한다는 글

이다.

24 (A) 상반되는 내용이 나오므로 Though (B) 예를 들고 있으므로 For example이 적절하다.

25 (A) 뒤에 복수 명사 'places'가 나오므로 a few, (B) 뒤에 결과가 이어지므로, '이유'를 나타내는 Since가 적절하다.

26 ⓐ weigh → weighs ⓔ another → the other

27 개미는 군집을 이루어 살며 개미들의 종류와 하는 일 등을 말하고 있으므로 ③번이 적절하다.

28 'Ants do not have lungs but breathe through small holes in their bodies.'라고 했다.

Lesson 2 (중간)

01 ④	02 ③	03 ④	04 ④	05 ④	06 ③	07 ⑤
08 ①	09 ①	10 ⑤	11 ②	12 ①	13 ⑤	

14 (1) since (2) though 15 ② 16 ① 17 ②

18 One million ants are as heavy as a human being.

19 ④	20 ③	21 ③	22 ③	23 ⑤	24 ④	25 ②
26 ④	27 ②	28 ①	29 ③, ⑤			

01 (A) 무언가를 가방이나 상자에 넣는 것은 'pack(싸다)', (B) 다리가 6개이고 보통 날개가 있는 것은 'insect(곤충)'이다.

02 (C)에는 'sensitive(민감한)'가 적절하다.

03 'I'll join you.'라고 한 후 '새와 곤충을 싫어한다'는 말은 어색하다.

04 'I'll join you.'라고 했다.

05 간접의문문의 어순은 '의문사+주어+동사'이다.

06 '선호'를 묻는 질문이며 (C) 다음에 그 질문에 답하므로 (C)가 적절하다.

07 'I'll go hiking because we can see wild birds and insects in the woods.'라고 했다.

08 • 현재완료에 어울리는 since(~ 이래로)
• '이유'를 나타내는 since(~ 때문에)가 적절하다.

09 ⓑ running → run ⓒ making → made
ⓓ moved → moving ⓔ sit → sitting

10 ⓔ는 'beehive'를 가리키지만, 나머지는 'chestnut tree'를 가리킨다.

11 간접의문문의 어순은 '의문사+주어+동사'이다.

12 'I'm trying to choose a picture for my story in the school newspaper.'라고 했다.

13 ① solved →solving ② covering → covered

③ waited → waiting ④ building → built

14 (1) 뒤에 '이유'가 나오므로 since (2) 뒤에 상반되는 내용이 나오므로 though

15 while → since, Until → Though

16 guess의 목적어와 are의 주어 역할을 할 수 있는 what이 적절하다.

17 'They use a special chemical to communicate.'라고 했다.

18 as ~ as ...: …만큼 ~한(동급 비교)

19 (A) 상반되는 내용이 연결되고 있으므로 '양보'의 접속사 Though, (B) 예를 들고 있으므로 For example, (C) 뒤에 결과가 이어지므로, '이유'를 나타내는 Since가 적절하다.

20 개미들이 '어떻게 의사소통을 하는지'에 관한 글이다.

21 'A queen lives up to five years, but worker bees only live for about seven weeks'라고 했다.

22 'They use a special chemical to communicate.'라고 했다.

23 'An ant has two stomachs.'라고 했다.

24 개미들이 군집을 이루어 살며 개미들의 종류와 하는 일 등을 말하고 있다.

25 ⓐ has → have ⓓ produces → produce 또는 to produce

26 (A)와 ⓑ, ⓒ, ⓓ: 관계대명사 ⓐ: 지시형용사 ⓔ: 접속사

27 개미들이 얼마나 많은지에 대한 글이다.

28 'a human being'을 수식하는 역할을 해야 하므로 weighing이 적절하다. 앞에 'which is'가 생략된 것으로 생각해도 된다.

29 'there are about one million ants for every human in the world', 'Though each ant hardly weighs anything, one million ants are as heavy as a human being'이라고 했다.

Lesson 3 (기말)

01 ③	**02** ③	**03** ①	**04** ②	**05** ④	**06** ③
07 That makes sense.					
08 ③	**09** ①	**10** ②	**11** ⑤	**12** ④	**13** ②	**14** ②
15 ①	**16** ④	**17** ⑤	**18** ④	**19** ④	**20** ③	**21** ①
22 ⑤	**23** ②	**24** ②	**25** ④	**26** ②	**27** ⑤

01 matter: 지장, 어려움, 걱정(명사), [보통 부정·의문] 중요하다, 문제가 되다(동사)

02 ① appear → disappear ② impossible → possible ④ bad → good ⑤ small, high → large, low

03 'All we need is a ball to play basketball.'이라는 대답이 나올 수 있는 것은 '이유'를 묻는 ①번뿐이다.

04 (C) 10대 때 시간제 일자리를 갖는 것이 좋다고 하자 (A) 그 이유를 묻고 (D) 이유를 답하고 (B) 일리가 있다고 하는 순서가 자연스럽다.

05 have butterflies in one's stomach: 조마조마하다, 가슴이 두근거리다

06 'What makes you say that?'은 '이유'를 묻는 표현이다.

07 make sense: 의미가 통하다[이해가 되다], 타당하다[말이 되다]

08 약간의 스트레스는 도움이 되었다는 말에 이어 ⓒ 이유를 묻고 ⓑ 이유를 답하고 ⓓ 알겠다며 다른 방식으로도 도움이 되었는지 묻자 ⓐ 기억력을 높이는 데 도움을 주었다고 답한다.

09 'I'd like to ~'는 '~하고 싶다'라는 의미로 주제를 소개할 때 쓸 수 있는 표현이다.

10 'What makes you say that?'은 '왜 그렇게 말하는 거야?'라는 의미로 '이유'를 묻는 표현이다.

11 ① has → have
② Have Aidan been worked → Has Aidan been working
③ has been not → has not been
④ have preparing → have been preparing

12 2월에 시작해서 아직까지 하고 있으므로 현재완료진행형으로 나타내고 'have been ~ing'의 형태로 쓴다.

13 tell a lie: 거짓말하다, tell+간접목적어+직접목적어

14 so ~ that 주어 can = ~ enough to, so ~ that 주어 cannot = too ~ to

15 바르게 배열하면 'My grandfather is so old (A)that he can't (B)travel long distances.'이다. 그러므로 세 번째와 여섯 번째 올 단어는 that과 travel이다.

16 positive(낙관적인, 긍정적인)는 'hopeful and pleasant' 정도가 되어야 한다.

17 'While I fish, I'm so focused that I can leave all my worries behind.'라고 했다.

18 친구들과의 문제는 세 번째가 아닌 두 번째이다.

19 ⓐ 또 다른 나머지의 일부를 나타낼 때 'Still others'로 쓴다. ⓑ 추가하고 있으므로 Besides(게다가)가 적절하다.

20 (A) break one's promise: 약속을 깨뜨리다 (B) at the

top of one's lungs: 목청껏, 큰 소리로 (C) positive: 긍정적인 negative: 부정적인

21 친구들이 때때로 스트레스를 줄 때 미나가 어떤 음식을 먹기 좋아하는지는 알 수 없다.

22 엄마가 스트레스를 해결하는 방법에 관한 글에서 친구가 뉴욕에 산다는 것은 관계없는 내용이다.

23 (A) deal with: ~을 다루다, 처리하다 (B) 사람을 선행사로 하는 주격 관계대명사 who나 that (C) about의 목적어와 bothers의 주어 역할을 할 수 있는 관계대명사 what

24 바르게 배열하면 'so scary that I scream a lot'이다.

25 ⓑ와 ④: 효과가 있다 ① 일 ② 일하다 ③ 작품 ⑤ 작동하다

26 정해지지 않은 것 중에서 some: 일부 others: 나머지 중 일부 still others: 또 다른 나머지 중 일부

27 'Here are some stories about people who suggest different ways.'라고 했으므로 ⑤번이 적절하다.

Lesson 3 (기말)

01 ④	02 ①	03 ④	04 ②	05 ⑤	06 ③	07 ④
08 ⑤	09 ③	10 ②	11 ⑤	12 ①	13 ⑤	14 ③
15 ①	16 ③	17 so	18 ②	19 ④	20 ⑤	21 ①
22 ②	23 ③	24 ①				

01 (A) neatly: 깨끗이, 말쑥하게 (B) angry: 화난, 성난 (C) lessen: 줄다[줄이다]

02 at the top of one's lungs: 목청껏, 큰 소리로

03 beside: ~의 곁[옆]에 besides: 그 밖에, 게다가, ~ 외에(도)

04 'What makes you say that?'은 '이유'를 묻는 표현이다.

05 (D) 약간의 스트레스는 도움이 되었다는 말에 이어 (C) 이유를 묻고 (A) 이유를 답하고 (B) 알겠다며 다른 방식으로도 도움이 되었는지 묻자, 기억력을 높이는 데 도움을 주었다고 답하는 마지막 문장으로 이어지는 순서가 적절하다.

06 have butterflies in one's stomach: 조마조마하다, 가슴이 두근거리다

07 'I got stressed when I had an exam, but at the same time it made me focus and try harder.라고 했다.'

08 숲에서 새와 곤충을 볼 수 있기 때문에 쇼핑을 갈 것이라는 말은 어색하다.

09 댄스 동아리 가입을 권하는 말에 '싫다'고 했으므로 그에 맞는 이유에 해당하는 ③번이 적절하다. have two left feet: (특히 춤을 추거나 운동을 하는 모습이) 아주 어색하다[발이 마구 엉기다]

10 과거에 시작한 일이 현재까지 진행되고 있으므로 현재완료진행형으로 나타낸다. had를 has로 고쳐야 한다.

11 ① waited → waiting
② have been playing → played
③ very → so
④ what → that

12 ② know는 진행형으로 쓰이지 않는다. ③ for → since ④ read → reading ⑤ interviewed → interviewing

13 10대들이 스트레스를 받는 요인들에 대한 글이다.

14 도빈이의 누나가 학업 때문에 많은 스트레스를 받으면 도빈이가 어떻게 느끼는지는 알 수 없다.

15 (A) 'When she's so stressed that her life looks gloomy, she cleans her room.'이라고 했다. (B) 'When she's under stress, she writes "Me Time" on her calendar. This means she takes some time out for herself.'라고 했다.

16 ① won → win
② could → could not
④ cannot → can
⑤ enough strong → strong enough

17 so ~ that ...: 너무 ~해서 …하다. 보통 '~' 자리에는 형용사나 부사가 나오며 명사가 나올 경우에는 so 대신에 such를 쓴다.

18 'he's been looking for a job for some time'이라고 했다.

19 at the top of one's lungs: 목청껏, 큰 소리로

20 글의 마지막에서 'Here are some stories about people who suggest different ways.'라고 했다.

21 (A) 다음의 It이 주어진 문장의 내용을 가리키므로 (A)가 적절하다.

22 도빈이의 엄마가 도빈이에게 스트레스를 준다는 언급은 없다.

23 'Problems with friends took second place with 15.3%.'라고 했으므로 ⓒ에는 'friends'가 와야 한다.

24 (A) 다음부터 주어진 문장의 good news를 언급하고 있으므로 (A)가 적절하다.

01 ④	02 ③	03 ②	04 ②	05 ①	06 ③	07 ⑤
08 ④	09 ⑤	10 ③	11 ④	12 ③	13 ③	
14 if[whether] they speak Chinese						
15 ④	16 ②	17 ④	18 ②	19 ⑤	20 ④	21 ①
22 ④	23 ④	24 ④	25 ③	26 ②		

01 'collect - collection'은 '동사 - 명사'이다.

02 다른 건축가들에 의해 사용되는 것이므로 used가 적절하다.

03 앞에서 6월 7일이 너무 짧다고 했고, 뒤에서 6월 11일까지 마실 수 있다고 했으므로 ②번이 적절하다.

04 a. 'It's also good for your health.'라고 했다. f. 곤드레밥을 먹고 계산서를 요구하며 곤드레밥이 정말 좋았다고 했다.

05 계산서를 요구하자 식사를 맛있게 했는지 묻고 곤드레밥이 정말 좋았다고 했으므로 ①번이 적절하다.

06 간접의문문의 어순은 '의문사[if/whether]+주어+동사'이다. I wonder if ~: ~인지 아닌지 궁금하다.

07 '곤드레밥 조리법을 드릴까요?'라는 말에 'Yes'라고 했으므로 ⑤번이 적절하다.

08 'It also digests well.'이라고 했다.

09 안경을 두고 왔다는 말에 이어 (D) 6월 7일까지 마셔야 한다고 알려주고 (C) 기한이 더 긴 게 있는지 궁금해 하고 (B) 하나 찾았다며 6월 11일까지 마실 수 있다고 하자 (A) 그걸로 사겠다며 고맙다는 말로 이어진다.

10 'I wonder if there's one that lasts longer.'라고 한 것은 유통기한이 너무 짧아서이며 질문의 답으로 이 이유를 말하고 있으므로 첫 번째 우유를 사지 않은 이유를 물어야 한다.

11 best-before date: (식품 등의) 유통 기한

12 ③번에 쓰인 if절은 '조건절'이므로 미래시제가 아닌 현재시제로 써야 한다.

13 ③번에 쓰인 if절은 '조건절'이며 나머지는 '명사절'이다.

14 의문사가 없는 간접의문문은 'if[whether]+주어+동사'의 어순으로 쓴다.

15 주어진 문장의 however로 (D)의 앞 문장과 상반되는 내용이므로 (D)가 적절하다.

16 'The building where the market is housed is bigger than 120 soccer fields.'라고 했다.

17 (A) the place가 선행사이므로 where (B) 사기 전에 땄을 것이므로 before (C) 이유를 말하고 있으므로 Because가 적절하다.

18 therefore로 (B) 앞 문장의 결과를 이끌고 있으므로 (B)가 적절하다.

19 1. 'You may wonder whether you can buy just a few flowers at the market. Sadly, you cannot,'이라고 했다.

2. 'The building where the market is housed is bigger than 120 soccer fields.'라고 했다.

3. 'Every day, around 20 million flowers are traded and shipped to all corners of the world.'라고 했다.

20 (A) 과거부터 시작해서 현재도 진행 중이므로 현재완료나 현재완료진행시제, (B) 주어 역할을 해야 하므로 동명사나 to부정사가 적절하다.

21 (C) places를 선행사로 하는 where, (D) 확정적인 사실이 아니므로 '~인지 아닌지'를 의미하는 if나 whether가 적절하다.

22 거래되는 꽃의 종류에 대한 언급은 없다.

23 ① 네덜란드 사람들 ② 수 천 개의 ③ 약 2천만 송이의 꽃 ⑤ 조금

24 앞 문장의 결과가 나오므로 therefore가 적절하다.

25 ③번은 '조건절'을 이끌고 있지만 (나)와 나머지는 '명사절'을 이끄는 if이다.

26 'out of'는 '~의 안에서 밖으로, ~ 바깥에'의 뜻으로 어색하다. 'alive' 정도로 쓰는 것이 적절하다.

01 ⑤	02 ③	03 ②	04 ③	05 ④	06 ②	07 ③
08 ⑤	09 ④	10 ①	11 where		12 ⑤	13 ②
14 ③	15 ②	16 ②	17 ④	18 ②	19 ①	20 ③
21 ⑤	22 ②	23 ⑤	24 ①	25 ⑤	26 ⑤	27 ①
28 ④	29 ④	30 ②				

01 모두 '나라(명사) - 나라의, 나라 사람[말]의(형용사)' 관계인데 ⑤번은 반대로 되어 있다.

02 순서대로 • method • seems • digest • discover가 들어간다.

03 'Do you want me to ~?'는 도움을 제안하는 표현이다.

04 'I wonder if ~'는 궁금한 점을 묻는 표현이다.

05 'Do you want me to ~?'는 도움을 제안하는 표현이다.

06 간접의문문은 '의문사[if/whether]+주어+동사'의 어순이다.

07 'It opens every five days'라고 했으므로 19일이다.

08 계산서를 요구하자 식사를 맛있게 했는지 묻고 곤드레밥이 정말 좋았다고 했으므로 ⑤번이 적절하다.

09 ① curious → wonder, leaves → left
② crowded → covered ③ house → digest
⑤ national → natural

10 ② when → where ③ why → when
④ which → where ⑤ how → 삭제

11 the town을 선행사로 하는 관계부사 where가 적절하다.
in which = where

12 각 문장의 의미상 그리고 어법상 보어로 쓰이는 절과 목적어와 주어로 쓰이는 절을 이끌 수 있는 것은 whether이다.

13 ⓐ do 삭제 ⓒ making → made ⓓ were → was
ⓕ during → since

14 순서대로 • 맞음 • 맞음 • will you → you will • is it → it is • 맞음

15 간접의문문은 '의문사[if/whether]+주어+동사'의 어순이다. guess의 경우 의문사를 문두에 써야 하나 'Yes'나 'No'로 답할 수 있는 경우 '의문사+주어+동사'의 어순으로 쓴다.

16 찜질방을 방문해 보라는 내용의 글이다.

17 가장 인기 있는 찜질방에 대한 언급은 없다.

18 try: 시도해 보다('좋은지 알맞은지 등을 보려고 써 보거나 먹어 보다'라는 뜻)

19 easy on: ~에 관대한, 부담이 안 되는

20 주어진 문장의 however에 주목한다. (C)의 앞 문장과 상반되는 내용이므로 (C)가 적절하다.

21 'If you have not had a meal'에서 앞 문장과 반복되는 'you have had a meal'을 생략한 것으로 'If you have never eaten a meal'로 쓸 수 있다.

22 앞 문장과 상반되는 내용이 이어지므로 however가 적절하다.

23 ⓐ Thai people traded goods on rivers
ⓑ floating markets
ⓒ Damnoen Saduak Floating Market ⓓ noodles

24 'You can buy local foods and traditional gift items directly from boats.'라고 했다.

25 '전통'은 '세대에 걸쳐 전해 내려온 문화적 신념이나 관습'이다.

26 'The market was built in 1455 in Istanbul. Back then, the market had two big buildings'라고 했다.

27 (A) rise: 일어서다(자동사) raise: 재배하다
(B) transcribe: 베끼다, 복사하다 transport: 수송하다,

운반하다
(C) wholesale: 도매 retail: 소매

28 'The building where the market is housed is bigger than 120 soccer fields.'라고 했다.

29 with A: A(함)에 따라(서)
crowded with: ~으로 붐비는

30 Damnoen Saduak Floating Market은 수상 시장이므로 (A)에는 boats, (B)에는 'some of them have come back and kept the tradition alive'라고 했으므로 tradition이 적절하다.